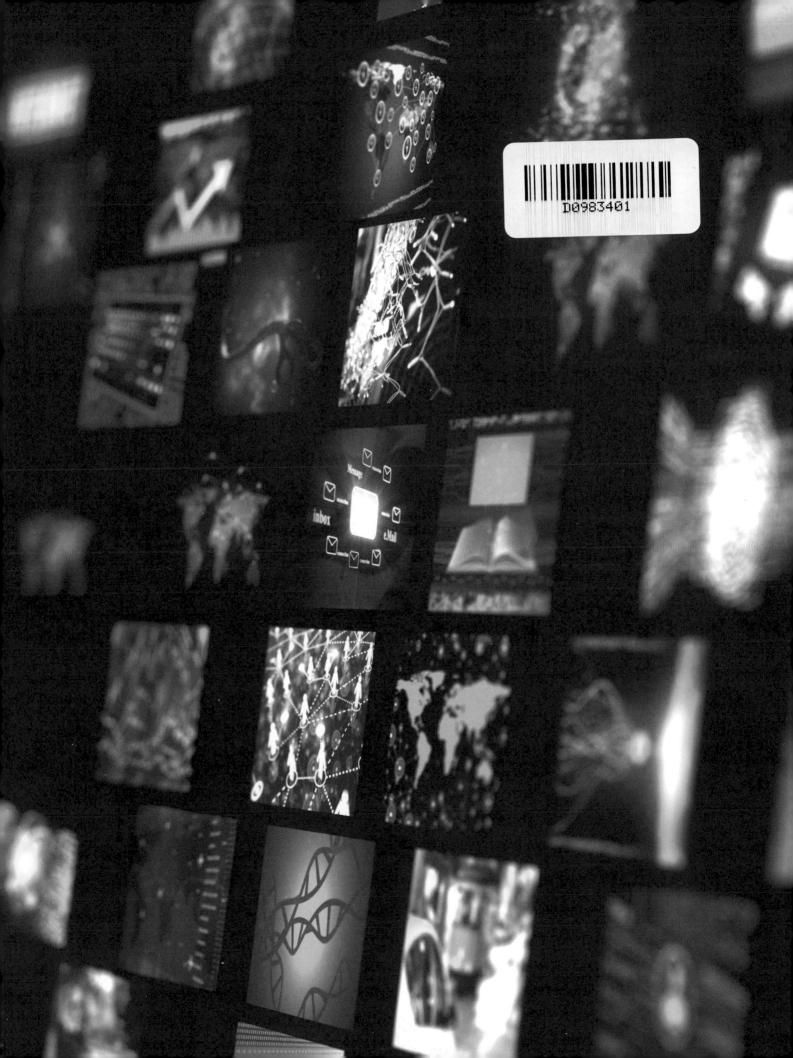

GILBERT D. HARRELL

MARKETING
CONNECTING WITH CUSTOMERS

2017e

Marketing: Connecting with Customers- 2017e

By Gilbert D. Harrell

This book was previously published by: Pearson Education, Inc.

The work contained herein is the 2017 edition produced by Chicago Education Press, LLC.

Printed in the United States of America

10 9 8 7 6 5 4 3 2

CASE BOUND: ISBN 13: 978-0-9905178-9-4

SOFT COVER: ISBN 13: 978-0-9835986-9-5

Executive Editor: Karen Sadler

Design: Troy Miller

Cover Images: ©istock.com/Danil Melekhin; ©istock.com/Rawpixel Ltd; ©istock.com/Cathy Yeulet; ©iStock.com/andresr

CHICAGO EDUCATION PRESS

Chicago Education Press, LLC
27 N. Wacker Drive, Suite 390
Chicago, IL 60606-2800
USA

www.chicagoeducationpress.com

To Susanna (my wife), Rachael, Katherine,
Nicole and the twins — Olivia and Oliver

CONTENTS

CHAPTER 1

MARKETING: CREATING & CAPTURING VALUE

CHAPTER 2

THE MARKETING STRATEGY & PLANNING PROCESS

CHAPTER 3

THE GLOBAL MARKETING ENVIRONMENT

CHAPTER 4

MARKETING INFORMATION & RESEARCH

CHAPTER 5

UNDERSTANDING CONSUMER BEHAVIOR

CHAPTER 6

UNDERSTANDING BUSINESS MARKETING

CHAPTER 7

CREATING CUSTOMER SATISFACTION & LOYALTY

CHAPTER 8

SEGMENTATION, TARGETING & POSITIONING

CHAPTER 13

MASS COMMUNICATION: ADVERTISING, SALES PROMOTIONS, & PUBLIC RELATIONS

CHAPTER 14

PERSONAL SELLING

CHAPTER 15

SUPPLY CHAIN MANAGEMENT & CHANNELS

CHAPTER 16

RETAILING, DIRECT MARKETING & WHOLESALING

CHAPTER 17

PRICING OBJECTIVES & INFLUENCES

CHAPTER 18

PRICING STRATEGIES

ABOUT THE AUTHOR

Gilbert D. Harrell, Ph.D.

Gilbert D. Harrell, Ph.D., is Professor of Marketing in the Eli Broad College of Business and Graduate School of Management at Michigan State University. Professor Harrell has been featured by Business Week as one of the top American educators in leading business schools. He has received The John D. and Dortha J. Withrow Teacher-Scholar Award which is presented to members of the business school faculty who have achieved the highest level of distinction for service to Michigan State University through excellence in teaching and scholarship; the Phi Chi Theta Professor of the Year Award; and the Golden Key National Honor Society Teaching Excellence Award as the top teacher at Michigan State University. He has taught over 50,000 students in the undergraduate, MBA, Executive MBA and Ph.D. programs at MSU. Professor Harrell is a highly respected consultant with business clients from around the world.

Professor Harrell earned his Ph.D. at The Pennsylvania State University, where he was elected to the Phi Kappa Phi Honorary and the American Marketing Association Consortium. He earned his bachelor's and master's degrees at Michigan State University. He lives with his wife, Susanna, near the campus of Michigan State University. They are frequent travelers on Study Abroad missions and enjoy all aspects of college life.

PREFACE

Introduction

Marketing has a huge influence on how well our economy serves its many constituents. Whether the constituent is a business, consumer, or government, marketers connect with these customers billions of times each day to form our global market-based economy. Customers receive goods and services that contribute to more vibrant lives; in exchange marketers generate profits necessary to build amazing businesses. With lasting, loyal connections, outstanding value is created—a win-win for all involved. In a nutshell, the theme of this book, "Connecting with Customers," is about how these connections are made and what value is generated.

The exchange of value at the core of marketing connections is an incredibly complex process! The American Marketing Association, the largest association of marketing professionals, divides the field into 17 special interest groups (SIGs), including consumer marketing, entrepreneurial marketing, global marketing, innovation, technology, societal marketing, marketing communications, marketing research, marketing strategy, relationship marketing, retailing, pricing, selling and sales management, services marketing, sports and sponsorship marketing and other subjects. In turn, each SIG delves deeply into the subject to explore and comprehend its multifaceted interconnections with the whole of marketing. This text is designed to provide the reader with a basic comprehension of the most up-to-date concepts and ideas that excellent organizations use to make fundamentally sound marketing decisions in many of these arenas.

As consumers we all experience a vast amount of marketing. We are immersed in it where we live, work and play! It is safe to say that marketing activities directly or indirectly involve the bulk of the American and world economy. While marketing might appear to be dominated by social media, advertising, promotion and selling, much of it is also about less apparent aspects such as business strategy, marketing research, forecasting, product innovation, technology and pricing. As students dig more deeply into the field, most become fascinated by marketing's incredible importance to businesses of all types. And many students visualize the huge number of exciting career opportunities at the heart of our market-based economy.

All business functions undergo change, but marketing operates at warp speed. In fact, a great brand like Starbucks or Amazon grows, evolves and endures because outstanding marketing dominates the thinking of executives, managers and employees who understand that sustainable competitive advantage comes from being innovative, fresh and ground breaking. So many of the marketing concepts we will explore in this text describe ways to make really innovative decisions that lead to lasting connections with customers.

The world of contemporary marketing changes very rapidly! The overarching goal of this text is engage you, the reader, with compelling, relevant and pragmatic content that represents the best current marketing ideals and practices. This new edition of Marketing; Connecting with Customers has been updated with over 3,000 new examples, statistics, quotations and concepts—nearly all from 2016 sources. This is particularly impressive because the book underwent a similar revision only two years ago.

Acknowledgements

I especially want to thank Troy Miller, Executive Director, Chicago Education Press, and Karen Sadler, Executive Editor, for their remarkable work on this edition. I am deeply indebted to Karen for many outstanding contributions. She carefully and creatively researched sources, seamlessly integrated examples and skillfully edited the entire text to craft a comprehensive, engaging work that students will enjoy. I am also indebted to Troy for his impressive contributions that include designing a new, exciting visual appearance using vivid graphics, illustrations, notations and pictures. He developed the perfect visual content to complement exciting ideas and concepts. Troy also managed the process to insure that all parts of the project came together on a very aggressive schedule. Karen and Troy insured that the text sets the standard for being up-to-date with a lively presentation, yet sophisticated readability. John Wilson, Business Director, Chicago Education Press, has my appreciation for his excellent project support, timely oversight and management.

Also my thanks to Roger Calantone for his ongoing enthusiasm of this text, which is used by many of our MSU students. I also want to recognize colleagues at Michigan State University for being part of a stimulating, enjoyable environment, including: Forest Carter, Dave Closs, Bix Cooper, David Frayer, Rick Simonds, Doug Hughes, Tomas Hult, Rich Spreng, Ahmet Kirca, Glen Omura, Dale Wilson, Tom Page, Clay Voorhees, Brenda Sternquist, Hang Nguyen, Irina Kozlenkova, Ayalia Ruvio, Stephanie Mangus, Michael Brereton, and Keith Ferguson to name a few. Also, many executives in the business world have provided important dialog, including Neil Ferranti, Bruce Leech, Pete Pendergast, Dan Wolf, Jake Lestan, Dan Ahearn, Jenn Johnson, Pete Macking, Stephanie Kalil, Kevin Hamilton, Marco Ten Bruggencate, Lynn Wallace and others. I also want to recognize previous Eli Broad School of Business Dean, Stefanie Lenway, for supporting MSU student use of an earlier edition featuring IBM Watson content. Additionally, I thank Gary Frazier for contributions to an earlier edition, although due to prior commitments he was unable to participate in this edition.

Faculty from over 50 different universities contributed in-depth reviews of earlier editions. Many of their excellent suggestions have been incorporated into this edition:

David Andrus	*Kansas State University*
Bob Balderstone	*Western Melbourne Institute of TAFE (Australia)*
Richard Brand	*Florida State University*
Jim Brock	*Susquehanna University*
Bruce Buskirk	*Pepperdine University*
William Carner	*University of Texas at Austin*
George Chrysschoidis	*University of Wales*
Howard Combs	*San Jose University*
John Cronin	*Western Connecticut State University*
Bernard Delagneau	*University of Wales*
Peter Doukas	*Westchester Community College*
Jim Dupree	*Grove City College*
John Durham	*San Francisco State University*
William Flatley	*Principia College*
James S. Gould	*Pace University*
Joyce Grahn	*University of Minnesota at Duluth*
Robert F. Guinner	*Arizona State University*

Pola Gupta	*University of Northern Iowa*
Lynn Harris	*Shippensburg University*
Benoit Heilbrunn	*Le Groupe ESC Lyon/Lyon Graduate School of Business (France)*
George Kelley	*Erie Community College*
Stephen Koernig	*California State University at Fullerton*
Rex Kovacevich	*University of Southern California*
Frank Krohn	*SUNY Fredonia*
Felicia G. Lassk	*Western Kentucky University*
Ken Lawrence	*New Jersey Institute of Technology*
Chong S. K. Lee	*California State University at Hayward*
Marilyn Liebrenz-Himes	*George Washington University*
Elizabeth Mariotz	*Philadelphia College of Textiles and Science*
Mike Mayo	*Kent State University*
Gary McCain	*Boise State University*
G. Stephen Miller	*St. Louis University*
Herbert Miller	*University of Texas at Austin*
Mark Mitchell	*University of South Carolina*
David Mothersbaugh	*University of Alabama*
Robert O'Keefe	*DePaul University*
Cliff Olson	*Southern State College of SDA*
Stan Paliwoda	*University of Calgary*
Eric Pratt	*New Mexico State University*
Abe Qastin	*Lakeland College*
Zahir Quaraeshi	*Western Michigan University*
Mohammed Rawwas	*University of Northern Iowa*
Deborah Reed Scarfino	*William Jewell College*
A.J. Taylor	*Austin Peay State University*
David Urban	*Virginia Commonwealth University*
Anthony Urbaniak	*Northern State University*
Simon Walls	*Western Washington University*
Mike Welker	*Franciscan University*
Ken Williamson	*James Madison University*
Mark Young	*Winona State University*
George Zinkham	*University of Houston*

Special gratitude is expressed to Peter D. Bennett, my valued mentor, who contributed greatly to my enthusiasm for marketing. He passed away on January 4, 2016 in State College, Pennsylvania. Peter retired in 1997 after a distinguished career at The Pennsylvania State University. In addition to being a positive force in the American Marketing Association, he was an outstanding Chairman of the Marketing Department, Senior Associate Dean of the Smeal College of Business and President of the Penn State Senate. Peter was a terrific teacher who believed in the philosophy that learning should always be fun; his students were fortunate beneficiaries.

Finally, I want to take this opportunity to thank my wife, Susie, and our family for the joy they bring to life everyday!

Gil Harrell
East Lansing, Michigan

CHAPTER *01*

Marketing:
Creating & Capturing
Value

STARBUCKS®

When you walk into a Starbucks, you're not just walking into a coffee shop...you're walking into the "Starbucks Experience." You know you'll get great coffee drinks in comfortable surroundings, served by enthusiastic partners (employees), produced by a tech-saavy company that cares about our world. Since 1971 when Starbucks opened its first coffee shop in Seattle, it has transformed the concept of a coffee house into an international fixture. How did this happen?

Simply put, Starbucks knows how to embrace and connect with its customers, its community and its environment. Consumers continue to respond with overwhelming loyalty through repeat business; today the company has more than 24,000 stores in 70 countries, annual revenue of over $19 billion, and is ranked number six on Fortune's 2016 list of Most Admired Companies.

A great part of the company's success can be attributed to its effectiveness, efficiency and agility; Starbucks is constantly making changes to be relevant to its markets and customers. For example, young adults, aged 18 to 24, account for approximately 40 percent of Starbucks' sales. Starbucks positions itself as a place college students can meet friends, hang out, study, and write papers. Starbucks appeals to this consumer directly through current technology, focusing on social networking and actively cultivating a "cool" image.

Busy, professional urbanites, aged 25 to 40, account for another 49 percent of sales. Status symbols, such as Starbucks, are important to these consumers. For this market, Starbucks positions itself as a modern, customer-oriented, community-involved, and environmentally-friendly company. Many locations now offer an "after work" evening menu, featuring craft beer, wine, and small plates, such as Truffle Mac & Cheese. So how does Starbucks connect with all these customers?

A large part of the answer lies in three words: global digital marketing. Starbucks has an online community in social media platforms such as Twitter, (11.7 million followers) Facebook (over 36 million "likes") , Instagram (8.9 million followers), LinkedIn (690,000 followers), Pinterest (251,400 followers), and YouTube (over 30 million views). In April 2016, the new Starbucks Emoji keyboard app was introduced for

SCAN & WATCH

Starbucks has perfected the concept of connecting with customers.

communication among texting fans. Customers can also engage with the company and fellow customers at the popular www.mystarbucksidea.com or @MyStarbucksidea to submit ideas for offering new products, improving the customer experience and expanding community involvement And, of course, Wi-Fi with the Starbucks Digital Network is always free in company stores.

Starbucks is continually innovating to keep its position as the world's leading coffee cafe. On the Starbucks mobile app, customers can order and pay for a drink, including a tip for the barista, then walk into a store minutes later and pick up their beverages. Want Starbucks brought to your office? If you work in the Empire State Building, Starbucks Green Apron Delivery is on it! Within 30 minutes of ordering and paying on line, you'll be holding your coffee. Delivery is also available through Starbucks' partnership with Postmates in major U.S. cities.

Understanding customers and creating value for them is how Starbucks continues to thrive while accomplishing its mission to "inspire and nurture the human spirit – one person, one cup, and one neighborhood at a time."

Sources: www.academia.edu/3836383, website visited May 4, 2016; www.marketwatch.com/investing/stock/SBUX/financials, website visited May 4, 2016; www.fortune.com/worlds-most-admired-companies, website visited May 4, 2016; www.investopedia.com/articles/markets/092915/why-starbucks-expanding-its-evening-menu.asp, website visited May 4, 2016; www.news.starbucks.com/news/starbucks-green-apron-delivery-empire-state-building, Oct 15, 2015, website visited May 4, 2016; www.starbucks.com, website visited May 3, 2016; www.sloanreview.mit.edu/article/how-starbucks-has-gone-digital, website visited May 4, 2016; www.wsj.com/articles/starbucks-sheds-light-on-delivery-service-plans-1426705107, March 18, 2015.

LO 01 Understand the concept of marketing, including its definition, purpose and role in creating exchanges.

LO 02 Contrast the periods of marketing evolution from its early history through the five marketing eras.

LO 03 Explain the marketing strategy process, including the Four P elements that create the marketing mix.

LO 04 Understand the six key forces that influence how organizations create and capture value.

LO 05 Realize how marketing affects you.

The Concept of Marketing

Successful companies set themselves apart from others by doing an exceptional job of creating and capturing value for customers. They are extraordinary marketers. They understand the marketing concept, use a full range of marketing tools and techniques, and help customers experience the satisfaction that occurs when products match their needs and wants. Every time satisfaction occurs, value is created. Value instills customer loyalty and lasting relationships. This is what marketing is all about!

Today's business environment is global, diverse and ethically challenging. It is based on serving customers in ways unimaginable just a short time ago. Marketing is about much more than just selling a product; it is about providing value to customers in ways that are deeply rewarding for them. Marketing is also about serving the needs of society and accomplishing the goals of the organization. It includes researching potential customers' needs and wants; understanding competitors' strategies; developing appropriate goods and services; communicating with the market; creating, selecting and managing channels to reach customers; and pricing to deliver superior customer value. It is about satisfying customers so they will reward the business with loyalty necessary to reach organizational objectives.

For example, Starbucks has become a fixture in your world at home and abroad. Why? Because the company excels at marketing and connecting with customers. It has created exceptional brand loyalty; it's ethically and socially responsible, focusing on community and sustainability; it understands and accommodates diversity, and its employees—from the CEO to the baristas—share a single goal: create value. Organizations like Starbucks know you have plenty of choices, so they practice marketing at its highest level to win your business.

This chapter introduces marketing concepts. As it presents ideas, it references chapters that discuss those ideas in more detail, providing a brief overview of the book. It begins by defining marketing and discussing its purpose, including how marketing creates and facilitates economic exchanges, followed by a discussion of how marketing has evolved. Then a section on the marketing strategy process introduces the basic elements used to build a marketing plan. Next are descriptions of six factors that are major influences on the practice of marketing. Finally, the chapter ends with a note about how marketing affects you on a daily basis, and the possibility of making it a career.

LO 01

What is Marketing?

What do you think of when you hear the word "marketing?" Is your impression positive or negative? Most people have been exposed to advertising, point-of-purchase displays and personal selling, so marketing is often considered to be the promotion and sale of existing products. However, excellent marketing is much more extensive, beginning long before a product exists. This allows all marketing decisions, including promotion, to be made with customer needs and wants in mind. Marketing extends far beyond a purchase to ensure customer satisfaction and loyalty. You can gain a good idea about the extent of marketing by understanding each element in its definition.

The American Marketing Association (AMA) defines **marketing** as the activity, set of institutions and processes for creating, communicating, delivering and exchanging offerings that have value for customers, clients, partners and society at large.[1] As an introduction to marketing, the first part of this chapter discusses the definition in depth.

MARKETING

The activity, set of institutions, and processes for creating, communicating, delivering, and exchanging offerings that have value for customers, clients, partners, and society at large.

> Marketing is the activity, set of institutions and processes for creating, communicating, delivering and exchanging offerings that have value for customers, clients, partners and society at large.

THE ACTIVITY

Marketing activity focuses on understanding the needs and wants of customers and engaging in competitive behavior to satisfy those needs and wants. Organizations that do this well tend to grow and prosper. The quest to understand and satisfy customers provides the basis for a competitive system that dramatically benefits society. Because needs and wants are numerous, diverse and dynamic, there are unlimited opportunities for marketing.

CUSTOMER ORIENTATION

An organizational philosophy that focuses on satisfying consumer needs and wants.

NEED

A fundamental requirement, the meeting of which is the ultimate goal of behavior.

Understand the Needs and Wants of Customers Understanding customer needs and wants is central to marketing activities; it creates the foundation on which value is created and lasting relationships are built. Knowing that, today's successful marketers embrace an organizational philosophy called **customer orientation**, which focuses on satisfying customer needs and wants.

Needs and wants are not the same. A **need** is a fundamental requirement and meeting it is the ultimate goal of behavior. Of course, there are many needs, from those that allow survival to those that produce personal enrichment. A need becomes apparent when there is a gap between a desired

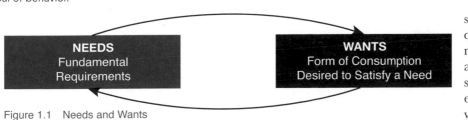

Figure 1.1   Needs and Wants

state and an actual state. For example, you need proper nutrition on a regular basis to have a healthy and energetic body. When nutrition drops below a desired state, your body signals the deprivation and you feel hungry. When the need is satisfied, the hunger goes away. Needs represent what people and organizations must have to survive and thrive. The degree to which needs are satisfied determines the quality of life for all people and organizations.

A **want** is the specific form of consumption desired to satisfy a need. Therefore, a want is simply one of many desires a person may have to help fulfill a particular need. For instance, hunger can be satisfied with a candy bar, an orange or a chicken sandwich. Taken a step farther, a consumer may want a Snickers® bar or a Sunkist® orange or a McChicken® sandwich.

Like people, organizations have objectives that must be met. Companies operating to make a profit must earn a sizable return on the owners' investment or they will go out of business. Nonprofit companies have other needs; The Red Cross, for example, must help increasing numbers of disaster victims to meet its organizational objectives. Every organization needs customers or clients—the people they serve. There are many ways to obtain them, as well as specific types of suppliers, employee characteristics and profit objectives. The aerospace company, Boeing, addresses the need of United Airlines for aircraft by designing planes the airline will want with attributes that satisfy United's *needs*. Figure 1.1 shows the relationship between needs and wants.

Potential customers try to satisfy wants in ways that produce the greatest amount of need satisfaction. This makes wants dynamic. Marketing leaders facilitate and adjust to change rapidly by learning how to serve customers in new and creative ways. Marketers that learn how to best serve customers can gain tremendous competitive advantages.

Competitive Behavior Unless a company is a monopoly, it has market competition. Strong marketers work hard to compete, and they measure success by the way their customers judge them, especially relative to competitors. Competition is the key to our economic system. You see aggressive global competition occurring every day: Coke vs. Pepsi, McDonald's vs. Burger King, Samsung vs. Apple, Duracell vs. Energizer, and Crest vs. Colgate are just a few examples.

Perhaps you've recently seen Verizon's "A Better Network as Explained by Colorful Balls" ad campaign. Individual colors represent Verizon and direct competitors: AT&T, Sprint and T-Mobile. The balls run down a course with each one representing a first place finish in a Rootmetrics 2015 U.S. wireless network report.[2] The campaign immediately sparked rebuttal ads from T-Mobile and Sprint, claiming Verizon's ad was misleading.

Verizon Wireless

You Tube SCAN & WATCH ▶

Verizon Wireless "A Better Network as Explained By Colorful Balls."

Sometimes companies will use a person with whom its target market identifies to competitively market a product. For example, Villanova Head Basketball Coach Jay Wright is known for being a good decision maker, so Unilever's Dove Soap created a commercial for its Men+Care Clean Comfort to directly compete with market leader Old Spice High Endurance Pure Sport. The ad shows a Dove representative interviewing Coach Wright. When asked if he would choose Old Spice soap that "cleans," or Dove soap that "cleans and protects against dryness," Wright, without hesitation, chooses Dove.[3]

Even nonprofit groups compete. Mail-order catalogs from the Art Institute of Chicago, the Smithsonian Institution and Boston's Museum of Fine Arts all vie for your purchases. The United Way, the American Cancer Society, and the Humane Society compete for your discretionary income, and political parties compete for your donations. This competition makes nonprofit marketing more important than ever. Like businesses for profit, nonprofit businesses win customers by being more effective, efficient and agile.

EFFECTIVENESS

An organizational philosophy that focuses on satisfying consumer needs and wants.

EFFICIENCY

The ability of an organization to execute activities with minimal waste of time and money.

AGILITY

The flexibility and speed with which organizations can identify or create new wants and take action to satisfy them.

Effectiveness occurs when the organization's activities produce results that matter to consumers. **Efficiency** means operating with minimal waste of time and money. Baxter International, a hospital products company with more than $16 billion in annual sales, is successful on both counts.[4] First, it recognized that its customers, hospitals, were spending too much money storing and distributing supplies. Baxter developed an electronic ordering system to indicate which supplies a particular hospital requires on a daily basis and where in the hospital the supplies should go. This system is effective because it meets the wants of Baxter's customers better than the competition. It is efficient because it saves both the hospitals and Baxter substantial amounts of money and time. In many cases, hospitals choose Baxter as their only supplier, which leads to higher sales and profits for Baxter.

Agility is the anticipation of market dynamics and speed of response to changing customer desires and competitors' actions. Organizations that possess agility continually sense and explore marketplace opportunities. McDonald's prides itself on its ability to evolve; one of the company's core values states, "We are a learning organization that aims to anticipate and respond to changing customer, employee, and system needs through constant evolution and innovation."[5]

SET OF INSTITUTIONS

MARKET

All the individuals and organizations with potential desire and ability to acquire a particular good or service.

BUSINESS-TO-CONSUMER (B2C) MARKETING

When organizations sell to individuals or households that buy, consume, and dispose of products.

BUSINESS-TO-BUSINESS (B2B) MARKETING

When a business purchases goods or services to produce other goods, to support daily operations, or to resell at a profit.

The most basic set of marketing institutions is comprised of a market with buyers and sellers who want to exchange value. A **market** consists of all the organizations and individuals with potential desire and ability to acquire value—that is, to own a particular idea, good or service. Generally, we talk about marketing products, which are usually goods that are manufactured or services that are performed. Marketing can also be applied to any idea that can be used in an exchange of value. These include, for example, marketing events, causes, people, and places. Ideas, goods and services are exchanged in business-to-consumer markets, business-to-business markets, nonprofit markets and internal markets.

Business-to-consumer (B2C) marketing occurs when organizations sell to individuals or households that buy, consume and dispose of products. Leading consumer marketers include such companies as Procter & Gamble, Johnson & Johnson, General Mills, Hewlett-Packard, and Nike.

You know the products of these companies very well. You have probably already purchased or used many of them and will continue to do so over the years. Because you buy, consume and dispose of products such as these daily, you are an important part of consumer marketing. Consumer marketing is often referred to as B2C, business-to-consumer, because businesses like Nike market to consumers like you. We will learn more about consumer marketing throughout this book.

Business-to-business (B2B) marketing occurs when a business purchases goods or services to produce other goods, to support daily operations, or to resell at a profit. Although there are many more consumers than companies, business-to-business purchases far outweigh the consumer market in dollar amount.

Organizations belong to either the public or private sector. The public sector consists of federal, state and local government organizations. The private sector includes industrial firms, professionals, retailers and service organizations. Utility companies, which provide water, electricity, gas and waste disposal, fall between the public and private sectors because they are regulated by the government but may be privately owned. Most of these organizations rely on business-to-business marketing to sell and purchase goods or services.

For example, Dell uses LinkedIn groups to give its B2B marketing campaign an advantage over competitors. Using this social media platform with more than 430 million members, Dell has successfully linked over 10,000 professionals in the fields of IT, Engineering and Consulting. Seventy percent of the LinkedIn group members are top management, corporate executives, and business owners. This gives Dell direct access to the key decision makers of its target market, and the exposure will likely influence purchasing decisions of group member companies. Additionally, Dell gains a network of professionals related to its core business that can improve its operations and buying decisions.[6] In Chapter 6, we will explore many of the topics involved in business-to-business marketing.

NONPROFIT MARKETING

When an organization does not try to make a profit but instead attempts to influence others to support its cause by using its service or by making a contribution.

Nonprofit marketing occurs when an organization does not try to make a profit but instead attempts to influence others to support its cause by using its service or by making a contribution. It is generally used to benefit a particular segment of society. Marketing has many applications in the not-for-profit sector. Churches, museums, hospitals, universities, symphonies and municipalities regularly create marketing plans in an effort to be more consumer-oriented. Do-Something.org is a nonprofit organization running a number of different campaigns to "make the world suck less." With 5.3 million members in 130 countries, it is one of the world's largest nonprofit organizations for youth and social change. Recent campaigns were successful in cleaning up 3.7 million cigarette butts, getting Merriam-Webster to change its racist definition of "nude," convincing Apple to include non-white emoji options, and donating five million pairs of jeans to homeless youth. The nonprofit's promise "Any cause, anytime, anywhere" resonates with young adults and inspires them to take a grassroots approach to issues impacting everyday life. DoSomething.org connects with its members through a free mobile app, feeding current news and campaigns to the palm of the hand. It is then up to its members to turn the news into action, and share with the world how they are helping to make it a better place.[7]

DoSomething.org is a non-profit organization connecting with millions of members around the world.

Like businesses that seek profit, nonprofit organizations want to please their constituents, and they have competition. Although they may not be motivated by profit, many are interested in obtaining revenues that equal or exceed expenses, requiring a full range of marketing knowledge. Chapter 10 discusses nonprofit marketing in greater detail.

INTERNAL MARKETING

When managers of one functional unit market their capabilities to other units within their own organization.

Internal marketing occurs when managers of one functional unit market their capabilities to other units within their own organization to provide customer satisfaction. This type of marketing addresses the needs and wants of internal customers, the employees of the firm, so they can ultimately contribute to external customers who are the end users of a company's products or services. For example, Dr. Lew Dotterer, Director of Learning and Organizational Development at Sparrow Health System in Lansing, Michigan, is responsible for maintaining the knowledge and skills of employees in all units of the system. Applying marketing techniques, he first identified the key customers: doctors, nurses, administrators and so forth. Next, he researched each group to determine its learning needs. He then created educational programs to address the specific needs of each group and promoted these programs throughout the organization. Through internal marketing, one functional unit was able to help employees in other units to better serve Sparrow's external customers (patients).

PROCESSES

Marketing is composed of many ongoing processes which are used to manage complex, changing phenomena. New competitors enter the market, customers change, and the economic climate shifts. What works today may be a blunder tomorrow. Consequently, those who practice marketing need to take a long-term view of events. They must focus on the enduring, systematic management of change, rather than a single transaction. Marketers look for patterns, trends and surprises that signal what is likely to happen in the future, while still being responsive to current circumstances. In fact, marketing has its greatest value when it helps to guide organizations in highly dynamic environments

> Marketers look for patterns, trends and surprises that signal what is likely to happen in the future.

Marketing involves the process of planning and providing a guidance system for companies. Planning sets direction before action takes place; it addresses what is to be accomplished and how to accomplish it. Competitors force each other to make strategic marketing plans, to innovate, and to ultimately develop ways to better satisfy customer needs and wants. Later we will see that plans are created for a whole organization as well as for select products.

Marketing is also responsible for processes involved in executing or carrying out the plan. Marketing manages people and events in line with the plan, which serves as a guide. To carry out plans, marketing must acquire and develop many of the organization's human resources. It may be necessary to draw not only from the marketing department, but also from other functions within the company, such as sales, finance and engineering.

For firms to stay on the leading edge, they must focus on market-oriented product development processes and innovation. Consider how Apple used a marketing process for the introduction of the iPhone, which was the first to introduce an integrated mobile phone, MP3 player, camera, and internet connectivity in one device for state-of-the-art media communication. Through marketing processes, the company has continued to introduce enhanced products based on customer wants. The iPhone 6 Plus model uses a dual-core A8 chip for faster graphics with improved browsing and gaming experiences. Its upgraded retina display is now 5.5 inches, and its 8MP iSight camera has sensors to automatically adjust pictures and shoot videos in HD with the option of time lapse. It also was the first to introduce 3D touch, which revolutionized the way people interact with a one-dimensional surface. The iPhone 7 with an iOS 10 is expected to have even more enhanced features with a new design. Apple's agility to respond to market demand through innovation continues to create strong customer loyalty.

As you can imagine, successful execution of any marketing process requires the involvement and cooperation of many people and functions from within an organization. Consequently, marketing usually means working in groups rather than working alone.

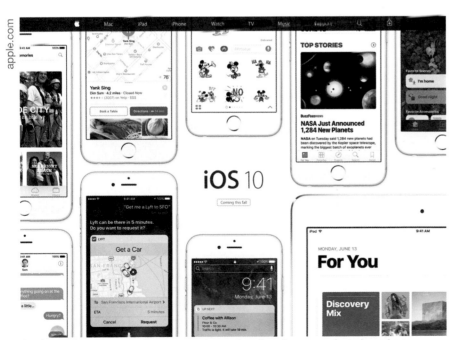

Apple employs the marketing process to continually enhance products based on customer wants.

Effective marketers are energetic, determined, creative managers who can focus on market-oriented, product development processes and innovation.

CREATING, COMMUNICATING & DELIVERING

Harvard Professor James Culliton in 1948 described the business executive as a "decider," an "artist," and a "mixer of ingredients" who sometimes follows a recipe as he or she goes along, sometimes adapts a recipe to the ingredients immediately available, and sometimes experiments with ingredients no one else has tried. This description gave Neil Borden, another noted Harvard marketing professor, the idea that there is a list of elements the marketer mixes together. He called these elements the **marketing mix.**[8] In 1960, Michigan State University Professor E. Jerome McCarthy, another pivotal figure in the development of marketing thinking, grouped these elements into four categories that are today known as "the four Ps" of marketing: product, price, promotion and place.

The four Ps are classification titles for a lot of what happens in marketing. For example, product development, branding, packaging and service are included in the product area. Sales, leasing and credit terms are part of pricing. Advertising, personal selling, and social media are included in promotion. Distribution, logistics, retailing and direct marketing are part of place.

Each of the four Ps will be discussed in detail later in the book. What's important to remember is that they are part of the marketing mix that marketers develop for a product or service. Each element can be controlled, or altered, as necessary. Perhaps as a marketing manager you decide the price of your product is too high and you're losing sales to a new, competitive product. As part of the marketing team, you can change the price of your product, or bundle (package) it with accessories. Maybe you create a new advertising campaign on social media. It's through this mixing process that marketers arrive at the right recipe to create, communicate and deliver value to customers.

MARKETING MIX

The four controllable variables (product, price, promotion and place) that are combined to appeal to a company's target markets.

MARKETING MIX
4Ps
OF MARKETING

01	PRODUCT
02	PRICE
03	PROMOTION
04	PLACE

EXCHANGES CREATE VALUE

Value occurs for customers and for the organization only when an exchange occurs. An **exchange** is a process in which two or more parties provide something of value to one another. At the most basic level, an exchange generally involves a seller who provides a good or service to a buyer for money or some other item. Most exchanges are much more complex than that, involving several parties in a social system exchanging all kinds of items.[9]

Relationship marketing is the development and maintenance of successful relational exchanges. It involves interactive, ongoing, two-way connections among customers, organizations, suppliers and other parties for mutual benefit. For example, Unilever Group's Dove Hair conducted a survey which revealed that only 10 percent of women respondents said they "feel proud" of their naturally curly hair. It also found that only four in ten girls with curly hair think their hair is beautiful. Dove, in an effort to help women inspire future generations to love their curls, launched the #LoveYourCurls campaign. As a part of the campaign, Dove created a powerful video that shows women and girls how to celebrate their curly hair. The video quickly went viral and within a few months it was shared and viewed by more than ten million people.[10]

Emotion is a key ingredient in relationships, so in addition to providing logical reasons for buyers to prefer particular brands, marketers involve customers by being

EXCHANGE

The process in which two or more parties provide something of value to one another.

RELATIONSHIP MARKETING

The development and maintenance of successful relational exchanges through interactive, ongoing, two-way connections among customers, organizations, suppliers, and other parties for mutual benefit.

trustworthy, supportive and a part of their lives. Coca-Cola Worldwide President of Marketing, Mary Minnick, captured this idea: "Historically, we thought 'enjoyment' was great taste. But it's a very complex 'need' state. We don't just want to entertain customers, we want Coke (brands) to be more relevant, an integral part of consumers' everyday lives. We want to build a relationship with consumers, not hold a mirror up to them."[11] Relationship marketing builds customer loyalty, a critical goal that dramatically improves business performance.

Marketers need to be sensitive to the fact that not all customers are looking for strong relationships in all exchanges. However, there is a clear trend showing that, in recent years, marketing has evolved from transaction-based exchanges toward relationship-based exchanges. The change goes far beyond the interaction of an organization with its customers; suppliers and other parties also play roles. The relationships range from informal to contractual or even ownership. On the informal level, incentives make it difficult or inconvenient for customers to switch to a new organization. For example, Land Rover has a club for customers that publishes a newsletter and sends invitations to off-road rallies. Service managers routinely call customers to see how their Land Rover Discovery is performing.[12]

Marketing brings the many parties together and facilitates exchanges. This provides utility, which in turn creates value. Utility is a term economists use to describe the want-satisfying potential of a good or service. There are four fundamental types of utility: form, place, time and ownership.

Form utility occurs when knowledge and materials are converted into finished goods and services. Marketing provides form utility when it guides decisions about what products to create. When McDonald's created grilled chicken salads with low-fat salad dressing as alternatives for health-conscious consumers, the company provided form utility. Beech-Nut, the nation's third-largest baby-food manufacturer, has just launched 40 new products that have no additives or preservatives. Its independent research revealed that 70 percent of parents make some of their baby food at home because they believe the supermarket products are overprocessed, contain too many additives, or are unhealthy for their baby.[13] Generally, the marketing function is responsible for specifying what form utility the final product should possess, and it works closely with research and development (R&D), engineering, manufacturing and other units.

Place utility makes goods and services conveniently available. Fresh bananas on a remote tree are not nearly as want-satisfying as those at a local supermarket, convenience store or restaurant. Their accessibility makes them worth much more at those locations than where they are grown. Marketing brings products to customers for the sake of convenience. When FedEx delivers more than ten million shipments a day to more than 220 countries and territories at a guaranteed time, it is providing place utility.[14]

Time utility makes goods and services available when they are wanted. Netflix is very popular because it allows subscribers to watch shows and movies at their convenience. This consumer versatility enables Netflix to connect with customers worldwide. The company currently has over 81.5 million members, 42 percent of whom are outside of the United States.[15]

Amazon Prime also offers outstanding time utility. Prime members get free two-day shipping with all Prime orders and free same-day in select areas. A future drone delivery system from Amazon, PrimeAir, promises to have your package safely delivered to your front door in 30 minutes or less.[16]

Ownership utility makes it possible to transfer the title of goods and services from one party to another. The most obvious way is through cash trans-

FORM UTILITY

A want-satisfying value that is created when knowledge and materials are converted into finished goods and services.

PLACE UTILITY

A want-satisfying value that is created by making goods and services conveniently available.

TIME UTILITY

A want-satisfying value that is created when goods and services are made available when they are wanted.

OWNERSHIP UTILITY

A want-satisfying value that is created by making it possible to transfer the title of goods and services from one party to another.

Courtesy of Amazon

Amazon PrimeAir, a concept awaiting regulatory clearance, promises package delivery in 30 minutes or less.

actions, but credit card purchases and leasing are other means. Later we will learn how this functions on an international scale. Even airplane travel is a form of ownership utility. By leasing a seat (buying a ticket), you can possess the vast resources of the air transportation system during the time it takes to reach nearly any destination on the planet. Marketing has progressed by finding better ways to produce increasing amounts of utility.

CUSTOMERS, CLIENTS, PARTNERS & SOCIETY

Customers and Clients **Customer value** refers to what consumers perceive they gain from owning or using a product when weighed against the cost of acquiring it. We explore customer value in Chapter 6. **Satisfaction** refers to the consumer's overall rating of his or her experience with a company and its products. **Loyalty** is a measure of how often, when selecting from a product class, a customer purchases a particular brand. In combination, satisfaction and customer value help create customer loyalty. Satisfaction and loyalty are more fully explored in Chapter 7. Loyal customers provide a continuous revenue stream through repeated purchases of a brand. They also provide word-of-mouth of their satisfaction, which is one of the most effective and inexpensive forms of promotion.

For example, to increase customer satisfaction, Xerox's Total Satisfaction Guarantee allows unsatisfied customers to return any equipment and Xerox will replace it without charge.[17] Hampton Hotels led the industry when it became the first national hotel brand to offer guests an unconditional 100-percent satisfaction guarantee. "It's a philosophy we continue to live by today. Our guarantee...Friendly service, clean rooms, comfortable surroundings every time. If you're not satisfied, we don't expect you to pay. That's our commitment and your guarantee. That's 100% Hampton."[18]

A level of satisfaction strong enough to create product loyalty requires an organizational commitment to customer value in every aspect of the business.

© Hampton Hotels

Hampton's satisfaction commitment -- The 100% Hampton Guarantee.

Partners (Organization and its Stakeholders)
All organizations have objectives. Many focus on financial measures such as profit margins and return on investment to evaluate performance. In order to stay in business, companies must make money when they fulfill consumer needs. Profit provides the financial fuel that allows companies to innovate and grow. Nonprofit organizations, in contrast, use measures such as donation levels, membership and services provided to evaluate performance.

Although nonprofit organizations must be effective and efficient, by definition they do not seek profit as a primary goal. Still, they strive to satisfy their constituents in a cost-effective way. For example, the national organizations for Boy Scouts and Girl Scouts have rigorous financial goals. They often strive for growth in sales and in number of members, as well as certain levels of customer satisfaction relative to competitors.

Both private and public companies work to increase the value of the organization to its stakeholders. Stakeholders of an organization include employees, customers, suppliers, and shareholders. The single most important role of the marketing effort is to increase stakeholder value by establishing and implementing an effective marketing strategy. This can be accomplished in many ways. For example, it can involve focusing on a new set of customers, expanding the organization's base, or focusing on the types of customers that the company has targeted in the past, relying on loyalty and its established reputation.

Increasing the value of the organization can also be achieved by introducing an entirely new product. For example, Smith Klein Beecham created a vaccine for Lyme disease in an attempt to limit new cases of the disease. The organization was able to increase the value to all stakeholders: its employees, its customers, its suppliers and its stockholders. Creating value for the organization and its stakeholders is an important part of marketing.

Society Marketing offers great value to society. It stimulates demand, promotes innovation, and improves life by providing an array of goods and services that benefit every citizen. The marketing industry has also provided a significant percentage of the population with employment. When marketing decisions contribute to the profit of firms, they fuel economic growth. Today, leading edge companies also accomplish their objectives through the concept of sustainability.

SUSTAINABILITY

The steps and processes organizations undertake to manage growth without detrimentally affecting the resources or biological systems of the earth.

Sustainability consists of the steps and processes that organizations undertake to manage growth without detrimentally affecting the earth's resources or biological systems. It is the fundamental concept of meeting the needs of today without compromising the ability of future generations to meet their needs.[19] As consumer awareness of environmental sustainability increases, organizations have focused on marketing their sustainable initiatives. Some organizations are doing this by offering green products to consumers. Green products provide energy-saving options or inflict minimal damage on the surrounding environment. Other organizations may focus on reducing waste and emissions.

For example, S.C. Johnson & Sons, the maker of popular household cleaning products such as Windex, Pledge and Drano, implemented a sustainability process called Greenlist. Through Greenlist, the company searches for the most environmentally friendly inputs and raw materials. By reformulating Windex brand glass cleaner, S.C. Johnson & Sons cut 1.8 million pounds of volatile organic compounds (VOCs) from the product while giving it 30 percent more cleaning power.[20] Environmental sustainability is becoming more important to consumers, and therefore organizations are placing greater emphasis on it in order to connect with customers.

The Evolution of Marketing

Marketing activities, in the broadest sense, can be traced to the trading and bartering that occurred thousands of years ago. The ancient Egyptians had vending machines as early as 200 B.C.! But it wasn't until the 1500s in England and the 1600s in Germany and North America that modern marketing began. Most people lived in rural areas and produced all necessary goods themselves. Nevertheless, enterprising business people—early marketers— discovered they could make money by providing luxury items to the upper class and more practical goods to others in the population.

Although large trading companies had existed for centuries, many merchants and craftsmen built their businesses by satisfying individual customers. People often bought their shoes from a cobbler who knew the exact dimensions of their feet, their preferred shoe style, and their ability to pay. During the late 1700s and early 1800s, major improvements in production and transportation, along with growing urbanization, fostered the development of mass marketing. **Mass marketing** is the mass production, mass distribution and mass promotion of a product to all buyers. A free-enterprise system based on competition began to develop.

MASS MARKETING

The mass production, mass distribution, and mass promotion of a product to all buyers.

Starting in the late 1800s, advertising, marketing research, improved physical distribution methods and retailing were used to help find and develop markets for mass production. Unlike the days when the consumer came into direct contact with the producer, more goods began to be purchased through an intermediary. The producer had no contact with

the end user. During the 20th and 21st centuries, the focus of marketing has evolved through five eras: the production era, the sales era, the customer era, the value era and the social media era, depicted in Figure 1.2.

1900s to 1920s	1930s to 1960s	1960s to 2000	2000 to 2010	2010 to Present
Production Era	Sales Era	Customer Era	Value Era	Social Media Era

Figure 1.2   Eras of Marketing Since 1900

THE PRODUCTION ERA

PRODUCTION ORIENTATION

Historical marketing period that emphasized new products and the efficiency of production.

During the production era, companies focused on ways to make products in mass quantities. They achieved production economies that often led to lower prices. This **production orientation** emphasized developing new products and creating them with efficiency. Businesses were primarily concerned with ways to speed physical production. Manufacturers did not address the consumer until after the goods had been made. They assumed a good product would sell itself. Salespeople were more interested in helping the manufacturer take orders than in helping the customer. Demand for these new lower-priced products was often greater than supply, which led to the growth of large manufacturing organizations.

Henry Ford's approach is a prime example of production orientation. Until Ford came along, automobiles were made one at a time in small factories. Often each car was unique. Ford standardized the design of the Model T and mass-produced it on an assembly line. This dramatically reduced costs and made cars affordable to more people. Production was company-oriented without consideration of customer preferences; every car that came off the assembly line was identical. When asked by a reporter if people could have different colored cars, Ford replied that "people can have any color they want, as long as it's black."

Ford Company / Public Domain

Ford's innovative technique of using assembly lines transformed the automobile industry and dramatically reduced costs.

THE SALES ERA

As production methods improved and more firms entered markets, competition increased. Eventually, the supply of many products outpaced demand. Since businesses had more goods than their regular customers could buy, the need for personal selling and advertising arose. The sales era focused on ways to sell more effectively. This period was spurred on by the Great Depression of the 1930s, when spending power was drastically reduced. Consumers resisted purchasing nonessential goods and services, so organizations developed sales forces and sales tactics to overcome customer resistance.

SALES ORIENTATION

Historical marketing period that emphasized that consumers must be convinced to buy.

The **sales orientation** emphasized that consumers must be convinced to buy. Consumer tastes, preferences and needs did not receive much consideration. Rather, companies tried to shape consumers' ideals to fit the attributes of the products offered.

After World War II, a vastly different economic environment emerged in the

SELLER'S MARKET

The marketing environment in which scarcity of products lets the seller control the market.

BUYER'S MARKET

The marketing environment in which an abundance of product lets the buyer control the market.

United States. The country was moving from a **seller's market**, in which scarcity of products lets the seller control the market, to a **buyer's market**, in which abundance of products lets the buyer control the market. This forced companies to begin placing emphasis on customer satisfaction.

THE CUSTOMER MARKETING ERA

In the 1960s, the customer marketing concept evolved to emphasize customer satisfaction, value and loyalty. Instead of selling whatever products they had, organizations began to determine consumer needs and wants and then coordinate processes to create products or services that would satisfy those needs and wants.

Led by the efforts of President John F. Kennedy, legislators began to be more responsive to consumer rights. Throughout the 1960s and '70s, government agencies and private consumer protection groups advanced this cause. Successful companies realized they could gain a competitive edge by treating customers fairly. They also became keenly aware that a loyal repeat buyer is more profitable than a one-time buyer (which you will learn more about in Chapter 7). Businesses began to realize that customer satisfaction was paramount.

During the '80s, foreign competition threatened U.S. companies, and strategic planning became widely accepted. The role of marketing was elevated from understanding consumer behavior to assessing customer expectations, learning about competitors' practices, and determining how to make the organization an industry leader in a continuously changing world.

In the early 1990s, business executives began building teams designed to focus an organization's resources on customer satisfaction. Even today, achieving customer satisfaction requires all departments of an organization to work together while remaining focused on the goal. The organization that can form fast, flexible, powerful teams is most capable of competing in global markets. An organization must be designed to maximize both the speed of its responsiveness to customers and its ability to work as a team.

THE VALUE MARKETING ERA

VALUE-DRIVEN ORGANIZATIONS

Organizations that implement the marketing concept by ensuring that all parts of the organization make the maximum contribution toward creating value for the customer.

A natural extension of customer marketing is value marketing. **Value-driven organizations** implement the marketing concept by ensuring that all parts of the organization make the maximum possible contribution toward creating value for the customer. They make sure that every part of the organization has a clear focus on its customers, researching their satisfaction and loyalty to the company. Value-driven organizations also make sure that all the costs they incur over the long run provide at least as much value in customer-want satisfaction.

Today, organizations want lasting relationships so that customers become loyal, repeat buyers, not just one-time purchasers. How do marketers develop such relationships to create on-going value for customers? They use processes of target marketing, positioning and development of the marketing mix. Then with value-driven marketing practices, they respond to customer needs and wants. For example, when environmental sustainability became an important public issue, many companies devoted new resources to the "go green" effort because it was important to their customer base. When all parts of an organization strive for maximum customer value, stakeholders benefit and the company thrives.

> Today, organizations want lasting relationships so customers become assets of the organization, not just one-time buyers.

THE SOCIAL MEDIA ERA

Today, technology enables marketers to connect with consumers through social media channels that didn't exist even a few years ago. Smart phones and mobile devices provide

Social media has become an integral part of businesses marketing strategies.

immediate access to the internet and apps link consumers to a specific company's site instantaneously. Apple's iWatch is one of the newest extensions of technology through which businesses and consumers can interact.

Interaction may take place in any number of social mediums: Facebook, Twitter, Instagram, YouTube, LinkedIn, Google+, and Pinterest, among others. The benefits are immense. In a recent survey of 2800 marketers, 92% said that social media is important for their business.[21]

Social media marketing usually focuses on efforts to draw attention to featured content and encourages users to share it with their social networks. If the content is successful, the message can spread from user to user at incredible rates. Typically the message resonates well with users because it comes from a known source, instead of the company or brand itself.

Social media has become a platform for organizations to increase communication, create brand awareness, elevate customer service, and move customers through the buying cycle. A study conducted by E-tailing Group shows that Facebook posts influence 31 percent of respondents' buying behaviors, while Twitter has an impact on 17 percent of customers. The report indicates that consumers use social media to get reviews about products and services.[22]

For marketers, social media is a dream come true. All of a sudden consumers can be reached in far greater numbers at substantially lower costs—sometimes at no cost—with minimal barrier to entry. In Chapter 13 we'll explore how social media has changed the landscape of marketing. Throughout the book we'll also explore how companies are changing the social media landscape with innovative ideas like Groupon, LivingSocial, and FourSquare. Resulting revenue from purchases is good, but exposing a large group of customers to a company's product or service is even more valuable. The social media era offers marketers an entirely new way of connecting with customers to create and capture value.

The Marketing Strategy Process

The marketing concept is implemented through the marketing strategy process, a series of steps an organization takes to interface with the rest of the world. Figure 1.3 illustrates the steps of the marketing strategy process: situational analysis, target marketing, positioning and marketing mix decisions. An overview of each step is included here, and detailed discussion of each step is in Chapter 2.

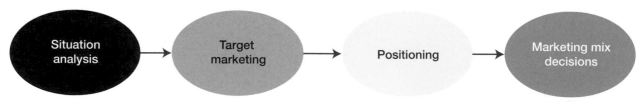

Figure 1.3   Marketing Strategy Process

Situation Analysis Situation analysis includes all the marketing activities required to understand the global marketing environment, customers' needs and wants, and competition. It provides the context around which plans are created, altered, and adjusted. It includes analysis of the marketing environment (covered in Chapter 3), an assessment of customer needs and behaviors (covered in Chapters 5, 6, and 7), and the competition. Understanding the situation requires a thorough knowledge of consumer behavior or, in business-to-business marketing, of organizational buying behavior. Understanding consumer behavior gives marketers insight into why buyers respond to goods and services as they do. As we will see in Chapter 6, consumer behavior involves more than just purchasing patterns. It also includes the ways in which consumers perceive and use information and how they arrive at feelings of satisfaction and dissatisfaction. Organizational buying behavior is more complex in terms of the functions and personnel involved in the buying decision, and marketer relationships with these buyers are often more direct. Chapter 6 covers organizational buying in the context of business-to-business marketing. An important function of the situation analysis is to provide information that helps marketers decide where to focus, or *target*, marketing efforts.

Target Marketing Most markets have a wide range of customers, and attempting to satisfy all of their needs and wants isn't feasible. Consequently, leading organizations divide customers into groups with similar characteristics. Then they select one or more of these groups with high demand potential, called target markets, toward which they concentrate marketing efforts and resources. Leading companies identify potential market segments by using research methods discussed in Chapter 4. Nike has used target marketing to focus attention on college sport teams, many of which prominently display the Nike swoosh on their uniforms. When fans see the brand worn by their favorite teams and players, they are more likely to purchase Nike gear for themselves. At nike.com, fans can purchase athletic gear to look just like their favorite player. Chapter 8 explores target marketing in depth.

dickssportinggoods.com

The Michigan State men's basketball team unveiled Nike ALWAYS REPPIN' shirts during the 2016 NCAA Tournament.

PRODUCT

Any physical object, service, idea, person, event, place, or organization offered to satisfy consumers' needs and wants.

Positioning Consumers often perceive well-known brands as having a certain image or reputation. While this perception exists in consumers' minds, marketing organizations undergo a deliberate process, called positioning, to influence it. Nike says, "Just do it," reinforcing the image of an aggressive, action-oriented company. It's no accident that both amateur and professional athletes perceive Nike as producing high-quality products that help athletes perform to their maximum potential. Everything Nike does is designed to create this impression, including the use of outstanding athletes such as Kobe Bryant and Lebron James to promote the brand. Chapter 9 examines positioning strategies in more detail.

Marketing Mix Decisions Once the target market is selected, marketing mix decisions have to be made. How do you go about blending the elements into an appealing mix? Clearly, there needs to be a focus and a purpose. That's where the target market enters the picture. Since it is composed of similar customers, one marketing mix is created to address the overall group. Adjustments to individual customers can then be made within this framework. Figure 1.4 illustrates elements of the marketing mix and target marketing. The marketing mix is based on product, place, promotion and pricing decisions.

Product A **product** is any physical object, service, idea, person, event, place or organization offered to satisfy consumers' needs and wants. Product strategy includes decisions about how to manage current products, determine which need development, and decide which to phase out. It thereby determines the portfolio of goods and services the organization provides to the market. Equally

The Marketing Mix

Product
Positioning
Price
Target Market
Customer Needs and Wants
Place
Promotion

Figure 1.4 The Marketing Mix

important for many companies is the establishment of brands and the creation of brand equity (the value associated with a brand). Marketers carefully establish brand names to effectively communicate their products' unique attributes and protect their reputation. For example, Pepsi introduced Pepsi MAX, a soft drink with zero calories, while preserving the original Pepsi flavor. Propel, a Pepsi company product, is offering many different flavored waters. While the consumer shift toward healthier alternatives may account for the new beverages, these products keep Pepsi current in the changing environment. Both products are a part of the company's product strategy. Techniques for making product decisions will be discussed in Chapter 11, "Product Innovation and Management."

PLACE

Providing products where and when they are needed, in the proper quantities, with the greatest appeal, and at the lowest possible cost.

DISTRIBUTION CHANNEL

A set of independent organizations that make a good or service available for purchase by consumers or businesses.

PHYSICAL DISTRIBUTION

The movement of products through the channels to consumers.

RETAILING & DIRECT MARKETING

Selling products directly to end users.

PROMOTION

Setting objectives to be attained, creating messages and forms they will take.

PRICE

Setting prices to reflect the value received by customers and to achieve volume and profit required by the organization.

Place **Place** strategy is developed to serve customers by providing products where and when they are needed, in the proper quantities, with the greatest appeal, and at the lowest possible cost. The first task is to determine which distribution channels to use. A **distribution channel** is a set of independent organizations that make a good or service available for purchase. Some companies sell directly, such as your local dry cleaner, whereas others use longer channels with more members. For example, a company may sell to wholesalers, who sell to retailers, who sell to you. This becomes increasingly complex in global markets, where numerous channel members are required to move products to customers around the world. **Physical distribution** is the movement of products through the channels to consumers. Companies need order entry systems, transportation, and shipping and inventory storage capacity. Sophisticated information systems are creating some extremely innovative ways of serving customers better.

Retailing and direct marketing provide direct contact with customers. Retailing involves selling products directly to end users, often in retail outlets such as Jimmy John's or Walmart. Chapter 15, "Supply Chain Management and Channels," and Chapter 16, "Retailing, Direct Marketing, and Wholesaling," address the place strategy.

Promotion **Promotion** involves communicating with customers in a variety of ways. The promotion strategy includes determining the objectives to be attained, as well as creating messages and the forms they will take. In addition, the communication mechanism or media must be selected. Will two-way communication be used, such as personal selling, the phone or internet, or will one-way radio, television or other media carry the message? Since many messages are carried by numerous media, these decisions can be complex and tremendously interesting. Marketers have a vast number of options when developing promotions, such as training and managing a sales force or creating advertising. Because these mechanisms work together, coordination is vital. The promotion strategy is addressed in Chapter 12: "Integrated Marketing Communications," Chapter 13: "Mass Communications: Advertising, Sales Promotions, and Public Relations," and Chapter 14: "Personal Selling."

Price **Price** strategy affects nearly every part of a business. The objective is to set prices to reflect the value received by customers and to achieve the volume and profit required by the organization. When prices are too high, customers are dissatisfied and refuse to buy, or will switch to a competitor. When prices are too low, companies don't have money to cover costs, invest in new development, and provide a fair return to owners. Pricing must focus on determining value, which is based on what customers expect and desire and what competitors charge, as well as the unique qualities of the products. Marketers must also determine how their prices will influence the volume sold relative to the competition, and what competitors are likely to do with their prices. Prices not only need to be set but also must be communicated and administered. Will warranty charges be extra? What is charged for the base product or add-on? What financing is available? These questions must be answered and factored in. Pricing strategy is explored in Chapter 17, "Pricing Objectives & Influences," and Chapter 18, "Pricing Strategies."

Forces Important to Create & Capture Value

The future will center around better ways of creating value for customers. How marketers create and capture value for customers is embodied in the six supporting themes of this book. They are:

- Technology
- Relationships
- Global forces
- Diversity
- Ethics
- Sustainability.

These six key forces, depicted in Figure 1.5, will reappear throughout the book; they are the foundation on which marketers build lasting connections.

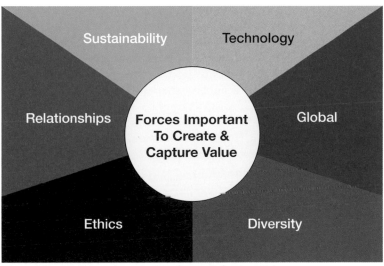

Figure 1.5   Six Forces Important to Create & Capture Value

CREATING AND CAPTURING VALUE THROUGH TECHNOLOGY

New technology is all around us, but two types are particularly noteworthy: (1) product technology that leads to the development of new goods and services, and (2) the internet, which facilitates two-way global connectivity with customers. Additionally, we will discuss the concept of a marketspace, which is bringing many of these technological forces into a single focus.

Product Technology **Product technology** is technology that leads to the development of new goods and services. Product technology provides the raw material that fuels improvements in our standard of living. Examples of innovative technology that has produced radically new goods and services are everywhere. Nanotex, a Crypton Company, applies nanotechnology to fabrics, which changes the molecular structures of fibers to create improved performance and comfort in five textile technology segments: repellency/stain resistance, moisture management, odor control, static elimination and wrinkle free. The technology also has applications in other industries, such as energy, high-tech, building and construction, medical, and paints.[23] Cellular systems support telephone calls, fax and data transmissions, as well as global positioning from moving vehicles everywhere. Digital television and flat-screen technology support in-home theater systems that rival movie theaters. And although there are many practical and ethical issues, we can clone the "best" sheep, tomatoes and viruses.

The Internet We tend to think of marketing as activities that occur in a physical **marketplace**, a physical arena where marketing exchanges take place. With new developments in technology, however, it is also possible to market goods and services in **marketspace**, an electronic space where business occurs. Marketspace transactions take place via the internet, interactive television, online gaming, shopping channels, 800 numbers and others. You can visit your local music store and buy music or movies—or visit iTunes online and purchase digital music, television shows and movies. Some new artists or the organizations behind them use marketspaces to expand their audience, encouraging them to sample music free of charge.

PRODUCT TECHNOLOGY

Technology that spawns the development of new goods and services.

MARKETPLACE

A physical arena where marketing exchanges take place.

MARKETSPACE

An electronic space where business occurs.

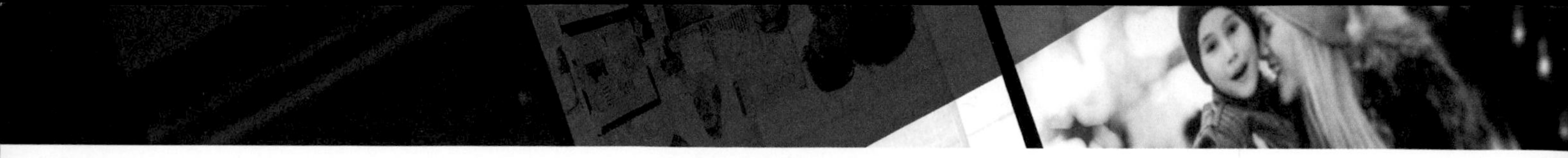

Information about virtually any product in existence can be found on internet marketspaces. For example, are you interested in features and reviews of the new Go-Pro video camera? No problem. You'll find plenty of information on Amazon, You-Tube, social media, and many other marketspaces of your choice.

You can experience music from around the world in a few clicks. Many streaming services such as Pandora provide free, personalized music. These freeware marketspaces offer visual, audio and interactive advertising to users along with music. Marketing in spaces like Pandora is relatively new but can be extremely successful.

Other new marketspaces like podcasts have produced a huge amount of new interest to marketers. Advertising during the podcast "Serial" was a boost for the email marketing software company MailChimp because of a 20 second ad featuring a child mispronouncing 'MailChimp' as 'MailKimp.' The ad went viral and Jason Klein, co-founder and co-CEO of analytics firm ListenFirst Media said, "The substantial lift MailChimp saw in organic conversation over Serial's other two advertisers indicates that they're effectively and efficiently engaging their listeners, as the majority of conversation reflected listener satisfaction with 'MailKimp' ad's return."[24]

Some predict that the growth of marketspace will eventually result in the eradication of marketplaces. Indeed, U.S. online retail sales are expected to reach $414 billion in 2018.[25] Although this is significant growth, the eradication of marketplaces altogether is unlikely; technology does not offer the social dimension of shopping in a marketplace, where consumers can interact with store personnel and other shoppers. Some consumers prefer to physically touch, test, compare and try on products. Marketspaces can use media to provide a similar experience with certain products.

For example, if you want to buy a shirt from J. Crew, its website will let you magnify the shirt to see the smallest of details, such as stitching and buttons; it also provides front and back views of the shirt. For some customers, this is enough information to make a purchase decision. Other products, such as tools and strollers, are still more likely to be purchased only after a consumer personally inspects them. Nonetheless, technology has dramatically changed marketing. The convenience of shopping in a marketspace provides incredible options to consumers to review and purchase goods and services. This unlocks challenges but unlimited potential to marketers!

STRATEGIC ALLIANCES

A partnership formed by two or more organizations which commit resources to achieve a common set of goals.

CREATING AND CAPTURING VALUE THROUGH RELATIONSHIPS

Before the production era, marketers embraced customer orientation. They created products on demand for specific customers. Manufacturers and customers did business directly, building relationships on a personal level. As mass production took root and more levels of distribution channels were added—including retailers and wholesalers, the consumer's voice was heard less and less. In an effort to become more connected to their markets, organizations today are enthusiastically embracing relationship marketing. Figure 1.6 describes a continuum of marketing exchanges from pure transactions to repeated transactions to relationships.[26]

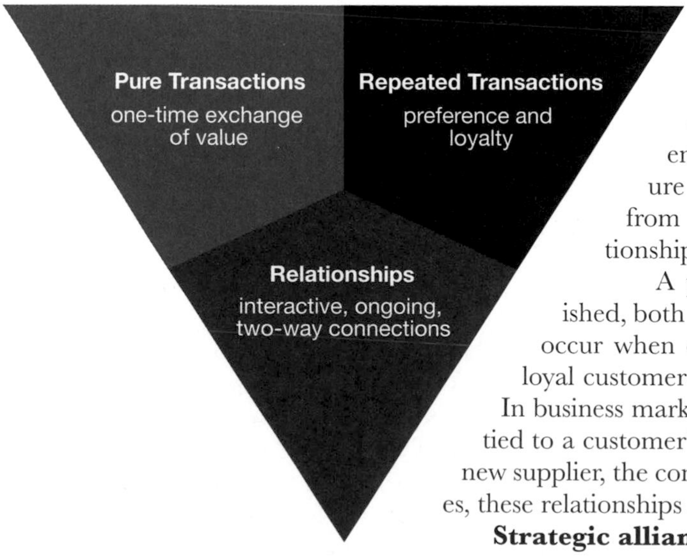

A pure transaction occurs only once. When it is finished, both parties go their separate ways. Repeated transactions occur when customers have strong preferences, often becoming loyal customers. Relationships create an even stronger connection. In business markets, suppliers develop computerized systems that are tied to a customer's manufacturing processes. If the customer selects a new supplier, the computer system will also need alterations. In some cases, these relationships are based on long-term contracts and partnerships.

Strategic alliances occur between firms in which each commits re-

Figure 1.6   Types of Marketing Exchanges

Pure Transactions
one-time exchange of value

Repeated Transactions
preference and loyalty

Relationships
interactive, ongoing, two-way connections

sources to achieve a common set of objectives. In 2016, General Motors and Lyft announced a strategic alliance in which GM will invest $500 million dollars in the ride-sharing service. Currently Lyft's biggest competitor is Uber. Initially the companies will offer

short term rentals of GM cars to Lyft drivers, and eventually GM's development of autonomous (driverless) cars and Lyft's software that matches drivers to passengers with routing and payment information will create a new service of cars that operate themselves. "We had a really common view of the future" with Lyft, said GM President Dan Ammann in an interview with Reuters. Both companies believe ride-sharing is how consumers will first experience autonomous cars, and they plan to be at the forefront of this global, automotive technology.[27] Some alliances may involve actual ownership arrangements. In these cases, several parties form an organization that is owned jointly.

GM and Lyft announced a strategic alliance that will provide drivers with short term rentals of GM cars.

CREATING AND CAPTURING VALUE GLOBALLY

The global marketplace is tremendously attractive to organizations ready to expand beyond domestic sales. The United States reigns as the world's third largest exporter of merchandise, grossing approximately $1.6 trillion per year. China leads the world with annual exports of approximately $2.3 trillion.[28] Marketers should not ignore or lose sight of the importance of a global organization. Compared to domestic firms, global companies have an increased customer reach and a better understanding of diversity and competition. They can also offset economic downturns by implementing appropriate strategies based on environmental conditions at the time.

The global marketplace can be very complex. Brand awareness of companies like McDonald's and Starbucks penetrates cultures, which is an advantage for promoting product sales. But cultural differences and barriers including language, currency, infrastructure, laws and regulations, consumer preferences, and negotiating styles all need to be fully understood in the global marketplace. The same understanding applies to marketing through digital technology, which has grown exponentially and has a tremendous impact on global marketing. Currently, more than 3.17 billion people worldwide access the internet, up from 394 million in 2000.[29]

Creating value to this immense global market requires marketers to understand and be sensitive to the different preferences and needs of all customers, which we will discuss throughout this book.

CREATING AND CAPTURING VALUE THROUGH DIVERSITY

Professor Warren Plunkett teaches what he calls the "new golden rule." The traditional golden rule states that you should do unto others as you would have them do unto you, but that assumes all people are the same. In an increasingly diverse society, you must be sensitive to differences. People from different cultures or backgrounds don't necessarily have the same perceptions, needs and wants. Plunkett's new rule is: Do unto others as they would have you do unto them. In other words, as a marketer, you must remember to satisfy your customer on the basis of your customer's desires and social norms—not your own.[30]

As marketers move to a more personalized, one-on-one connection with customers, it is imperative to understand and respect diversity among customers, because no two are alike. As you will learn in Chapter 5, some commonalities exist within various subcultures and social classes. But marketers today are much more sensitive to the needs of a diverse population.

When marketing to ethnic groups, it is important to distinguish between ethnic background and ethnicity. A person's **ethnic background** is usually determined by birth and related to one or more of four elements: country of origin, native language, race, and religion. Hispanics are an ethnic group, but members have diverse interests and beliefs depending on country of origin, length of time in the United States, geographic placement, and other factors.

ETHNIC BACKGROUND

Subculture membership usually determined by birth and related to one or more of four elements: country of origin, native language, race, and religion.

©iStockphoto.com/franckreporter

ETHNICITY

The amount of identification an individual feels with a particular ethnic group.

Ethnicity is an individual identifying with a particular ethnic group. According to Lafayette Jones, president and CEO of Segmented Marketing Services, Inc., marketers should "look at the market not in terms of black and white, but in terms of true ethnicity. We use terms like 'African American' because these terms really describe what we're talking about, without the social and political implications of race. … Every culture has its own food, music and religious practices. They're diverse in competition, flavorings, attitudes and expressions."[31]

In Chapter 5, we'll look more specifically at ethnic markets because understanding how to market to subcultures will determine a company's success in the future. The three largest subcultures in the U.S. (Asian Americans, Hispanics and African Americans) are expected to spend about $2.4 trillion for goods and services in 2018.[32] According to Nielsen, multicultural buying has increased 415% since 1990. By 2030, the non-Hispanic white population will be declining annually, and all U.S. growth will be multicultural.[33] The ethnic market's size, buying power and growing clout will expand the challenges of marketing and require marketers to consider the immense importance of cultural groups.

These are just a few of the diverse customers you will be learning about in this book. It is both profitable and rewarding for marketers to connect and build relationships with every type of customer. By acknowledging, understanding, and accommodating the needs of diverse groups, companies develop a larger base of loyal customers for future business.

CREATING AND CAPTURING VALUE ETHICALLY

Today, most marketers understand the importance of social responsibility and ethical behavior. In fact, ethical initiatives by businesses have more than doubled in the past five years. Responsible marketers make decisions with a clear code of ethics in mind and consider the standards of conduct for an organization. A worldwide poll conducted by Environics International asked 25,000 people in 23 countries to name the factors that most affected their impressions of individual companies. A majority mentioned factors related to social responsibility (e.g., labor practices and business ethics) and felt that companies should go beyond the traditional goals of "making a profit, paying taxes, and providing employment."[34] Ethics and social responsibility are two directly related forces, but they are not the same.

MARKETING ETHICS

The application of moral standards to marketing decisions, behaviors, and institutions.

Ethics
Marketing ethics deal with the application of moral standards to marketing decisions, behaviors and institutions.[35] Nearly every area of marketing has significant ethical dimensions that raise difficult questions. Throughout this book, we will evaluate many ethical situations, including issues of fairness, equity, conflict of interest, privacy, confidentiality and product safety. You will also find that every area of marketing can present an ethical dilemma, including product development, promotion, distribution and pricing.

In order to promote ethical behavior in each area of marketing, both large and small businesses implement a code of conduct, sometimes referred to as value statements or management integrity statements. These may provide a wide range of guidelines, depending on the beliefs and values of a particular organization. For example, Johnson & Johnson established one of the first codes in 1947. It embodies a commitment to ethical business practices as well as a responsibility to consumers, employees, the community and shareholders. You will learn more about Johnson & Johnson in Chapter 2.

Responsible organizations don't simply implement a code of ethics; they make it clear that ethics are a priority by communicating standards to employees. An ethical organization requires the support of top management, and many companies aim to manage beyond compliance by exceeding the standards defined by federal, state, and local regulations.

Because the marketing function within an organization relies heavily on interaction with customers, it is often subject to public scrutiny. This emphasizes the power of ethics as a force in making business decisions. Over the long run, organizations with a strong ethical culture and code of conduct likely will be better equipped to handle ethical dilemmas.

SOCIETAL MARKETING CONCEPT

The marketing concept extended to include satisfying the citizen as well as the consumer.

Social Responsibility
Many people believe that a socially responsible business must satisfy the needs of customers in ways that provide profits to the owners or meet other requirements outlined by the owners. Some argue that profits represent the response of consumers to businesses that best serve their needs. As mentioned previously, social responsibility and ethics are closely related. The **societal marketing concept** seeks to balance customer satisfaction against corporate profits and the well-being of the larger society. It extends the marketing concept to include satisfying the citizen as well as the customer. Social responsibility reflects "the consequences of a person or firm's acts as they might affect the interest of others."[36]

Method considers social responsibility when developing naturally safe cleaning products.

Method, one of the fastest-growing privately owned companies proves that successful products can also be responsible. Makers of safe and effective home cleaning products, Method eliminates hazardous chemicals and replaces them with natural ingredients like coconut, soy and palm oils. The company's humanifesto uses clever statements like "role models in bottles," and "good always prevails over stinky" to help describe its pursuit of social responsibility.[37]

Many companies are well known for their commitment to social causes and for acting in the best interest of the citizen as well as the consumer. Consider Ben & Jerry's, which contributes about $2 million each year to charitable causes. Its initiatives include innovative recycling, energy saving and waste reduction. The company incorporated its dedication to societal marketing into this part of its mission statement: "to operate the Company in a way that actively recognizes the central role that business plays in society by initiating innovative ways to improve the quality of life locally, nationally, and internationally."[38]

CREATING AND CAPTURING VALUE THROUGH SUSTAINABILITY

Most people believe that sustainability pertains strictly to environmental issues. However, the Brundtland Commission outlined in its classic report, "Our Common Future," that sustainable development is a complex process involving three components: the environment, economy and society. It is important to understand that these elements are closely linked. The environment is where we live, while economic and social development are the actions we take to improve our conditions within the environment.[39]

How does this relate to creating and capturing value? Increased environmental concerns among consumers lead them to assess an organization's value not only by its products but how its products and processes affect the environment. Therefore, marketers must be good at positioning their products globally and in sustainable ways.

As a direct marketing company, L.L.Bean publishes several catalogs each year. It responds to the related environmental impact by controlling paper and sustainable forest management. Bean's requires that 90 percent of the fiber in its catalogs be sourced through a credible certification system and contain 10-20 percent recycled fiber. The company gives preference to suppliers who share commitments to environmental stewardship, and in particular those who source from the United States.[40]

The result of consumer environmental consciousness has been the creation of green marketing campaigns by many organizations, such as the marketing of eco-friendly products or processes, or marketing efforts using eco-friendly methods. For example, S.C. Johnson and Sons markets how its manufacturing facilities use waste methane gas, a byproduct of decomposition in landfills, for energy. It also uses biofuel, wind power, and solar power to support its effort to reach a 2016 goal of 33 percent global renewable energy use.[41] Marketers must weigh the importance of sustainability to its customers and implement a strategy accordingly. Throughout this book, you will learn of different companies undertaking environmental initiatives in order to create and capture value for customers.

Anthony22 / CC BY-SA 3.0

L.L.Bean is an organization well known for its environmental stewardship.

LO 05 Marketing: Your Involvement

By now it should be clear that marketing affects you in many ways. Your exploration of marketing begins from several angles: the prospective marketer, member of a target market, customer, and citizen. Each of these roles gives you a slightly different point of view, which can lead to the development of valuable marketing skills. One in three of you will be in a job that directly involves marketing. Whatever career you choose—working for a political campaign, a nonprofit organization, a religious organization, or a Fortune 500 company—will require an understanding of marketing.

In a sense, you are already a marketer through your everyday actions. You market yourself when you apply to schools or pursue a scholarship. You are a marketer when you seek election to an organization or attempt to influence its members. You are a marketer when you interview for an internship or job. In all likelihood, you will be applying marketing in a professional sense in the future, regardless of your college major or job title.

You also belong to a target market, which makes you tremendously important to other marketers. You are part of a target market when political candidates appear on popular TV shows to ask for your votes, when a TV network produces a show designed to appeal to you, and when sports teams, theme parks and movies compete for your entertainment dollars.

Marketing affects you through your role as a customer. You are a customer every time you purchase. You are a loyal customer when you have a strong preference that results in your repeated purchases of a company's goods or services. You are part of a marketing relationship when a company that knows you by name wants to customize its actions to fit your desires.

Finally, marketing pertains to you as a citizen. You are affected by marketing when McDonald's selects paper over Styrofoam packaging to reduce pollution. You are affected when Mothers Against Drunk Driving (MADD) reduces your chance of injury from a traffic accident through legislation. You are affected when General Motors designs a Cadillac that is completely recyclable.

Marketing is a relevant, fun subject! You encounter it every day. When you compare products and prices, you're a marketer. When you order from Amazon or any on-line company, you encounter marketing from the second you enter the site until you receive the product. Often you're asked for feedback after your product arrives! This is all marketing. Marketing affects what you buy, what you do, where you go. It touches your life directly in countless ways, and it always will.

Marketing: Your Career

A career in marketing can take you in many different directions because marketing is multi-faceted and diverse. As you've already learned, marketing affects everyone everyday. As you participate in career fairs and apply for jobs, you're marketing yourself! Everything matters...your research of potential companies, your grades, your resume, your appearance, your attitude, your personality, your skill set, and your follow through. If you send a thank you note to a recruiter, you're marketing; you're engaging in value-added after the contact, just like companies do when they follow through after a sale or potential sale by soliciting customer feedback and satisfaction levels or sending a "we value your business" thank you. Marketing yourself is really no different than marketing a product; you need to develop a plan, implement the plan, then evaluate the plan and determine if changes are required.

The diversity of marketing career opportunities is huge. Perhaps you'll be a summer marketing intern who gathers research for a small, independent marketing firm. Perhaps you'll intern for a large company such as Amazon, Nike or General Motors. Perhaps you'll enter the field as a marketing support representative for

©iStockphoto.com/andresr

A career in marketing offers constant change, challenge, and growth opportunities.

a multinational corporation such as Apple, IBM or Procter & Gamble.

Once you've entered the marketing field in some capacity, you have multiple options to consider. Do you want to be a product or brand manager? Do you want to be in direct sales, sales management or customer service? Perhaps strategic planning, retailing, or new product development interests you. What about advertising and promotion...or social media marketing? Digital technology is giving rise to marketing positions unheard of just a few years ago. If you're more oriented toward research and analytics, perhaps you'll want to try marketing research and data management. The opportunities are vast.

Consider how some of the greatest marketing success stories began. Steve Jobs was just 20 years old when he grasped the marketing potential of the small computer he and Steve Wozniak built in his parents' garage. Four years later, in 1979, sales ballooned to $200 million.[42] Today, Apple is considered the world's most valuable company with 2015 revenue reaching nearly $234 billion.[43]

Mark Zuckerberg was a 19-year old college sophomore at Harvard University in 2004 when he started "theFacebook" in his dorm room. Since then Facebook has transformed the internet, social media, marketing and people's daily lives. Zuckerberg's personal net worth is now over $51.6 billion, while Facebook's 2015 revenue hit nearly $18 million.[44]

Mark Zuckerberg, CEO of Facebook, transformed a dorm room idea into the world's largest social media network.

Ben Cohen and Jerry Greenfield took a $5 correspondence course in ice cream making from Penn State, and, with a $12,000 investment, in 1978 they opened their first ice cream scoop shop in a renovated gas station in Burlington, Vermont.[45] Twenty two years later, they sold Ben and Jerry's to Unilever for $326 million.[46]

These are just a few examples of unknown people who transformed initial ideas into products and developed successful marketing strategies to create and communicate value to customers. Not all entrepreneurs are this successful. In fact, the majority of new products fail to exceed first-year sales benchmarks. But marketing offers an array of options to consider when you begin thinking about a career.

It is also a good path for company advancement. About one in five, or 20 percent, of current Fortune 500 Chief Executive Officers (CEOs) began their careers in sales and marketing roles.[47] Anne Mulcahy was named CEO of Xerox after being with the company for 24 years, with 16 of those years spent in sales/marketing.[48] There is an argument that in order to run an organization you need to know it from the bottom up. So, while the average annual starting salary for marketing positions is $54,100, realize that the potential for upward mobility is enormous.[49]

We hope that this edition of Marketing: Connecting With Customers will inspire you to become interested in marketing as an important element in business, society, and everyday life. Perhaps the subject will appeal to you enough to consider the field as a possible career path, or perhaps it will simply strengthen your business acumen. Either way, you will find that marketing is, and will remain, a part of your life!

Chapter Summary

Objective 1: Understand the concept of marketing, including its definition, purpose and role in creating exchanges.

Marketing is an organizational function and a set of processes for creating, communicating, and delivering value to customers and for managing customer relationships in ways that benefit the organization and its stakeholders. By definition, it is the activity, set of institutions and processes for creating, communicating, delivering and exchanging offerings that have value for customers, clients, partners and society at large.

The purpose of marketing is to identify the needs and wants of customers within markets and to create customer value in ways that will ensure the long-run success of the organization by making connections between companies and customers. Many people refer to the purpose as the marketing concept. Marketing works by creating valuable exchanges that provide utility. Utility is produced when products are created or adjusted, when goods and services are placed so consumers can discover and acquire them, when products are delivered at the right time, and when the transfer of ownership is facilitated.

Objective 2: Contrast the periods of marketing evolution from its early history through the five marketing eras.

Marketing has progressed through five eras: the production era, the sales era, the customer marketing era, the value marketing era and the social media era. As the names suggest, the production era focused on ways to efficiently mass-produce new products, while the sales era focused on getting people to buy products. The customer marketing era moved management's attention toward satisfying customer needs and wants. The value driven era required every part of an organization to create maximum value for its customers. Today, the social media era has significantly improved the efficiency and effectiveness of how companies communicate to customers *and* how customers communicate to companies. Digital marketing focuses on enriching people's lives through the use of technology.

Objective 3: Explain the marketing strategy process, including the four marketing mix components: price, product, place and promotion.

The marketing strategy process has four steps: situation analysis, targeting, positioning and marketing mix decisions. Situation analysis provides information about the marketing environment and specific company elements. It is based on insights gained from the use of marketing information systems and marketing research. Targeting occurs when groups of customers with identifiable characteristics are selected for attention. Targeting helps focus resources. The best marketing strategies do an excellent job of addressing the needs and wants of customers within these targets. Positioning is used to determine what impression the marketer wants customers within a target segment to possess regarding the organization or its products.

By blending the four elements of the marketing mix —product, price, place and promotion—marketing decisions are made to support the positioning strategy. A product is developed to satisfy a want or need of consumers. A price for the product is established to reflect the value customers will realize and to achieve organizational price/volume objectives. Place refers to how the product will be made available to target market customers. Promotion refers to how the company will communicate the offering and its benefits to the target market. These elements are within a company's control; they can be changed in response to market conditions.

Objective 4: Understand the six key forces that influence how organizations create and capture value.

Marketing is influenced by relationships, technology, ethics, diversity, globalization and sustainability. Today, more organizations are implementing the marketing concept by forging relationships with valued customers. These relationships are creating customer loyalty and repeat business that help an organization achieve its objectives.

Product technology develops radically new goods and services, and process technology makes it possible to be more responsive to customers by altering how marketing occurs. The Internet is a particularly noteworthy technological advance because it brings us new distribution, communication, scanning and research capabilities. The global economy affects all customers and competitors. Consequently, global factors must be considered when making marketing decisions. Ethics and social responsibility are also important forces because they help guide many marketing decisions. Ethics involve making decisions based on what is right and wrong. Social responsibility involves decisions that affect citizens, customers, and the environment. Finally, supporting sustainability enables a company to work toward protecting the environment, the economy and society in general.

Objective 5: Explain how marketing affects you.

You are intimately involved in marketing. You are already a marketer, a member of a target market, a customer, and a citizen. Marketing pertains to you personally, and you begin your study of the subject having already experienced many of its facets. Professionally, marketing is important with any major or career you choose. In a sense, you are often a marketer when you attempt to advance yourself or your opinions. Along with other people similar to yourself, you are part of a target market toward which certain marketers direct their attention. As a customer, you experience the actions of marketers. As a citizen, you are impacted positively and negatively by many organizations whether or not you purchase their products. You may decide to pursue one of the many fields in marketing as a career, or it may be a natural extension of a product that you create. The opportunities for advancement in the field of marketing are immense.

Review Your Understanding

1. What is marketing? What are the key elements in its definition?
2. What are the four basic areas (types of markets) in which marketing is typically applied?
3. What is utility? What are the four types of utility involved in marketing exchanges?
4. What is the difference between a need and a want? Give examples of each.
5. What is the marketing concept? What are its three key aspects?
6. What are the stages in marketing evolution? Describe each of the five marketing eras.
7. What is a marketing strategy? Describe each of its four steps.
8. How do product, place, promotion and price decisions form the marketing mix? Give examples of each decision.
9. What are the six key forces shaping marketing in the 21st century? Describe each.
10. How does marketing affect you? List three examples of how you are the recipient of marketing and three examples of how you market to others.
11. Why is marketing a viable choice to consider when choosing a career path?

Discussion of Concepts

1. Describe marketing, highlighting examples from your daily life that illustrate each of its four aspects.
2. Identify one company with which you are familiar and describe four ways in which it provides utility.
3. Discuss the activities involved in implementing the marketing concept. How do they pertain to customers, competitors and the marketing organization?
4. Describe the steps in developing a marketing strategy. Why is it important to target prior to positioning? Why is positioning important prior to marketing mix decisions?
5. Compare and contrast the various eras of marketing, assessing the role each era played in reaching the current social media era.
6. Discuss the six key forces shaping marketing today by explaining how each helps to create and capture value.
7. Describe how marketing affects you from three angles: how people/companies market to you, how you market yourself to people/companies, and what career opportunities are available in the field of marketing.

Key Terms & Definitions

1. **Agility:** The flexibility and speed with which organizations can identify or create new wants and take action to satisfy them.
2. **Business-to-Business (B2B) marketing:** When a business purchases goods or services to produce other goods, to support daily operations or to resell at a profit.
3. **Buyer's market:** The marketing environment that exists when an abundance of product lets the buyer control the market.
4. **Business-to-Consumer (B2C) marketing:** When organizations sell to individuals or households that buy, consume, and dispose of products.
5. **Consumer orientation:** An organizational philosophy that focuses on satisfying consumer needs and wants.
6. **Customer value:** What consumers perceive they gain from owning or using a product over and above the cost of acquiring it.
7. **Distribution channel:** A set of independent organizations that make up a good or service available for purchase by consumers or business.
8. **Effectiveness:** The degree to which an organization's activ-

ities produce results that matter to consumers.
9. **Efficiency:** The degree to which activities are carried out without waste of time or money.
10. **Ethnic background:** Subculture membership usually determined by birth and related to one or more of four elements: country of origin, native language, race, and religion.
11. **Ethnicity:** The amount of identification an individual feels with a particular ethnic group.
12. **Exchange:** A process in which two or more parties provide something of value to one another.
13. **Form utility:** A want-satisfying value that is created when knowledge and materials are converted into finished goods and services.
14. **Internal marketing:** When managers of one functional unit market their capabilities to other units within their own organization.
15. **Loyalty:** A measure of how often, when selecting from a product class, a customer purchases a particular brand.
16. **Market:** All the individuals and organizations with potential desire and ability to acquire a particular good or service.
17. **Marketing:** The process of planning and executing the

conception, pricing, promotion, and distribution of ideas, goods, and services to create exchanges that satisfy individual and organizational objectives.

18. **Marketing ethics:** The application of moral standards to marketing decisions, behaviors, and institutions.

19. **Marketing mix:** The four controllable variables—product, price, promotion, and place (distribution)—that are combined to appeal to a company's target markets.

20. **Marketplace:** A physical arena where marketing exchanges take place.

21. **Marketspace:** An electronic space where business occurs.

22. **Mass marketing:** The mass production, mass distribution, and mass promotion of a product to all buyers.

23. **Need:** Fundamental requirements the meeting of which is the ultimate goal of behavior.

24. **Nonprofit marketing:** When an organization does not try to make a profit but instead attempts to influence others to support its cause by using its service or by making a contribution.

25. **Ownership utility:** A want-satisfying value that is created by making it possible to transfer the title of goods and services from one party to another.

26. **Physical distribution:** The movement of products through the channels to consumers.

27. **Place:** Providing products where and when they are needed, in the proper quantities, with the greatest appeal, and at the lowest possible cost.

28. **Place utility**: A want-satisfying value that is created by making goods and services conveniently available.

29. **Price:** Setting prices to reflect the value received by customers and to achieve volume and profit required by the organization.

30. **Product:** Any physical object, service, idea, person, event, place, or organization offered to satisfy consumers' needs and wants.

31. **Product technology:** Technology that spawns the development of new goods and services.

32. **Production orientation:** Historical marketing period that emphasized new products and the efficiency of production.

33. **Promotion:** Setting objectives to be attained, creating messages and forms they will take.

34. **Relationship marketing:** The development and maintenance of successful relational exchanges; it involves interactive, ongoing, two-way connections among customers, organizations, suppliers, and other parties for mutual benefit.

35. **Retailing & direct marketing:** Selling products directly to end users.

36. **Sales orientation:** Historical marketing period that emphasized that consumers must be convinced to buy.

37. **Satisfaction:** The customer's overall rating of his or her experience with a company's products.

38. **Seller's market:** The marketing environment that exists when scarcity of products lets the seller control the market.

39. **Societal marketing concept:** The marketing concept extended to include satisfying the citizen as well as the consumer.

40. **Strategic alliances:** A partnership formed by two or more organizations for a new venture.

41. **Sustainability:** The steps and processes organizations undertake to manage growth without detrimentally affecting the resources or biological systems of the earth.

42. **Time utility:** A want-satisfying value that is created when goods and services are made available at a desired time.

43. **Value-Driven organization:** Organizations that implement the marketing concept by ensuring that all parts of the organization make the maximum contribution toward creating value for the customer.

44. **Want:** A specific form of consumption desired to satisfy need.

References

1. www.ama.org, website visited March 3, 2016.

2. www.globenewswire.com/news-release/2016/02/18/811649/10160163/en/RootMetrics-Releases-2nd-Half-2015-US-Mobile-Network-Performance-Review, website visited May 10, 2016.

3. Jay Wright soap commercial, www.youtube.com, website visited May 10, 2016.

4. Form 10-K for BAXTER INTERNATIONAL INC, Annual Report, February 26, 2015.

5. McDonald's Values, www.aboutmcdonalds.com, website visited March 13, 2016.

6. "Case Study: Dell Builds Brand Equity with Business Solutions Exchange LinkedIn Group," www.linkedselling.com, February 6, 2014; www.linkedin.com/company/dell, website visited May 28, 2016.

7. www.dosomething.org, website visited March 3, 2016.

8. Culliton, James W., The Management of Marketing Costs, cited in Borden, Neil H., "The Concept of the Marketing Mix," Journal of Advertising Research, June 1964, pp. 2-7.

9. Bagozzi, Richard P., "Marketing as Exchange," Journal of Marketing, October 1975, pp. 32-39.

10. Nina Bahadur, "Dove's 'Love Your Curls' Campaign Celebrates Girls' Curly Hair," The Huffington Post, January 20, 2015.

11. Kathleen Sampey, "Coke Unveils Global Strategy," Adweek, December 7, 2005.

12. www.roversclub.org, website visited March 25, 2016.

13. Stacy Finz, "Homemade baby food biting into sales," San Francisco Chronicle, May 13, 2014.

14. www.fedex.com website visited March 25, 2016.

15. Letter to Shareholders - First Quarter 2016, www.netflix.com, website visited May 25, 2016.

16. www.amazon.com, website visited May 25, 2016.

17. www.xerox.com, website visited May 25, 2016.

18. www.facebook.com/Hampton, website visited May 25, 2016.

19. The President's Council on Sustainable Development.

20. www.scjohnson.com, website visited March, 16, 2016.

21. Michael A. Stelzner, "How Marketers Are Using Social Media to Grow Their Businesses," Social Media Examiner, May, 2015.

22. Ibid.

23. Constance Gustke, "Nanotechnology Now an Unseen Success," CNBC.com, May 29, 2012; www.nano-tex.com, website visited March 14, 2016.

24. www.adweek.com/new/advertising-branding/how-mailchimp-bene-fiting-return-serial-168691.

25. Allilson Enright, "U.S. online retail sales will grow 57% by 2018," www.internetretailer.com, May 12, 2014.

26. Webster, Frederick, E., "The Changing Role of Marketing in the Corporation," Journal of Marketing, October 1992, pp.1-17.

27. Trousdale, Steve, "GM, Lyft announce $500 million by automaker and strategic alliance," Reuters.com, January 4, 2016, website visited May 14, 2016.

28. CIA World Factbook, www.cia.gov, website visited March 15, 2016.

29. http://www.statista.com/topics/1145/internet-usage-worldwide, website visited June 3, 2016.

30. Plunkett, Warren, Instructor's Manual for Supervision, 7th ed. (Boston: Allyn & Bacon, 1993), pp. 6-7.

31. Mogelonsky, Marcia, Everybody Eats: Supermarket Consumers in the 1990s (Ithaca, NY: American Demographic Books, 1995), pg. 185.

32. www.latinodonorcollaborative.org/wpcontent/uploads/2015/12/Multicultural-Economy-2013-SELIG-Center.pdf, website visited July 13, 2016.

33. www.nielsen.com/content/dam/corporate/us/en/reports-down-loads/2015-reports/the-multicultural-edge-rising-super-consum-ers-march-2015.pdf, website visited July 13, 2016.

34. "Great Expectations," Across the Board, January 1, 2000.

35. Laczniak, Gene R., Murphy, Patrick E., Ethical Marketing Decisions: The Higher Road (Boston: Allyn & Bacon, 1993), pg. 3.

36. Bennet, Peter D., Dictionary of Marketing Terms (Chicago: American Marketing Association, 1995), pg. 267.

37. www.methodhome.com, website visited June 5, 2016.

38. "Activism," Benjerry.com website visited June 5, 2016.

39. Our Common Future: Report of World Commission on Environment and Development, United Nations, 1987.

40. www.llbean.com/customerService/aboutLLBean/environment.html, website visited May 23, 2016.

41. www.scjohnson.com, website visited June 5, 2016.

42. Jen Wieczner, "Apple Takes Back Title of World's Most Valuable Company," Fortune, February 3, 2016.

43. "Apple-Reports-Record-Fourth-Quarter-Results," Apple Press Info, www.apple.com, website visited June5, 2016.

44. www.forbes.com/profile/mark-zuckerberg, website visited May 27, 2016.; quotes.wsj.com/FB/financials/annual/income-statement, website visited May 3, 2016.

45. www.benjerry.com/about-us#1timeline, website visited May 25, 2016.

46. Gelles, David, "How the Social Mission of Ben & Jerry's Survived Being Gobbled Up," The New York Times, August 21, 2015.

47. Sanders, Jeffrey S., "The Path to Becoming a Fortune 500 CEO," Forbes, December 5, 2011.

48. Lisa Vollmer, "Anne Mulcahy: The Keys to Turnaround at Xerox," Stanford Business, www.gsb.stanford.edu, website visited May 24, 2016.

49. "Top-Paid Business Majors", www.naceweb.org, website visited May 23, 2016.

CHAPTER 02

The Marketing Strategy

& Planning Process

Coca-Cola

Coca-Cola, the world's leading manufacturer, marketer and distributor of nonalcoholic beverages, has an unprecedented ability to fit into people's lives. Its global footprint is staggering, with more than 500 brands and 3,800 products served 1.9 billion times daily in more than 200 countries. Its broad beverage portfolio includes soft drinks, sparkling drinks, bottled water, sports drinks, energy drinks, juices, teas and coffees. It's ranked by Interbrand as the world's third most valuable brand in 2016.

How has Coca-Cola thrived for 130 years? Quite simply, the company connects with customers. Today, a large market for Coke is driven by 18-30 year-old Millennials who are altruistic, entrepreneurial and tech savvy, so Coke is constantly creating new marketing strategies to stay relevant with this consumer group. If social media platforms are an indication of success, then Coca-Cola is on the right track. It currently has over a million likes on Facebook, over 750,000 followers on both Twitter and LinkedIn, 21,000 followers on Instagram and over six million views on YouTube. CEO Muhtar Kent understands the importance of brand-building initiatives to stay connected with consumers. "Our productivity initiatives are on track, as is our commitment to increase media investments in key markets," Mr. Kent told analysts. "We are delivering more and better quality marketing by focusing on increased efficiency and effectiveness."

For example, Coca-Cola has always promoted its brand in association with happiness. Whether it's "Share a Coke," "Taste the Feeling," or "Open Happiness," the company positions its products as relaxing, refreshing and satisfying. In summer of 2015, retail displays of Coca-Cola bottles across the country featured 250 of the most popular names among teens; in summer of 2016, the company swapped out first names for song lyrics, such as "Lean on me,""We are the champions," and "Celebrate good times, come on!" Fans can also visit ShareaCoke.com to choose from a list of lyrics to customize bottles, and they can also access digital images to share on social media or add to the #ShareaCoke Photo Gallery. The popular site will also continue to customize 8-ounce glass bottles and six-packs of Coca-Cola with names and inspiring messages for personal events like graduations and weddings.

During 2016 Coke will roll out its new "One-Brand" strategy, which is designed to unite all Trademark Coke prod-

Coca-Cola's new "One Brand" strategy features its iconic Red Disk to visually unite the brand worldwide.

ucts—Coca-Cola, Diet Coke/Coca-Cola Light, Coke Zero and Coca-Cola Life—under a single visual identity system anchored by the iconic Coca-Cola Red Disc. The strategy is in packaging. According to James Sommerville, VP of Global Design for Coca-Cola, "Packaging is, in essence, our most visible and most valuable owned media asset. While TV commercials, digital communication and billboards are extremely effective and important, consumers physically touch a Coca-Cola bottle or can. These new packaging designs signal a shift in our visual language in which the classic Red Disc is more prominent than other elements associated with the brand. Consumers will see the Coca-Cola Red Disc in all global markets at the end of our 'Taste the Feeling' TV ads, in our print ads and on our billboards. Using this same device on packaging completes the picture."

Coca-Cola's success is a direct result of the company's dedication to creating innovative marketing strategies to differentiate itself from competitors and appeal to consumers. As you've learned, components of the marketing mix are controllable, and strong marketers frequently change elements of the mix in anticipation of market conditions. This is agility! It's also why Coca-Cola ranks as the most effective marketer in the world, according to the prestigious 2016 Effie Effectiveness Index. The marketing strategy and planning process will be critical to achieving its 2020 Vision of doubling system revenues this decade, while continuing to connect with customers and increase brand loyalty.

Sources: coca-colacompany.com/our-company, accessed May 24, 2016; Moye, Jay, "Share a Coke and a Song: Summer Campaign to feature Lyrics on Packaging," Coca-ColaCompany.com, Front Page, March 31, 2016; Moye, Jay, "Marketing to Millennials," Coca-ColaCompany.com, Front Page, Oct. 29, 2013; Tam,Inti, "Behind Coke's new makeover," Marketing-Global, April 20, 2016, www.marketing-interactive.com/behind-cokes-new-makeover, accessed May 23, 2016; Zmuda, Natalie, "Coca-Cola Maintains Marketing Spend Amid Sluggish Demand," Advertising Age, July 22, 2014.

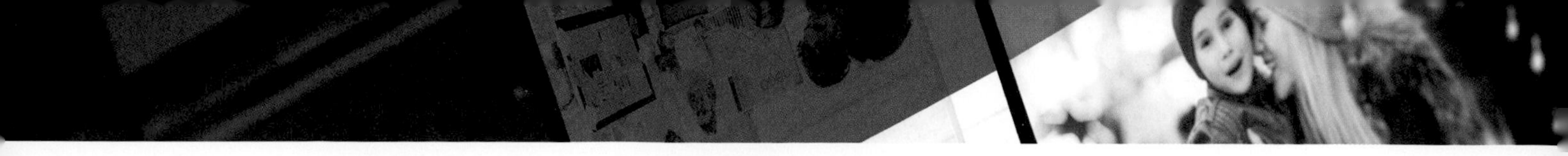

LO 01 Explain how each level of the strategic marketing planning process is related. Define components at each level.

LO 02 Describe the four elements of an organization's vision that provide guidance for all actions.

LO 03 Integrate components of the strategic marketing plan with the vision.

LO 04 Understand why elements of the marketing mix must be integrated, and outline the steps of the marketing control process.

LO 05 Identify the four major ways that organizations enter and develop global markets.

LO 01

The Strategic Marketing Planning Process

VISION

Statement of an organization's operating philosophy including core values, business definition, strategic direction and strategic infrastructure.

STRATEGIC MARKETING PLAN

The document describing the company's objectives and how to achieve them in light of competitive activities.

MARKETING MIX PLANS

Plans for how each part of the marketing mix will help to achieve the strategic marketing plan goals.

Marketing can be described as philosophy, as strategy and as tactics. Leading-edge businesses such as Coca-Cola, Eli Lilly and Johnson & Johnson develop marketing plans that address each of these aspects to help them connect with customers. So do smaller companies. Figure 2.1 outlines the type of planning that corresponds with each level of marketing, including the people who usually implement it.

Marketing as philosophy is embodied within the organization's **vision**. It is usually developed by top executives, and it articulates the codes of conduct guiding organizational behavior, what customer value will be delivered, specific strategic objectives, and the resources that will be required. The vision describes the fundamental contributions the business intends to make to society, its position relative to competitors, and the attributes that make the organization unique. Those developing the statement may seek input from all organizational levels.

Marketing as strategy is formalized in the **strategic marketing plan,** a document describing the company's objectives and how to achieve them in light of competitive activities. Essentially, this plan outlines the decisions executives have made about how to accomplish their vision. The strategic marketing plan generally requires input and guidelines from marketing executives and a planning team of top- and middle-level personnel.

Marketing as tactics refers to precisely how each part of the marketing mix (product, price, promotion and place) will be managed to meet requirements of the strategic marketing plan. **Marketing mix plans** are developed by specialists in each component, such as product managers, advertising managers, logistics personnel and sales personnel.

In a small company, the owner may perform all of these plan-

Marketing Aspect	Type of Planning	Responsibility
Marketing as philosophy	Vision	Top executive and top management team
Marketing as strategy	Strategic marketing plan	Marketing executive and other members of the strategic marketing team
Marketing as tactics	Marketing mix plans	Managers responsible for product, price, promotion, and place programs

Figure 2.1   Strategic Marketing Planning Hierarchy

Figure 2.2   Marketing Planning Hierarchy

ning roles, whereas in a larger company several hundred people may be required. You will find that companies tend to blend philosophy, strategy and tactics into a range of planning, but all three will be present in varying degrees, depending on what is most appropriate for a given organization. The hierarchy in Figure 2.2 describes what takes place as companies develop plans that address the three marketing aspects. Each of the major components of the vision, strategic marketing plan, and marketing mix plans is explored in the following sections. The final portion of this chapter focuses on the strategies companies use to enter and build strength in foreign markets.

LO 02

The Vision

Successful companies have a vision that focuses marketing efforts purposefully. The vision helps maintain consistent direction despite volatile market environments. When President John F. Kennedy said, "...I believe this nation should commit itself to achieving the goal, before this decade is out, of landing a man on the Moon and returning him safely to the Earth," he created an effective vision. He provided a picture that inspired the U.S. space program, largely because the vision was simple, clear and easy to remember. If Kennedy had described the enormity of the challenge in detail (how many people were needed, what talents they must possess, what type of equipment would be required), it's doubtful the venture would have succeeded. Instead, Kennedy's vision was fulfilled in 1969, when Neil Armstrong took "one small step for man, one giant leap for mankind," and walked on the moon.

If you visualize your life now and in five years, 15 years, and beyond, you are forming a personal vision. To make that vision a reality, what values will guide your behaviors? What will you contribute to people around you? What is your idea of excellence? What skills and attributes do you possess or will you develop? Organizations have to answer the same questions.

President John F. Kennedy delivering his historic vision to a joint session of Congress on May 25, 1961.

This is the visioning process. Discovering the vision is critical for companies (or people) that wish to deliver superior value.

The corporate vision provides a common understanding of what the organization is trying to accomplish in the broadest sense. Most company visions are composed of four parts: a set of core values, a business definition, a strategic direction, and a strategic infrastructure.

CORE VALUES: THE ETHICAL FOUNDATION

Core values describe the type of behavior expected from a company's employees. They are the articulation of ethics and social responsibility, which were discussed in Chapter 1. Whole Foods Market considers its values the underpinning of its company culture and says, "We're not just about selling groceries; we believe we have a responsibility toward all people involved in our business." The company commits to selling the highest-quality natural and organic products available, satisfying and delighting customers, supporting team member excellence and happiness, creating wealth through profits and growth, caring about communities and the environment, creating ongoing win-win partnerships with suppliers, and promoting the health of stakeholders through healthy eating education.

By sustaining these core values, Whole Foods believes it will preserve what has made it special since its beginning, regardless of how large the company becomes.[1] Employees believe that if they do this, business will be grounded on a firm foundation. Core values often express the company's philosophy about societal well-being, good corporate citizenship and treatment of employees.

A core value of Johnson and Johnson (JNJ) is to put people first. It prides itself in "caring for the world...one person at a time." Operating with this credo since the company was founded in 1886, JNJ has grown to 265 companies in 60 countries.[2]

Core values provide an ethical guide that may be particularly useful in a crisis. It's possible that Johnson & Johnson would not even be around today if it had waivered from its core values when Tylenol capsules laced with cyanide were linked to several deaths in the early 1980s. However, JNJ followed the core values outlined in its credo and responded immediately by removing all Tylenol products, reimbursing customers and repackaging the product by adding a foil seal to the bottle opening and a plastic seal around the outside of the bottle. In doing so, Tylenol became the first product in its industry to use new tamper-resistant packaging just six months after the crisis occurred.

Courtesy of Whole Foods Market

Whole Foods Market considers its values the underpinning of its company culture.

JOHNSON & JOHNSON CREDO

- We believe that our first responsibility is to our customers.
- Our second responsibility is to our employees.
- Our third responsibility is to our management.
- Our fourth responsibility is to the communites in which we live. We must be a good citizen.
- Our fifth and last responsibility is to our stockholders. Business must make a sound profit. When we operate according to our principles, stockholders should realize a fair return.
- We are determined with the help of God's grace to fulfill these obligations to the best of our ability.

Johnson & Johnson core values are stated in its credo.
Adapted from Johnson & Johnson "Our Credo"

Competitors immediately followed suit. Because it adhered to its core values, Tylenol revolutionized the industry and became a respected market leader.[3]

eBay's community philosophy has provided customer-creating value satisfaction across the world to the 100 million members who buy and sell on its marketplace. The company's online culture uses the following five principles to connect with customers and create value for the e-Bay community:

- We believe people are basically good.
- We believe everyone has something to contribute.
- We believe an honest, open environment can bring out the best in people.
- We recognize and respect everyone as a unique individual.
- We encourage you to treat others the way you want to be treated.[4]

BUSINESS DEFINITION (MISSION)

The **business definition**, also referred to as the company mission, describes the fundamental contributions the organization provides to customers. The mission of clothing company Patagonia is "to build the best product, cause no unnecessary harm, and use business to inspire and implement solutions to the environmental crisis."[5] Patagonia continually demonstrates environmental consciousness, including the use of eco-friendly dyes and materials, energy-efficient computer configurations, and power conservation in product development and manufacturing. In the health care industry, Sparrow Health System's mission, "to improve the health of the people in our communities by providing quality, compassionate care to everyone, every time," has remained consistent for more than 110 years.

Noted scholar Ted Levitt has had a tremendous influence on how companies develop their business definition. In a classic Harvard Business Review article, "Marketing Myopia," he explains why customer orientation is absolutely critical to a company's business definition. **Marketing myopia** occurs when executives focus on their company's current products and services rather than on benefits to consumers.

Part of Patagonia's mission is to deliver the best products without causing harm to the environment.

Levitt uses U.S. railroads as an example. They didn't stop growing when the need for passenger and freight transportation declined; they continued to expand. They got into trouble because they saw themselves as being in the railroad business supplying a product rather than in the transportation business offering a service. Trucking and airline companies took customers away from railroads because they better met their needs. In addition, the railroads' failure to focus on customers meant they also failed to make themselves more competitive.

If the railroads had defined their business as transportation, they would have likely retained a strong influence in the market even with the introduction of alternative methods. Levitt adds that "the entire corporation must be viewed as a customer-creating and customer-satisfying organization. Management must think of itself not as producing products but as providing customer-creating value satisfactions."

An organization's business definition should be stated in basic, benefit-rich terms and

> An organization's business definition should be stated in basic, benefit-rich terms and should focus on consumer benefits, not product features.

should focus on consumer benefits, not product features. It should always answer this question: "What business are we really in?" For example, Johnson & Johnson sees itself in the business of bettering lives. It innovates with this in mind and participates in multiple environmental partnerships, such as the World Research Institute, a research organization dedicated to finding ways to protect the earth.

STRATEGIC DIRECTION (INTENT)

STRATEGIC DIRECTION

The desired leadership position of an organization and the measures used to chart progress toward reaching that position.

Strategic direction is the desired leadership position of an organization and the measures used to chart progress toward this position. Strategic intent is another term for strategic direction: "Strategic intent captures the essence of winning."[6] Strategic direction addresses the competitiveness of the organization and often sets specific growth, profit, share or scope goals relative to the competition and market opportunities.

Strategic direction may identify competitors by name or by industry. Facebook's strategic direction is aimed at overtaking Microsoft in advertising revenue. Volkswagen's "Strategy 2018" is geared to be the most successful automaker in the world.[7] Coca-Cola's "2020 Vision" is a roadmap for doubling revenues this decade.[8] Strategic direction may guide organizations toward becoming one of the largest in an industry. General Electric wants to be either a leader or close follower in each venture it pursues. Google, Mozilla and Microsoft's strategic directions each involve a battle for dominance of the web. Microsoft's Internet Explorer web browser dropped from the top spot in market share after a steady decline to Mozilla Firefox and Google Chrome.[9] In 2008 Internet Explorer controlled nearly 70 percent of the market. Today, it continues to lose users and only holds approximately 11 percent of the market. Firefox holds about 15 percent of the market, Safari holds 10 percent and Chrome has captured 57 percent.[10]

STRATEGIC INFRASTRUCTURE

STRATEGIC INFRASTRUCTURE

The corporate configuration that produces the company's distinctive or core competencies and provides the resources necessary to satisfy customer wants.

Executives must develop and organize the company's **strategic infrastructure**, the corporate configuration that produces the company's distinctive or core competencies and provides the resources necessary to satisfy customer wants. This often means dividing the business into functional units and determining which core competencies to develop. The idea is to focus energy on specific goods, services and talents necessary to create customer value in specific market segments.

STRATEGIC BUSINESS UNIT (SBU)

A part of the firm that can be managed separately for marketing purposes; it may be a division, a product or product line, a distinct group of customers, or a unique technology.

Strategic Business Units (SBUs) Most medium and large companies have several strategic departments or units. A **strategic business unit (SBU)** is a part of the firm that can be managed separately for marketing purposes; it may be a division within the company, a separate brand or product line, a distinct group of customers, or a unique technology. Johnson & Johnson (JNJ) has three SBUs: consumer and medical devices, pharmaceutical, and diagnostic. The consumer and medical SBU concentrates its efforts on marketing consumer products such as Band-Aids, No More Tears shampoo, and Tylenol. The pharmaceutical SBU mainly markets prescription drugs to the health-care industry. The diagnostic SBU produces sutures, surgical equipment, and medical supplies for physicians, dentists and others. Coca-Cola has many SBUs, including coffees, energy drinks, juices and juice drinks, soft drinks, sports drinks, teas and waters.[11]

Consider the corporate structure illustrated in Figure 2.3. It has two divisions: ground transportation and air transportation. The ground transportation division is divided into SBUs according to products (motorcycles, trucks and cars), types of mar-

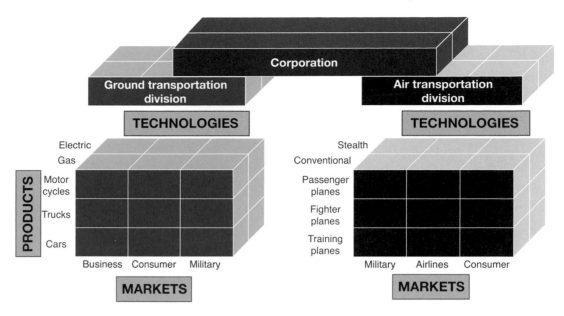

Figure 2.3 Corporate Structure with Small Business Units (SBUs)

kets (business, consumer and military) and technology (electric and gas). The air transportation division is divided similarly (products are passenger planes, fighter planes and training planes; markets are military, airlines and consumers; technologies are conventional and stealth).

The total SBUs possible for this company is 36, but not all combinations would make sense, such as an SBU the produces stealth passenger planes for civilian consumers. There are several ways to structure the SBUs in this company. Grouped by technology there would be four: electric, gas, conventional and stealth, based on products, there would be six: motorcycles, trucks, cars, passenger planes, fighter planes and training planes; and based on type of market, there would be four: airlines, other businesses, consumers and military. Some companies form SBUs by product line. Market-oriented companies, however, usually form SBUs on the basis of specific market segments.

The SBUs of a company can be considered a portfolio...similar to companies in a stock portfolio. When a company has multiple SBUs like JNJ or Coca-Cola does, it needs to decide how to allocate resources to each unit, just like a broker decides what stocks to buy, hold or sell, based on relative strength and market conditions. Companies sometimes use a portfolio planning approach to make these decisions. A **portfolio planning approach** is a technique to measure the contribution each SBU makes to the overall performance of a division or company.

PORTFOLIO PLANNING APPROACH

A technique to measure the contribution each SBU makes to the overall performance of a division or company.

Assessing SBUs: The Growth-Share Matrix One of the most popular portfolio planning approaches was developed by The Boston Consulting Group, an international management consulting firm, which created a matrix to help companies decide how to allocate resources to their SBUs based on two factors—company competitiveness and market attractiveness—as determined by relative market share and growth rate, respectively. The growth-share matrix, shown in Figure 2.4, uses market growth as a measure of opportunity and the company's market share as a measure of resource strength. SBUs are placed in the matrix according to their scores on these two dimensions. The purpose of evaluating a company's portfolio with the BCG matrix is to determine which SBUs generate the most cash and which ones require the most cash, so that a company

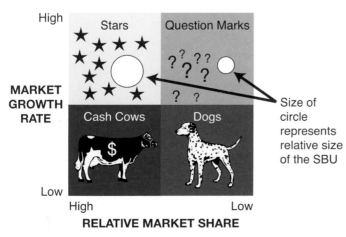

Figure 2.4 Boston Consulting Group Growth-Share Matrix

The Marketing Strategy & Planning Process **39**

can adjust its resource allocations to develop the best marketing strategy. For this to be successful, marketers need to understand market opportunities and the strength of their organization's resources relative to competitors.

Let's consider the BCG matrix using brands that you'll probably recognize from Unilever Corporation.[12] Stars are high market share/high market growth SBUs. They're a lot like movie personalities—give them attention and expect a lot of success! Two of Unilever's "stars" are Dove and Lipton. Dove is the world's top cleansing brand and Lipton is the world's best-selling tea brand.[13] Neither of these brands is new; in fact they've been around for a long time. But like most "star" SBUs, the company continues to invest cash in them and improve the brands to continue earning high returns.

Cash cows are high market share/low market growth SBUs that should be milked for cash to reinvest in more profitable stars. Although the market is growing at a very low rate, the SBU has enough market share to generate substantial cash flow. Companies want at least one product in this category and often have more, since revenues from these products can support the development of other "stars." Two huge "cash cows" for Unilever are Hellmann's mayonnaise (America's #1 mayonnaise brand) and market leader Q-tips.

Market leader Hellman's mayonnaise is a cash cow for Unilever.

Dogs are low market share/low market growth SBUs and typically provide less than desirable returns. They're often considered competitively disadvantaged and unlikely to generate profits. They may actually consume resources, becoming cash drains that create negative value for the company. Slim Fast is an example of a "dog" that Unilever had held for years until finally deciding to sell the brand.[14]

Question marks, or problem children, are low market share/high market growth SBUs. Although they're in a market that is growing quickly, most have not yet achieved competitive advantage or begun generating substantial revenues. Managers need to decide whether to invest more money into these questionable SBUs and hope they become "stars," or get rid of them so they don't become "dogs" and drain cash. Unilever brands that you might find in this quadrant are Omo laundry detergent (also sold as Wisk) and gourmet tea brand T2.

Once SBUs or products are classified, the BCG matrix helps managers decide where to allocate resources. For example, let's say a company decides to take a "question mark" and make it a "star" because of its market share potential. The cash resources to do that would be taken from "cash cows" and invested into the question marks.

A company should regularly evaluate its SBU placements in the matrix. It's a fluid model; positioning will often change as consumer preferences, technology, and competitors change. When a product or SBU shifts from one quadrant to another, marketing managers need to alter their marketing strategies accordingly to make the overall portfolio more profitable.

Assessing SBUs: The Attractiveness-Strength Matrix
The growth-share matrix is useful, but it fails to address competitive behavior or the dynamic characteristics of the market. To obtain a larger picture, some marketing strategists use the attractiveness-strength matrix. As illustrated in Figure 2.5, the marketer first examines such factors as market size, market growth, competitive pressure, price levels and government regulation to develop a composite industry attractiveness score. Next, the marketer as-

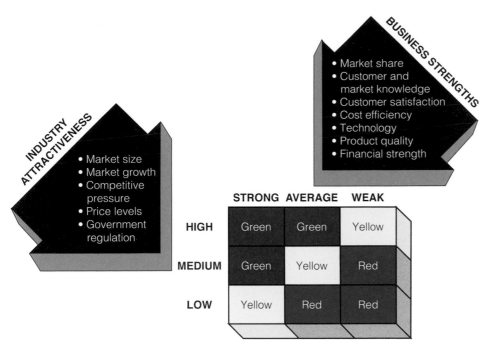

INDUSTRY ATTRACTIVENESS
- Market size
- Market growth
- Competitive pressure
- Price levels
- Government regulation

BUSINESS STRENGTHS
- Market share
- Customer and market knowledge
- Customer satisfaction
- Cost efficiency
- Technology
- Product quality
- Financial strength

	STRONG	AVERAGE	WEAK
HIGH	Green	Green	Yellow
MEDIUM	Green	Yellow	Red
LOW	Yellow	Red	Red

Figure 2.5 The General Electric Attractiveness-Strength Matrix

sesses the business strengths of each SBU based on estimates of the company's market share, customer and market knowledge, customer satisfaction with the company, cost efficiency, level of technology, product quality, and financial strength. Each SBU is then graphed in the matrix based on these several measures.

The attractiveness-strength matrix uses colors to signal whether executives should stop (red), be cautious (yellow) or go ahead (green) with the SBU. Unfortunately, during the 1960s and '70s, "red" SBUs were sometimes categorically denied the resources required to compete, dooming them to failure. At the same time, "green" SBUs were allowed to charge ahead, regardless of the vision of the company. All that was important was the amount of investment required and the SBU's potential return.

Today, portfolio-planning tools are considered useful indicators, not predictors. Even SBUs that fall in the same category may require vastly different management strategies. Portfolio techniques are helpful in identifying the current business situation, but they are inappropriate for making resource allocations. These, as we shall see later, should be made only after the strategic marketing plan has been developed. Because portfolio techniques say little about strategy, they should be used simply as a first step in strategic marketing.

CORE COMPETENCIES

The unique resources a company develops and promotes as its specialty to create distinct customer value; the fundamental building blocks of competitive advantage.

Core Competencies **Core competencies** are the unique resources a company develops and promotes as its specialty to create distinct customer value. They help an organization to distinguish itself from rivals, and they often lead to lower costs. Core competencies are the fundamental building blocks of competitive advantage. They evolve. They help in developing new goods and services and can determine the future of an organization.

McDonald's core competencies in food distribution and preparation enable it to reproduce precisely the same taste, texture and service millions of times a day, anywhere in the world. The chain also added competencies in coffee-based drinks in order to compete with Starbucks. These core competencies give McDonald's the competitive advantage of consistent quality and world recognition associated with the brand.

FedEx has developed a core competency in logistics management. The company represents the benchmark of delivery speed and reliability. Through its computerized information and tracking system technology, the location of any package worldwide can be located within seconds. A competitive advantage for FedEx lies in the fact that its slogan "When it absolutely, positively has to get there overnight" is synonymous with the brand.

Core competencies form the foundation of the success of any one SBU and also span several SBUs or corporate divisions. Marketing's role is to interpret market forces so that the proper core

Courtesy of FedEx

Fedex developed sophisticated package tracking technologies into a core competency.

competencies can be developed to provide maximum benefit to consumers in the marketplace. When they succeed, companies are rewarded with the profit necessary to support continued improvement and growth.

An understanding of core competencies is necessary to comprehend how technology is shaping marketing practices. Through the rapid growth of technologies, companies build millions of products and services that produce superior customer value. The many types of core competencies can be grouped into five categories: (1) base technologies, (2) process technologies, (3) product technologies, (4) people systems and (5) information systems.

Base Technologies Base technologies refer to a broad innovation that a given organization is especially effective at harnessing, or even one it pioneered. The best base technologies are adaptable and can be applied to several different products. For example, one of Canon's core competencies, vision optics, can be used to deliver outstanding cameras, copiers and other inventive products. Dow Chemical - Dupont, known for basic chemistry, has developed multitudes of industrial and consumer products. General Dynamics is skilled in the wave technology necessary for radar and other types of vision systems. General Electric has spent billions of dollars developing its extensive knowledge of physics. Base technologies can be applied simultaneously to a number of diverse industries and product areas.

Process Technologies Process technologies allow the firm to produce quality products in the most effective and flexible manner possible. Marketing's job is to make sure that the development of processes is consistent with market trends and is in the best interest of customers. In an effort to decrease time customers spend waiting for their orders, fast food companies often use hand-held wireless devices at the drive-thru during peak hours to input customer orders. Today, the same companies are turning to smartphone apps to expedite order placement. These process technologies significantly reduce the amount of time customers wait for their food.

Product Technologies A company's ability to create new goods and services is supported by product technologies. Many organizations have worked hard to develop competency in moving quickly from the idea stage through a series of well-defined steps to commercialization. Others follow the leader, copying competitors' products, sometimes improving upon them slightly. Followers benefit from the innovation of leaders without having to invest substantially in developing their own product technology.

The cellphone industry, for instance, has been dramatically affected by changes in technology. Motorola, formerly the market leader in the industry, lost significant share to competitors as rivals introduced smartphones with advanced technologies. Apple took an early lead in the market leaving competitors like Samsung and LG scrambling to gain market share. In the U.S., Apple continues to lead with 40 percent of the total smartphone market but Samsung is catching up. Samsung holds 30 percent of the market and LG has been able to capture 10 percent.[15] On a global scale, Apple and Samsung are in a constant battle to gain the highest market percentage. The industry leader will be the company that consumers believe offers the best technology, customer service and value.

Courtesy of Samsung

Samsung's Galaxy S7 edge delivers some of the best technology in the industry. For those looking for extra storage, the phone can be expanded to an amazing 200GB.

People Systems The procedures that provide the human connection between companies and consumers are called people systems. Johnson and Johnson's website offers a specific section titled "our stories," which recounts customers' stories of how Johnson and Johnson products have made a difference in their lives. Johnson and Johnson employees also share stories of successes and failures they have faced in bringing new products, ideas and services to their customers.[16]

The Walt Disney Company has always placed high value on its team of employees. Walt once said: "The whole thing here is the organization. Whatever we accomplish belongs to our entire group, a tribute to our combined effort. I feel that there is no door with which the kind of talent we have cannot be opened." Today Disney has updated those sentiments: "The Disney name—and the image it conveys—is one of our greatest assets, second only to the people who have contributed their talents and dreams toward the achievement of the goals we have set for ourselves."[17] The importance of Disney's employees is reflected in the organization's retail operation. To foster a spirit of teamwork, employees are called cast members; they refer to the customers as their guests. On the retail floor, they are onstage; in the storeroom, they are backstage. Such role playing helps employees keep the desired goal in mind: exceed guests' expectations.[18]

Courtesy of Walt Disney Company

To foster a spirit of teamwork, Disney employees are called cast members and refer to customers as their guests.

Information Systems An information system that is robust enough to give an organization a competitive advantage is a core competency. Historically, companies were located close to their customers, so they could feasibly research their markets firsthand. Even executives talked directly with customers. Today, the situation is very different because of the increasing diversity of products, customers, competitors and geographical distances in a global marketplace. Information processing technologies are especially important in global marketing because they provide vast amounts of data almost instantly. Companies that don't possess this core competency are at a dramatic competitive disadvantage.

UPS has an extensive information system in which each parcel handled requires many data elements that are transmitted over a optic cable network supported by satellite and wireless communication. This network is called UPSnet.[19] It facilitates the complex logistics involved in transporting millions of parcels each week from different origins to recipients around the world. These systems also allow better, faster communication with third parties, speeding international shipping and the time necessary to clear customs.

The Strategic Marketing Plan

In an organization, many people, not just the marketing department, have at least some responsibility toward developing and executing strategic marketing plans. As noted scholar and business consultant Frederick Webster Jr. says: "Everyone in the firm must be charged with responsibility for understanding customers and contributing to developing and delivering value to them."[20] Marketing is so pervasive in customer-focused, competition-driven companies that teams from diverse areas of the firm (such as accounting, engineering and manufacturing) often work together with marketers to implement it.

In the past, the planning process included only marketing personnel. Today, strong marketers generally assemble a **cross-functional planning team**. This team works together and ideally contributes a total understanding of the market and the organization's capabilities.[21] Just as relationships with stakeholders outside the company are important, so are internal relationships. Since each member of the planning team has a unique perspec-

CROSS-FUNCTIONAL PLANNING TEAM

Employees from several areas responsible for developing the company's strategic marketing plan.

TITLE	RESPONSIBILITY
Marketing	Development of strategic plan and team leader
Engineering	Technological product development
Manufacturing	Efficient manufacturing
Finance	Financial modeling of strategies
Marketing Intelligence	Estimate competitor strengths, vulnerabilities
Marketing Research	Customer and consumer requirements
Sales	Potential sales strategies
Promotion and Advertising	Support program development
Procurement	Available supply partners and costs
Human Resources	Union and employee relations
Logistics	Distribution systems approaches
Accounting	Analysis of cost data

Figure 2.6   A Cross-Functional Strategic Planning Team

STRATEGY

The development and/or deployment of resources with the intent of accomplishing goals and objectives in a competitive arena.

STRATEGIC WINDOW

The time during which market needs and the competencies of the firm fit together to create a significant opportunity.

LOW-COST STRATEGY

Strategy based on efficiency with objective to be the low-cost leader, thereby allowing the company to have higher margins than competitors and pass savings on to customers through lower prices.

tive, these people must bring all parts of the picture together. Figure 2.6 identifies each person's functional area and a short description of the function's responsibility.

WHAT IS STRATEGY?

For decades, the definition of strategy has been debated among business scholars. Even the military has a unique definition of the term ("the art of meeting the enemy in battle under advantageous conditions"). Although there are several "correct" definitions of strategy, we will use the following: A **strategy** is a company's long-term plan of how to use resources for pursuing goals and objectives in competitive arenas. Companies have limited human, financial, geographical and technological resources, so executives must determine how to best use those resources to accomplish organizational goals. Note that "competitive arena" implies the presence of competitors. They all have their own goals to achieve, and some of them overlap and affect each others' ability to succeed. The idea of strategy is to win outright by serving customers better through relationships and technology, with attention to diversity, global dimensions, sustainability and ethics.

Strategy is not just about beating the competition. It also involves seizing the moment to make changes when appropriate. Observe any group of planners and you're sure to hear someone refer to the **strategic window**. Derek Abell, noted business strategist, coined the term to describe the moment when requirements of the market and competencies of the firm fit together to create a significant opportunity.[22] Now, more than ever, the strategic window is important. Products and technologies change so rapidly that organizations must be prepared to respond quickly when opportunities arise to gain sales and market share. Companies slow to respond often find their product(s) sitting in inventory after spending millions of dollars on product development.

For example, after Apple introduced its iPad tablet, a host of competitors quickly followed: the HP Touchpad, the Dell Streak, the 16GB BlackBerry PlayBook, all of which have since been shelved.[23] Savvy marketers know that the strategic window is open for a relatively short period as consumers consider new technology. During this short time, organizations can and should create sustainable strategies to win customers, create value and gain market share.

In the next section we'll explore three of the most common types of marketing plan strategies: low-cost, differentiation and customer intimacy. Then we'll explore the idea of sustainable competitive advantage, which is what a company may gain through successful strategic marketing.

Low-Cost Strategy A **low-cost strategy** focuses on winning through efficiency. The objective is to be the low-cost leader, which allows the company to have higher margins than competitors and to pass some savings on to customers through lower prices. There are many ways to gain a favorable cost position:

- *Process technology* Invent a low-cost way to create and deliver a product.
- *Product design* Create a product that provides the same level of functionality with lower cost than predecessors or competitors, often through new materials or miniaturization.

The low-cost strategy used by Dollar Tree stores is successful because of low-cost suppliers.

- *Consolidation of the value chain* Combine several steps of the value chain into one.
- *Low-cost suppliers* Reduce costs by purchasing materials and other inputs at lower prices.
- *Location* Put facilities in low-wage areas or nearby markets to lower distribution costs.
- *Economies of scale and scope* Produce more and market in a larger area so costs are spread over more units and customers.[24]

DIFFERENTIATION STRATEGY

Strategy based on delivering customer value in a way that clearly distinguishes the product from competitors; works through effectiveness.

Differentiation Strategy A **differentiation strategy** involves delivering customer value in a way that clearly distinguishes the product from its competitors. Differentiation works through effectiveness by giving superior benefits or reducing customer cost rather than price. There are several ways to achieve differentiation.

- *New functional capabilities* Create products that do new things.
- *Improved performance* Make products that work better.
- *Product tailoring* Make products that more closely suit the needs of select groups.
- *Lower Costs* Make products that are more energy efficient, require less maintenance, or are less expensive to operate.

CUSTOMER INTIMACY STRATEGY

Strategy based on delivering value through superior empathy for customers and solutions tailored to specific customer needs.

Customer Intimacy Strategy A **customer intimacy strategy** is based on delivering value through superior empathy for customers and solutions tailored to specific customer needs. Intimacy requires developing close relationships with the customer. There are several ways to achieve this:

- *Add value* Assume responsibilities such as updating and supporting products at the customer's site.
- *Mass customization* Use a process that creates products precisely to the specifications of individual customers.
- *Information* Collect and maintain databases regarding customers' product usage.
- *Product bundling* Develop product configurations specifically suited for individual customers.

SUSTAINABLE COMPETITIVE
ADVANTAGE

A lasting ability to outperform all
competition in a particular market
or industry.

Sustainable Competitive Advantage **Sustainable competitive advantage** is a strategy that develops when companies are able to create a lasting ability to outperform all competition in a particular market or industry. Sustainable competitive advantage is derived from a company's strong core competency. Competitors generally try to copy it or create their own, but the advantage can't be readily duplicated...otherwise it wouldn't be sustainable. Organizations that create sustainable advantages have less volatility and better long-run performance.

- *Strong research and Innovation* Become an industry leader through research and innovation.
- *Brand Popularity* Create a brand that is recognized and respected throughout the world.
- *Corporate reputation* Develop the polished reputation of being a world-class corporation with high standards.
- *Superior Product or customer support* Provide a superior or unique product at an affordable price with great customer service.

LO 03 Components of the Strategic Marketing Plan

Guided by the corporate vision, the strategic marketing plan essentially describes how to accomplish that vision. Keep in mind that many organizations are complex and may have more than one strategic marketing plan. General Electric has a strategic marketing plan for the company itself and additional ones for divisions of the organization, such as aircraft engines and lighting. It even developed a separate plan for its participation as a worldwide partner of the 2016 Olympic Games in Rio.

Courtesy of GE

GE LED fixtures at the 2016 Rio de Janeiro Olympic site will save half a million dollars in energy costs compared to fluorescent technology. (Source: GE)

The planning team has to address five areas: objectives, situation analysis, target markets, positioning, and integration of the marketing mix. The first step is to state the objectives the business will pursue and the specific goals it expects to obtain. The second step is a situation analysis, which describes the current business environment and how well the company will be able to compete in it. The third step is to determine target markets to identify which customers the organization will serve. The fourth step is to decide positioning relative to competitors—the image the organization wants customers to have about it and its products. The fifth step is to develop plans for each aspect of the marketing mix and integrate these into the overall strategic plan.

We will discuss each step in detail following this logical order, but as actual plans are developed, the various steps usually interact with one another. For example, objectives are stated first but may later be changed to reflect information revealed during the situation analysis. Finally, like a baseball pitch, a good strategic marketing plan needs follow-through or control measures that provide feedback on how well the plan is working.

OBJECTIVES

The strategic marketing plan must support the business definition stated in the organization's vision. Since the objectives are an outgrowth of the vision, they tend to be stated up-front. But they must take into account all of the remaining parts of the plan as well, so objectives might be recast as strategies emerge during subsequent steps in the planning process. Companies usually set objectives in terms of desired profit, market share or total sales. Profit is the most common choice and may be stated in various ways, such as return on investment, cash flow (amount of cash returned to the business), or profit margins. Market share refers to a proportion relative to competitors that the company captures: the percentage of customers within a given market, the percentage of dollars spent on similar products, or the percentage of all similar product units that are sold (unit sales). Finally, businesses determine a total sales objective, defined as either a dollar amount or a quantity of products sold. Most organizations state objectives in these ways, but many may add others: number of loyal customers, customer retention rates, and customer satisfaction scores.

Often, it's appropriate to state very specific objectives such as "44% market share by 2020." Notice that objectives always provide a time frame and must be verifiable (meaning it will be clear whether or not the objective has been met). You will see why this is important when we discuss the marketing control process.

SITUATION ANALYSIS

All marketing activities required to understand the marketing environment, customer needs and wants, and the competition are examined in the situation analysis. This analysis predicts market conditions for the period that the strategic marketing plan is in effect. If the plan extends through 2020, for example, then predictions should be made up to that time. Developing possible scenarios generally requires bringing together data and expertise from different parts of the company to provide an accurate picture.

The situation analysis can be very elaborate or fairly simple, depending on the circumstances. At a minimum, it should give the planning team a general idea about the future, including potential size of the market, types of customers, competitors, technology, channels of distribution, economic conditions, governmental regulations, and the resources the company will have at its disposal, both globally and in individual countries.

As a final step in the situation analysis, the planning team must determine how well the company's skills and resources match the predicted market opportunities. This is typically called a **SWOT analysis**, which is an acronym for strengths, weaknesses, opportunities and threats. An example is shown in Figure 2.7.

Strengths and weaknesses are defined by such measures as market share, number of loyal customers, level of customer satisfaction and rate of success with new products. Strengths describe the unique resources or circumstances that can be used to take advantage of opportunities. Weaknesses suggest aspects of the organization or product that need improvement or, if that is not possible, ways to minimize any negative effects. Opportunities indicate advancements that can be made in new or existing markets. They identify areas in which the organization can gain competitive advantages.

SWOT ANALYSIS

An analysis of strengths, weaknesses, opportunities, and threats to determine how well a company's skills and resources match the predicted market opportunities.

Strengths

Assess good use of competencies and results in the market:
- Share increase
- High loyalty and satisfaction ratings
- Excellent sales force
- Unique products, services

Opportunities

Assess areas where advantage may be gained:
- Add a new product
- Promote to new segment
- Sell more to existing customers
- Use a new form of distribution to reach new markets

Weaknesses (Constraints)

Assess poor use of competencies and results in the market:
- Share decrease
- Disloyal customers
- Not enough salespeople
- Product launch delays

Threats (Vulnerability)

Assess external forces that may prevent the company from accomplishing its objectives:
- Competitor with a new technology
- New government regulations
- Changing customer preferences

Figure 2.7   An Example of SWOT Analysis

The threats section describes how the competition, new technology, the business environment or government may possibly impede the company's development.

Companies are constrained by their weaknesses and are vulnerable to threats. When the government eliminated the use of certain environmentally hazardous resins in the manufacture of recreational boats, irate customers complained that colors faded in the sun. White didn't fade, but the lack of color reduced much of the excitement of new models and designs, convincing many customers to stop purchasing designer-style boats for that reason. Today, technological breakthroughs in environmentally friendly but stable colors have eliminated this threat.

TARGET MARKETING

Once the situation analysis is complete, the planning team determines the characteristics of viable customer groups. Businesses cannot be "all things to all people;" given their competencies, they must choose which segments have the greatest potential.

Target marketing is the process of selecting which market segments the firm will emphasize in attempts to satisfy customers better than its competitors. Many consumer businesses target Millennial customers, also known as Generation Y (born in the 1980s and 1990s). As marketers are well aware, Millennials are 75.4 million strong and spend about $200 billion a year.[25] The group is considerably more tech oriented and design savvy than its predecessors. "With this generation, everything has to be visual and contextual. … They will form impressions about a product based on how it looks and what it does, not what advertisers say about it," says Kit Yarrow, Professor of Psychology and Marketing at Golden Gate University and author of the book *Gen BuY*.[26]

This market is also getting a lot of attention from companies such as Toyota, Honda, Ford, Volkswagen and Saturn. Ford was one of the first automobile companies in the U.S. to target Millennials, using the Ford Focus. Ford specifically aimed at winning Millennial customers by providing a vehicle with a Sync sound system, affordable pricing, and fashionable design. Other companies followed suit with powerful factory stereo systems, faster designs, and sporty interiors.

Today, Ford is using social media as a main source to reach out to Millennials. It recently launched a campaign including free Ford Focus iOS and Android emoji keyboards along with sticker packs for Kik, PalTalk and Tango mobile messaging apps. "Our Ford Focus stickers and branded emoji keyboard reach an audience that has embraced the concept of personalizing their communications with friends and making their favorite brands a part of that dialogue," said Angie Kozleski, Global Digital Communications Manager, Ford Motor Company.[27]

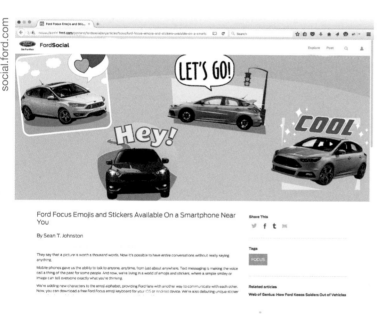

social.ford.com

Ford Focus Emojis and Stickers Available On a Smartphone Near You

By Sean T. Johnston

FordSocial announces Ford Focus emojis and stickers for social media, a way of targeting Millennials.

POSITIONING

Planning teams often decide to pursue different positioning strategies with different target market segments. **Positioning**, as you recall, refers to creating a perception in the minds of consumers about the company and/or its products relative to competitors. A more common word for positioning is image—the thoughts and perceptions that a brand evokes in people. For example, Tiffany & Co. wants to convey an image of high quality and status. If consumers see the company that way, then the marketing team has been successful in its positioning efforts.

VALUE PROPOSITION

A statement of the compelling reason(s) customers should select a brand.

Positioning is closely related to **value proposition**, which is a statement of the compelling reason(s) customers should select the brand. For example, the value proposition for Advanced Micro Devices Inc. (AMD) is simple: AMD offers superior products at competitive costs and industry-standard products at lower costs. Sometimes a value proposition is simply a tagline. BMW promotes "the ultimate driving machine." Target promises "pay less expect more."

"Everyone is after everyone's business. The mind of your customer or prospect is the battleground and that's where you win or lose," says Jack Trout, author of numerous marketing books and president of Trout & Partners, Ltd. According to him, "Just as each product needs to be positioned in the mind (of consumers) against competitors, so does a company need to be positioned. Customers want to know where you're going. So do your employees."

INTEGRATING THE MARKETING MIX

Once the desired positioning is established, the marketing mix—product, place, promotion, and price—must be integrated to make the strategy happen. It's the tactical part of the strategic marketing planning process. An effective strategy incorporates all elements of the mix in order to produce a unified effort to achieve the company's marketing objectives.

This is how successful companies maintain their market positions. As previously mentioned, Disney offers multiple products, including amusement parks, MGM Studios, Epcot Center, Blizzard Beach, Discovery Island and others. Each provides a high-quality experience, whether for vacations, weddings or business meetings.

Disney is constantly adding new *products* in order to remain relevant to lifestyles of its target markets. The company carefully chooses theme park locations that are easily accessible to consumers (*place*). The variety of *pricing* options—deluxe, moderate and economy—allows customers to choose options that are best for them. And Disney takes care to promote its products to a variety of customers. It also makes information about its products readily available online and through thousands of travel agents around the world. Some promotion is aimed directly at children, some at young singles, and some at married couples traveling without children. This communicates to consumers that Disney parks are for everyone. The company's integrated strategy is clearly paying off: Disney's annual sales are more than $45 billion and rising.[28]

MARKETING CONTROL PROCESS

Procedures designed to provide feedback on how well the marketing strategy is working.

Once the marketing mix is integrated and the marketing plan is implemented, results need to be studied. Is the plan effective? Is it working as expected? The **marketing control process** evaluates how well the strategy marketing plan is working. Members of the planning team assemble to determine whether they are reaching objectives. As described in Figure 2.8, the team first reviews the original objectives, including sales volume projections, order quantities, customer loyalty and satisfaction rates, and market share projections. These objectives are compared to the actual results for each target market segment and the total—which is why objectives should be measurable and verifiable, as stated earlier. This procedure is often called metrics, or metering (measuring) what actually happened.

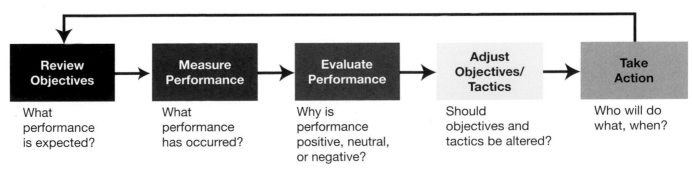

Figure 2.8   The Marketing Control Process: Assessing the Strategic Marketing Plan

By comparing actual results to the stated objectives, the team assesses the organization's performance. During these reviews, the planning team looks for trends and areas of strength or weakness. For example, sales and market share may be higher than expected because competitors were late in launching a new product, or sales may be low because the company's price was too high compared to competitors' prices. An unclear cause for results points to a need for more intensive marketing research.

Next, the team may decide to take corrective action by adjusting elements of the plan or the marketing mix. If results are strong, then objectives (such as revenue or unit sales) may be increased. If not, objectives may be lowered, but the team usually resists this step because it can be viewed as a sign of weakness.[29]

Adjustments to the plan usually are tactical rather than strategic, done through changes in the marketing mix elements. A change in overall strategy requires a more involved and lengthy process. Sometimes teams need to start over from the beginning with a brand new plan. In either case, time is critical. One executive says that adjusting plans and taking action can be "like changing a flat tire on a moving automobile." It happens rapidly in companies that are flexible, efficient and competitive.

Marketing Mix Plans

Companies need a plan for each part of the marketing mix: product, place, promotion and price. The plan for each element often is developed within specific functional areas of marketing, such as the product development department. In some cases, all of these plans are combined into one. Individual mix elements will be covered in detail in subsequent chapters, but a brief discussion of the major issues is provided here. Figure 2.9 illustrates some of the questions marketers consider when developing plans for each aspect of the marketing mix. This list is far from comprehensive; companies need to consider their specific environments in deciding how to address each element.

Plans for the marketing mix components encompass both strategies and tactics. For example, the decision to enter a new product area or distribution channel is strategic. Changes to an existing product or the addition of a new retailer in distribution are tactical. Tactics are used to achieve strategies. Strategies are long-term and broad in scope; **tactics** are short-term, well-defined actions suited to specific market conditions. Strategies describe how a company will compete to serve customers, whereas tactics specifically describe who will do what, how, where and when.

Companies usually employ several tactics to accomplish a given strategy. McDonald's strategy is to provide high-quality, value-priced food and friendly, fast service to families. One tactic is to have a child enticing "playground" at some of its restaurants. Another is personal appearances by Ronald McDonald and colorful packaging of children's meals that include toys associated with popular cartoons or movies, such as Angry Birds, Skylanders Superchargers and the Powderpuff Girls.[30]

Subway, which targets a more adult audience, pursues a

TACTICS

Short-term actions and reactions to specific market conditions through which companies pursue their strategy.

Marketing Mix Element	Types of Decisions
Product	What new products/services should we introduce? Which ones should we drop? What are our objectives with each product/service? Are any new technologies available to improve our product/service?
Place	Where do our customers shop? Should our product/service be available at all these places or just a few? Should we sell directly to our customers or through middlemen, such as retailers, wholesalers, or dealers? How should we ship the product—by rail, truck, air, ship, or others?
Promotion	What are our promotion objectives? Are we trying to create awareness, encourage purchases, or others? What medium should we use: social media, television or radio advertising, coupons, free trials, personal selling, public relations campaign, or a combination of these?
Price	What type of message do we want to send out? What is our overall pricing philosophy? Do we want to exceed, meet, or underprice our competitors? Is our price consistent with the amount of value we deliver to our customers?

Figure 2.9 Examples of Marketing Mix Decisions

strategy of preparing customized sandwiches quickly. Its assembly line tactic allows patrons to build their own sandwiches from a variety of breads, meats, cheeses, vegetables and condiments. Another aspect of the Subway strategy focuses on providing healthy alternatives to other fast-food restaurants. Its efforts paid off when the tactic of Subway's five-dollar foot-long deal became a huge hit, leading to an explosion of business.[31] The company's specific tactic to pre-slice and weigh the meat element of the sandwich, leaving only toppings to be added, expedites the process while still enabling patrons to create unique sandwiches of their choice.

Both of these franchises employ strategies that make use of their core competencies. It would be tactically inconsistent for McDonald's to add expensive, gourmet items to its menu or for Subway to offer complicated, full-course meals. Each has capitalized on its core competencies by supporting them with innovative tactics. As a result, McDonald's is the 2016 number one ranked chain in the U.S., and Subway is the number two ranked chain, according to Franchise Direct. [32]

PRODUCT PLANS

A company may sell physical goods (such as automobiles or textbooks) or intangible services (a college education, legal counsel or health care). Many companies sell both. In the business world, "product" has come to mean physical goods as well as services. Unless specified otherwise in this text, we shall use product to mean either goods or services.

Product decisions are critical for most companies, and they are among the most difficult to make. Marketers must help determine which products or product lines to develop for the target market and which ones to drop. Because products go through a life cycle, product strategy decisions are ongoing. Most organizations use systematic processes to develop and manage products over their life cycles, including decisions regarding product attributes, warranties, package design, and customer service features.

PRODUCT LINE

Closely related products marketed by the organization.

CC BY 2.0

Red Velvet Oreo cookies is a limited edition product in Nabisco's product line.

A **product line** consists of several closely related products marketed by an organization. For example, Nabisco offers many different types of snack foods, including Oreo cookies, Fig Newtons, Chips Ahoy!, and Ritz crackers; each of these is a separate product line. Items are constantly being added, such as seasonal Oreo cookies with different colored fillings.

Marketers must take consumers into account when making product decisions. Each year, Coach, the maker of handbags and fine accessories, interviews more than 60,000 customers through online questionnaires, phone surveys and face-to-face encounters. The information has helped executives spot trends and extend the Coach brand beyond the traditional leather bags. After hearing customers complain that they couldn't find decent carry-on luggage for weekend getaways, Coach launched its successful Signature Stripe travel bags.[33]

Product plans challenge marketers to continuously monitor, assess and make decisions based on the ever-changing environment. Technological products go through a very rapid life cycle, requiring marketers to make frequent and sometimes difficult product decisions. For example, in the video game industry, leaders have changed often, from Atari and Coleco to Sega and Nintendo to Sony and Microsoft.

Samung's VR technology powered by Oculus could be pioneering the next big gaming experience.

Now the mobile game industry has reached $29 billion in revenue and is expected to reach $45 billion by 2018, surpassing the traditional console game industry.[34] In response to this trend, traditional console game companies are increasing graphic and sound hardware, and continually innovating with new products and features. The Nintendo Wii introduced motion controls, bringing new interest and technology to the industry. Microsoft launched Kinect, a motion sensor that was touted to change the gaming industry forever. Nintendo quickly refocused to duel screen controllers and Sony decided virtual reality (VR) would be the next "game-changer."

Taking note from Sony, Facebook quickly jumped into the action and acquired VR technology company Oculus for $2 billion.[35] The modest but bold acquisition sent the industry into a frenzy, sparking Samsung, Sony, Google, and HTC to all make VR a priority to meet the market first.[36] Samsung won the race with the release of a Oculus-powered headset, but time will tell which company's technology will prevail. This rapid shift in technologies will likely keep the game industry, and its marketers, working to position their companies for the next major change.

PLACE PLANS

DISTRIBUTION CHANNELS

A set of independent organizations involved in making the product available to the target market.

Distribution channels are the set of independent organizations involved in making the product available to the target market. A channel describes the route a product follows as it moves from manufacturer to consumers. First, marketers must determine where target customers shop: malls, shopping centers, downtown areas, discount outlets, online or by telephone. People also shop in many different types of stores: supermarkets, merchandise marts, hyperstores, specialty shops and outdoor markets. In each area of the world, consumer shopping patterns are unique. Parisians buy bread baked daily at small shops located throughout the city. The Japanese prefer to purchase fresh fish, caught within hours of eating, from small neighborhood retailers. Suburban Americans often shop once a week and freeze many items for use days or even weeks later. They like one-stop supermarkets within driving distance. Obviously, it's important for marketers to know where consumers prefer to shop for the types of products or services that their company makes.

PHYSICAL DISTRIBUTION

The movement of finished products through channels of distribution to customers.

Physical distribution (or logistics) involves getting the right product, in the right condition, to the right customer, at the right time, for the minimum cost. This is one of the fastest-growing and most important areas of business. Annual spending on supply chain logistics services has reached $3 trillion globally. Apple alone spent $10.5 billion on additional supply chain robots and machinery in 2013.[37]

Physical distribution decisions can greatly affect the profitability of the company. For example, excess inventory in the channel increases storage costs. The marketing team is responsible for ensuring inventory keeps flowing through the channel. Recent data from financial information company Sageworks Inc. shows that delayed customer payments and slow-moving inventory are tying up private companies' cash for 16 percent longer than just three years ago. "Their cash is tied up in inventory as well as receivables, and that has a significant effect on cash flow and, consequently, a significant effect on how much they can use for capital expenditures or new jobs," said Michael W. McNeilly, Sageworks' Director of Advisory Services.[38]

PROMOTION PLANS

The third element of the marketing mix, promotion, provides information about a company's product or service in an effort to encourage target customers to buy it. Marketers develop integrated marketing communications by coordinating advertising, sales promotion, personal selling, and public relations to get consistent messages to the target market. These messages provide information necessary for the decision process. Promotion also increases demand for products, describes unique product characteristics, and helps build customer loyalty by creating expectations and reinforcing buying decisions.

Even marketers who traditionally used narrow communication channels have expanded their audience through increased promotions. Broadway shows were traditionally only advertised in theater directories. Today, ads appear everywhere, including on water towers and subways. The musical "Hamilton," a hip-hop rendition about the life of American Founding Father Alexander Hamilton, became a smash hit on Broadway. The electrifying "Hamilton" performance at the 2016 Grammys created a flurry of praise on social media, drawing further attention to the show. The cast's recent performance at the White House was introduced by President Obama himself. Within a few months of its release, the YouTube video of the performance reached well over a million views. Promoters for the show are now benefiting from its 11 Tony Awards, advertising this feat on social media and the official "Hamilton" website. The website also has links to ticket sales, special sneakpeak videos from the cast and crew, and a store where fans can buy merchandise.[39]

Official White House Photo by Pete Souza

President Obama greets the cast and crew of "Hamilton."

PRICING PLANS

Price is how much money customers must pay for the product. It sends strong signals to buyers. When Reebok aerobic shoes were first introduced into the women's market segment, demand was disappointing. The product was priced incorrectly—in this case, too low. When Reebok raised its prices, demand increased. Consumers often equate low prices with poor quality, whereas higher prices signal high quality, and perhaps something unique or difficult to obtain. Porsche raised prices in the American market. Ralph Lauren found it worked with men's and women's clothing. The perfume industry has used this technique since its inception.

In other cases, price increases can be devastating to sales volume. Think about the airline industry, with many different providers offering service between the same cities. What do you think would happen to ticket sales at United Airlines if it raised its prices above those of Delta? Unless United offered a unique benefit to justify the additional cost, demand would start dropping. That's why a price shift in one airline triggers shifts in others.

Connecting Globally:
Entering World Markets To Capture Value

Once the domain of a few corporate giants, global marketing is fast becoming a requirement for most companies. Why? First, world markets offer tremendous opportunities. Many foreign market segments are larger and growing more rapidly than segments in the United States. Second, for better or worse, U.S. business is no longer safe from global competitors. Most U.S. companies are in some form of competition with foreign ones, even in local markets. The United States' relatively few restrictions on foreign entry provide opportunities for that competition. Third, a company intent on becoming an industry leader must operate globally or be placed at a severe competitive disadvantage.

GEOGRAPHIC SCOPE

World trade has skyrocketed in recent years: U.S. exports exceed $1.6 trillion annually. The United States also imports a large amount of foreign goods and services, approximately $2.4 trillion each year.[40] From a planning standpoint, marketers must identify the **geographic scope** of the strategy, which is the extent of a company's international activities. Generally, geographic scope is divided into four categories, as outlined in Figure 2.10.

International	Operating in one or a few foreign markets
Regional	Operating within countries in close proximity, such as North America, Europe, Scandinavia, or the Pacific Rim
Multinational	Heavy involvement in a few countries located in various regions such as Italy, South Africa, and Japan
Global	Operating in nearly all world markets

Figure 2.10   Geographic Scope

International Scope When a company conducts business in one or a very few foreign countries, it has an international scope. Generally, international companies treat foreign business as a supplement to their domestic operations rather than as a strategic necessity. Yet expansion in even one country can provide useful experience for further global activity at a later date. Some of the top players in the U.S. agriculture industry are keeping a close eye on Cuba for international growth, now that the U.S. could lift the trade embargo established in 1962. Cubans, who for the most part grow crops without pesticides, could also benefit by being able to tap into the American organic market.[41] Other types of U.S. businesses like airlines, hotel chains, and telecommunication firms are interested in expanding to Cuba as well. "Cuba is a very romantic and sexy market right now," said Alana Tummino, director of policy at Council of the Americas.[42]

Regional Scope A company with operations in several adjacent countries has regional scope. In essence, regional companies are competing within one large market that crosses national borders, generally only in one area of the world. Regional operations tend to be efficient because the markets are close together. The benefits of large market size, combined with localized production and distribution provide a viable strategy. This was the approach of Starbucks as it expanded outside the United States. The company opened its first Pacific Rim outlet in Tokyo and from there expanded into other nations in the Asian-Pacific region, including Singapore, Hong Kong, Taiwan and Indonesia.

Multinational Scope When companies operate in several countries around the world, unrestricted by region, their scope is multinational. For example, Westinghouse Process Control sells services to electric utilities in the United States and several selected countries in many regions of the world. However, Westinghouse has decided to avoid marketing to certain countries in several areas. Multinational companies carefully choose their target areas and use an appropriate method of operation (if any) for each area of the world.

Global Scope Operations in nearly all countries around the world constitute a global scope. Kenichi Ohmae, previous global consultant for McKinsey & Company, describes global scope with the mental image of hovering like a satellite over the earth.[43]A global market reaches nearly all countries. Differences as well as similarities among market areas are recognized, so that similar segments of buyers in various regions can be targeted with a universal image.[44]

Global businesses develop totally integrated strategies that maximize competitiveness worldwide over the long term. The Quaker Oats Company has committed to this type of integrated global strategy. Its Quaker International Branding Program is designed to ensure that the Quaker name means "healthy," no matter where you live. The company has a basic advertising, packaging and promotion plan that is tailored to meet local conditions. This helps keep the Quaker image consistent around the globe.

Coca-Cola is another truly global company. It operates in over 200 countries and has invested over $75 billion together with global bottling partners since 2010.[45] The feature article at the beginning of this chapter identifies Coca-Cola's new "One Brand" strategy, which is designed to globally unite all Trademark Coke products—Coca-Cola, Diet Coke/Coca-Cola Light, Coke Zero and Coca-Cola Life—under a single visual identity system anchored by the iconic Coca-Cola Red Disc. The company has recently sought growth opportunities in China, India and Africa. It has had a presence in those markets for a while, but global marketing—like national marketing—requires the same diligence in constantly looking for ways to connect with customers to increase sales, market share and loyalty.

Global marketing is based on the notion that consumers around the world are behaving more alike and that modern technology has created a degree of commonality. Travel and communication have exposed more and more people to the same types of goods and services. Global companies appreciate the differences in consumer preferences, shopping behavior, cultural institutions, and promotional media, but they believe that these preferences and practices can and will become more similar.[46]

The Quaker image is consistent around the globe.

Export	Send products abroad for resale
Foreign Licensing and Franchising	Agreements that permit foreign companies to produce and distribute merchandise, often using trademarks and/or selected merchandising and customer delivery approaches
Overseas Marketing and Production	A marketing infrastructure and/or production facilities abroad
Foreign Strategic Alliances and Joint Ventures	The shared ownership of operations by two or more local and foreign companies (joint venture) or the pooling of resources by two or more companies for the purpose of competing as one entity (strategic alliance)

Figure 2.11   Approaches for Entering and Building Foreign Markets

STRATEGIES FOR FOREIGN MARKET ENTRY

There are several different approaches for entering and developing markets. Small companies may use only one or two methods, due to resource limitations or a focused target market, whereas larger companies may use several simultaneously. Figure 2.11 outlines the four most important approaches.

Exporting Exporting is the least risky and most common form of international marketing. Exporting sends domestically manufactured products into foreign countries for resale. Exporting is a relatively easy way to enter foreign trade for two reasons: the investment is lower than other meth-

EXPORT INTERMEDIARIES

Domestic or foreign firms with specialized experience in exporting activity.

TRADING COMPANIES

Large intermediaries that facilitate the movement of goods in and out of countries.

FOREIGN LICENSING

Assigning the rights of a patent, trademark, or manufacturing process to a foreign company for a fee, often called a royalty.

FRANCHISING

A special type of licensing arrangement whereby the marketer provides not only the product, technology, process, and/or trademark but also the entire marketing program.

ods, and most governments offer support to help companies enter their markets.

Still, establishing an export arrangement can involve many complicated details. That's why many firms choose to engage **export intermediaries**, which are firms with specialized experience in exporting activity. There are two types of intermediaries: indirect and direct. Indirect export intermediaries are located in the domestic market and help send products abroad. They specialize in knowledge about foreign customs, regulations affecting businesses and products, laws, and market conditions. Direct export intermediaries are located in the foreign market. Since they are very familiar with the local business environment, they can help clients in special ways, such as offering unique government contacts. Intermediaries can be very beneficial because they assume many of the risks involved with distribution. At the same time, the exporting company must give up a significant amount of control over how its product is distributed.

Trading companies are large intermediaries that facilitate the movement of goods in and out of countries. For example, Koch is an international trading company that aids in the sale of essential goods to and from a variety of regions, such as food, clothing, building materials, fuel, and other commodities. In order to provide customers a diverse array of products and commodities, Koch companies have access to major international trading regions around the world and employs over 100,000 people across more than 60 countries. [47]

Foreign Licensing and Franchising **Foreign licensing** assigns the rights to a patent, trademark or manufacturing process to a foreign company for a fee, often called a royalty. Licensing allows companies to gain entry into a foreign market at almost no cost or risk, but control of the marketing strategy is turned over to the licensee. **Franchising** is a special type of licensing arrangement whereby the marketer provides the product, technology, process and/or trademark, as well as most of the marketing program. In nearly any major city around the world, you are likely to find McDonald's, KFC and Taco Bell, or Holiday Inn, Hilton and Marriott. They are there because local entrepreneurs have bought the franchise. Franchising allows companies to maintain marketing control while passing along many of the costs, risks, and responsibilities to the foreign licensees. These franchises often function quite autonomously from the parent company but benefit from being part of a large corporation.

Overseas Marketing and Production Also called subsidiaries, overseas marketing and production operations are owned by a parent company in foreign countries. They can be a small office or a large, elaborate production facility. A subsidiary operation may simply assemble finished goods or may function as an independent business, responsible for product development, manufacturing, marketing and so on. For example, General Motors operates assembly plants for automotive components in Mexico, while its German and British subsidiaries produce entire automobiles.

McDonald's and KFC franchises on the colorful streets of Hong Kong.

Concrdialme / CC BY-SA 3.0

Another company entering foreign markets through production is Mars Corporation, maker of Snickers and M&M's. Via its wholly-owned subsidiary, Mars International India, Mars is investing over $160 million in a new factory at Pune, India. This will be the company's first chocolate factory in India. The project is expected to help the local economy in Pune by generating over 200 direct and 1000 indirect jobs, while allowing Mars to grasp a share of the chocolate industry that's growing at 20% every year.[48]

Subsidiaries can be very costly to establish and very risky to operate, since the owner is liable for any mishaps. Foreign operations also are subject to a host of circumstances beyond the company's control. For example, several oil companies lost billions of dollars when their Iranian subsidiaries were closed after the invasion of Kuwait. The major advantage of a subsidiary is that the parent company retains control and can carry out its own strategy while benefiting from a presence in foreign markets.

Foreign Strategic Alliances and Joint Ventures

Strategic alliances involve partnership. Sony, for instance, develops many of its innovative computer and communications products through strategic alliances and joint ventures with companies in the United States. A **joint venture** occurs when two companies combine resources for a new venture. They are formed to provide products and services more competitively than a single organization could do independently. Typically, a foreign joint venture has one company in each of two countries, but more partners or countries are possible. National laws often require any business to have a certain percentage of domestic ownership.

When the Soviet bloc dissolved, joint ventures were formed rapidly as foreign firms attempted to gain access to these markets. Often, the first strategy was to buy ownership, as Volkswagen did in the Czech Republic. The Germans beat out other contenders, such as Renault of France, and acquired a significant percent of the Czech auto leader Skoda.

Global strategic alliances are joint ventures with that involve international actions by two or more companies, each contributing an agreed amount of resources. The arrangement often resembles a well-funded startup operation. This approach may be preferred when competition is tough or technology and capital requirements are relatively large for one partner.

For example, General Motors has global alliances with Suzuki, Isuzu and Fiat. Ford has alliances with Volkswagen and Nissan, Daimler-Chrysler with Mitsubishi and Honda. General Mills created an alliance with Nestlé in Europe, called Cereal Partners Worldwide (CPW), to compete against Kellogg's growing global share. They agreed to pool part of their product lines and distribution system. Etisalat, one of the largest telecommunications companies in the world, and GE Healthcare recently signed a Memorandum of Understanding (MoU) to mark its strategic alliance. The joint initiative aims to improve synergies between health care and telecom, setting the highest standards for health care in the United Arab Emirates (UAE).

Some companies are competitors in certain regions of the world, but not in others, and they may choose to form a global strategic alliance in those areas. Toshiba, for example, has allied with a number of firms in the United States (United Technologies, Apple, Sun Microsystems, Motorola, and National Semiconductor) as well as a number of firms in Europe (Olivetti, Seimens, Rhore-Poulenc Ericcson, and SGS Thomson). Notice that many of these are rivals in various markets, but each works with Toshiba.

Whether its scope of operations is global or local, a company needs in-depth knowledge of its target markets in order to shape the strategic plan and meet its goals. In the next chapter, we will look at the global marketing environment and the forces that influence a company doing business in it.

JOINT VENTURE

An alliance of two companies that combine resources to provide products and services more competitively than either could do independently.

Solomon203 / CC BY-SA 4.0

The Ford Pronto is actually a re-badged Suzuki Carry ST through a global strategic alliance between Ford and Lio Ho in Taiwan.

Chapter Summary

Objective 1: Explain how each level of the strategic marketing planning process is related. Define components at each level.

Strategic marketing flows from a company's vision, to the strategic marketing plan, to the marketing mix plans. The vision describes what the organization is trying to accomplish in the broadest sense. It includes the organization's marketing philosophy. The strategic marketing plan is developed in line with the vision by a cross-functional team representing several business areas, such as manufacturing, accounting, finance and engineering. The plan describes the company's goals and states how the company will achieve them. Specialists in each component of the marketing mix prepare a plan for that area.

Objective 2: Describe the four elements of an organization's vision that provide guidance for all actions.

The vision statement expresses the company's core values, business definition, strategic direction and strategic infrastructure. Core values reflect the company's beliefs about the types of behavior acceptable from employees and the company as a whole, as well as its relationship to employees, customers and society in general. A business definition (also known as a mission statement) describes the contributions a company seeks to make to customers and society.

It is important to avoid marketing myopia when developing a mission statement. Marketing myopia occurs when executives focus on the company's goods and services rather than on the benefits these goods and services provide to consumers. Strategic direction is the desired leadership position of an organization as well as the measures used to chart progress toward reaching that goal. It captures the "essence of winning" and addresses the competitiveness of the organization.

A company's strategic infrastructure consists of both strategic business units and core competencies. SBUs can be managed using portfolio planning tools, such as the growth-share matrix or the attractiveness-strength matrix. Core competencies are the unique resources a company develops and employs to create superior customer value. They are the fundamental building blocks of competitive advantage and can be developed in one or more of the following areas: base technologies, process technologies, product technologies, people systems or information systems.

Objective 3: Integrate components of the strategic marketing plan with the vision.

The strategic marketing plan describes how to accomplish the vision for a particular part of the business. It has five components: objectives, situation analysis, target marketing, positioning and integration of the marketing mix. Objectives are developed in line with the vision and the situation analysis. They state aims regarding profit, market share and total sales, as well as customer satisfaction and loyalty.

The situation analysis describes the marketing environment for the period in which the plan is in effect. It gives all the information required to estimate possible business scenarios, including market size, customer characteristics, competitors and technology. A key part of the situation analysis is to examine strengths, weaknesses, opportunities and threats (SWOT). The target marketing phase focuses on select groups of consumers who the company will pursue through marketing efforts in order to win them as customers. In the positioning phase, the image of the organization relative to the competition is developed. The final step is to integrate the marketing mix plans to accomplish the overall strategy. It is important to consider the total effect of the marketing mix, rather than a single element.

Objective 4: Understand why elements of the marketing mix must be integrated and outline the steps of the marketing control process.

Plans for each part of the marketing mix are usually developed by specialists in the respective areas. Often a separate plan is created for product, place, promotion and price, but sometimes these plans are combined. Plans for any of these elements are both strategic and tactical. Strategies are long term and broad in scope, whereas tactics are short-term actions suited to specific market conditions. Several tactics may be used to carry out a single strategy.

To determine whether the strategic marketing plan is accomplishing the intended objectives, a marketing control process is needed. It has five steps. First, the original performance objectives are reviewed. Second, measures indicate what performance has occurred. Third, performance is evaluated by interpreting the results obtained and looking for any trends. Fourth, the planning team decides if actions or objectives should be altered. Fifth, the strategy proceeds as planned or another course is developed and implemented.

Objective 5: Identify the four major ways that organizations enter and develop global markets.

Organizations enter and develop global markets through 1) exporting, 2) foreign licensing and franchising, 3) overseas marketing and production, and 4) joint ventures and strategic alliances.

Exporting involves sending domestically manufactured products into foreign markets. It is usually a low risk and low cost way to enter markets. There are businesses that specifically assist other companies that want to establish an exporting operation. Foreign licensing and franchising simply assign the rights to a patent, trademark or process to a foreign company. Overseas marketing and manufacturing involve setting up operations in a foreign country. This requires the commitment of direct investment in a foreign country. Strategic alliances and joint ventures involve sharing resources with a partner to enter markets. Often the partner has strong contacts in the country or region where the venture takes place. Joint ventures can simply involve contracts between companies or shared ownership of new organizations. In some cases, these joint ventures require huge investments and substantial risks.

Review Your Understanding

1. What are the elements of the marketing planning hierarchy?
2. What are the components of a vision?
3. What is marketing myopia? How is the company's mission related to myopia?
4. In what ways can strategic business units be structured?
5. What is the portfolio planning approach?
6. What are the two methods discussed in this chapter for assessing SBUs? Explain each.
7. What are core competencies? Give examples of five types.
8. Which people in an organization create the strategic marketing plan?
9. What is the difference between a strategy and a tactic? How do they work together?
10. Explain how core competencies relate to sustainable competitive advantage.
11. What are the components of the strategic marketing plan? Describe each.
12. What are the elements of a SWOT analysis?
13. How are marketing mix plans strategic and tactical?
14. What is the marketing control process, and what are its five steps?
15. In what four ways can an organization enter foreign markets? Describe each.

Discussion of Concepts

1. Define strategy. Define tactics. How is strategy related to tactics? What strategy do you think Coca-Cola is following? What tactics is it using to support this strategy?
2. How are a company's core values, business definition, strategic infrastructure and strategic direction interrelated? Do you think it is important for a company to develop an explicit statement about each of these?
3. Imagine that the following companies describe their business as shown: (a) Black & Decker: drills and sanders; (b) Sherwin-Williams: paint; (c) Schwinn: bicycles; (d) U.S. Post Office: mail delivery. Do you think these companies are suffering from marketing myopia? How may they better define their business?
4. Why is it important for a company to have a well-defined strategic direction? In your opinion, what may happen to a company that lacks strategic direction?
5. How would you assess the contribution made by each strategic business unit? Do you think it is important for technology to be shared among SBUs? Why or why not?
6. Who should be involved in the development of a strategic marketing plan? Why?
7. What is the purpose of a situation analysis? What type of information should be included?
8. Why do most companies engage in some type of target marketing? What market do you think Nintendo is targeting with its handheld DS product line?
9. What are the advantages and disadvantages of a company entering a foreign market?

Key Terms & Definitions

1. **Business definition:** Describes the contributions the business makes to customers and society; also called the company mission.
2. **Core competencies:** The unique resources a company develops and promotes as its specialty to create distinct customer value; the fundamental building blocks of competitive advantage.
3. **Core values:** A set of statements describing the type of behavior expected of the company and its employees.
4. **Cross-functional planning team:** Employees from several areas responsible for developing the company's strategic marketing plan.
5. **Customer intimacy strategy:** Strategy based on delivering value through superior empathy for customers and solutions tailored to specific customer needs.
6. **Differentiation strategy:** Strategy based on delivering customer value in a way that clearly distinguishes the product from competitors; works through effectiveness.
7. **Distribution channel:** A set of independent organizations involved in making the product available for purchase.
8. **Export intermediaries:** Domestic or foreign firms with specialized experience in exporting activity.
9. **Foreign licensing:** Assigning the rights of a patent, trademark or manufacturing process to a foreign company for a fee, often called a royalty.
10. **Franchising:** A special type of licensing arrangement whereby the marketer provides not only the product, technology, process, and/or trademark but also the entire marketing program.
11. **Geographic scope:** The extent of a company's international activities.
12. **Joint venture:** An alliance of two companies that combine resources to provide products and services more competitively than either could do independently.
13. **Low-cost strategy:** Strategy with objective to be the low-cost

leader, thereby allowing the company to have higher margins than competitors and pass savings on to customers through lower prices.

14. **Marketing control process:** Procedures designed to provide feedback on how well the marketing strategy is working.

15. **Marketing mix plans:** Plans for how each part of the marketing mix will help to achieve the strategic marketing plan goals.

16. **Marketing myopia:** A focus on company products rather than on how these products benefit consumers.

17. **Physical distribution:** The movement of finished products through channels of distribution to customers.

18. **Portfolio planning approach:** A technique to measure the contribution each SBU makes to the overall performance of a division or company.

19. **Positioning:** Creating an image or perception in the minds of consumers about the organization or its products relative to the competition.

20. **Product line:** Closely related products marketed by the organization.

21. **Strategic business unit (SBU):** A part of the firm that can be managed separately for marketing purposes; it may be a division, a product or product line, a distinct group of customers, or a unique technology.

22. **Strategic direction:** The desired leadership position of an organization and the measures used to chart progress toward reaching that position.

23. **Strategic infrastructure:** The corporate configuration that produces the company's distinctive or core competencies and provides the resources necessary to satisfy customer wants.

24. **Strategic marketing plan:** The document describing the company's objectives and how to achieve them in light of competitive activities.

25. **Strategic window:** The time during which market needs and the competencies of the firm fit together to create a significant opportunity.

26. **Strategy:** A company's long-term plan of how to use resources for pursuing goals and objectives in competitive arenas.

27. **Sustainable competitive advantage strategy:** A lasting ability to outperform all competition in a particular market or industry.

28. **SWOT analysis:** An analysis of strengths, weaknesses, opportunities and threats to determine how well a company's skills and resources match the predicted market opportunities.

29. **Tactics:** Short-term actions and reactions to specific market conditions through which companies pursue their strategy.

30. **Target marketing:** The process of selecting which market segments the organization will emphasize in attempts to satisfy customers better than its competitors.

31. **Trading companies:** Large intermediaries that facilitate the movement of goods in and out of countries.

32. **Value proposition:** A statement of the compelling reason(s) customers should select a brand.

33. **Vision:** Statement of an organization's operating philosophy including core values, business definition, strategic direction and strategic infrastructure.

References

1. Whole Foods Market, Mission & Values, www.wholefoodsmarket.com, website visited April 24, 2016.
2. www.jnj.com/about-jnj, website visited April 3, 2016.
3. Berge, T., "The First 24-Hours," Cambridge, MA: Basil Blackwell, Inc., 1990.
4. "Our Community," eBay, www.ebay.com, website visited March 20, 2016.
5. "Patagonia Company Information: Our Reason for Being," www.patagonia.com, website visited February 20, 2016.
6. "Strategic Intent," Harvard Business Review, May-June 1989, pg. 64.
7. www.volkswagenag.com, website visited March 20, 2016.
8. www.coca-colacompany.com/our-company/mission-vision-values, website visited March 20, 2016.
9. StatCounter Global Stats, http://gs.statcounter.com, website visited April 26, 2016.
10. Ibid.
11. www.coca-cola.com, website visited April 22, 2016.
12. www.themarketingagenda.com/2014/09/20/unilever-bcg-matrix, website visited May 7, 2016.
13. www.unileverusa.com/brands-in-action/detail/Dove-/298217; www.unileverusa.com/brands-in-action/detail/Lipton-/295859, websites visited May 7, 2016.
14. www.telegraph.co.uk/finance/newsbysector/retailandconsumer/10960347/Unilever-tightens-belt-with-Slim-Fast-sale.html, website visited May 7, 2016.
15. "Apple's Market Share is Swindling: Samsung's Smartphone Sales Increase in the U.S.," www.inquisitr.com, February 10, 2016.
16. www.jnj.com, website visited March 4, 2016.
17. Recruiting brochure for the Disney Store.
18. Ibid.
19. Rodrigue, Jean-Paul, "UPS: Logistical Management of Distribution Networks," The Geography of Transport Systems, www: people.hofstra.edu/geotrans/eng/ch5en/appl5en/ch5a2en.html, accessed June 16, 2016.
20. "The Changing Role of Marketing in the Corporation, Journal of Marketing, October 1992, pg. 14.
21. Schmidt, Jeffery B., Montoya-Weiss, Mitzi M., Massay, Anne P., "New Product Development Decision Making Effectiveness: Comparing Face-to-Face Teams and Virtual Teams," Decision Sciences, Fall 2001.
22. Abell, Derek F., "Strategic Windows," Journal of Marketing, July 1978, pg. 21.
23. "iPad Competitors From Samsung, Sony, And RIM Leak; Retina Display Galaxy Tab Coming?", The Huffington Post, www.huffingtonpost.com, August 1, 2012.
24. Porter, Michael, Competitive Advantage: Creating and Sustaining Superior Performance (New York: The Free Press, 1985.)
25. Fry, Richard, "Millennials overtake Baby Boomers as America's largest generation," Fact Tank, Pew Research Center, April 24, 2016.
26. "Gen Y: The Next Generation of Spenders," Destination CRM, http://www.destinationcrm.com, website visited March 3, 2016.

27. "Ford Puts Millennials in Focus with New Emoji Campaign," swyft-media.com, website visited May 26, 2016.

28. www.hoovers.com, website visited March 3, 2016.

29. Schmidt, Jeffery, Ph.D. dissertation, Michigan State University, 1996.

30. www.happymeal.com, website visited May 26, 2016.

31. "The diabolical geniuses behind Subway's 'five-dollar foot-long' song," Slate, www.slate.com, site visited March 5, 2016.

32. www.franchisedirect.com/top100globalfranchises/rankings/, website visited May 23, 2016.

33. "The 50 best stocks of the S&P 500," BusinessWeek, April 30, 2007.

34. www.digi-capital.com/news/2015/05/games-leaders-to-dominate-45-billion-mobile-games-revenue-forecast-by-2018, website visited June 5, 2016.

35. www.recode.net/2016/3/24/11587234/two-years-later-face-books-oculus-acquisition-has-changed-virtual, website visited June 5, 2016.

36. Ibid.

37. Neil Hughes, "Apple investing record $10.5 billion in supply chain robots & machinery," http://appleinsider.com, November 13, 2013.

38. "Companies' cash tied up in inventory, slow payers," Forbes, www.forbes.com, May 25, 2012.

39. www.hamiltonbroadway.com, website visited June 17, 2016.

40. CIA World Factbook, www.cia.gov/library, website visited May 23, 2016.

41. Amy Mayor, "Vilsack: U.S. Relationship With Cuba Begins With Agriculture," http://kcur.org, June 4, 2016.

42. Kate Linthicum, "U.S. companies line up to do business in Cuba,"Los Angeles Times, March 25, 2016.

43. Ohmae, Kinichi, The Borderless World (New York: Harper Business, 1990), pp. 17-31.

44. Calantore, Roger J., Kim, Daekwan, Schmidt, Jeffery B., Clavusgil, S.T., "The Influence of Internal and External Firm Factors on International Product Adoption Strategy and Export Performance," Journal of Business Research, April 19, 2004.

45. www.coca-cola.com, website visited May 28, 2016.

46. Erickson, David A., "Standardized Approach Works Well in Establishing Global Presence," Marketing News, October 7, 1996, pg. 9.

47. www.kochoil.com, website visited May 3, 2016.

48. www.mars.com/global/press-center/press-list/news-releases, "Mars On Track to Open First Chocolate Factory in India," March 2015, website visited May 23, 2016.

CHAPTER 03

The Global
Marketing Environment

MARS

Scan to learn more about Mars and "The Five Principles" it follows.

If any company knows about change, it's Mars Corporation—makers of M&M's. The colorful, bite-sized chocolates have been one of the world's most recognizable candies for generations. M&M's were first produced in 1941 and sold exclusively to the U.S. military to supplement troops' rations during World War II. The candy's hard coating kept the chocolate from melting and made it easy to transport. When the war was over, soldiers returned home and clamored for more M&M's. Mars responded and began selling to the public in 1948.

Since then, Mars has consistently scanned its marketing environment and made changes to keep the brand successful. As it turns 75 this year, Tracy Massey, president of Mars North America, emphasizes the importance of change. "We have always been very brand and customer focused, and the biggest change we are making is further driving customer centricity throughout our business." Specifically, the company is currently focusing on Millennials—the demographic cohort following Generation X. Most Millennials were born between the early 1980s and 2000. They are comfortable using technology, they prefer brands that have a social presence, they are health conscious, and they generally distrust traditional advertising.

Focused on Millennials as a target market, Mars Corp. is making changes to keep the brand relevant for that market segment. It connects with customers through digital marketing and social media sites such as YouTube, Facebook, Instagram (@mmschocolate), Pinterest and Twitter, where each M&M's color has its own account. Check out #mmsgreen! Mars does a great job of choosing highly visible promotion channels, such as the Superbowl and ABC's The Bachelor to reach large numbers of its target market. "This is the perfect partnership because both Yellow and The Bachelor are irresistible," said Seth Klugherz, senior director of M&M's. "Yellow also knows a thing or two about worrying about being picked—in fact, only 1 in 100 peanuts is lucky enough to find its way into a bag of M&M's Peanut." The Bachelor, and variations of it, were among the top ranked shows watched by Millennials in 2015.

Understanding Millennials allows Mars to connect with the segment. For example, since health is important to Millennials, the company has proactively announced its commitment to removing artificial colors from all of its candies over the next five years. The company promises complete transparency in its ingredients and nutritional analysis through the transition. Having a party? The popular www.mymms.com site consistently draws Millennials, among others, who want to order personalized M&M's for special occasions like graduations, weddings and baby showers. Of course, Mars will create product innovations…new flavors, new textures, special colors, new packaging, and new advertising campaigns. But consumers can be sure that the traditional brown and yellow bags filled with original colored M&Ms will always exist. They represent consistency and success!

For the same reasons, Mars will continue to operate on its Five Principles foundation, which has united the brand for the last 75 years. It is the world's leading confectionery company, producing seven of the world's 20 best-selling chocolate snacks. It's a family-owned, $33 billion business employing over 70,000 associates at 230 sites in 73 countries. Despite its size, the company connects with customers by understanding them, and it recognizes the importance of changing strategy and marketing mix plans to meet customers' evolving preferences. Market awareness and marketing creativity will continue to produce sweet rewards for Mars in the global market.

Sources: www.csnews.com/product-categories/candy-snacks/mm's-brand-looks-love-bachelor, website visited June 5, 2016; www.mars.com/global/press-center/press-list/news-releases, website visited June 5, 2016; www.usatoday.com/story/money/2016/03/03/mms-75th-anniversary/81173224/, website visited June 5, 2016.

LO 01 Describe the marketing environment, and explain the purpose of environmental scanning.

LO 02 Learn how stakeholders can affect a company in achieving its objectives.

LO 03 Explain why understanding industry competition is important in an environmental analysis.

LO 04 Identify the six components of the global macroenvironment, and explain why each is important to a company's marketing strategy.

LO 05 Discuss the factors that influence ethical marketing decisions.

LO 06 Understand how digital marketing is changing the global marketing environment.

The Concept of The Global Marketing Environment

The entire landscape of global marketing has changed drastically. In the mid 1900s, U.S. companies were basically content to make profits on their home turf, marketing to customers through traditional advertising channels, and growing domestic sales or market share.

Doing business in other countries was complicated and costly because of barriers such as language, communications, customs, culture, currency, values, safety, tariffs, shipping and political uncertainty. So, for the most part, U.S. companies chose to develop domestic markets rather than going abroad.

Fast forward to today, and it's a different world! The introduction of digital technology and the internet has revolutionized the global marketing environment. Now communications are immediate, as is the transfer of information and data. Transportation, delivery and supply chains are managed in logistics software. As a result, most U.S. companies have *some* participation in the global marketspace.

In this chapter, we explore the two environments that affect how a company creates and captures value: the microenvironment and the global macroenvironment. You will learn that a company's response to its environment can determine its success or failure. Some organizations are reactive; they adjust marketing strategies after environmental changes occur. That can be dangerous, since it may be too late to construct a successful new strategy. Other organizations are proactive; they anticipate environmental changes before they occur and adjust their strategies in advance. Successful companies are almost always proactive!

The Marketing Environment

LO 01

MARKETING ENVIRONMENT

The sum of all factors that affect a business.

ENVIRONMENTAL SCANNING

Collecting and analyzing information about the marketing environment in order to detect important changes or trends that can affect a company's strategy.

The **marketing environment** is the sum of all factors that affect a business. Figure 3.1 depicts the marketing environment surrounding our theme: creating and capturing value. First is the microenvironment, then the all-encompassing global macroenvironment. An organization has to be sensitive to its environment; many factors can dramatically influence it. These create opportunities, but they can also limit the company from pursuing its desired strategy. **Environmental scanning** collects and analyzes information to detect any trends that can affect a company's strategy. It can be performed by the company itself, by a professional or industry association, or by a consulting organization that specializes in forecasting.

Through scanning the environment, Ford monitors the technological needs and wants of its market in order to deploy state-of-

Figure 3.1   The Marketing Environment

the-art advances in its vehicles. One new feature is Sync 3, an in-dash connected car platform to roll out in 2016. It is designed to be more intuitive than the current MyFord Touch system and will offer a number of new features. A recent study by Deloitte and Michigan State University assistant professor Clay Voorhees found that Generation Y consumers (Millennials) are highly focused on in-dash technology, with 59 percent declaring it the most important part of a vehicle's interior to them.[1]

The internet is an extraordinary environmental scanning tool. It enables marketers to retrieve press releases, news stories, online magazines, journals, newspapers and company websites highlighting product offerings, as well as technical and financial data. It also allows real-time streaming of product launches and important events. A skilled marketing analyst can sometimes glean competitive company strategies from this information.

Getting information about the market is much faster and easier on the internet than through other methods. The U.S. Bureau of the Census website (census.gov) provides demographic information, and online magazines such as American Demographics (demographics.com) identify cultural trends. When scanning for legal or regulatory information, marketers can check many government sites. For example, data on pending designs can be found at the U.S. Patent Office website (uspto.gov). The most authoritative sources for economic and demographic information about foreign countries are globalEDGE™ (globaledge.msu.edu), the CIA (cia.gov) and Economist Intelligence Unit (eiu.com) websites. The internet also offers research opportunities, surveys and other means for studying online behavior and surfing habits.

Courtesy of Ford

The Sync 3 in-dash connected car platform is likely an important upgrade for Millennials.

All this is used extensively to collect marketing information, which we will discuss in Chapter 4.

Depending on its size and resources, a company may choose to do its own environmental scanning, or it may outsource its environmental scanning to a third party. Companies that specialize in competitive intelligence—part of environmental scanning—even offer subscriptions to access data they have assembled. GE Information Services (Global Exchange) and Factiva (a Dow Jones & Reuters Company) are two leading providers of these services.[2]

The Microenvironment

The **microenvironment** is made up of the forces close to the company that influence how it connects with customers. As you'll notice in Figure 3.2, stakeholders and industry competition are part of the microenvironment. Stakeholders, as the name suggests, have a stake in an organization. Marketers need to understand stakeholders and recognize that marketing decisions affect them; in turn, the influence of stakeholders affects companies. Since companies interact with stakeholders on a daily basis, marketers need to consider their wants and needs when making decisions.

Competition is another force that impacts an organization daily. Competitors challenge your organization—sometimes you win, and sometimes they win. In either case, healthy competition is beneficial because it stimulates innovation and change. An organization must consider its competitors and stakeholders in nearly every major marketing decision.

MICROENVIRONMENT

RELATIONSHIPS WITH STAKEHOLDERS
- Customers
- Owners
- Employees
- Suppliers
- Intermediaries
- Action groups
 (& Others)

COMPETITIVE INDUSTRY
- Competitors
- Competitive groups

Figure 3.2   The Microenvironment

RELATIONSHIPS WITH STAKEHOLDERS

Any group or individual, other than competitors, that can influence or be influenced by an organization's actions is a **stakeholder**, including customers, owners, shareholders, employees, suppliers, intermediaries, and action groups. In the previous chapter we stressed the importance of building relationships with customers. In this chapter we focus on building relationships with other stakeholders.

Marketers form interactive, ongoing, two-way connections with stakeholders so they will be a positive influence on the organization. Stakeholders can help serve customer needs and wants, as well as help accomplish other objectives of the organization. Consequently, marketers try to act in the long term interest of all the firm's stakeholders. Because one organization can have a diverse array of stakeholders with conflicting objectives, this can be difficult. Therefore, companies try to find a balance that will satisfy all stakeholders when creating marketing strategies and objectives. Let's examine some of these stakeholders.

> Marketers form interactive, ongoing, two-way connections with stakeholders so they will be a positive influence on the organization.

Customers Customers are the most important part of a company's microenvironment. Without them, there would be no reason to be in business. As the late Peter Drucker, considered one of the fathers of business management, once said, "Because

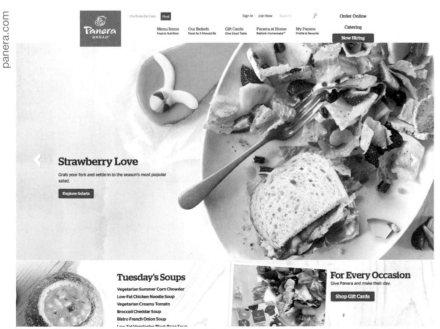

L.L. Bean provides a 100% satisfaction guarantee as part of its commitment to superior customer service.

the purpose of business is to create a customer, the business enterprise has two—and only two—basic functions: marketing and innovation."[3] An organization's mission, vision, strategic marketing plan and marketing mix all focus on creating value for customers and connecting with them. Once the initial connection is made, the real value to a company is in developing customer loyalty for repeat business and referrals.

L.L.Bean has focused on customers as stakeholders since it opened in 1912. Says President Steve Smith, "Our commitment to superior customer service is the very foundation of our brand. L.L. (Bean) introduced the company's Golden Rule, which is 'Sell good merchandise at a reasonable profit, treat customers like human beings and they'll always come back for more.' Leon strengthened that philosophy by making our customers stakeholders of the business. That sentiment and commitment is as strong today as it ever was. In an increasingly competitive industry and ever-evolving marketplace, L.L.Bean still stands out as the benchmark for customer service."[4]

Owners Whether public or private, an organization operates to benefit its owners, or shareholders. For companies, these benefits are derived by increasing the value of the business—making substantial profit. In nonprofit organizations, the benefits usually relate to helping constituents. For example, members of the Sierra Club are concerned about a safe and healthy community, smart energy solutions to combat global warming, and protecting America's wild places. The club urges members to contact political leaders about environmental issues and endorses candidates who support its goals.[5]

Shareholders have purchased, been given or inherited a share of the business. Typically, owners either represent themselves or are represented by a board of directors, which is charged with the responsibility to speak for all the owners. Marketers need to understand the goals, risks and reward levels acceptable to owners, who only invest in a company that continues to reach its objectives.[6]

For example, Panera Bread Company's stock price increased 100 percent in a single year. It took an aggressive and somewhat risky market approach by introducing several new menu items and announcing plans to open 500 new stores. Panera continues to grow at an impressive rate and now operates 1,997 bakery-cafes in 46 U.S. states and Ontario, Canada.[7] These actions produced results in line with shareholders' expectations, so shareholders were willing to hold the stock, and, in some cases, buy more at market price.

Employees Employees are also key stakeholders. Their livelihood depends on the company. Since every employee helps to create and deliver value to the end consumer, each has a very important influence on the organization. When marketing managers create marketing plans, they need to consider employees in other

Panera Bread Company is meeting shareholder expectations and growing the business at an impressive rate.

departments of the company, such as management, finance, accounting, logistics, engineering, purchasing, legal, R&D, and operations. Usually employees in each of these departments contribute to developing elements of the marketing mix that supports the strategic marketing plan.

W. L. Gore & Associates Inc., a top 100 company to work for, emphasizes the importance of a company's internal environment. Founder Bill Gore created an organization with no chains of command or pre-determined channels of communication. Employees are called "associates," communicate directly with each other and are accountable to fellow members of multi-disciplined teams. Instead of bosses, "sponsors" guide associates to reach team objectives in an environment that combines freedom with cooperation and autonomy with synergy. "We work hard at maximizing individual potential, maintaining an emphasis on product integrity and cultivating an environment where creativity can flourish," says Terri Kelly, the company's new president and CEO. "A fundamental belief in our people and their abilities continues to be the key to our success, even as we expand globally."[8]

SUPPLIERS

Organizations that provide a company with necessary services, raw materials, or components.

Suppliers

Suppliers are stakeholders who provide a company with necessary resources to produce its goods and services. Very few organizations can exist without suppliers, who also can be a major factor in creating customer satisfaction. For example, Ford relies on more than 1,300 production suppliers to provide many of the parts that are assembled into Ford vehicles. Another 11,000 suppliers provide a wide range of goods and services, from production equipment to computers to advertising.[9] If you like the dashboard, seats or electronics on the new Ford F-150, chances are a supplier worked with Ford to design it. Suppliers manufacture many of the components that go into vehicles--no matter what brand.

Since they are specialized in their product, suppliers are an excellent source of new technology and are likely to speed the introduction of the latest designs and techniques. Suppliers give access to technology and expertise that an organization could not obtain with its own resources. For example, DuPont is a supplier of extremely advanced materials to NASA and the European Space Agency, giving the programs the ability to reach higher and farther than ever before. NASA's New Horizons space probe recently flew by Pluto and into small, but dangerous space rock. The probe is armored with bullet-resistant Kevlar® from DuPont, which allowed it to sustain in the brutal environment. The European Space Agency used insulation blankets made from DuPont™ Kapton® polyimide films to protect instruments on the Rosetta space probe, which helped make it possible to land on a comet. Dupont is a supplier that is continually pushing technologies, allowing its customers to achieve new and amazing things.[10]

Companies rely on suppliers, so when suppliers have their own problems, it can mean trouble. Failure to develop and maintain good working relationships with suppliers can have consequences too. In May 2014, Wolverine Packing Co. issued a recall for 1.8 million pounds of ground beef after people were sickened during a fifteen-state E. coli outbreak. If the food makers had better visibility with their suppliers, the recall may have been avoided.[11]

Dupont delivers innovation to the market through expertise in science, chemistry, biological and engineering.

INTERMEDIARIES

Stakeholders who move products from the manufacturer to the final user.

Intermediaries

Intermediaries are independently owned organizations that serve as links to move products between producers and end users. They have an important influence on organizations because they dramatically extend the ability of marketers to reach customers at home and abroad. Book wholesalers and campus bookstores help publishers sell textbooks to students. Beverage manufacturers such as Gatorade, Dole and Ocean Spray use intermediaries to deliver their goods to stores that sell them to the final consumer. Kawasaki, Sea-Doo and Honda market their personal watercrafts through dealerships.

There are several different terms used for marketing intermediaries. They include: retailer, wholesaler, distributor, dealer, agent, broker and middleman. Some intermediaries specialize in international markets, using their unique skills and capabilities to give a company global reach. For example, when a company wants to connect with customers in an untapped, emerging market, it might use an intermediary with special expertise in that market to provide access. The intermediary provides a marketing channel of distribution; it helps to make products available to customers.

ACTION GROUP

A number of people who support some cause in the interest of consumers or environmental safety.

Action Groups **Action groups** are stakeholders that support some cause in the interest of consumers or environmental safety. Hundreds of action groups act as "watchdogs," making sure that companies keep the interests of people and the environment in balance with those of profit.

A vocal and well-known environmental advocate, former Vice President Al Gore, is fighting to stop global warming and solve the climate crisis. His Climate Reality Project works to raise awareness of the ongoing dangers posed by our present climate, and he is calling for action through his website, AlGore.com. Gore's book, *Our Choice*, describes his take on the real solutions to global warming through his experiences. The Our Choice app allows you to interact with graphics, animations and video.[12] Gore is also the Chairman of the Board for the Alliance For Climate Protection, which is committed to finding and implementing comprehensive solutions for the climate crisis.[13]

Global warming action groups will sometimes organize protests to raise awareness.

Tony Webster / CC BY 2.0

Marketers are very aware of consumer groups that frequently criticize the pursuits of business. A marketer may have to make difficult decisions when there is a conflict between the desires of action groups and other stakeholders. For instance, the Washington D.C. Center for Gay, Lesbian, Bisexual and Transgender People is a member of Walmart's affiliate program. When the American Family Association learned of this, it initiated a national boycott, claiming that the deal suggests Walmart executives believe "the homosexual agenda is worthy of their support." Nevertheless, Walmart did not give in to protesters, stating that it forges business partnerships with many minority organizations to help it attract a diverse array of suppliers. While stressing its support for diversity and nondiscrimination, Walmart said in its statement that it "will not make corporate contributions to support or oppose highly controversial issues unless they directly relate to our ability to serve our customers." In response to Walmart's comments, The American Family Association later abandoned the boycott.[14]

Action groups can also help marketers gain positive publicity and may help businesses make a greater contribution to society. In recent years, NFL players have supported Breast Cancer Awareness Month by wearing pink equipment, such as cleats, wristbands and gloves, during the month of October. Merchandise and footballs used during the games are later autographed by players and auctioned to benefit the American Cancer Society.[15]

INDUSTRY COMPETITION

The word *competition* brings to mind an image of two giant companies vying against each other. However, competition also involves companies of differing types and sizes. Well-established and new companies, along with suppliers and customers, form an industry structure that dictates the intensity of competition. Competitors may be individual companies or an industry as a whole.

The competitive environment can be marked by intense change, making it difficult to successfully launch a new product.[16] It is important for companies to assess the risks and ask the following questions: Who are our existing rivals? What new competitors may emerge? What is the relative strength of suppliers and buyers within the industry? Finally, what substitutes are likely to appear? The answers give a complete picture of the overall nature of competition within an industry. Figure 3.3 depicts the forces that shape the competitive environment.

Existing Firms Marketers need to thoroughly understand their competition. They need to know how each competitor campaigns against their company and others in the industry. An effective marketer examines each rival's strategy in terms of current and potential products, pricing, promotion and distribution. They also identify key customers and suppliers, the types of technologies used, current performance, and strengths and weaknesses. From all this information, the marketing manager attempts to determine the plans of every competitor and how each will react to changes that the marketing manager proposes.

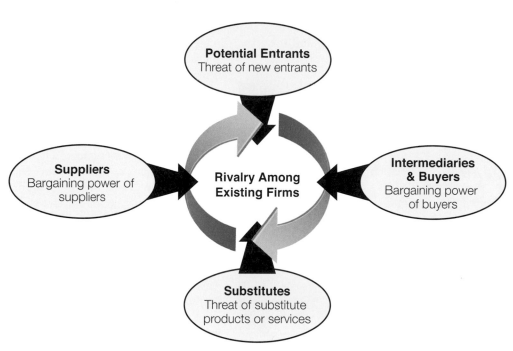

Figure 3.3 Forces Driving Industry Competition
Source: The Free Press, a division of Simon & Schuster, from Competitive Strategy: Techniques for Analyzing Industries and Competitors, by Michael Porter. Copyright 1980

Potential Entrants At any time a company may enter an industry with similar products. Recently, 3,231 new snack, cookie and cracker products, including 382 types of potato chips, were introduced in a single year.[17] This is not a welcome statistic to established competitors such as Lays and Pringles, but one advantage is that aggressive marketing by several companies will often draw attention to the overall product category and cause industry-wide sales to increase. New competitors are not always upstart companies, but are sometimes established ones branching into a new market. Taco Bell's entry into the breakfast market with innovative products like the waffle taco required new strategies by the leader, McDonald's, which responded with a promotion offering a free cup of coffee with a breakfast purchase. McDonald's tactic appears to have worked in the short term, as its breakfast sales rose 1.2 percent just one month after Taco Bell's entry.[18]

SUBSTITUTE PRODUCT

Any good or service that performs the same function or provides the same benefit as an existing one.

Substitutes A **substitute product** is any good or service that performs the same function or provides the same benefit as an existing one. For example, who competes

able to consumers, businesses and countries. An understanding of consumer economic factors such as income, spending behavior, spending power and wealth dispersion is essential in assessing opportunities that may emerge. Global marketers also must be familiar with the economic features of the world's major trading blocs.

Consumer Income and Spending Behavior Benjamin Franklin once said that only two things are certain in life: death and taxes! Taxes certainly influence how much money a person has available to spend on products and services. Let's see how.

GROSS INCOME

The total amount of money earned in one year by an individual, household or business.

DISPOSABLE INCOME

The income consumers have left after paying taxes.

DISCRETIONARY INCOME

The amount of money consumers have left after paying taxes and purchasing necessities.

Gross Income is the total amount of money earned in one year by an individual, household or business. Our discussion will focus on individuals and households. According to the Census ACS survey, the median household income for the United States was $53,657 in 2014.[25] **Disposable income** is the money consumers have left after paying taxes, and many marketers prefer to use this as the measure of consumer wealth. People spend some of their disposable income on necessities, such as food, clothing and shelter; anything left over is called **discretionary income**. Marketers of nonessentials, such as vacation packages, sports cars, jewelry and electronics, target consumers' discretionary income.

Rapidfire / CC BY-SA 3.0

Vacation packages offered by cruise lines like Carnival are targeting consumers' discretionary income.

Just as important as the amount of income is the willingness—*propensity*—of a person or household to spend it. According to the U.S. Bureau of the Census, the average income of the top fifth of households rose 38 percent in the past 10 years, the middle class has declined and the poor have remained static. Marketers have seized these numbers and taken the opportunity to focus on promoting nonessential, luxury items to consumers with higher discretionary income. Other marketers have found a significant opportunity in attracting consumers with less discretionary income through outlets like the Dollar Store, the Dollar Tree and Family Dollar.

SPENDING POWER

The ability of the population to purchase goods and services.

GROSS DOMESTIC PRODUCT

The total market value of all goods and services produced by a country in a single year.

Spending Power and Wealth Dispersion Marketers must realize that a large population does not always provide a large marketing opportunity. A key factor to consider is **spending power**, or the ability of people to purchase goods and services. A common measure of spending power is the gross domestic product of a country. **Gross domestic product (GDP)** is the total market value of all final goods and services produced for consumption during a given period by a particular country. The European Union has the highest GDP, at approximately $15.65 trillion, followed closely by the United States at $15.29 trillion. The next closest GDP is China ($11.44 trillion), followed by India ($4.51 trillion) and Japan ($4.49 trillion).[26]

When the GDP of every nation is added together, the sum is the gross world product (GWP). Today's GWP is about $70.16 trillion. That figure is not spread equally among countries, however. The United States accounts for about 21 percent of the GWP. Considering that the United States has less than five percent of the world's population, this is a high figure. In comparison, with 36 percent of the world's population, China and India contribute about 22 percent to GWP (China at sixteen percent and India at six percent).[27]

Many marketers do not look solely at GDP, because it does not indicate how much

> Many marketers do not look solely at GDP, because it does not indicate how much each person in the country has to spend.

each person in the country has to spend. For example, Mexico and Sweden have approximately the same GDP, but we know that the standard of living is lower in Mexico than in Sweden. Because Mexico has a larger population, a smaller portion of GDP is allocated to each inhabitant. Consequently, many marketers use GDP per capita ("per person") to assess the standard of living. This way, they can estimate the living conditions of a country's individuals.

Even GDP per capita has limitations, because it ignores the dispersion of wealth within a country. Often there are a few rich people and many, many poor ones. In Brazil, for example, the richest 10 percent of the population controls 46 percent of the wealth. In the United States, that figure is 29 percent.[28] In Japan and Spain, the dispersion of wealth is much more even.[29]

Trading Blocs The world's three major trading blocs—North America, Europe and the Pacific Rim—are shown in Figure 3.5. Often called the world's economic superpowers, they are expected to compete for the mastery of international markets well into the 21st century. Combined, these three regions are responsible for about 80 percent of the world's economic activity. Customers in the superpower triad buy, for instance, a great majority of all computers and consumer electronics. The triad contains over a half billion consumers with converging preferences. Among others, IBM, Motorola and Gucci are found nearly everywhere in the triad. Today, each of these blocs is basically equal in terms of economic activity, but current trends point toward shifts. The Pacific Rim is growing most rapidly, followed by Europe, then North America.

Despite their collective power, the triad's constituent economies are not without difficulties. Many of these countries have a mature economy, rising social welfare costs, an aging population, and escalating research and development costs.[30] Let's look at each of the trading blocs in more detail.

North America When the United States, Canada and Mexico entered into the North American Free Trade Agreement (NAFTA), they created the largest single market in the world. The objective was to make all three nations more globally competitive by combining their strengths. The United States and Canada have capital, skills, technology and natural resources; Mexico has low-cost labor. Proponents of NAFTA believe efficient North American companies will be able to offer lower-priced products to consumers. Overall, the open market means removal of tariffs and other trade barriers, increased investment opportunities, stronger protection of intellectual property, and more environmentally sound business practices. Today, the NAFTA market boasts a total gross domestic product of more than $18 trillion.[31]

NAFTA is not without crit-

NORTH AMERICA	EUROPE		PACIFIC RIM
Canada	France	Portugal	South Korea
USA	Spain	Greece	Singapore
Mexico	Germany	Ireland	Japan
	Denmark	Luxembourg	China
	Italy	Belgium	Taiwan
	Austria	Netherlands	Hong Kong
	Sweden	Finland	
	Cypress	Latvia	
	Czech Republic	Lithuania	
	Estonia	Malta	
	Hungary	Poland	
	Slovenia	Slovakia	
	Romainia	Bulgaria	

Figure 3.5   The Three Superpower Trading Blocks

Flag of the North American Free Trade Agreement countries

ics. Companies are becoming more mobile, and some will go where labor is less expensive. If U.S. technology does not create enough high-paying jobs at home, U.S. workers will ultimately be fighting for low-paying jobs with fewer benefits.

Europe The European Union (EU) has tremendous economic relevance in Europe and around the world. Its goal is to eliminate barriers that restrict the flow of people, goods, services and money within the union. The objective is to restructure Europe economically so that it can better compete against the United States, Japan and other developed nations. The EU members include Austria, Belgium, Bulgaria, Cyprus, the Czech Republic, Denmark, Estonia, Finland, France, Germany, Greece, Hungary, Ireland, Italy, Latvia, Lithuania, Luxembourg, Malta, the Netherlands, Poland, Portugal, Romania, Slovakia, Slovenia, Spain, and Sweden. Great Britain withdrew from the EU in June of 2016.[32]

MAASTRICHT TREATY

Consists of 282 directives that eliminate border controls and customs duties among members of the European Union.

The **Maastricht Treaty** consists of 282 directives that eliminate border controls and customs duties, strengthen external borders, establish a single European currency, coordinate defense and foreign policy, unify product standards and working conditions, protect intellectual property, and deregulate many industries, including telecommunications, airlines, banking, and insurance. This will make it much easier to move products from one region to another. Eventually, companies will be able to create more unified marketing strategies for business operations in the EU; today, its different market environments can make strategic planning difficult.

Pacific Rim The Pacific Rim (PAC Rim), which comprises much of East Asia, is named for the ocean it borders. It is made up of Japan and the four "dragons:" South Korea, Singapore, Taiwan and China (including Hong Kong), and it is known for its enormous manufacturing potential. Depending on the outcome of attempts at economic reform, Thailand, Malaysia and Indonesia could join soon. Economic integration in the PAC Rim is based primarily on market forces, not a formal agreement such as NAFTA. Much of the growth in East Asia has been spurred by Japanese investors, such as Matsushita Electric, which has established major operations in Southeast Asia. China has experienced at least an eight percent annual growth rate since 2000, making it the fastest-growing area in the region.[33]

Asia-Pacific Economic Cooperation, or APEC, is a forum for 21 Pacific Rim countries to cooperate on regional trade and investment in the Asia Pacific region. These members account for approximately 40 percent of the world's population, 54 percent of world GDP and about 44 percent of world trade.[34]

Despite the recent downturn, East Asia has undergone explosive economic growth in the past few decades. China has averaged an annual growth rate of nearly ten percent since 1996, making it the fastest growing area in the region.[35] Asian nations are feeding their home markets with the net gain in money received from other economies, which is possible when a country exports more than it imports. The domestic markets are increasing in size as companies and workers earn more money. With cash reserves of several hundred billion dollars and personal wealth, they can buy large amounts of goods from other countries.

General Agreement on Tariffs and Trade and the World Trade Organization In 1947, the General Agreement on Tariffs and Trade (GATT) was founded under the United Nations. GATT is responsible for many of the current trade agreements among its 155 members. This organization has successfully negotiated significant reductions in trade restrictions and import duties that countries would otherwise impose in their own interests. GATT has successfully reduced import duties and tariffs from more than 40 percent in 1947 to less than five percent today. In 1995, GATT was absorbed by the World Trade Organization (WTO), which will carry out the traditional role of GATT. The WTO deals with a broad range of issues, including pollution, tariffs, trade agreements and trade disputes.

Natural Resources The availability of natural sources of wealth (which can be minerals, vegetation, wildlife, water and others) within a given region or nation is an important economic factor. For example, the U.S. Pacific Northwest provides a rich source of timber for the paper and construction industries, while countries in the Middle East control approximately 65 percent of the world's crude oil. In both cases, natural resources provide income to the area's inhabitants. Resource availability affects a marketer's pricing strategy. If a company operates a large plant in an area where energy or raw materials are expensive, production costs will be high, and its pricing plans must be set accordingly.

When seeking natural resources, companies must balance corporate objectives with preservation of the natural environment. The practice of fracking has brought the importance of this balance to light. Fracking is the process of drilling down into the earth to release the gas inside the earth's rock with a high-pressure mixture of water, sand and chemicals. The term fracking refers to how the rock is fractured apart by the high pressure mixture. Fracking allows drilling firms to access difficult-to-reach resources of oil and gas.

In the U.S. it has substantially boosted domestic oil production and driven down gas prices. Some estimates predict that as a result of fracking, the U.S. and Canada will have gas for about 100 years, and it has presented an opportunity to generate electricity at half the CO2 emissions of coal.[36]

Yet, the practice is highly controversial. Fracking uses enormous amounts of water, which has to be transported to the fracking site, at substantial environmental cost. Environmentalists argue that the potentially carcinogenic chemicals used can escape and contaminate groundwater around the fracking site. Debate continues to circle around whether the pollution incidents are the result of human error or a dangerous technique. Clearly, marketers of oil and gas have to weigh all aspects of the issue during the strategic marketing planning process to make the best decision for their company and their stakeholders.[37]

Some experts believe fracking is extremely harmful to our environment. You can learn more at dangersoffracking.com.

Companies also have to consider environmental regulations that might threaten current business practices or create new opportunities. For example, the Strategic Environment Initiative (SEI) recommends that the government provide tax breaks to companies using environmentally-friendly technologies and levy high taxes on those using older, unsafe methods. This has encouraged companies to come up with innovative ways to reduce emissions. In the product area, for example, companies can retrofit antipollution devices or engineer more environmentally-friendly designs.

The environment has become an increasingly prominent factor for marketers to consider because stakeholders are rewarding companies that practice sustainability to protect our environment. When it became known that the chlorofluorocarbons (CFCs) released from aerosol cans were thinning the ozone layer, many companies switched to pump spray bottles. Starbucks adopted a new beverage sleeve, made with 34 percent less raw fiber material and 25 percent more post-consumer content. The company says the "EarthSleeve" will save 100,000 trees. [38] McDonald's replaced styrofoam containers with carton board made from recycled and controlled wood forestry sources. Visit just about any popular company's website or social media site and you'll find space dedicated to promoting its sustainability commitment and actions.

DEMOGRAPHIC ENVIRONMENT

DEMOGRAPHIC ENVIRONMENT

The statistical data used to describe a population.

The **demographic environment** consists of the data that describe a population in terms of age, education, health and so forth. Marketers examine such information to gain an understanding of current opportunities and discover trends that may indicate future opportunities. Some frequently studied demographics include population size and density, urbanization and age structure.

Population There are approximately 7.3 billion people in the world, and there are expected to be over 9.8 billion by 2050.[39] If marketing opportunities were defined solely by population size, then the prospects would be bright indeed! However, marketers need to look at trends *within* populations to get a more accurate picture.

Population growth is determined by the number of live births plus the number of immigrants entering a country. The birthrate, which is measured as the number of live births per 1,000 people, is increasing throughout the world, but the rate of increase has begun to slow. Still, there are about 256 worldwide births per minute, or 4.3 births every second.[40] At the same time, advances in medicine and technology mean that people are healthier, and the number of deaths per 1,000 people is decreasing. Longer life spans combined with births result in an even larger world population.

Movement from one country to another redistributes the world's population, and the United States is gaining considerable numbers this way. Although U.S. immigration laws have become more restrictive, immigration is still expected to contribute as much to U.S. population growth as natural births. The multicultural population is over 30 percent today and is expected to climb to 54 percent of the total U.S. population by 2050.[41]

The U.S. population is expected to grow to 349 million in 2025 and to 403 million in 2050.[42] As with the world population, the average annual growth rate is expected to decrease by nearly half from 1.1 percent in the 1990s to around .54 percent by 2045. This predicted decline, which would be the lowest growth rate in U.S. history, is attributed to numerous factors, including the general aging of the population, increased age at first marriage, delayed childbearing, a growing proportion of childless couples, and a greater participation of women in the labor force who choose not to have children.[44]

The United States Census has a continuous live population clock on its website

POPULATION DENSITY

The concentration of people within some unit of measure, such as per square mile or per square kilometer.

Density A country with a large population may seem to offer a large marketing opportunity, but it is important to know where those people live. **Population density** refers to the number of people within a standard measurement unit, such as a square mile. Canada has more than 34 million people and 8.9 people, on average, per square mile. Yet, because three-quarters of Canadians live in a few large cities, such as Quebec and Toronto, large areas of the country are quite sparsely populated. Singapore's population of about 5.6 million is highly concentrated, with an average of over 20,000 people per square mile.[44]

When people are concentrated, it's easier and more cost effective to reach them with advertising campaigns and products. When they are spread out, however, traditional marketing can be difficult, time-consuming and expensive. Consider the Pacific Rim countries, where many more people live in the coastal regions than inland, or Australia with its sparsely populated Outback. Delivering products to consumers in the thinly populated areas takes far more effort than delivering to consumers in a city. Even promoting products can be more difficult; billboards aren't seen by as many people, and magazine subscribers are spread out. Organizations have historically concentrated marketing efforts on densely populated areas for those reasons. Today, technology has created new and important ways to reach consumers through the internet and social media, so population density is becoming less of a constraint.

With wide-spread use of the internet, population density is less of a constraint for marketers.

URBANIZATION

The shift of population from rural to urban areas.

AGE COHORT

A group of people close in age who have been shaped by their generation's experience with the media, peers, events, and society at large.

Urbanization **Urbanization** refers to the population shift from rural areas to cities. About half of the world's population lives in an urban area, including the vast majority of some countries' populations. In Germany, for example, 74 percent of the population lives in urban areas; in Singapore, 100 percent.[45] In the United States, four out of five people live in or near a city. Over a quarter of the U.S. population is concentrated in the 10 largest metropolitan areas, with New York City (20 million), Los Angeles (13.3 million), and Chicago (9.5 million) at the top.[46] Urbanization is significant to marketers for three important reasons. First, as noted earlier, it is easier to reach a concentrated population because advertisements and promotions get much greater exposure. Second, as a group, people in cities tend to have enough income to purchase luxuries and support the arts, such as opera or theater. Third, people in urban areas tend to demand a wider variety of products than do rural residents.

Age Structure Because generations differ in their tastes, age-related marketing research has become popular. An **age cohort** is a group of people close in age who have been shaped by their generation's experience with the media, peers, events and the larger society. Often these cohorts are divided by birth year into five groups. "Matures" were born between 1909 and 1945, "Baby Boomers" between 1946 and 1964, "Generation X" between 1965 and 1976, "Generation Y," or Millennials, between 1977 and approximately 1995, and, finally, "Generation Z" from approximately 1996 to today. Research reveals substantial differences among them in values, tastes and needs.[47] In this text you will read about many companies that are currently focusing on Millennials as a target market.

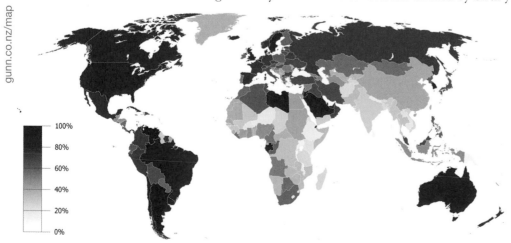

100%
80%
60%
40%
20%
0%

Global representation of percent of urbanized population.

Globally, the population's average age is less than 25 years and getting younger. Many countries, such as Mexico, have rapidly growing populations that contribute to this statistic. In some industrialized nations, however, the picture is different. Children constitute a declining proportion of the German population, which is aging slowly but is older than the U.S. population, with a median age of 46.1.[48] Today the median age in the United States is 37.6; by 2030, almost 20 percent of the population will be age 65 or older. This is partly due to the baby boom after World War II, which will affect U.S. demographics for many years. In addition to varying by history, the U.S. age distribution also varies according to race. About 80 percent of Americans are Caucasian, but that percentage increases with age. Among the 12.9 percent of all Americans who are African American, nearly 15 percent are younger than ten. Sixteen percent of Americans are Hispanic, and 20 percent of them are younger than ten..[49]

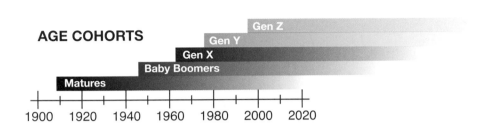

AGE COHORTS

Now that U.S. Baby Boomers are migrating into senior life status during which spending power is substantial, marketers are focusing on connecting with these older consumers; this age group currently makes up 44 percent of the population but controls 70 percent of its disposable income. There's even been a surge in gray-haired models as companies try to appeal to the Boomer demographic, who want to see versions of themselves, not twentysomethings, in ads. Even youth-oriented clothing retailer American Apparel has hired "seasoned" model Jacky, who sports long gray hair and laugh lines.[50] In the years ahead, marketers will face the growing task of serving an aging market and addressing its unique concerns. You will learn more about age structure and how to use it for segmentation in Chapter 8.

CULTURAL ENVIRONMENT

CULTURAL ENVIRONMENT

The learned values, beliefs, language, symbols, and patterns of behavior shared by people in a society and passed on from generation to generation.

The **cultural environment** consists of the learned values, beliefs, language, symbols and behaviors shared by people in a society and passed on from one generation to the next. Culture includes morals, values, religion, art, customs, traditions, folkways, technology, myths and norms. These and other characteristics distinguish different societies, define the way we think about ourselves and the world, what we want, and how we behave. Marketers must be in touch with the cultural environment because it helps them to make stronger connections with diverse customers. This connection has even been made between culture and environmental practices. For example, a study about Chinese consumers' green purchase behavior found that the traditional, collectivist, and nature-oriented Chinese culture has a positive impact on Chinese consumers' attitude toward green purchases.[51]

SELF-REFERENCE CRITERION

The unconscious reliance on values gained from one's own socialization when trying to understand another culture.

Most people are socialized to be part of the culture in which they were raised. The socialization process is so strong that even marketers may be influenced by their own learned values when trying to understand another culture. This is called the **self-reference criterion**, and it is not always acceptable to rely on it. For example, most people in the United States would not think twice about eating a candy bar as they walk down the street, but in Japan this is considered impolite. In China, when people approach a bus, the first person is expected to buy tickets for the group. It is easy to embarrass yourself and others in a foreign culture unless you take the time to understand it.

Because of people's tendency to use the self-reference criterion, it's often difficult to assess opportunities in other countries, but global success requires precisely that. McDonald's targets the same audience around the world—young families with children—but the basic concept is adapted to local cultures. For example, in Singapore, customers can order

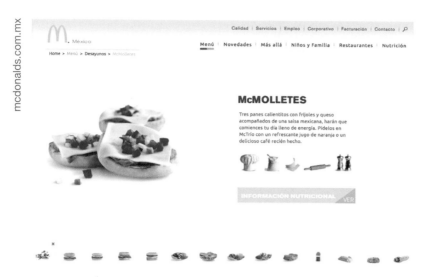

In Mexico, McMolletes are a breakfast staple at McDonald's.

a burger served on toasted rice cakes instead of a bun. In Mexico, customers enjoy McMolletes—refried beans, cheese and pico de gallo on an English muffin.[52] Understanding different cultures has helped McDonald's establish itself in the new global market.

Edward Hall, a specialist in cross-cultural management research, notes that perceptions of time, space, property, friendships, agreements, and negotiations cause the greatest misunderstanding between people of different cultures.[53] In order to succeed in global marketing, companies need to acknowledge and understand these differences.

Perceptions of Time It's also important to consider a culture's perception of time, which communicates several subtle points. For example, in some cultures the most significant decisions are given the greatest amount of time. In contrast, Americans tend to operate within deadlines, and time is a scarce resource to be used efficiently. In the United States, if visitors are kept waiting, then they infer that they are unimportant. In a Latin culture, schedules are not rigid, and it is acceptable to use time more flexibly. More recently, many Latin American countries have redefined time for business. In some cultures, a very long time may pass between customer awareness of a product and the actual purchase, something marketers need to plan for in these regions. In cultures where decisions are made quickly, this time frame is usually much shorter.

Size and Space In the United States, size is equated with importance; the larger and taller a building, the greater the degree of perceived status. The dean of a college of business is likely to be located in a spacious office on the top floor; the university president is likely to have a larger office in a taller building. In contrast, the French try to place important executives close to the scene of action, where their influence can be most strongly felt.

The distance between people during conversations also can be culturally related. In many Latin cultures, people show friendship by talking closely, sometimes within two or three inches of each other. In the U.S., a distance of three to five feet is usually considered respectful. Marketers must be sensitive to space when promoting products in different regions. In commercials, advertisements materials, and social media sites, the wrong interpersonal distance among the actors or models could deliver the wrong message.

Negotiations and Agreements Business agreements may have different meanings in various parts of the world. In highly legalistic cultures, they must be written and signed prior to acceptance. In other cultures, legal documents are viewed as inconveniences; more important is a meeting of the minds, sealed with a handshake.

When Americans consult a lawyer, visit a doctor or take a taxi, they assume the charge will be at the going rate, something that cannot be taken for granted in other cultures. For example, in the Middle East, it's best to settle the charge in advance or the person providing the service is likely to set an arbitrary price. It is important to know a culture's stance on payment and agreements when developing a pricing strategy for your products. Whereas a predetermined price is expected in the United States, bartering is part of the social process elsewhere, and a preset price upsets or offends consumers.

Different cultures have different ways of conducting meetings and negotiations, too. For example, German people tend to speak loudly when sharing ideas, whereas Japanese people tend to speak softly. The Portuguese generally dislike confrontation and are offended by overly exaggerated gestures. In France, the use of first names in business meetings can be interpreted as rude and disrespectful, as is an overly strong handshake. In fact, French business etiquette dictates that handshakes should be initiated by the highest ranking person at a meeting unless a woman is included...in which case she is expected to extend her hand first.[54] In the U.S., business meetings and negotiations often begin with small talk to establish rapport. Many other cultures, however, consider this practice offensive. As a general rule, avoid topics such as salary, age, family and hobbies when conducting business in foreign cultures.

LEGAL/REGULATORY ENVIRONMENT

LEGAL / REGULATORY ENVIRONMENT

International, federal, state, and local regulations and laws, the agencies that interpret and administer them, and the court system.

Almost all marketing decisions are affected by laws and regulations. The **legal/regulatory environment** is comprised of international, federal, state and local regulations and laws, the agencies that interpret and administer them, and the court system. It also includes the ethical standards and theories that guide marketing decisions. This environment reflects long-standing political and economic philosophies and varies dramatically from one country or region to another. It indicates the general outlook of government toward business practices and ethical issues. It also includes the effect that legal/regulatory decisions can have on an organization, individuals, and society as a whole. Marketers need to be aware of this environment so they can estimate how tolerant or cooperative the government will be with their company's operations.

In the United States, several agencies are charged with the responsibility of regulating businesses to comply with the intentions of major laws, the most important of which are listed in Figure 3.6. These agencies must interpret laws and develop policies and procedures to gain compliance. In some cases, the agency only sets guidelines so businesses can self-regulate within them. Businesses that step out of line may be taken to court by the agency. In other cases, a company's product needs to obtain approval from an agency. For example, the Food and Drug Administration (FDA) must approve all drugs prior to their release in the United States.

Although the U.S. legal and regulatory sphere covers hundreds of specific practices, for our purposes these can be divided into four basic types: laws promoting competition, laws restricting big business, laws protecting consumers, and laws protecting the environment.

U.S. Laws Promoting Competition During the 1800s and early 1900s, a few U.S. enterprises grew to the point of monopoly. Companies such as Standard Oil and Pennsylvania

Consumer Products Safety Commission (CPSC)
• Enforces regulations to protect consumers from being harmed by products.

Environmental Protection Agency (EPA)
• Regulates business actions to prevent damage to the environment.

Federal Communication Commission (FCC)
• Regulates communications on telephone, radio, television, and other aspects including allocations of frequencies.

Federal Trade Commission (FTC)
• Enforces laws to prevent unfair or deceptive marketing practices.

Food and Drug Administration (FDA)
• Enforces laws to maintain safety in food and drug products.

Figure 3.6   Federal Agencies Regulating Marketing

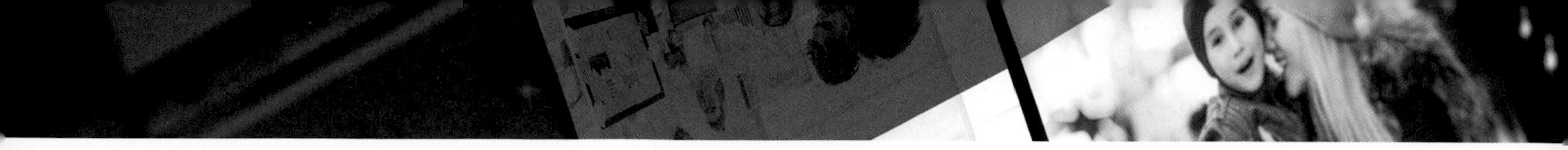

Railroad could exercise economic control over smaller firms, in many cases forcing them into bankruptcy by temporarily lowering prices. In 1890, due to a strong political movement led by Midwestern farmers, Congress passed the Sherman Antitrust Act, which prohibits business practices designed to create monopolies or restrict trade across state lines or internationally. The Sherman Antitrust Act laid the foundation for many related laws. The premise behind them is that fair competition allows more companies to serve the market, which in turn keeps prices down and provides more choices to consumers. As you can see from Figure 3.7, many laws since 1890 have been enacted to ensure fair competition.

Sherman Antitrust Act (1890)
Outlaws monopolies and any business practice that restricts interstate or international commerce.

Federal Trade Commission Act (1914)
Declares as unlawful "unfair methods of competition in or affecting commerce, and unfair or deceptive acts or practices in or affecting commerce."

Clayton Act (1914)
Prohibits mergers and acquisitions that may "substantially lessen competition or tend to create a monopoly"; outlaws tie-in and exclusive dealing arrangements; allows violators to be held criminally liable.

Robinson-Patman Act (1936)
Developed primarily to protect small retailers. Amends the Clayton Act. Makes it illegal to sell "commodities of like grade and quality" to competing buyers at different prices if it will restrict competition. Also makes it illegal knowingly to receive an illegal price break.

Miller-Tydings Act (1937)
Protects interstate fair-trade (price fixing) agreements from antitrust prosecution.

Wheeler-Lea Act (1938)
Outlaws the pursuit of unfair or deceptive practices or actions.

Antimerger Act (1950)
Prevents corporate acquisitions or mergers that may substantially reduce competition.

Figure 3.7 U.S. Laws Promoting Competition

U.S. Laws Restricting Big Business

The U.S. approach to competition has tended to restrict company size and power. The Federal Trade Commission (FTC) has explored numerous accusations of monopolistic control. For example, Johnson & Johnson proposed a $16.6 billion acquisition of Pfizer's health-care division. The proposal underwent extensive review by the FTC for a possible violation of the Federal Trade Commission Act and monopolistic activity. The FTC ruled that the acquisition would be allowed.[55]

CARTEL

A group of businesses or nations that work together to control the price and production of a particular product.

Some countries have laws that favor monopolies and cartels, which are outlawed in the United States. A **cartel** is a group of businesses or nations working together to control the price and output of a particular product. You've probably heard of a cartel called OPEC, Organization of the Producing Export Countries, which tries to manage the supply of oil in an effort to set the price of oil on the world market. One of its goals is to avoid fluctuations that could affect the economies of both producing and purchasing countries. The U.S. government has recognized that laws intended to provide a fair environment for domestic competition can be restrictive and sometimes put American companies at competitive disadvantages in the global market. So, in the late 1970s, the Department of Justice began to lighten its enforcement of traditional antitrust laws.

U.S. Laws Protecting Consumers

Recall that the early economic philosophy in the United States was typically caveat emptor: "Let the buyer beware." Essentially, consumers were responsible for protecting themselves against the unscrupulous acts of sellers. The Pure Food and Drug Act and the Meat Inspection Act, both introduced in 1906, were the first attempts by government to protect consumers. For four decades, regulations concentrated on making the food supply safe. Then they extended to regulating products such as automobiles and toys, and eventually protecting consumers from misleading and deceptive advertising.

By 1960, the consumer movement was so powerful that President Kennedy issued the Consumer Bill of Rights. This enforced the idea that it was not up to the consumer alone to assess the quality and safety of a product. The Consumer Bill of Rights guaranteed consumers:

Pure Food and Drug Act (1906) - Regulates the manufacture and labeling of food and drugs.

Meat Inspection Act (1906) - Permits federal inspection of companies selling meat across state line and allows for enforcement of sanitary standards.

Lanham Trademark Act (1946) - Outlaws misrepresentation of goods and services sold across state lines; forces trademarks to be distinctive.

Automobile Information Disclosure Act (1958) - Forces auto manufacturers to disclose the suggested retail price of their new cars, which keeps car dealers from inflating prices.

National Traffic and Safety Act (1958) - Provides a set of automobile and tire safety standards.

Fair Packaging and Labeling Act (1966) - Permits the FTC and FDA to create standards for packaging and labeling content.

Child Protection Act (1966) - Makes illegal the sale of dangerous toys and children's articles as well as products creating a thermal, mechanical, or electrical danger.

Federal Cigarette Labeling and Advertising Act (1967) - Requires cigarette manufacturers to label cigarettes as dangerous. Outlaws use of television media for cigarette advertisements.

Truth-in-Lending Act (1968) - Also called the Consumer Credit Protection Act. Forces lenders to disclose in writing, before the credit transaction: (1) the actual cash price, (2) the required down payment, (3) how much cash is being financed, (4) how much the loan will actually cost, (5) estimated annual interest rate, and (6) penalty for late payments or loan default.

Fair Credit Reporting Act (1970) - Allows consumers to see free of charge a copy of their credit report. Forces credit reporting agencies to remove any false information. Protects the confidentiality of the consumer.

Consumer Product Safety Act (1972) - Created the Consumer Product Safety Commission. It collects and disperses information on all consumer goods except automobiles, food, and a few others. It also has the authority to develop and enforce product standards, when deemed necessary.

Consumer Goods Pricing Act (1975) - Prevents retailers and manufacturers from entering into certain types of price maintenance agreements.

Magnuson-Moss Warranty/FTC Improvement Act (1975) - Requires the company or individual who offers a warranty to explain fully what the warranty covers and what its limitations are. This information allows consumers to file a lawsuit if the warranty is breached.

Equal Credit Opportunity Act (1975) - Forces creditors to disclose the reason for any credit denial. Credit cannot be denied on the basis of sex, marital status, race, national origin, region, age, or receipt of public assistance.

Fair Debt Collection Practice Act (1978) - Prohibits debt collectors from using harassment, abuse, or deceit when collecting a debt.

Toy Safety Act (1984) - Allows the government immediately to remove dangerous toys from the market.

Children's Television Act (1990) - Limits number of commercials aired during children's programs. Nutritional Labeling and Education Act (1990) - Requires nutrition labeling on food products.

Americans with Disabilities Act (1991) - Prohibits discrimination against people with disabilities in employment, transportation, public accommodations, communications, and governmental activities.

Do-Not-Call Implementation Act (2003) - Allows the FTC to collect fees from telemarketers for the implementation and enforcement of the national Do-Not-Call Registry.

Consumer Product Safety Improvement Act (2008) - Establishes consumer product safety standards and other safety requirements for children's products and reauthorizes and modernizes the Consumer Product Safety Commission.

Family Smoking and Prevention and Tobacco Control Act (2009) - Restricts tobacco marketing and sales to youth, requires smokeless tobacco warning labels, ensures "modified risk" claims are supported by scientific evidence and requires disclosure of ingredients in tobacco products.

Data Broker Accountability and Transparency Act (2014) - Prohibits data brokers from collecting or soliciting consumer information in deceptive ways and allows consumers to access and correct their information to help ensure maximum possible accuracy. Allows consumers to opt out of having their information collected and sold by data brokers for marketing purposes.

Figure 3.8 Consumer Protection Laws

- The right to choose freely from a variety of goods and services.

- The right to be informed about specific products and services so that responsible purchase decisions can be made.

- The right to be heard when voicing opinions about products and services offered.

- The right to be safe from defective or harmful products and services when used properly.

There are numerous consumer protection laws (see a partial list in Figure 3.8), and marketers need to know which ones affect their industry. Consumer safety legislation has a direct effect on important marketing decisions, such as product design, label information and design, and advertising claims. Interest in consumer safety has provided opportunities for marketing as well. For example, the development of seat belts, air bags, shatterproof windshields, anti-lock brakes, and other features were a direct result of consumer safety concerns.

But marketers need to manage safety-related features carefully. Consider the effect of air bags on marketing in the auto industry. Although air bags have saved more than 37,000 lives since 1987, they have also caused hundreds of deaths—eight of which are linked to the recent Takata airbag recall.[56] As a result, Ford Motor Company was the first to introduce less forceful air bags in 1998. Since the 2006 model year, all passenger cars and light-duty trucks are equipped with sensors that identify children and very small adults to restrict deployment of the airbag, or do so with less force. The Buick Lucerne uses airbag technology that identifies both size and position of the occupant and adjusts the airbag's size and force accordingly.[57]

The Global Marketing Environment   83

U.S. Laws Protecting the Environment By the early 1960s, people were consuming the world's natural resources at an alarming rate. The most basic resources—air and water—were often so polluted that they were unfit to sustain life. Although little was done internationally, the U.S. Congress enacted the National Environmental Policy Act in 1969 to direct environmental protection activities. The following year, the Environmental Protection Agency (EPA) was formed so that one agency would be responsible for enforcing all federal environmental regulation.

U.S. companies are required to adequately disclose potential environmental threats from their operations. The EPA maintains that those responsible for environmental contamination must pay for the cleanup and subsequently protect citizens' health. The EPA's Water Alliances for Volunteer Efficiency (WAVE) seeks to encourage commercial businesses and institutions to reduce water consumption while simultaneously increasing efficiency, profitability and competitiveness. WAVE is a part of the EPA's long-standing effort to prevent pollution and reduce demand on America's water and energy infrastructure.[58]

The EPA is also responsible for protecting human health. It reacted to the recent Flint, Michigan, water crisis in which city drinking water was deemed unsafe to consume because of high levels of lead leaching from the pipes and city infrastructure. The EPA assembled the Flint Safe Drinking Water Task Force, comprised of scientists and technical experts, to make recommendations to the City of Flint and state officials. It also oversees corrosion control and tests drinking water throughout the city to ensure it is safe to consume. The crisis is far from over, but the EPA will in instrumental in the repair and maintenance of the Flint water infrastructure.[59]

Samples collected from water taps in Flint, Michigan, led the EPA to create the Flint Safe Drinking Water Task Force.

Environmental groups such as the Audubon Society, Greenpeace and the Sierra Club have drawn attention to numerous environmental disasters and are actively seeking remedies and legislation to repair or avert damage.

LO 05

ETHICAL ENVIRONMENT

Questions of ethics are not always straightforward. In many countries bribery is regarded as highly unethical, but in others it is considered standard business practice. There is an important difference between what is legal and what is ethical. To determine legality, you must examine the relevant law. If the meaning is unclear, then a court may have to interpret it. Without a precedent, you may have to assess whether the action would be deemed legal or illegal.

Ethical issues are not so easily defined. Is it ethical for a pharmaceutical company to charge a price for a new drug that is much higher than the cost to produce it? After all, the company has poured millions into R&D and is trying to recoup its investment. Yet the high price makes the drug unaffordable to many people who desperately need it to survive. Is the drug company acting unethically?

The matrix in Figure 3.9 shows that marketing decisions may fall into one of four categories: legal and ethical, illegal and ethical, legal and unethical, or illegal and unethical.

The appropriate behavior is easy to assess when the proposed action is clearly

	Legal	**Illegal**
Ethical	Market FDA-approved cold medicine	Market a safe AIDS vaccine not yet approved by the FDA
Unethical	Market a harmful drug banned by the FDA in a country with no drug review agencies	Market contraband drugs

Figure 3.9   Ethics Situations

legal and ethical (acceptable) or clearly illegal and unethical (unacceptable). However, legality and ethics are open to different interpretations, so marketers must be sensitive to issues in both categories.

Perhaps the most difficult circumstances occur when legal and ethical standards conflict. Some people place more weight on the ethical side ("Should we do it?"), others emphasize the legal ("Can we do it?"), while still others believe it is best to altogether avoid any actions that are either illegal or unethical. Most laws that affect business are interpreted in the courts, which set precedents to be followed. Every legislative session can create new laws that lead to new regulations, which often require new court decisions to set new precedents. As with every other environment, the legal field is constantly changing and marketers need to keep in step with it.

Many companies have developed a code of ethics for employees. This helps ensure that everyone in the company is following the same set of ethical standards. For instance, eBay took action against the unethical slaughter of endangered elephants by banning all ivory from its website. Senior regulatory counsel Jack Christin from eBay's blog "eBay Ink" explained, "Due to the unique nature of eBay's global online marketplace and the growing complexity of the rules and regulations surrounding the sale of legal ivory, we will be moving from a ban on cross-border sales to rolling out a complete ban of the sale of ivory on eBay."[60]

Ivy Allen / USFWS

This photograph taken by the United States Fish and Wildlife Service shows the result of unethical slaughtering of endangered elephants.

The American Marketing Association is also committed to promoting the highest level of professional ethics for its members through its Statement of Ethics. As you read the Statement, notice how it emphasizes the importance of marketers being honest and acting with integrity. It covers basic responsibilities, what a customer should be able to expect from an exchange, and ethics surrounding the marketing mix areas of product, promotion, place, and price—as well as in marketing research and relationships with others.

In its preamble to the statement, AMA emphasizes that "as marketers, we recognize that we not only serve our organizations but also act as stewards of society in creating, facilitating and executing the transactions that are part of the greater economy. In this role, marketers are expected to embrace the highest professional norms and the ethical values implied by our responsibility toward multiple stakeholders."

ETHICAL NORMS

As marketers, we must:

1. Do no harm. This means consciously avoiding harmful actions or omissions by embodying high ethical standards and adhering to all applicable laws and regulations in the choices we make.

2. Foster trust in the marketing system. This means striving for good faith and fair dealing so as to contribute toward the efficacy of the exchange process as well as avoiding deception in product design, pricing, communication and delivery of distribution.

3. Embrace ethical values. This means building relationships and enhancing consumer confidence in the integrity of marketing by affirming these core values: honesty, responsibility, fairness, respect, transparency and citizenship.

ETHICAL VALUES

Honesty — to be forthright in dealings with customers and stakeholders. To this end, we will:

» Strive to be truthful in all situations and at all times.
» Offer products of value that do what we claim in our communications.
» Stand behind our products if they fail to deliver their claimed benefits.
» Honor our explicit and implicit commitments and promises.

Responsibility — to accept the consequences of our marketing decisions and strategies. To this end, we will:

» Strive to serve the needs of customers.
» Avoid using coercion with all stakeholders.
» Acknowledge the social obligations to stakeholders that come with increased marketing and economic power.
» Recognize our special commitments to vulnerable market segments such as children, seniors, the economically impoverished, market illiterates and others who may be substantially disadvantaged.
» Consider environmental stewardship in our decision-making.

Fairness — to balance justly the needs of the buyer with the interests of the seller. To this end, we will:

» Represent products in a clear way in selling, advertising and other forms of communication; this includes the avoidance of false, misleading and deceptive promotion.
» Reject manipulations and sales tactics that harm customer trust.
» Refuse to engage in price fixing, predatory pricing, price gouging or "bait-and-switch" tactics.
» Avoid knowing participation in conflicts of interest.
» Seek to protect the private information of customers, employees and partners.

Respect — to acknowledge the basic human dignity of all stakeholders. To this end, we will:

» Value individual differences and avoid stereotyping customers or depicting demographic groups (e.g., gender, race, sexual orientation) in a negative or dehumanizing way.
» Listen to the needs of customers and make all reasonable efforts to monitor and improve their satisfaction on an ongoing basis.
» Make every effort to understand and respectfully treat buyers, suppliers, intermediaries and distributors from all cultures.
» Acknowledge the contributions of others, such as consultants, employees and coworkers, to marketing endeavors.
» Treat everyone, including our competitors, as we would wish to be treated.

Transparency — to create a spirit of openness in marketing operations. To this end, we will:

» Strive to communicate clearly with all constituencies.
» Accept constructive criticism from customers and other stakeholders.
» Explain and take appropriate action regarding significant product or service risks, component substitutions or other foreseeable eventualities that could affect customers or their perception of the purchase decision.
» Disclose list prices and terms of financing as well as available price deals and adjustments.

Citizenship — to fulfill the economic, legal, philanthropic and societal responsibilities that serve stakeholders. To this end, we will:

» Strive to protect the ecological environment in the execution of marketing campaigns.
» Give back to the community through volunteerism and charitable donations.
» Contribute to the overall betterment of marketing and its reputation.
» Urge supply chain members to ensure that trade is fair for all participants, including producers in developing countries.

DIGITAL MARKETING

The global population today is almost completely connected by technology. This presents incredible opportunities for businesses to connect with more customers than ever before. Throughout this text you will learn how digital marketing has changed the global marketing environment; it is infused in most every company's effort to connect with customers locally, nationally and around the world.

Digital marketing is the promotion of products or brands in one or more forms of electronic media.[61] It is the most current term for what you may know as internet marketing, or e-marketing. Organizations that conduct commercial transactions over the internet are part of e-commerce, which is now referred to as the digital marketing economy, or traditionally referred to as the internet marketing economy.[62]

Digital marketing can be divided into two sectors. **Business-to-consumer (B2C) e-commerce** is trade involving businesses selling to consumers over the internet. **Business-to-business (B2B) e-commerce** is trade involving internet sales in which businesses sell to other businesses, including governments and organizations.

The internet is structured to facilitate these transactions. Search engines, such as Google and Yahoo, serve B2C marketing, whereas ZDNet and Marketsite.net are more B2B oriented. Web market makers facilitate buying and selling; Ebay and Priceline, for example, support B2C marketing, while Bloomberg and ChemConnect serve the B2B markets. Finally, product service providers such as Amazon and Walmart deliver to the B2C market while Cisco and Dell deliver to the B2B market.

This structure is user friendly for both markets, which is why growth is soaring. U.S. consumer retail e-commerce sales (e-sales) are increasing by approximately 14 percent annually, much higher than total retail sales of four percent. The mobile e-commerce market is growing quickly, too. Recent forecasts predict global e-commerce sales made on mobile devices will top $638 billion in 2018. To put that in perspective, it's roughly the size of the world's entire e-commerce market in 2013.[63]

The dramatic online consumer spending increase has a direct impact on the B2B sector. Typical B2B buyers are also consumer buyers outside of work. They're aware of Amazon, Zappos, eBay, and other e-commerce giants. With those positive and common online experiences in their personal life, they begin to expect the same experiences at work. When the office runs low on toner, why would they call vendors for pricing, search dusty

DIGITAL MARKETING

Promotion of products or brands in one or more forms of electronic media.

BUSINESS-TO-CONSUMER (B2C) E-COMMERCE

Trade involving businesses selling to consumers over the Internet.

BUSINESS-TO-BUSINESS (B2B) E-COMMERCE

Trade involving Internet sales in which businesses sell to other businesses, including governments and organizations.

Mobile e-commerce sales are quickly catching PC e-commerce sales, and marketers must create new ways to connect with these customers

catalogs and phone in orders, instead of just jumping on Amazon and having it delivered to the office door the next day? B2B sellers must be very aware of these shifts and adapt as quickly and effectively as the B2C sellers or they could miss out on huge opportunties.[64] There is no doubt that both the B2B and B2C e-commerce markets demand serious attention from marketers!

Cloud computing also enhances B2B and B2C e-commerce. Cloud computing is a general term used to incorporate a variety of information services and applications remotely operated by users across the web. It allows companies to access scalable computing power and intelligent networks, while reducing labor needs, physical space and energy consumption.[65] Salesforce.com sells its customer relationship management (CRM) system over the cloud, eliminating the requirement for businesses to download bulky software and create in-house databases. Other companies have created cloud computing products, including Amazon Web Services, Google AppEngine and Microsoft Azure, Zoho, and Rackspace, offering both B2B and B2C solutions.[66]

VALUE OF THE INTERNET TO BUYERS AND SELLERS

According to Forbes, the B2B e-commerce market will grow to $7.6 trillion and the B2C e-commerce market will grow to $3.2 trillion by 2020.[67] That makes a total global e-commerce market of $10.8 trillion in 2020, compared to an estimated $1.316 trillion in 2014.[68] What explains this massive growth of e-commerce?

As Figure 3.11 indicates, both buyers and sellers receive great value from e-commerce. Compared to traditional channels, buyers get more information, greater convenience, wider customized selection, and better prices. Marketers have access to more customers, reduced supply-chain costs, efficient two-way communication with customers, and the ability to personalize messages and products.

Figure 3.11   Internet Marketing Benefits

Value to Buyers *Better Information*

The internet enables buyers to obtain a great deal of information about products, including availability, costs, attributes and use instructions, as well as information about manufacturer warranties and service. Some sites provide comparison shopping, helping users find the right product configuration at the lowest price. In many cases, before selecting an item, potential buyers can see other customers' opinions of the product. At Amazon.com and BestBuy.com, for example, readers can browse customer reviews based on a five-star system prior to making a buying decision. Travelers can also learn what others thought of a hotel or destination with the Travel Advisor on-line rating system. Digital technology gives consumers more information to make informed decisions than ever before.

Greater Convenience Shopping at home or in the office via computer reduces the amount of travel and time associated with in-store purchases. Buyers in rural or remote communities benefit by saving a lengthy trip to a store. In urban and suburban settings, buyers can avoid traffic congestion, and long checkout lines. In addition, savings in gasoline and other vehicle costs can be substantial, not to mention the social benefits of less auto pollution and congestion. Many companies offer free shipping for orders placed on line.

UberPrints.com offers a wide selection of products that customers can custom design and print at very reasonable prices.

Wider Selection and Customization

Online buyers can choose from a wide selection of products, and if that's not enough, they can customize their own. Retail outlets may carry only certain brands and sizes, but online sources offer all possible configurations for buyers to compare. Even scarce products, such as an obscure book, can be found very quickly. If the book's in print, you'll likely find it on Amazon. At the same time, more customization is possible, because buyers can interface with a seller's manufacturing facilities, which in turn are networked with suppliers, so sellers can build or manufacture on demand. UberPrints.com will print customer designed t-shirts, hats, and more at incredibly low prices and no minimum order. Many custom bicycle shops allow users to build their own bike online and have the finished product delivered to their doorstep in weeks or even days.

Better Prices Due to the efficiency and competitive nature of the digital marketing economy, shoppers may benefit from lower prices. One company asks: "Would you like to buy this camera [a popular brand is shown] at $169 or $149 or $129? Shop at MySimon.com." Internet retailers tend to be driven by price because many buyers shop online specifically to save. The pioneers of e-commerce used a low-price strategy to attract business in what was a new and unfamiliar market at the time. This strategy is still popular. Online shoppers jump from site to site with a few key strokes, and they've come to expect competitive prices. The contact retailer, 1-800-CONTACTS, guarantees to match any online competitive price; a buyer simply provides the competitor's name to a company rep, via phone or online, and the rep pulls up the competitor's site to verify pricing. Search engines make the benefit of such a pricing policy especially easy and advantageous for buyers.

Value to Sellers *Access to More Customers*

On the seller side of the market, internet businesses have access to a world of customers. A firm in Chicago can communicate with a potential customer in India as easily as with one next door. B2B and B2C has grown by leaps and bounds, which means that more businesses and customers are being brought together in more uniquely personal ways than ever before. The internet keeps sellers available to buyers 24/7, and digital technology allows a business or consumer to shop for products from anywhere. The days of sitting at a desktop computer as the only way to shop online are gone.

The Apple App Store is an example of how sellers gain access to huge numbers of customers. It has more than 1.2 million apps available, from simple games to time-management helpers to guitar tuners. Each represents a seller. The App Store—which now also includes software for the Apple Watch and Apple TV—exceeded revenue of $20 billion for 2015, an increase of more than 40% in sales from 2014, and there are expectations for even larger profits in the coming years.[69]

There are more than three billion people around the world with internet access, accounting for more than 40 percent of the world's population. That's a major increase from the mere one percent penetration that existed 19 years ago. [70] Obviously, not all users make web purchases. In fact, only eight percent of retail sales are made online.[71] Many shoppers go online to do research but still prefer to purchase in an actual store. In the reverse scenario, some shoppers will go to stores to try on clothing or shoes, or check out high-end items, then buy them for less online, in a practice known as "showrooming." Showrooming is particularly common for items $100 or more, and it has hit appliance and electronics stores particularly hard with lost sales.[72]

Increased Loyalty through Customization While the ability to customize products online is a value to buyers, it's also a value to sellers. Companies are finding it boosts sales and brand loyalty. A survey by Bain & Company showed that customers who had customized a product online engaged more with the company. They visited its website more often, stayed on the page longer, and were more loyal to the brand.[73]

The Share a Coke campaign allows you to customize your own bottles for five dollars.

In the footwear industry, customers who designed their own shoes gave companies a 50% higher Net Promoter Score[SM] (NPS®)—a standard measure of customer loyalty—than customers who bought generally manufactured shoes from the same company.[74] Higher NPS scores indicate higher sales, referrals and customer loyalty.

Customization is helping companies reach the lucrative demographic of Millennial shoppers, who demand more individualized products than older consumers. This segment adopts new preferences easily, and it's closely tied to social media for tracking trends and styles. You may recall in the feature article at the beginning of this chapter we mentioned M&M's website, mymms.com, where people can customize M&M's by color, message and even image! In the Chapter 2 feature you learned that Coca-Cola also customizes bottles and cans for special events through its website, shareacoke.com. These are both popular sites for Millennials who host events like graduation parties, showers and weddings, and guests instantly become potential customers because the products are such hits!

Online customization is likely to increase significantly as marketers look for new ways to create and capture value for customers. Brooks Brothers is a retailer that offers men the option of customizing their own suits. Ken Seiff, executive vice president of direct and omni-channel marketing at Brooks Brothers, says, "In general, customers who buy customized products are more satisfied and more valuable."

SUPPLY CHAIN COSTS

Costs associated with procuring goods and services from suppliers and with distributing products from businesses to consumers.

Reduced Supply Chain Costs The internet marketing economy reduces not only the **supply chain costs** associated with procuring goods and services from suppliers, but also the costs of distributing products to consumers. Savings occur throughout the supply chain, including lower inventory costs due to better demand forecasting, streamlined manufacturing, warehousing, and transportation. Better communication among all members of the value chain reduces errors.

Dell has been successful in the computer server market by integrating its supply chain through the internet. For example, Dell allows purchasers to specify precisely which computer configuration they want by providing the option to "Build Your Own" computer.[75] All members of Dell's supply chain are connected online and are given intensive information linked to customer demand. This allows each supplier to operate efficiently while knowing the context of the customer's requests and supplying precisely what Dell customers want.

Two-Way Communication A significant benefit of digital marketing for marketers is how efficiently it facilitates two-way communication. It is a constant bridge between customers and companies. Social media sites facilitate personalization and customization of both products and messages. Marketers can gather opinions and test reactions to marketing activities. Perhaps you've visited mystarbucksidea.com that you read about in Chapter 1. The dialog between customers and the company is fascinating.

Digital marketing also enables companies to collect data on a buyer's purchases, which reveals the buyer's preferences and buying patterns. In turn, companies can direct personal communications and product offerings to that same consumer. Amazon has been doing this with great success for years. And online customers can chat with a company rep, customize an order, pay for it, and choose how they want it delivered. Digital marketing has completely changed the marketing environment for business and customer communication. We will discuss this topic more throughout the text.

Chapter Summary

Objective 1: Describe the marketing environment and explain the purpose of environmental scanning.

The marketing environment is the sum of all factors that affect a business. The factors are divided into two groups: the microenvironment and the global macroenvironment. The microenvironment includes factors that marketers interact with regularly. Consequently, the microenvironment influences and is influenced by marketing. The global macroenvironment includes factors that marketers must take into account when making decisions. However, marketers seldom influence these factors.

Together, the two environments can facilitate or inhibit organizations from reaching their objectives. Environmental scanning is the process of collecting and analyzing information about the marketing environment in order to detect important changes or trends that can affect a company's strategy. Proactive organizations use results of environmental scanning to anticipate changes in the marketing environment and plan accordingly. The internet is a particularly useful tool for gathering current data about the environment.

Objective 2: Learn how stakeholders can affect a company in achieving its objectives.

Stakeholders are important parts of the microenvironment and directly participate in accomplishing the organization's goals. They include owners, employees, suppliers, intermediaries and action groups. Stakeholders participate with the organization in order to accomplish their own goals; consequently, marketers must take their desires into consideration when making decisions.

Because owners are entitled to a fair return on their investment, companies need to make a substantial profit, and nonprofit organizations must accomplish the goals established by their owners or sponsors. Employees critical; happy employees produce happy customers. Suppliers provide necessary services, raw materials and components. They also provide technology in specialized areas. Suppliers have a dramatic influence on a company's customers. Intermediaries help move products between a producer and the end user. They may contact customers directly, so a good working rela-

tionship between the company and the intermediary is important. Action groups are "watchdogs" that keep the interests of the environment and people in balance with profit seeking. They can help marketers interface better with society.

The relationship between marketers and stakeholders is fluid. Marketers must be sensitive to stakeholders' desires because the organization is dependent on them to achieve objectives. In turn, stakeholders need to support the organization in reaching its objectives or it wouldn't exist.

Objective 3: Explain why understanding industry competition is important in an environmental analysis.

An understanding of industry competition provides an integrated picture about the major forces that determine competitive intensity. Competition involves single competitors and groups of company types that compete. We look at the rivalry among existing firms to understand one-on-one competition. Potential competitors are also considered, because firms enter and exit industries. At the same time, substitute products can play a role, especially when new technologies bring new ways to perform old functions. The bargaining power of buyers and suppliers determines how a company competes. Suppliers have more power when there are few suppliers and many buyers. All of these aspects of industry competition need to be understood in order to build appropriate marketing strategies.

Objective 4: Identify the six components of the global macroenvironment, and explain why each is important to a company's marketing strategy.

The global macroenvironment is being influenced by six key forces. The technological environment provides knowledge and tools that companies can acquire to produce better products. By phasing in new technology, progressive companies stay abreast of the best ways to create customer value. Economic factors are also important. Changes in income and spending power and other factors help determine which countries have the ability to purchase. The world has three major trading areas. The regions offer large markets, but they also compete against one another. The natural resources environment also comes into play. It provides raw materials and must be protected. Global demographics are changing. Shifts in population density and dispersion are important, as are age shifts. It is important to grasp the cultural environment and to view things from other perspectives. The values, beliefs and behaviors of others may differ from your own. Finally, the legal/regulatory environment is complex. Laws must be interpreted and followed. They help promote competition, influence business size, protect customers and protect the environment.

Objective 5: Discuss the factors that influence ethical marketing decisions.

Marketers often face ethical dilemmas, particularly when legal and ethical standards conflict. Many companies have developed codes of ethics for their employees to help ensure that everyone in the company is following the same standards. The American Marketing Association publishes a Statement of Ethics that covers the basic responsibilities of marketers It stresses the importance of honesty, fairness, respect, transparency, citizenship and professional responsibility.

Objective 6: Understand how digital marketing is changing the global marketing environment.

Technology connects people and markets around the world and digital marketing connects buyers and sellers. Both business-to-consumer and business-to-business organizations rely on digital technology to connect with markets. The business-to-business sector is growing more quickly than the business-to-consumer sector. The internet and digital marketing together have changed the marketing landscape for buyers as well as for marketers, who can more easily connect with customers to create and capture value.

Review Your Understanding

1. What is environmental scanning and what technology is being used for it today?
2. What is the microenvironment and what are its elements?
3. What is the global macroenvironment and what are its components?
4. Who are stakeholders and why are they important? List five different types of stakeholders.
5. What are the elements of industry competition? Describe each.
6. Why is the technological environment important?
7. What are the elements of the economic environment? List three aspects that are influencing global marketing.
8. What are the three major trading blocs in the world economy?
9. What demographic trends are influencing marketing?
10. What is the self-reference criterion? What are some cultural differences to be aware of?
11. What are the types of laws that affect marketing?
12. What is the difference between unethical and illegal behavior?
13. What is digital marketing?
14. What are four ways the internet brings value to buyers?
15. What are four ways the internet brings value to sellers?

Discussion of Concepts

1. Suppose that IBM and Microsoft announced plans to merge into one company. Would U.S. laws allow this to happen? Why? Do you think that other countries around the world would have the same reaction?
2. What is culture, and how does it affect marketing? Can you think of any products that are successful in the United States but would fail in Japan because of cultural differences?
3. The chapter discussed changes that Starbucks and McDonald's, among others, have made for sustainability. Identify additional companies that have altered practices or products to protect the environment, and explain those changes. What types of legislation do you expect in the future? What could be the potential effects of such legislation on corporate marketing? ?
4. Do you think that General Motors should invest a significant amount of money in research and development projects? Why or why not?
5. In recent years, discount stores such as Walmart and Target have become extremely large and powerful. How does this affect industry structure and competitive intensity?
6. As the director of marketing for Dow Chemical Company, you are required to interact regularly with a number of different publics. List these publics, the concerns that each might have, and how you would address each of those concerns.
7. What effect do you think the Euro has had on trade among the three superblocs? Which trading relationships are most affected and how?
8. Which do you feel is more important — ethics or the law? Why?
9. If the internet hadn't been developed, how would business marketing be different than it is today? If digital technology hadn't been developed, how would your life be different than it is today?
10. What are the advantages and disadvantages of technology in the field of marketing?
11. In what ways does the internet provide value to buyers and sellers?

Key Terms & Definitions

1. **Action Group:** A number of people who support some cause in the interest of consumers or environmental safety.

2. **Age cohort:** A group of people close in age who have been shaped by their generation's experience with the media, peers, events and society at large.

3. **Business-to-business (B2B) e-commerce:** Trade involving Internet sales in which businesses sell to other businesses, including governments and organizations.

4. **Business-to-consumer (B2C) e-commerce:** Trade involving businesses selling to consumers over the Internet.

5. **Cartel:** A group of businesses or nations that work together to control the price and production of a particular product.

6. **Cultural environment:** The learned values, beliefs, language, symbols and patterns of behavior shared by people in a society and passed on from generation to generation.

7. **Demographic environment:** The statistical data used to describe a population.

8. **Digital marketing:** the promotion of products or brands in one or more forms of electronic media.

9. **Discretionary income:** The amount of money consumers have left after paying taxes and purchasing necessities.

10. **Disposable income:** The income consumers have left after paying taxes.

11. **Economic environment:** The financial and natural resources available to consumers, businesses and countries.

12. **Environmental scanning:** Collecting and analyzing information about the marketing environment in order to detect important changes or trends that can affect a company's strategy.

13. **Global macroenvironment:** The large external influences considered vital to long-term decisions but not directly affected by the company itself.

14. **Gross domestic product (GDP):** The total market value of all goods and services produced by a country in a single year.

15. **Gross Income** The total amount of money earned in one year by an individual, household or business.

16. **Intermediaries:** Stakeholders who move products from the manufacturer to the final user.

17. **Legal/regulatory environment:** International, federal, state, and local regulations and laws, the agencies that interpret and administer them, and the court system.

18. **Maastricht Treaty:** Consists of 282 directives that eliminate border controls and custom duties among members of the European Union.

19. **Marketing environment:** The sum of all factors that affect a business.

20. **Microenvironment:** The forces close to a company that influence how it connects with customers.

21. **Population density:** The concentration of people within some unit of measure, such as per square mile or per square kilometer.

22. **Self-reference criterion:** The unconscious reliance on values gained from one's own socialization when trying to understand another culture.

23. **Spending power:** The ability of the population to purchase goods and services.

24. **Stakeholder:** A group that can influence or be influenced by the firm's actions.

25. **Substitute product:** Any good or service that performs the same function or provides the same benefit as an existing one.

26. **Suppliers:** Organizations that provide a company with necessary resources to produce its goods and services.

27. **Supply chain costs:** Costs associated with procuring goods and services from suppliers and with distributing products from businesses to consumers.

28. **Technological environment:** The total body of knowledge available for development, manufacturing and marketing of products and services.

29. **Urbanization:** The shift of population from rural to urban areas.

References

1. "Gen Y's embrace of hybrids may be auto market's tipping point," http://news.msu.edu, January 18, 2012.

2. www.factiva.com and www.gegxs.com, websites visited February 22, 2015.

3. Trout, Jack, "Peter Drucker on Marketing," Forbes, July 3, 2006.

4. www.llbean.com/customerService/aboutLLBean/company_information.html, website visited May 25, 2016.

5. Sierra Club, www.sierraclub.org, website visited March 13, 2015.

6. Laczniak, Gene R., Murphy, Patrick E., Ethical Marketing Decisions: The Higher Road (Boston: Allyn & Bacon, 1993), pp. 14-15.

7. www.panerabread.com, website visited March 29, 2016.

8. Kiger, Patrick J., "Small Groups, Big Ideas," Workforce Management, February 27, 2006, pg. 1, 22-27.

9. Ford Sustainability Report, 2013-14, www.ford.com, website visited May 14, 2016.

10. "Blanketing Space with DuPontTM Kevlar®," Dupont News, www.dupont.com, December 18, 2015.

11. Jonel Aleccia, "College Student Sickened in Big Beef Recall: Lawsuit," NBC News, May 27, 2014.

12. "'Our Choice': Al Gore's New Book Follows On 'Inconvenient Truth'," Huffington Post, www.huffingtonpost.com, website visited March 19, 2015.

13. www.allianceforclimateprotection.org, website visited March 19, 2015; www.algore.com, website visited March 19, 2015.

14. Geewax, Marilyn, "Gay link prompts call for Walmart boycott," The Austin American-Statesman, November 11, 2006. Crary, David, "Conservatives abandon planned boycott of Walmart over outreach to gay groups," Associated Press, November 22, 2006.

15. "NFL Supports Breast Cancer Awareness Month with A Crucial Catch Campaign," www.nflcommunications.com, 2015.
16. Anthony, C., Bendetto, D., Calantone, Roger, Schmidt, Jeffrey, "New Product Activities and Performance: The Moderating Role of Environmental Hostility," J Product Innovation Management, 1997.
17. "SWEETS and SNACKS 2012 Trends: Sharing Sweets, Mango Mania, Healthy Snacking," Business Journals, www.bizjournals.com, May 8, 2012.
18. John Kell, "McDonald's so far unfazed by latest entrant in breakfast war," Fortune, May 8, 2014.
19. "Corporate Fact Sheet," www.walmartfacts.com, website visited April 22, 2015.
20. Merck Annual Report, www.merck.com, website visited May 22, 2016.
21. Schubarth, Cromwell, "Intel tops chip R&D spending, but industry research gowth slowing." Silicon Valley Business Journal, January 26, 2016.
22. www.intel.com, website visited May 1, 2016.
23. Deal, Terrence E., Kennedy, Allan A., Corporate Cultures: The Ethics and Rituals of Corporate Life, Massachusetts: Addison-Wesley Publishing, 1982, p. 8.
24. "Why Culture is Key," Booz & Company, www.booz.com, Winter 2011, website visited May 13, 2016.
25. www.census.gov, website visited June 14, 2016.
26. www.cia.gov, website visited May 1, 2015.
27. Ibid.
28. "What Latin America Can Teach Us," New York Times, www.nytimes.com, website visited May 1, 2015.
29. "Wealth distribution: Which nations are the best?," Rediff, www.rediff.com, website visited May 2, 2015.
30. "Becoming a Triad Power: The New Global Corporation," International Marketing Review, Autumn 1986.
31. www.cia.gov, website visited May 2, 2015.
32. www.europa.eu, website visited May 2, 2015.
33. www.chinability.com/GDP.htm, website visited May 21, 2016.
34. www.apec.org, website visited May 21, 2016.
35. www.tradingeconomics.com/china/gdp-growth-annual, website visited June 6, 2016.
36. "What is fracking and why is it controversial," BBC News, December 16, 2015.
37. Ibid.
38. "Starbucks' new environmentally friendly coffee-cup sleeve validated by Western Michigan University paper program," MLive, www.mlive.com, July 12, 2012.
39. www.prb.org, website visited May 2, 2016.
40. www.cia.gov, website visited May 2, 2016.
41. Chang-Hoan Cho, Ph.D., John Holcombe & Daniel Murphy, "Multicultural Marketing in Contemporary U.S. Markets," www.greenbook.org/marketing-research.cfm/multicultural-marketing, website visited May 29, 2014.
42. http://esa.un.org/unpd/wpp/, website visited May 2, 2015.
43. Bennett, Claudette, "Current Population Reports (Washington, DC: Bureau of the Census, U.S. Department of Commerce," January 1995, pg. 2.
44. CIA World Factbook, www.cia.gov, website visited May 2, 2016.
45. Ibid.
46. www.census.gov, website visited May 2, 2016.
47. Fry, Richard, "Millennials overtake Baby Boomers as America's largest generation," FactTank, Pew Research Center, April 25, 2016.
48. CIA World Factbook, www.cia.gov, website visited May 2, 2015.
49. www.census.gov, website visited May 2, 2015.
50. "Are Baby Boomers an Invisible Goldmine for Marketers?", Forbes, www.forbes.com, August 10, 2012; "Gray-haired models growing in popularity as baby boomers age," Boston.com, www.boston.com, July 24, 2012.
51. Chan, Ricky Y. K., "Determinants of Chinese consumers' green purchase behavior," Psychology & Marketing, Vol. 18, Issue 4, pgs. 389-413, April 2001.
52. "McDonald's food you can't get here," Chicago Tribune, www.chicagotribune.com, website visited May 2, 2015.
53. Hall, Edward T., "The Silent Language in Overseas Business," Harvard Business Review, May-June 1960, pg. 87.
54. www.businessculture.org/western-europe/business-culture-in-france/meeting-etiquette-in-france, website visited June 13, 2016.
55. "0610220 Johnson & Johnson and Pfizer Inc," Federal Trade Commission, www.ftc.gov, website visited May 2, 2015.
56. "Everything you need to know about the Takata airbag recall," www.consumerreports.org, website visited June 25, 2015.
57. www.buick.com, website visited May 2, 2015.
58. www.epa.gov/nscep, website visited June 12, 2016.
59. www.epa.gov/flint/flint-safe-drinking-water-task-force, website visited June 12, 2016.
60. www.businessdictionary.com/definition/digital-marketing.html, website visited May 28, 2016.
61. "eBay Bans Ivory Trading to Protect Endangered Elephants," Environmental News Service, October 22, 2008.
62. Mahadevan, B., "Business Models for Internet-based E-Commerce," California Management Review, 42 Summer 2000, pg. 56.
63. Cooper Smith, "US E-Commerce Growth Is Now Far Outpacing Overall Retail Sales," http://www.businessinsider.com, April 2, 2014.
64. Brian Walker, "Why E-Commerce Still Isn't Clicking with B2B Executives," Forbes, May 6, 2014.
65. Service Management and Cloud Computing, www-01.ibm.com, website visited February 11, 2010.
66. Armbrust, M., Fox, A., Griffith, R., et.al. "Above the Clouds: A Berkeley View of Cloud Computing," UC Berkely Reliable Adaptive Distributed Systems Laboratory, http://radlab.cs.berkeley.edu/, website visited May14, 2015.
67. Sarwant Singh, "B2B eCommerce Market Worth $6.7 Trillion by 2020: Alibaba & China the Front-Runners," Forbes, November 6, 2014.
68. Thad Reuter, "Global e-commerce will increase 22% this year," Internet Retailer, December 23, 2014.
69. Keizer, Gregg, "Apple's cut of 2015 App Store revenue tops $6B," Computerworld, January 6, 2016.
70. www.internetworldstats.com, website visited May 24, 2016.
71. www.strategyand.pwc.com/perspectives/2015-retail-trends.
72. "Showrooming Challenges Brick-and-Mortar Retailers," Practical eCommerce, www.practicalecommerce.com, July 25, 2012.
73. Spaulding, Elizabeth and Perry, Christopher, "Making it personal: Rules for success in product customization," Insights, September 16, 2013, www.bain.com/publications/articles/making-it-personal-rules-for-success-in-product-customization.aspx, website visited June 16, 2016.
74. Ibid.
75. www.dell.com, website visited May 20, 2016.

CHAPTER *04*

Marketing
Information & Research

P&G

YouTube SCAN & WATCH ▶

P&G produces many of the common household items you use every day.

What began as a small, family-operated business in the 1830s has grown into the largest consumer products corporation in the world. Procter & Gamble (P&G) brands serve over four billion people today! You probably use many of them, such as Tide, Bounce, Cascade, Dawn, Crest, and Gillette.

"The Consumer is Boss" is the mantra that CEO A.G. Lafley instills throughout P&G, and to learn about its consumers the company devotes massive resources. It's one of the few companies with a division dedicated solely to learning about consumers and markets, a self-proclaimed "secret weapon." The Consumer and Market Knowledge (CMK) division conducts thousands of research studies annually and also invests hundreds of millions each year in consumer understanding. Through print, email, social media and personal meetings, CMK promotes new products, offers free samples and conducts surveys. It uses the survey information to analyze trends, target customers, adjust advertising campaigns and generate ideas for new products. CMK also gathers data about consumer and shopper decision processes, market and retailer dynamics, external influences, and marketing opportunities.

P&G recently built a $300 million research and development facility in Ohio, dedicated solely to beauty products. The Beauty Innovation Center includes laboratories, pilot plants and space to conduct focus groups with consumers regarding new P&G beauty products (current brands include Head & Shoulders, Old Spice and Olay). It's designed to provide interactive marketing information and research for P&G. The company also relies heavily on social media for gathering information through sites like Facebook (5,548,000 likes), Twitter (148,000 followers), and Instagram (19,000 followers), which encourage two-way communication between the company and its consumers. Monitoring social media gives P&G marketers a chance to gain valuable insights from informal exchanges between customers.

Its dedication to learning about consumers is constant; how it goes about that learning is fluid. P&G was ranked the number one company for innovative market research by the GreenBook Research Industry Trends (GRIT) Report, a leading surveyor of the market research industry. In the report, P&G was cited as innovative, future thinking and on the cutting edge of research. Specifically, the company was applauded for focusing on human emotion as it pertains to consumer behavior, and using new methods for analyzing qualitative data.

Procter & Gamble is truly a global company that relies on extensive marketing information and research. It even launched an immersion research program called "Living It," in which its marketing managers submerge themselves in daily life with customers in developing nations. The P&G managers spend time to learn and understand what's important to their customers in life, as well as their desires, aspirations, and needs for current or potential P&G products. P&G invests hundreds of millions annually in market research and consumer understanding, more than any other company in the world. As a result, stakeholders continue to reap rewards, with most recent worldwide sales exceeding $75 billion.

Sources: Christopher Freeburn, "Procter & Gamble Brings Back 'Consumer Is Boss' CEO," InvestorPlace, May 24, 2013; Barrett J. Brunsman, "P&G to build massive R&D center in Mason," Cincinnati Business Courier, March 17, 2015; Peter Sims, "How Google and P&G Approach New Customers, New Markets," Harvard Business Review, March 02, 2009; http://www.greenbookblog.org/2015/04/08/the-15-most-innovative-market-research-clients-grit-spring-2015-sneak-peek, website visited June 28, 2016; www.pg.com, website visited May 23, 2016.

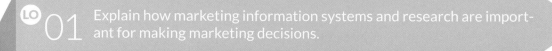

LO 01 Explain how marketing information systems and research are important for making marketing decisions.

LO 02 Recognize how data is transformed into useful information for marketing purposes.

LO 03 Explain the steps of a typical marketing research process.

LO 04 Describe widely used marketing research techniques.

LO 05 Explore technology's effect on marketing information and research.

LO 06 Understand the ethical considerations of marketing information and research.

LO 01

The Concept Of Marketing Information & Research

To connect with customers, companies need information. They need information about who their customers are, who their *potential* customers are, what's important to them, who is competing for their business, and what changes will likely occur in the marketplace. This is a lot of information for marketers to gather!

According to IBM, 90% of the data in the world today has been created in the last two years alone, thanks to technology.[1] Technology has brought many changes to marketing research, and it has greatly increased the amount of data available to a company for learning about its markets and its customers. Global internet access, social media, and mobile tracking devices all provide new ways for companies to gather information.

This data can be extremely beneficial in learning about a company's markets and adjusting strategies to better connect with customers. It can also be a problem. Sometimes there's so much data available that managers don't know how to sort through it to extract the most relevant information. To help decision makers, most companies carefully structure the way data are collected, stored and made available through marketing information systems and marketing research.

A marketing information system (MkIS) is a set of procedures and methods for the regular, planned collection, analysis, and presentation of information for use in making marketing decisions. A significant portion of that data is generated through marketing research. **Marketing research** is the formal assembly and analysis of data about specific issues relating to marketing products and services. According to the American Marketing Association, marketing research is the function that links the consumer, customer, and public to the marketer through information—information used to identify and define marketing opportunities and problems; generate, re-

MARKETING INFORMATION SYSTEMS (MkIS)

A computerized system used to collect and analyze the data needed for marketing decisions.

MARKETING RESEARCH

The formal assembly and analysis of information about specific issues surrounding the marketing of goods and services.

Figure 4.1   Marketing information and Decision Making

fine, and evaluate marketing actions; monitor marketing performance; and improve understanding of marketing as a process. Marketing research specifies the information required to address these issues, designs the method for collecting information, manages and implements the data collection process, analyzes the results, and communicates the findings and their implications.[2]

Simply put, when there's little or no information available about a particular marketing situation, organizations should conduct research on the problem. Marketing research addresses a specific issue with a clearly identified objective regarding marketing strategy. Once the research is completed, it's typically saved as part of the marketing information system. Figure 4.1 shows the relationship of the MkIS and marketing research to marketing decision making.

Marketing Information Systems & Data

Marketing information systems often include a **marketing decision support system (MkDSS)**, which allows decision makers to access raw data from the MkIS and view it in a useful form. A typical marketing decision support system consists of a computer database, data retrieval and modeling software, and a user-friendly graphical interface. Let's say that a marketing manager wants to know how the price of the company's downhill skis compares to that of a competitor. The information is probably in the MkIS on a store-by-store basis, but it would be difficult and time consuming for the manager to sort through it and put it into a usable form. Instead, an MkDSS performs the task quickly. Let's say the marketing manager wants to compare average prices of its Elite skis to its biggest competitor, Snowflake, for the previous 12 months in the state of Colorado. Within seconds the MkDSS could produce a line chart or a bar chart in vivid colors to show the comparison. The marketing manager then has useful data for making decisions about the product's marketing mix elements.

A **transaction-based information system (TBIS)** is a specialized type of MkIS that serves as an electronic link between a firm and its customers, distributors and suppliers. Originally designed for ordering, billing, shipping and inventory control, these systems are now designed to provide data on customer preferences, loyalty, sales trends and an array of marketing issues. As part of an initiative to streamline communications, Walmart requires all of its suppliers to adopt Applicability Statement 2 (AS2), a company-created connectivity standard designed to standardize trading and facilitate data interchange over the internet.[3]

To develop a solid marketing information system and design a useful MkDSS, an organization needs to assess its marketing information needs. This assessment begins by identifying the types of executive decisions, what information will help make them, and the best formats and timetables for presenting it. Figure 4.2 describes the types of questions used to assess marketing information needs.

MARKETING DECISION SUPPORT SYSTEM (MkDSS)

A coordinated collection of data, systems, and techniques by which an organization gathers and interprets relevant information from business and the environment and turns it into a basis for marketing action.

TRANSACTION-BASED INFORMATION SYSTEM (TBIS)

A computerized link between a firm and its customers, distributors, and suppliers.

1. What decisions are made, with what frequency?
2. What information helps make those decisions?
3. What information is currently supplied?
4. What additional information is required?
5. What information is currently generated that is unnecessary?
6. How should the information be displayed to be most useful?
7. What sources of information would be useful to receive on a regular basis?

Figure 4.2   How to Determine Marketing Information Needs

TURNING DATA INTO INFORMATION

In order to comprehend marketing information systems and marketing research, it is important to understand how data becomes information useful for decision making. Keep in mind that data and information are not the same. Data are raw facts and statistics. **Information** is composed of data that have been analyzed and put in useful form, as depicted in Figure 4.3. It is difficult to draw marketing conclusions from data in simple tabular form. In other words, market analysts and researchers need to interpret data—turn them into information—to assist managers and executives in making efficient, informed decisions.

Types of Data	Data Analysis	Information and Decision Making
External and internal Primary and secondary	Data sorting Statistics Models	Marketing planning Marketing mix decisions Performance monitoring

Figure 4.3   How Data Becomes Information

Types of Data Data provides the starting point from which marketing information is derived. **Data** can be any set of facts or statistics obtained from outside (external) or inside (internal) the company. **Primary data** are those gathered for the first time for a particular issue being addressed. **Secondary data** are obtained from sources that have already gathered the data. Since primary data can be costly and time-consuming to gather, secondary data are far more common and easy to attain with today's technology. The price tag can still be expensive, though, costing thousands of dollars for access to studies by primary researchers.

External data comes from outside the company. Popular external databases include LEXIS®-NEXIS®, Dow Jones Interactive, Hoover's Online and Dialog. They provide raw data as well as articles, newsletters, breaking news stories, financial reports and nearly any other type of data imaginable. For specific needs, there are sources such as Forrester Research Group's Technographic Data, which provides continuous surveys of 260,000 households in North America and Europe. Technographic Data gives valuable survey information on how consumers think about, buy and use technology in the categories of devices and media, health care, financial services, retail, and travel... information that many companies need to make marketing mix decisions.[4]

To track competitors, some companies use Nexis®, which provides news, company and industry content by using over 26,000 news sources from around the world.[5] For research of business customers, Dun & Bradstreet (D&B) can provide information on almost 130 million businesses in 190 countries.[6] D&B can provide in-depth financial and operational reports on most of the companies in its database. These databases are rarely free; companies charge either for time online or for each piece of data, such as a name or news release.

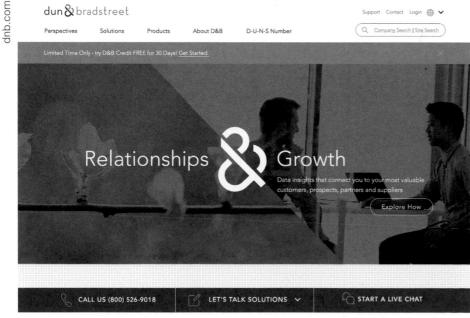

dnb.com

Dun & Bradstreet provides data insights that connect businesses with customers,

INTERNAL DATA

Data obtained from within a company.

Internal data is obtained from within a company. It includes consumer and market information that may come from many sources within the business. For example, the accounting department often has detailed records of sales, costs and revenue generated by each product. In some cases, these figures are available for each market segment. The manufacturing and shipping or logistics departments track production schedules, amount of capacity utilized, shipping dates, and inventory levels. In many companies, the supply-chain management department provides detailed records of the flow of goods into the company and out to each customer, including the frequency of orders, stock levels and purchase rates. The marketing department will usually have data about type and frequency of sales calls, orders received from each location, advertising schedules, customer demographics, website visits and social media interaction.

Data Analysis Data analysis transforms material into a usable form, so analysts can develop insights. It usually involves data sorting, statistics and models. Data sorting uses several tools for grouping data. For example, Burger King may want to know sales by time of day to determine whether certain items are more popular at certain times.

Statistics help describe data in more detail or illustrate how representative certain occurrences are relative to overall patterns. Most information systems have readily available statistical packages that can be applied to the data. In some cases they simply count frequencies of occurrence or describe using cross-tabulations or averages. Gannett Co., a leading international news and information company, hired The Advanced Marketing & Media Group (AMM Group) to provide it with an advertising performance measurement system. The AMM Group is a marketing technology business that uses technological innovation to help companies capitalize on marketing performance. The system it created for Gannett Co. will be designed to "offer its advertisers an opportunity to measure marketing return on investment across Gannett media assets, including newspapers, television stations, websites and mobile devices." This information system will add value to the company by unifying statistical marketing data.[7]

> Data analysis transforms material into a usable form, so analysts can develop insights.

INFORMATION IS FOR DECISION MAKING

Using information is not easy; however, it's absolutely critical to have good information if you expect to develop a good marketing strategy. In the past, marketers often relied on their experience and intuition. Instinct and prior knowledge remain useful tools today, but the world is more complex, and organizations need to get as much information as possible about their market. Good information helps executives make key marketing decisions. Marketing information plays a key role in marketing planning, marketing mix decisions and performance monitoring.

Marketing Planning Marketing planning requires input about customers, competitors, market trends, technology, channels of distribution and economic conditions. Marketing information helps marketers make better decisions about which segments to target and how to position the organization in response to competitors. Marketing planning should always place priority on complete, fact-based data, not opinion or conjecture. Most planning teams have a marketing information specialist who collects relevant information and shares it with the team.

Marketing Mix Decisions Marketing information is necessary for making decisions about any component of the marketing mix. In fact, decision methods have been developed for each of the individual components (product, place, promotion and price). Radius

Global Market Research is one consulting firm that provides in-depth research and analysis to help clients make informed decisions on product ventures.[8] There are several others, as well.

Product Decisions Marketing information on new products is essential. Marketing information monitors test markets, helps monitor customer satisfaction with goods and services, forecasts technology trends, and indicates when to introduce new products or phase out old ones. JCPenney conducted in-depth research in order to determine the needs of "the missing middle," defined as middle-income married women between ages 35 and 54. The company did a telephone survey of 900 women asking them about casual clothes. It also conducted video interviews with 30 women for up to six hours, recording their feelings about fashion and shopping preferences. The research shows the target women have a more casual lifestyle, want to look trendy without sacrificing quality, and crave something suitable for relaxed occasions. As a result, JCPenney launched two lines of moderately priced casual clothes, one by designer Nicole Miller.[9]

Nicole Miller's clothing line meets the needs of "the missing middle."

Place Decisions Marketing information helps with place decisions such as determining the appropriate distribution channel, either directly to consumers or through intermediaries, such as wholesalers and retailers. It can be used to identify specific distributors or the inventory requirements for selected channels. One form of marketing information tracks every item sold in every store.

At Amazon, users can shop online, yet still receive personal attention. Customers are encouraged to log in with each visit so the company can access the user's previous purchases to create a recommended product list to cross sell items. Attention to customization and personalization has elevated Amazon to a dominant position in the market because customers are satisfied and respond with return visits. At the same time, Amazon executives are able to track the sales of all items to the smallest detail. Once executives gain a good understanding of market phenomena, they are able to make quality decisions regarding the distribution of products and services.

Promotion Decisions In order for a promotion campaign to accomplish desired objectives, it needs to deliver the proper combination of advertising, personal selling, and other approaches, which require a great deal of information. For advertising, decision makers need to determine the most effective numbers of internet, mobile, print, television and radio ads to reach targeted consumers. Internet advertising is continuously growing as an explosion of companies race to compete. Google now holds an impressive 54 percent of the online advertising market.[10]

Information is available regarding the number of target audience members that can be reached by each media, including variations by type of television programming, time of day and region of the country. The Nielsen Company provides data to help marketers decide what times and during which programs ads are most likely to reach a target market. There is even available data that determines the cost for each airing of a promotion.[11] Information about promotion variations, such as the use of in-store coupons, is also available and helpful.

Price Decisions Because prices send strong signals to the market about the value of a product, information on pricing is critical for almost every marketing decision. Walmart and Toys "R" Us advertise that they will meet or beat (local) competitors' prices. They monitor local competition and collect competitors' ads, feeding the information into a centralized marketing information system. Automobile companies look not only at the prices of major competitors but also at finance and leasing terms. Information is collected about the effectiveness of cash discounts and rebates as well as the likelihood of buyers switching from one brand to another at various price points. The airline industry, whose profits are highly sensitive to volume, continually monitors how price affects demand in local, national and international markets. Internet ticket sellers such as Expedia.com and Travelocity.com are especially helpful in this regard, as commercial websites are an excellent source of consumer information.

Performance Monitoring

The third area supported by marketing information is performance monitoring. This helps managers make sure that plans and programs are progressing as scheduled. Information is required to track progress, identify unexpected obstacles, make corrections to accomplish objectives, determine customer satisfaction levels, and provide valuable feedback.

"Without indicators like increased sales or market share gain, we really have no way of knowing how effective our plan for a brand really is," says Dana Anderson, media buyer for United Airlines at Leo Burnett Company Inc., a major advertising agency. Marketing information also tells how well an advertising plan meets specific marketing objectives, like an increase in brand awareness or an improved image of a brand relative to competitors. And today, nearly every organization monitors customer service levels and requires information on how well it is meeting them. Where does information like this come from?

Outside rating services can provide unbiased information on how consumers evaluate performance. You're probably familiar with the Nielsen ratings, which usually appear weekly in publications such as USA Today. Nielsen Media Research, the leading international television information services company, monitors thousands of homes. A Nielsen People Meter is installed to monitor tuning records for every channel: the time of day, duration of tuning, and which household members are watching. The result is television show rankings, weekly ratings, and season-to-date rankings. Nielsen also provides reports on consumer trends including television, books, music, social media, video games, health and beauty, alcohol, snacks and more.[12]

Nielsen data can provide insights to forecast consumer trends and growth opportunities.

The Marketing Research Process

Marketing research is a key aspect of the organization's ability to make good marketing decisions. It starts with a clear understanding of the problem or opportunity to be addressed and ends with an interpretation of findings to recommend a marketing action.

A decision is a choice between two or more alternatives. As individuals, we make many decisions each day: what to wear, what to eat, what shampoo to buy, when to study, what classes to take, what internship to apply for, and so forth. Some decisions are easier than others. Marketers also have to make decisions each day. They are responsible for using corporate resources effectively and acting responsibly for shareholders. Therefore, they try to improve the likelihood of making good decisions by using a structured process called the marketing research process. The six steps of the marketing research process are shown in Figure 4.4 and described in the following sections.

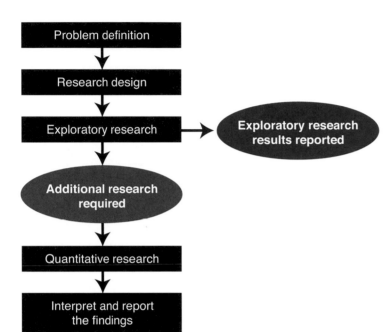

Figure 4.4   The Marketing Research Process

PROBLEM DEFINITION

A highly respected marketing research executive for Pfizer Corporation once said, "Never begin a research process with a search for market information. Always start by understanding the decisions to be made and the managerial circumstances surrounding those decisions." This isn't as easy as it sounds, but it's a critical step in the research process. As Albert Einstein said, "The formulation of a problem is often more essential than its solution."[13]

The marketing researcher and key decision makers should work together to accurately specify the problem. The researcher usually must ask probing questions to determine the extent of the problem and the time and resources available to address it.

A researcher needs to carefully isolate the symptoms from the actual problem. For instance, if Pepsi's sales were to experience a sudden decline, that would be a symptom, not the source. The real problem may be a new promotional campaign by Coca-Cola that Pepsi has failed to address, or a shift in its marketing toward a new product offering. Just as a fever is a sign of the flu, declining sales are usually a sign of a deeper problem. Once the problem is isolated, the variables or factors causing it can be identified. Defining the problem is necessary before any marketing research begins.

RESEARCH DESIGN

RESEARCH DESIGN

An outline that identifies what data to collect, how to collect it, and how it will be analyzed.

EXPLORATORY RESEARCH

Research designed to clarify the problem and suggest ways to address it.

QUANTITATIVE RESEARCH

Research designed to provide the information needed to select the best course of action and estimate the probable results.

PILOT STUDY

A small-scale project that allows the researcher to refine and test the approaches that eventually will be used.

A **research design** is an outline that identifies what data to collect, how to collect it, and how it will be analyzed. The research design is, in effect, a master plan for the research project.

Most designs call for two types of research: exploratory and quantitative. **Exploratory research** clarifies the problem and searches for ways to address it. The research is meant to provide details to what little information already exists. It may include methods such as interviews, group discussions, and trial studies to gain more information. **Quantitative research** provides the information needed to select the best course of action and forecast probable results. Research generally starts with an exploratory study, may include a pilot study phase, and ends with quantitative research. A **pilot study** is a small-scale project that allows the researcher to refine and test the approaches that will ultimately be used.

EXPLORATORY RESEARCH

Exploratory research enables investigators to gain a better understanding of the issues. Specifically, it helps to:

- Determine the exact nature of the problem or opportunity
- Search for causes or explanations for the problem
- Define the magnitude of the problem
- Create hypotheses about underlying causes
- Describe why or how the causes may affect the situation
- Understand competitors' actions and reactions
- Estimate how courses of action may affect the market.

Exploratory research seeks information that will enlighten marketers in the decision-making process. It generally begins by finding and reviewing secondary data. This information has already been collected, so it's usually the quickest and most cost-effective way to get started. Primary data are usually required at some point, but sometimes information from secondary sources is enough. A simple Google search for sports sites reveals 621 million results for baseball, 700 million for basketball, and 1.66 billion for football.[14] By starting with exploratory research, companies can learn a lot about sports, such as how fans follow the game, how leagues, teams, and players market themselves, and what products and services sports fans buy.

Although exploratory research seldom reveals the best solution, it helps to define the problem and identify options. Exploratory research is conducted with focus groups, interviews, projective techniques, observation, and case analysis. Each is discussed next.

FOCUS GROUP

A group, usually composed of eight to twelve people, whose opinions are elicited by an interviewer to provide exploratory insights into a problem.

Focus Groups A **focus group** usually involves eight to twelve past, present or prospective customers whose opinions provide qualitative insights about a company's product or service. This approach is particularly useful in clarifying problems with a company's products, services, advertising, distribution channels and the like. It's possible to gather a wide range of information about customers' feelings on these subjects and discover the reasons for their attitudes or purchase behaviors. Researchers ask questions and encourage participants to interact with one another to discover unexpected attitudes, behaviors and ideas that may suggest innovative marketing strategies. In a sense, the group interviews itself. The social interaction often yields insights that could not be obtained through one-on-one interviews.

Frank Luntz, a highly respected communication professional in America, founded Luntz Global, offering focus group services to provide business and political insights. Luntz advises many Fortune 500 companies in areas like international expertise, crisis management, ad creation and testing, product development and employee satisfaction. Pioneering the "Instant Response" focus group, Luntz can moderate a carefully selected group to provide real-time measurements of human emotions. Each participant is equipped with a wireless dial, calibrated from 1 to 100, which is used to measure relative favorability of what the participant sees and hears. The technology can be used in a number of applications

Luntz Global conducts focus groups for many Fortune 500 companies.

but perhaps most famously for measuring the success of political debates and television ads. Luntz "Instant Response" focus group data is often revealed to news sources after political debates and SuperBowl ads have aired.[15]

When selecting participants for a focus group, it's generally best to choose them all from similar demographics, since common experiences provide the basis for more in-depth discussion. Researchers can cover other groups in future focus groups, since just one is rarely enough to obtain an accurate sampling. The researcher should use several groups to ensure that the results are fairly representative. Even though many individuals may be involved, the unit of analysis is the group and not the individual. Six groups with eight people each, in effect, yields six interviews, not 48.

DEPTH INTERVIEWS

A relatively unstructured conversation that allows the researcher to probe deeply into a consumer's thoughts.

PROJECTIVE TECHNIQUES

A technique that enables respondents to project their thoughts onto a third party or object or through some type of contrived situation.

Depth Interviews **Depth interviews** are relatively unstructured conversations that allow researchers to probe into a consumer's thought processes. Often they are used to investigate the mechanisms of purchase decisions. Although the discussion may appear casual to the participant, the skilled researcher exerts a great deal of control, subtly discovering the participant's attitudes, opinions or motivations. The marketer uses these results both as individual case studies and as comparative data to examine commonalities among respondents.

What personal needs and wants would be fulfilled if you owned a Mustang?

Projective Techniques **Projective techniques** enable respondents to project their thoughts onto a third party, or through some type of contrived situation. This is often done using word associations, sentence completion and role playing. Because projective approaches do not require respondents to provide answers in a structured format, people are more likely to interpret the situation creatively and in the context of their own experiences and emotions. When asked directly why they purchase a particular item, they may describe a far more rational process than the one that actually occurs. For example, if a recent college graduate is asked why she would purchase a Ford Mustang, she may cite performance, gas mileage and overall value of the product. But if asked to describe the personal needs and wants to be fulfilled by a Mustang, she may say things like status, self-esteem and the need to be noticed.

OBSERVATION

A research technique in which researchers simply watch the participants they are studying.

Observation **Observation** is a technique in which researchers simply watch the participants. In one classic study, researchers stationed themselves in both crowded and uncrowded supermarkets to see if buying behavior differed. In less crowded stores, shoppers tended to use the information on labels and shelves, whereas in crowded conditions they tended to make decisions more quickly. This exploratory observation was followed by a more formal survey that enabled the researchers to draw conclusions about buyer behavior in crowded situations.[16]

Structured observation is made through mechanical means. Tachistoscopes measure visual stimuli, while galvanometers record electrical resistance in the skin, associated with sweating and other responses. Special cameras often are used to study eye move-

> In less crowded stores, shoppers tended to use the information on labels and shelves, whereas in crowded conditions they tended to make decisions more hastily.

ment as a subject reads advertising copy. By observing pupil dilation, blinking and eye tracking, it is possible to judge what receives attention in ads, packaging or the internet.

Case Analysis **Case analysis** takes a few select examples and studies them in depth. This technique is particularly appropriate for complex buying and competitive situations. For example, how industrial companies make decisions for particular components or capital goods is often studied this way. A single researcher may spend several days interviewing a firm's employees who purchase and use the product in question. In addition, buying policies, documents and actual purchase history are investigated. When researchers give this treatment to enough companies (perhaps 10), they start to get a larger picture of how suppliers are selected. The information can help suppliers determine the appropriateness of various marketing approaches.

Case analysis can also be used to study the competition. Researchers may select two or three activities of key competitors and examine them in depth. By knowing all aspects of the strategies used to introduce a couple of products, researchers can assess competitors' strengths and weaknesses and also predict how they might behave in the future with other products. Researchers can also use competitors' sales and expense figures to set benchmarks for their own organization.

QUANTITATIVE RESEARCH

Quantitative research provides information that helps decision makers select the best course of action and estimate the probable results. Rigorous statistical procedures allow researchers to estimate how confident they can be about their conclusions. Since quantitative research uses widely accepted methods, duplicating the study should arrive at approximately the same results. Certain techniques also indicate how closely the results represent the views or attitudes of the whole population at large, not just the sample studied.

Quantitative research played an enormous role in the successful positioning and launch of Kimberly-Clark's Expressions facial tissue line. With increasing competition from a new product line of super soft tissues by Procter & Gamble, the company began looking for an innovative way to increase market share for its Kleenex brand.

Through quantitative research, it found that the second most important feature to consumers behind softness was the box design. Nearly 37 percent of buyers said they disliked the look of tissue boxes and often hid them in closets or bathrooms. Product testing in eight U.S. cities revealed consumer preferences for six styles: traditional, country, Southwestern, contemporary, Asian and Victorian. The new designs were a great success, partly because marketers took the time to learn the opinions of consumers.[17] Recently, Kleenex brand teamed up with Disney to create new boxes for kids, including a line of Frozen™ inspired designs.

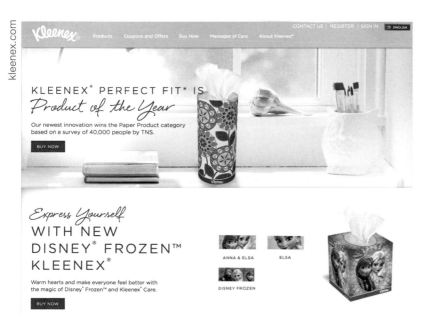

kleenex.com

Quantitative research revealed that the second most important feature of tissues behind softness was the box design.

Quantitative research usually follows the **scientific method** to prevent faulty conclusions. The scientific method is a systematic way to gather, analyze and interpret data in order to confirm or refute a prior conception. First, researchers develop a **hypothesis** about an issue based on a limited amount of information. A hypothesis is a tentative assumption about a particular event or issue. Second, rigorous tests are conducted to determine whether the hypothesis is supported by the information.

Let us say we have an idea that more people shop in malls on the weekend because they're not working, so we hypothesize that malls will generate greater sales volumes on Saturday and Sunday than on weekdays. We then gather information to test the hypothesis. The key is for researchers to state beforehand what they believe the results may be and why. This enables appropriate data to be gathered and analyzed to determine whether the hypothesis is true.

Data-Collection Methods

Two of the most common methods for collecting quantitative data are experiments and surveys. **Experiments** usually take place either where the marketing problem occurs or in a laboratory setting that is contrived to match research needs. To test new packaging for a pain reliever, for example, the manufacturer may invite consumers to "shop" in a simulated supermarket. In that way shopping patterns can be observed to see whether the packaging is eye-catching. Experiments are often used for **causal research**, which attempts to show a cause-and-effect relationship between two events. One of the most important forms of causal research is test marketing. A test market provides a limited trial of a product strategy under realistic conditions.

Surveys are the most popular way to collect data. When researchers want to ensure that each subject is asked for the same information, they prepare a written survey questionnaire. It is a measurement device, much like a thermometer or a ruler. Two common units of measure for questionnaire items are the points along Likert scales and bipolar adjective scales.

Likert scales allow the intensity of feelings to be expressed and tend to provide information about a person's attitude toward something. Subjects are asked to indicate the extent to which they agree or disagree with each statement in the survey. The Likert scale shown in Figure 4.5 has five points (units of measure). A seven-point scale is sometimes used, adding "somewhat disagree" and "somewhat agree" on either side of the middle point.

Bipolar adjective scales allow respondents to choose along a range between two extremes. Figure 4.6 shows a typical bipolar adjective scale. In general, there are three, five, or seven points in the scale. This scale is used frequently in marketing research, likely because it can cover a wide range of

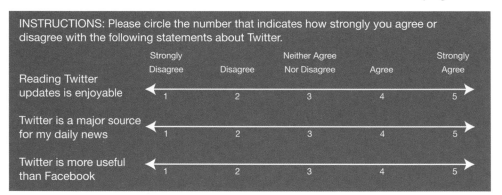

INSTRUCTIONS: Please circle the number that indicates how strongly you agree or disagree with the following statements about Twitter.

	Strongly Disagree	Disagree	Neither Agree Nor Disagree	Agree	Strongly Agree
Reading Twitter updates is enjoyable	1	2	3	4	5
Twitter is a major source for my daily news	1	2	3	4	5
Twitter is more useful than Facebook	1	2	3	4	5

Figure 4.5   A Typical Likert Scale

INSTRUCTIONS: Please put an X in the space that most appropriately indicates your feelings about shopping at Gap

	Very	Moderately	Slightly	Neither One nor the Other	Slightly	Moderately	Very	
Inexpensive	___	___	___	___	___	___	___	Expensive
Helpful Salespeople	___	___	___	___	___	___	___	Unhelpful Salespeople
High-quality Products	___	___	___	___	___	___	___	Low-quality Products

Figure 4.6   A Typical Bipolar Adjective Scale

opinions with relatively few questions.

The wording of an item can make quite a difference. A classic example occurred in the 1980s during the battles between Burger King and McDonald's. Burger King asked respondents: "Do you prefer your hamburgers flame-broiled or fried?" When Burger King's method of flame-broiling was preferred three to one, the chain aggressively publicized this in an ad campaign. The results were completely different when McDonald's researchers asked: "Do you prefer a hamburger that is grilled on a hot stainless-steel grill or cooked by passing the warmed meat through an open-gas flame?" McDonald's frying method received a clear majority. When the question was modified to include the fact that the gas-flame burgers were warmed in a microwave oven prior to serving, McDonald's won seven to one.[18]

Administering Surveys A survey can be administered through personal interviews, mall intercepts, telephone, mail or the internet. Each technique has benefits and disadvantages, as shown in Figure 4.7. The researcher needs to select the method most appropriate for the current project.

	Personal Interviews	Mall Intercepts	Telephone	Mail	Internet/ Social Media
Speed of Completion	Slowest	Fast	Fast	Moderate	Fastest
Response Rate	High	Moderate	Moderate	Low	Moderate
Quality of Response	Excellent	Good	Good	Limited	Good
Interviewer Bias	High	Moderate	Moderate	Low	Low
Geographic Reach	Limited	Limited	Excellent	Excellent	Excellent
Cost	Very expensive	Moderate	Moderate	Inexpensive	Inexpensive

Figure 4.7   Comparative Advantages of Interviews, Mall Intercepts, Telephone Surveys, Mail Questionnaires and Internet Surveys

Personal Interviews Personal interviews require face-to-face, two-way communication between the interviewer and the respondent. This method is particularly useful in probing complex answers or observing the respondent's behavior. The setting usually is comfortable, and the respondent is given undivided attention.

One benefit of personal interviews is the high participation rate. It's unlikely that any questions will go unanswered, and props or visual aids can be used. But there are several disadvantages. Subjects may be influenced by the interviewer, and they give up anonymity when meeting face-to-face, so they may withhold information or answer in unnatural ways. Interviewing is expensive, since professionals must be trained and then transported to the various locations.

Mall Intercepts Mall intercepts, as the name implies, occur at a shopping mall, and the interviewer chooses respondents on some objective basis, such as every fifth person encountered. Mall intercepts are simple to conduct, and data can be collected quickly and cost-effectively. Interviewers can ask questions about actual purchases during some specified period, which helps determine actual behaviors as well as opinions and attitudes. One variation of this method is a shopping basket study, or simply looking at what a consumer purchases during a particular trip to the store. Grocery stores often want this kind of information in order to identify which products are purchased together, the total amount of spending, and the shopping patterns of individuals while in the store.

Telephone Surveys Telephone surveys offer speed and relatively low cost. Using banks of telephones, marketers can contact a large number of people at approximately the same time. This method is particularly effective with professionals, who tend to be articulate and willing to discuss matters over the telephone. By prearranging the call, it's possible to gain considerable cooperation from respondents. Another advantage of the telephone is that a follow-up call can be arranged easily if the individual cannot respond at that moment. It can also provide a personal relationship with the consumer you might not be able to achieve through other methods.

A major drawback of telephone interviews is the large number of unlisted numbers, which makes it very difficult to obtain a valid sample. Many consumers have done away with landlines, using cell phones as their primary phone lines. The Federal Trade Commission also issued the National Do Not Call Registry, which prevents organizations from contacting numbers on the list. The Millennial generation is far less apt to take unknown calls than previous generations. In fact, Millennials are less likely to take any call that might take them off task or interrupt their social life.[19] Younger generations are also much more aware of telephone phishing and scams, making it difficult to gain trust with those surveyed. In addition, phone surveys have an obvious limitation if respondents are required to see something, like evaluating ads or product renderings.

NATIONAL DO NOT CALL REGISTRY

Mail Surveys In mail surveys, a questionnaire is sent directly to the respondent's home or place of business. An advantage is that people can answer at their own pace and at a convenient time. Mailed questionnaires can be extremely useful for surveying professionals, who have a high response rate and tend to give thoughtful answers. Publishers regularly survey professors by mail concerning textbooks they have adopted, teaching methods, and their ideas about innovative materials that can be created. Associations often obtain good response quality and return rates from membership surveys by mail.

Many techniques are used to encourage people to answer mail questionnaires. Including an explanatory cover letter or small incentive can increase return rates. Research also reveals that the rate can be boosted considerably by multiple prior notifications, while sending only one has no influence. Mailing a second survey has a significant effect on response rates as well.[20]

According to a study reported in *Industrial Marketing Management*, surveys get better receptions when sponsored by a legitimate organization, such as a professional association. The mean response rates for the questionnaires from a university and an honor society sponsor were significantly higher than for those sponsored by a marketing research firm and an unidentified source.[21] The greatest problem with mail questionnaires is that many people simply refuse to answer them. This causes significant problems for researchers, since those who do respond may differ from the rest of the population. For example, people may be motivated to answer because they intensely like or dislike a product, whereas other people don't respond because they're indifferent about the product.

Internet Surveys Many researchers use the internet to gain individuals' participation in surveys. The main advantage of using the internet instead of traditional methods is that the information is available very quickly. Additionally, researchers can survey a greater number of people with a lower cost compared to written and mailed surveys, and data can be analyzed as they are collected.

There are four main types of online surveys:[22]

1. *Pop-up surveys:* When a user leaves a website, another window, containing a questionnaire, pops up on the screen. Internet users have the option of either completing the survey or closing the browser window. The response rate for this type of survey ranges from 15 to 45 percent.

2. *Email or web surveys:* Via e-mail, a company can invite someone to participate in an online questionnaire. The response rates for these surveys range from 25 to 50 percent and are usually completed by the user in two to three days.

3. *Online groups:* A research company can organize what is essentially a focus group discussion on internet chat rooms.

4. *Consumer-generated media:* Researchers can get information from discussions with individuals on blogs, forums, podcasts and email portals like gmail.

Recognizing that the quality of online survey data is a major concern for market researchers, the TrueSample Quality Council was formed in 2008. The Council includes several market research industry leaders such as Procter & Gamble, General Mills, Microsoft, Samsung, Nestle and Unilever. It has established a set of Online Consumer Research Quality Guidelines for research suppliers to follow if they want corporate marketing researchers to purchase consumer research from them.[23]

Best Buy Cares Survey gives customers a chance to win a $5,000 shopping spree for completing the survey.

Marketers also monitor discussions on their company websites and social media sites to gather information about current and prospective customers. Many companies encourage customers to fill out an online registration form after buying a product. The form usually solicits certain personal demographic information, such as age, income and interests, in exchange for an incentive. This gives companies a profile of their customers, which is invaluable for marketers. For example, when you pay for a purchase at a Best Buy store, the cashier makes it a point to show you the portion of your receipt that has an online address for its Best Buy Cares Survey. The incentive to complete it is a chance to win a $5000 Best Buy shopping spree. By providing an incentive, the company gets a higher rate of participation in the survey, which means more useful comments about a store's atmosphere, a customer's overall shopping experience, and information about you...the customer![24] Marketers then use this information in the strategic planning process.

SAMPLING

POPULATION (UNIVERSE)

All the individuals or organizations relevant to the marketing research project

SAMPLING FRAME

A list of people in the universe who potentially could be contacted.

Surveys are conducted to gain insights about the groups of consumers or companies being studied. The **population (universe)** is composed of all the individuals or organizations relevant to the marketing research project. For example, if the a company wants to know the average number of jobs a U.S. resident holds during the first 10 years out of high school, the relevant population is all U.S. residents age 28 or older—millions of people. The company could attempt to interview all of them, but that would be impractical, if not impossible, and far too costly. Researchers have developed methods for surveying a subset of people from whom they draw inferences about the larger population.

The first step is to obtain a **sampling frame**, which is a list of people in the universe who potentially could be contacted. From this, researchers select the **sample**, a group of people who are asked to participate in the research.

There are two categories of samples: probability and nonprobability. In a **probability sample**, the chance of selecting a given individual can be calculated. One popular method is **simple random sampling**, whereby each individual has an equal chance of being chosen (say, every third name is selected). Another is **stratified random sampling**, whereby each individual within a selected subgroup of the sample has a known chance of selection (say, every third household with income of $50,000 or more). This method is often used in marketing, since much research focuses on market segments. If some form of random sampling is adopted, then statistics can be used to determine the likelihood that responses from the sample will be similar to the responses of the larger population.

When using **nonprobability samples**, the researcher does not know the likelihood of selecting a particular respondent. The two most common types are judgment and convenience samples. **Judgment samples** are chosen by the researcher based on the belief that these people represent a majority of the study population. For example, a researcher may decide to draw the entire sample from one "representative" city, even though the population includes all cities. When using this method, the researcher must be confident that the chosen sample is truly representative of the entire population.[25] **Convenience samples** are composed of people who happen to come along, such as shoppers in a given store at a certain time or travelers passing through an airport. Convenience samples are relatively inexpensive, and the selection can be purposely unrepresentative, such as interviewing only females. In general, this method does not provide data reliable enough for quantitative research. Even probability samples can become like convenience samples if care is not taken regarding the smallest details, such as when interviews are conducted. Tom Brokaw, renowned broadcast anchor, once remarked that election polls could not be taken on Friday night because the results would be skewed since so many people go out that evening.

Convenience samples can also be used to survey internet users. Researchers use one-time surveys that invite participation from whoever sees the survey invitation online, or they may rely on panels of respondents who volunteer to participate in the panel. These surveys are subject to the same limitations facing other surveys using non-probability-based samples: the relationship between the sample and the population is unknown, so there is no way to know the margin of error which would indicate how representative the sample is of the population as a whole.[26]

INTERPRET AND REPORT FINDINGS

Once the research is completed, results are reported to the appropriate decision makers. No matter how sophisticated or reliable, marketing research is of little use unless it can be easily understood by the decision makers who act upon it. Most managers and executives have little experience with research techniques and little interest in learning about them. Thus, presentation of understandable research results is an important skill for marketing researchers. Good research moves succinctly from data to information to insight. Unfortunately, to demonstrate the hard work that has gone into a project, many researchers give too much extraneous data. A report that describes each table in extensive detail is not likely to meet the needs of executives; instead, the information should be presented in simple, easy-to-understand information so decisions can be mad based upon it.

Experience pays off in interpreting research. When the Museum of Fine Arts (MFA) in Boston held focus groups on an upcoming exhibition of Winslow Homer's works, the researchers found that the public did not know much about the artist and might not attend. A museum executive used her experience, including the MFA shop's sales records of items linked to Homer, to indicate that while the public may not know his name, it knows his pictures and would turn out for the show. Because the museum relied on the executive's experience to help interpret the focus group, it was able to create a blockbuster event.

On the other hand, sometimes research is right when the experts are wrong. Ford didn't listen to marketing research in the mid-1950s. The Edsel was built with features that consumers said they wanted, but the car itself did poorly in several rounds of consumer testing. Ford went ahead anyway, believing it could push the car with a strong sales force. The mistake cost about $350 million (in 1950s dollars)!

There is some debate about whether marketing researchers should recommend action. Whether marketing researchers make recommendations must depend on the total data available, the inclinations of the researcher and the desires of decision makers. In keeping with team spirit, most executives would like knowledgeable people to provide as many insights as possible. If recommendations are made, then the circumstances they are based on should be clear.

The Ford Edsel was an enormous failure because the company ignored its own marketing research.

Who Does Marketing Research?

The first commercial research department was founded in 1911 at the *Saturday Evening Post*, when Charles C. Parlin completed his now-famous study of Campbell's soup consumers. He undertook the research because Campbell's executives refused to purchase advertising in the Post, believing that its working-class readership did not represent a significant market for the company. The soup sold at 10 cents a can, a cost they believed only wealthy consumers could afford. By counting cans in the garbage from different neighborhoods, Parlin proved they were wrong. He showed that canned soup was bought mainly by the time-constrained working class, whereas the wealthy enjoyed homemade soup prepared by servants. Campbell's became a big advertiser in the magazine and one of the top brand names in the United States.

Charles C. Parlin's study of Campbell's soup consumers proved the company was targeting the wrong market segment.

In-Company Research Most large companies have a formal in-company marketing research department. In fact, nearly all consumer product manufacturers, retailers, wholesalers, advertising agencies and publishers have such a department. The majority were created within the last decade.

In-company marketing research departments are often headed by experienced personnel who report to top executives. The research staff usually includes project directors, analysts and specialists. The project director is responsible for designing projects, which may be conducted within the department or by outside agencies. The position of analyst is an entry-level job with the function of interpreting specific types of data for select decisions. Analysts are usually part of a marketing team from several units or divisions, although they report directly to the head of their department. Marketing research specialists have expertise in one aspect of a project, such as survey design, data collection, statistics, modeling or marketing science.

Marketing research has developed to a point where few organizations have employees that cover the full range of skills required to conduct state-of-the-art research. Consequently, research is conducted by both in-house personnel and outside agencies, which may or may not work together. Data collection is a particularly broad field, and many companies are in the business of offering that service to others. Even if external agencies are used, however, most companies still need internal staff to help identify the research problem and interface with the outside agency.

External Research Companies often hire out marketing research. As Figure 4.8 shows, conducting research can be a very lucrative business. Outside agencies include consulting companies, full-service research firms, specialty research firms and syndicated data companies. Such consulting companies often conduct all phases of marketing research for clients with whom they have an ongoing relationship, as well as with new clients who have unique information needs. Full-service firms focus on all aspects of data collection and analysis, and their personnel can handle the entire project. Specialty research firms concentrate on certain aspects of a project. There are more than 180 research firms in the United States, and U.S. companies spend more than $7 billion annually on external research.[27] Some only conduct surveys, relying on others to supply questionnaires and even others to perform data analysis.

Rank	Organization	Headquarters	Total Research Revenue (Millions)
1	Nielsen	New York, NY	$3,606.0
2	IMS Health	New York, NY	$1,127.0
3	Kantar	Danbury, CT	$ 973.0
4	IRI	New York, NY	$ 605.0
5	Ipsos	Chicago, IL	$ 552.0
6	Westat	Rockville, MD	$ 491.4
7	GfK	New York, NY	$ 345.9
8	comScore	Reston, VA	$ 268.3
9	The NPD Group	Port Washington, NY	$ 231.1
10	J.D. Power	Westlake Village, CA	$ 181.0

Figure 4.8 Top 10 U.S. Research Organizations
Source: "Top 50 Market Research Organizations," Marketing News, June, 2016, pg. 45.

Certain specialty research firms help marketers better understand diversity or particular segments. Companies such as Nielsen, IMS Health and Kantar earn hundreds of millions of dollars in research revenue each year.[28] Syndicated data companies also research one type of information or a single industry. For example, the Bureau of the Census and the Bureau of Labor Statistics are experts on census data and use the data to model various scenarios for clients. Neurocommunication Research Laboratory specializes in customized information about how broadcast and print advertisements trigger the maximum responses in viewers.

Because marketing research is critical for good decision making but expensive to conduct, most companies build a long-term association with one or more outside sources. This enables the agency to become familiar with the typical problems faced by the organization and to establish a good working relationship with in-company marketing research staff.

Technology's Effect on Marketing Information and Research

Technology has brought many changes to marketing research. Today's marketers can acquire and analyze information faster than ever before. Technology has also made it easier to connect with an increasing number of customers and information sources. In the past, marketing research was a relatively static process in the face of constantly changing markets. Now marketers can track the marketplace in real time, quickly collecting data and converting it into useful information. Technology, particularly regarding big data and internet searches, has not merely hastened the research process, it has made it more convenient, accurate and essential.

BIG DATA

BIG DATA

An umbrella term for the vast amount of data continually generated by society which can be analyzed to reveal trends, patterns and predictions relating to human behavior and interactions.

Big data is an umbrella term for the vast amount of data continually generated by society which can be analyzed to reveal trends, patterns and predictions relating to human behavior and interactions. It is especially valuable to marketers. Technology has made it possible to collect data on nearly every human endeavor, including social activities and a myriad of actions that shape how individuals go about their daily lives. Aaron Fuller, principal consultant at Superior Data Strategies, writes: "When the alarm on your smartphone goes off, you might sync your FitBit, check your Facebook account or scan your email. You haven't even been awake for five minutes, and already you're immersed in big data."[29]

Coca-Cola generates petabytes of data from different sources. Multi-channel retail data, customer profile data from loyalty programs, social media data, supply chain data, competitor data, bottling partner sales and shipment data are just some of the origins of data that Coca-Cola compiles and analyzes to add value to the company and its stakeholders.[30]

Can big data make orange juice? It can at Coca-Cola. The company uses it to create consistency in each batch of its Minute Maid Pure Squeezed orange juice. Since oranges have peak flavor for only a few months a year, Coke had to find a way to produce the same taste year round. The solution is in what's called Coke's Black Book model. The Black Book is an algorithm that includes detailed data about flavors that make up an orange, consumer preferences, acidity, sweetness, and so forth. That data is incorporated with external factors such as weather, crop yields and cost factors.[31]

The result? Consistent tasting orange juice. This wouldn't be possible without technology and big data. In fact, Coca-Cola's Chief Big Data Insights Officer, Esat Sezer, has said, "Innovation for us means differentiated capabilities, either in revenue growth management, in sales and customer services, or in the supply chain—big data has influences across all of these and is a vital component of our business." [32]

Marketing research and information technology specialists are tapping into big data at an unprecedented rate using analytical tools to better understand the marketing landscape. The ability to quickly dissect consumer insights through big data can have a huge impact on business strategies and marketing decisions. Three types of analytics are used to reduce—or *mine*—big data into manageable, usable information for marketers: descriptive analytics, predictive analytics and prescriptive analytics.

Descriptive analytics Descriptive analytics explore what has happened in the marketplace, providing performance indicators linked to marketing strategy and consumer/business response. Descriptive analytics condense information into smaller chunks, making it more understandable and usable. Dr. Michael Wu, chief scientist of San Francisco-based Lithium Technologies, estimates that "more than 80% of business analytics, most notably social analytics, are descriptive."[33]

The information presented in marketing dashboards is derived from descriptive analytics. This online marketing dashboard is an example of how digital marketing managers

©iStockphoto.com/Mikko Lemola

Tapping into consumer insights through big data can have a huge impact on business strategies and marketing decisions.

Marketing dashboards are derived from descriptive analytics.

track their marketing metrics. Since online marketing uses multiple channels, a dashboard such as this is designed to provide an overview of six important marketing channels: website performance, digital advertising, social media, lead generation, revenue generation and email marketing.[34] Companies customize their marketing dashboards to present big data as usable information.

Predictive analytics Predictive analytics is the process of mining historical data to forecast future events or trends. [35] It is another step in data reduction that uses statistical and forecasting techniques to predict what is likely to happen given different conditions and actions. In the healthcare industry, predictive analytics is used to determine if a patient is likely to have diabetes, heart failure or other diseases.

Historically, marketers have tried to use past performances to guide the direction of new programs and predict the results. For example, predictive analytics might be able to indicate specific consumer purchasing in response to a new marketing strategy. Dr. Michael Wu says: "You basically take data that you have to predict data you don't have."[36] The ability to track digital behavior through online clicks, coupled with social media communication, allows marketers to know the profiles of people most likely to buy from them.

Prescriptive analytics is an emerging technology that goes beyond descriptive and predictive analytics. Prescriptive analytics can be used to recommend one or more courses of action and shows the likely outcome of each decision. It helps optimize the use of resources and solve complex problems that improve processes such as retail space usage, medical treatment, manufacturing and supply chains.[37]

Despite the impressive technologies available today for analyzing big data, further advancements are critical to help humans interpret data more efficiently, which is why global spending on big data technology is predicted to reach $48.6 billion by the end of 2019.[38] Investments in technologies to turn raw data into useful information will ultimately reduce costs and risks of business and marketing innovations. Many believe we are just scratching the surface in a revolution where data collection and analytics give organizations of all sizes the ability to be more creative, efficient and agile in business and marketing.

INTERNET SEARCHES

The internet is an excellent source of marketing data. In fact, it is sometimes referred to as the world's largest resource library. It contains information on literally millions of topics and is updated instantly. The trick is to sift through all of it to find what you need. Marketers do this through the use of search engines such as Google, Yahoo! or Bing. Google is expanding its search capabilities to include off-line library content in online search results. All 14 universities of the Big Ten consortium joined Google's efforts, adding more than 10 million volumes of material to Google's collection. Books are scanned and digitized, and when a user searches a key word, the Google results will show information about the book and a few sentences that display that search term within the book. Google estimates there are approximately 130 million unique books in the world, and it plans to scan all of them by the end of the decade.[39]

Google estimates there are approximately 130 million unique books in the world, and it plans to scan all of them.

Global Marketing Research

Global marketing research involves the same six step process as any other kind of research, from defining the problem to interpretation and presentation of results. Usually the same techniques are employed as well: interviews, focus groups and surveys. In the global marketplace, these are often done online. However, the level of difficulty increases exponentially when conducting global marketing research.

It's not always easy to locate secondary data in foreign countries. Some national governments simply don't collect certain information. For example, Ethiopia and Chad don't gather population statistics.[40] Many developing countries lack mechanisms for collecting data about retail and wholesale activities. Even if secondary data are available, they may be incomplete or inaccurate. The data may also be manipulated by the government for political reasons.

For instance, some countries report an artificially low inflation rate. In developing countries, data are likely to be based on estimates or outdated processes.[41] Industrialized nations usually have sophisticated collection procedures, at least for basic statistics on population and economic activity. One resource that marketers can utilize is globalEDGE™. It was developed by MSU-CIBER at Michigan State University as the ultimate international marketing research tool. GlobalEDGE™ has up-to-date information on 200 countries including maps, governmental information, key statistics and history, as well as economic, stock market and country-specific marketing resources and news.

When secondary data are difficult to find, global research may require the collection of primary data. This comes with challenges for even large companies because of various language and cultural differences. It's difficult to ensure an exact translation, especially when slang is used. Many researchers use a technique called back translation: the research question is translated into the foreign language by one person, and then it

> When secondary data is difficult to find, global research often requires the collection of primary data.

is put back in the original language by a second person. This helps to catch any errors. It certainly saved an Australian soft-drink company hoping to market its product in Hong Kong. Its slogan, "Baby, it's cold in here," translated into Chinese as: "Small mosquito, on the inside it is very cold."[42]

When Gerber started selling baby food in Africa, it used the same packaging that had become synonymous with the brand in the U.S., featuring the classic image of a baby on the front. Gerber didn't realize, though, that companies routinely put pictures on a label to represent what's inside since English isn't the primary language of all African countries! In Taiwan, the Pepsi slogan "Come alive with the Pepsi Generation" was translated as "Pepsi will bring your ancestors back from the dead."[43] Proper marketing research would have caught these mistakes.

Gathering data through surveys can be a particular challenge for marketers. Countries vary widely in their laws, norms, values and customs pertaining to data collection and access. Some countries officially prohibit survey research (North Korea and Burma/Myanmar).[44] While a survey conducted in one country might encounter a few obstacles, a larger, multi-nation survey will encounter many more.

For example, once the survey instrument is translated, the equally difficult task of finding participants begins. In Mexico, there are only 20 (unreliable) phones lines per 100 citizens.[45] In Brazil, mail often gets delayed in customs. Even if mail reaches an intended recipient, the survey must take into account literacy levels. Individual interviews can also present challenges because of cultural differences. For example, people in some cultures consider it embarrassing to discuss personal hygiene, such as which shampoo or soap they use. Others tend to avoid discussing personal finance and money issues.

Nevertheless, companies that avoid global marketing research find themselves in trouble. Global marketing research is becoming more and more prevalent as companies expand their scope of operations. Concurrently, technological advances enable greater collection of data in less time and at a lower cost than ever before. This presents great opportunity for marketers!

LO 06 Ethical Considerations of Marketing Information and Research

J. D. Power is paid by automakers to provide research on customer satisfaction, the results of which are used in publications to promote autos. Some magazine editors receive "consulting fees" from auto companies and write reviews of car performance. These are certainly legal practices, but are they ethical?

J. D. Power is paid by automakers to provide research on customer satisfaction, the results of which are used in publications to promote autos.

With the information explosion comes the potential for deceptive research that can be used to sway consumer opinion. Historically, studies were sponsored by scientists, the federal government and academic institutions. Today, with government and universities on tight budgets, private companies fill the void with so-called objective research for hire. Corporations, litigants, political candidates, trade associations, lobbyists and special-interest groups can buy research to use as they like.[46]

A study by the Boston Center for Strategy Research revealed that some marketing managers believe market research is likely to reflect biases rather than present objective information. They also believe much of it is conducted to confirm a preconceived conclusion or validate a client's position. In other words, it arrives at the desired outcome, no matter what the facts may indicate. Research of this nature is confirmatory, not exploratory.[47]

The scientific method is supposed to prevent this type of bias, because anyone duplicating a study or experiment should come up with the same results. More and more of the information available to consumers is created to sell a product or advance a cause, though; buying and selling information to advance a private agenda demonstrates how the modern sense of truth may be warped.[48] Companies obviously want their products portrayed in a positive light, and privately sponsored studies often downplay negative information.[49] This becomes an ethical or legal problem if information that indicates potential harm to customers is suppressed.

Although consumers are increasingly suspicious about "facts," they often have little basis for questioning them. The average consumer does not have enough personal knowledge to dispute the research that almost daily shapes our beliefs about social, political, economic and environmental issues. That is why many groups exist to assist and protect consumers. Interested in truth, objectivity and accuracy, these groups consist of representatives from industry, individual companies, academia and the government. They have taken action to regulate the content of information and to defend the average consumer from distorted messages. Some industries have collectively formulated policies in order to reduce litigation, prevent mandatory regulation and increase consumer trust. Still, questionable information finds its way to consumers.

Consider a study sponsored by Procter & Gamble, the leading maker of disposable diapers. For several years, the company had been fighting a public relations battle against environmentalists and the cloth diaper industry. Environmentalists pushed cloth diapers, and their sales skyrocketed; more than a dozen state legislatures were considering various regulations for disposable diapers. Under pressure, Procter & Gamble decided to finance a public policy study. The researchers found that disposable and cloth diapers were environmentally equivalent, when factors such as energy and water use were taken into account. P&G's public relations improved, as did their diaper sales.

Concurrently, Gerber Products, the largest supplier of cloth diapers at the time, closed three plants and laid off 900 workers. Gerber's CEO said: "There was a dramatic change in the cloth diaper market caused by reduced environmental concern about disposable diapers."[50] Procter & Gamble won back lost market share and gained, at least temporarily, acceptance of disposables. Today, new companies have emerged to make cloth diapering a popular option again. bumGenius cloth diapers are designed to make cloth diapering easy for every-day people while being wallet and planet friendly. In fact, buying cloth diapers instead of disposables can save up to $1200 and prevent up to one ton of landfill waste before a child is potty trained.[51]

bumgenius.com

Jules · Accidental · Albert · Alicia · Armadillo · Audrey · Ballet · Carroll · Chaplin · Chico · Clementine · Countess · Dazzle · Eiffel Tower · Free Spirit · Glimmer · Grasshopper · Harper · Hummingbird · Jelly · Jet Setter · Jolly · Kiss · Louis · Love · Lovelace · Marie · Martin · Mirror · Moonbeam

Buying cloth diapers instead of disposables will save up to $1,200 and prevent up to one ton of landfill waste before a child is potty trained.

Although a marketer may occasionally benefit from biased information, those who connect ethically are more likely to create a profitable long-term relationship based on trust and loyalty. Often, as a company seeks to build such relationships, it must first answer two questions: What customers are we trying to reach and how do we reach them? One concern for parents is the ethical use of information about children under the age of 18. The Children's Online Privacy Act of 1998 covers targeting children. In response, Kibu.com has promised to keep all information regarding its 13- to 18-year-old target market private.[52]

Another dimension of the ethical use of marketing research information lies in information obtained about the internet and its users. Privacy is an important issue for most internet users. The Online Privacy and Disclosure Act of 2003, passed in California, requires all commercial entities that collect personal information online to clearly post a privacy policy and makes it unlawful for an online entity to violate it.[53]

Chapter Summary

Objective 1: Explain how marketing information systems and research are important for making marketing decisions.

You can't connect with customers if you can't locate, understand and respond to them. A marketing information system is critical in making informed decisions about nearly every aspect of marketing. It is used to systematically collect and analyze data to support decision making. An MkIS often includes a marketing decision support system (MDSS), which puts information in convenient forms for executives to use. An MkIS is ongoing and encompasses all information. Marketing research is conducted to address a particular opportunity, problem or issue surrounding the marketing of goods or services. Information derived from marketing research is used by marketers in planning, marketing mix decisions and performance monitoring.

Objective 2: Recognize how data is transformed into useful information for marketing purposes.

Data and information are not the same. Data must be translated into information before they are useful for decision making. External data come from outside the firm, and internal data originate from within the firm. Both types are stored in databases so they can be retrieved through a computer. Primary data are collected for the first time to address a specific issue. Secondary data already exist and can typically be accessed immediately online by a broad range of users. Once data are assembled, they must be analyzed through data sorting, the use of statistics and models. All of this is done with particular issues and decision areas in mind. The data becomes useful once it is transformed into information and presented in understandable ways, such as charts and graphs, that are often part of a marketing dashboard.

Objective 3: Explain the steps of a typical marketing research process.

The marketing research process starts with the problem definition, which focuses on the needs of decision makers to ensure that the research will be useful. The research design is then based on what decisions need what information, what data and data sources will provide that information, and how the data will be collected and analyzed. Next, exploratory research helps investigators better understand issues by defining problems, searching for possible explanations, and creating hypotheses. Quantitative research yields information to help decision makers select the best course of action. Because it is quantitative, estimates usually can be made of the likely results of actions. This requires appropriate measurement and sampling. The last steps are to interpret and report results. Experience and insight are useful at this stage because the same information can be interpreted in various ways.

Objective 4: Describe widely used marketing research techniques.

Exploratory research techniques include focus groups, depth interviews, projective techniques, observation, and case analysis. A focus group usually has eight to twelve people. Several sessions must be used since the group, not individuals, provide the data. Depth interviews are one-on-one conversations. Researchers spend a lot of time probing a few respondents about their opinions and actions. With projective techniques, subjects are asked to analyze contrived situations or to give opinions about how they believe others may respond. Observation provides insights by watching consumers in a range of situations. Finally, case analysis is the study of a few situations in depth. It is particularly useful for benchmarking. Quantitative research often involves using the scientific method. Surveys and test markets are common in this type of research. Survey data are usually collected from a sample of the population. Questionnaire design is important and should be objective in an attempt to capture authentic information. Likert scales or bipolar adjective scales are frequently used in questionnaires.

Objective 5: Explore technology's effect on marketing information and research.

Both internal and external marketing research is being dramatically influenced by technology. It facilitates the faster collection and analysis of greater quantities of information than was possible in the past. The internet also enables more efficient and less expensive interaction with customers than traditional information collection methods. Surveys must be carefully translated, and data collection is often difficult. Still, global research is becoming more and more important as companies compete in global marketing.

Objective 6: Understand the ethical considerations of marketing information and research.

There are many ethical issues surrounding marketing research. One problem is that it sometimes can reflect the biases of marketers. When research is conducted to confirm or validate a position, the results are not likely to be objective. The scientific method can eliminate this type of bias. A number of groups exist to prevent the manipulation of marketing research. They are interested in accuracy and want to protect consumers.

The use of loyalty cards, membership cards, and credit card linked transaction details provides valuable information to marketers and companies in general. However, some consumers are worried about why this data is collected and how it could eventually be used.

Review Your Understanding

1. What is a marketing information system (MkIS)? What is a marketing decision support system (MDSS)? What is a transaction-based information system (TBIS)?
2. What is marketing research? How is it different from a marketing information system? How are data transformed into information? What are the three steps?
3. What are the differences between primary and secondary data?
4. What are the three major uses of marketing information?
5. What are the steps in a typical marketing research project?
6. What is exploratory research? List five exploratory research methods.
7. What is quantitative research? Name two quantitative methods.
8. Give two challenges associated with global marketing research.
9. What are the pros and cons of each type of survey data collection?

Discussion of Concepts

1. How is a marketing information system used? Describe the two components of a typical MkIS.
2. What is the difference between data and information? Why is it important for marketers to provide executives with information rather than data?
3. Explain the objective of the marketing decision support system.
4. List and describe the four types of information an MkIS provides. Why is each type important for decision making?
5. Describe each step of the marketing research process. Why is it critical to lay out each step in detail prior to beginning any research project?
6. Select a marketing problem and design a suitable marketing research approach to address it.
7. After completing an exploratory research study, how would you decide whether quantitative research is in order?
8. What would be the major considerations in developing a marketing research capability for a small company?
9. Under what circumstances would you consider it to be ethical to withhold marketing research from interested consumers? When would it be unethical?

Key Terms & Definitions

1. **Big Data:** An umbrella term for the vast amount of data continually generated by society which can be analyzed to reveal trends, patterns and predictions relating to human behavior and interactions.
2. **Case analysis:** The in-depth study of a few examples.
3. **Causal research:** Research that attempts to prove a cause-and-effect relationship between two phenomena.
4. **Convenience sample:** A sample composed of people who happen to come along, such as shoppers in a store at a given time, whoever answers the doorbell, or travelers passing through an airport.
5. **Data:** Facts or statistics obtained from outside or inside the company.
6. **Database:** A collection of data that can be retrieved by a computer.
7. **Depth interview:** A relatively unstructured conversation that allows the researcher to probe deeply into a consumer's thoughts.
8. **Experiment:** A test conducted under controlled conditions in order to prove or disprove a marketing hypothesis.
9. **Exploratory research:** Research designed to clarify the problem and suggest ways to address it.
10. **External data:** Data obtained outside the company.
11. **Focus group:** A group, usually composed of eight to twelve people, whose opinions are elicited by an interviewer to provide exploratory insights into a problem.
12. **Hypothesis:** A tentative assumption about a particular event or issue.
13. **Information:** Data that has been analyzed and put in useful form.
14. **Internal data:** Data obtained within the company.
15. **Judgment sample:** A sample selected by the researchers or interviewers based on their belief that those chosen represent a majority of the study population.
16. **Likert scale:** A scale that measures the respondent's intensity of agreement with a particular statement.
17. **Marketing decision support system (MkDSS):** a coordinated collection of data, systems, and techniques by which an organization gathers and interprets relevant information from business and the environment and turns it into a basis for marketing action. MkDSS is usually part of a marketing information system.
18. **Marketing information system (MkIS):** A set of procedures and methods for the regular, planned collection, analysis, and presentation of information for use in making marketing decisions.
19. **Marketing research:** The formal assembly and analysis of information about specific issues surrounding the marketing of

goods and services.

20. **Nonprobability sample:** A sample in which the likelihood of selecting a particular respondent from the sampling frame cannot be calculated.

21. **Observation:** A research technique in which researchers simply watch the participants they are studying.

22. **Pilot study:** A small-scale project that allows the researcher to refine and test the approaches that eventually will be used.

23. **Population (universe):** All the individuals or organizations relevant to the marketing research project.

24. **Primary data:** Information collected for the first time.

25. **Probability sample:** A sample in which the chance of selecting a given individual from the sampling frame or population can be calculated.

26. **Projective technique:** A technique that enables respondents to project their thoughts onto a third party or object or through some type of contrived situation.

27. **Quantitative research:** Research designed to provide the information needed to select the best course of action and estimate thc probable results.

28. **Research design:** An outline that identifies what data to collect, how to collect it, and how it will be analyzed.

29. **Sample:** The group participating in a research project that represents the entire population of potential respondents.

30. **Sampling frame:** A list of people in the universe who potentially could be contacted.

31. **Scientific method:** A systematic way to gather, analyze, and interpret data in order to confirm or reject a prior conception.

32. **Secondary data:** Information that already has been collected.

33. **Simple random sampling:** A sampling technique in which each member of the study population has an equal and known chance of being chosen.

34. **Stratified random sampling:** A sampling technique in which each member of a selected subgroup of the population has an equal chance of selection.

35. **Transaction-based information system (TBIS):** A computerized link between a firm and its customers, distributors, and suppliers.

References

1. www-01.ibm.com, website visited May 22, 2016.
2. www.ama.org/AboutAMA/Pages/Definition-of-Marketing.aspx, website visited June 28, 2016.
3. Fusaro, Dave, "Meeting Wal-Mart's Mandates," www.foodprocessing.com, website visited April 16, 2016.
4. www.forrester.com, website visited May 22, 2016.
5. "Nexis®—News, Company & Industry Content for Business Intelligence," LexisNexis, 2013.
6. www.dnb.com, website visited May 22, 2016.
7. "Gannett Selects the AMM Group to Provide Advertising Performance Measurement System," Reuters. www.reuters.com, website visited May 22, 2016.
8. Radius Global Market Research. www.radius-global.com, website visited May 23, 2016.
9. Byron, Ellen, "New Penney: Chain Goes for 'Missing Middle,'" The Wall Street Journal, February 14, 2005, pg. B1.
10. Jerin Mathew, "Google to dominate search ad market in 2015 with 55% global revenue share," International Business Times, April 1, 2015.
11. www.acnielsen.com, website visited May 16, 2016.
12. www.nielsen.com, website visited May18, 2016.
13. Einstein, A.; Infeld, L., The Evolution of Physics (New York: Simon & Schuster, 1942), pg. 95.
14. www.google.com, website visited May 19, 2016.
15. www.luntzglobal.com, website visited May 19, 2016.
16. Harrell, Gilbert D.; Hutt, Michael D.; Anderson, James C., "Path Analysis of Buyer Behavior Under Conditions of Crowding," Journal of Marketing Research, February 1980, pg. 47.
17. www.meridianai.com/success_product_kimberly-clark.html, website visited May 15, 2016.
18. Burke, Kenneth, "10 Reasons Millennials Aren't Answering Your Phone Calls," www.textrequest.com, November 24, 2015, website visited June 29, 2016.
19. Marshall, Christy, "Have It Your Way with Research," Advertising Age, April 4, 1983.
20. Schmidt, Jeffery B.; Calantone, Roger J.; Griffin, Abbie; Montoya-weiss, Mitzi M., "Do Certified Mail Third-Wave Follow-Ups Really Boost Response Rates and Quality?" Marketing letters 16:2, 2005, pp. 129-141.
21. Girard, Peter, "Alloy's Online/Offline Dividends," Catalog Age, May 2000, pg. 12.
22. Cross, Richard, "Real-Time and Online Research Is Paying Off," Direct Marketing, May 2000, pg. 61.
23. "Buyers Guide to Online Research Quality: Your Checklist for Standardizing Quality," www.truesample.com, website visited May 25, 2016.
24. "Best Buy Customer Voice Survey," Best Buy, www.bestbuycares.com, site visited May 15, 2016.
25. www.statpac.com/surveys/sampling.html, website visited May 23, 2016.
26. www.pewresearch.org/methodology/u-s-survey-research/collecting-survey-data, website visited May 28, 2016.
27. Honomichl, Jack, "Strong Progress, U.S. research firms see healthy growth in '04," Marketing News, June 15, 2005, pg. 3.
28. "Top 50 U.S. Research Organizations," Marketing news, June 15, 2005, pg. 4.
29. Aaron Fuller, "Why Small business Needs to Understand Big Data," FOCUS Magazine, Small Business Association of Michigan, May/June, 2015, p10.
30. www.datafloq.com/read/coca-cola-takes-refreshing-approach-big-data/425, website visited June 6, 2016.
31. Stanford, Duane, "Coke Engineers Its Orange Juice—With an Algorithm," Bloomberg.com, January 31, 2013.
32. "Coca-Cola's Juicy Approach to Big Data," BusinessIntelligence.com, July 29, 2013.
33. Jeff Bertolucci, "Big Data Analytics: Descriptive Vs. Predictive Vs. Prescriptive," InformationWeek, December 31, 2013.
34. www.klipfolio.com/resources/dashboard-examples/marketing/online-marketing-dashboard, website visited June 1, 2016
35. www.birtanalytics.actuate.com, website visited May 30, 2016.
36. Jeff Bertolucci, "Big Data Analytics: Descriptive Vs. Predictive Vs. Prescriptive," InformationWeek, December 31, 2013.
37. Hugh J. Watson, "The Business Case for Analytics," BizED, AACSB

International, May/June 2013.

38. www.cio.com/article/3004512/big-data/idc-predicts-big-data-spending-to-reach-48-6-billion-in-2019.html, website visited June 26, 2016.

39. Joab Jackson, "Google: 129 Million Different Books Have Been Published," www.pcworld.com, website visited May 27, 2016.

40. Henessey, Jeannet, Global Marketing Strategies, 3rd ed. (Boston: Houghton Mifflin, 1995), pg. 202.

41. "The Good Statistics Guide," Economist, September 11, 1993, pg. 34.

42. Onkvisit, Sak; Shaw, John J., International Marketing, 2nd ed. (Upper Saddle River, New Jersey: Prentice Hall, 1993), pg. 398.

43. Bush, Ian; Damminger, Rachelle; Daniels, Lisa Marie; Laoye, Elizabeth, "Communication Strategies: Marketing to the 'Majority Minority,'" Villanova University Publications, 2005.

44. ccsg.isr.umich.edu/datacoll.cfm, website visited June 3, 2016.

45. www.cia.gov, website visited May 19, 2016.

46. Crossens, Cynthia, Tainted Truth: The Manipulation of Fact in America (New York: Simon & Schuster), 1994, pg. 19.

47. "Respondents Assail Quality of Research," Marketing news, May 8, 1995, pg. 14.

48. Crossens, Tainted Truth, pg. 14.

49. Ibid., pg. 19.

50. Kluger, Jeffrey, "Poll Vaulting," Discover, May 1995.

51. "Cloth Diapers: Truth, Facts and Benefits for Infant and Family," Children's Hospital Los Angeles, www.chla.org, website visited May 15, 2016.

52. "They Know What Girls Want," Marketing News, March 27, 2000, pg. 3.

53. Swartz, Nikki, "California Passes Online Privacy Bill," Information Management Journal, Lemexa: September/October 2004, Vol. 38, Iss. 5, pg. 11.

CHAPTER *05*

Understanding
Consumer Behavior

The Home Depot does an excellent job of building customer connections.

The do-it-yourself home improvement industry was revolutionized when Bernie Marcus and Arthur Blank opened the first Home Depot in 1978. As one of the largest retailers in the world, Home Depot is the "go-to" store for customers who want to make home improvements. It has 2274 stores located throughout the United States, including the Commonwealth of Puerto Rico and the territories of the U.S. Virgin Islands and Guam, Canada, and Mexico. Over 385,000 well-trained, customer-oriented sales associates provide knowledge on everything from how to lay tile, install faucets, use power tools, build fences and grow plants. Each store carries more than 40,000 products and is tailored to the local market's climate and style.

In his commencement address to the 2015 graduating class of Michigan State's Broad College of Business, Home Depot's Chairman of the Board and CEO, Craig Menear, stressed the company's commitment to its customers...from executives to cleaning staff. He said most organizations use a pyramid structure with customers on the base, then middle management, then executives at the top. Home Depot, however, inverts the pyramid in all communications and actions so that customers are higher on the pyramid than even the president or CEO. Every employee is trained to treat customers like "the boss." This attitude permeates the organization.

Customer commitment has made Home Depot the success it is today. For many people, a home is the biggest financial investment they make and improvements can be costly and stressful, so the company strives to make those improvements as easy as possible. The company targets three market segments. The first is the do-it-yourself customer. For this segment, the company provides free "how-to" clinics every Saturday and Sunday for common household projects, and unlimited consultation with its sales people. The second segment is the do-it-for-me customer, who personally purchases the materials but hires a third

party for installation/building. Home Depot provides independent contractors to complete a range of installation services once a product is purchased. Finally, the company caters to professional customers through will-call services, expanded credit programs, equipment rental and merchandise selection.

Home Depot has found a huge following on social media at sites like Pinterest, where over 1000 ideas are displayed for modeling, organizing, and painting projects. The company's Facebook page has more than 2 million likes

Today, Home Depot is transforming the home improvement industry through the aggressive introduction of the Eco-Option brand. Recognizing increased customer awareness of the environment, the company has labeled every product that benefits sustainable forestry, energy efficiency, healthy homes, clean air and water conservation. It also gives preferential buying treatment to suppliers who sell wood and wood products that come from managed forests that meet strict sustainable guidelines. Home Depot has always done an excellent job of building strong, lasting relationships with customers, suppliers, and employees. Today, that commitment is stronger than ever, earning Home Depot the #39 spot on Forbes' list of The World's Most Valuable Brands.

Sources: www.homedepot.com/phoenix.zhtml?c=63646&p=irol-newsArticle&id=1345670, website visited April 11, 2016; www.homedepot.com/ecooptions/index.html, website visited April 11, 2016; www.bloomberg.com/research/stocks/snapshot/snapshot_article.asp?ticker=HD; www.forbes.com/companies/home-depot; www.pinterest.com/explore/home-depot, website visited April 11, 2016.

LO 01 Learn how different types of purchases dictate customer involvement levels.

LO 02 Explain the five steps of the Consumer Decision Making Process.

LO 03 Describe the five psychological factors that influence consumer behavior.

LO 04 Explain how social factors such as culture, subculture, social class, reference groups and family help explain consumer behavior.

LO 05 Identify how technology affects consumer behavior.

LO 06 Discuss the ethical dilemmas marketers encounter when appealing to consumers.

The Concept of Consumer Behavior

More than ever, consumers and markets are diversifying. The challenge for cutting-edge organizations is to enhance the life experiences of consumers with products that live up to their expectations. To understand customers, marketers must understand the psychological and social factors that determine their decisions. Leading organizations are bundling their knowledge of all these factors into systematic ways of influencing customer satisfaction, loyalty and relationships. Discovering and delivering value requires a thorough understanding of consumer behavior.

Consumer behavior involves the actions individuals and households take in discovering, evaluating, acquiring, consuming, and disposing of products. Consider the key parts of that definition. First, it looks at both actions (what people do) and decision processes (how they think and feel). Marketers want to know how often shopping occurs and for what reasons. Second, the definition refers to individuals and households. Usually an individual makes the purchase, but those decisions are often related to household considerations. When a mother shops, she may buy Pepsi for one person, Coke for another, bottled water for a third, and so forth. Third, evaluating, acquiring and consuming products are important parts of the process, but we need to remember that consumer behavior starts with discovery and proceeds through disposal.

Figure 5.1 provides an overview of the main topics covered in this chapter. We begin with the relationship between consumer involvement and decision making. Then we incorporate five psychological factors that influence consumer behavior and the social influences that affect the decisions of individual consumers. In the last sections, we look at ways in which technology is used to track consumer behavior, as well as ethical issues to consider when trying to persuade consumers.

CONSUMER BEHAVIOR

Involves the actions and decision processes of individuals and households in discovering, evaluating, acquiring, consuming and disposing of products.

Figure 5.1   Understanding Consumer Behavior

Consumer Involvement and Decision Making

Decision making and involvement are closely related processes. Involvement is a function of how important, complex and/or time-consuming a purchase may be. Decision making varies with the degree of involvement. For high-involvement purchases, the consumer is likely to devote time and attention to each of the five steps in the decision process. Understanding both concepts and how they relate provides insight into how and why consumers behave as they do.

CONSUMER INVOLVEMENT

LOW-INVOLVEMENT PURCHASE

A routine buying decision.

HIGH-INVOLVEMENT PURCHASE

A complex buying decision made after extensive thought.

Think about the difference between buying a box of breakfast cereal and a new home. Which purchase would you spend more time researching and generally care more about? Some purchases are more important to consumers than others. A **low-involvement purchase** requires only simple decision making; choosing cereal, soap, soft drinks and similar items doesn't require much thought. In making these purchases, most people choose the same brand every time they shop, which underscores the importance of brand awareness. **High-involvement purchases** demand more extensive and complex decision making. Buying a car, a computer or even a television requires a good deal of thought. The product is expensive and you will likely own it for a long time. Nontraditional products often fall in this category. An extreme example of high-involvement purchases involves Curtco Robb Media LLC, which publishes magazines such as The Robb Report and Showboats International. These magazines advertise such nontraditional products as Yves Saint Laurent's Waterproof Loafers; private jet-rental providers; vacation homes overlooking the Old Course in St. Andrews, Scotland; and luxury yachts. These magazines tout themselves as a one-stop resource for the luxury lifestyle. However, many high-involvement products are more frequently purchased items like jeans, jewelry and automobiles. What requires high involvement for one person might be a low-involvement purchase for another.[1]

Figure 5.2 shows how involvement influences decision making. The level of involvement with any product depends on its perceived importance to the consumer's self image. High-involvement products tend to be tied to self image, whereas low-involvement products are not. A middle-aged consumer who feels (and wants to look) youthful may invest a great deal of time in her decision to buy a sport-utility vehicle instead of a sedan. However, when purchasing an ordinary light bulb, she may buy without thinking, because the purchase has nothing to do with self image. On the other hand, if she sees herself as a "green" consumer, her desire for energy conservation might get her to

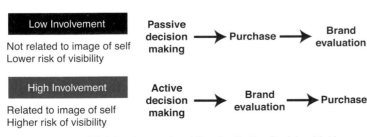

Figure 5.2   Low/High Involvement and Passive/Active Decision Making

think a lot about which type of light bulb to buy. Generally, the more visible, risky or costly the product, the higher the level of involvement.

Involvement also influences the relationship between product evaluation and purchasing behaviors. With low-involvement products, consumers generally purchase and try them first and then form an evaluation. With high-involvement products, they first form an evaluation (expectation), and then purchase. Consumers do not actively research low-involvement products, instead they form an opinion of them through commercial advertisements or conversations with friends. This is called **passive learning,** which characterizes the passive decision-making process. Only when they acquire and use the product do they learn more about it. In contrast, consumers investigate high-involvement products through **active learning**—part of an active decision-making process—in order to form an opinion about which product to purchase.

Figure 5.3 shows that products fall on a continuum between low and high involvement. Moving toward the high end, decisions are made about more expensive, permanent and complex products that also are more related to self-concept. Consumers give these purchases more thought.

Figure 5.3   Examples of Products on an Involvement Continuum

CONSUMER DECISION MAKING

For a better understanding of consumer buying behavior, marketers have broken the decision process into the five steps shown in Figure 5.4 (along with examples). Consumers making low-involvement purchases may skip the first three steps altogether. As involvement increases, each step takes on greater importance, and more active learning occurs.

Problem recognition occurs when a consumer becomes aware of an unfulfilled desire, or need. In a low-involvement situation, such as the purchase of a song, you might immediately go to a source such as iTunes and casually select recordings by two or three of your favorite artists. Or, if you're thirsty, you might simply run out and buy a soft drink. In a high-involvement purchase, the recognition of a need may arise long before it is acted upon. For example, if you live in an apartment with a spouse and three children, you may recognize that you really need to get a house, but the cost may prevent you from acting on your need for several years.

The **information search** consists of thinking through a situation, recalling previous experiences stored in memory (internal search), and probably seeking information from friends, salespeople, advertisements, online services, publications such as Consumers Reports, and other sources (external search). Each source has its benefits and drawbacks; experience is an effective learning device, but you may not have enough firsthand informa-

STEPS IN DECISION MAKING

EXAMPLES IN ERIN'S PURCHASE

Problem recognition

Erin's old Ford Explorer is giving her trouble, so she starts thinking about a new vehicle.

Information search

Erin decides what she likes or dislikes about her old Explorer. She talks with family and friends and searches Internet sources on vehicles.

Alternatives evaluation

Erin establishes some decision rules (price, features, styling), test drives several vehicles, and evaluates her options.

Purchase decision

Erin decides on a Ford Escape Hybrid and determines that leasing will work best for her.

Purchase evaluation

Friends and family like the car, which reinforces Erin's decision. Interaction with the Ford dealer after the sale is positive.

Figure 5.4   The Consumer Decision Making Process

ALTERNATIVES EVALUATION

Use of decision rules that attempt to determine which product would be most likely to satisfy goals.

PURCHASE DECISION

The decision of whether or not to buy and which competing product to buy, which is made after carefully weighing the alternatives.

PURCHASE

The financial commitment to acquire a product.

PURCHASE EVALUATION

The process of determining satisfaction or dissatisfaction with a buying choice.

tion. An external search is beneficial, but friends may have preferences different from yours, salespeople may push the product that earns them the highest commission, and ads are often incomplete.

Alternatives evaluation is based on decision rules about which product or service is most likely to satisfy goals. These rules are personal; that is, they vary according to what the individual consumer considers important. At this point, complex thinking is likely to occur. Using the results of the information search, the consumer weighs the pros and cons of each choice.

The **purchase decision** emerges from the evaluation of alternatives. A consumer may decide to save the money instead or spend it on a different item altogether. He or she may play it safe by deciding to purchase a small amount for trial purposes, or by deciding to lease rather than to buy. The decision to buy often occurs some time before the actual **purchase**—the actual financial commitment and transaction made to acquire the product. It may take time to secure a mortgage or car loan, or the dealer may be temporarily out of stock.

The **purchase evaluation** stage results in satisfaction or dissatisfaction. Buyers often seek assurance from others that their choice was correct. Positive feedback reinforces the consumer's decision and affirms expectations, making it more likely that he or she will make a similar purchase in the future.

Psychological Factors That Influence Consumer Decisions

Although the decision-making process appears straightforward, it is influenced by many psychological factors. The most important are: (1) motivation, (2) perception, (3) learning, (4) attitudes and (5) information processing.

J. Howard Miller, Westinghouse / Public Domain

This 1942 Westinghouse poster was produced to boost morale in factories where women were working during World War II.

MOTIVATION

Marketers first conducted "motivation research" during the 1950s and early 1960s in an attempt to identify buyers' subconscious reasons for purchasing various products. This work has since been discredited, because it was based on a very limited theory and poor research techniques. The pioneering psychoanalyst Sigmund Freud suggested that most human behavior is determined not by conscious thought but by unconscious urges, passions, repressed feelings and underlying desires. Based on these beliefs, motivation researchers proposed ideas such as men purchasing a convertible as a substitute for a mistress, and women making cakes as a symbol of giving birth. About the best that can be said for this early work is that it inspired marketers to develop new methods of researching motivation. Today, motivation theories are much sounder, and they provide several basic insights for marketers.

MOTIVATION

Motivation is an internal force that directs behavior toward the fulfillment of needs. It involves the needs (or goals) a person has and the energy that is triggered to drive the person to action. The needs that underlie motivation can be classified as either biological or psychological. Biological needs have been called primary or innate needs, because they seem to exist in all people, regardless of environment. Needs in this category include food, water, shelter, fresh air and at least some degree of comfort. Products such as Evian spring water, Kellogg's Special K, and Fruit of the Loom t-shirts were developed in direct response to this type of need.

Psychological needs are often called secondary or learned needs, because they result from socialization. Needs in this category include friendship, a sense of self-worth and achievement or self-fulfillment. The U.S. Army slogan "Be all that you can be" appeals directly to psychological needs.

Maslow's Hierarchy of Needs Abraham Maslow's famous classification is often used by marketers to help categorize consumer desires. According to Maslow, five basic needs underlie most human goals. He ranked them in a hierarchy to indicate that higher-level needs tend to emerge only after lower-level needs are satisfied. Figure 5.5 illustrates Maslow's hierarchy in the form of a pyramid.

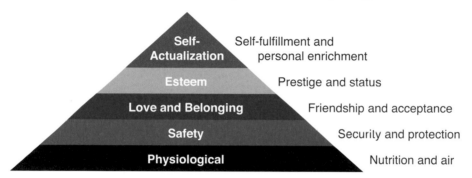

Figure 5.5   Maslow's Hierarchy of Needs
Source: Adapted from Abraham H. Maslow, Motivation and Personality, 2nd ed. Copyright 1970 by Abraham H. Maslow. Reprinted by permission of Harper & Row Publishers, Inc.

At the base of the pyramid are physiological needs essential to survival, such as food, clean air and water, warmth, and sleep. Businesses tend to market products that fulfill physiological needs only if they meet higher level needs as well, such as Evian water. Water is the basic, physiological need, but the name "Evian" draws on one's need for esteem.

On the next level is the need for safety, which includes basic security and freedom from physical abuse. These needs are both biological and psychological. Insurance companies appeal to them with such slogans as "Nationwide is on your side."

The third level of the pyramid is the need for companionship, love and belonging. Family and friends are instrumental in satisfying this need. Advertisements for Kay Jewelers play on our need for human interaction, love and belonging. You are even told at the end of every commercial that "Every kiss begins with Kay®."

The fourth level is the need for esteem, which comes from prestige, status and self-respect. Many consumers maintain and exhibit their social status through high-visibility products. Designer labels or symbols on clothing and recognizable automobile designs are two ways marketers have attempted to fulfill this need.

The final level of Maslow's hierarchy is the need for self-actualization. As people begin to feel physically satisfied, safe and secure, accepted, and esteemed by others, they may need a higher level of personal satisfaction, spurring them to develop themselves and their abilities. Education is direct-

Kay Jewelers connects with viewers through love and belonging.

Type	Description	Sample Situation	Possible Marketing Response
Approach-Approach	Two objectives are desired, but the consumer cannot have both.	Toothpaste ↙ ↘ Health with fluoride — Sex appeal with breath freshener	***Provide both benefits:*** Toothpaste with fluoride and a breath freshener.
Avoidance-Avoidance	The consumer must choose between two undesirable alternatives.	Muffler repair ↙ ↘ Depleted savings — Bothersome exhaust noise	***Stress unpleasantness of one alternative to get desired action:*** Muffler ads that emphasize how embarrassing a defective muffler can be or that offer financing or delayed payments.
Approach-Avoidance	The consumer's goal has both positive and negative aspects.	College education ↙ ↘ Hard work and expense — Greater earnings opportunities	***Emphasize positive benefits of desired action:*** A college ad campaign that illustrates how long-term earnings compare for a college graduate and a nongraduate.

Figure 5.6   Types of Motivational Conflict

ed toward this need by helping people attain knowledge and experiences that improve self-worth, sharpen talents, and promote personal growth. Self-actualization also may come from coaching youth soccer or playing in a basketball league. Backpacking, writing, skiing, painting and composing are other examples. The Marine Corps has a new ad titled "The Sound of Chaos" and depicts troops heading into battle, then challenges the viewer, "Which way would you run?"

APPROACH-APPROACH CONFLICT

Motivational conflict that occurs when a consumer desires two objectives but cannot have both.

Motivational Conflict People are motivated to attain some ends and avoid others. In marketing terms, consumers approach activities that help them attain desired outcomes but avoid activities that have negative consequences. Yet, because human needs and wants are so varied, consumers may be faced with outcomes that combine both desirable and undesirable features. Three types of such motivational conflict have been identified: approach-approach, avoidance-avoidance, and approach-avoidance. These are summarized in Figure 5.6.

Approach-approach conflict occurs when a consumer desires two objectives but cannot have both. Suppose you are interested in purchasing a new Dodge vehicle that offers great fuel-efficiency but also SUV carrying capacity. You have two desirable options, but unless you can afford to buy a both a Dart and a Durango, you will have to buy one or the other. Dodge attempts to circumvent the conflict with its mid-size crossover Journey. It gets 26 mpg on the highway and still has room for life. It is targeted at consumers who want to combine good gas mileage with storage capacity in one vehicle.[2]

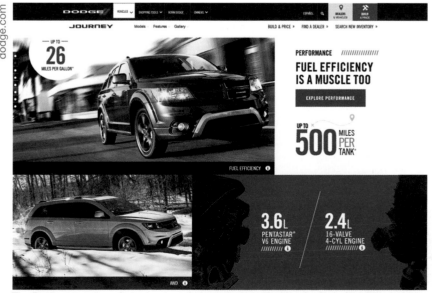

dodge.com

The Dodge crossover Journey appeals to customers looking for fuel efficiency and lots of cargo space.

AVOIDANCE-AVOIDANCE CONFLICT

Motivational conflict that occurs when consumers must choose between two undesirable alternatives.

APPROACH-AVOIDANCE CONFLICT

Motivational conflict that occurs when a consumer desires an alternative that has positive and negative qualities.

PERCEPTION

The process of recognizing, selecting, organizing, and interpreting stimuli in order to make sense of the world around us.

Avoidance-avoidance conflict results when a choice must be made between two undesirable alternatives. Elaine's car has a bad muffler, but the repairs will deplete Elaine's savings account. She wants to avoid spending money; however, she also wants to avoid driving around with a bad muffler. Elaine will have to resolve this conflict by selecting the least adverse choice. Midas Muffler offers a Midas Lifetime Guarantee option for mufflers for as long as a vehicle is owned. The appeal is to consumers who don't want engine problems yet also don't want to spend extra money on maintenance.

Approach-avoidance conflict occurs when a consumer desires an alternative that has positive and negative qualities. If Andrew lifts weights at the gym, his body will be stronger, but at the cost of time-consuming strenuous exercise and an expensive gym membership. Many types of purchases cause approach-avoidance conflict because they have drawbacks, side effects or other undesirable features. In a way, all purchases can be considered a mixed blessing, since the buyer must forfeit some money eventually. Consider the Army National Guard, which may offer tuition assistance and enlistment bonuses, but requires training obligations and a period of service. The approach-avoidance conflict for people who join involves positive rewards in exchange for hard work and sacrificed time.

By understanding motivational conflicts, marketers can respond with new products as well as advertising, pricing and distribution plans that help minimize buyers' concerns.

PERCEPTION

Human beings use their sensory organs to see, hear, smell, taste, and touch an almost infinite variety of sensations. The sensations are caused by stimuli—the sound of a jackhammer, the fragrance of a flower, the texture of a fabric, and so on. **Perception** is the process of recognizing, selecting, organizing and interpreting these stimuli in order to make sense of the world around us.

We are constantly receiving stimuli, and can only process a limited number of them. Consumers must select—either consciously or subconsciously—which stimuli to focus on. Typically, this selection occurs in four stages: selective exposure, selective attention, selective comprehension and selective retention. At each stage, one may lose messages, due to conscious or subconscious screening. Figure 5.7 illustrates the perception process.

Selective Exposure U.S. companies spend more than a billion dollars every day in hopes of communicating messages to consumers. However, a large portion of these messages are screened out in the first stage, when consumers choose whether to ignore or receive the message. How often do you reach for the remote and channel surf when-

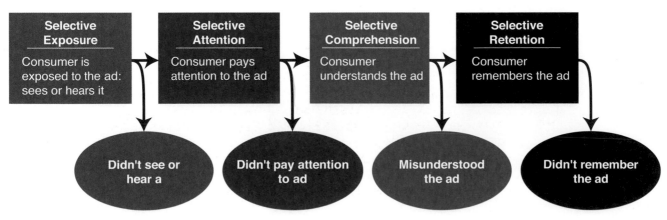

Figure 5.7   Perception Process

SELECTIVE EXPOSURE

Consumer's ability to seek out or avoid information.

SELECTIVE ATTENTION

When people pay attention to messages that are consistent with their attitudes and beliefs and ignore messages that are not.

ever an ad appears on television? Marketers call the consumer's ability to seek out or avoid information **selective exposure**. For example, Gatorade advertises on television with very unique commercials portraying athletes competing. These ads are placed in media often viewed by consumers interested in fitness and extreme sports. Non-athletes are not exposed to this information.

Selective Attention
Consumers pay attention to only a small percentage of messages. Noticing every one of them would lead to mental exhaustion from information overload, so consumers are extremely skilled at screening out irrelevant messages.

Through **selective attention,** people have a strong tendency to pay attention to messages that are consistent with their attitudes and beliefs and ignore messages that are not. Democrats listen more often to Democratic than Republican politicians, and vice versa. Similarly, consumers pay attention to advertising for products they have already purchased or intend to purchase. They screen out much of the information that conflicts with their experience or goals because it is irrelevant and distracting. One of the most important challenges faced by any marketer is gaining the consumer's attention. Without it, the message—no matter how well crafted—will have no effect on the intended target.

A good example is the ineffectiveness of smoking prevention campaigns. Forty-four million American adults continue to smoke, despite millions of dollars spent in anti-smoking campaigns trying to dissuade them. Even with warnings from the U.S. Surgeon General and proof that each year 480,000 Americans die prematurely from a tobacco-related illness, tobacco use remains the leading preventable cause of death in the United States.[3] Smokers may tune into advertisements about their brand but ignore prevention ads. This selective attention reinforces the likelihood that they will continue to smoke, since they choose not to heed the health warnings.

CoverGirl

Ellen Degeneres makes a great spokesmodel to appeal to middle-aged women.

To help gain attention, a marketer initiates the message in a way relevant to the consumer—by using a known sports figure, a common activity, an attractive person or humor, while allowing the consumer to relate the brand to this central figure by association. It's important to maintain attention by keeping the ad meaningful or interesting to the consumer. Procter & Gamble's choice to use talk-show sensation Ellen DeGeneres as a spokesmodel for its CoverGirl line was a good one; Ellen's daily show is popular with middle-aged women, which makes her a recognizable and appealing face for the company's SimplyAgeless line of products.

SELECTIVE COMPREHENSION

The tendency to interpret products and messages according to current beliefs.

Selective Comprehension
Marketers must take care to ensure that consumers understand their products and messages in the way intended. **Selective comprehension** refers to consumers' tendency to interpret messages with their biases. If a message runs counter to a consumer's strong beliefs, then the consumer is less likely to even attempt to hear the complete message. Consumers are likely to reject any information that contradicts their current beliefs or past behaviors. That is why marketers usually keep ads simple and avoid controversial images. A notable exception is political ads, since selective comprehension can work in the marketer's favor.

SELECTIVE RETENTION

The tendency to remember messages that are consistent with one's attitudes and beliefs, and forget those that are not.

Selective Retention
Selective retention is the tendency to remember messages that are consistent with one's attitudes and beliefs, and forget other messages that are not. The

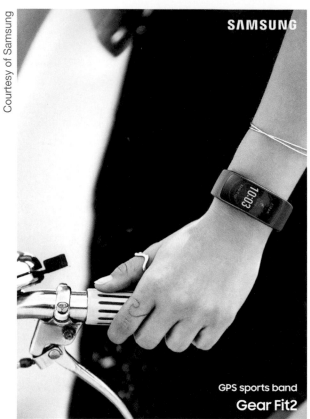
Courtesy of Samsung

Samsung's Gear Fit2 will not only count your steps, but map your miles with the built-in GPS system.

way information is understood determines whether or not a person "selects" to retain it. Once information is retained, it is held until replaced or altered. Old information may be forgotten when new, conflicting messages are received, or it may be reshaped if the new information is more consistent with the person's beliefs or goals.

For instance, Joan currently owns a Samsung smartphone as well as a Samsung television, and she is happy with both. So when she decided to purchase a fitness tracker, Samsung's Gear Fit2 was her first choice. One of Joan's good friends, however, had recently purchased a FitBit fitness band, and he insisted that it was a much better deal than the Gear Fit2, which he deemed way too expensive in comparison. After reading a blog about the cost of fitness trackers, Joan learned that Samsung is not the highest priced product. As a result, she discards the idea that the Samsung fitness tracker is too expensive and retains the information that she's always been happy with Samsung and it's not the most expensive fitness band.

Subliminal Perception Since our conscious perceptions selectively and routinely filter messages, is it possible to bypass that level and market to the consumer's subconscious? Subliminal perception means that you see or hear messages without being aware of them. The belief in subliminal persuasion began in 1957 in a New Jersey movie theater. Market researcher Jim Vicary coined the term "subliminal advertising" after claiming to flash the messages "Drink Coca-Cola" and "Eat Popcorn" on the screen too quickly to be recognized by the naked eye. According to him, the messages still registered in the brain, resulting in sales increases of 18% for Coke and almost 60% for popcorn. Researchers were never able to replicate his study, and he later admitted to making up the data.[4]

Today, consumer researchers continue to investigate the influence of subliminal messages and behavior. A psychology study set out to determine whether self-improvement audio samples really help people lose weight, improve memory, raise self-esteem or quit smoking. Researcher Anthony Greenwald found that roughly half of the people who listened to the audio claimed improvement in the area specified on the label. But the labels had been deliberately switched, so any effect had to be attributed to the power of suggestion, not to the audio itself.[5] Even after this study, there is debate over the effectiveness of subliminal messages. Still, advertising agencies continue to push the envelope and attempt to submit messages that are considered taboo and subliminal to the general public.

LEARNING

The process in which people learn to acquire and use products starts at an early age and develops throughout life. It is through learning that consumers select the patterns of behavior that determine when, where, and how they purchase, consume, and discard goods. **Learning** is any change in consumers' behavioral tendencies caused by experience. There are two basic types of learning: cognitive and behavioral. Cognitive learning, often used in high-involvement purchases, emphasizes perception, reason and problem solving. The five decision steps outlined in Figure 5.4 deal with this type of learning. Behavioral learning occurs through either classical or operant (sometimes

LEARNING

Any change in consumer behavior caused by experience.

called instrumental) conditioning when consumers react to external events. Behavioral learning primarily concerns what consumers do, not what they are thinking.

Classical Conditioning Classical conditioning gets its name from an early (and, therefore, classical) experiment by the Russian physiologist Ivan Pavlov in the 1920s. He presented meat paste to a dog, and the dog salivated. He then presented the paste while ringing a tuning fork, and the dog again salivated. Pavlov repeated this several times. He found that the dog would salivate at the ring of the tuning fork, even with no meat paste present.[6] The basic idea behind **classical conditioning** is that people can learn to respond to one stimulus in the same way they respond to another if the two stimuli are presented together.

Classical conditioning is used extensively in marketing. Think for a minute about a Gatorade ad that shows athletes training while covered in sweat. Marketers want viewers to connect Gatorade with athletic prowess in much the same way that Pavlov's dogs associated the tuning fork with meat paste. The marketers' desired result is that consumers will drink Gatorade at the stimulus of an intense workout or game. Gatorade continually reinforces this with taglines like "Gatorade: created to help replace what you sweat out," and "The best fuel the best." One recent ad campaign, "Sweat it to Get it," featuring Payton Manning, takes it a step further by implying that you can't purchase or drink Gatorade without breaking a sweat first.

Often, it is aspects of advertising (stimuli) that influence a consumer's evaluation of a product, more so than the product itself. Marketers claim that music helps define the emotional appeal of a certain brand. Classical music, for example, is often used to convey an aura of comfort, luxury and distinctive taste.[7] It is often played in spas and luxury hotel lobbies. The Gap also pays close attention to its audio identity. In one San Francisco location, Gap shoppers can use Rockbot's mobile apps to help customize the music they hear while shopping at the store. Rockbot lets customers choose the music that plays at a restaurant, bar or business, right from their smartphones. Because of its early success, Google Ventures has invested in the company with hopes it will be successful enough to fully acquire into Google proper.[8]

Marketers need to understand that consumers may generalize stimuli or discriminate among them. **Generalization** occurs when people make the same response to different stimuli. **Discrimination** occurs when consumers make different responses to different stimuli. For instance, when oat bran cereals were first found to reduce cholesterol levels, the oat bran image was generalized to other bran cereals, such as Raisin Bran. With experience, however, consumers began to discriminate, aided by advertisers. The Quaker Oats Company distinguishes its oat bran from other bran products, saying "Oats contain soluble fiber that binds with and helps remove some of the cholesterol which can clog your arteries and lead to heart disease."[9]

To take advantage of a strong brand name, marketers establish visual consistency across categories. The various products in ConAgra's Healthy Choice line, including pasta sauces, cereals, breakfast bars, frozen dinners and ice cream, are branded under the distinctive green Healthy Choice label. Consumers can readily identify the brand and many are likely to generalize the health benefits its image conveys, attributing them to a wide range of ConAgra's products.

CLASSICAL CONDITIONING

After two stimuli are presented together repeatedly, people learn to respond to one in the same way as the other.

GENERALIZATION

Making the same response to different stimuli.

DISCRIMINATION

Making different responses to different stimuli.

Courtesy of Gatorade

THE BEST FUEL THE BEST

Gatorade uses classical conditioning to get consumers to drink its sport drinks when working out.

Marketers also try to take advantage of a buyer's ability to discriminate among brands. For example, McDonald's names its products "Mc," as in the case of the Egg McMuffin and the McFlurry, to ensure that its food is associated only with McDonald's.

Operant Conditioning Even before Pavlov gained fame, Edward Thorndike, a noted psychologist, published work showing how rewards encourage certain responses and punishment discourages others. Behavior that is intermittently rewarded (positive or negative reinforcement) will be repeated in the expectation of eliciting the reward. Behavior that is punished will be avoided and diminish in frequency. Psychologist B. F. Skinner later termed this type of conditioning "operant" because the learning occurs as the subject responds to or "operates on" the environment. Thus, **operant conditioning** is the use of reinforcement or punishment to shape behavior. Today, marketers know that consumers associate positive and/or negative consequences with the items they consume.

Positive reinforcement can take place in different ways, the first being a product satisfying a need or want. If you drink Sierra Mist and your thirst disappears, then your action was reinforced, increasing the likelihood you'll reach for Sierra Mist the next time you're thirsty. Knowledge is the second source of reinforcement, and many organizations publish magazines to feed consumers information that supports their business: American Airlines has *American Way Magazine*, the National Hockey League publishes the online magazine *Impact*, and the Humane Society of the United States has *All Animals*.[10] These offer information that will reinforce purchases and stimulate new interests while maintaining brand loyalty. A third way consumer behavior can be reinforced is by seeing results. For example, Weight Watchers members are encouraged to attend weekly meetings to support other members in their area. Each member has a "weigh-in" to track his or her progress, and the group leader provides tips on subjects such as reducing emotional eating. Eating right and living a healthy lifestyle actually becomes reinforcement because consumers know they are making progress toward getting in shape.[11] Yet another way companies reward purchasers and encourage repeat purchases is the frequent-customer card promotion. Biggby Coffee offers its customers a frequent buyer card that rewards them with one free beverage for every 12 purchased. A consumer can feel punished (and subsequently become less receptive or outright reject the company) by a product that fails to perform as advertised, a service agent who acts in a curt, unfriendly manner, or even news stories that cast a corporation in a bad light and undermine the consumer's pride in owning its products.

biggby.com

Biggby Coffee rewards customers and encourages repeat purchases with the use of frequent buyer cards.

ATTITUDES

An **attitude** is a combination of a consumer's thoughts, feelings and intentions toward some object. Attitudes are often described as consumer preferences—a like or dislike for products or product characteristics. Marketers usually think of attitudes as being the sum of three dimensions: cognitive, affective and behavioral. The **cognitive** aspect

AFFECTIVE

Emotional feeling of like or dislike.

BEHAVIORAL

Tendency to act positively or negatively.

BELIEF

A conviction that something is true or that descriptive statements are factual.

refers to knowledge about product attributes that is not influenced by emotion; the **affective** component relates to the emotional feelings of like or dislike; the **behavioral** element reflects the tendency to act positively or negatively.

Figure 5.8 shows how attitude can affect the purchase of a mountain bike. Attitudes are important because they help us understand why consumers take a particular action. Note that attitudes are not the same as beliefs: A **belief** is a descriptive thought or conviction that expresses an opinion about the characteristics of something. For example, a consumer may believe that a rapid-fire shifter is a feature of a Specialized brand bicycle. Beliefs may help shape attitudes but don't necessarily imply like or dislike. Attitudes also influence beliefs: If rapid-fire shifters increase the price, then a consumer who dislikes high cost may believe they are not a very useful feature.

Consumers frequently form attitudes to help evaluate whether products and brands fit into their lifestyle. These attitudes are drawn from a broad range of ideas, not just the characteristics of a product. Generally, marketers use their knowledge of consumer attitudes to make sure that strategies are consistent with consumer tastes and preferences. For example, fast-food chains are using more naturals ingredients, including chicken and beef, in an effort to lure health-conscious Millennials. Hardee's and Carl's Jr. recently announced they will use natural chicken breasts in their sandwiches; McDonald's is testing similar chicken in it's Chicken McNuggets.[12]

Product Attribute	ATTITUDE COMPONENT		
	Cognitive (Does the bike have this attribute?)	Affective (Do I like this attribute?)	Behavioral (Am I likely to buy this bike?)
Rapid-fire shifters	Yes	Like very much	Very positive
Light weight	Yes	Like very much	Very positive
Rigid frame	Yes	Neither like nor dislike	Neutral
Durability	No	Like somewhat	Somewhat negative
Vibration absorption	Yes	Like somewhat	Somewhat positive
High cost	Yes	Dislike somewhat	Somewhat negative

Figure 5.8 Attitudes About a Mountain Bike Purchase

From time to time, marketers attempt to change consumer attitudes, usually by influencing one of the three components. A common approach is to use promotion to influence the cognitive component. This may involve claims of product superiority such as the Calloway Golf Club claim "a better game by design."

Marketers also try to influence the affective component of consumer attitudes. For example, as the health and fitness craze swept the United States, many people developed a dislike for beef, believing it to be high in fat and cholesterol. The industry launched a campaign showing that beef is nutritious and easy to prepare, hoping to make consumers feel good about eating it. "Beef. It's what's for dinner" became a recognizable slogan for millions of Americans in the 1990s. Despite the efforts, sales have continued to decline since 1976, when beef consumption peaked at 94.4 pounds per person. Today, healthier eating and higher beef prices have dropped the consumption to 57.5 pounds, a 39 percent decline.[13]

To change the behavioral aspect of consumer attitudes, companies will sometimes offer a coupon or free sample. This may involve claims of product superiority like claiming that your brand or product is clearly better than the nearest competitor.

INFORMATION PROCESSING

INFORMATION PROCESSING

The process whereby consumers acquire, store, and evaluate the data they use in making decisions.

Information processing refers to ways in which consumers acquire, store and evaluate the data they use to make decisions. The human mind has a remarkable ability to process (understand and apply) the information it takes in. Perception, motivation, behavioral learning and attitudes are integrated into the human thought system, which processes data to arrive at goal-directed behaviors. The key to information processing is the encoding of information and its use in memory.

ENCODING

The process of converting information to knowledge.

Encoding **Encoding** is the process of converting information to knowledge. The brain is sometimes described as having two relatively distinct ways of encoding information.[14] These enable it to handle pictorial, geometric and nonverbal information as well as verbal, symbolic and analytical thinking. The mind combines all of this information and produces integrated perceptions.

The mental images encoded as thoughts are held in "picture" form called episodes. Human memory represents concepts such as aesthetics, tastes and symbolic meaning in the form of a mental image that one can "feel." Ads and other phenomena are also likely to be retained as episodes.[15] Nike traditionally creates highly visual ads, targeting consumer emotions or values (often with dynamic imagery associated with competitive spirit). Nike appeals to consumers by focusing on professional athletes or athletic activities, and then ties their products and brand to those values. The "Swoosh" symbol actually represents the wing of the Greek goddess of victory, Nike.[16] The logo is a highly recognized trademark that elicits these desired effects because it is an episode encoded in the consumer's brain.

Verbal encoding occurs when words or symbols are stored in semantic memory. General knowledge, facts and principles gleaned from experience are held there. Many believe that the brain stores information such as package size, the meaning of brand names, and prices in this way. For example, advertisements for Johnson & Johnson's baby products use facts to appeal to concerned mothers. One ad states that Johnson's Baby Wash is the number one choice of hospitals.[17] Many mothers may form an impression in their semantic memory based on this information and call upon it later to make a purchase decision.

Marketers must remember that consumers in all markets encode both verbal and pictorial information.[18] In the early stage of information processing, the pictorial tends to dominate, giving way to verification and more analytical thoughts as the process continues. Striking images, memorable music and general creative advertisement will catch a consumer's attention. Then they're likely to consider the facts and details of product messages.

MEMORY

The brain function that stores and recalls encoded information; includes sensory, short-term, and long-term capacities.

Memory **Memory** is the brain function that stores and recalls encoded information (knowledge). There are three types of memory: sensory, short term and long term. Each operates differently and can be considered a separate step in the process of memory formation.

The first and most basic stage is sensory memory, which takes in an almost unlimited amount of encoded information. These sensory impressions are forgotten within a fraction of a second. But when attention is focused on a few stimuli, sensory information about them is transferred to short-term memory, where it can be coded and interpreted.

Short-term memory interprets what is sent from sensory memory. It usually can hold information for only a short time, and its capacity is much smaller than that of sensory memory—about four to seven chunks of information at once.[19] A chunk is a unit of organized information that can be recalled to solve specific problems of short duration.

Different people focusing on the same object may form very different chunks. A first-time buyer of a used car is likely to have a more difficult time than a person who has purchased several. For example, the experienced buyer probably will ask for past service receipts to learn about repair history, whereas the novice may not think of it.

In long-term memory, a vast amount of information may be held for years or even indefinitely. It remains there until replaced by contradictory information through a process called interference. For example, you go to your favorite restaurant and receive a poor meal or poor service. This interferes with your positive memory of the place, and you then reclassify it to a lower status. Once a brand is stored in long-term memory, consumers can add relevant information to help with future choices.

Pixar's imaginative feature film 'Inside Out' is set inside a little girl's brain, where Joy and Sadness become guardians of her memories.

Social Factors That Influence Consumer Decisions

Social factors have a great influence on how individual consumers and households behave. Consider something as simple as a pair of earrings. In some societies, children's ears are pierced at birth; other societies frown on ear piercing altogether. Some social groups regard earrings as a symbol of wealth and refinement; others consider them showy and in poor taste. They can be worn long-term or changed daily, and indicate status, membership or taste. Different social influences affect people's purchase decisions, but marketers focus on culture, subculture, social class, reference groups and family.

> Different social influences affect people's purchase decisions, but marketers focus on culture, subculture, social class, reference groups and family.

CULTURE

CULTURE

The learned values, beliefs, language, symbols, and patterns of behavior shared by people in a society that are passed on from generation to generation.

Perhaps the most pervasive influence on human beings is culture. **Culture** is the learned values, beliefs, language, symbols and patterns of behavior shared by people in a society and passed on from generation to generation. It produces manners and actions that are often taken for granted as the "appropriate" way.

Culture changes very slowly unless outside forces intervene. Historically, such forces have included political and religious wars and natural disasters. Today, global economics and technology are having enormous effects, as the swift exchange of ideas is making global culture more uniform. For example, the hugely popular NBC comedy *The Office* is an adaptation of a BBC show first broadcast in the UK that ran for two seasons. The original stories have already been sold in 80 countries worldwide, making it the most successful BBC comedy export of all time.[20] However, globalization extends beyond just entertainment. Banks, investment firms and credit card companies exchange capital and important knowledge-based information 24 hours a day, taking advantage of this emergent world culture.

By taking cultural values into account, companies adjust to the particular customs of people in different societies. **Values** are the shared norms about what is considered appropriate to think and do. Marketers need to understand values so their actions don't oppose what consumers in a given market consider acceptable. For a company like Whirlpool, a global provider of kitchen appliances and related products, it would be important to know how different societies view and utilize their kitchens. In Sweden, for example, the cooking facilities are more prized areas of the house, as indicated by the fact that utensils are often given as gifts and subsequently shown proudly to guests. On the other hand, in India, the kitchen is not usually shown to guests but serves as a strictly functional space. Thus, Swedes might be interested in more upscale kitchenware and appliances, while people in India might prefer space-saving, practical items.[21]

VALUES

The shared norms about what is right to think and do; what culture considers to be worthy and desirable.

SUBCULTURE

SUBCULTURE

A subset of people with shared values within a culture.

Understanding a culture provides marketers with an overall picture, but they also need more specific information. A **subculture** is a group of people with shared values within a culture. In the United States, these groups may be defined by ethnicity, age, religion, geographic location, and national origin. In this section we will focus on ethnicity and look at three groups: Hispanic, Asian and African-American consumers.

An ethnic subculture can be a very broad category. For example, the U.S. Hispanic community includes Cubans, Puerto Ricans, Mexican Americans, Tejanos and Chicanos, among others. Within such groups are further distinctions—low or high ethnicity, length of time in

Marketers know that ethnic subgroups are much more likely to buy branded products and spend more for what they perceive as quality.

the United States, place of birth, and place of residence, to name a few. A marketer can narrow this down to a very specific target, such as Cubans with high ethnicity living in New York City.

Marketers know that ethnic subgroups are much more likely to buy branded products and spend more for what they perceive as quality. Immigrants are often perplexed by the wide variety of choices, so they tend to stick with the major brands they knew at home.

Groups with strong ethnicity form some of the most important subcultures. You will learn that marketers are interested in identifying segments of the population with common needs, wants, and buying behaviors, since they can develop a single strategy to appeal to that entire segment. This encourages marketers to seek out segments with high ethnicity: Since they identify strongly with particular values and traditions, they are likely to have similar behavior in many aspects.

Hispanic Consumers
Hispanics are a booming subculture. Their number is growing rapidly due to births and immigration. There are more than 53 million Hispanics in the U.S. and the Hispanic buying power approaching $1.5 trillion.[22] These numbers make the Hispanic community a very important target for marketers since they are the nation's largest ethnic minority.

Because Latinos share Spanish as a common language (except for Brazilians, who speak Portuguese), radio or television stations that broadcast in Spanish are obvious media choices for promotional messages. Although many Hispanics are fluent in English, most marketers believe that it is better to sell in Spanish. According to a pilot study by Skunkworks of New York, advertisers can gain a 20 percent increase in sales among Hispanics simply by advertising on Spanish-language network television.

According to a New York Times article, English-language television is struggling to attract the nation's more than 50 million Latinos. Argentina's win against the United States in the 2016 Copa America Centenario soccer semi-final gained 4.8 million viewers on Univision and Univision Deportes, better than the 3.29 million viewers watching the same event on Fox Sports 1.[23] Univision is an extremely important network for reaching the Hispanic audience. Some believe it is the key to who will win the next presidential election. Interestingly, the Republican National Committee did not select Univision to air the 2016 presidential debates. Jorge Ramos, the top anchor on Univision and Fusion, says "the new rule in American

Argentina's win against the United States in the 2016 Copa America Centenario soccer semi-final gained 4.8 million viewers on Univision.

politics is that no one can make it to the White House without the Hispanic vote... so we still expect all candidates from both parties to talk to us on Univision and Fusion."[24]

Fantástico is a free mobile-optimized site that provides Latino consumers with a ticket-purchasing experience that is entirely in their native language.

Many companies are starting to recognize opportunities to address the growing Hispanic market. Schramm Marketing Group recently announced its newest venture, Fantástico, a free mobile-optimized site that provides Latino consumers with a ticket-purchasing experience entirely in their native language. "Currently, there is no real mobile option for U.S. Spanish-speaking consumers to purchase tickets online in their native language from any of the major ticket retailers," said Joe Schramm, Founder and Managing Partner, Schramm Marketing Group. "Spanish-speaking ticket buyers who want to attend a concert, show or sporting event have to resort to waiting in line at a box office or at a local 'tienda' retailer to get their tickets. Fantástico will provide Latino consumers with an equal opportunity to purchase tickets on the mobile devices they use the most, and in the language they speak."[25]

Asian American Consumers Asian Americans constitute the fastest growing subculture in the United States. The Census Bureau estimates that the Asian American population will grow to 40.6 million, or nine percent of the total population, by 2050.[26] This segment is well educated, affluent, and geographically concentrated. It generally has a propensity to spend more than other ethnic groups, especially on technology.

The median household income for Asian Americans is 28 percent greater than total U.S. median income, which means the segment typically has higher discretionary income to spend. A recent Nielson report called Asian Americans "significant, sophisticated, and savvy." [27] More than 70 percent of Asian American consumers have smart phones, a higher percentage than any other American ethnic group. Bill Imada, founder and chairman of IW Group, an advertising agency specializing in Asian American markets, says "Social media continues to change the landscape on how marketers reach and engage with Asian and Asian-American consumers." Mobile chat applications like Kakao, Viber, Tango, WeChat and WhatsApp have become popular in the Asian American community. According to Tommy Ng, general manager at Admerasia,"…a large portion of us use a mobile chat app to communicate with our family/friends back in our home country."[28] The ability to recognize and adapt to these cultural paradigms will enable companies to both reach and capture this savvy consumer base.

As with all ethnic groups, marketers must pay careful attention to the nuances of cultural and linguistic differences. Chinese, Filipino, and South Asian consumers are all unique, and strategies to connect with them should reflect appreciation of their individual culture by customizing content and imagery for each group. The potential embarrassment of addressing a segment incorrectly causes some companies to avoid subculture markets altogether. Asian Americans currently make up only 5.6 percent of America's population, but that small proportion contains a wide variety of culture and language differences, making it a challenge to tap effectively.[29] In order to reach Asian-American consumers, marketers need to be aware of what's important to them—information learned through marketing research—and tailor marketing mix plans accordingly. Using generic or stereotypical marketing is a mistake with any subculture.

I Have to Deal with Stereotypes

kev

Subscribe 2,903,462

+ Add to   → Share   ••• More

YouTube SCAN & WATCH ▶

3,967,918 views

👍 40,265   👎 2,320

Inspiring almost four million viewers, Kevin Wu's viral videos brought stereotypes and popular Asian culture to light in a comical and powerful way.

Celebrity YouTube sensation kevjumba (Kevin Wu), well known to Asian Americans, confronted these stereotypes in some of his early videos nearly a decade ago. Inspiring almost four million viewers, his viral videos brought stereotypes and popular Asian culture to light in a comical and powerful way.[30] Now a successful blogger and TV personality, Kevin has influenced the way companies connect with Asian Americans. Marketers who want to attract this segment should be aware of subculture phenomenons, such as kevjumba, to stay apprised of social and cultural differences that can affect business decisions.

Some companies focus attention on the Asian American subculture during important cultural holidays, such as the Asian Lunar New Year. Hallmark Cards, for example, has developed a line of Lunar New Year greeting cards. According to Kim Newton, marketing manager for Hallmark's Ethnic Business Center, "We wanted to make sure we chose cards that are appropriate for the domestic market but still tie ethnic consumers to who they are. Our goal is to help them keep cultural traditions alive during the holidays that are important to them." Whereas Hallmark's advertising is a large-scale effort, Honest Tea is also realizing the value of the Asian-American market and increases promotion of its products during the Lunar New Year.[31]

African American Consumers African Americans represent about 13 percent of the total U.S. population and are expected to have an annual buying power of $1.3 trillion by 2017.[32] According to the Buying Power of Black America, a study conducted by Target Market News, African Americans are increasing their expenditures in various consumer markets, from books to automobiles, making them a market of growing importance. In addition, they are savvy with internet usage and active on social media; a recent Pew Internet study found that 22 percent of African Americans use Twitter at a high level, compared with 16 percent of white users.[33]

In fact, Black Twitter (#blacktwitter) has emerged as a powerful subculture of the social media giant. Meredith Clark, a doctoral candidate at the University of North Carolina at Chapel Hill, wrote a dissertation on Black Twitter, comparing it to "Freedom's Journal," the first African-American newspaper in the United States. Armed with a social or political agenda, the group of devoted Twitter followers can be quite influential.[34] The group is credited for killing a book deal for a juror in the trial of George Zimmerman, who was acquitted in the shooting death of unarmed black teenager Trayvon Martin. Black Twitter is also the reason for the demise of Zimmerman's attempt to appear in a celebrity boxing match.[35]

Some companies are seeking to market goods directly to African Americans by focusing on African American culture, much like Hallmark has done through its cards and e-cards celebrating Kwanzaa. However, some consumers are concerned about the lack of major advertising to African Americans outside of January and February, when Martin Luther King Jr.'s birthday and Black History Month are celebrated.

It's prudent for marketers to be cognizant and sensitive toward issues and traditions of all subcultures. The African American community is distinct and "marketers should develop advertising and promotions specifically targeted to the African American community, rather than assuming general-market advertising is enough because this ethnic group speaks English."[36]

SOCIAL CLASS

SOCIAL CLASS

A grouping of people whose members share similarities in interests, values, behaviors and wealth.

The third major social influence on consumer behavior is social class. A **social class** is a grouping of people whose members share similarities in interests, values, behaviors and wealth. The United States tends to recognize four major social classes in its population, as shown in Figure 5.9. Why do marketers care about social class? Because it can have a significant effect on consumer spending habits. Perhaps the most obvious effect is the level of disposable and discretionary income of each social class. Generally, the upper class has the ability to purchase more consumer goods than those with less income, and those goods are of higher quality. [37]

Figure 5.9   Major Social Classes

People within a social class tend to have the same buying behavior and prefer the same brands. For example, a corporate marketing manager for Walmart will realize that advertising a product special in Conde Nast or Fortune magazine is probably not going to be as effective in reaching its target customers as advertising in a local Sunday flyer. Why? Because Condé Nast and Fortune magazines both target readers in the upper class and the upper middle class; those segments are not target markets of Walmart. The working class is, however, and people in it tend to wait for weekly flyers to arrive before they determine what they'll buy in a given week.

Global Social Class Dimensions Marketers increasingly look at social class from a global perspective. In some societies, such as India, South Africa and Brazil, class distinctions are clear, and status differences are prominent. In others, such as Australia, Denmark and Canada, differences are less extreme. In countries with strong class differences, where people live, the cars they drive, the restaurants they frequent, the sports in which they participate, the type of clothing they wear, how much they travel, and where (or whether) they go to college are largely determined by social class.

Class associations also have a great impact on commercial activity, particularly in business-to-business relations. For example, the president of a French company expects to deal only with the top executives of another firm. More than once, U.S. companies have failed at marketing in France because they did not know or ignored this, sometimes offending French executives by sending low-level managers to important meetings, other times losing stature by sending high-level executives to communicate with mid-level French managers. In a country with a more homogeneous class structure, such as Sweden or Denmark, it is not uncommon for executives from all levels to work as a team, so Americans of various ranks are accepted as well.

Marketers study global social class dimensions in order to understand consumer profiles, habits, interests, and purchasing behavior. For example, three national surveys costing more than $30 million were mailed to more than 24 million British homes by ICD Marketing Services. The research was designed to give insight into consumer preferences for cars, finance, travel, and other purchases. [38]

REFERENCE GROUPS

REFERENCE GROUPS

A set of people whose norms and values influence a consumer's behavior.

Another major influence on consumer behavior is reference groups. We all live with, depend on and are nurtured by other people. We influence and are influenced by those with whom we have frequent contact, such as friends, coworkers, and family members. We also are influenced by people we know only indirectly through the mass media. Research shows that groups have an immense effect on the purchasing behavior of their members, including their search for and use of information, their response to advertisements, and their brand choices. [39]

Reference groups are people whose norms and values influence a consumer's behavior. Consumers depend on them for product information, purchase comparisons, and

ASSOCIATIVE REFERENCE GROUPS

A group with which people want to identify.

DISSOCIATIVE REFERENCE GROUPS

A group with which people do not want to identify.

rules about correct or incorrect buying behavior. In a college fraternity, for instance, each member is unique, but the group has certain norms and standards.

Marketers distinguish between two types of reference groups. **Associative reference groups** are considered desirable to belong to, even by those who are not part of one. In contrast, **dissociative reference groups** are those to which people do not want to belong. The same reference group can be associative to some people and dissociative to others. For example, The Gap chose its name because many younger people wanted to actively dissociate from parents and other older people not deemed "cool." Teens may choose these bands as associative or dissociative reference groups.

On the other hand, famous faces can also be a positive reference group. For example, country and pop superstar Taylor Swift recently donated $4 million to the Country Music Hall of Fame to help establish the Taylor Swift Education Center, which will teach children about country music.[40]

Advertisers capitalize on the human tendency to rely on groups. In one form or another, groups are a part of almost all mass media advertisements and are used in many personal selling presentations. One Revlon campaign used a diverse collection of celebrities to create an atmosphere of intrigue playing to the characteristics of each celebrity. Recent Revlon spokespeople have included Halle Berry, Olivia Wilde and Emma Stone to target a number of different reference groups.[41]

Promotions that appeal to associative tendencies, such as consumers' dreams and hopes for the future, command a good deal of attention. Consider the number of advertisers that use famous spokespersons to deliver their messages about products, particularly targeted toward a younger audience. Respected professional athletes are often members of associative reference groups. LeBron James has become a highly marketable athlete due to his exposure in the NBA and his ability to connect with a youthful audience. "King James" appeared as number 18 on Forbes' 2015 Celebrity 100 because of influential endorsements with large companies like Nike, McDonald's, Coca-Cola and State Farm.[42]

The Gap store name came about because many younger people wanted to dissociate from parents and other "uncool" people.

THE FAMILY

How much has your family influenced the way you behave, speak, or dress? Often, the family in which you grow up—known as your family of orientation—teaches you certain purchase habits that continue throughout your life. Many consumers buy the same brand of soap, toothpaste, mayonnaise, laundry detergent or gasoline that their mother or father did. Those consumers later start their own families, called the family of procreation, which also influences purchase habits.

The family is especially important to marketers because it forms a **household**, which is the standard purchase and consumption unit. If you do not already have a household, you are likely to purchase or rent a home, buy appliances and durable goods, and require banking and insurance services. In other words, your household will be a consumption unit.

Not all households consist of a mother, a father, and children. Many have only one person, or several nonrelatives, or a single parent with children. This section, however, focuses on the traditional nuclear family. Marketers generally look at three important aspects:

- How do families make decisions as a group?
- What roles can various members play in a purchase decision?
- How does family purchase behavior change over time?

HOUSEHOLD

Family members (and occasionally others) who share the same housing unit; for marketers, the standard purchase and consumption unit.

Family Decision Making Family decision making is "one of the most under-researched and difficult areas to study within all of consumer behavior."[43] How does your family make buying decisions? Most purchases are probably conceived and carried out by one member with little influence from the others. These are called autonomous decisions. In other cases, several family members may be involved. These are called joint decisions.

Marketers must remember that gender roles affect how family decisions are made. Decisions are termed *"syncratic"* when both spouses are jointly and equally involved; *"autonomous"* when either one of them makes the decision independently; and *"husband- or wife-dominant"* depending on which one has the influence. Research has found that gender especially affects financial decisions and that men and women approach finances differently. In general, men perceive themselves as advisers, active in business and in influencing their friends' financial decisions. Men are more likely to take independent financial risks, and they often place value on ego-gratifying opportunities. Women are less likely to take risks and are more open to advice from friends and others. Directing marketing activities to the wrong person in the household could be as wasteful as directing them to the wrong market segment altogether.[44] For this reason, it's important for marketers to understand the decision-making roles within a family.

Family Purchasing Roles When children ask a parent to buy a certain type of cereal, they are influencing the purchase, but the parent still makes the final decision. In contrast, when teenagers go to the mall to buy clothing, while they certainly may be influenced by their parents, they usually make the final decision. Family members play certain roles in certain purchases and play different roles for different products. There are five key roles:

- *Initiator:* First suggests that a particular product be purchased.
- *Influencer:* Provides valuable input to the decision-making process.
- *Decision maker:* Makes the final buying decision.
- *Purchaser:* Physically goes out and makes the purchase.
- *User:* Uses the product.

The role a consumer plays is not always obvious. For example, women no longer rely on a husband or boyfriend to take care of home repairs and construction. Retailers such as Home Depot are now actively targeting this segment that spends $50 billion a year on hand tools, power tools and other equipment.[45] Children have a significant effect on family decisions. In fact, for certain products, the marketer may decide to focus on them rather than parents. Johnson & Johnson is among the many companies that market toward children. The company offers kid-friendly "easy-grip" bars of soap, body wash in scents such as "tropical blast" and detangling spray that smells like strawberries.[46] Cereal manufacturers also recognize the important role young children play. Eye-catching boxes and cartoon characters are designed to appeal directly to children. General Mills cereals often targets kids using games or prizes as an incentive to purchase. Other common methods include limited editions featuring new flavors and shapes, or popular cartoons, athletes and movies.[47] Children continue to influence their parents' purchasing decisions as they grow, but their interests may shift to other products such as clothes, video games, and such services as family vacations or restaurant chains.

General Mills has released four collectible Star Wars boxes, featuring a Droid Viewer prize.

Family Life Cycle As families age, they progress through a series of predictable stages, each presenting unique problems and situations to address. An understanding of each stage gives marketers powerful insight into the needs and expectations of families.

Only a few decades ago, everyone was expected to move in orderly progression from youth, to marriage, to childrearing, to retirement. Today, the picture is more complex because of widespread divorce and single parenting, as shown in Figure 5.10. What's important for marketers to understand is that a family's needs and purchase decisions vary at each stage.

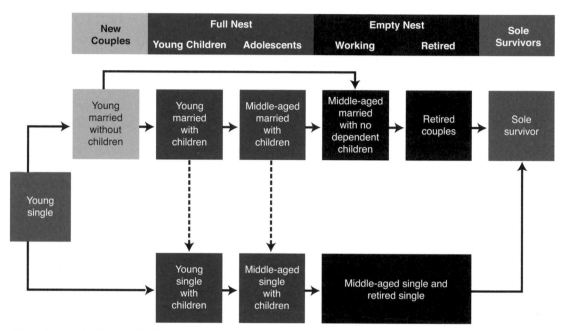

Figure 5.10   The Family Life Cycle

Young Singles Young singles are in the process of setting up their first household. Items they buy tend to be easily transportable from one location to another as living arrangements change or they find a new job. During this stage, courtship activities make social events, recreation and entertainment important. They may also look into purchasing advanced education or training to equip themselves for a career. This market category, when combined with middle-aged singles and sole survivors, has shown high growth.

New Couples Young married people without children generally try to build an economic foundation for later responsibilities. By combining resources, a new couple may have enough discretionary income to enjoy recreational activities while still saving for the future. This group spends more than other households on furnishings, new vehicles, and alcohol.

Full Nesters Caring for children consumes a great deal of time and resources, whether the guardian is single, married or divorced. Household budgets for full nesters increase for nearly every category of purchase, and new expenses emerge: diapers, day care, toys, lessons, glasses, braces and so forth. As children reach adolescence, their sports activities may cost from several hundred to several thousand dollars per year. Many families prepare for the cost of college, which can consume a large amount of annual household income. The government has recently noted the increase in student loan debt, which has now surpassed credit card debt for the first time ever. The current administration is trying to make college more accessible by doubling investments in Pell Grants, expanding education tax credits, and maintaining lower student loan interest rates.[48] Of course, purchase behavior will differ according to family structure—traditional family, divorced parent, widowed parent, or single parent. The latter group often has limited spending power. A divorced or widowed parent may have some child support or death benefits to ease the burden a little, but often he or she must often work long hours to make ends meet and has very little free time. In traditional families, both parents usually work to provide for their children.

Working Empty Nesters This category consists of three types of consumers: middle-aged singles, married couples with no children, and married couples with grown children who have left home. These households are in their prime wage-earning years: According to the U.S. Census Bureau, the median income of people aged 45 to 54 is $67,992, the highest income bracket of any one group. Some 75 percent of Americans in their fifties still work, whereas the baby boomers who were born between 1946 and 1964 make up the largest segment of the U.S. population with nearly 80 million people.[49] Without children around, empty nesters are free to travel, pursue hobbies, and explore new lifestyle options. As baby boomers turn 50, this market will grow even more.

Retired Empty Nesters Americans aged 65 and older have considerably more purchasing power than the average American and over the next 20 years, this market is expected to grow by 30 percent. This wealthier group has changed the image of the retired couple over the last decade. Retirees are now viewed as financial investors willing to assume some risk, mobile and daring, physically active and health conscious, and willing to pamper themselves. It was once thought that advertising dollars were wasted on this segment, but this idea has reversed: It's a powerful niche that is targeted in television programming and advertising campaigns. The wealthy elderly are the focus of luxury cruise lines, automobile manufacturers and land developers.

Sole Survivors Sole survivors are men and women whose spouse has died, as well as older singles who never married. Their net worth and buying power have increased over the past two decades. A number of sole survivors are senior citizens, who are targeted heavily by marketers with products such as home health care and websites like CareScout.com.[50] Companies that produce television fitness programs and diet supplements also target the elderly.

Using Technology to Track Consumer Behavior

Technology not only helps marketers better understand consumers, it also directly influences how companies build relationships. If you are reading this book, chances are you're a member of Gen X, Gen Y (Millennials) or Gen Z, and therefore you're very comfortable using technology. Whether it's taking an online survey, contributing to an online focus group, or interviewing on Skype for a job, the fact that technology is involved probably doesn't phase you at all.

What implications does this have for marketing? Dozens of Internet survey groups such as CyberAtlas, Nua and Jupiter Communications maintain up-to-date databases and news sites with information on Internet demographics, advertising effectiveness and industry-wide web spending and usage. These groups allow marketers to effectively track consumer behavior. American internet usage is remarkable with an average of nearly 5.1 hours a day per person. That is well ahead of the 4.2 hours spent watching television.[51] Even more telling, the average person spends 50 minutes a day on Facebook. This is nearing the amount of time a person spends eating in a day.[52] Social media sites like Facebook provide marketers an audience that is easily targeted.

The NPD Group maintains an "Online Panel" of consumers, demographically selected, who participate in continuous surveys of the web. For a fee, companies can access

Online Panel reports, including attitude and usage studies, longitudinal tracking, as well as product and concept reviews. Together with names, addresses, and other data requested when a website is accessed, such research provides a reservoir of information about consumers.[53]

Marketers also make use of web-tracking software that allows them to track every website a surfer visits and to compile information such as purchases made. The resulting silhouette, or profile, provides the kind of precision targeting that marketers so eagerly desire. Google Analytics is an excellent example of web-tracking technology. This free tool is an enterprise-class web analytics solution that gives site owners rich insights into traffic and marketing effectiveness. The easy-to-use features allow users to see and analyze traffic data in an entirely new way. The main statistics Google Analytics provides include the length of time visitors stay at the specific site, where they live, and what pages of the website are most popular.[54]

Recently stores have begun to use mechanical instruments in stores to track consumer behavior. Mondelez International—formerly known as Kraft—has starting to embed little sensors and data analytics into grocery and retail shelves. These will track the demographic data of passing shoppers—age, gender, height and weight—to profile the audience of Mondelez' snack-food, which includes Ritz, Chips Ahoy, Oreos, and Toblerone. The "smart snack shelf" will have weight sensors to tell when you pick up a snack, and if you are undecided, it'll bombard you with coupon information, an advertisement for the snack, and so on. [55]

Almax EyeSee Mannequins use both cameras and microphones in store mannequins to track shopper behavior.

Almax, an Italian company, has a really bizarre addition to the let's-spy-on-the-customer mix: the EyeSee Mannequin, which buries both cameras and microphones in those already sketchy store mannequins to track shopper behavior. American Apparel is working on more experimental applications like using heat maps to chart how customers move around a store and to identify repeat customers. And Nordstrom experimented tracking customer movements by following the WiFi signals generated from smartphones, but they eventually ended the effort when customers complained.[56]

It's only a matter of time before new technologies provide marketers with most any details they want to know about consumer behavior. Digital technology, smartphones and the desire of companies to learn everything possible about their markets will fuel this new area. Hopefully companies *and* consumers will both benefit.

LO 06 The Ethics Of Influencing Consumer Behavior

For a long time, marketers have used sexual themes to heighten brand awareness and influence consumers. Today, ethical questions are being raised about some of these promotions, which many people find offensive. Procter & Gamble set up a "sex task force" to examine its policy toward sexually suggestive magazine articles and cover headlines. With nearly $500 million in magazine advertising per year, Procter & Gamble was concerned that it was overly connected with risqué content in magazines such as Cosmopolitan and Glamour.[57]

Controversial promotion risks losing consumers in the selective comprehension phase of perception. Some people screen out ads altogether that conflict with their values. At the same time, controversy generates free publicity, which can result in positive or negative impacts to a company. Ben & Jerry's liberal political view was controversial enough for three angry conservatives to launch their own brand of ice cream, Star Spangled Ice Cream, to target conservative consumers. Flavors included Iraqi Road, I Hate the French Vanilla and Smaller GovernMINT.[58] Italian shoe company Geox S.p.A. donated several pairs of its anti-foot sweat system shoe to the Pope, hoping that they might be able to capitalize on a photograph of the Pope wearing the company's shoes. Although the Pope does not receive money for endorsing products, his use has created marketing opportunities. The Pope also owns Bushnell sunglasses and a specially engraved Apple iPod. These kinds of endorsement pursuits are seen as being unethical by some consumers and may result in backlash from the Pope's followers.[59]

Although consumers are free to seek out or avoid information, people often feel that children should not be exposed to objectionable images. When these are plastered on billboards or the side of a bus, it's hard to avoid them. M&M's maker, Mars, has an ongoing target of no advertising to children on TV and no advertising on any of its digital media sites to children under 12. It was the first food company to announce a global commitment to stop advertising food, snack and confectionery products to children younger than 12.[60] Mars does not support sporting events, nor does it place snack vending machines in primary schools.

Still, marketers face a challenge when deciding whether to promote a product with a sexual theme or shock tactics. They must weigh the risk of losing customers and crossing ethical boundaries against the advantages of gaining attention and strongly influencing purchase behavior. Consider the magazine Cosmopolitan. It's readily available as you wait in line to check out at the grocery store. Its cover story titles and provocative models have led many stores to either put a cover shield over the magazine holder, or move the magazine to another section of the store where kids aren't likely to see it.

Then there's the issue of marketers intruding on customer privacy. For example, loyalty cards are scanned each time you make a purchase at a favorite store. Even grocery stores know exactly what you buy, because you probably signed up for a "gas card" or a "perks card." Panera Bread asks for your "MyPanera" when you order. Starbucks asks for your "Starbucks Rewards" card. These companies aren't just tracking purchases, they're tracking purchases by you and your demographic. That's why coupons or "rewards" you receive are customized to your preferences. Even NetFlix tracks consumer selections and viewing habits, including preferred genre, how many times a show is paused, what time of day, and from what devices. Why? So it can influence its subscribers with additional products or services that will appeal directly to them.[61] Is this ethical? Is it beneficial to consumers? Or are companies amassing too much big data about people? What do you think?

Many of the factors that influence consumer decision making also play a role in the buying decisions of businesses because businesspeople are, after all, individuals with psychological motivations, perceptions and attitudes. However, business buying behavior is quite different from consumer buying behavior. Business-to-business transactions follow formalized procedures, involve many persons and functions, and require more personalized communication with the selling firm.

mms.com

OUR PROMISE

As a responsible manufacturer, we need to check your age to ensure that we adhere to our commitment to market our brands responsibly.

Please enter your date of birth:

mm | dd | yyyy | Let's go!

For more information about how we only promote our products responsibly, please follow the link to the Mars Marketing Code. For more information about our Marketing Code, please click here.

Mars has an ongoing target of no advertising to children on TV and no advertising on any of its digital media sites to children under 12.

Chapter Summary

Objective 1: Learn how different types of purchases dictate customer involvement levels.

Marketers know that an understanding of consumer behavior lies at the heart of nearly every successful strategy for connecting with customers. Consumer behavior is the actions and decision processes of individuals and households in discovering, evaluating, acquiring, consuming, and disposing of products. Consumers behave differently in low- and high-involvement purchasing situations. When involvement is high, they use an elaborate five-step decision process, and their attitudes are learned actively. When involvement is low, they make choices without much effort, and learning is passive.

Objective 2: Explain the five steps of the Consumer Decision Making Process.

The five steps of the consumer decision making process are: problem recognition, information search, alternatives evaluation, purchase decision, and purchase evaluation.

Problem recognition occurs when a consumer becomes aware of an unfilled desire. For example, a person is thirsty so he goes to the store to buy a drink. *Information search* involves thinking through a situation by recalling information stored in memory or obtaining it from external sources. In our example, the person thinks about what he's had to drink in the past that sounds good to him now. *Alternatives evaluation* is based on decision rules about which product is most likely to satisfy goals. In our example, the consumer is tired and has a test later in the day, so he decides to buy either a Monster or a Mountain Dew for the caffeine. Next, the *purchase decision* emergences from the evaluation of alternatives. In our example, the consumer decides to purchase a Monster drink, so he pays for it and leaves the store. *Purchase evaluation* is the process of determining whether one is satisfied or dissatisfied with a purchase. When the customer opens the Monster can and begins drinking it, he sighs, feeling satisfied that he made a good decision.

Objective 3: Describe the five psychological factors that influence consumer behavior.

The five important psychological factors influencing consumer behavior are motivation, perception, learning, attitudes and information processing. Motivation is an internal force that directs behavior toward the fulfillment of needs. Marketers often use Maslow's hierarchy to categorize needs. Consumers may experience one of three forms of motivational conflict: approach-approach, avoidance-avoidance, or approach-avoidance. Perception is the process of recognizing, selecting, organizing and interpreting stimuli in order to make sense of the world around us. It occurs in four stages: selective exposure, selective attention, selective comprehension and selective retention. Learning is any change in behavioral tendencies due to previous experience. The two basic types of learning are cognitive learning and behavioral learning. Behaviors can be learned

(conditioned) by classical conditioning and operant conditioning. Attitudes have cognitive, affective, and behavioral components. Information processing involves encoding and memory processes. The human brain encodes information differently depending on the type of data. It processes nonverbal, emotional and visual concepts in one way, while it handles general knowledge, facts and justifications in another. Memory consists of sensory, short-term and long-term memory.

Objective 4: Explain how social factors such as culture, subculture, social class, reference groups, and family influence consumer behavior.

Subcultures are groups that display similar values and behaviors that diverge from the surrounding culture. Social class is a relatively stable division into groups based on such factors as interests, values, behavior, and wealth. Reference groups provide norms and values that become the perspectives which influence consumer behavior. Associative groups are ones with which people want to be associated, whereas dissociative groups are ones with which people do not want to identify. Families have a profound influence on consumer behavior.

Objective 5: Identify how technology affects consumer behavior.

From a marketing standpoint, technology allows an immediate and easy connection with consumers through online surveys and focus groups, chats, marketing emails and social media. It also provides massive amounts of data about consumer spending patterns, preferences and feedback, which in turn becomes useful information for future marketing strategies and plans. Retailers use scanners at checkout counters to track shoppers' purchases. Recently, supermarket "smart snack shelves" have begun to track consumer behavior when purchasing snack foods, so marketers know exactly what type of consumer comprises their demographic.

From a consumer's perspective, technology—particularly digital marketing—enables quick gathering of information for a potential purchase and purchase options, as well as in-store availability. It also provides competitive shopping at the touch of a key. Finally, technology allows a person to download an online coupon for a store he or she is about to enter. When consumers have discount coupons for an item, they are more apt to purchase the item.

Objective 6: Discuss the ethical dilemmas marketers encounter when appealing to consumers.

Companies are generally taking a more ethical marketing approach in response to stakeholder demands. Of particular concern is the effect marketing has on children. Proactive companies like Mars are carefully monitoring marketing programs to insure they are not designed to target children. Procter & Gamble set up a "sex task force" to insure its promotions weren't considered sexual. Retailers of certain magazines now conceal the cover to prevent children from being exposed. Then there's the dilemma of how much information marketers should be allowed to collect about individual consumers. Is your information safe? Do you know who keeps it? How will it be used in the future?

Review Your Understanding

1. What is involvement? How does it influence passive and active learning?
2. Describe the five steps in decision making.
3. What is motivation? Describe Maslow's hierarchy of needs.
4. Describe the four elements of the perception process.
5. What is learning? Describe cognitive learning and two types of behavioral learning.
6. What are attitudes? What are their three components? How does knowledge of the components help in creating attitude change strategies?
7. What is information processing and how does it work?
8. What social influences are most important to marketers? List and define each.
9. Why is social class important to marketers? Be specific.
10. What ethical dilemmas do marketers encounter when trying to attract consumers?

Discussion of Concepts

1. Identify several subcultures in the United States. Which companies consider them target markets? Why?
2. Why must marketers distinguish between a person's ethnic background and ethnicity?
3. How does social class affect consumer behavior? Which social classes exist in the United States?
4. What are the different ways families make purchase decisions? How do these affect marketing?
5. Imagine that you are the marketing manager for the Audi TT sports car. What product features would you include to meet each of the five types of needs described by Maslow's hierarchy? (For example, air bags might fulfill the safety need.)
6. What types of motivational conflict might be associated with the purchase of this Audi TT? How would you try to resolve the conflict?
7. What ethical dilemmas do marketers face when trying to sway consumers to become customers?
8. How are companies responding to concerns from stakeholders about ethical and unethical practices of influencing consumer behavior. How are consumers vulnerable and how are they protected by the legal environment. What changes would you expect, if any, in future U.S. legislation?

Key Terms & Definitions

1. **Active learning:** Learning in which substantial energy is devoted to thinking about and elaborating on information.
2. **Affective (component of attitude):** Emotional feeling of like or dislike.
3. **Alternatives evaluation:** Use of decision rules that attempt to determine which product would be most likely to satisfy goals.
4. **Approach-approach conflict:** Motivational conflict that occurs when a consumer desires two objectives but cannot have both.
5. **Approach-avoidance conflict:** Motivational conflict that occurs when a consumer desires an alternative that has positive and negative qualities.
6. **Associative reference groups:** A group with which people want to identify.
7. **Attitude:** A combination of a consumer's thoughts, feelings and intentions toward some object.
8. **Avoidance-avoidance conflict:** Motivational conflict that occurs when consumers must choose between two undesirable alternatives.
9. **Behavioral (component of attitude):** Tendency to act positively or negatively.
10. **Belief:** A conviction that something is true or that descriptive statements are factual.
11. **Classical conditioning:** After two stimuli are presented together repeatedly, people learn to respond to one in the same way as the other.
12. **Cognitive (component of attitude):** Knowledge about a product's attributes not influenced by emotion.
13. **Consumer behavior:** The actions and decision processes of individuals and households in discovering, evaluating, acquiring, consuming, and disposing of products.
14. **Culture:** The learned values, beliefs, language, symbols, and patterns of behavior shared by people in a society that are passed on from generation to generation.
15. **Dissociative reference groups:** A group with which people do not want to identify.
16. **Discrimination:** Making different responses to different

17. **Encoding:** The process of converting information to knowledge.

18. **Generalization:** Making the same response to different stimuli.

19. **High-involvement purchase:** A complex buying decision made after extensive thought.

20. **Household:** Family members (and occasionally others) who share the same housing unit; for marketers, the standard purchase and consumption unit.

21. **Information processing:** The process whereby consumers acquire, store, and evaluate the data they use in making decisions.

22. **Information search:** Thinking through a situation by recalling information from stored memory or obtaining it from external sources.

23. **Learning:** Any change in consumer behavior caused by experience.

24. **Low-involvement purchase:** A routine buying decision.

25. **Memory:** The brain function that stores and recalls encoded information; includes sensory, short-term, and long-term capacities.

26. **Motivation:** An internal force that directs behavior toward the fulfillment of needs.

27. **Operant conditioning:** The use of reinforcement or punishment to shape behavior.

28. **Passive learning:** Learning in which little energy is devoted to thinking about or elaborating on information.

29. **Perception:** The process of recognizing, selecting, organizing, and interpreting stimuli in order to make sense of the world.

30. **Problem recognition:** Becoming aware of an unfulfilled need or desire.

31. **Purchase:** A financial commitment to acquire a product.

32. **Purchase decision:** The decision of whether or not to buy and which competing product to buy, which is made after carefully weighing the alternatives.

33. **Purchase evaluation:** The process of determining satisfaction or dissatisfaction with a buying choice.

34. **Reference groups:** A set of people whose norms and values influence a consumer's behavior.

35. **Selective attention:** The tendency to pay attention to messages that are consistent with one's attitudes and beliefs and ignore messages that are not

36. **Selective comprehension:** The tendency to interpret products and messages according to current beliefs.

37. **Selective exposure:** The tendency to seek out or avoid information sources.

38. **Selective retention:** The tendency to remember only certain information and forget other information.

39. **Social class:** A relatively stable division of society based on education, income, and occupation.

40. **Subculture:** A subset of people with shared values within a culture.

41. **Values:** The shared norms about what is right to think and do; what a culture considers to be worthy and desirable.

References

1. www.robbreport.com, website visited June 14, 2016.
2. www.dodge.com, website visited May 13, 2016.
3. U.S. Department of Health and Human Services, "The Health Consequences of Smoking—50 Years of Progress," A Report of the Surgeon General. Atlanta: U.S. Department of Health and Human Services, Centers for Disease Control and Prevention, National Center for Chronic Disease Prevention and Health Promotion, Office on Smoking and Health, 2014.
4. Vivian, John, The Media of Mass Communication (Boston: Allyn & Bacon, 1993), pg. 296.
5. Spangenberg, Eric R.; Greenwald, Anthony G., "A Field Test of Subliminal Self-Help Audiotapes: The Power of Expectancies," Journal of Public Policy & Marketing, Fall 1992, Vol. 11, Issue 2, pp. 26-36.
6. Pavlov, Ivan, Conditioned Reflexes: An Investigation of the Physiological Activity of the Cerebral Cortex, trans. G.V. Anrep (London: Oxford University Press, 1927.
7. "Stand By Your Fans," Advertising Age, April 29, 1996, pg. M1.
8. "Google Ventures continues to precede acquisition with Divide," Slash Gear, May 19, 2014.
9. www.quakeroatmeal.com, website visited April 8, 2016.
10. http://www.americanwaymag.com, www.nhl.com/intheslot/read/impact, www.humanesociety.org, websites visited April 8, 2016.
11. "What Happens at a Meeting?" Weight Watchers. www.weightwatchers.com, website visited April 8, 2016.
12. Woodyard, Chris, "More fast food goes 'natural' to lure Millennials," USA Today, June 23, 2016, p. 5B.
13. Sarah Schoenborn, "Per capita meat consumption predicted lower for 2013; Prices moderately higher," www.agriview.com, February 21, 2013.
14. Hansen, Flemming, "Hemispherical Lateralization: Implications for Understanding Consumer Behavior," Journal of Consumer Research 8, June 1981, pp. 23-36.
15. Holbrash, Morris B.; Moore, William L., "Feature Interactions in Consumer Judgments of Verbal Versus Pictorial Presentations," Journal of Consumer Research 8, June 1981), pg. 103.
16. "Nike Logo," Logo Blog, www.logoblog.org, website visited March 29, 2015.
17. www.johnsonsbaby.com, website visited April 11, 2016.
18. Piave, Allan, "A Dual Coding Approach to Perception and Cognition," Modes of Perceiving and Processing Information (Hillsdale, New Jersey: Laurence Erlbaum, 1978), pg. 16.
19. Simon, Herbert A., "How Big Is a Chunk?" Science, February 8, 1974, pg. 183.
20. "The Office remade for French TV," news.bbc.co.uk., website visited April 11, 2014.
21. Fielding, Michael, "In One's Element," Marketing News, February 2006, Vol. 40, Issue 2, pg. 15.
22. Alan Gomez, "Voices: Fast-growing Hispanic market tough to tap," USA Today, February 28, 2014.
23. Christopher Harris, "USA vs. Argentina semi-final nets 8 million viewers," World Soccer Talk, www.worldsoccertalk.com, June 22, 2016.

24. Michael Calderone, "Univision, Biggest Spanish-Language Network, Shut Out Of Republican 2016 Debates," The Huffington Post, February 15, 2015.
25. "Fantástico to Revolutionize the Online Ticket-Buying Experience for U.S. Hispanics," BUSINESS WIRE, June 16, 2016.
26. www.census.gov, website visited June19, 2016.
27. Yuriy Boykiv, "How BuzzFeed Is Winning With Asian-Americans," Advertising Age, August 05, 2015.
28. Lily Chen, "What's Next In Advertising to Asian Americans?," Asian Fortune, April 30, 2014.
29. www.census.gov, website visited June19, 2016.
30. www.youtu.be/nbZ9zJ22WfQ, YouTube, website visited June 19, 2016.
31. Gates, Kelly, "Marketers Tie into Asian Lunar New Year," Brandmarketing, May 2000.
32. www.census.gov, website visited April 12, 2015; "Britni Danielle, "African Americans Have $1.1 Trillion in Buying Power, Are We Putting Our Money to Good Use?," Clutch Magazine, February 11, 2014.
33. Pew Internet, www.pewinternet.org, website visited June 14, 2016.
34. Jesse J. Holland, "Black Twitter Emerging As Major Force In A Technological Civil Rights Age," Associated Press, March 11, 2014.
35. Janelle Griffith, "DMX, George Zimmerman 'celebrity boxing match' canceled," The Star-Ledger, February 9, 2014.
36. Brumback, Nancy, "Ethnic Markets Are Growing Up," Brandmarketing, July 2000.
37. "Social Classes." Boundless Marketing. Boundless, May 26, 2016. www.boundless.com, website visited June 23, 2016.
38. "Giant Lifestyle Survey to Hit U.K.," December 4, 1996, www.adage.com.
39. Peter, J.P.; Olson, Jerry C., Consumer Behavior and Marketing Strategy, 3rd ed, (Homewood, Illinois: Richard D. Irwin, 1993.
40. "Taylor Swift donates 4 million to charity. Wow," Sugarscape, www.sugarscape.com, May 18, 2012.
41. www.revlon.com, website visited April 14, 2016.
42. www.forbes.com, website visited April 14, 2016.
43. Wilkie, William L.; Moore-Shay, Elizabeth S.; Assar, Amardeep, Family Decision Making for Household Durable Goods (Cambridge, Massachusetts: Marketing Science Institute, 1992), pg. 1.
44. Plank, Richard E.; Greene, Robert C. Jr.; Greene, Joel M., "Understanding Which Spouse Makes Financial Decisions," Journal of Retail Banking, Spring 1994, Vol. 16, Issue 1, pp. 21-36.
45. Kwiatkowski, Jane, Women take on home improvement projects, big and small, McClatchy Tribune Business News, Washington, March 8, 2008.
46. www.drugstore.com, website visited April 14, 2016.
47. Kellogg's, hwww.kelloggs.com, website visited April 14, 2016.
48. www.whitehouse.gov, website visited April 14, 2016.
49. DeNavas-Walt, Carmen; Proctor, Smith, "Income, Poverty and Health Insurance Coverage in the United States: 2008.
50. www.carescout.com, website visited April 11, 2016.
51. "Facebook Users Average 7 hrs a Month in January as Digital Universe Expands," The Nielsen Company, February 16, 2010.
52. Shea Bennett, "28% of Time Spent Online is Social Networking," Social Times, www.adweek.com, January 27, 2015.
53. www.internetnews.com, website visited May 12, 2016.
54. www.google.com/analytics, website visited May 12, 2016.
55. Kerwin, Anne M.; Neff, Jack, "Too Sexy? P&G 'Task Force' Stirs Magazine Debate," Advertising Age, April 10, 2000, www.adage.com.
56. Beth Stackpole, "You're Being Watched: New Tech Turns Store Shelves into Stalkers," www.blog.hubspot.com, website visited June 21, 2016.
57. "Companies in the Crossfire," BusinessWeek, April 17, 2006, Issue 3980, pg. 30.
58. Meichtry, Stacy, "Does the Pope Wear Prada," Wall Street Journal, April 25, 2006, pg. B1.
59. www.bustle.com/articles/7113-smart-shelves-to-hit-your-local-store-by-2015-thanks-to-mondelez-international, website visited June 21, 2016.
60. www.mars.com/global/doing-our-part/marketing principles/marketing-brands-responsibly, website visited June 21, 2016.
61. https://cmsreport.com/articles/using-big-data-to-track-consumer-behavior 12414, website visited June 21, 2016.

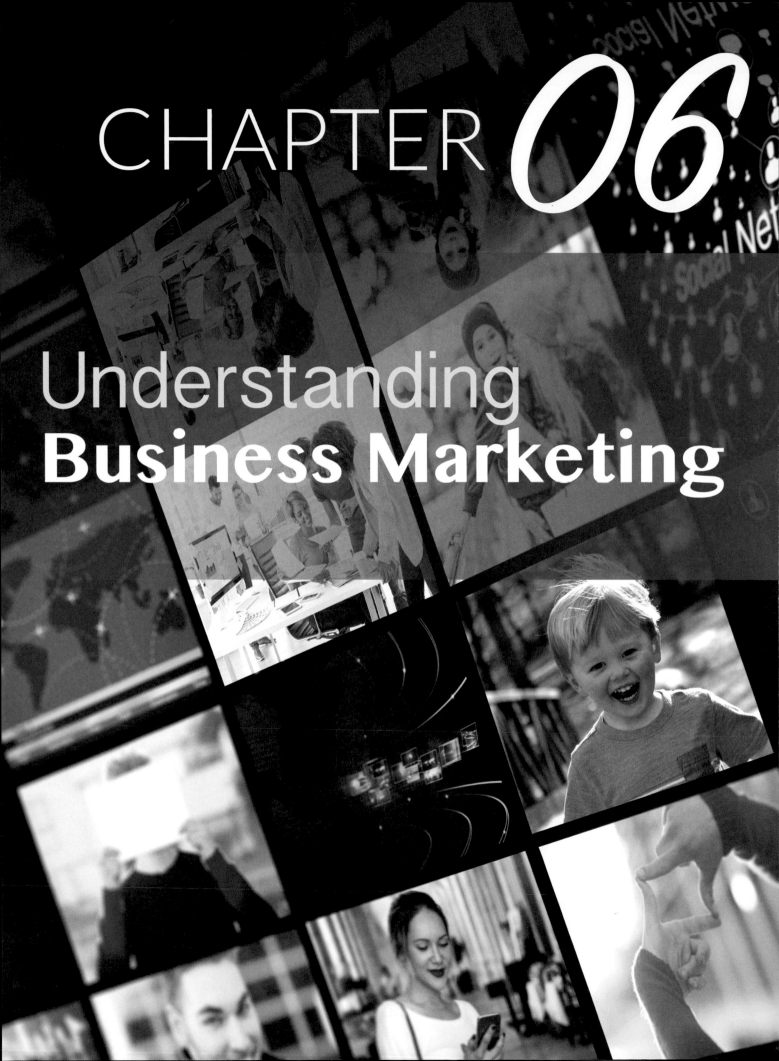

CHAPTER *06*

Understanding
Business Marketing

Intel is repositioning its brand image as a partner in diversified technology pursuits to make people "feel good" about the company and its products.

Before Intel, few computer users knew or cared about the microprocessor powering their PC or Mac. In 1992, the company began one of the most revolutionary corporate branding campaigns in history with "Intel Inside." Never before had an electrical component company tried to create brand identity with end users who it doesn't even sell directly to, let alone in a commodity market such as computer chips. Yet, Intel's share of the microprocessor market quickly climbed to almost 80 percent.

The approach that Intel took to gain end users' trust relied heavily on building a cooperative marketing strategy and advertising budgets with PC makers like Dell and Hewlett-Packard. Part of the deal that Intel struck with manufacturers was that if the Intel logo was included on a marketing piece, then it would share the cost of advertising. The result? The Intel logo became as recognizable as Windows. The move shook up the entire microprocessor industry, transforming it into both a consumer and business-oriented company.

Today Intel is trying to shift its brand image of simply producing processors that make your computer run faster to being known as a partner in diversified technology pursuits. The company has formed an internal creative group called Agency Inside that will have 90 employees by the end of 2016, with a goal to produce videos and digital media to showcase the company's role in these new, exciting pursuits.

For example, a newly released video shows a woman in India with an epileptic son who used an Intel Edison (a minicomputer the size of a stamp) in designing a glove that can detect oncoming epilepsy seizures before they occur. Another shows the making of Drone 100, a collaboration with Ars Electronica FutureLab, which became a Guinness world record event. Yet another shows facial projection mapping, a project with Nombumichi Asai and Studio WOW, that turns a woman's face into a projection easel. Perhaps you saw this technology when Lady Gaga and Intel partnered to create a revolutionary performance at the 2016 Grammy Awards. All of these Intel "Experience Amazing" videos can be found on YouTube. The QR code above will direct you to a fascinating overview of today's Intel!

So far, these two and three minute videos are distributed and promoted through social media, as well as through Intel's own publication, iQ. Obviously Intel wants to sell more microprocessors, the foundation of its business. The role of Agency Inside is to make that happen by influencing consumers' perception of the company.

Meanwhile, the majority of Intel chips are embedded in computers, tablets, and mobile applications, and they're used in most all industries. Retail solutions developed in collaboration with HSN, Kraft Foods and Macy's use Intel-based technologies to provide customized shopping experiences, and Intel will clearly continue to influence how brands engage and connect with consumers in all areas. This powerhouse leader in the B2B market consistently innovates and has rewarded shareholders with a 2767% return on investment since 1992. It is currently ranked #17 on Forbes list of the World's Most Valuable Brands.

Sources: www.forbes.com/powerful-brands/list, website accessed July 20, 2016; Noel Randewich, "Analysis: As PC era fades, good times may be over at Intel," Reuters, October 14, 2012; Walker, Rob, "Intel Tells Stories That Go Beyond Chips," Advertising, June 26, 2016; www.intel.com, website visited June 15, 2016.

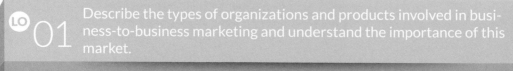

LO 01 Describe the types of organizations and products involved in business-to-business marketing and understand the importance of this market.

LO 02 Understand the link between consumer demand and business-to-business marketing.

LO 03 Describe the organizational buying process.

LO 04 Know how buyer-seller relationships work, including informal and contractual partnerships.

LO 05 Learn what functions and roles within organizations influence the purchase of a broad range of products.

LO 01

The Concept of Business-to-Business Marketing

Intel, Dow Chemical Company and General Electric are just three examples of businesses that market directly to other companies. The other companies are their customers, who buy very large quantities of their product(s). This on-going, business-to-business relationship is dependent on a strong customer connection with personalized service and attention.

A variation of that marketing scale is Market Data Retrieval. MDR has been selling data-rich marketing information and communication tools to colleges and universities for over 40 years. MDR doesn't normally sell directly to students or other consumers, but directly to schools and other businesses in need of such services.[1] This chapter describes the challenges of business-to-business marketing and its importance to the global economy. Business-to-business (B2B) marketing is the marketing of goods and services to other businesses, governments and institutions.

Total B2B sales are about five times greater than total business-to-consumer (B2C) sales. On the surface, this seems paradoxical, because most goods and services ultimately benefit the consumers who pay for them. However, consumer products result from a variety of components and processes, going through several different organizations before reaching the final consumer. Think about a product like an Apple iPad. Dow Chemical, for example, purchases petroleum to create a special plastic used for the case. A plastics manufacturer purchases the raw material from Dow to use in its manufacture of the case. The computer chips and communication components are manufactured by other suppliers like Intel. Corning supplies a tough, scratch-resistent glass called Gorilla Glass to protect the device from wear and tear. Each manufacturer adds some value to the process, and eventually Apple has a finished product to sell to consumers in the B2C arena. At each B2B step, increasing amounts of money, time and effort are spent on marketing. What the first party in the chain contributes is charged to the next party, which is included in the price to the next party as it moves along the chain.

In other cases of B2B marketing, a finished product is simply sold and re-sold along the line until it reaches the end consumer. For example, a deck of playing cards is purchased by a wholesaler, who resells it to a retailer such as Kmart, who then sells it to the final consumer, with each step requiring time, money and effort. In still other cases, one company sells products directly to another for its own internal use; Products in this type of B2B marketing include copy machines, laptop computers and paper tablets.

Many types of organizations buy business products. For example, General Motors and Ford (B2C companies) have several thousand suppliers that support their auto divisions. Other profit and nonprofit organizations—from Fortune 500 to small private firms—do the same and add to this total volume. Finally, the government market makes purchases nearly as large as all private organizations combined, ranging from country road repairs to army boots to toothbrushes. The business market offers tremendous opportunities, and upon graduation, most business students enter the B2B arena. Key aspects of the business-to business market are shown in Figure 6.1.

Figure 6.1   Connecting with Customers Through B2B Marketing

DERIVED BUSINESS MARKET DEMAND

Derived demand means that the amount of sales for business-to-business products ultimately depends on (is derived from) consumer demand. For example, when Xbox sales increase, so does the need for materials, components and subassemblies. The first (original) demand occurs among consumers and is reflected in the business-to-business market. This ripple effect is felt throughout the supply chain, and it drives economic growth.

Certain products are so essential that they are less responsive than others to changes in the economy. **Inelastic demand** refers to products so necessary that a change in price has relatively little effect on the quantity demanded. If the price of sugar or another cola ingredient rises, it's doubtful that Coke or Pepsi will use less of it in making their product. The cost has little to do with their decision about what to buy, although it may affect the price charged to consumers.

Some business products are highly sensitive to changes in consumer demand. We see the **accelerator principle** operating when a small fluctuation (increase or decrease) in consumer demand has a larger effect on business demand. Suppose that the economy is sluggish. In an effort to save money, consumers are closely watching their energy consumption by turning off lights when not in use, running the air conditioner as little as possible, and so forth. A few dollars saved by each customer in the area will have a noticeable effect on the local power plant's revenue. Even a small drop in consumer demand may be enough to force the plant to postpone the purchase of multimillion-dollar equipment. Of course, if consumer demand exceeds expectations by only a little, the result may be blackouts, power outages or the need to buy energy from outside the system.

LO 02

DERIVED DEMAND

A demand, such as the demand for business-to-business products, which depends ultimately on the demand of end customers.

INELASTIC DEMAND

Demand that is influenced little by price changes.

ACCELERATOR PRINCIPLE

A small increase or decrease in consumer demand has a larger effect on business demand.

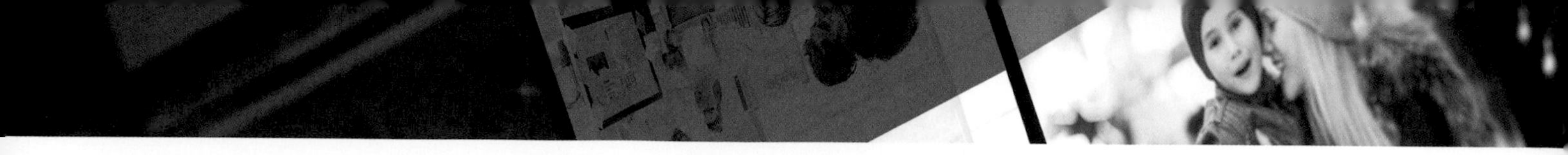

Category	Examples of Organizations	Purchase Examples
Commercial	Fabricators	Raw materials
	Component manufacturers	Component parts
	Processors	Processing equipment
	Original equipment manufacturers	Transportation
	Designers	Consulting services
Extractor	Agriculture	Fertilizer and pesticides, seeds
	Forestry	Heavy- and light-duty equipment
	Mining	Pipe
	Drilling	Aircraft and transportation
	Water	Real estate, mining rights
		Products for resale
		Loading equipment
Trade	Retailers	Computer systems
	Wholesalers	Buildings/real estate
	Dealerships	Advertising
		Transportation
		Warehousing
		Pharmaceuticals
		Equipment
Institutions	Hospitals	Food
	Schools	Consulting
	Day care centers	Health care
	Banks and finance organizations	Suppliers
	Insurance	Computer systems
	Churches	
	Charities	
Utilities	Electric utilities	Nuclear fuel
	Gas utilities	Power generation equipment
	Water and waste disposal plants	Electric components
		Motors
		Computers
		Chemicals
		Testing equipment
Transportation & Telecommunications	Airlines	Fuel
	Trucking	Equipment
	Rail companies	Computers
	Telephones	Real estate
	Cellular	
Government Federal	Senate and House	Consulting
	Judicial	Offices
	Agencies	Forms
	Military	Computers
		Energy
		Aircraft
		Radar communications
State and Local	Highway commissions	Health care items
	Health and social services	Food
	Schools and universities	Logistics
	Prisons	Equipment
	Police	Energy
	Libraries	Books
	Parks and recreation	Sports equipment
	Museums	Restoration

Figure 6.2   Types of B2B Markets

TYPES OF MARKETS

The business market is divided into the seven categories shown in Figure 6.2 and further described below. Each category is composed of organizations with similar business circumstances and general purchasing requirements.

Commercial The **commercial market** category consists of organizations that acquire goods and services that are then used to produce other goods and services, eventually creating finished products used by consumers. For example, Pulte, the nation's largest home builder, has hundreds of suppliers of construction products used to build houses. These, in turn, have other suppliers. All the marketing activities leading up to and including the sale of goods and services to Pulte are part of the commercial market.

Extractor The **extractor industries** category includes organizations that obtain and process raw materials, as in forestry or mining. Extractor companies are separated from the commercial segment because they acquire much of their supply from the earth, which requires expensive equipment such as drilling rigs and instrumentation. These industries consume a wide variety of products in vast quantities. Many of the companies in this category have global operations, such as Exxon-Mobil and BP.

The public is often especially demanding of extractor organizations to be environmentally sensitive, but this also provides these organizations unique opportunities to market ecological products. EnviroGroup is a firm that provides both consulting and testing services. Its expertise in vapor intrusion evaluation and mitigation helps clients deal with the technical, regulatory and risk communication challenges presented by vapor intrusion— an emerging focus of environmental agencies. With its expertise and advanced equipment, EnviroGroup manages environmental issues for clients worldwide.[2]

Trade The **trade industries** category is made up of organizations that acquire or distribute finished products to businesses or to consumers. It includes retailers, wholesalers and other intermediaries. These companies play an important role in the "place" component of the marketing mix. The importance of a reseller, a company that purchases a product and sells it in the same form for profit, has been gaining more and more recognition recently. The computer industry, for example, is now emphasizing the role of resellers in distribution and increasingly relies on them to install and service products, granting consumers the freedom to get computer maintenance at a location of their choice. Apple realizes the benefits of reselling and expanded its offerings to resellers by extending its build-to-order (BTO) capabilities to them, allowing customers to order custom-built computers from their preferred reseller.[3]

LARABAR products contain Fair Trade Certified coffee and cocoa.

In many cases, resellers repackage products to suit the needs of particular market segments. Humm Foods, the creator of LARABAR, uses Fair Trade Certified coffee and cocoa in its products. The certification ensures that the practice that goes into farming both coffee and cocoa "enables sustainable development and community empowerment by cultivating a more equitable global trade model that benefits farmers, workers, consumers, industry and the earth."[4]

COMMERCIAL MARKET

Organizations and individuals that acquire goods and services to produce other goods and services sold to an end consumer for profit.

EXTRACTOR INDUSTRIES

Industries that obtain and process raw materials.

TRADE INDUSTRIES

Industries comprised of organizations that acquire finished products and distributes them to others

INSTITUTIONS

Public and private organizations that provide services to consumers.

UTILITIES

Companies that distribute gas, electricity and water.

TRANSPORTATION & TELECOMMUNICATIONS

Companies that provide passenger and freight service and/or local and long-distance telephone service.

Institutions The **institutions** category covers public and private organizations that provide health, education and welfare services to consumers. It includes universities, hospitals, churches, nursing homes and museums. Institutional buyers purchase a broad range of products with funds of their own or from third parties, such as donors, insurance companies and government grants.

Institutions that rely largely or entirely on third-party funding must be especially prudent with their purchases, so potential suppliers need to take this into account when marketing to them. Solvay Chemical, for example, is a company that provides numerous chemical products for a number of industries including the pharmaceutical industry. In this industry, they provide products to hospitals and other businesses, requiring them to pay careful attention to the money they use so that they can charge accurate prices to their market.

Utilities The **utilities** category is composed of companies that distribute gas, electricity and water. Once highly regulated by the government, utilities now have the opportunity to operate more like private organizations. Public service commissions continue to provide oversight, however, because even private utilities are considered to be part of the public sector to some degree. Consolidated Edison and Florida Power & Light are huge buyers of business products. General Electric sells billions of dollars in nuclear fuel, power generation equipment and design services to public and privately owned utilities like Consolidated Edison and Florida Power & Light.

Transportation and Telecommunications **Transportation and telecommunications** make up another business market category. The transportation portion is composed of companies that provide passenger and freight service such as Union Pacific Railroad and United Airlines. Telecommunications companies supply local and long-distance telephone service as well as cable and broadcasting: CBS, AOL Time Warner and AT&T are some examples. Like utilities, this category was once subject to extensive government regulation that has been relaxed in recent years.

Although there are relatively few companies in this category, their purchases are huge. The cable and broadcast companies purchase satellite capacity, equipment and a huge range of services necessary to develop state-of-the-art telecasting.

GOVERNMENT MARKET

Market category including federal, state, and local government units.

Government Markets In the United States, the subdivisions in the **government market** category are (1) the federal government, (2) the 50 different state governments and (3) 8,700 local governments. Honeywell, a diverse company with many different services, markets to these government sectors by providing "government experts" to assist their customers with the challenges that come from navigating the demands of government while getting what they need.[5]

LARGE PURCHASES IN B2B MARKETS

Unlike B2C marketers, who sell a relatively small amount to a large number of buyers, business marketers choose to sell a large amount to a few customers. Often the price of a single item is high, like the cost of a corporate jet or a new information technology system for a company. In other cases, the buyer purchases a huge number of a lower priced item. For example, if EDS wins an order to replace computer work stations for a client, each work station might cost a little more than $1,000, but the total price tag could easily be several hundred million dollars. In some cases, these sales are great enough to affect the companies' stock price. For example, when FedEx bought $3.5 billion of Boeing aircrafts, it had to back out of a deal with Boeing's competitor Airbus. Boeing's stock price increased by five percent in a single day, a huge win for Boeing's marketing team.[6]

FedEx's Boeing aircrafts are large purchases in the B2B market.

BUSINESS MARKET LINKAGES: THE SUPPLY CHAIN

SUPPLY CHAIN

The linkage of organizations involved in the creation and delivery of a product.

TIER

The degree of contact between the supplier and the OEM.

The **supply chain** links organizations involved in the creation and delivery of a product. Figure 6.3 is a simplified diagram of the supply chain for automobiles. The original equipment manufacturer (OEM), such as Toyota, is in the middle of the chain, with supply activities occurring on both sides. In B2B marketing, the word "**tier**" refers to the degree of contact between suppliers and the OEM. For example, there are third-tier suppliers (extractors who process steel from ore), second-tier suppliers (manufacturers of components such as wiring), and first-tier suppliers (makers of computer chips). The first tier is a direct supplier to the OEM such as LEAR Corporation which sells sophisticated electronic systems to auto manufactures like Ford.

Supply chain management involves establishing or improving linkages to maxi-

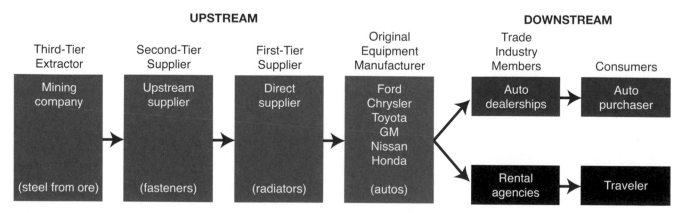

Figure 6.3   An Example of the Supply Chain in the Automotive Industry

mize efficiency and effectiveness. Marketers view the supply chain in terms of activities that need to be coordinated to provide the greatest value to the consumer, who is at the end of the chain. For example, UPS is more than a $50 billion company with an extremely successful supply chain that delivers goods to more than 200 countries worldwide. It developed a unified organization called UPS Supply Chain Solutions. This system offers logistics, global freight, financial, and mail services to improve customers' profitability.[7]

GLOBALIZATION OF BUSINESS MARKETS

Because strong business-to-business marketers realize their success is tied to their clients' success, there is a lot of potential for overseas marketing. Companies such as International Data Group (IDG), the world's leading technology media, events and research company, is capable of providing multi-country coverage. IDG Communications, a division of the company, has globally branded product lines that extend to over 280 million consumers in 97 countries. IDG marketing services connect tech buyers and sellers around the world.[8] Global brand identity is as important in B2B marketing as in consumer marketing. JP Morgan, a highly recognized financial services firm in the United States, launched a global branding campaign to expand its customer base to include younger, high-tech and web-based firms.[9]

Organizational Buying

BUYING DECISIONS

Businesses decide whether to buy from suppliers or make the product in-house. When businesses decide to use a supplier, they then determine the best choice among competitors. Business consumers have to make many decisions about their own plan and potential suppliers before selecting one.

MAKE OR BUY DECISION

The decision whether to supply products in-house, or to purchase them from other businesses.

OUTSOURCING

Purchasing products and services from other companies.

The Make or Buy Decision The **make or buy decision** occurs when an organization determines whether to supply products or services in-house (the make decision) or to buy them from other businesses (the buy decision). The buy decision results in outsourcing from a supplier, which allows the buying company to focus on investments and its core business. An organization must evaluate its need for direct control over production or quality, and the costs associated with supplying internally versus externally. Other issues include supplier reliability, design secrecy and workforce stability.

The Outsourcing Decision **Outsourcing**, the purchasing of products and services from other companies, has become widely popular. In fact, Dun & Bradstreet estimates that outsourcing is now a $4 trillion a year business globally.[10] Of the 300 largest global companies, about three-quarters use it as a strategy. The Global Outsourcing 100 listed in Fortune magazine are judged on four key characteristics: size and growth, customer references, organizational competencies, and management capabilities. Headquartered in Denmark, ISS is currently ranked as the best outsourcing service provider in the world.[11] It offers a wide range of services including facility management, cleaning, support, property management and maintenance,

Courtesy of ISS

ISS offers outsourcing services like facility management, cleaning, property management and security.

TYPE	DESCRIPTION	PEOPLE INVOLVED
Straight rebuy	Reorder from current supplier	One purchasing agent
Modified rebuy	Evaluate alternative suppliers of a product purchased before or a new or different product from a current supplier	Purchasing agent plus one or a few others
New task	First-time purchase of a product	Many people from several areas of the organization

Figure 6.4   Organizational Buying Situations

catering, and security. To do this on a global scale, ISS will outsource to organizations that can do a job better, faster, cheaper, or all three. It also looks to outsourcing partners to become a source for innovation and to help create new ways of improving business.[12] Outsourcing reduces need for in-house expertise and cuts costs, allowing companies to focus resources on primary business activities. Essentially, this allows B2B buyers to extend their enterprise by using the specialized talents and resources of suppliers.

Outsourcing may involve the purchase of a product on a routine basis, after evaluating a current product or supplier, or when purchasing a product for the first time. These three kinds of situations—straight rebuy, modified rebuy, and new task situations—are summarized in Figure 6.4. A **straight rebuy** is a purchase that the organization is very experienced at making, to the point of routine. For example, an exclusive furniture manufacturer may purchase leather for its sofas from only one supplier, which has a reputation for the highest quality. The two organizations have done business for years, and the manufacturer has made hundreds of purchases. In this case, a buying decision may take less than a week and involve only one or two people from each organization. In fact, it's normal for a purchasing agent to handle the entire transaction.

Suppose that the furniture manufacturer is dissatisfied with the leather supplier or doesn't want to depend on only one. A **modified rebuy** situation involves purchasing a familiar product from an unfamiliar supplier or a new product from a familiar supplier. A modified rebuy usually requires more personnel, time and energy.

Finally, let's say the furniture manufacturer decides to add a line of fabric sofas. This **new task situation** involves purchasing an unfamiliar product from an unfamiliar supplier. Because there is a great deal at risk, many people will likely provide input to the decision process, which may take several weeks, months or even years.

Competitive Bidding Some organizations use competitive bidding, especially for larger purchases. They want to get the lowest price rather than establish long-term relationships with suppliers. Most government purchases are required by law to use competitive bidding. Many companies, such as General Motors, have purchasing rules that require a minimum number of bids—usually three—for certain types of purchases. Even these companies will often make exceptions, as long as all parties agree and the justification is documented. In straight rebuy situations in the private sector, competitive bids are seldom required. Since both modified rebuys and new task situations often involve unfamiliar suppliers, bidding is likely to take place with either. In any of these cases, if the amount is very large, then the bidding procedure will probably be used.

Competitive bids may be sealed or negotiated. For the sealed bids, each seller is given a request for quotation (RFQ), which describes all of the product and purchase specifications. The responses are due on a given date, when envelopes are opened, and the lowest bidder is awarded the order. Negotiated bids are much more flexible, often allowing suppliers to be present and to comment on the results.

STRAIGHT REBUY

A routine purchase with which the organization has considerable experience.

MODIFIED REBUY

Purchase of a familiar product from an unfamiliar supplier or a new or different product from a familiar supplier.

NEW TASK SITUATION

Purchase of an unfamiliar product from an unfamiliar supplier.

Web Auctions For competitive bidding, the auctions need to have enough bidders in the same place at the same time. The internet has solved this problem, as there is no need for bidders to meet together physically; they simply need to be online while the auction is in process. Web auctions are conducted online and match buyers and sellers around the world. They are powerful and efficient to both buyers and sellers on two levels. First, they provide in-depth information that enhances bidders' understanding of the products. Buyers are more comfortable and feel that they can properly assess the products when they have adequate time to research. The fact that sellers, on average, obtain higher winning bids from web auctions than other formats is telling of the buyers' comfort levels. The second is that the web can increase the numbers of bidders. This helps the seller, leading to a higher winning bid. It also helps prevent an auction failure; when bids do not meet a designated price, the seller can later agree to accept a lower bid.[13] eBay has more than 145 million buyers and sellers on its online marketplace—the world's largest—which keeps competition healthy. In Q1 2016, the company reported $20.5 billion in total value of successfully closed transactions. Many of these buyers and sellers are B2B companies.[14]

LO03 STEPS IN THE ORGANIZATIONAL BUYING PROCESS

An organization may go through eight different stages when making a buying decision, but every purchase does not require all of them. New task situations may involve all eight, modified re-purchases fewer, and straight re-purchases the fewest. The eight possible steps in the organizational buying process are shown in Figure 6.5.

Problem recognition occurs when the buying organization realizes that a situation can be improved by acquiring a good or service. Potential problems include unsatisfactory materials, mechanical failure, or development of a new product that requires new equipment. The organization identifies the characteristics needed from the new product such as reliability, price, range and durability. Next, the organization prepares product specifications, which are usually technical and very detailed: precise dimensions, tolerances, quantity or the objectives of a consultant's study are included.

Unless it has been decided to make the product in-house, the search for suppliers now begins. Some may have been involved in the previous stages, but the organization usually looks for more to be certain no options are missed and to encourage price competition. New products and straight rebuys are both sought as necessary. During the proposal solicitation and supplier selection stage, the buying organization invites bids and assesses these according to the criteria set forth in the specifications. The lowest price usually wins, especially in the government sector, but such considerations as a reputation for quality and reliability may enter as well.

Figure 6.5 Steps in the Organizational Buying Process

When a supplier has been selected, the buying organization negotiates the final terms of the agreement, called order routine specifications. At this point, fine-tuning of the agreement may occur. During the purchase and use of product stage, the buyer signs the contract, takes the delivery and begins to evaluate whether the product does the job as anticipated. At this point, follow-through by the seller is critical to resolve any problems that may arise. The final step is performance review and feedback. After making a formal analysis, the buyer lets the supplier know how well the product meets the needs of the organization.

As the buying organization moves through this process repeatedly, creeping commitment may occur. If there is consistent satisfaction with a seller's products, the two parties may begin to build a lasting relationship. In that case, the buying process becomes simpler for both organizations, as modified or straight rebuys are more likely.

LO 04

RELATIONSHIPS BETWEEN BUYERS AND SELLERS

Relationships grow in phases as the buying and selling organizations learn to work together. A marketer that understands the buyer's strategies, problems, and opportunities can help the company become more competitive. "With knowledgeable professional buyers, multiple decision makers, and fewer overall customers to choose from, B2B marketers have a more complex task than many realize," commented Nick Kaczmarek of Dow Chemical. Marketers who effectively understand buying organizations are considered valuable members of their customers' supply chains.

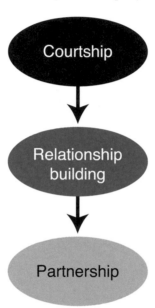

Figure 6.6   Building B2B Partnerships

Business relationships are not established overnight. It may take weeks, months or even years for the companies to understand and trust each other. There is a typical process involved (as illustrated in Figure 6.6) that consists of three phases: the courtship phase, the relationship-building phase, and the partnership phase. For example, a first-time customer of UPS will purchase only a few of their warehousing or shipping services. As the business comes to realize that UPS services are core aspects of the buyer's ability to satisfy its own customers, it purchases more services. Over time it is not unusual for UPS to supply all of a buyer's warehousing and transportation needs. UPS's high-technology information systems are not the only reason; UPS works to understand each customer's business thoroughly. This means that strategies and plans must be shared freely, and the client must trust UPS to keep them confidential. In many cases, UPS even helps customers develop the strategies and plans.

The Courtship Phase During courtship, purchasers express their desires to sellers. This phase often begins when a seller is placed on the buyer's approved supplier list, which means it meets at least minimum standards. The criteria usually include financial health, size, licensing qualification, and delivery capabilities.

Unlike many people, businesses tend to look before they leap. Each company is trying to understand the other's requirements, so there are many discussions about product specifications, product design and order routines. After what can be a great deal of time, the social distance begins to narrow. Often the buyer will grant the supplier a small order to test the waters, including the response to any problems that occur. In addition, the effectiveness of a solution depends on a customer's willingness to adapt to a supplier's offerings, and share relevant internal operations and political considerations with a supplier.[15]

Courtesy of UPS

UPS attempts to build relationships that might someday turn into partnerships.

The Relationship-Building Phase

The buyers and sellers work together for the first time in the relationship-building phase, which strengthens the bond between them. Unlike consumer marketing, business-to-business marketing tends to involve customizing the product, its delivery and its terms and conditions to each individual buyer. Buyers often grow to rely on suppliers for additional expertise, especially regarding new technologies. That is why trust, loyalty and compromise become so important in organizational buying activities. Due to the complexity and technical nature of most organizational purchasing, buyers and sellers must learn to work together, sometimes even adjusting their own internal practices to better satisfy the other's needs. Understanding the customer—and *its* customers—is critical.

During the relationship-building phase, the purchasing organization does not always have the upper hand. In fact, the relationship is sometimes said to be symmetrical, which occurs when the buyer and the seller have equal power.[16] Both frequently feel a very strong need to interact in order to explore all options before signing a contract, especially if they are considering a formal partnership. Sellers generally offer information to help buyers formulate ideas about the purchase decision, while buyers provide information that helps the sellers do a better job of matching products to needs.

The Partnership Phase

After several purchases have been completed satisfactorily and long-term agreements are reached, the partnership phase begins. Because the buyer and seller have extensive experience with each other, they spend less time on the relationship itself and more time on ways to improve the productive aspects of the exchange, until it becomes routine. The seller may become an exclusive supplier or blanket orders may guarantee that the buyer will purchase a certain amount within a certain period.

The seller can commit resources to the buyer because it is assured that the business relationship will continue. Chrysler, for example, gets 70 percent of the value of its vehicles from its regular suppliers. Jeffrey Trimmer, formerly director for operations and strategy in the Chrysler Group Procurement & Supply Organization at DaimlerChrysler, says that the company's challenge is how to continue with its suppliers while using the internet to facilitate that relationship and to identify and foster technology developments.[17] In many cases, computerized order entry systems are developed to link the buyer with the seller's manufacturing facilities. Nearly all big box retailers like Walmart give suppliers such a link. Vender-managed inventory, or VMI, is an order entry system that allows suppliers to monitor inventory and replenish stock without prior approval from the retailer. Through this close relationship with its suppliers, Walmart and other big box retailers can keep costs down and speed product distribution to avoid lost sales.[18]

Sometimes business relationships become permanent. For example, in 2004, NBC and Vivendi Universal Entertainment combined to create NBC Universal. While this was the start of their official partnership, the two companies had worked together for decades, starting with the 1950 television premiere of "Stars Over Hollywood." Since then, the two companies have collaborated to produce hit television series such as "Miami Vice," "30 Rock" and "The Office." The company also owns and operates numerous cable channels, motion picture companies, and branded theme parks. The newest theme park, "The Wizarding World of Harry Potter," brings the magic of the screen to real life with a full-scale Diagon alley, complete with store fronts, Gringotts Bank, and other familiar haunts from the mind of J.K. Rowling. This long-lasting relationship has helped enhance NBC Universal's platform as one of the leading media and entertainment companies worldwide.[19]

Hogwarts Castle at NBC Universal's "Wizarding World of Harry Potter."

Ethics and Business Relationships Unethical decisions can have a destructive effect on business relationships. Purchasing agents are often very familiar with the trade secrets, production plans and technologies of sellers. Misuse of this information has both ethical and legal implications. Employees may have trade secrets that need to be protected even if the employee takes a job with a new company. A former Intel employee, for example, was recently given a sentence of up to 20 years in prison for fraud due to taking trade secrets with him as he moved to Advanced Micro Devices, Intel's main competitor. While in the process of transferring from Intel to AMD, Biswamohan Pani accessed data from Intel about one of its microprocessors. The value of the material he was found guilty of illegally accessing was between $200 and $400 million.[20]

Coca-Cola concentrate contains the company's most important secret ingredients, hidden behind the general term "natural flavors."

Turning over trade secrets to a competitor is a serious breach of ethics with numerous repercussions. It tarnishes reputations, requires time and money in legal disputes, and creates friction between the buyer and supplier. An individual who steals and betrays company information may face serious criminal charges. Consider former employees of Coca-Cola that conspired to sell trade secrets to rival Pepsi for $1.5 million. They were discovered and exposed in an undercover sting by the FBI and ultimately had to pay fines in excess of $40,000 and were sentenced to serve eight- and five-year federal prison sentences.[21] Coca Cola goes to great lengths to protect its trademarked secret formula. Coca-Cola archivist, Phil Mooney, says "The formula for Coca-Cola may be the most closely guarded secret in the history of American commerce." The most important part of the Coca-Cola formula, the concentrate, is so secret it is unknown where it is produced. Even bottling plants are unaware of the ingredients contained in the concentrate.[22]

FUNCTIONS INVOLVED IN BUSINESS PURCHASES

Many employees are important to the purchasing process. Because of their different functions, they do not have the same motives for purchasing and do not use the same criteria. This section highlights functions most often involved in organizational buying: purchasing agents, functional managers, and the buying center.

Laterally, people at about the same level of management but from different functional areas (such as purchasing, engineering, production, sales and marketing) may take part in a purchasing decision. Although their status is roughly similar, each has a particular area of expertise and influence. Imagine that several vice presidents meet to select a strategic marketing consultant. Comments by the vice presidents of manufacturing and purchasing are certainly valuable, but the vice president of marketing probably will have the most influence on the final decision.

Vertically, people at different management levels within one functional area may participate in a buying decision. For example, the need for a new piece of equipment may be pointed out by a production floor worker to the foreman, who relays this to the production manager. The production manager seeks approval from the plant manager. If the purchase is costly, then the vice president of manufacturing or even the company president might be involved. If not, then the production engineer may have authority to approve the purchase.

Purchasing Agents Purchasing agents help buy a broad range of products most effectively. They establish and enforce purchase procedures, negotiate, and interact with suppliers. Through training programs, purchasing agents can learn how to obtain the best delivery schedules, prices and financing, while still meeting product specifications.

Purchasing agents are extremely important executives in some major corporations. In others, they simply process procurement requests. This function has received more attention in recent years, partly because of restricted supply in some industries and a greater general recognition of the cost savings from effective purchasing. College programs emphasizing the buying function have been developed, and graduates with this specialized education are finding increasing opportunities in global purchasing.

Functional Managers Functional managers have a position in a specific operational area of the buying organization. At one time or another in their career, most will be involved in negotiations to buy equipment or supplies. Typically, they come from the following areas:

- Administration (including accounting and finance): Help evaluate the cost effectiveness of projects.

- Design engineering: Buy equipment and material for products the company is marketing.

- Research and development: Look at basic materials and supplies rather than specific applications.

- Manufacturing: Often responsible for production equipment and processing approaches.

- Technical specialists: Advise others regarding the best brands and suppliers for a particular product type.

BUYING CENTER

The group of people from the buying organization who make a purchase decision.

The Buying Center A group of people in the organization who make a purchase decision form the **buying center**. These people may play one of six important roles: gatekeeper, information seeker, advocate, linking pin, decision maker or user. It's important to note that buying center membership changes, depending on the type of purchase being considered. Often the selling organization that wins the order is the one that has made contact with each of the buying influencers. Figure 6.7 depicts the buying center roles.

Figure 6.7 The Buying Center

GATEKEEPER

A person within the buying center who controls the flow of commercial (outside) information into the buying organization by screening all potential sellers and allowing only the most qualified to have access to decision makers.

Gatekeepers A **gatekeeper** controls the flow of commercial (outside) information into the buying organization. Purchasing agents have been referred to as gatekeepers because they are often the first people that sales representatives contact. They are responsible for screening all potential sellers and allowing only the most qualified to gain access to key decision makers. When dealing with unique or complicated products, a specialist can serve as the gatekeeper. For example, the head of engineering may recommend that only suppliers with which the company has a working relationship should be contacted for engineering consulting services.

Experienced salespeople and gatekeepers will make efforts to understand each other and their organizations, and they will take action in the best interests of both. If the relationship is cooperative, a gatekeeper can efficiently direct a salesperson to the appropriate decision maker.

GATEKEEPER
I control flow of outside information by screening commercial contacts with other members of the buying center.

Information Seekers A great deal of information about products, competitors and suppliers is required for major purchases. **Information seekers** locate data that they or others can use during the purchasing process. Often the purchasing department is responsible for obtaining lists of firms or alternative types of products, but this task can also be performed by others. Think about the fundamental changes technology has brought to business-to-business marketing. Virtually every company in the world maintains a website to provide information about itself. The web can satisfy some of an information seeker's needs in only seconds.

INFORMATION SEEKER

A person within the buying center who locates data that can be used during the purchasing process.

INFORMATION SEEKER
I locate data about products, competitors, and suppliers to be used during the purchasing process.

The role of an information seeker differs from that of a gatekeeper. The former looks for sources of information, whereas the latter tends to reject sources of information and limits the number of people and companies allowed access to the buying firm. Naturally, marketers can make the job of the information seeker easier by clearly presenting relevant product data in an accessible way.

ADVOCATE

A person within the buying center who exercises a powerful influence over group decisions.

Advocates The **advocate** exercises a powerful influence over buying center decisions. Advocates are the most active participants in group discussions, have high status and play a leadership role. They often obtain their power from the amount of interaction they have with outside organizations and from their expertise on particular topics. Advocates sometimes use their position to inhibit the communications (or recommendations) of less powerful people in the organization. Thus, they may support one seller's offering while restricting the influence of competitors' presentations. Consequently, sellers often seek high-status, knowledgeable and articulate people within the buying organization to help promote their products. If salespeople are to succeed, then one or more advocates must take their side during purchase deliberations.

ADVOCATE
I provide group leadership to support (or not support) specific solutions and suppliers.

LINKING PIN

A person within the buying center who establishes contact among functional areas within the buying organization.

LINKING PIN
I establish contacts among functional areas involved in the buying center.

Linking Pins Contact among the functional areas involved in a buying center is provided by **linking pins**. Linking Pins are employees who have the confidence of management and work on teams. Teams are linked together by people, who are members of more than one team. People in more than one group are called "linking pins." They are particularly important to marketers of products that require cooperation among several parts of the buying company, such as electronic data-processing and telecommunications equipment. Linking pins communicate with one another both formally and informally. In many cases, information from the seller to one linking pin is then spread throughout the buying organization. A cooperative linking pin makes the seller's job easier, so savvy sellers try to endear themselves to earn approval from the linking pin(s) in an organization who can help their cause.

Decision Makers Sometimes it is difficult for the seller to identify **decision makers**, the people with authority to make or at least approve the purchase decision. It is also hard to determine when the decision is actually made. Often the selling organization wins enough support from the buyer to obtain the order by building the relationship over time, which is called creeping commitment. In competitive bidding situations, the decision to purchase occurs when the envelopes are opened. In these cases, however, much depends on how the specifications are drawn up in the first place. Some salespeople work closely with the buying organization at that stage to tilt the specs and ultimate decision in their favor.

DECISION MAKER

A person within the buying center who has the authority to make or approve a purchase decision.

DECISION MAKER
I have the authority to make or approve purchases.

Often the salesperson can identify exactly who will make the buying decision. In some organizations the decision maker is the purchasing agent. In most cases, however, the choice is made by a buying committee or by someone who has budgetary authority and long-term experience with the product. Salespeople are invited to make a presentation or to supply information so that the committee or a committee member can decide.

Users Users purchase and operate the product in question. In manufacturing firms, for example, they are the employees who operate or service production equipment. When components are purchased, the **users** assemble the parts. In hospitals and other health care facilities, users may be nurses, physicians or the technicians who operate medical equipment. In other professional organizations, they may be programmers or technical support staff who interface with computers. There are almost as many types of users as there are job descriptions, and their influence on the purchasing process varies.

USER

A person within the buying center who actually uses the product.

USER
I actually use the product, initiate purchasing changes and provide feedback.

Users with a high degree of expertise may help develop product specifications. They are especially important in the last phase of the buying process, follow-through. The sophisticated salesperson values user feedback, in turn providing them with information to make the product function as smoothly as possible.

The decision-making process of the buying organization is affected by a number of factors including background of buying center members, information sources, product factors, company factors, joint decisions and conflict resolution.

INFLUENCES ON ORGANIZATIONAL BUYING BEHAVIOR

The buying process is seldom the same from one firm to the next, or even from one purchase to the next within a given firm. In each case, the decision-making process of the buying organization is affected by a number of factors.[23]

Background of Buying Center Members The background of the buying center members affects the buying process. Purchasing agents, engineers, users and others in the organization have expectations that are formed largely by their experiences. These expectations, in turn, influence the criteria used for decision making. Specialization has a great deal to do with how people look at problems. Engineers, for instance, are highly trained in technical areas and are likely to judge a product accordingly, while financial managers are inclined to evaluate products on the basis of profitability.

Role orientation, which refers to the way people see themselves, is also a factor. Position or rank within the organization obviously can have an effect—one vice president among several lower-level managers has a stronger say in buying center decisions. Finally, personal characteristics play a role. The lifestyles, interests, activities and general opinions of buying center members affect the buying process.

Information Sources Organizational buying is influenced by the sources of information: salespeople, exhibitions and trade shows, direct mail, press releases, journal advertising, professional and technical conferences, trade news, word of mouth and others. Like direct selling, exhibitions provide one-on-one contact with a company's target audience. Although sales calls generally reach only a small number of potential customers each day, exhibitions can reach dozens more each hour.

The internet is particularly significant in business-to-business marketing. Websites enable organizations to promote brand values, reduce printing costs, attract and qualify prospects and leads, and foster customer loyalty. Sites also can expand the customer database, provide customer service, showcase and sell products.

Product Factors: Time and Risk Product and company factors tend to influence the organizational buying process. **Product factors** include time pressure and perceived risk. Time pressure relates to the speed with which a purchase must be made. When several members of the buying organization are involved in the decision, more time is required to make it. Perceived risk refers to what can be lost rather than gained when making the purchase.

Five types of uncertainty or risk aversion have been identified among buying organizations:

1. *Acceptance uncertainty:* Buyers are not sure of their need for a product.
2. *Need uncertainty:* The buying organization has not yet established product specifications.
3. *Technical uncertainty:* Buyers are unsure about the performance of a product in their own particular environment.
4. *Market uncertainty:* Buyers are unsure of the possible offerings from which they can select.
5. *Transaction uncertainty:* Buyers are unsure about the terms of the sale and product delivery.

When uncertainty is high, buyers strive to reduce perceived risk by either purchasing less or learning more. Decreasing the amount at stake means smaller orders or a reluctance to pay top prices. When much is at stake, the risk of the purchase decision may affect others in the organization.

Company Factors Three company factors have particular influence on the purchasing process: the organization's orientation, its size, and its degree of centralization. An organization's orientation, or dominating function, is very important. Some companies are production oriented, others marketing oriented, while still others let finance or accounting control the decisions. When marketing dominates, sales factors tend to be very important in making purchase decisions. In production-oriented organizations, production factors are most important. In finance-oriented organizations, decisions are likely to be made on the basis of cost and other financial concerns. The seller must understand the organization's orientation in order to determine the basis for purchasing decisions and which members of the buying center are most influential.

The size of the organization is also likely to influence the number of people involved in purchasing. In very small companies, the purchasing process is typically informal, with the final decision made by a single high-ranking executive. Very large organizations use a formal purchasing process, and decisions are often made by members lower in the managerial structure.

Finally, highly decentralized organizations are likely to give various departments or divisions the autonomy to make their own purchases. Even these companies, requiring accountability, have formal buying procedures that can involve red tape.

Joint Decisions and Conflict Resolution Whenever several people are involved in decision making, there is a potential for conflict. Purchase decisions are no exception and can be affected by how conflict is handled. When it occurs, members of the buying organization negotiate with one another to arrive at a solution. These negotiations can be influenced by task or non-task motivation.

Task motivation refers to solving the organization's problem, whereas non-task moti-

PRODUCT FACTOR

A factor such as time or perceived risk that influences the organizational buying process.

vation refers to the personal needs of the buying group members. Organizations usually attempt to use problem solving and persuasion to make a decision in the company's best interest. Non-task-oriented approaches to conflict involve bargaining and politicking. Each party is attempting to "get its own way" without considering the organization's goals or engaging in open communication. Sellers who are sensitive to the prevailing negotiating mode can plan their approach accordingly.

PROBLEM SOLVING

A task-oriented method of conflict resolution whereby all parties agree to put the organization's goals first.

PERSUASION

A task-oriented mode of handling conflict in which persons with different goals attempt to convince the others that their goal should take precedence.

BARGAINING

A non task-oriented mode of handling conflict in which one person obtains his or her goal by agreeing to allow the other's goal to prevail at another time.

POLITICKING

A non task-oriented mode of handling conflict in which personal ego needs take precedence over problem solving.

Problem solving in the buying context occurs when all decision makers agree on the goals of the particular purchase. Sellers address those goals and show how their product can help meet them. The fact that all parties agree to this method usually indicates the process will be straightforward.

Persuasion occurs when buying center members do not agree on purchase goals, and each tries to convince the others that his or her own goals should take precedence. In the case of buying a computer, for example, the purchasing agent may consider cost most important, whereas a user may put software compatibility first. When the two discuss the merits of the various trade-offs, they are engaging in persuasion. The seller needs to understand both parties and address both sets of goals.

Bargaining occurs when people in the buying center cannot arrive at a solution. Through dialogue, one person may try to obtain his or her preferred product by agreeing that someone else can choose the supplier for a different product. The supplier needs to make sure to address all individuals who might ultimately be in a good bargaining position.

Politicking occurs when buying center members of the organization have strong ego needs. In their search for power or self-esteem, they place their own goals before those of the organization as a whole. Such people are looking for support rather than the most functional purchase choice. What usually results is a "pecking order" within the buying firm, in which an employee's influence on the purchase is proportional to his or her status in the company. The superiority of a product is irrelevant if a buyer's ego is more important to him or her. Sellers must be very sensitive to personalities if they wish to conduct business under this circumstance.

Chapter Summary

Objective 1: Describe the types of organizations and products involved in business-to-business marketing and understand the importance of this market.

A large number of companies sell most of their products to other companies, which is known as business-to-business marketing. In total volume, business-to-business marketing is much larger than consumer marketing. Types of business markets include the commercial market, extractor industries, trade industries, institutions, utilities, transportation and telecommunications, and government markets. These markets can be segmented according to company demographics, geographic scope, buying approach and product/technology. Multiple steps bring the final product to consumers as businesses sell materials and processes to each other along the supply chain.

Objective 2: Understand the link between consumer demand and business-to-business marketing.

Business markets rely on derived demand to create opportunities for their products. When consumers purchase more, businesses buy more in order to produce more. The demand for business goods and services tends to be inelastic, which means that a price change does not greatly affect the types of products purchased. The accelerator principle recognizes that some business goods and services are highly sensitive to changes in consumer demand.

Objective 3: Describe the organizational buying process.

Organizations make purchases to support their production requirements and business needs. Buying decisions often start with the make or buy decision. Decisional situations in outsourcing include straight rebuy, modified rebuy, and new task situations. The buying process can involve as many as eight steps: problem recognition, need description, product specification, supplier search, proposal solicitation and supplier selection, order routine specification, purchase and use, and performance review and feedback. Good buyer-seller relationships are key to facilitating the process.

Objective 4: Know how buyer-seller relationships work, including informal and contractual partnerships.

The buyer-seller relationship between businesses develops over time, usually in three sequential phases: courtship, relationship building, and partnership. During courtship, buyers express their desires to sellers, who, in turn, propose products to satisfy the buyer's needs. In relationship building, the two parties work together for the first time, customizing the product, its delivery and conditions. In the partnership phase, long-term agreements are reached either informally or contractually, and close cooperation develops lasting relationships.

Objective 5: Learn what functions and roles within organizations influence the purchase of a broad range of products.

Different functional areas may be involved in business purchases, ranging from operational units to a purchasing department. The group of people who make a purchase decision forms the buying center. Having different backgrounds and functions in the company, they have different buying motives and use different criteria in evaluating products. Purchase decisions may be made laterally, through the interaction of people from different functional areas, or vertically, at one or more levels in the corporate hierarchy. Various buying center members play different roles: gatekeeper, information seeker, advocate, linking pin, decision maker and user. It is important that the salesperson identifies exactly who will make the purchase decision, whether it is the purchasing agent, a buying committee or someone with budgetary authority.

Review Your Understanding

1. What is business-to-business marketing? How does it differ from consumer marketing?
2. List the types of business-to-business markets.
3. What is the supply chain? Give an example.
4. What is derived demand? Inelastic demand? How do they apply to business markets?
5. What are two ways globalization affects business marketing?
6. What is a make or buy decision?
7. What are three types of decisional situations in outsourcing?
8. What are the steps in the organizational buying process?
9. List the phases in buyer-seller relationships.
10. List six functions performed in the buying center.
11. What are purchasing agents? Functional managers?
12. List and explain five types of purchase uncertainty.

Discussion of Concepts

1. Why is business-to-business marketing larger than consumer marketing? Explain the process of business-to-business marketing.
2. The private sector is composed of several classes of organizations. List examples of these classes, along with companies in each, and explain their importance within business-to-business marketing.
3. Explain the accelerator principle and how it is used in to business-to-business marketing. Give an example.
4. When making a purchase, an organization generally goes through a number of steps. Describe these and explain why some purchases require more steps than others.
5. Describe an informal partnership and a contractual partnership. What are the advantages and disadvantages to both buyer and seller of each type? How does price-only purchasing come into play?
6. Why are many employees within a buying organization essential to the purchasing process? Explain the different levels of involvement in business purchases. What roles do purchasing agents and functional managers play?
7. Several roles that people play within the buying center are essential to the purchasing process. Define these and explain why they are necessary. Is one more important than the other? Which has the most influence on the purchase decision?
8. Numerous factors influence the buying process. Explain the relevance of each in purchase decisions.

Key Terms & Definitions

1. **Accelerator Principle:** A small increase or decrease in consumer demand has a larger effect on business demand.
2. **Advocate:** A person within the buying center who exercises a powerful influence over group decisions.
3. **Bargaining:** A non task-oriented mode of handling conflict in which one person obtains his or her goal by agreeing to allow the other's goal to prevail at another time.
4. **Buying center:** The group of people from the buying organization who make a purchase decision.
5. **Commercial market:** Organizations and individuals that acquire goods and services to produce other goods and services sold to an end consumer for profit.

6. **Decision maker:** A person within the buying center who has the authority to make or approve a purchase decision.

7. **Derived demand:** A demand, such as the demand for business-to-business products, which depends ultimately on the demand of end consumers.

8. **Extractor industries:** Industries that obtain and process raw materials.

9. **Gatekeeper:** A person within the buying center who controls the flow of commercial (outside) information into the buying organization by screening all potential sellers and allowing only the most qualified to have access to decision makers.

10. **Government market:** The federal, state, and local governments in their role as purchasers of goods and services.

11. **Inelastic demand:** Demand that is influenced little by price changes.

12. **Information seeker:** A person within the buying center who locates data that can be used during the purchasing process.

13. **Institutions:** Public and private organizations that provide services to consumers.

14. **Linking pin:** A person within the buying center who establishes contact among functional areas within the buying organization.

15. **Make or buy decision:** The decision to supply products in-house or to purchase them from other businesses.

16. **Modified rebuy:** Purchase of a familiar product from an unfamiliar supplier or a new or different product from a familiar supplier.

17. **New task situation:** Purchase of an unfamiliar product from an unfamiliar supplier.

18. **Outsourcing:** Purchasing products and services from other companies.

19. **Persuasion:** A task-oriented mode of handling conflicts in which persons with different goals attempt to convince the others that their goals should take precedence.

20. **Politicking:** A non task-oriented mode of handling conflict in which personal ego needs take precedence over problem solving.

21. **Problem solving:** A task-oriented method of conflict resolution whereby all parties agree to put the organization's goals first.

22. **Product factor:** A factor such as time or perceived risk that influences the organizational buying process.

23. **Straight rebuy:** A routine purchase with which the organization has considerable experience.

24. **Supply chain:** The linkage of organizations involved in the creation and delivery of a product.

25. **Tier:** The degree of contact between the supplier and the OEM.

26. **Trade industries:** Industries comprised of organizations that acquire finished products and distribute them to others.

27. **Transportation & Telecommunications:** Companies that provide passenger and freight service and/or local and long-distance telephone service.

28. **User:** A person within the buying center who actually uses the product.

29. **Utilities:** Companies that distribute gas, electricity, or water.

References

1. www.schooldata.com, website visited April 12, 2016.
2. www.envirogroup.com, website visited April 12, 2016.
3. www.apple.com, website visited April 12, 2016.
4. www.larabar.com, website visited June 14, 2016.
5. www.honeywell.com, website visited June 14, 2016.
6. Frost, Laurence/Associated Press, "National-World Business," The Albuquerque Tribune, November 8, 2006.
7. "Global Commerce and Transportation," UPS. www.ups.com, website visited March 13, 2016.
8. "Corporate Profile," IDG, www.idg.com, website visited March 13, 2016.
9. www.jpmorgan.com, website visited June 13, 2016.
10. "Outsourcing History," www.issworld.com, website visited June 13, 2016.
11. www.iaop.org, website visited June 13, 2016.
12. "Introduction to ISS," www.issworld.com, website visited June 13, 2016.
13. Hanson, Ward; Kalyanam, Kirthi, "Internet Marketing & e-Commerce," 2007, pg. 410; Milgrom, Paul, "Auction and Bidding: A primer," Journal of Economic Perspectives 3, Summer 1989, pg. 3.
14. eBay, www.ebay.com, website visited June 13, 2016.
15. Tuli, Kapil R.; Kohil, Ajay; Bharadway, Sundar G., "Rethinking Customer Solutions: From Product Bundles to Relational Processes," Journal of Marketing, Vol. 71, No. 3, July 2007.
16. Hakanson, Hakan; Wootz, Bjorn, "A Framework of Industrial Buying and Selling," International Marketing Management 8, 1979, pp. 39-49.
17. Kachadourian, Gail, "DCX Relies on Supplier Innovations," Automotive News, June 19, 2000, pg. 28.
18. www.vendormanagedinventory.com, website visited June 23, 2016.
19. www.nbcuni.com, website visited June 13, 2016.
20. Gareth Halfacree, "Ex-Intel engineer pleads guilty to IP theft," bittech, April 10, 2012.
21. Day, Kathleen, "Three Accused in Theft of Coke Secrets," Washington Post, July 6, 2006; "Two Sentenced in Coke Trade Secret Case," CNN Money, May 23, 2007.
22. "Coca Cola Trade Secrets" YouTube video featuring National Geographic, www.youtube.com/watch?v=MJ6wO5igfAI, website visited June 21, 2016.
23. Sheth, Jagdish N., "A Model of Industrial Buyer Behavior," Journal of Marketing 37, October 1973, pp. 50-58.

CHAPTER *07*

Creating Customer
Satisfaction
& **Loyalty**

THE RITZ-CARLTON®

You Tube SCAN & WATCH

The Ritz-Carlton holds impeccable standards and is a leader in customer satisfaction.

One of the world's most attentive companies to its customers is The Ritz-Carlton. Upon your first stay, you feel like you're the most important guest in the hotel. When you return, you'll feel like you never left. Everyone from the bellhop to the front desk clerk will address you by name. Requests and preferences from previous stays are carefully noted by employees in the company's sophisticated information technology system.

That means if you stay at a Ritz-Carlton in Seoul, South Korea, and request to have green tea and blueberry scones in your room, then when you visit a Ritz-Carlton anywhere else in the world, there will automatically be green tea and blueberry scones waiting in your room when you arrive. These small touches form a cornerstone of the Ritz-Carlton strategy.

Dedication to extraordinary customer service distinguishes the brand and continues to deepen its customer loyalty. The Ritz-Carlton has won the Malcolm Baldrige National Quality Award multiple times—only one other company has received this award more than once, and no other hotel has ever won it. Recently Ritz-Carlton was named to the Condé Nast Gold List 2016 and received the J.D. Power 2015 Luxury Travel Award. Its customer loyalty reputation also earned it a spot on Forbes' 2015's Brands With The Most Loyal Customers.

How has the Ritz-Carlton accomplished this success? It starts at the top, with a team of senior executives who meet every week to review quality issues. This includes the company's products, services, customer satisfaction, loyalty, growth, profits, and evaluation of the competition. In fact, Ritz executives spend 25 percent of their time working on quality-related issues. However, the ultimate responsibility for delivering customer value depends on its 32,000 employees who complete 120 hours of on-the-job training in their first year. Every employee is given a "preference pad" to record the personal preferences of Ritz customers. Employees record obvious guest requests like the type of room preferred, but they also catch smaller details like requests for down pillows, extra towels and whether the guest took apples or bananas from the fruit basket. This information is used to provide more personalized service to each customer during future stays.

The Ritz-Carlton Hotel's impeccable standards continue to make it an industry leader of customer satisfaction, repeat business and loyalty. With a customer satisfaction rate of 97 percent, it is a perfect example of how core values form a company's ethical foundation, as we discussed in Chapter 2. Consider the following Ritz-Carlton Credo to understand why customer service and satisfaction makes it one of the most customer-loyal brands in the world.

The Credo

The Ritz-Carlton Hotel is a place where the genuine care and comfort of our guests is our highest mission.

We pledge to provide the finest personal service and facilities for our guests who will always enjoy a warm, relaxed, yet refined ambiance.

The Ritz-Carlton experience enlivens the senses, instills well-being, and fulfills even the unexpressed wishes and needs of our guests.

Source: www.ritzcarlton.com, website visited June 19, 2016.

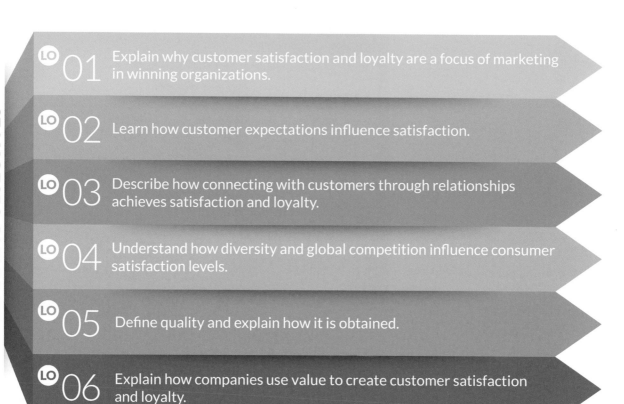

LO 01 Explain why customer satisfaction and loyalty are a focus of marketing in winning organizations.

LO 02 Learn how customer expectations influence satisfaction.

LO 03 Describe how connecting with customers through relationships achieves satisfaction and loyalty.

LO 04 Understand how diversity and global competition influence consumer satisfaction levels.

LO 05 Define quality and explain how it is obtained.

LO 06 Explain how companies use value to create customer satisfaction and loyalty.

LO 01

The Concepts of Customer Satisfaction & Loyalty

People have unlimited choices about where to spend their money. Ultimately, the decision depends on how much value they perceive they're getting for what they pay. Companies that consistently produce high value are likely to have satisfied customers who reward them with loyalty and repeat purchases. Winning organizations go to extremes to create customer satisfaction because they know that satisfaction leads to loyalty, which is the single most important factor in extraordinary business performance. And when it comes right down to it, satisfied and loyal customers are the key to sustainability and growth for any business.

Leading companies focus a good deal of effort on satisfaction and loyalty, but how do they achieve these two goals? The process begins with producing quality products that consumers want. When quality products perform as expected, a company creates value that leads to satisfaction. Remember that satisfaction doesn't rest on value in product performance alone; customers have to feel they're getting value from their entire purchase experience. From the first contact with a representative or salesperson, all the way through to customer support and service after the sale, the customer must be satisfied if loyalty is to develop.

A significant amount of marketing research is dedicated to measuring customer satisfaction and loyalty because customer satisfaction ratings are an especially useful indicator of an organization's performance. In fact, surpassing a competitor in satisfaction ratings is often a strategic objective.

What is customer satisfaction and loyalty? What is value and quality? How do relationships and technology affect these factors? As a marketer, you need a strong foundation in these concepts and this chapter will give you a good start. It begins by exploring the importance of satisfaction and loyalty. Next, we look at how customer expectations affect satisfaction and then we tie all of these elements together by describing how relationships promote satisfaction and loyalty. By the end of the chapter, you'll realize that satisfaction and loyalty usually go hand in hand, and companies prosper as a result.

Key Aspects of Satisfaction and Loyalty

CUSTOMER SATISFACTION

A customer's positive, neutral, or negative feeling about the value received from an organization's product in specific use situations.

Customer satisfaction is a customer's positive, neutral or negative feeling about the value received from an organization's product in specific use situations. In the past, product innovation was the major way to gain a competitive edge. Now, new products are copied by rivals, often within a few weeks or months, and the life span of new products is declining rapidly. Thus, organizations need to look beyond the immediate sale and focus on achieving the highest level of customer satisfaction if they want loyal customers and repeat business. Favorable satisfaction ratings not only boost sales but can also have a dramatic effect on overall company performance.[1]

Customer loyalty refers to how often, when selecting from a product class, a customer purchases a particular brand. Customer satisfaction is a critical ingredient in building loyalty, and loyalty is essential to the long-term survival of an organization. It is estimated that companies lose 10 to 30 percent of their customers annually, and even more in the online world.[2] At this rate, few firms can achieve acceptable volume or profit without a strong base of loyal buyers. This is the point of the "80/20 Rule." The "80/20 Rule" is a well-known guideline used by marketers for growing their businesses by con-

CUSTOMER LOYALTY

A measure of how often, when selecting from a product class, a customer purchases a particular brand.

centrating on their most lucrative customers. It suggests that 80% of a company's profits are generated by 20% of its customers.[3] When marketers can identify the characteristics of the 20% of customers who are generating the 80% of sales, it knows its target market. It then looks for more customers with the same characteristics to further increase sales. This 20% of satisfied, loyal customers helps a company's performance because these customers provide on-going sales and referrals to increase revenues, they are less concerned about price because they like the company, and they help reduce the organization's costs because little advertising is required to keep them aware of the brand. One study found that a one percent improvement in customer retention will improve firm value by five percent.[4] Therefore, a company's top 20% of customers is golden!

Sales to Increase Revenues The revenue stream from one lifetime customer can be tremendous. A loyal buyer of Starbucks may spend thousands of dollars, and a corporate buyer of Boeing aircraft equipment may invest billions of dollars. When you view the amount a customer buys over the lifetime of a relationship, you can see why customer retention is vital to an organization's prolonged success. In fact, many organizations develop compensation systems that offer pay incentives to executives and employees who contribute to customer satisfaction and loyalty.

Courtesy of Amazon

Jeff Bezos, founder of Amazon.com, says:
"If your brand is based exclusively on price,
you're in a fragile position..."

CUSTOMER LIFETIME VALUE (CLV)

The amount of profit a company expects to obtain over the course of a customer relationship.

COST STRUCTURE

The amount of resources required to produce a specific amount of sales.

CUSTOMER EXPECTATIONS

Consumer beliefs about the performance of a product based on prior experience and communications.

The importance of satisfied customers for revenue generation is magnified by their influence on other buyers. If a typical customer purchases a new car once every four years and influences one new buyer each year, the loyal, satisfied customer can be worth nearly $1 million in revenues and more than $100,000 in profit. Some companies calculate the **customer lifetime value (CLV),** which is the amount of profit an organization expects to obtain over the course of a customer relationship. For example, assume you are a marketing manager for a large bicycle equipment manufacturer. One of your customers, Trek, purchases about $80,000 in equipment each month. If Trek becomes dissatisfied and selects another supplier, how much will it cost your company? At $80,000 per month for 12 months, Trek purchases $960,000 annually. Assuming you earn a profit of 15 percent, that equals $144,000 per year. Over two decades, your company would forfeit more than $2.8 million in pure profit and $19.2 million in revenue. If the same problem that dissatisfied Trek results in the defection of other key customers, you face huge losses.

Less Concern About Price Customer satisfaction has become a key to making sales at appropriate prices. Jeff Bezos, founder of Amazon.com, commented on the role of price: "We're known for competitive prices....that's very important online. But we're also known for great customer experience and great customer service. If your brand is based exclusively on price, you're in a fragile position, but if your brand is about great prices and great service and great selection, that is a much better position."[5]

Essentially, creating satisfied customers through service and experience is often more important and successful than trying to create satisfied customers through price. In general, customers are willing to pay more because they are certain that the higher price is due to extra value or benefits. Consider the frequent traveler who chooses to fly United, even if it charges more for a particular route, because he wants to accumulate enough miles in his Mileage Plus account to become a Platinum member and get free upgrades. Or the businesswoman who always rents from Hertz because she likes to choose which car she takes from the Gold Plus Rewards aisle. Loyal customers such as these are less reactive to price increases. They'll stay with a company because they perceive a benefit from it. The result is higher profit margins for the company.

Reducing Organization Costs The percentage of loyal, satisfied customers is a very important determinant of an organization's costs and revenues. In addition to generating sales, loyal customers affect the **cost structure**, which is the amount of resources required to produce a specific amount of sales. Depending on the industry, the cost of acquiring a new customer is usually five to 25 times more expensive than keeping an existing one.[6] In fact, loyal customers are often responsible for a company's seemingly disproportionate amount of profit. Loyal customers don't require high costs to retain, and they are likely to either demonstrate or tell others about their satisfaction with the company, prompting them to give the company a try. Some of these first-time purchasers may become loyal customers and, in turn tell others.

CUSTOMER EXPECTATIONS

Customer expectations play an important role in determining satisfaction. **Customer expectations** are consumer beliefs about the performance of a product based on prior experience and communications. A consumer will be dissatisfied with a company that falls short of expectations, but delighted with one that exceeds them. In both cases, customers are emotionally charged by their experience; the delighted are more likely to be loyal, and the dissatisfied are more inclined to switch.

Customer expectations are based on personal experience, observation of others, company actions, advertising and promotion. Customers also expect companies to offer services to support their purchase decisions. For example, because it is difficult for people to assess the quality of products in a catalog, companies such as Williams-Sonoma and Crate & Barrel make it easy for people to return products that do not meet their expectations. Some companies even offer free return shipping when a customer isn't pleased with a purchase.

Higher and more varied expectations result when competition is intense. One Starbucks customer found the company pulling out all stops when a licensed store, not corporate owned, refused to honor a 10 percent corporate discount. Angered, he called Starbucks customer service and explained his frustration to the corporate representative. The representative told the customer he wanted to "make me whole, and give me an experience nothing short of fantastic." Expecting a free drink coupon, the customer was floored when he was mailed a $50 Starbucks card.[7]

A company benefits from exceeding customer expectations, but it also raises those expectations for the future. Similarly, each change in product, price, promotion or distribution can affect expectations. Companies have both competitors' efforts and consumer expectations to exceed, and it is a challenge to continually win over consumers without raising their expectations to unrealistic levels.

CUSTOMER DEFECTIONS AND COMPLAINTS

CUSTOMER DEFECTIONS

The percentage of customers who switch to another brand or supplier

Organizations look at **customer defections,** the percentage of customers who switch to another brand or supplier. Customer satisfaction often creates loyalty, but loyal customers are not always highly satisfied, and satisfied customers are not always loyal. In some cases, customers continue to purchase a brand that doesn't fully meet expectations because defecting would be difficult or an alternative would be no better. In other cases, satisfied customers defect because they simply want to try something new. Consumers have degrees of satisfaction; they may be pleased by some aspects of a product, but not others. One study showed that 40 percent of all customers, though satisfied, would be willing to switch to a competitor, whereas highly satisfied customers are much less willing to do so.[8] The point is that just focusing on satisfaction isn't enough. You must build a bond of loyalty based on a relationship.

Figure 7.1 illustrates that, in a classic study completed in Sweden, 65 percent of customers defect primarily because they are dissatisfied with the way they are treated and 15 percent defect because of dissatisfaction with the product itself.[9] The remaining defect because they prefer a different product or for unrelated reasons. As this study indicates, treating people with respect is especially important when attempting to win their loyalty. The positive consequences of loyal customers can be seen everywhere and range by industry. A study by Temkin Group revealed that TV and internet service providers have very few loyal customers in comparison to retailers and hotels. Companies such as DirectTV or Comcast would likely experience fewer defections if more emphasis was put on building a valuable relationship with its customers.[10]

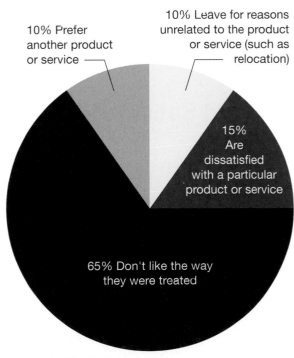

Figure 7.1   Why Customers Leave
Source: Eugene W. Anderson, Claes Fornell and Donald R. Lehmann, "Customer Satisfaction, Market Share and Profitability: Findings from Sweden," Journal of Marketing 58 (1994): 53.

Companies committed to customer satisfaction will deal with any complaints they receive in a way that still leads to overall satisfaction. On average, nine of every 10 customer problems that are discovered and resolved immediately will result in satisfaction and loyalty, with seven of those 10 customers willing to do repeat business with a company that makes a clear effort to resolve a problem. In fact, the average customer will tell five people about an effectively resolved problem, but may inform nine to 20 people about a negative experience or poor service.[11] This suggests that customers who complain and receive satisfactory attention are often more satisfied than those who don't complain at all.

Companies that respond to customer feedback and complaints are rewarded with customer loyalty and repeat business. They create a relationship through customer service. Companies that don't often do more harm than simply losing a customer. Perhaps you remember Dave Carroll, a young musician, who created the now-iconic "United Breaks Guitars" YouTube video after United Airlines damaged his Taylor guitar and would not address his claim and numerous complaints. The video quickly spread and is nearing 16 million views today. After the video went viral, United Airlines realized its mistake. It tried everything in its power to get Dave to remove the video, even offering him payment. The company's reaction was too late for Dave, though. He proceeded to post two additional YouTube videos that would further tarnish the airline's reputation and stock price.

"United Breaks Guitars" is the result of United Airlines refusal to address Dave Carroll's claim and complaints.

In retrospect, the entire situation could have been avoided if United Airlines had simply responded to his initial complaint. Instead, United lost a customer for life, and its image was tarnished with each YouTube hit. Taylor Guitars, on the other hand, seized the marketing opportunity to increase its sales by cleverly using the video to promote its brand through social media. It also rewarded Dave with a brand new Taylor guitar. To see the video, go to YouTube and search for "United Breaks Guitars" or scan the QR code on the left.[12]

LO 03 Relationships Build Satisfaction & Loyalty

Just a few years ago, marketers were content to sell to new customers with the goal of increasing sales faster than competitors. When one company's sales rise faster than all others, that organization's market share increases. Today, most companies realize that customer loyalty may be far more important than just market share.

When you decide that you like a product, you tend to buy it repeatedly, recommend it to friends, and endorse it through social media. The product becomes sort of a fixture in your life. It can be something as small as a favorite brand of coffee, or a computer, or a vehicle. Very few organizations can survive without loyalty and repeat business from customers. If an organization is forced to rely on single transactions, its costs escalate, and in many cases the company fails. Even companies that market products bought once in a lifetime depend on loyalty. The hospital that markets its heart surgery capabilities relies on positive word-of-mouth from loyal customers. Likewise, a Harley-Davidson dealer that sells a customer that one and only "dream machine" still builds the relationship after the sale. The customer tells friends and other prospective buyers of the experience, and they develop a positive perception of Harley Davidson's customer relations.

In 1983, Harley established the Harley Owners Group (H.O.G.) for Harley riders across the nation to share their passion and pride for their Harleys. Today, there

Harley has built incredible relationships and loyalty through the Harley Owners Group (H.O.G) which has over a million members worldwide.

are over a million H.O.G. members worldwide.[13] How many companies have relationships so strong that consumers are willing to tattoo the brand or logo on their bodies, as thousands of devoted Harley customers have done? While few companies connect with their customers to the extent of Harley-Davidson, it's clear that an effective connection creates a personal bond.

That's what Harley-Davidson wants. When you buy a Harley, your new motorcycle is cleaned and polished to perfection. Your salesperson makes sure to take time, without interruptions, to discuss all of the features of your new purchase and answer any questions you may have. Typically, a personal phone call from your salesperson, followed by a letter, provides the initial follow-through to begin furthering the relationship.

For a different demographic, BabyCenter.com, a one-stop shopping and information website for expectant and current mothers, allows users to set up personalized profiles with their children's names and birthdays. This allows the company to track demographic information and email relevant information regarding products, child development and safety to the parent, all based on the child's birth date. Therefore, just before a child's birthday, BabyCenter.com automatically emails the mother about an appropriate and exciting birthday gift or about an important developmental milestone, increasing the probability that the mother will remain a customer.

CREATING A PERSONAL RELATIONSHIP

By its very nature, a relationship reflects the personal connection between two or more parties. While the core concept of marketing is to address customer needs and wants, marketers should seek to go beyond a minimalist effort and produce customer satisfaction and loyalty. Although not every customer seeks a relationship with every purchase, establishing one is typically the best way to address needs and wants. Involvement with customers is key in relationship marketing. More and more companies are embracing social media as a primary means to build relationships with customers. Proper social media management will enhance trust, increase communication and feedback, and develop a personal relationship that provides an emotional con-

BUILDING SOLID RELATIONS FOR LASTING SUCCESS

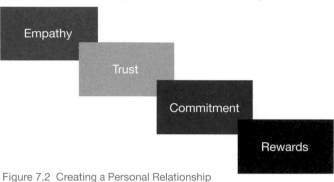

Creating A Personal Relationship

Empathy

Trust

Commitment

Rewards

Figure 7.2 Creating a Personal Relationship

nection. Figure 7.2 lists empathy, trust, commitment and rewards as important aspects of creating personal relationships, which is true whether we are looking at consumer, B2B or other markets.

Empathy Empathy is the ability to put yourself in someone else's shoes, or from a marketing position, to understand the perspective of a consumer or another organization. Companies that build effective relationships and create inviting cultures often dedicate extensive marketing research to understanding consumers. But empathy works best when customers know that they are understood—that the organization has accurate knowledge of their circumstances. Marketers communicate this empathy in nearly everything they do. For example, when a customer calls a pharmacy to renew a prescription but doesn't have the prescription number, the pharmacy can either look up the number or tell the customer they can't do anything without it. Pharmacies that willingly research the number are customer oriented. They demonstrate empathy by going the extra mile to find the prescription number.

In addition to showing empathy through customer service, companies can also do so by being compassionate about the environment. A company's efforts to reduce its harmful impact on the environment show consumers its concern for the well-being of the community. Apple strives to preserve the earth by limiting environmentally harmful compounds, such as elemental forms of bromine and chlorine, in its materials and manufacturing processes. Even the aluminum enclosures on the popular MacBook Pro and other products are toxin-free and highly recyclable. Apple's packaging designs use post-consumer pulp fiber and vegetable-based inks. Even iTunes gift cards are made from 100 percent recycled paper. The steps Apple is taking to provide a greener environment for its customers helps it form a long-lasting personal relationship with consumers.[14]

Trust Trust is being able to rely on another party to perform as promised in the way you expect. The communications of marketers are filled with promises. According to recent study, when customers trust a brand, 83 percent will recommend the company to others and 82 percent will continue to use that brand.[15] Like people, companies that keep promises earn trust. Providing great service, being transparent, and remaining consistent also help to build trust. These are tremendously important elements in building lasting connections with customers.

Commitment Commitment occurs when companies go out of their way to deliver beyond what they promised in order to ensure customer satisfaction. When things go wrong, they work hard to fix them. This is particularly critical to relationships over time. For example, The Home Depot pledges to help its neighbors in troubled times with its "Team Depot." The company partnered with the American Red Cross to provide assistance in nearby communities to prevent disasters. The three-year joint venture is a $6.6 million program to teach one million people about emergency preparedness. The companies also work together if a disaster

After a tornado outbreak in Texas, "Team Depot" pitched in to deliver necessities like water and supplies, board up broken windows, clear debris and fix fences.

occurs. After one recent tornado outbreak in Texas, hundreds of Team Depot volunteers pitched in to deliver necessities like water and supplies, board up broken windows, clear debris and fix fences. The Home Depot is deeply committed to its communities and customers, thus forming a trusting relationship.[16]

Rewards Relationship marketing creates connections that make it unnecessary or difficult for customers to switch to competitors. It rewards loyalty. In order for relationship marketing to work, companies must understand customers so well that competitors have little chance of new or unique offers that would entice a trial. This means that companies must be willing to provide superior value for their best customers. Louise O'Brien and Charles Jones, vice presidents with the successful consulting firm, Bain & Company, say that if companies want to realize the benefits of loyalty, they must admit that "all customers are not equal ...a company must give its best value to its best customers. That is, customers who generate superior profits for a company should enjoy the benefits of that value creation. As a result, they will then become even more loyal and profitable."[17]

Starbucks is attempting a slight variant on this approach with its customer loyalty program, "My Starbucks Rewards." You earn one Star every time you pay with your Starbucks Card or the new mobile app, and as you collect Stars, you move up to bigger benefits. A few Stars can earn you free refills on brewed coffee and tea or free flavored syrups. With more Stars, you can receive a Personalized Gold Card and special offers via email.[18]

Courtesy of Starbucks

Starbucks' mobile app allows you to collect and manage your rewards with your smartphone.

DIVERSITY, GLOBAL COMPETITION & SATISFACTION

The diversity of tastes and preferences presents opportunities for customer-centered marketers. Diversity helps explain why companies with the highest overall sales sometimes have lower satisfaction ratings than smaller companies. The latter can design products and services for very narrowly defined segments and can focus all of their attention on those customers. These companies may have lower market share but score high satisfaction points with a select few customers. As companies gain share by selling to more people, their products and services must appeal to more diversified customers with a broader range of expectations, something that requires a great deal of flexibility. Achieving satisfaction in the face of growth requires using the broadest range of marketing tools and techniques. If an organization expects impressive satisfaction scores, then it must understand all forms of diversity better than even its smallest competitors.

The success of a product or service in one market segment will not automatically transfer to consumers in another segment. The diverse nature of consumers makes universal buying preferences and behaviors very unlikely. Companies such as Coca-Cola, McDonald's, Apple and J.Crew address the individual wants and needs of people by acknowledging their unique differences. Attention to the diversity of consumers is often reflected in better market share and product sales. When McDonald's expanded to the Philippines about 25 years ago, few expected the local, Jollibee fast-food chain to survive. However, Jollibee reacted by first copying McDonald's business model and then tailoring its menu to better serve the preferences of the local market. It introduced a slightly sweeter hamburger,

Jollibee tailors its menu to appeal to the preferences of the local Filipino market.

a Philippine-style Burger Steak with rice, and a kids spaghetti plate. Today, Jollibee is the widest store network in the Philippines with over 900 locations, and it has even opened 34 stores to compete with McDonald's in the United States.[19] Its success in the U.S. is largely due to strategic placement of stores across California and other areas with a high concentration of Filipinos.[20]

Groups based on ethnicity have such tremendous buying power that marketers have begun to recognize the advantages of addressing each group individually, to the point where many organizations have departments and positions for this very purpose. At Kraft, for example, there is a director of ethnic marketing. Today, most of the largest firms in the United States have created diversity management positions in an effort to modify corporate culture to reflect the growth of minority segments.

The success of global companies is highly dependent on customer satisfaction. Throughout the 1960s and '70s, domestic firms dominated the U.S. market. By the early '80s, U.S. businesses were under the false impression that they could sustain success without making any major adjustments, which led to the neglect of changing customer needs and satisfaction. Many foreign companies spotted this weakness and entered U.S. markets quickly, putting great stock in customer satisfaction. Some of the strongest U.S. companies saw their market shares plummet because foreign rivals gained strong customer satisfaction ratings. Honda and BMW are examples. These foreign competitors raised consumer expectations for quality and speed of service to new levels and often at substantially lower overall prices. Essentially, foreign competitors created new levels of customer satisfaction in the U.S. market.

Quality Creates Satisfaction & Loyalty

Quality can be a catalyst for companies trying to create customer value. Overall, products are getting better and more functional, while costs are staying the same or even decreasing. Leading companies know they have to deliver quality products to stay competitive in the marketplace and keep customers satisfied. In this section we'll look at how some successful organizations focus on quality to ensure customer satisfaction and loyalty.

QUALITY & SATISFACTION

QUALITY

The degree of excellence in a company's products or services.

Quality describes the degree of excellence in a company's products and services. It is an essential component to achieving customer satisfaction and loyalty. As such, companies known for quality are very consistent in their products as well as in their customer service.

Patagonia is a good example. If you own Patagonia gear, you will undoubtedly notice the quality woven into each garment. Many customers find themselves so devoted to the gear they have a hard time disposing of it even after it has been damaged or worn. Suppose your favorite Patagonia fleece has traveled to many parts of the world with you, including a thru hike along the Appalachian Trail. The fleece that has

patagonia.com

BETTER THAN NEW

You[Tube] SCAN & WATCH ▶

Patagonia offers garment repair services to fix your favorite worn or torn item. Watch this YouTube video to see stories of why Patagonia goods are so loved.

shared your life passions of traveling and adventure, and given you warm hugs for months on a trail, may well become an emotional attachment. This is how Patagonia has been able to use quality as a distinguishable asset to secure customer loyalty.

In many markets, quality is so important that if products do not meet a certain standard, they simply won't have a chance of succeeding in the market. As more companies build quality into their products, quality alone ceases to provide a differential advantage. Quality has become a more complex concept. For some time, many consumers bought Japanese cars because they were perceived to be of much higher quality than U.S. brands. Today, most experts believe that U.S. vehicles are equal in quality to Japanese cars and that U.S. manufacturers are even beginning to take the lead in new areas of quality, such as design and performance. Luxury automobiles like Jaguar are often perceived as quality vehicles, but a quick look at Consumer Reports might find the repair record below average, indicating poor quality to some people.

SUBJECTIVE ASSESSMENT OF QUALITY

The degree to which a product does what consumers expect it to do.

OBJECTIVE ASSESSMENT OF QUALITY

An evaluation of the degree to which a product does what it is supposed to do.

Assessments of Quality

Subjective assessment of quality indicates to what degree the product does what consumers expect it to do. After an extensive review of a number of studies, one expert defined quality as "the consumer's judgment about a product's overall excellence or superiority."[21] From this perspective, different groups may evaluate quality altogether differently. When asked, adults may say Wendy's is higher in quality than McDonald's, whereas children may have the opposite response. Health-conscious people might rate both items as low in quality. We all want quality goods and services, but each of us may view quality as being slightly different. Our perceptions of quality can shift depending on circumstances, preferences and tastes.

Suppose you have the opportunity to eat at Wolfgang Puck's legendary restaurant *Spago*. Eating a gourmet meal at the premier five-star restaurant, you will likely view quality differently than you would at McDonald's. In this case you might define quality by uniqueness, superior ingredients, and variety. Restaurants such as *Spago* take a very different path than McDonald's to achieve their standard of quality.

Objective assessment of quality indicates to what degree the product does consistently what it's supposed to do. If you get an urge for a Big Mac® and can even taste its flavor in your mouth, then you might define quality by consistency. Have you ever wondered why McDonald's Coke tastes better than other restaurants? There are many conspiracy theories believing Coca-Cola provides an exclusive formula or a secret ingredient like cinnamon. However, McDonald's follows the guidelines set by Coca-Cola, but implements them with meticulous detail in each location to ensure consistency. Water and syrup are pre-chilled before entering fountain dispensers with the ratio of syrup set to compensate for melting ice. McDonald's drinks are run through proper filtration, and the wider straw is intended to allow the flavors to hit all of your taste buds. With hamburgers and soft drinks, it's possible to develop objective assessments of quality in the form of standards, such as fat and salt content or amount of carbonation and syrup ratio. McDonald's has perfected consistency to such a degree that we perceive it as quality.[22]

Even objective assessments are open to interpretation, particularly in a global setting. For example, German and Japanese products are manufactured to precise

ExpyB / CC BY-SA 3.0

Customers tend to rate Coca-Cola at McDonald's high in quality due to objective assessment.

specifications and will not perform in excess of their rating. If a product is rated to lift 1,000 kg, it will do precisely that and no more. In contrast, a similar U.S. product in some cases has a safety factor of 1.5, so the product will lift 1,500 kg. The extra capacity is a sign of quality in the United States but not in many other markets. Consequently, even measures of so-called objective quality are created in response to the subjective desires of various groups.[23]

Static and Dynamic Quality There are two other ways to categorize quality. **Static quality** results when an accepted practice is perfected. Many companies have processes designed to produce items to given quality standards that approach perfection. **Dynamic quality** results when a major change makes the existing standard obsolete. For example, Kodak once dominated the photography and film business by continually improving its extremely high-quality 35mm film. As consumers shifted to digital cameras and film became obsolete, Kodak's efforts to achieve static quality became irrelevant. A revolution had taken place as digital camera companies created value through change, a dynamic quality shift. Time will tell if hand-held digital cameras will face a similar shift with the increased camera technology and popularity of smartphones.

Focusing activities on static quality can divert resources from new ventures, and there seems little point in perfecting technology that is about to become obsolete. At the same time, dynamic quality shifts cannot be forced; the technology needs to be ready and the market prepared. The task falls to marketers to discover what will be new and relevant, and what customers consider to be high quality. Marketers develop estimates of what attributes customers use to define quality, what quality standards must be met, and what various segments are willing to pay for quality.

User-submitted Quality and Satisfaction Ratings You may not consider product ratings on Amazon or other retail sites as "satisfaction ratings" or "quality ratings," but in fact these ratings can contain both. Think about the last time you shopped on Amazon or a website containing user ratings. Did these ratings impact your purchase decision? Chances are they did...either consciously or subconsciously. User ratings can have a huge impact on product sales and can also affect the brand itself. A product seen with only a few "stars" on Amazon can impact a company much more than the product itself. It is easy for consumers to assume that one poorly rated product can mean the entire brand is poor in quality, satisfaction and service.

Online product reviews, which were popularized by companies like Amazon, can offer a level playing field for unbiased viewpoints on a product or service. While they can open the door for unwanted negative publicity, they can also offer introspective feedback and offer a touch point for companies to address problems they might not have been aware of. This creates an avenue to improve products and interact with customers.

As you might know, user reviews are not always reliable and don't always reflect the actual quality of the product. Negative reviews are sometimes written by disgruntled customers, who may have had a bad experience with shipping, a missing part, or trouble with assembly of the product. We also know there are perceptions of quality that may play a role. For instance, suppose someone purchases a Bluetooth speaker for ten dollars and reviews the product with one star, citing poor sound quality. Another person might purchase the same product for their child (who

shutterstock.com / kasahasa

User-submitted ratings can be unreliable when rating quality and satisfaction.

STATIC QUALITY

Quality that results when individuals or organizations perfect an accepted practice.

DYNAMIC QUALITY

Quality that results from a change that makes an existing standard obsolete.

might not care about the sound quality) and review it with five stars, citing excellent design.

Another reason ratings or reviews are unreliable is because of fakes. Teams of people are sometimes hired to write unethical or dishonest reviews to boost the ratings of products. A recent study by Best Reviews, which looked at 488 different products listed on Amazon, discovered that nearly 240,000 of the 360,000 users gave the products a five-star rating.[24] This would be a difficult feat for almost any single product, if all respondents were verified purchasers. Google Play Store and Apple App Store have similar issues. Both of the companies use ranking algorithms that place apps with better scores higher on the charts. According to Cult of Mac, app developers looking to get a boost in ratings and rankings can find services claiming to offer a guaranteed five-star rating or a week in the App Store's Top 10 for around $65,000 per week.[25]

QUALITY AWARDS

To encourage companies to improve their quality and competitiveness, various governments have established awards for companies with the most outstanding quality initiatives. Two very distinguished annual awards are the Deming Prize in Japan and the Malcolm Baldrige National Quality Award in the United States. Other companies use these award winners for benchmarking their own operations. **Benchmarking** is the systematic evaluation of the practices of excellent organizations to learn new and better ways of serving customers.

The Deming Prize Everyone has heard of quality inspectors—people who examine finished products as they roll off the assembly line and remove defective goods before they are sold to customers. In the early 1900s, most companies used inspectors as their main source of quality control. Little or no effort was devoted to correcting the manufacturing problems that caused product defects.

In the 1950s, Dr. Edward Deming took a new approach to the issue. He applied the idea of **statistical quality control**, a concept he learned while a statistician at AT&T's Bell Laboratories, to manufacturing. Statistical quality control involves using statistics to isolate and quantify production line problems that may cause defects, improving the overall process, not just the final product. The Japanese openly embraced Deming's philosophy, and this is viewed by many as one of the reasons for Japan's tremendous economic success during the 1970s and '80s. Deming's work transformed Japan from the maker of inferior products to one of the most powerful economies in the world. To honor Deming's contributions, the Japanese created the Deming Award as their highest recognition of quality.

To help business managers implement quality initiatives within their organization, Deming outlined 14 key points, listed in Figure 7.5. Deming insisted, moreover, that top management be involved and supportive. If quality initiatives receive only lip service, without action, they will not be successful.

BENCHMARKING

The systematic evaluation of practices of excellent organizations to learn new and better ways to serve customers.

STATISTICAL QUALITY CONTROL

The use of statistics to isolate and quantify production line problems that may cause product defects.

EDWARD DEMING'S 14 POINTS OF QUALITY

1. Create constancy of purpose for improving products and services.
2. Adopt the new philosophy.
3. Cease dependence on inspection to achieve quality.
4. End the practice of awarding business on price alone; instead, minimize total cost by working with a single supplier.
5. Improve constantly and forever every process for planning, production and service.
6. Institute training on the job.
7. Adopt and institute leadership.
8. Drive out fear.
9. Break down barriers between staff areas.
10. Eliminate slogans, exhortations and targets for the workforce.
11. Eliminate numerical quotas for the workforce and numerical goals for management.
12. Remove barriers that rob people of pride of workmanship, and eliminate the annual rating or merit system.
13. Institute a vigorous program of education and self-improvement for everyone.
14. Put everybody in the company to work accomplishing the transformation.

Figure 7.5   Edward Deming's 14 Points of Quality
Source: Adapted from The New Economics for Industry, Government, Education by W. Edward Deming, by permission of MIT and The W. Edward Deming Institute. Published by MIT, Center for Advanced Educational Services, Cambridge, MA 02139. ©1993 by the W. Edward Deming Institute.

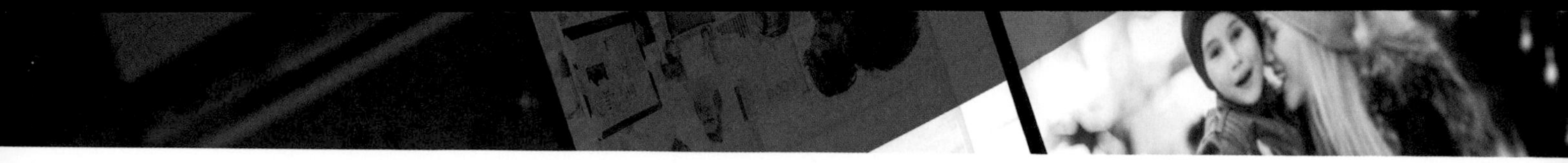

The Malcolm Baldrige National Quality Award U.S. businesses have been late to emphasize quality. During the same period that the Japanese excelled in implementing quality initiatives, U.S. firms slipped dramatically in quality. Congress finally moved to establish a quality award for U.S. firms, named after the late Malcolm Baldrige, an advocate for quality and a former secretary of commerce. While considering the passage of the Malcolm Baldrige National Quality Improvement Act, the U.S. Senate Committee on Commerce, Science and Technology observed: "Strategic planning for quality improvement programs is becoming more and more essential to the well-being of our nation's companies and our ability to compete effectively in the global marketplace. Such an award would parallel the prize awarded annually in Japan."[26]

The 1987 legislation was enacted by Congress to encourage U.S. businesses and other organizations to practice effective quality control in the production of goods and services. At the time of its passage, the Senate and House produced a declaration reiterating the need for an incentive program for U.S. businesses and affirming that these businesses had been considerably challenged by foreign competitors. Slow growth in productivity had, in some industries, resulted in annual losses of as much as 20 percent of sales revenues. It was evident that U.S. businesses needed to learn more about the importance of quality.

The **Malcolm Baldrige National Quality Award** is widely acknowledged as having raised quality awareness and practice among U.S. companies. Some consider the Baldrige an important catalyst for transforming U.S. business because it promotes quality excellence, recognizes achievements by companies that effectively improve quality, and supplies a guideline that business, industry, government and others can use to evaluate their quality improvement efforts.

A key criterion that winners must meet is "customer-driven excellence." Performance and quality are judged by the organization's customers. Thus, the organization must take into account all product and service features, and figure out how to best present them to provide customer value. This leads to customer acquisition, satisfaction, preference, referrals, retention, and loyalty. Customer-driven excellence means much more than reducing defects and errors, merely meeting specifications, or reducing complaints. In addition, *how* organization responds to product defects, service errors, or mistakes is crucial for retaining customers and building customer relationships."[27]
Figure 7.6 lists companies that have most recently received the Malcolm Baldrige Na-

MALCOLM BALDRIGE NATIONAL QUALITY AWARD

A program designed to raise quality awareness and practice among U.S. businesses.

MALCOLM BALDRIGE NATIONAL QUALITY AWARD WINNERS

2008	Poudre Valley Health System	**2011**	Concordia Publishing House
	Cargill Corn Milling North America		Henry Ford Health System
	Iredell-Statesville Schools		Schneck Medical Center
2009	Honeywell Federal Manufacturing & Technologies		Southcentral Foundation
	MidwayUSA	**2012**	Lockheed Martin Missiles and Fire Control
	AtlantiCare		MESA Products Inc.
	Heartland Health		North Mississippi Health Services
	VA Cooperative Studies Program Clinical Research Pharmacy Coordinating Center		City of Irving, Irving, TX
		2013	Pewaukee School District
			Sutter Davis Hospital
2010	MEDRAD, Warrendale	**2014**	PricewaterhouseCoopers Public Sector Practice
	Nestlé Purina PetCare Co.		Hill Country Memorial
	Freese and Nichols Inc.		St. David's HealthCare
	K&N Management, Austin		Elevations Credit Union
	Studer Group, Gulf Breeze	**2015**	MidwayUSA
	Advocate Good Samaritan Hospital		Charter School of San Diego
	Montgomery County Public Schools		Charleston Area Medical Center Health System
			Mid-America Transplant Services

Figure 7.6   Winners of the Malcolm Baldrige National Quality Award

THE RITZ-CARLTON

The Ritz-Carlton is the only two-time Malcom Baldrige National Quality Award winner in its service category.

tional Quality Award.

The Ritz-Carlton Hotel Company was an award winner in 1992 and 1999, making it the only two-time winner in its service category.[28] The Ritz-Carlton's quality success comes from its dedicated focus on customer service. Its outspoken goal is to "Understand Customers in Detail" by relying on extensive data gathering and the dissection of key points where customer satisfaction problems generally occur. The Ritz-Carlton maintains a database of almost a million customer files, which enables hotel staff to anticipate needs of returning guests and to make sure in advance that requests are honored.[29]

LO 06 Creating Satisfaction & Loyalty Through Value

Customer-centered marketing requires the development of unique competencies to satisfy customers within selected target market segments and to build their loyalty. Many parties are involved in creating customer satisfaction and eventual company loyalty. Additionally, to improve customer satisfaction and loyalty, leading-edge companies operate ethically to fulfill commitments and involve employees and customers in performance-improving efforts.

EMPLOYEE & CUSTOMER INVOLVEMENT

It's difficult to imagine making customers satisfied without having employees who are highly involved in the process. In turn, satisfied employees are much more likely to produce satisfied customers than are disgruntled employees, so the organization itself needs to ensure that employees feel appreciated. Strong companies involve the entire organization and its customers in efforts to improve performance in ways that will promote customer satisfaction. IBM integrates customers into its improvement planning process by inviting consumers from around the world to give direct input to top-level strategic planners. Executives at Procter & Gamble take time to interview consumers at grocery stores and answer customer service calls, while Hewlett-Packard recruits customers to assist in developing new products. All of these companies demonstrate how interaction between consumers and an organization's employees help ensure that the customer is a primary focus.[30]

The job of satisfying consumers cannot be left to the marketing or sales manager alone. Achieving customer satisfaction is nearly impossible without a well-defined process for focusing the entire organization on the customer. As with the most important marketing functions, everyone must participate, from top management to the workers on the factory floor. In fact, most companies that are serious about improving satisfaction consider it critical to involve their top managers. They sit in on meetings about customer satisfaction and demand that everyone "walk the walk"—not just discuss issues, but develop plans to address them. Compared to other organizations, managers in these companies spend more time talking with customers, and compensation structures often are based more on satisfying customers than on meeting short-term financial goals. Furthermore, all functional areas are involved in customer satisfaction, including marketing, sales, engineering, accounting and purchasing. Other channel members, such as manufacturers' representatives, wholesalers and distributors, are often part of the effort. The result is a customer-centered organization working to create satisfied purchasers.

The biggest mistake most companies make is to assume they know what their customers want without asking them. Unfortunately, most companies that guess do so incorrectly. For a true understanding of what consumers want, a company must establish a dialogue with not only current customers and those who have defected, but those of competitors and other potential purchasers. One way to achieve involvement is through formal marketing research, such as interviews or surveys. Another way is through social media channels. It's enlightening and invaluable for marketers to read what consumers are saying to other consumers about their companies. Several industry leaders astutely include customers on their product planning teams.

INTEGRATED SUPPLY CHAIN

SUPPLY CHAIN

All the activities that organizations undertake to deliver value to the customer, such as working with suppliers and distribution through convenient channels.

The **supply chain** is composed of all the activities that organizations undertake to deliver value to the customer, such as working with suppliers, and distribution through convenient channels. A simple supply chain starts by identifying customer needs. Most people seek products that perform as desired, portray the image they want, are easy to purchase and are priced fairly. Companies then identify the process required to deliver this value and ensure that each step of the process is carried out in quality fashion.

Many activities contribute to the process of achieving customer satisfaction. These include the procurement of raw materials as well as the manufacture and delivery of products to retailers and others in the channel of distribution. All functional areas — purchasing, operations, manufacturing, marketing, sales, and so on — are involved in delivering customer value and must clearly understand the customers of the final product. Many separate organizations may be involved in the process as well, and the respective organizations need to empathize with each other and the final customer.

Although customers have very little knowledge of these activities, they shape the quality of goods and services as well as the price that will be charged in the marketplace. For example, Banana Republic's customers want a quality product at a reasonable price, so Banana Republic takes that into account when considering the costs of manufacturing locations. In the same manner, the cost of Banana Republic's raw materials, its ability to deliver products efficiently to retail outlets, the effectiveness of its research and development, and many other activities affect the overall quality of the goods and services the company can provide to its customers. Even the quality of the commercials and print ads are important, since they largely shape the image of the

Banana Republic's competitiveness depends to a great degree on its ability, and the ability of its suppliers and distributors, to perform well on all the factors that influence the amount of value delivered to the marketplace.

brand. Banana Republic's competitiveness depends to a great degree on its ability, and the ability of its suppliers and distributors, to perform well on all the factors that influence the amount of value delivered to the marketplace. All organizations in the chain must behave with the intent of creating satisfaction for others in the chain in order for consumers to benefit to the greatest degree possible.

MONITORED SATISFACTION RATINGS

SATISFACTION RATINGS

Ratings provided by testing agencies that compare purchase and/or performance satisfaction of specific products or market segments.

Because satisfaction contributes so much to the success of an organization, it is no surprise that marketers are very interested in measuring satisfaction. **Satisfaction ratings** provide a way for consumers to compare brands, enable testing agencies to determine how well products perform, and allow companies to monitor how satisfied consumers are with their goods and services.

You may have used a rating system to help choose a smartphone, an insurance policy or even a college. Consumers have been sensitized to the importance of satisfaction by publications like Consumer Reports, which routinely rates many products, and Motor Trend, which rates autos. In the smartphone industry, J.D. Power and Associates' annual U.S. Wireless Smartphone Satisfaction Study measures factors like performance, physical design, features, and ease of operation. In 2016, Apple devices rank highest in overall satisfaction among Sprint, T-Mobile and Verizon Wireless wireless customers, while Samsung devices rank highest among AT&T customers.[31]

The American Consumer Satisfaction Index (ACSI) is a quarterly rating that measures customer satisfaction in seven sectors of the economy broken down into 10 economic sections.[32] Even the U.S. government has entered the scene by sponsoring the Malcolm Baldrige National Quality Award, which is given to outstanding U.S. firms based partially on customer satisfaction.[33] We will discuss this award in more detail later in the chapter.

Competitive advantage is earned by companies that anticipate and adjust quickly to market forces. In Chapter 3 you learned that environmental scanning is one way companies learn about forces that might affect their businesses. Another important source of information is feedback from customers about their experience with a product or service. A **customer satisfaction measurement program** is an ongoing survey of customers (and competitors' customers) for the purpose of obtaining estimates of satisfaction. Simply looking at sales data can tell us whether more or fewer products are purchased, but it doesn't reveal much about underlying reasons for behavior. Consequently, in addition to sales data, companies should measure customer satisfaction and loyalty rates. Marketers must not only measure their own company's performance but also that of their competitors. A company can work hard to build relationships through consumer satisfaction, yet it may still lose customers if a competitor suddenly improves its customer relationships through value and performance...sometimes in the form of guarantees.

CUSTOMER SATISFACTION MEASURE-MENT PROGRAM

An ongoing survey of customers (and competitors' customers) for the purpose of obtaining estimates of satisfaction.

The best consumer satisfaction program in the world is worth very little unless it feeds into the strategic and operational planning of the company. Customer feedback about satisfaction levels is shared with employees in all departments so they can make internal adjustments to improve overall company performance. Functions at all levels of the organization must be willing to work toward the common objective of satisfying customers. One of the most important aspects of a marketing executive's job is to motivate the entire organization to focus decisions and actions on improving customer satisfaction.

ETHICAL CONSIDERATIONS

A company's relationship with consumers doesn't end with the purchase of a product. In fact, it's just beginning. Once a consumer uses a product, he or she will either be satisfied or dissatisfied with the purchase. Satisfaction levels depend on expectations. For example, if a customer buys a gym membership, and everything about her experience with the membership is great, then she is satisfied with her purchase decision. If the gym changes its operating hours, stops offering the SPIN class she really likes and expected, and frequently has inoperable equipment, then she will be disappointed with her purchase decision. When performance matches or exceeds customer expectations, satisfaction levels are high. Conversely, when performance does not match expectations, dissatisfaction occurs.

When selling products, companies have an ethical responsibility to accurately represent a product and its capabilities. Overselling a product will lead to dissatisfaction and returns. If a salesperson says a print cartridge will last for 1000 copies, but it runs dry after 400, customers are dissatisfied and feel they've been misled. Either the salesperson wasn't trained properly, or the company is sharing wrong information. Either situation involves unethical behavior.

But when a product has been represented properly and customers purchase it based on real expectations, what happens when things go wrong? Many organizations that promise satisfaction and quality believe they have an ethical responsibility to compensate customers when product quality falls short of expectations. Even when a defect isn't obvious but a customer is unhappy, companies will repair or replace a product as a goodwill gesture toward building customer satisfaction and loyalty. Proactive, customer-oriented companies will always make the situation right for customers. This is how they gain loyalty.

A few sections ago we discussed Patagonia's commitment to repairing favorite clothing for long-time customers. It doesn't matter if the garment is three years old or 30 years old. As a gesture of goodwill, the company will repair or replace the garment. L.L. Bean has the same policy: "Our products are guaranteed to give 100% satisfaction in every way. Return anything purchased from us at any time if it proves otherwise." Lands' End promises: "From sheets to slacks, if you're dissatisfied with any item, simply return it to us at any time for an exchange or refund of its purchase price. We mean every word of it. Whatever. Whenever. Always. But to make sure this is perfectly clear, we've decided to simplify it further: Guaranteed. Period." Many other companies boast a 100% satisfaction guarantee, including Orvis, Eddie Bauer, Costco, Oxo, Craftsman, Hampton Inn, Hilton Garden Inn, Cutco, Dr. Martens, JanSport, and Vermont Teddy Bear. [34]

Even a treasured "best friend" can be guaranteed for life if it's a Vermont Teddy Bear.

On a daily basis you hear or read about companies offering customer satisfaction. If you're not happy with your coffee, a Starbucks barista will remake it or any other drink you want. If you don't like your Domino's pizza, it will be remade and redelivered free of charge. Meijer, a regional supermarket chain, has a reputation for exceptional customer service. Today even some colleges believe that the promise of a quality education should be backed by a guarantee.

Henry Ford Community College in Dearborn, Michigan, became the first school to offer a guarantee for its graduates. It provides up to 16 semester hours of further training if an employer feels a graduate lacks the expected job skills. Another popular educational school called App Academy is a software development program in San Francisco and New York City that requires no tuition payment until a graduate gets a job. [35]

Of course, many businesses offer satisfaction guarantees. We just discussed some of the exceptional ones offered by outstanding companies. Others make it more difficult for the customer to collect on such a guarantee, but generally it's in a company's best interest to pay off with little hassle. That's what builds satisfaction and loyalty.

Despite the satisfaction that results when a customer problem is handled well, a number of companies have tightened their rules and changed generous exchange policies. Best Buy, for example, now charges a restocking fee for returns without a receipt. Walmart has changed its open-ended return policy to one with a 90-day limit. Verizon will accept phone returns up to 14 days after purchase but requires a $35 restocking fee.

Customers are partly responsible for these changes. Imagine people returning goods actually purchased at a garage sale or bringing back clothes worn for an entire season. Or what about customers who pull items off store shelves and bring them to the counter for a refund? Nintendo has received returned game boxes containing underwear, soap and even a lizard. Although these are extreme examples, stores have tightened return policies to help prevent fraud in an effort to keep costs low.

According to a recent study, U.S. merchants are incurring $191 billion in fraud losses each year, so the stricter policies may seem reasonable.[36] The important consideration, however, is consumer response. If returning a defective or unwanted good is difficult, then customers develop a negative feeling about the company. It is important for all employees to understand how customer satisfaction contributes to the overall health of the organization. That requires their involvement in understanding the value of customer evaluations, both negative and positive, including why items get returned. Proactive, customer-oriented companies will always try to make the situation right for customers. The need to be customer focused in today's fluid marketing environment has never been more important. Creating customer satisfaction and loyalty is imperative to the future success of any company.

Chapter Summary

Objective 1: Explain why customer satisfaction and loyalty are a focus of marketing in winning organizations.
Satisfied, loyal customers generate profits because they are responsible for a large percentage of sales and are less costly to develop than new customers. Loyal, satisfied customers also influence others to buy products. Similar to product innovation, customer satisfaction has become a key to competitive advantage. In addition, satisfaction ratings help consumers compare products. Finally, loyal, satisfied customers will pay more and are less concerned about price and price increases.

Objective 2: Learn how consumer expectations influence satisfaction.
Customers form impressions about how well companies perform in relation to expectations. If performance falls short, then customers become dissatisfied. They may defect from a company because of perceived poor performance or because they think the company does not treat them well in attempting to rectify the situation. Conversely, when customers are pleased, their expectations for future purchases are likely to increase. When loyal customers become dissatisfied, they are likely to complain. If their complaint is handled quickly, then their satisfaction and loyalty may increase.

Objective 3: Describe how connecting with customers through relationships achieves satisfaction and loyalty.
The personal connection produces loyalty. Relationships are built, first, on empathy—the ability to understand another party and communicate that understanding. Second, trust is important, that is, insuring that products and customer service perform in line with expectations. Third, commitment is required. Commitment means making sure that the customer is better off because of the relationship. Finally, rewards increase satisfaction and loyalty. Many companies are finding rewards help to increase repeat business, while also providing valuable customer demographics and buying behavior patterns for company marketers at virtually no cost.

Objective 4: Understand how diversity and global competition influence consumer satisfaction levels.
Diverse customers have different expectations. Creating satisfaction requires paying close attention to various tastes and preferences. Many companies have created units to address specific groups. The variations in customer tastes and preferences are particularly challenging for large companies that want to gain high satisfaction scores. They still need to address each specific segment to achieve high ratings. Satisfaction scores have historically been higher for some foreign companies in this country, reflecting their attention to quality. This has helped them gain a market foothold. Now that U.S. companies also are stressing quality and satisfaction, their scores are improving in marketing to foreign countries.

Objective 5: Define quality and explain how it is obtained.
Quality is the degree of excellence in a company's products or services. It can be assessed subjectively or objectively, and it can be

categorized as static or dynamic. Subjective assessments indicate to what degree the product does what consumers expect it to do. Objective assessment indicates to what degree the product consistently does what it's supposed to do. Static quality is when an accepted practice is perfected. Businesses must be careful not to focus only on static quality. Dynamic quality results when a major change makes the existing standard obsolete, and it is also important. Both build value. Benchmarking is the practice of businesses evaluating their operations in comparison to excellent organizations. It is used by companies that want to increase quality and value. Very frequently, businesses that win the Deming Prize and the Malcolm Baldrige National Quality Award are considered "benchmarks" of quality that other companies try to emulate.

Objective 6: Explain how companies use value to create customer satisfaction and loyalty.
Achieving customer satisfaction requires the commitment of everyone involved with an organization to place customer interest at the forefront of all decisions. This includes internal employees as well as external contributors at every level of the supply chain. The united goal must be to create value through satisfaction. Companies rely on satisfaction rankings to monitor how satisfied consumers are with their goods and services. These rankings may be done through traditional methods with the customer using surveys and focus groups, or through social media. In creating customer satisfaction and loyalty, companies need to exhibit value to the customer through the practice of ethical behavior. Portraying a product accurately, and following through with customer service is important; many customer-oriented companies also offer 100% satisfaction guarantees to achieve this goal.

Review Your Understanding

1. What is customer satisfaction? What is loyalty? What are four reasons for an organization to stress loyalty and satisfaction? Explain each.
2. How do you calculate the lifetime value of a customer?
3. What are customer expectations? Why do customers defect? Why are complainers often your most loyal customers?
4. What are the three elements that form the personal basis of relationships? Explain each. How do companies reward loyal customers?
5. What are companies doing to address satisfaction with diversi-

fied customers?
6. Why is satisfaction important in global marketing?
7. What is customer-delivered value? Explain.
8. What is the value chain? Explain.
9. What are objective and subjective assessments of quality? Static and dynamic quality?
10. What is TQM, and what are its four critical components?
11. What is benchmarking?
12. What are the Deming Prize and the Malcolm Baldrige National Quality Award?

Discussion of Concepts

1. Why should companies focus on both satisfaction and loyalty? Why is satisfaction alone inadequate?
2. Imagine that you are the marketing director of a local company. How would you use the concept of customer-delivered value to improve the marketing for a product?
3. Discuss how connecting with customers through relationships relates to satisfaction and loyalty.
4. If you observed a large percentage of customer defections from a business, what might be the causes? How would you investigate?

5. Is complaining behavior good or bad? Should you encourage customers to complain?
6. What would you recommend for an organization that wishes to connect with customers through relationships?
7. What is the relationship between quality and customer value? How is quality attained?
8. Do you feel companies should allocate a great deal of effort to apply for the Malcolm Baldrige National Quality Award? Why or why not?

Key Terms & Definitions

1. **Benchmarking:** The systematic evaluation of practices of excellent organizations to learn new and better ways to serve customers.
2. **Cost structure:** The amount of money required to pro-

duce a specific amount of sales.
3. **Customer defections:** The percentage of customers who switch to another brand or supplier.
4. **Customer expectations:** Consumer beliefs about the per-

formance of a product based on prior experience and communications.

5. **Customer Lifetime Value (CLV):** The amount of profit a company expects to obtain over the course of a customer relationship.

6. **Customer loyalty:** A measure of how often, when selecting from a product class, a customer purchases a particular brand.

7. **Customer satisfaction:** A customer's positive, neutral or negative feeling about the value received from an organization's product in specific use situations.

8. **Customer satisfaction measurement program:** An ongoing survey of customers (and competitors' customers) for the purpose of obtaining continuous estimates of satisfaction.

9. **Dynamic quality:** Quality that results from a change that makes an existing standard obsolete.

10. **Malcolm Baldrige National Quality Award:** A program designed to raise quality awareness and practice among U.S. businesses.

11. **Objective assessment of quality:** An evaluation of the degree to which a product does what it is supposed to do.

12. **Quality:** The degree of excellence in a company's products or services.

13. **Satisfaction ratings:** Ratings provided by testing agencies that compare purchase and/or performance satisfaction of specific products or market segments.

14. **Static quality:** Quality that results when individuals or organizations perfect an accepted practice.

15. **Statistical quality control:** The use of statistics to isolate and quantify production line problems that may cause product defects.

16. **Subjective assessment of quality:** The degree to which a product does what consumers expect it to do.

17. **Supply chain:** All the activities that organizations undertake to deliver value to the customer, such as working with suppliers, and distribution through convenient channels.

References

1. Spreng, Richard, American Marketing Association, Conference Proceedings, Chicago: 1999, Vol. 10, pg. 208.
2. JoAnna Brandi, "The Real Costs of Losing Customers," http://www.refresher.com/the-real-costs-of-losing-customers, website visited June 9, 2016.
3. Lavinsky, Dave, "Pareto Principle: How to Use It To Dramatically Grow Your Business," Forbes/Entrepreneurs, January 20, 2014.
4. Gupta, Sunil, Lehmann, Donald R., Stuart, Jennifer Ames, "Valuing Customers," Journal of Marketing Research, Vol. 41, Issue 1, February 2004.
5. "We Interrupt This Issue to Remind You That the Internet Is Big," Wired, www.wired.com, website visited June 15, 2016.
6. Amy Gallo, "The Value of Keeping the Right Customers," Harvard Business Review, October 29, 2014.
7. "Unexpected Starbucks Apology Overflows Your Rewards Card With Delicious Credits,", www.consumerist.com, website visited June 18, 2016.
8. "Beyond Satisfaction," CMA Management, March 2000, pp. 14-15.
9. Carr, Clay, Front Customer Service (New York: John Wiley and Sons, 1990), p. 31.
10. "2014 Temkin Loyalty Ratings", www.customermanagementiq.com, website visited June 20, 2016.
11. Carr, Front Customer Service, p. 19.
12. "A Public Relations Disaster: How saving $1,200 cost United Airlines 10,772,839 negative views on YouTube," www.sentium.com, website visited June 29, 2016.
13. www.harley-davidson.com/content/h-d/en_US/home/owners/hog/membership-benefits.html website visited June 22, 2016.
14. "Apple and the Environment," www.apple.com/environment, website visited June 16, 2016.
15. Marjorie Adams, "Three Ways To Build Customer Trust" Forbes, www.forbes.com, website visited June 16, 2016.
16. "Rebuilding Hope & Homes," The Home Depot, http://corporate.homedepot.com, website visited June 16, 2016.
17. "Do Rewards Really Create Loyalty?" Harvard Business Review, May-June 1995, p. 75.
18. www.starbucks.com, website visited June 22, 2016.
19. www.jollibee.com.ph, website visited June 25, 2016.
20. www.jollibeeusa.com, website visited June 25, 2016.
21. "Consumer Perceptions of Price, Quality and Value: A Means-End Model and Synthesis of Evidence," Journal of Marketing, July 1988, p. 2; Vandermerwe, Sandra, "How Increasing Value to Customers Improves Business Results," Sloan Management Review, Fall 2000, pp. 27-37.
22. www.mcdonald's.com, website visited June 23, 2016.
23. Czinkote, Michael R., Kotabe, Masaki, Mercer, David, Marketing Management, 1997, pg. 273.
24. Jason Cipriani, "Why You Shouldn't Trust All Amazon Reviews," Fortune, March 14, 2016.
25. Steven Tweedie, "This disturbing image of a Chinese worker with close to 100 iPhones reveals how App Store rankings can be manipulated," Business Insider, February 11, 2015.
26. Malcolm Baldrige National Quality Improvement Act of 1987, report of the Senate Committee on Commerce, Science and Technology on HR 812 (Washington DC: US Government Printing Office, 1987).
27. Malcolm Baldrige National Quality Program, "Criteria for Performance Excellence," 2010, pg. 1.
28. www.ritzcarlton.com, website visited April 24, 2016.
29. www.quality.nist.gov, website visited March 12, 2016.
30. Naumann, Earl, Customer Value Toolkit, Thomson Executive Press, 1994.
31. Press Release "Wireless Charging and Fingerprint Scanner Technology Amp Up Smartphone User Satisfaction, Says J.D. Power Study," J.D. Power and Associates. www.jdpower.com, April 21, 2016.
32. www.theacsi.org, website visited June 17, 2016.
33. "Judges Panel of the Malcolm Baldrige National Quality Award," Federal Register, July 21, 2000.
34. www.consumerreports.org/cro/news/2014/09/15-american-companies-that-offer-great-guarantees/index.htm, website visited June 24, 2016.
35. www.appacademy.io, website visited June 21, 2016.
36. Deloitte CIO Journal Editor, "Using Analytics to Detect Retail Fraud," The Wallstreet Journal, March 17, 2014.

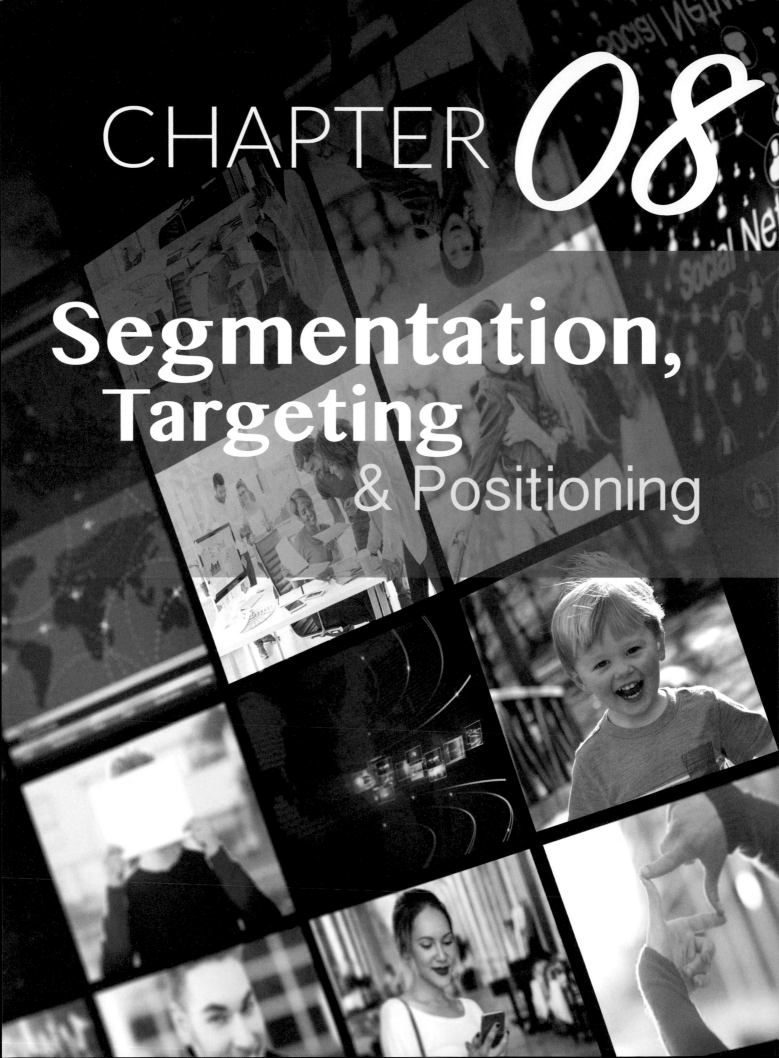

CHAPTER 08

Segmentation, Targeting & Positioning

Dell understands how to target segments that will help its business succeed.

Michael Dell and his team have long understood that different segments of customers have different computing requirements. For example, many families buy lower-priced PCs for daily household needs such as homework and entertainment, whereas, corporations need more sophisticated workstations to complete more complicated tasks. Similarly, an entrepreneur with a simple website does not need the high-end server that a large hospital requires to power its sprawling internal and consumer sites with vast databases of information. With these differing needs in mind, Dell's marketers use geographic, demographic and behavioristic variables to segment the consumer and organizational markets for computers and servers.

Using the geographic variable of national boundaries, Dell has segmented the world market and created product offerings for dozens of countries. Each geographic area has a tailored website, presented in the local language, which features hardware, software, services and online content specifically geared to that market's interests and requirements. In addition, Dell divides its overall market into consumer, business, government and institutional segments. The consumer segment consists of consumers who buy for personal and home-office use.

Responding to stiff competition from HP, Lenovo, and Apple, Dell was forced to depart from its direct B2C sales approach and begin selling its computers at Walmart. Now, Dell partners with retailers to sell its products at many locations worldwide, including Best Buy and Staples.

Positioned as a company with great supply chain efficiencies to sell established technologies at low prices, Dell was lacking the research and development to be a truly innovative company like its thriving competitors—who were selling to new and emerging segments. To combat declining PC sales and razor thin margins on technology outsourced by Dell, the company decided to target the prized big-business segment—customers whose annual hardware purchases may total millions of dollars.

Other segments targeted by Dell are the healthcare industry, government agencies, education and e-commerce. Dell has also forged alliances with a number of specialized suppliers to offer a complete menu of products and services to large hospitals for staff and administrative use. Within the government market, Dell targets federal government agencies (in the U.S. and other countries) separately from state and local government agencies. Within the education market, Dell targets K-to-12 schools separately from administrators, faculty and students of colleges and universities. Dell's ability to target market segments in line with its marketing strategy continues to create value for its customers.

Sources: www.dell.com, website visited June 21, 2016; www.youtube.com/watch?v=97scnB7c4t4, website visited June 24, 2016.

LO 01 Explain the advantages of market segmentation and how it differs from mass marketing and product differentiation.

LO 02 Describe how to segment a market and select a target market.

LO 03 Explore the three basic target marketing strategies: undifferentiated, differentiated and concentrated marketing.

LO 04 Explain the steps in positioning, and describe several approaches marketers use to create valuable, lasting images of their products.

MARKET SEGMENTATION

The process of defining and subdividing a large market into clearly identifiable segments having similar needs, wants, values and buying behavior.

MARKET SEGMENT

A homogeneous group of consumers with similar needs, wants, values, and buying behavior.

TARGET MARKETING

The selection of specific homogeneous groups (segments) of potential customers for emphasis.

The Concepts of Segmentation, Targeting and Positioning

If every consumer had the same wants and needs, marketing to the masses would be easy! However, that's not reality. People are unique and businesses have to determine how to reach the consumers most likely to want their products. So how does a business decide who those consumers are? They use a process called market segmentation.

Market segmentation is the process of defining and subdividing a large market into clearly identifiable segments having similar needs, wants, values and buying behavior. These segments vary in size and amount of opportunity they present. Market segments are the result of market segmentation; a **market segment** is a homogeneous group of consumers with similar needs, wants, values and buying behavior.

Because it would be difficult to appeal successfully to each segment, companies select certain ones that they think will be most profitable for their marketing efforts. This is called **target marketing**. For example, Great Lakes Crossing in Auburn Hills, Michigan, is an outlet mall with many entertainment attractions. The mall appeals to the entire family, with stores such as Bass Pro Shops Outdoor World, Disney Store Outlet, Saks Fifth Avenue Off 5th, Neiman Marcus Last Call Clearance Center, and Victoria's Secret Outlet. In addition to shopping, the mall has family-oriented entertainment options including a movie theater, an indoor amusement park and restaurants like Rainforest Café and Toby Keith's I Love This Bar & Grill. It is targeting value-conscious families who want to make shopping an experience everyone in the family can enjoy.[1]

greatlakescrossingoutlets.com

Great Lakes Crossing is a mall targeting value-conscious families who want to make shopping a fun experience for the entire family.

POSITIONING

Creating an image or perception in the minds of consumers about the organization or its products relative to the competition.

SEGMENTATION

Identifying and understanding the characteristics of potential customers.

TARGET MARKETING

Selecting customers to serve and focusing resources to serve them.

POSITIONING

Establishing how customers will view your organization relative to competitors. Gaining a positive image.

Figure 8.1   Connecting With Customers by Identifying, Selecting and Relating to Them

Positioning is the creation of an image, reputation or perception in the minds of consumers about the organization or its products relative to competition. Great Lakes Crossing has positioned itself as a one-stop destination with "something for everyone." The company appeals to customers in the target segments by adjusting products, prices, promotional campaigns, services, and distribution channels to be consistent with its positioning strategy. Great Lakes Crossing has identified a segment of value-conscious families and positioned itself as a dominant retail outlet and entertainment destination, attracting customers from throughout the Midwest and Canada. This provides an advantage over competitors that offer only traditional retail stores.

Segmentation, target marketing and positioning give organizations the means to connect with customers by identifying and understanding their characteristics, by directing resources to meet their needs and wants, and by creating an image of how they will view the organization. Let's say a company simply compiles data on consumers, averages them, and tries to develop one brand that appeals to the average consumer. In the U.S. marketplace alone, there are over 318 million people.[2] Averages for certain demographic characteristics such as age, gender, income, location, and so forth, are easy to determine, but what about ethnic origin, home life or taste in music, clothing and food? The "average" American represents few, if any, real people. Efforts to connect with this mythical average consumer probably wouldn't have appeal for many customers, making an "average" in this sense rather useless to marketers. Instead, marketers use segmentation to identify and understand characteristics of potential customers, target marketing to define unique consumer groups they want to focus resources on engaging, and positioning to establish a unified image of the product relative to the competition.

To be a leader, companies know that they must connect with customers by identifying, selecting and relating to them in innovative ways. That's why it is crucial to apply the above concepts in sequence, as shown in Figure 8.1. The activities required to accomplish each stage are described in the sections that follow. Under market segmentation, we include descriptions of mass marketing and product differentiation as general marketing approaches that are contrasted with the more preferred segmentation methods. We also introduce several ways to identify diverse market segments. The section on target marketing describes how to select targets and focus resources where they will accomplish the most. The last section explains positioning. It also describes how to reposition when conditions change.

LO01 Market Segmentation

Most successful companies are very conscious about targeting specific market segments. The objective of market segmentation is to design a marketing mix that precisely matches the expectations of customers in the targeted segment. Identifying key segments offers unique opportunities for marketing based on meeting specific customers' needs.[3] Historically, there has been a movement from mass marketing to product differentiation to market segmentation, targeting and positioning. In the following sections, we'll explore how these approaches differ.

SEGMENTATION VERSUS MASS MARKETING

We know from Chapter 1 that many companies once pursued mass marketing, which is the mass distribution and mass promotion of a product to all potential customers. The objective of mass marketing is to reach as many people as possible with the same marketing approach. Coca-Cola, introduced in 1886, pioneered this strategy and was successful in reaching most consumers with the same product formula, price, promotion and place (distribution) strategy.

hydrate the hustle

drink up ◐ ◐ be inspired

Coca-Cola acquired Glaceau, maker of the popular Vitaminwater, to compete in the water and energy drink markets.

Although mass marketing was useful decades ago, competition that appeals to consumer diversity prevents this from being a viable strategy for most organizations to use today. Segmentation is a much more effective way to market. Today, Coca-Cola's success depends on recognizing the tremendous diversity of the market. In an effort to expand its presence in the water and energy drink markets, Coca-Cola acquired Glaceau, maker of the popular Vitaminwater, in a deal at the time valued at more than $4 billion.[4] The company also owns popular beverage brands such as Illy Issimo coffee, which is targeted toward a much different market segment.[5]

SEGMENTATION VERSUS PRODUCT DIFFERENTIATION

PRODUCT DIFFERENTIATION

A marketing strategy with which companies attempt to make their products appear unique relative to the competition.

Eventually, companies realized that mass marketing didn't provide enough variety and they began to adopt a product differentiation strategy. **Product differentiation** makes a product appear unique relative to others, whether produced by the same company or the competition. This uniqueness is then used as a major factor in appealing to customers. The belief is that by offering choices, the company will attract more of the mass market. Notice that product differentiation implies recognition that consumers may want variety. But unlike market segmentation, the leading dynamic is a difference in the product, not in buyer characteristics. Coca-Cola was highlighted in Chapter 4 because of its extremely effective use of the differentiation strategy.

The pain-reliever market is also dominated by product differentiation. Aspirin comes in plain formula or with caffeine, buffered or not, with or without sleep aids, with or without a cold remedy, and in standard or extra strength. You can also find it in caplet, liquid, tablet, chewing gum or capsule form, coated or noncoated, flavored or not. The objective is to offer an aspirin for every conceivable preference. This might go unnoticed by consumers if companies didn't promote attention to it through advertising.

It is important to keep in mind the distinction between product differences and market segments. Market segments are made up of people and organizations, not defined by product names. Consequently, market segments are described according to their distinguishing characteristics, not according to the products they buy. Misunderstanding this distinction is a common and often costly flaw for the marketing strategist.

For example, a marketing consultant once asked the chief engineer of an air-conditioning manufacturer to describe the company's target segments. The engineer responded with product categories: heavy, medium and light-duty units. When asked questions about the characteristics of current and potential buyers, the engineer had little knowledge. The consultant knew immediately that this client did not fully understand market segmentation, a key reason customers were buying fewer of the engineer's new products. When executives equate product categories with market segments, they tend to focus attention on what they want to make, which may not meet customer requirements. The result is often products that please the people who make them but disappoint customers.

SEGMENTATION VARIABLES

HOMOGENEOUS GROUP

Buyers with similar characteristics.

HETEROGENEOUS GROUP

Buyers with diverse characteristics.

SEGMENTATION VARIABLE

Any distinguished market factor that can vary, such as gender, age or income.

The market as a whole is **heterogeneous,** meaning it has many types of buyers. Market segmentation divides the total market into **homogeneous** subgroups or clusters with similar characteristics, which can then be studied individually. Without a well-focused picture of the market, it's virtually impossible to create a powerful marketing strategy. Essentially, segmentation allows marketers to focus on relevant aspects of potential buyers. It's a critical step in connecting with customers.

How is segmentation done? First, the marketer selects a way to categorize potential customers into subgroups. A **segmentation variable** is any descriptive characteristic that helps separate potential purchasers into groups. Examples include gender, age and income. Second, variables are then subdivided into categories. For example, within the gender variable, the two categories are male and female. Categories may be very broadly or very narrowly defined. Income can be classified generally as low, moderate and high, or more specifically as, for example, up to $10,000, $10,001 to $30,000, $30,001 to $50,000, $50,001 to $70,000, and above $70,000.

Think about how colleges segment students for recruiting and admissions. Like companies, they do this to gain a better understanding of potential customers. At the most basic level, the segmentation variables are grade-point average in high school, SAT or ACT scores, and high school class rank. These variables can be subdivided into categories, as shown in Figure 8.2. The categories then can be grouped together in various ways to form several market segments, which often are named descriptively. For example, the market segment in the third categories column of Figure 8.2 might be called the "cream of the crop." Or students with above-average SAT/ACT scores but in the bottom of their class and with a low GPA might be the "underachiever" market segment.

Variable	Categories		
High School GPA	Below 2.0	2.0–3.5	3.6–4.0
SAT/ACT Score	Below average	Average	Above average
High School Class Rank	Lowest 25%	Middle 50%	Top 25%

Figure 8.2 Segmenting the College Market

Most colleges add other variables, and these can dramatically change the segmentation structure. For example, what seems to be a fairly uniform market turns out to be a lot of segments. From our example in Figure 8.2, 27 market segments emerge (three GPA categories, three SAT/ACT categories, three class rank categories). Adding just two residence categories (in and out of state) would produce 54 segments.

Variables need to be chosen carefully, because each segment must meet certain criteria to be useful to a marketer. Figure 8.3 outlines guidelines for effective market segmentation. Segmentation typically is based on geographic, demographic, diversity, psychographic and behavioristic factors, as well as benefits sought.

Geographic Segmentation One of the most common ways to analyze a market is by geography. This strategy works well when companies market to customers in a particular area, or when consumers have different preferences based on where they are located. For example, seasonal products like winterwear and beachwear are often marketed to geographic segments. Winterwear is promoted from early fall to January in the Midwest and northern regions of the U.S., but not in warm climates. In contrast, beachwear is marketed year-round in Florida, California and Hawaii, and marketers don't waste time targeting those geographical areas with promotions for winterwear.

Effective Market Segmentation

→ Members should have similar needs, wants, and preferences, because these are what marketers want to understand and influence.

→ Members should have similar information-gathering and media usage patterns, because these allow marketers to communicate with the segment.

→ Members should have similar shopping and buying patterns, because marketers then can find efficient places to sell and service their products.

→ The number of members should be large, because marketers need to generate a profit.

→ Data about the segments should be available, because marketers need to know about customers in order to build marketing strategies.

Figure 8.3 Effective Market Segmentation

Certain foods also have specific geographic markets in the U.S. For example, seafood is marketed more heavily along the east and west coasts, where supply is fresh all year. McDonald's offers seasonal seafood meals, including lobster rolls, in select markets like New England. This is an example of regional segmentation based on geographic consumer preferences and product availability. [6] The same is true of chili peppers in the Southwest and grits in the South and Southeast regions.

Geography can reveal interesting facts, too, such as the disparity between the size of men's suits. In New York, the most typical size is 42 regular; in Paris, 40 regular; in San Francisco, 38 regular; and in Chicago, a strapping 44 long![7] If you were a marketer of men's suits, how would that information affect your marketing mix plans?

Global companies often segment their markets by city. Coca-Cola knows that soft-drink consumption relates to population size. With the exception of New York City and Los Angeles, all metropolitan areas of more than 10 million are located outside the United States, which is a simple reason for Coca-Cola and other large companies to market globally. A city's population size alone doesn't always provide enough segmentation information, so marketers consider other factors. Some metropolitan areas are known for their industry expertise: in Hollywood, it's movies; in Silicon Valley, it's computer software/technology, and in Philadelphia, it's pharmaceuticals. Auto components suppliers, such as Bosch and Eaton Corporation, know that virtually all major buying decisions by auto manufactures are made in fewer than 20 cities located in a handful of countries. A presence in Stuttgart, Detroit, Los Angeles, Wiesbaden, Paris, Osaka and Seoul gives suppliers substantial global coverage.

Analytics allow researchers to cluster consumers in groups based on different variables. Using a small number of variables to explain consumer purchases in product categories, organizations develop site strategies for grocery stores, drugstores, department stores, big-box retailers and apparel companies. An understanding of segments in regions is used to adjust merchandising and identify local challenges to customize product offerings.[8]

ZIP CODE SEGMENTATION

Division of a market into specific geographic locations based on the demographic makeup of the ZIP code area.

DEMOGRAPHIC SEGMENTATION

Division of the market according to such characteristics as gender, family life cycle, household type, and income.

ZIP code segmentation divides the market according to the demographic makeup of the ZIP code area. Nielsen Claritas is a leader in the use of ZIP codes for consumer segmentation. It uses many customer characteristics to describe geographic locations even deep within ZIP codes in more specific neighborhoods and in some cases to individual households. As the population shifts, Nielsen Claritas and other similar firms adjust their data and the descriptive names they give to specific segments. For example, the most important city residents no longer are the older, mostly white "Urban Gold Coast" people in neighborhoods like Chicago's Lakeshore Drive and Boston's Beacon Hill. Instead, young, tech-savvy, highly educated singles and couples are driving the vitality of cities and live in places like Chicago's Lincoln Park. These young professionals read fewer printed newspapers and magazines in favor of online content, so they are no longer called the "Young Literati." Now, they're called the "Young Digerati."

Demographic Segmentation

Demographic segmentation divides the market into segments based on characteristics such as gender, family life cycle stage, age, income and diversity. This is a popular segmentation method because the information is readily available and consumers' preferences and usage rates are usually predictable based on demographics. An added benefit is that it's relatively easy to project the composition and size of demographic segments for the next five, ten or even 15 years. Consequently, this kind of segmentation is an excellent tool for long-range strategic planning as well as short-term marketing.

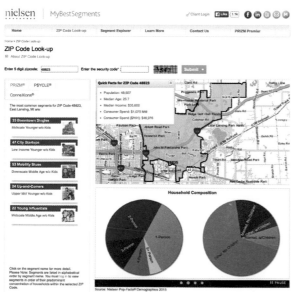

Nielsen Claritas offers a free tool to discover segments by ZIP code. Go to www.claritas.com/MyBestSegments to see segments at your ZIP code!

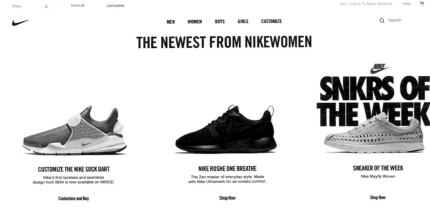

NikeWomen.com uses gender segmentation to market products geared toward female athletes.

nikewomen.com

Segmentation by Gender Men and women have different buying behaviors. Marketers need to adapt their techniques in order to reach each gender. Nike does just that with NikeWomen.com, a website especially geared toward female athletes. Shoppers can sort by product category, sport, or featured articles such as bra and pant guides, seasonal style guides, news releases, and the Nike Training Club, where members benefit from an even more personal experience.[9] By focusing on the specific values and lifestyles of women, marketers can more effectively reach an entire gender of the population. Even the auto industry has a long history of targeting women. A 1907 ad for a Franklin automobile showed women in long skirts behind the wheel and the caption, "Notice how much room there is to get in or out of the driver's side." In 1930, Chrysler research found women to be a "potent factor" in 75 percent of new car purchases, and themes focusing on them were credited with raising company sales by 33 percent. By 1948, all major automakers were advertising in *Women's Home Companion*, the most popular women's magazine at the time. The issue has never been whether to segment by gender...just *how* to address women. Chrysler formed a Women's Advisory Committee composed of 30 women from disciplines such as finance, manufacturing and marketing. The company pioneered driver's side sliding doors and integrated child seats on its minivans.

Men also make unique purchases. Traditionally those purchases included sports tickets, hunting and fishing equipment, and auto supplies. Today, men are increasingly buying personal care products that were at one time targeted only to women. The global market for men's grooming products is expected to reach $43.6 billion by 2020.[10] The men's skincare market continues to grow, with increased demand for moisturizers and anti-aging creams. Dollar Shave Club took a new approach to reach the personal care market. Michael Dubin, the co-founder and CEO of Dollar Shave Club, launched a hilarious social marketing campaign on YouTube, where his first commercial, costing only $4,500, has now reached over 22 million views. The company quickly found success selling razors and blades through a monthly membership program. For as little as one dollar a month, members will receive a basic razor and enough blades to last for a month. The company challenged traditional brands by questioning the need for shaving technologies like flashlights, vibrating handles, and a ridiculous num-

dollarshaveclub.com

Dollar Shave Club members will receive a basic razor and enough blades to last for a month.

ber of blades. Dollar Shave Club now offers a variety of men's care products, including shaving cream, body cleanser, face moisturizer, and hair pomade.[11]

Segmentation by Family Life Cycle Stage Families pass through stages, from young single adults, to marriage, to childbearing, to later life. The next chapter describes the specific categories in depth, but for now, it's important to note that these family stages are excellent segmentation categories. Several of the wireless service providers market packages of multiple cellphones to families, particularly parents with teenagers. Being able to stay in touch with their children and knowing where they are is comforting to parents. But cellphones serve many other purposes too. According to a study by Context, a company that uses anthropologists to study consumer trends, cellphones and smartphones have become a primary mode of socializing for teens. "Next time a teenager says, 'Mom, if I don't have a phone...' or 'Dad, if I don't have a phone, I'm going to be a nobody,' they are being serious," said Robbie Blinkoff, Context's principal anthropologist.[12]

Segmentation by Age Age cohorts are people of similar age and life experience. Heroes, music and even economic times are somewhat unique for each generation. Tastes, preferences, and product choices reflect those differences. Other generational similarities include physical capacity and earning power. You've probably heard of some of these segments.

Bill Gates, born in 1955, is a prominent business person in the Baby Boomer generation.

People with higher spending power, born before World War II, are sometimes called Matures or WOOFS (Well-Off Older Folks). This age cohort is often the target of major marketers. JCPenney has a clothing line called Easy Dressing, which uses Velcro fasteners instead of buttons and zippers. Barnes & Noble carries large-print paperbacks, and travel agencies market special trips for the elderly.

Baby Boomers are between 52 and 70 years old and were the largest generation until recently being surpassed by a peak in Millennials. The Baby Boomer generation, which is named for the boom in births after WWII, consists of consumers with rising incomes and higher standards of living than previous generations. There were an estimated 74.9 million Boomers in 2015. By 2050, the Boomer population will dwindle to 16.6 million.[13] Some notable Baby Boomers include Elton John, Bill Gates and former Presidents George W. Bush and Bill Clinton.

Gen X, the "Baby Busters," will peak in purchasing power around the time the Boomers retire. A survey of 3,000 U.S. citizens indicates that Generation X has saved more for retirement than previous generations. Part of this could be attributed to their lack of confidence in the social security system. In 1979, when the oldest Gen Xers were teenagers, 62 percent of workers relied on the traditional pension. Today, 63 percent of workers find themselves covered only by voluntary 401(k) plans.[14] Social security payments that Baby Boomers have made over the years have gone to pay benefits to current social security recipients, so little of what the Boomers actually paid will remain when they retire. That issue is spurring efforts to change the social security system in the United States.

Generation Xers have a lower net worth than their parents had at the same age. Because of income limitations, this generation stays home more and spends less.[15] As the Boomers retire, there is concern that the more frugal Gen Xers will consume less and will be burdened by the need to support the aging Boomers, who will require retirement subsidies and help with health care.

Generation Y, commonly referred to as Millennials, is the demographic group following Generation X; its members were born roughly between the early 1980s and mid 1990s. Millennials have witnessed a lot of affluence on television and in movies.

Taylor Swift, born in 1989 (hence her recent "1989" album name), is a Millennial celebrity.

Generation Z is the first group to be born with complete technology: PCs, tablets, mobile phones, games, MP3 players, the internet and social media.

They are aware of huge incomes of athletes, executives and coaches. Perhaps the most notable characteristic of this generation is that it grew up using technology and feels very comfortable around it. Consequently, marketers have been able to connect with this segment by using the Internet, social media and digital marketing.

Millennials, ages 18-34, totaled approximately 75.4 million in 2015, surpassing the Baby Boomer population. Immigrants add more numbers to this group than any other. Its population is expected to peak in 2036 at 81.1 million, and retreat (due to mortality) to 79.2 million in 2050.[16]

Marketers have recognized the importance of targeting this savvy group of consumers, a segment that was largely ignored in the past. It is the largest, most educated, diverse, and tech-proficient generation. However, as Millennials reach their mid-30s and increase their spending, marketers will need to focus on new and creative ways to capture this segment's attention because it generally distrusts traditional advertising. Social media and digital marketing will continue to play a major role in connecting with this market.[17]

Generation Z is the demographic group following Millennials (Generation Y). It represents people born roughly in the late 1990s to the present. The oldest members of Gen Z are still teenagers, but they already have a buying power of $44 billion, and it's growing steadily. That influence, coupled with the fact that they are approximately 26% of the population, makes marketers pay attention to the segment.[18]

It is the first group to be born with complete technology: PCs, tablets, smart phones, games, MP3 players, the internet and social media. This generation is creative, highly collaborative and extremely adept at technology. Members of it are more likely to live at home, rely on financial assistance from their parents, and trust their friends' opinions before believing traditional marketing methods.

This generation believes it is extremely important to invest in its future, with 84 percent of young adults striving to achieve at least $1 million in retirement before they stop working.[19] Holding a significant amount of income at its discretion, this group displays financial sophistication and is a prime target for marketers. Companies need to discover how to connect with Gen Z based on what's important to its members.

Age is a useful segmentation variable for high-technology services. As you would expect, most internet users are educated and earn incomes. Women outnumber men online, and their habits vary by age. Women ages 24 to 35 spend most of their time on sites that provide information and advice, whereas girls ages 2 to 11 visit television and learning websites most often. The growth rate of the female population online has outpaced the overall online growth rate. All categories except females ages 18 to 24 experienced a significant increase in their number of users online. Because of this shift in online usage, companies will certainly target women, keeping in mind the age-specific differences in their use of the internet. Comscore, Nielsen, MediaMetrix and Quantcast studies indicate that women are the driving force of social media, a trend marketers can't ignore. In business-to-consumer (B2C) marketing, female purchasing power is clear: Groupon reports 77 percent of its customers are women.[20]

Segmentation by Income Segmentation by income is based on income and spending patterns. This information is easy to attain, so income is a commonly used method for segmenting markets. It's often used by marketers of automobiles, clothing, travel, food and financial services.

Toyota segments its market for car buyers and offers a product for each group, such as Lexus for higher income buyers, Camry for middle income buyers and Corolla for the lower income market. Coach targets only high income clients, while H&M targets middle and lower income consumers. When diners enter LeBernardin in New York City for lunch, they expect to pay about $80 per person. What income segment does that restaurant target?

The Dollar Store offers every product in its stores for $1. The corporate marketing strategy to capture the lower and middle income segment has been extremely successful; it now operates over 5400 stores in 48 states. The company prides itself in addressing the needs of its customers: "Especially during these tough economic times, we continue to offer our customers products they need at extreme values." [21]

Segmentation by Diversity Some people hesitate to segment markets based on ethnic heritage, race or religious factors, but the world's tremendous diversity cannot be ignored. Marketers know that the character of many markets is dramatically influenced by these factors. What marketers need to consider is that a given ethnic group is heterogeneous.

African Americans, Hispanics and Asian Americans account for much of the current population growth in the United States. Within 25 years, each group will be approximately the same size—about 42 million people. Compared to the general population, African Americans will grow at about twice the overall rate, Hispanics at 4.5 times the rate, and Asians at more than eight times the rate. Whites will increase at about 60 percent the rate of other groups.[22] High ethnicity results in attractive market segments.

Minorities represent approximately one-third of the U.S. population, and the Bureau of the Census estimates that figure will rise to nearly 53 percent by 2050.[23] Minorities are now a majority in one of every six U.S. cities. Most immigrants settle in urban areas along with people from their home country, creating concentrations of ethnic populations.[24]

Currently, the U.S. Hispanic market consists of approximately 50 million individuals, making up 16.7 percent of the U.S. population. With a 3.3 percent increase per year, it is also the fastest growing market. The second-largest group is African Americans (40 million) followed by Asians (15 million), American Indians and Alaska natives (4 million) and Hawaiians/Pacific Islanders (1 million).[25] Total spending power of Hispanics is a considerable $670 billion, a number that is growing at twice the annual rate of non-Hispanics. Kellogg Co., the nation's most dominate cereal maker, recently boosted its marketing to Hispanics by 60 percent. Tony the Tiger's well-known growl, "They're g-r-r-reat!" has been changed to "G-r-r-riquisimos!" in Spanish language promotions.[26]

DE-ETHNICIZATION

The process whereby a product formerly associated with a specific ethnic group is detached from its roots and marketed to other cultures.

De-ethnicization occurs when a product formerly associated with a specific ethnic group is detached from its roots and marketed to other cultures. For example, Sriracha is a spicy chili dipping sauce originating in Thailand. Huy Fongs Foods brought a Sriracha recipe to America in 1980, initially supplying only Asian restaurants near Chinatown in Los Angeles.[27] The sauce was such a hit with locals that it quickly expanded to other markets. Today, Sriracha is well known to most Americans, and is a staple pantry item in many homes. In fact, the sauce is so popular that Huy Fong Foods conducts no advertising because demand has outpaced supply since the company was formed.[28] Other examples include salsa (Mexico), spring rolls (China) and bagels (Poland).

Steven Depolo / CC BY 2.0

When Sriracha was introduced to the U.S. market in 1980, the product experienced de-ethnicization.

Psychographic and Lifestyle Segmentation Psychographic and lifestyle segmentation links geographic and demographic descriptors with a consumer's behavioral and psychological decisions. Psychographic variables used alone are often not very helpful to marketers; however, they can be quite powerful when joined with demographic, geographic and other data. Lifestyle is a person's distinctive mode of living. It describes how an individual spends his or her time and money and what aspects of life he or she considers important. The choice of products, patterns of usage, and the amount of enjoyment a person gains from being a consumer are all part of lifestyle. Consider the difference between people who are physically fit from exercise and proper nutrition and those who are out of shape from high-fat diets, smoking and sedentary living. Messages such as "Just do it!" or "No pain, no gain" are received very differently by these two groups. Of course, since there are so many lifestyles, the trick is to identify them in the context of a company's marketing strategy.

Psychographics are marketing approaches and tools used to identify lifestyles based on measures of consumer values, activities, interests, opinions, demographics and other factors. Classifying lifestyles emerged from a Roper/Starch Worldwide survey of about 2,000 Americans for insights into views about money. Seven distinct profiles were discerned: hunter, gatherer, protector, splurger, striver, nester and idealist. The hunter takes risks to get ahead and equates money with happiness. The gatherer is better safe than sorry, a conservative investor. The protector puts others first and uses money to protect loved ones. The splurger is self-indulgent. The striver believes that money makes the world go around and equates it with power. The nester isn't very interested in money except to take care of immediate needs. The idealist believes there is more to life than money; material things aren't all that important.[29]

There are many ways to define lifestyles using psychographics, so marketers use a combination of research and creativity to develop useful segments. The best psychographic segmentation approaches are based on accepted consumer psychology and sound research methods. One of the most popular systems is SRI Consulting Business Intelligence's (SRIC-BI's) VALS™ systems. This second version of earlier research divides consumers into groups that think and act differently. VALS research found three major categories of consumers, each with a different primary motivation. Ideals-motivated consumers follow their own beliefs; achievement-motivated consumers are influenced by others; and self-expression-motivated consumers seek variety, action and risk-taking. In addition, VALS considers a consumer's resources, which are education, age, income, energy, self-confidence, eagerness to buy and health. Figure 8.4 illustrates the VALS segmentation system, and Figure 8.5 provides summary descriptions of the segments. The VALS battery of attitude items is used in survey research to discover the product choices, media preferences and leisure activities of each of the VALS consumer groups. Marketers, advertisers, media planners and new-product designers use VALS to discover who is naturally attracted to their product or service and then to design commu-

PSYCHOGRAPHICS

Marketing approaches and tools used to identify lifestyles based on measures of consumers' values, activities, interests, opinions, demographics, and other factors.

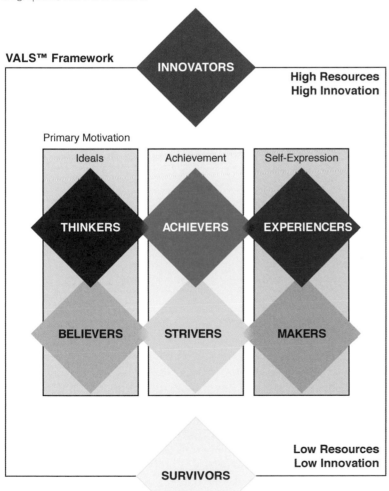

Figure 8.4   The VALS™ Segmentation System
Source: Printed with permission from SRI Consulting Business Intelligence (SRIC-BI), Menlo Park, California.

VALS™ Segment	Primary Motivation	Description	Portion of U.S. Adult Population
Innovator	Can express all three	High self-esteem, sophisticated, open to new ideas	10%
Thinker	Ideals	Information-seeking, reflective	13%
Believer	Ideals	Traditional, respect authority, risk-averse	16%
Achiever	Achievement	Goal-oriented, focus on career and family	13%
Striver	Achievement	Trendy, low self-esteem, resource constrained	11%
Experiencer	Self-expression	Stimulation-seeking, highly social	13%
Maker	Self-expression	Self sufficient in a hands on way, practical	12%
Survivor	No particular	Not active consumers, quiet, older	12%

Figure 8.5 Brief Descriptions of the U.S. VALS Groups
Source: SRI Consulting Business Intelligence (SRIC-BI); www.sric-bi.com/VALS

nication strategies, advertising and distribution plans that will be attractive to their particular consumer target. VALS refreshes its product media database twice a year. GeoVALS™ estimates the percentage of every VALS group living in each U.S. residential ZIP code. VALS systems have also been developed for Japan and the United Kingdom.

You can get your own VALS profile at www.strategicbusinessinsights.com. If you answer the questions on the VALS questionnaire, you'll find out whether you are an Innovator, Thinker, Believer, Achiever, Striver, Experiencer, Maker or a Survivor. Additionally, you can explore the types of media, products and services your profile prefers.

Behavioristic Segmentation Behavioristic segmentation groups consumers based on people's awareness, product and media uses, and actions. Past behavior is one of the best predictors of future behavior, so these variables require an understanding of what consumers have previously done. The variables include purchase volume, purchase readiness, ability and experience, loyalty, media habits and shopping behaviors.

Segmentation by Usage Rates When we discussed loyalty in Chapter 7, you learned about the 80/20 rule: 20 percent of buyers purchase 80 percent of the volume of any product. It's amazing how true this is for many products. Loyal (heavy) users can be extremely important to companies. Consequently, most marketers divide the market into heavy, moderate and light users, and then they look for characteristics that may explain why some people consume significantly greater amounts. It usually costs no more to reach heavy users than light users. In fact, sometimes it costs less because of their loyalty and assured, on-going business. Therefore, the marketing costs are lower per unit of sales. Still, marketing strategists need to realize that competition for heavy users can be fierce. If medium or light users are being ignored, they may provide a marketing opportunity.

Segmentation by Readiness For many products, potential users go through a series of stages that describe their readiness to purchase. There are six stages through which a consumer passes on the way to adopting a good or service: (1) Awareness of its existence, (2) Knowledge of its benefits, (3) Initial interest, (4) Preference over the competing products, (5) Conviction of its suitability to purpose, and finally (6) Purchase.[30] Knowing what stage the product is at in a consumer's mind helps marketers determine which promotional message or medium is most suitable for a marketing plan. This segment strategy is often used when a new product is being introduced to the market.

Segmentation by Ability and Experience The performance of products is determined by the ability or experience of its user. Consequently, ability is an excellent segmentation variable for almost any skill-based product. For example, the marketing of skis, tennis racquets, golf clubs and most other sports equipment is often targeted to ability segments. As performance requirements increase, new technologies release products with higher performance capabilities that generally require more skill. Organizations selling sports equipment and apparel might consider targets in a range of skill levels from non-athlete to professional.

Many times organizations use product differentiation to satisfy the needs of customers with different abilities or experience. Bridgestone Golf produces a range of

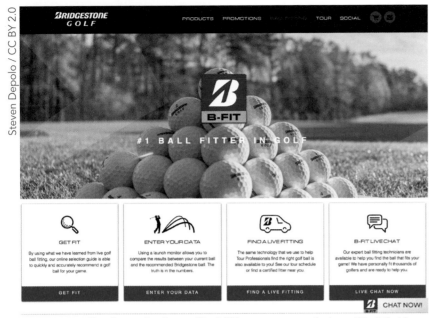

Bridgestone offers live and online golf ball fittings so you can find a golf ball that is best optimized for your swing and ability.

golf balls that can have an immediate impact on the performance of a golfer. Bridgestone's e5 model is engineered for moderate swing speeds, and its dimple technology helps combat hooks and slices common to amateurs. The e7 model provides a penetrating ball flight and unparalleled distance for golfers with higher swing speeds and more control of side spin.[31]

Segmentation by Loyalty As we have discussed, a key goal of firms is to create brand loyalty. Some consumers are naturally loyal to particular product categories. There are many ways to look at loyalty, but the most popular one segments consumers into three categories: switchers, moderately loyal and highly loyal. Switchers may select a separate brand with nearly every purchase. They may actually seek variety or they simply don't care which brand they buy. Moderately loyal customers have a preference for a brand but will switch if it is convenient to do so. Highly loyal buyers have strong preferences. In Chapter 7 we explored the highly loyal consumers of The Ritz Carlton Hotel services. Marketers should work to totally engage highly loyal buyers in social media networks, as well as to find an appropriate way to reward their loyalty. This type of segmentation may include more than the three main categories described.

Segmentation by Media and Shopping Habits A broad range of media and shopping habits can also be used to segment shoppers. For example, some people subscribe to cable, others don't; some prefer shopping in malls, others online, and so forth. These variables focus on the accessibility of target customers. Those who shop only in mall settings are reached differently from those who prefer catalog or online shopping at home. Shopping habits in the United States changed dramatically with the advent of e-commerce and digital technology. For example, the average shopper will go from spending two hours shopping online to spending closer to five hours online in the near future.[32] Online shopping will continue to increase as consumers become accustomed to larger selections, more competitors, lower prices and the convenience of shopping from home. Mobile marketing is exploding in growth, as we've discussed, and marketers are segmenting this group of consumers to target with mobile-friendly apps.

Another popular shopping habit marketers target is the likeliness of purchasing eco-friendly products. For example, Dell uses the "plant a tree for me" slogan to attract green-minded consumers to its products. This allows customers to make a donation while purchasing products. Dell will then plant a tree to offset CO2 emissions. Customers have already helped Dell plant more than 820,000 trees, making achievement of the 2020 goal to plant one million trees likely.[33] A recent survey conducted by Nielson revealed that three out of four Millennials are willing to pay more for products and services that come from companies that are committed to positive social and environmental impact [34]

Segmentation by Benefit Benefit segmentation divides the market into homogeneous groups based on the attributes consumers seek from a particular product class. Russell Haley popularized this method in the 1960s by dividing the toothpaste market into segments based on whether the consumer wanted flavor, brightness of teeth, dental health or low price. A benefit segmentation of auto buyers might group them according to the importance they place on economy, performance, styling or reliability. When a lot is known about the attitudes and perceptions of buyers, it is possible to develop a benefit profile of what product attributes are considered most important. This can be a useful step in segmentation, because customers in a benefit segment are likely to have other identifiable characteristics. For example, people who desire convenience are likely to be members of a dual-career family or single-parent household.

When only benefits are addressed, this technique is not always consistent with good segmentation procedures. Because the benefits are often described according to product characteristics, we learn very little about the buyers themselves. For example, you could say that Apple addresses the user-friendly computer benefit segment. Then again, you could say that Apple products are user-friendly. A good rule of thumb is that segments should not be defined solely by product characteristics. In fact, when benefit segmentation is based on product attributes, it may be confused with product positioning, which will be discussed later in this chapter.

BUSINESS MARKET SEGMENTATION

Although the business market is segmented using procedures much like those used to segment the consumer market, its distinctive characteristics are used to categorize business consumers on the basis of four dimensions: company demographics, geographic scope, buying approach, and product/technology. Each of these areas is described with examples in Figure 8.6.

Basis	Example
Company Demographics	
Industry	food, mining, automotive, computer
Company size	large, medium, small
Financial stability and profitability	strong, medium, weak
Channel	distributor, OEM, first tier, second tier
Ownership	private, public
Industry leadership	leader, close follower, laggard
Geographic Scope	local, regional, national, international, global
Buying Approach	
Centralization	centralized, decentralized
Functional involvement	finance, marketing, manufacturing
Partnering approach	bid, relationship oriented, contracts
Product/Technology	
Level of technology	high, medium, low
Configuration purchased	components, modules, subsystem
Design source	internal, external

Figure 8.6   Segmenting the Business Market

Segmentation by Company Demographics In describing a company, we usually think first about its demographics: industry, size, financial stability, place in the distribution channel and ownership. Industry is defined by the company's products. Ford, GM and Honda are in the automotive industry, whereas Mack and International are in the heavy truck industry. Large companies may have strategic business units (SBUs) in different industries. Johnson & Johnson, for example, makes consumer health-care products as well as medical supplies for professionals. The federal government's Standard Industry Classification (SIC) codes can help identify a company's industrial category. Industry classification reveals a great deal about an organization, such as the types of problems it will likely face, the kinds of products it purchases, its economic cycles and regulatory environment, and the types of competitive practices it is likely to encounter.

Company size is based on dollar amount or volume of sales, number of employees, or units produced. It affects purchase procedures and requirements such as delivery schedules and inventory capacity. Large firms often do much of their own engineering, and their purchasing departments use formal buying arrangements. Medium-sized companies may be interested in value-added services a seller can provide. Small firms often use less formal procedures and may want the seller's help with tracking and restocking inventory.

Another demographic characteristic is financial stability and profitability. Marketing to a company in financial difficulty comes with risks, and if the investment is substantial, delays in payments can cause the seller financial hardship. The profitability of a company is often used as an indication of its ability to pay, as well as other characteristics.

Channel membership refers to whether the organization is a distributor, original equipment manufacturer (OEM), or a tier supplier. Each type has significantly different needs. Distributors acquire to resell, OEMs want to develop a final product, and tiers have specific objectives depending on their position in the channel.

Ownership influences how organizations buy. Since private companies can set policies as they see fit, they use a variety of purchasing strategies. However, in the public sector, governmental units and utilities must follow very strict guidelines.

Segmentation by Geographic Scope

When we discussed geographic segmentation previously, it was in terms of locating clusters of targeted consumers. In the case of businesses, however, how they buy depends largely on the scope of their operations, whether local, regional, national, international or global. Pepsi has a global scope, so sellers must be able to think in terms of manufacturing plants around the world—and of reaching buyers who may come from various cultures.

> A centralized organization generally has one purchasing unit with very set policies, whereas a decentralized organization is likely to allow local buying decisions using various procedures and policies.

Segmentation by Buying Approach

Organizations also can be differentiated according to their buying approach. This takes into account their degree of centralization, what functional areas are involved, and what kind of partnering arrangements they have. A centralized organization generally has one purchasing unit with very set policies, whereas a decentralized organization is likely to allow more favorable local buying decisions using various procedures and policies. Functional involvement refers to a company's orientation: manufacturing firms use one set of criteria, whereas a financial institution or a consulting firm may use others. Partnering can range from simple bid purchases to a long- or short-term contract that may or may not contain detailed specifications and other requirements, such as an exclusivity clause.

Segmentation by Product/Technology

Product/technology can affect purchasing in numerous ways, but three of the more important segmenting strategies are based on level of technology, configuration purchased and design orientation. First, firms vary dramatically in technological capability. This is primarily due to their hiring, training, retention and technical practices. A high-tech firm has very different expectations than a low-tech firm. Consequently, marketing to each group is different. Second, buying configurations differ. Some companies want to purchase only components and base their decisions on price and delivery specifications. Others buy modules that already combine many components and make it easier to add the supplier's product at the time of manufacturing. Still others prefer to purchase a system that enhances the functionality of their products, as when Chrysler buys traction-control products from Tevis. This third variable is related in some ways to product design. Some organizations handle design in-house, some pay suppliers to take care of it, and others collaborate on it with suppliers. A company such as Delphi Automotive has extensive design capabilities but sometimes relies on suppliers for the design of certain components, modules, and systems.

Courtesy of Delphi

Delphi Automotive relied on supplier Ottomatika to provide all of the vehicle sensor technology for its first automated vehicle.

TWO COMMON SEGMENTING METHODS

Most markets are very complex, which can make the segmentation process difficult. There are many different types of customers and, as we have seen, literally thousands of variables can be used to segment them. Marketers typically use one of two approaches in selecting variables and grouping customers.

The **take-down segmentation method** starts with all consumers and seeks meaningful variables for subdividing the entire market. For example, the social media site Pinterest is primarily targeted to women. The virtual pinboard is significantly more appealing to women, who make up about 80 percent of the site's users. At least one-third of all women in the U.S. are using the platform and there are more than 70 million users globally. With an expanded test of ad products and targeting underway on Pinterest, users will likely see a lot more ads as the company tries to attract social media marketers. Various organizations like ABC Family, Expedia, Kraft and Target have realized the power of the platform and entered the market with paid advertisements called "Promoted Pins." These organizations are able to reach target consumers with extremely pertinent messaging, making Pinterest a valuable platform for advertising. [35]

The **build-up segmentation method** starts with a single potential customer and adds others with similar characteristics. Anyone without those characteristics is placed in a new segment, and the process continues. In other words, rather than the whole market, the focus is on one segment at a time. For example, Fancl, a Japanese line of natural hair and skin care products, is extremely successful with environmentally conscious women in Japan. To expand, it began marketing to Japanese women living in the United States. Now, Fancl is targeting American women by marketing both the idea of using natural products and of providing benefits. Fancl has expanded its product line to include makeup free of additives and preservatives, suitable for all skin tones targeted for the environmentally conscious women in Japan and America. [36] The build-up segmentation method is helping Fancl expand its business.

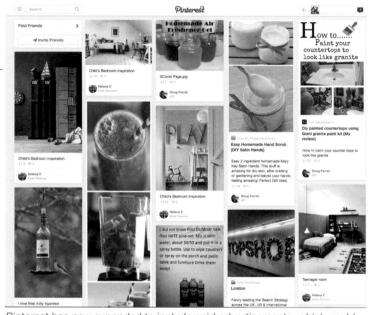

pinterest.com

Pinterest has now expanded to include paid advertisements, which could generate as much as $500 million by 2016.

Target Marketing

While segmentation is an analytical process, target marketing is a decision-making process. The company must choose the segment(s) on which it will focus its time and resources. At one extreme, a company will attempt to cover all segments, or at the other, it may choose only one. The Limited focuses on young, trendy women; Gerber on infants and young toddlers; McDonald's on families; and Lexus on quality-conscious, high-income adults. The Marketing Gazette feature on relationships (below), "Credit Card Co-Branding: New Shortcut to Hitting the Target Market," discusses a new spin on target marketing.

SELECTING TARGET SEGMENTS

How do companies decide which market segments to target? Once the segmentation scheme is developed, each group needs to be described, or profiled, in more detail. The **market segment profile** compiles information about a market segment and the amount of opportunity it represents. The profile may include (1) the number of current and potential buyers; (2) the potential number of products these buyers may purchase; (3) the amount of revenue the segment may provide; and (4) the expected growth rate. In addition to size and growth, other criteria used to select targets include competitive factors, cost and efficiency factors, the segment's leadership qualities and the segment's compatibility with the company.

Size and Growth Market segments vary considerably by size and growth rate. Although a segment must be large enough to generate revenues and profits, the biggest is not always the most attractive. The very largest segments may attract tougher competition. In the 1990s, Korean companies gained strong footholds in many countries (including the United States) by targeting smaller segments that other companies were ignoring. Not long ago, Haier, a global leader in appliances and consumer electronics, had a 26 percent share of the U.S. market for compact refrigerators, the kind often found in college dormitories and hotel rooms. It also had a 50 percent share of the low-end wine cellar market. Haier has a keen eye to identify and develop products for small segments. A quick search on Walmart's website will display 177 Haier products, many aimed at college students. These segments are large enough to support sustained marketing efforts and include Millennials, whose spending power will increase over time.[37]

Competitive Factors In general, the less competition within a segment, the better. Marketers must be aware not only of who is currently serving the segment but also of who is likely to do so in the future. A company may decide not to serve a particular segment in order to avoid particularly dangerous competitors. In other cases, a company may choose to challenge rivals. Church & Dwight decided to take on Procter & Gamble and Colgate-Palmolive by introducing its Arm & Hammer baking soda toothpaste, deeming the product just different enough to be successful with certain segments.

Cost and Efficiency Factors It is more efficient to target some segments than others. When Citibank set its sights on hiring chief financial officers of several worldwide corporations, costs ran into the millions for research, product development, and personal selling. This sounds expensive, but it was a very efficient use of funds. This extremely compact segment consists of a few known and very influential people, so all the marketing dollars could be aimed directly at the targets. If the message reaches all sorts of consumers, then the result is higher cost and reduced efficiency. For example, alcohol abuse prevention advertisements are seen by responsible drinkers and non-drinkers, not just the target audience.

Segment Leadership Qualities Some segments set the trend for adopting new ideas and products. Professional sports teams influence the dress and equipment of college athletes, who, in turn, influence high school teams. Marketers often choose a target segment with leadership qualities, hoping that other segments will follow suit.

Instagram has become a global social media giant, and companies have taken notice. Instagram "celebrities" include models, bloggers, trainers and influencers that have a large amount of followers, many of whom pay close attention to what the person is wearing and what brands they promote. It has become commonplace, for up-and-coming and premiere brands alike, to pay large sums of money to have these Instagram icons promote products and steer trends.[38]

instagram.com/kayla_itsines

Kayla Itsines, Australian fitness trainer, has 5.3 million followers on Instagram. Her inspirational fitness-related posts sometimes include branded products.

Honda's 1963 "You meet the nicest people on a Honda" ad appealed to the general population.

Compatibility Factors Companies often select segments they believe are particularly compatible with the company's vision, objectives and resources. Thus, to a significant degree, target segments reflect the qualities and character of the company. In the early 1960s, Honda recognized that Harley-Davidson was attracting niche customers rather than the general population. Honda took advantage of this by targeting younger, well-educated buyers with the theme "You meet the nicest people on a Honda." This segment was consistent with Honda's image. Other Japanese motorcycle companies, such as Yamaha and Kawasaki, did the same and captured a large number of U.S. customers.[39] Harley-Davidson has since softened its image to appeal to more segments in the market. With its emphasis on a lifestyle, buyers now include a broad range of customers. Harley-Davidson executives now make the point that "Nobody Needs a Harley," as they attempt to attract buyers by appealing to "wants" instead of needs by marketing all the features that promote excitement of owning a Harley.

FINDING NEW MARKETS TO TARGET

A major innovation occurs when companies discover new market segments. You can probably think of many examples. Kajeet Inc. discovered a novel way to market cell phones. The phones are designed specifically for kids and tweens, and they allow parents to set security settings for their kids on the go. The parents can restrict incoming calls and text messaging and monitor cell phone use online. These phones give parents piece of mind, assuring them that their children are always just a phone call away, while giving kids a sense of responsibility without the dangers of misuse that come with a normal cell phone. With a slightly altered approach, Kajeet tapped into a new market.

LO 03

TARGETING STRATEGY

The number of market segments and the relative amount of resources targeted at each.

TARGET MARKETING STRATEGIES

A **targeting strategy** defines the number of target markets and the relative amount of resources allocated to each. As shown in Figure 8.7, strategies usually fall within one of three categories: undifferentiated marketing, differentiated marketing and concentrated marketing. Niche marketing and mass customization are two other targeting strategies.

Undifferentiated	Differentiated	Concentrated
Single mass market	Several well-defined markets	Single well-defined market
One approach for all	Different approach for each	One approach for the particular market

Figure 8.7   Target Market Strategies

Undifferentiated Marketing Similar to mass marketing, **undifferentiated marketing** treats all customers the same. Companies look for needs and wants that are common to most potential customers and then try to design products that appeal to everyone. By focusing internally on a single or a few products, companies can streamline manufacturing, distribution and even promotion in order to improve quality and gain cost efficiencies. But the standardized product may fail to meet individual customer needs. For years, United Parcel Service (UPS) used this strategy, with users and the company alike benefiting from its efficient operations. Users, however, became upset by the company's inability to fulfill unique customer requirements. UPS had to adapt to continue to thrive, as you will see in the next section.

As long as companies keep their prices relatively low and competitive alternatives are unavailable, an undifferentiated marketing strategy can be successful. However, with the tough, widespread competition of today, it is an extremely difficult strategy to implement. Companies that once thrived are being threatened by rivals that use more targeted approaches, such as differentiated or concentrated marketing.

Differentiated Marketing **Differentiated marketing** serves each segment with marketing mix elements matched specifically to its desires and expectations. When Federal Express and others entered the market with differentiated strategies, UPS executives had to make a choice. Should the company settle for slowly eroding sales, or should it choose the risk, hard work and uncertainty of a new course? UPS decided on a differentiated marketing strategy. It carefully selected targets and designed services to meet their different needs. Some of its operations are applicable to all segments, such as its computerized tracking system and extensive aircraft fleet. Other elements differ, such as product mix, personal selling and pricing. This approach allows UPS to serve all its customers better.

The advantage of differentiated marketing is that needs and wants are better satisfied for each targeted segment. The disadvantage is that it may also cost more than undifferentiated marketing, because several marketing mix strategies are typically required. Differentiated marketing requires decentralized decision making. **Centralized decision making** involves a small group of executives who make all the major decisions for the whole company. **Decentralized decision making** permits numerous groups, each dedicated to a specific segment, to make the decisions for their particular segment. This gives marketers a lead role in the company, as they need to ensure that customers' needs and wants are considered in every decision. When UPS decided to engage in differentiated marketing, the first step was to strengthen its marketing capabilities. This meant educating large numbers of executives about the latest marketing techniques.

Concentrated Marketing Focusing the organization's marketing mix on one or two of the many possible segments is called **concentrated marketing**. Companies must make sure they have a great deal of knowledge about their core market segment, as this major target is called. Although most of the marketing is aimed at the core, substantial revenues and profits may be gained from other segments. This is because concentrated marketing often targets segments with leadership qualities, in the hope that they will influence other segments' purchasing behavior. Ralph Lauren has used concentrated marketing successfully to target high-income, well-educated professionals and their families. Wanting to emulate them, consumers in the non-core segment are drawn to Lauren products as well.

Concentrated marketing has worked extremely well for new companies or companies entering new areas of the world. By gaining a foothold in a core market, a company can build the financial strength, experience and credibility needed for expansion.

Niche Marketing A **niche** is a very small market that most companies ignore because they do not perceive adequate opportunity. For example, Mert's Meats in Okemos and Lansing, Michigan features Chairman's reserve beef from a Midwest distributor. The premium meat includes grass-fed ground beef and steaks, homemade sausages, free range chickens, and duck. The seafood selection includes salmon, crab, shrimp and prepared selections

Delectable seafood.

The USDA has certified that all of Mert's service case fresh beef is free of hormones and antibiotics. Ask Brandon about this and other fresh meat and seafood items.

Delicious Meats. Delectable Seafood. Delightful Service.

Mert's Meats targets a niche market with its specialty meats and foods.

such as stuffed clams and crusted tilapia. Decker Prescott, co-owner of Mert's Meats, says, "We can also bring specialty items in as customers ask and availability is there. We have the ability to fill a much needed niche." The store also stocks spices, sauces and limited local produce like asparagus, potatoes, and tomatoes. Mert's Meats has no desire to become a full-fledged grocer; it caters to the niche of consumers looking for premium and healthier cuts of meat. "We're just going to focus on meat—that's what we're best at," she said. "We can't compete with Kroger or Meijer, but we can do something they can't by keeping our emphasis on quality and personal customer service."[40]

When stores like The Home Depot, Menards and Lowe's move into smaller communities, local hardware stores inevitably fall into the niche category. Ace Hardware embraces the niche market by offering services big box stores traditionally fail at, outstanding customer service and knowledge of its products. Ace Hardware says, "...(we) offer a wide variety of paint, lawn and garden, tools, local niche services and virtually anything you'll ever need to fix, repair and maintain your home. And of course, Ace is most certainly the place with the helpful hardware folks!"[41] Despite being out-done by size and a wide diversity of products, Ace Hardware serves a market of homeowners that seek a more personalized experience and expertise in everything from key making to finding the correct replacement for your small engine part.

Mass Customization Probably the most important technological development for marketing is the personalization of mass merchandise. As mentioned previously, mass customization serves one or several markets while efficiently responding to the needs and desires of individual consumers. By creating a process that can respond to uniquely defined needs of targeted consumers, mass customization gives customers tremendous individualized attention. Companies can make affordable, high-quality products tailored to a customer's desires—but with the short cycle time and low costs associated with mass production.[42]

Nike has enjoyed success with mass customization. The company introduced NIKEiD, unique shoes that consumers create on its website. The consumer starts with a basic shoe and works from there, choosing the base and the accent colors. In addition, Nike allows each customer to put a personal "ID" on the shoe.[43]

In preparation for the 2016 Olympic games, NIKEiD launched a new line of customizations, including country flag, colors, and a personal message.

ETHICAL DIMENSIONS OF TARGETING

It makes sense that manufacturers should want to target age segments, but this brings controversy upon some companies, such as those in the tobacco industry. When e-cigarettes hit the market, it was believed to be a safer alternative to traditional cigarettes, but recent indications show that companies are targeting the young adult market with fruity flavors and clever advertising. A recent Congressional Report calls on the FDA to assert its authority over e-cigarettes, suggesting that advertisements should not be allowed on radio and television, and that manufacturers should be banned from marketing in ways that are designed to attract minors. The report prioritizes a ban on all sales of e-cigarettes to anyone under the age of 18. Many manufacturers are fighting back claiming they are simply offering a safer alternative to traditional cigarette smoking, although no long-term studies exist to support that claim.[44]

The tobacco industry has come under intense fire for similar reasons. With more than 400 cigarette brands available in the U.S., many of the products could not survive without appealing to very specific consumer groups. For example, American Tobacco Company's Misty and Philip Morris' Virginia Slims are both geared toward women. These brands effectively target subsets of the larger population. When R. J. Reynolds introduced a menthol cigarette for African Americans called Uptown, the result was public scrutiny and condemnation by the U.S. secretary of health and human services and numerous African-American and community groups. There were demands that the government bar tobacco companies from designing and promoting cigarettes targeted at this market segment. The fight stopped short of litigation when Reynolds agreed to cancel the brand at an estimated cost of $5 million to $7 million. Not all businesspeople believe this should have happened. Caroline Jones, president of a New York advertising agency owned predominantly by African Americans, said that it is insulting to ignore the African-American community and not target it. "Marketers could and should advertise products to blacks, and that includes cigarettes and alcohol as well as bread and candy."[45]

Are there differences between products such as Uptown cigarettes and Kmart's line of private-label health and beauty care items aimed specifically at African Americans? There are varying opinions among consumer groups and industry manufacturers. One thing is certain: tobacco and alcohol companies find it increasingly difficult to introduce, position and market their products to ethnic consumers.

More broadly, there are ethical concerns about targeting vulnerable consumer segments with particular products. These products include lottery tickets, weight-loss products, food supplements, fast food, insurance, and credit cards. Businesses operate to make a profit, but to be successful and remain viable, they have to balance profit objectives with the responsibility of making ethically sound decisions when choosing target markets.

China has several companies that rank in the world's top 10 turbine manufacturers.

Leaflet / CC BY-SA 3.0

GLOBAL TARGETING

Major U.S. and foreign companies often reach carefully targeted market segments outside of domestic markets. They sometimes spend vast amounts of resources to create a presence in areas with potential for significant growth. Chinese companies are trying to leverage their advances in wind power by exploring prospects in markets in Europe and the United States. China has several companies that rank in the world's top 10 turbine manufacturers, including Sinovel, Goldwind and Dongfang, who have seen rapid growth under Beijing's renewable energy law. Goldwind has already put several wind turbines on U.S. soil, with the first installed in Minnesota. Sinovel has an agreement with the Greek Public Power Corporation and Ireland's Mainstream Renewable Power to install wind turbines in

their respective countries. While China's domestic wind turbine market remains strong, competition is fierce and has slower demand than supply. Global targets may make the difference on which of these companies will succeed.[46]

Positioning Strategies

Once the segmentation process gives a clear picture of the market and the target marketing strategy is selected, the positioning approach can develop. Positioning is the process of creating in the mind of consumers an image, reputation or perception of the company and its products relative to competitors. Positioning aligns a marketing strategy with the way the marketer wants buyers in a given target market to perceive the value they will receive from the company's products.

Positioning helps potential customers understand what is unique about the company and its products relative to competitors. Most importantly, it helps buyers understand what a brand represents. **Product position** refers to the characteristics that consumers associate with a brand. For example, Snickers is positioned as the snack to give energy, while Milky Way provides comfort in every bar. BMW is positioned on prestige performance, while Mercedes projects prestige luxury.

THE POSITIONING MAP

A **positioning map** is a diagram of how consumers in a segment perceive specific brand elements they find important, giving marketers a picture of how their products are viewed. Essentially, the idea is to graph where each brand falls regarding important attributes relative to other brands. To understand this, consider Figure 8.8, which depicts a positioning map of a test group's perception of talk shows (the product). The graph depicts the combined results, using social enlightenment and intellect as anchors. Once the perceptions are plotted, most marketers want to know the consumer's ideal position. The ideal position is the one most preferred by consumers in a particular segment. Take a moment to consider other talk shows and where you would place them relative to the ones listed in the figure.

PRODUCT POSITION

The characteristics consumers associate with a brand based on important attributes.

POSITIONING MAP

A diagram of how consumers in a segment perceive specific brand elements they consider important.

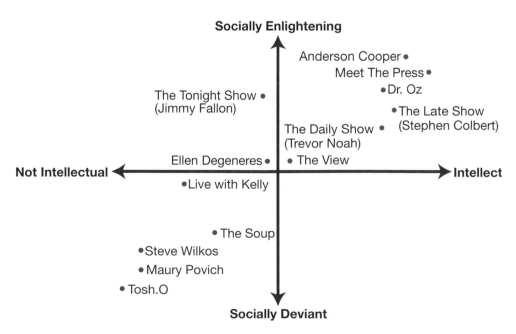

Figure 8.8   Examples of a Positioning Map: TV Talk Shows

POSITIONING BUSINESS PRODUCTS

In addition to the same positioning methods used by consumer marketers, business marketers look at three other product classifications: commodity, differentiated and specialty. Commodity products, as seen in Figure 8.9, are distinguishable from each other primarily through price and delivery reliability. The differentiated position requires buyers to evaluate, compare and contrast the products from various suppliers. The specialty position is for a unique product that can be customized to user needs.

Category	Commodity	Differentiated	Specialty
Product Characteristics	No hidden qualities, similar to other suppliers	Comparisons with other suppliers show advantages	Unique
Technology	Standard	State-of-the-art	Customized

Figure 8.9   Positioning of Business Products

Delphi markets auto components to various GM groups such as GMC, Cadillac and Opel, as well as to manufacturers around the world, such as BMW and Renault. Depending on the product line and target segment, Delphi uses all three positioning strategies. In some cases it positions products as cost-efficient, standard commodities, such as simple wire harnesses that connect parts of the electrical system. Delphi also markets brake systems that are differentiated from those of competitors and require state-of-the-art technology. In order to produce unique specialty products, Delphi works closely with designers at other levels. For instance, the company markets engine fuel systems that are both up to code and tailor-made for a consumer by collaborating with drive train designers.

STEPS FOR POSITIONING

Consumers' perceptions are influenced by how marketers choose to categorize a product. Music, for example, is categorized as rock, country, jazz, classical and so forth, whereas other dimensions help differentiate one artist or group from another. Consumers also evaluate a brand relative to others based on their impression of how similar they seem. Finally, they look at a brand according to their preferences—or how close it comes to their ideal position. The following steps can be used to position a brand.

1. Identify the attributes or characteristics used by buyers in a segment to understand brands.
2. Diagram the most important dimensions on a grid (map).
3. Locate the brand relative to others based on how it is perceived by buyers.
4. Identify the ideal position for buyers in the segment.
5. Determine the fundamental way to position the product.
6. Develop the marketing mix that supports the positioning strategy selected.

BASES FOR POSITIONING

David Aaker and J. Gary Shansby, two noted marketing scholars, have identified the following seven fundamental bases that marketers can use to position products. Each base is described in more detail next.

Positioning by Benefit   Benefits (attributes) can be used to describe the appeal of a product. For example, Procter & Gamble uses medical testimony to position Crest as a cavity-fighting toothpaste. Glad trash bags are positioned to be more durable than the competition. Fisher-Price toys are positioned as safe and educational. Energizer batteries are positioned to keep going and going.

Marketers must carefully select the benefits to associate with their product. Describing benefits that satisfy wants tends to work better than merely describing product attributes, because consumers can relate the benefits to themselves.

Positioning by Price or Quality

Sam Walton made billions by identifying underserved geographical market segments and then positioning Walmart as being consistently lower priced than competitors. Other retailers, such as Neiman Marcus, position themselves as high priced to signal higher quality. Another typical example of price vs. quality is the pharmaceutical industry. Branded drugs (usually marketed by firms that first develop them) are priced much higher than generics (usually marketed by companies that copy drugs when the patent expires). While the generics are positioned on price and the branded products emphasize quality, the products are basically the same.

Positioning by Time of Use or Application

Marketers frequently position products on the basis of how they are used or applied. Gatorade, Powerade, and All-Sport are positioned for drinking while exercising. Hot Pockets sandwiches and paninis are positioned as hot meals on-the-go.

Often sales can be increased by positioning a product for more than one use or application. For example, McDonald's discovered a huge opportunity when breakfast service was added. It recently expanded further by adding the McCafé coffee items to its selection.[47] Arm & Hammer increased baking soda sales by positioning the product as an odor fighter in the refrigerator, auto or cupboard, in addition to its uses in toothpaste, laundry and baking. V-8 juice, originally consumed at breakfast, is now infused with fruit and vegetable flavors to make it an "anytime" beverage.

Positioning by Product User or Spokesperson

Sometimes a product is associated with characteristics of its spokesperson. For example, Garnier Nutrisse uses Sarah Jessica Parker to position its hair products as classy and chic. Andre Agassi and John McEnroe, both considered tennis rebels in the 80's and 90's, were used to help position Nike athletic shoes as an alternative to the conservative models sold by competitors.

Sometimes spokespeople are not even real, such as Betty Crocker and Mr. Goodwrench. At other times, the person's area of expertise may be more significant than his or her identity as an individual. The Club, a device designed to prevent auto theft, was introduced in a national ad campaign by actual police officers.

Positioning by Direct Comparison

Nearly all customers develop impressions about a brand by comparing it to another, so marketers attempt to favorably influence impressions. In a few cases, competitors are named, although many marketers believe they should not be given "free" publicity. More often, the comparison is general—one brand is stronger, brighter and so forth than "the others." In an example some consider "classic," Apple created a series of commercials making direct comparisons to competitor personal computers. Apple's 2006-2009 "Get a Mac" campaign portrayed a man dressed in casual clothes introducing himself as a Mac ("Hello, I'm a Mac.") and another more formally dressed man introduces himself as a Microsoft Windows computer ("And I'm a PC."). The commercials showcased direct comparisons between the system components, software and features while poking fun at PC's inabilities to compete with Apple's more casual approach to meet consumer needs. At that time, Apple was striving to overtake the industry leading Windows PC, making it relevant to create a series of ads featuring a head-to-head, David vs. Goliath direct comparison. Apple won the battle, soon selling its computers based on new features and the perceived downsides of its primary competitor. [48]

Apple

Apple took on Windows' personal computers in a direct comparison advertising campaign.

Positioning by Product Class or Category Cereals can be categorized as natural or sweetened. Consumers are likely to position the natural cereals, such as All-Bran or Kashi, or sweetened cereals, like Frosted Flakes and Lucky Charms, relative to one another. But since they serve different purposes as breakfast, customers are not likely to compare Frosted Flakes and All-Bran. When a marketer is determining a positioning strategy, it is important that he or she understands how customers categorize products.

Positioning by Country of Origin A company's image can be affected by the mental association people make with its country of origin. We think of German precision engineering, Japanese cost and quality, Italian fashion, French taste and U.S. technology. Certain countries are associated with certain products: the United States with movies, Germany with beer, Japan with electronics, Belgium with chocolate, France with wine, and Italy with shoes. Companies may create a subsidiary in a nation associated with a product, or they may use a brand name that sounds like it's from that country.

REPOSITIONING

Repositioning is important for the longevity of a brand. It often rejuvenates a brand that might otherwise fade from lack of appeal. For example, some beer brands like Pabst Blue Ribbon (PBR) have repositioned several times. It had a tough-guy persona for years until it repositioned in the 1950's to be "The Fashionable Beer." PBR advertising campaigns appeared in high-end magazines like The New Yorker and Vogue with the tag line "Pabst Makes it Perfect." In the 1970's PBR made a Southern expansion in the U.S. and was even featured in a hit country song "Rednecks, White Socks, and Blue Ribbon Beer," by Johnny Russell. This redneck image would prove to plague PBR until it repositioned again in the last decade to be the beer of choice by hipsters and other urban groups.[49]

P&G's brand Old Spice also found huge success by repositioning. It was long viewed as an old-timer's brand with many remembering the classic aftershave bottle on the back of their grandfather's sink. P&G cleverly leveraged the masculinity and age of the brand in the new slogan "Experience Is Everything," and created bold new advertisements to appeal to a younger generation. The brand has continued with its bold and bizarre tactics using actors Isaiah Mustafa, Terry Crews, and now Thomas Beaudoin in a new campaign "Smell 'Em Who's Boss."[50] This particularly strange commercial is catching a lot of attention—it had over four million YouTube views in the first week of airing. The ad agency Wieden + Kennedy accompanied the campaign with this description: "Once there was a man who wanted to be the man. But that man lacked the confidence to be the man. Then along came Old Spice Swagger and Desperado. And soon that man smelled like the man. But not just the man. A better smelling version of the man."[51]

Old Spice

You Tube SCAN & WATCH

P&G repositioned Old Spice brand products through bold and bizarre campaigns. "Smell 'Em Who's Boss," seen above, captured over four million YouTube views in the first week of airing.

Repositioning may become necessary over time as competitive forces, customer preferences, and marketing environments change. It requires significant time and effort to replace past impressions with new ones. Whether a company is positioning a new product or repositioning an old one, the ultimate goal of its decision making is to persuade the targeted consumer to make a decision as well...the decision to purchase the product.

Chapter Summary

Objective 1: Explain the advantages of market segmentation and how it differs from mass marketing and product differentiation.

Mass marketing treats all customers as though they have the same needs and wants. A single marketing strategy is designed to appeal to all potential customers. This strategy does not generally work well, because customers with different characteristics have different needs and wants. Product differentiation is a strategy that alters products to stress their uniqueness relative to competitors. It recognizes that customers have differing needs and wants, but it doesn't start with an understanding of them. Market segmentation involves dividing a market into several smaller groups of buyers with similar characteristics so marketers can select which groups they can best satisfy. It gives an efficient focus to marketing resources. Most successful companies are very conscious about targeting specific market segments; it is advantageous for the customer because needs and wants are addressed, and it is advantageous for the company because it connects with the consumers who are most likely to buy the company's product.

Objective 2: Describe how to segment a market and select a target market.

Market segmentation separates potential customers into several groups or segments with distinctive characteristics. Customers within a segment should have similar needs, wants and preferences; they should have similar media habits and shopping and buying patterns; the group should be large enough to justify attention; and data about individuals in each segment should be available. Typical segmentation variables are geographic and demographic factors, ethnic and other diversity-related factors, psychographic and behavioristic factors, and desired benefits. Two common segmenting methods are the take-down method and the build-up method. The take-down method begins by selecting segmentation variables and assigning customers to the category in which they fit. The build-up method starts with the unique characteristics of one potential customer. Each time someone with unique characteristics is discovered, a new segment is added. Segments are selected as target markets based on such factors as size and growth potential, competition, cost and efficiency, leadership qualities and compatibility with the organization.

Objective 3: Explore the three basic target marketing strategies: undifferentiated, differentiated and concentrated marketing.

Undifferentiated marketing treats all customers alike and is similar to mass marketing. In order for this strategy to work, companies generally must have significant cost advantages. Differentiated marketing involves serving several segments but adjusting the marketing mix for each. It usually requires decentralized decision making. Concentrated marketing focuses on one segment or only a few. Companies can devote their resources to gain advantage within that specific group or groups. Because differentiated and concentrated strategies consider customer needs and wants, they are more effective than an undifferentiated strategy.

Objective 4: Explain the steps in positioning, and describe several approaches marketers use to establish valuable, lasting images of their products.

Positioning creates in the mind of consumers an image, reputation or perception of the company and its products relative to competitors. It helps customers understand what is unique about a company and its products. Marketers can use a positioning map to show how customers perceive products according to certain characteristics. For business products, a commodity, differentiated or specialty positioning strategy can be used. Products are often positioned by benefit, by price and quality, by the time of use or application, by user or spokesperson, by direct comparison with a competitor, by product class or by country of origin. Successful marketers use positioning to understand how consumers perceive their product. If perception is different than what a company desires, marketers will adjust the marketing mix in an effort to align consumer perception with company intent.

Review Your Understanding

1. Define mass marketing, product differentiation, and market segmentation. How are they different?
2. What are the steps in segmentation, targeting and positioning?
3. What variables are used to segment markets? Give examples of each.
4. What are the three basic marketing strategies associated with segmentation?
5. What is VALS™? What major categories of consumers does it profile?
6. What are the differences between the take-down and the build-up segmentation methods?
7. What characteristics are used to select target markets?
8. What is niche marketing, and how does it differ from mass customization?
9. What are positioning strategies? List three used in business markets.
10. What is a positioning map, and how do organizations use it to position products? Why is this a valuable tool for marketers?

Discussion of Concepts

1. Why do marketers use market segmentation to summarize information about large numbers of consumers? Why not just use averages?
2. Are segmentation techniques used by companies that follow a mass marketing strategy? A product differentiation strategy?
3. How does a company benefit by market segmentation?
4. Imagine that you are the marketing manager for a company that wants to produce a new line of men's and women's dress shirts. Which segmentation variables would be relevant for this market? What categories would you use? Describe five or six market segments that may emerge.
5. What is a segment profile? Develop one for each market segment you listed in question 3.
6. Which segments in question 3 would you select as target markets?
7. Once target markets are chosen, what different strategies might address them? Which would work best for your target markets in the above example?
8. Why is positioning important? What are some of the different ways to position dress shirts in your target markets?
9. Positioning is typically done relative to the competition. If you have no important competitors, then how can the concept still be useful?
10. Do you think there are any market segments that companies would not want to target, even if segmentation revealed they might be prosperous?

Key Terms & Definitions

1. **Build-up segmentation method:** Method that starts with a single potential customer's characteristics and adds a segment for each new characteristic found in other customers.
2. **Centralized decision making:** Management process in which a small group of executives makes all the major decisions for the whole company.
3. **Concentrated marketing:** Focusing the organization's marketing mix strategy on one or only a few of many possible segments.
4. **Decentralized decision making:** Management process in which numerous company groups, each dedicated to a specific segment, make decisions about their segment.
5. **De-ethnicization:** The process whereby a product formerly associated with a specific ethnic group is detached from its roots and marketed to other cultures.
6. **Demographic segmentation:** Division of the market according to such characteristics as gender, family life cycle, household type and income.
7. **Differentiated marketing:** Marketing to each of several segments with a marketing mix strategy matched specifically to its desires and expectations.
8. **Heterogeneous group:** Buyers with diverse characteristics.
9. **Homogeneous group:** Buyers with similar characteristics.
10. **Market segment:** A homogeneous group of consumers with similar needs, wants, values and buying behavior.
11. **Market segmentation:** The process of defining and subdividing a large market into homogeneous segments having similar needs, wants, values and buying behavior.
12. **Market segment profile:** Information about a market segment and the amount of opportunity it represents.
13. **Niche:** A very small market segment that most companies ignore because they fail to see any opportunity.
14. **Positioning:** Creating an image or perception in the minds of consumers about the organization or its products relative to the competition.
15. **Positioning map:** A diagram of how consumers in a segment perceive brands based on specific elements they consider important.
16. **Product differentiation:** A marketing strategy with which companies attempt to make their products appear unique relative to the competition.
17. **Product position:** The characteristics consumers associate with a brand based on important attributes.
18. **Psychographics:** Marketing approaches and tools used to identify lifestyles based on measures of consumers' values, activities, interests, opinions, demographics and other factors.
19. **Segmentation variable:** Any distinguishing market factor that can vary, such as gender, age or income.
20. **Take-down segmentation method:** Method that starts with a set of variables and assigns all consumers to one of them.
21. **Target marketing:** The selection of specific homogeneous groups (segment) of potential customers for emphasis.
22. **Targeting strategy:** The number of market segments and the relative amount of resources targeted at each.
23. **Undifferentiated marketing:** A strategy that views all potential customers as though they are the same.
24. **ZIP code segmentation:** Division of a market into specific geographic locations based on the demographic makeup of the ZIP code area.

References

1. www.shopgreatlakescrossing.com, website visited June 24, 2015.
2. www.census.gov, website visited June 24, 2015.
3. Raynor, Michael E., Weinberg, Howard, S., "Beyond Segmentation — Does your company want to satisfy a niche or gain a foothold in the market?" Marketing Management, November/December 2004.
4. Sorkin, Andrew, "Coca-Cola Agrees to Buy Vitaminwater," May 26, 2007, New York Times.
5. "Products," CocaCola, www.cocacola.com, website visited June 8, 2015.
6. Kokemuller, Neil, "Examples of Geographical Segmentation," Houston Chronicle, smallbusiness.chron.com/examples-geographic-segmentation-61612, website visited June 29, 2016.
7. Chicago, March 1996, pg. 22.
8. Rigby, Darrell K., Vishwanath, Vijay, "Localization: The Revolution in Consumer Markets," Harvard Business Review, April 1, 2006.
9. Nike, www.nikewomen.com, website visited April 9, 2015.
10. "American Men Get More Savvy," Business and Industry, Vol. 22, No. 6, March 21, 2005, pg. 21.
11. Adam Lashinsky, "The cutting edge of care," Fortune, March 9, 2015.
12. Batista, Elisa, "She's Gotta Have It: Cell Phone," www.wired.com, May 16, 2003.
13. Fry, Richard, "Millennials overtake Baby Boomers as America's largest generation," Fact Tank, Pew Research Center, April 25, 2016.
14. "Debt-squeezed Gen X," USA Today, www.usatoday.com, website visited April 12, 2015.
15. Palmer, Kimberly, "Gen X-ers: Stingy or Strapped," U.S. News and World Report, www.usnews.com, website visited April 14, 2015.
16. Fry, Richard, "Millennials overtake Baby Boomers as America's largest generation," Fact Tank, Pew Research Center, April 25, 2016
17. Judith Aguino, "Gen Y: The Next Generation of Spenders,"CRM Magazine, February 2012.
18. "4 Marketing Tactics for Appealing to Generation Z," Entrepreneur, www.entrepreneur.com/article/252923, website visited May 30, 2016.
19. www.mybudget360.com, website visited April 14, 2015.
20. Lee, Aileen, "Why Women Rule the Internet," www.techcrunch.com, March 20, 2011.
21. http://www.dollartreeinfo.com/about%2Dus, website visited June 13, 2015.
22. U.S. Census Bureau, www.census.gov, website visited April 9, 2015.
23. Hector Cordero-Guzman, "The 'majority-minority' America is coming, so why not get ready?," MSNBC, August 15, 2014.
24. McDermott, Michael J., "Marketers Pay Attention! Ethnics Comprise 25% of the U.S.," Brandweek, July 18, 1994, pg. 26.
25. http://quickfacts.census.gov, website visited June 19, 2016.
26. Magazine Monitor. "Sriracha: How a sauce won over the US," http://www.bbc.com/news, December 21, 2013, website visited June 21, 2016.
27. Roberto A. Ferdman, "The sad truth: Sriracha, the world's coolest hot sauce, is losing its edge," The Washington Post, February 10, 2015.
28. "Food Companies Targeting Hispanic Consumer," www.foxnews.com, website visited April 12, 2015.
29. Sullivan, Robert, "Americans and Their Money," Worth, June 1994, pg. 60.
30. www.businessdictionary.com/definition/buyer-readiness-stages.html, website visited July 3, 2016
31. Bridgestone e5, e6, and e7 Ball Review, www.thesandtrap.com, website visited June 8, 2015.
32. Burns, Enid, "Shoppers Shift to Online," ClickZ Network, www.clickz.com, website visited April 9, 2015.
33. www.dell.com, site visited April 13, 2016.
34. "Green Generation: Millennials Say Sustainability Is a Shopping Priority," Nielson, November 5, 2015.
35. Matt Kapko, "Pinterest Pins Revenue Plans on Ad Targeting," CIO, May 30, 2014.
36. www.fancl.com, website visited April 8, 2016.
37. Tarun KhannaKrishna G. Palepu, "Emerging Giants: Building World-Class Companies in Developing Countries," Harvard Business Review, October 2006 Issue.
38. Heather Saul, "Instafamous: Meet the social media influencers redefining celebrity," Independent, www.independent.co.uk, March 27, 2016.
39. Associated Press, "Biker Sues Harley-Davidson for Trying to Yank Business," The State News, April 10, 1996, pg. 6.
40. Allan I. Ross, "New in town," Lansing City Pulse, May 21, 2014.
41. www.acehardware.com, website visited June 19, 2016.
42. Weiss, Michael J., The Clustering of America (New York: Harper & Row), pg. 1.
43. "What is Nike+?", www.nike.com, website visited June 19, 2016.
44. Irvin Jackson, "E-Cigarette Ads Aimed At Underage Smokers: Congressional Report," www.aboutlawuits.com, April 15, 2014.
45. Dagnoli, Judann, "RJR's Uptown Targets Blacks," Advertising Age, December 18, 1989, pg. 4.
46. Sarah Murray, "Wind power in China: Turbine talent seeks overseas outlets," www.ft.com, September 28, 2011.
47. Zachary, G., "Strategic Shift," Wall Street Journal, June 13, 1996, pg. A1.
48. Tim Nudd, "Apple's 'Get a Mac,' the Complete Campaign," Adweek, April 13, 2011.
49. www.pabstblueribbon.com, website visited June 28, 2016.
50. Sylvia Ogweng, "Quebec-Born Actor Thomas Beaudoin Fronts New Old Spice Campaign," ET Canada, June 27, 2016.
51. Tim Nudd, "2 New Old Spice Guys Kick Off Hilariously Weird 'Smell 'Em Who's Boss' Campaign Thomas Beaudoin and Alberto Cardenas join the W+K madness," Adweek, June 27, 2016.

CHAPTER *09*

Brand Management
& Product Decisions

Richard Branson introduces Virgin Galactic's SpaceShipTwo.

Over the years, Sir Richard Branson's name has become synonymous with innovation, wealth and global appeal. Knighted by the Queen of England for his entrepreneurship, he is best known for Virgin Records, a label that signed such acts as the Rolling Stones, the Sex Pistols and Janet Jackson. In 1970, Branson founded *Virgin Group* and has since formed more than 200 companies, employing over 50,000 people in 34 countries. Virgin has been successful in a variety of markets, including mobile phones, transportation, travel, media, music and financial services. It has even dabbled in businesses such as bridal wear, soda, vodka, cars, cosmetics and vacations. Each area of business is under the umbrella of a core category: Lifestyle, Media & Mobile, Money, People & Planet, Music, and Travel.

Virgin's eclectic and broad business portfolio is well planned through extensive research and analysis. According to Virgin, it focuses on putting itself in the customer's shoes to see what can be improved. Each new customer-centric venture demonstrates the company's devotion to picking the right market and the right opportunity. Virgin is known for building great marketing strategies with excellent teams of executives.

Virgin understands that customers want fun and innovative choices that are both high in quality and affordable. In the mid '80s, Virgin Atlantic Airways was created to make transatlantic flights more appealing. The airline revolutionized the industry by extending passenger legroom and installing individual TV screens. Most major competitors followed years later.

Recently Virgin partnered with Microsoft to create a new sales tool called 'Ida', an Immersive Digital Adventure built using a Windows 10 app, to simulate an "Upper Class" journey. It starts with checking in at the Upper Class wing, moves to visiting the Heathrow Clubhouse and finishes on board as you wake up refreshed and ready to land.

The guided tour is viewed through a headset with narration, and the journey is brought to life with a high resolution 360-degree video as a part of the overall physical service experience. Virgin Atlantic sales experts will show the immersive reality on a Windows 10 tablet or phone with their corporate customers, adding a new dimension to the airline's approach at trade events and enabling customers to become part of the Virgin Atlantic experience from anywhere in the world.

Virgin Galactic, a sister company started by Branson, is taking innovation to new heights by offering space flights to civilians on its new SpaceShipTwo. Passengers reach 70,000 feet for a short sub-orbital journey to experience true weightlessness. The first 700 seats are already booked with Virgin Galactic at a cost of $250,000 each, but Virgin plans to eventually make the price more affordable to the general public.

Virgin's commitment to customers is the catalyst for its success. Its marketing strategies and plans are designed to exceed customer expectations through innovation and fun. Thanks to Virgin's vision, the brand will continue to inspire and capture value for its customers.

Sources: www.breakingtravelnews.com/news/article/virgin-atlantic-takes-guests-on-upper-class-flight-with-windows-10, website visited July 3, 2016; www.theverge.com/2016/2/19/11048534/virgin-galactic-space-shiptwo-unveiled-mojave-air-spaceport, website visited July 5, 2016; www.virgin.com, website visited June 28, 2016.

LEARNING OBJECTIVES

LO 01 Describe the major dimensions used by marketers to differentiate products from competitors.

LO 02 Define consumer and business product classifications based on how and why products are purchased and consumed.

LO 03 Know how organizations make product line decisions that determine what will be sold, including the degree of standardization chosen for global markets.

LO 04 Recognize that branding and brand strategies are important aspects of building and maintaining a brand name.

LO 05 Explain how to create brand equity.

LO 06 Discuss the legal and ethical issues surrounding brand and packaging decisions.

LO 01

The Concept of Products

When Harley-Davidson recently announced its radical new electric motorcycle prototype, dubbed Project LiveWire, a lot of skepticism surrounded the product as Harley traditionalists spoke out. "It's not going to make any noise," said Gigi Beaird, Chapter Director of Women on Wheels in the DeKalb County area. "I was surprised Harley was testing an electric model because it's the polar opposite of what they're known for."[1] Indeed, Harley has long been known for its size and sound, not for its sportiness and eco-friendly silence. Ashley Lambert, the marketing director at Woodstock Harley-Davidson says, "There is something to be said about sitting on a Harley-Davidson and hearing that 'pop-pop-pop-pop-pop' vibration underneath you and the sound and the roar of the bike."[2] The new bike is certainly a risk for Harley-Davidson, but the company understands that great risk can produce great rewards. Harley just might have the name and brand to bring legitimacy to the electric motorcycle industry, which is often regarded as a fad for a few niche buyers. It could also tap into a hard-to-reach market: younger, more progressive, thought-leading buyers. The jury may still be out for some, but for others the electric mo-

You Tube SCAN & WATCH

harley-davidson

Harley-Davidson introduces the electric motorcycle, dubbed Project LiveWire, to expand its product line in order to tap into the younger, progressive buyer segment.

GLOBAL PRODUCT LINE DECISIONS

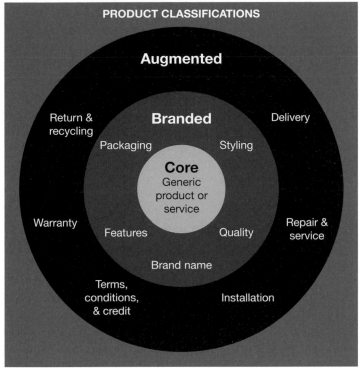

Figure 9.1   Concept of a Product

PRODUCT

Any physical object, service, idea, person, event, place, or organization offered to satisfy consumers' needs and wants.

CORE PRODUCT

The essential physical item or intangible service that the customer receives.

BRANDED PRODUCT

The core product plus the characteristics that allow the consumer to differentiate it from similar products.

torcycle has finally been validated.[3]

Product strategies provide an exciting challenge to marketers, since they affect nearly every aspect of a business. This chapter describes how products are managed from a marketer's perspective with particular attention to brand management, a critical component for most organizations. The next chapter focuses on goods, services, and non-profit marketing, then Chapter 11 addresses new product development.

Technically, a product is either a good or a service. For our purposes, however, a **product** is any physical object, service, idea, person, event, place or organization that can be offered to satisfy consumers' needs and wants. Products can be combined to perform important functions for individuals, families or organizations. In the broadest sense, anything that is purchased or sold can be considered a product. Corn, cornflakes and Kellogg's Corn Flakes are all products. A movie, a baseball game and an airplane trip are also products. For many people, the term *product* refers to a tangible item, but services are considered products as well. Services represent more than 68 percent of U.S. G.D.P., and about four out of five people in the U.S. are employed in service industries, such as restaurants, lodging, health care and law.[4]

Figure 9.1 presents the topics covered in this chapter. First we explore the three dimensions of how marketing experts describe products: core, branded and augmented. Then we discuss product classifications and consider global product line decisions. Next we'll take a look at branding, packaging and labeling. The chapter concludes with a discussion of ethical issues surrounding product safety and liability.

CORE PRODUCTS

A **core product** is associated with the basic function a consumer receives in the form of a physical item or intangible service. It could be a tennis racket, a subcompact automobile, a bowling center, a life insurance policy or a physical examination. The core product does not include the brand name, styling features, packaging or any other descriptive aspects.

A core product is often called the *generic product*, which means it conforms to the basic description. While some bicycles are suited for different terrains and activities, all of them have two wheels and function as a mode of non-motorized transportation. Another common example is generic pharmaceuticals, which refers to drugs sold without reference to a particular manufacturer. When the patent on an invented drug expires, other companies can simply copy the pharmacological formula and sell it as a generic drug. It usually costs much less than the branded drug since its price doesn't have to reflect the research or marketing costs associated with developing and introducing a new drug.

BRANDED PRODUCTS

A **branded product** is the core product plus characteristics organizations use to differentiate it from similar products. Most important is the brand name, although styling, quality, features and packaging are additional ways to distinguish brands. The branded product also can be called the identified product, because branding confers an identity just as a rancher's brand identifies a herd. Branded products not only carry the value of the core product but also have a distinctiveness that allows consumers to recognize and recall experiences with them. Nearly every global consumer recognizes the name Apple. In a recent international readers survey, Apple was ranked the brand with the most global impact. With its unique emphasis on innovation, simplicity and style, Apple-branded products have captured the eyes and dollars of consumers worldwide.[5]

Some branded products are identified purely by the need for the function they perform, such as Morton's salt. Distinctive style, such as the lines of a Porsche or a Corvette, can be an identified by features. The swoop back styling of a Beetle is a distinctive and identifying feature of Volkswagen. Brands like Maytag, which is now owned by Whirlpool Corporation, attempt to create identification through a product benefit such as reliability. For many decades, Maytag has successfully promoted its reliability by depicting a lonely repairman who never gets to visit a customer. Packaging can also distinguish a product, such as the instantly identifiable "Coke" bottle form and script, or the Tic Tac case. And, of course, a symbol like the iconic golden arches of McDonald's carries instant brand identification.

AUGMENTED PRODUCTS

An **augmented product** has characteristics that enhance value beyond that of the core and branded products. Delivery methods, warranty conditions and credit terms are ways to augment a product. A dishwasher from Sears can be delivered, installed, covered by a limited warranty and paid off on credit. Many products also require extensive installation, such as an in-ground swimming pool, which will likely need maintenance or repair after some use. That's why warranty conditions and the availability of service are significant in augmenting products.

Another aspect of augmentation is product **bundling strategy** that combines many products into a single offering. Stereo equipment, for example, can be sold as a system or as individual components. Maybe in the purchasing process, you find that Bose speakers sound better, but you prefer the Pioneer receiver, prompting you to purchase the components separately. Sony's strategy is to market an entertainment system with components specifically designed to work together, such as a Blu-ray player, speakers, TV and receiver.

As online shopping continues to increase, privacy and security are becoming very important ways to augment a product. Patagonia, for example, recognizes its customers' concern about confidentiality issues while shopping on its website. The company takes the initiative to ensure its customers' safety through high-security measures, making the consumer feel safe about shopping for its products online.[6] Amazon augments its products with satisfaction guarantees and Prime shipping

Green marketing is another form of augmentation. In particular, there is increasing demand for products that can be returned or recycled after their usefulness to the initial buyer has ended. A common example of recycling is automobiles that flow to the used car market and eventually into reclamation centers, where usable parts are extracted and raw materials such as metal and rubber are recycled. Toyota is working to promote its brand as environmentally conscientious. It was recently named the 2016 World Green Car. Says Bill Fay, group vice president and general manager, Toyota Division, "With a range of over 300 miles per tank, a refueling time of under five minutes, and emissions that consist only of water vapor, Mirai is leading the world forward toward a more sustainable future." [7]

CONSUMER PRODUCT CLASSIFICATION

Marketers divide products into the five categories: u nsought products, emergency products, convenience products, shopping products and specialty products.

Unsought Products **Unsought products** are not thought about frequently or perceived as very necessary. The desire is usually felt just briefly before purchase, such as novelties, T-shirts or "over the hill" gag gifts. They also include items that are important but unpleasant for many buyers to think about, such as long-term health care and cemetery plots. In any case, consumers don't seek information about these products, so it is essential for marketers to effectively promote them. In some cases, heavy promotion efforts, such as advertising and point of sales materials, may be required to persuade potential buyers to consider the item.

Impulse items make up a special category of unsought products, which as the name suggests, are often purchased on a whim. In most cases, impulse items are relatively inexpensive and have little to do with need fulfillment, other than the buyer's immediate enjoyment at the time of purchase. How many times have you been grocery shopping and tossed a box of Chips Ahoy! or Twinkies into your cart?

EMERGENCY PRODUCT

A product purchased due to an unexpected event and for which the consumer has an urgent need.

Emergency Products **Emergency products** are purchased when an unexpected event takes place and the consumer has an urgent need for a product. When an ambulance or tow truck is needed, the buyer is unlikely to compare prices and probably has little choice about the supplier. From the marketer's standpoint, it's crucial to have telephone numbers and other means of access available to buyers when an emergency occurs. A good example is the 911 service that local police, fire and ambulance agencies promote. American Express provides consumers with phone numbers that allow lost traveler's checks to be replaced immediately. Many automobile companies also provide toll-free numbers for emergency roadside service.

CONVENIENCE PRODUCT

A relatively inexpensive item that consumers purchase frequently and with minimum effort.

Convenience Products **Convenience products** are relatively inexpensive items that consumers purchase frequently and with minimum effort. Often they are referred to as staples, because people use them regularly. Examples include milk, toilet paper, gum, bottled water and so on. Convenience items are usually bought close to home, work or travel routes. Typically they are purchased only when the consumer's supply is low, such as when a tube of toothpaste is almost empty. One might take notice in the morning, and make a note to buy more on the way home from work.

Branding is very important for convenience products; buyers don't spend a lot of time selecting their purchases, so they gravitate toward the brands they know. The national drugstore chain CVS caters to purchasers by providing a one-stop shopping center for a multitude of consumer convenience needs. CVS also offers its own brand, which reduces purchase decision time as well as cost. Marketers must ensure that convenience items are widely distributed and prominently displayed with eye-catching packaging so they are quickly noticed and easily purchased.

SHOPPING PRODUCT

A purchase generally made only after the consumer has compared several alternatives.

Shopping Products **Shopping products** are generally purchased only after the consumer has compared the style, features, pricing, packaging and quality of several alternatives. Buyers compare prices to select the product providing the best value. Shopping products typically cost more and are purchased less frequently than convenience items; they include automobiles, televisions, appliances, furniture and clothing. Although people may do some pre-purchase planning at home, they are likely to visit stores to examine shopping goods, a desire that companies accommodate by often establishing stores near competitors. There may be several shoe stores in the same wing of a shopping mall, or several automobile dealerships in a row on the same street. This makes it easier for consumers to draw comparisons and increases the chance that one of the locations will make the sale.

Because shopping goods tend to be relatively durable, consumers don't want to be stuck with an unsuitable purchase for a long time. Selecting just the right piece of furniture to complement a room or finding an item of clothing that coordinates with one's wardrobe can require extensive shopping. Many people take along friends or family to help with the decision, and many do not feel comfortable making a major purchase without speaking with a salesperson. Many retailers and manufacturers recognize this and train their salespeople to identify buyers' needs and help them find exactly the right item.

Louis Vuitton is a premium brand that makes specialty products.

Specialty Products **Specialty products** have unique characteristics that provide unusual value to the purchaser, such as an association with the buyer's self-image. Consequently, customers are brand loyal and willing to travel long distances rather than settle for a substitute. Some examples are Movado watches, Gucci purses, Godiva chocolates, Louis Vuitton luggage and Armani suits. A lobster and filet mignon dinner, a dress from Saks Fifth Avenue, a stay at the Plaza Hotel or a luxury cruise also can be considered specialty items.

Most consumers spend a considerable amount of time on pre-purchase planning for specialty items. Because of the typically high cost of these items, both purchaser and retailers need to be highly involved to ensure that an ultimately satisfying purchase is made. To justify the expense of this service, marketers work hard to create customer loyalty. Repeat purchases generate enough profit over time to offset the cost of the first sale.

Service professionals often try to achieve the status of a specialty provider. There are physicians who practice only internal medicine, oncology or cosmetic surgery. The specialty classification signifies a great deal more value to most customers, which prompts certain types of lawyers, architects, consultants and accountants to charge more than their non-specialized counterparts. Buyers often seek these suppliers not only for their status but also because of the unique qualities of the product or service they provide.

BUSINESS PRODUCT CLASSIFICATION

Business products are purchased by an organization for its own use. The seven types listed in Figure 9.3 are grouped into three categories according to function: capital products, production products and operations products. These are the products needed to start a company and maintain it for the long term.

Capital Products **Capital products** are costly items that last a long time but are not part of any finished product. They usually are built or used to manufacture, distribute or support the development of other products. For accounting purposes, these items are depreciated over several years. Capital products are subdivided into installations and equipment.

Installations refer to house operations, and can also include office buildings, factories and distribution centers. Because they have a high cost and are intended to last for a considerable time, they are carefully selected by top management, and the involved salespeople possess technical expertise. Marketing generally requires a team approach, an understanding of the prospective client's business, and customization of the product to meet the unique requirements of each customer. Providers range from a small construction firm that may put up an office for a local dentist to companies such as Bechtel, a huge multinational. It has offices in most world regions and relies on mar-

Category and Type	Description	Examples
Capital Products		
Installations	Facilities that contain operations	Office buildings, factories, stores, distribution centers
Equipment	Items used to manufacture products and support the business	Drills, computers, desks, robots, lifts, trucks, airplanes
Production Products		
Raw materials	Substances in natural state	Crude oil, sand, gas, water
Processed materials	Basic substances used to manufacture products	Refined oil, steel, plastic, aluminum
Component Parts and Subassemblies		
Operations products	Products that are elements of other products	Brakes, transmissions, computer chips, switches, lights, cords
Operating services	Activities purchased to help run the business	Consulting, accounting, waste removal, employee food service
Operating supplies	Consumable items used by the business	Paper, pens, file folders, cleaning products

Figure 9.3   A Classification of Business Products

keting skills to find opportunities and win construction business globally.

Equipment is movable capital goods, such as drills, computers and forklifts, used to manufacture or maintain other products. ABB and AO Smith sell robotics designed for specific tasks to many types of manufacturers. General Motors (GM), Nissan and Toyota have purchased thousands of robots for welding alone; other functions include sorting, lifting and inspecting. Of course, products that bring information to businesses represent a huge equipment marketing opportunity. Companies such as Sun Microsystems sell computerized workstations for professional and clerical workers. These products are connected through elaborate networks that allow personnel around the globe to tie into the company system. Airline reservations in Japan, France, the United States and the Czech Republic are likely to be made this way. It is not unusual for equipment systems like these to be priced at hundreds of millions of dollars.

PRODUCTION PRODUCTS

Raw materials, processed materials, component parts, and sub-assemblies that become part of other goods.

Production Products
Production products — which include raw materials, processed materials, component parts and sub-assemblies — become part of other goods. Few manufacturers extract the raw materials or make all the components for a finished product. Instead, they rely on external suppliers to perform at least part of the task. Raw materials are basic substances used in the manufacture of products, such as ore to produce steel, or cotton and wool for textiles, oil for plastics, and soybeans for food products. Companies such as Archer-Daniels-Midland (ADM) claim that they "feed the world" because their agricultural products go into so many food items. Headquartered in Decatur, Illinois, the company's 31,000 employees work with crops such as oilseeds, wheat and soybeans. The harvested products are converted into food ingredients, animal feeds, chemicals and alternative fuel options. ADM serves as a vital link between farmers and the global community.[8] Processed materials undergo an intermediate treatment, such as refining, chemical combination, purification, crushing or milling, before reaching the manufacturer.

Component parts and subassemblies are manufactured goods that are elements of other products (like brake lines, components of antilock brake systems). Since these have several components and are part of still another product—vehicles—they are called subassemblies. Companies such as Eaton and North American Rockwell make components and subassemblies. Although each component is relatively inexpensive, manufacturing companies are likely to purchase large quantities at one time, numbering thousands or even millions of units.

Quality control and delivery of component parts can be very complicated, so successful companies must perform these operations at a high level of precision. Marketers stress this aspect of their product when selling to businesses, which usually is done by highly trained sales representatives.

Operations Products **Operations products** are purchased to help run the business but are not included in finished products. These range from very inexpensive items, such as paper clips, to an expensive product like nuclear waste removal from power plants. Operations products are subdivided into supplies and services. **Supplies** are consumable items that may seem relatively unimportant, but in total they can involve large sums. In banks, printed business forms alone often cost several hundred thousand dollars a year. Items such as pens, folders and cleaning products can contribute significantly to company costs. Even with increased use of the internet and more offices going paperless, Xerox found that the world prints about 2.8 trillion pages each year, with 45 percent of them read only once.[9]

Operations services are activities purchased to help run the business. Examples are legal, accounting, advertising and billing services. Accenture and McKinsey & Company all compete for lucrative contracts involving R&D, tactical and strategic plans and design of information systems, while companies like ARAMARK supply food services. Many companies subcontract other companies to help handle customer service; for example, if your Toshiba laptop computer needs to be repaired, UPS will pick it up, get it repaired, and return it to you within four days. By having a third party (UPS) handle its customer service, Toshiba was able to greatly reduce the repair turnaround time and increase customer satisfaction.[10]

Product Line Decisions

Product lines must be configured for domestic and global markets. Decisions about how many lines to carry, how many products will be in each line and the degree of standardization across markets shape the overall offering of an organization. A product line consists of closely related products marketed by a single organization. A company may have one line or several, but a single line usually focuses on the same type of benefit, such as hair care. An **item** is a specific version of a product within a product line. Each item, in turn, consists of several units, which refers to the specific product amount, container type and formula. Retailers call these stock keeping units (SKUs) to identify the variations they regularly have on their shelves.

Consider Procter & Gamble's Pantene product line for hair care. The Pantene brand has 113 items in its product line, which includes shampoo, conditioner, styling products and hair treatments.[11] Pantene's PRO-V product line is separated into categories made specifically for different types of hair (normal, dry, damaged, fine, smooth, curl and color treated). The products all have different levels of active ingredients designed to target specific hair issues, so consumers can choose the category of their hair type to get the best results.

Pantene is one of the leading hair care brands in the world. With the 2016 global hair care market estimated to be worth about $83.1 billion, P&G clearly has a vested interest in keeping the Pantene product line relevant to its customers worldwide, so brand managers constantly try to anticipate the next new product or product extention that will keep customers loyal to the Pantene brand.[12]

Product Depth and Breadth Most companies need to consider how broad and deep their product lines should be, as described in Figure 9.2. The **depth** of a product line refers to the number of items in it.

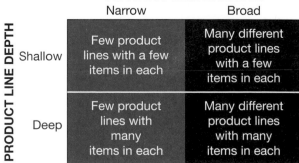

Figure 9.2   Product Line Depth and Breadth

BREADTH

The number of different lines a company markets.

Since the Pantene shampoo product line consists of many items, it is said to be deep. **Breadth** of product lines refers to the number of different lines a company markets. General Electric markets household products to consumers and nuclear power plants to foreign governments, as well as hundreds of other product lines, classifying it as very broad.

Hershey's candies can be considered a narrow and deep product line. Its products fall into a single category, candy, and there is a wide variety of items. Hershey's produces everything from their gourmet CaCao Reserve chocolate bar to Bubble Yum. In the pizza industry, Domino's Pizza has a broad and shallow product line. Domino's menu offers a wide variety of products that includes pizza, salads and drinks, with only a few choices in each category.

Most companies with a broad product line are large; smaller organizations usually lack the resources for competing across diverse product categories. Brunswick is a large company that uses a broad and deep product line strategy. It markets over 41 brands within five product lines: marine boats, marine engines, fitness, billiards and bowling. Popular boats such as Sea Ray and Boston Whaler, Mercury and Quicksilver engines, LifeFitness exercise equipment, and Brunswick Bowling & Billiards are all Brunswick brands.[13]

7-11 caries a broad and shallow product line.

Now think about 7-11. It carries a broad product line, but the variety of items within each is limited. For example, if you're looking for a box of macaroni and cheese, you'll find one choice on the shelf. You'll also find only one choice of ketchup, one choice of tissues, and one choice of laundry detergent. You might get to choose which energybar you want, or which brand of chips you want from the few sitting on the shelf...but your choice is very limited. In other words, 7-11 carries a broad and shallow product line. This is 7-11's business strategy.

It is entirely possible for companies to overextend their resources and make product lines too deep or broad, so they need to be adaptable and ready to restructure if necessary. Procter and Gamble has recently decided to divest 90-100 brands from its portfolio that are less profitable than others; P&G will become a simpler, more focused company of 70 to 80 brands, organized into about a dozen businesses and four industry-based sectors.[14] The company is narrowing its breadth and, in some cases, its depth so it can focus on its most profitable brands.

GLOBAL PRODUCT DECISIONS

The globalization of business creates several product-related dilemmas. Among the most critical is determining the optimal amount of standardization for individual products and lines across market regions. Different areas of the world vary greatly in terms of consumer and business purchasing approaches, media exposure, expectations, tastes and preferences. In addition, product standards and regulations, measurements and calibration systems, and economic factors vary immensely. Despite these differences, many firms like to standardize products to achieve economics of scale in R&D, production and marketing.

Standardization plays a major role in global company strategy. Companies often start by standardizing their suppliers to consolidate worldwide supply purchasing, improve material quality and reduce costs. By purchasing from a few similar suppliers, companies reduce product variations from region to region and develop relationships with their suppliers that enhance customer satisfaction.

Although product modifications usually center around conforming to local needs, the costs can be very high. Europe and the United States use different interfaces for electronics, so products made for one market simply will not work in the other. R&D costs to conform to standards run into the hundreds of millions for companies such as Siemens in Germany.

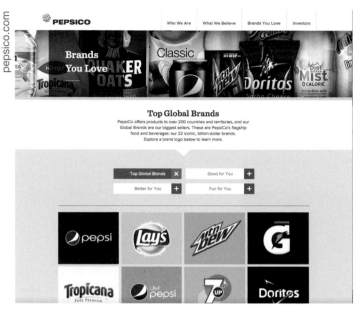

Pepsi's parent company, Pepsico, produces many popular products you may consume frequently.

The depth and breadth of a product line have a lot to do with successful global competition. Pepsi and Coca-Cola continually compete with each other to expand their product lines. Some believe Coke's global strategy of carrying a narrow, deep product line focused strictly on beverages, with geographic variations, is one reason for its success. Pepsi, in contrast, has a broader line that includes convenience food chains and has standardized its beverage line globally. Clearly, product line breadth and depth doesn't determine why one company outsells another, but the issue is important in developing global strategy. Although Coca-Cola remains the No. 1 beverage company with a deep product line, Pepsi is gaining in popularity through its other products. Pepsico recently acquired the South Beach Beverage Company, makers of SoBe, and Quaker Oats, maker of Gatorade, deepening its beverage offerings to include fruit blends, teas and energy drinks, in addition to its current Aquafina, All Sport, Lipton's Ice Tea and Frappuccino products. Coca-Cola has responded to Pepsi's expansion by purchasing Planet Java coffee, selling its own energy drink KMX, and experimenting with children's milk drinks. Coca-Cola also has its own brands of bottled water, sports drink, and root beer, in addition to other brands sold around the world. With Pepsi deriving 65 percent of its profits from its snack food line, including products such as Doritos, Cheetos and Sun Chips, Coca-Cola must continue to promote its beverage products in ways that capture buyers in order to retain its lead.[15]

Even some companies with deep domestic product lines find additions are necessary to compete internationally. Newell Rubbermaid, known for its large number of products, has its product lines divided to include products marketed globally, which account for approximately 28 percent of total revenues. Newell Rubbermaid implemented a global group product line strategy with four distinct product lines: cleaning, organization and decor; office products; tools and hardware; and home and family. The focus is to invest in strategic brands, reduce supply chain costs, strengthen the portfolio and streamline non-strategic selling, general and administrative (SG&A) expenses.[16] Experience with a deep and broad product line in the consumer, industrial and health care fields will be important as companies seek to connect with the needs and tastes of consumers in diverse regions.

Emerging economies such as China present their own problems from a product standpoint because large and risky investments in design and manufacturing are often necessary. For example, Caterpillar Inc., the world's largest maker of heavy machinery, opened 16 manufacturing facilities in China, with plans for nine more, based on projected economic growth in China's economy. However, that growth hasn't occurred, and company sales have slumped significantly, leaving huge facilities filled with new Caterpillar equipment idle.[17] Things may be starting to turn around now, though. "Infrastructure projects are starting and for the first time in a few years, we're seeing stronger demand from China," said Caterpillar Chief Financial Officer Brad Halverson.[18] Expanding product lines internationally increases a company's exposure to dynamic forces of the macroenvironment, as Caterpillar and so many other companies have learned.

BRAND

A distinguishing name or symbol to identify and differentiate products from those of competitors.

Brand Management

A **brand** is a distinguishing name or symbol that identifies and differentiates products from those offered by competitors.[19] Take a moment to try to name the top 10 brands in the world (check Figure 9.4 when you're done). No matter what criteria are used in creating such a list, the same brands tend to emerge as leaders.

Brands are very powerful concepts in business. They send strong signals about what a company represents, signals that can make or break a reputation. To a consumer, a trusted brand promises high quality, but a "tainted" reputation means poor quality or bad service. One study by Pricewaterhouse-Coopers found that 80 percent of online shoppers say that their purchasing decisions are strongly influenced by the need to buy brand-name products.[20]

Today, brands do far more than identify the manufacturer. They have become "personalities" with a character much greater than the products they represent. An early example of successful branding is Ivory soap, introduced in 1879 by Harvey Procter. With its claim of "99.44 percent pure," it has long been the leader of the soap market. Estimates suggest that the Ivory brand has brought more than $3 billion in profit to Procter & Gamble over the years. In some cases the brand name becomes the product itself to many people: Xerox, Band-Aid, Kleenex and Post-It Notes are synonymous with their functions. And such brands as Nabisco, Kellogg's, Kodak, Gillette, Campbell's and Goodyear have all outlived the specific items they represented when introduced. Although the products themselves may have changed with technology, customer preferences and modernization, the brand name has remained consistent.

Rank	2000	2016
1.	Coca-Cola	Apple
2.	Microsoft	Google
3.	IBM	Microsoft
4.	Intel	Coca-Cola
5.	Nokia	Facebook
6.	General Electric	Toyota
7.	Ford	IBM
8.	Disney	Disney
9.	McDonald's	McDonalds
10.	AT&T	General Electric

Figure 9.4   Top 10 Brands Worldwide
Source: Forbes — The World's Most Valuable Brands, 2016

Historically, brands were used to identify a product's manufacturer. They also protected both the customer and the producer by ensuring that the products met certain quality standards and came from a reputable source. Companies with early success in building brands include Procter & Gamble (P&G), IBM, McDonalds, Sony, American Express, Volkswagen, American Airlines, Pepsi and Kodak. Such companies created a brand perceived by consumers as having more intrinsic value.

In the 1960s, strategy was simple: the greater the perceived value, the greater the sales. This strategy is still used today, but companies must work hard to ensure that the products themselves provide the added value communicated by the name. Brand strategies help businesses such as Coca-Cola, Disney, Gillette and Intel develop and retain credibility with customers, and that shows no sign of changing. According to TNS Media Intelligence, a leading provider of market information, most advertising expenditures are brand related.[21]

TRADEMARKS

People tend to use the words "brand" and "trademark" interchangeably, but there are some notable differences. The brand name is the wording attached to the product. Adidas, Levis and Chiquita are brand names. The **trademark (brand mark)** is a word, phrase, symbol, or design that identifies and distinguishes the source of a good/service. The term "trademark" is often used to refer to both trademarks and service marks.[22] A

NBC's peacock logo was first created by designer John J. Graham in 1956. It has since undergone several changes to keep it current.

picture is called a trademark symbol, such as McDonald's golden arches; distinctively shaped letters are called a logo: IBM, HBO, GE. Other examples are NBC's peacock, Adidas's three stripes and Chrysler's five-pointed star.

TRADEMARK PIRACY

The brand name and trademark symbols or logos are protected by law if they are registered. That gives the owner sole right to use them any way he or she chooses. Just as most people want to protect their reputation, companies are careful to protect a brand from imitators or competitors. For example, a federal court in Milwaukee ruled that the Hog Farm, a motorcycle parts and repair shop, had infringed on the rights of Harley-Davidson, whose motorcycles are widely known as "hogs."

Apple secured a massive patent that could have turned the smartphone industry upside-down. It was granted a series of patents that include almost all of the user interface elements in smartphones, including the multi-touch system developed for its iPhone. Tim Cook, Apple's CEO, stated "From our point of view, it's important that Apple not be the developer for the world. We can't take all of our energy and all of our care and finish the painting, then have someone else put their name on it." While Apple wants proprietary standards, Google advocates the broadening of Standards Essential Patent (SEP) product category of patents, making these popular features that consumers know and love shared industry standards.[23]

Securing trademarks globally can be very tricky. The Wrigley Company wanted to trademark the name "Doublemint," which seems reasonable enough. But in Europe, at least, they can't do it. The ruling against Wrigley stated that the word "Doublemint" lacks an imaginative element.[24] If a company plans to market in Europe, its marketers should understand the Madrid Protocol, which explains how trademarks are registered and enforced in the European Union.[25] In advanced economies, trademark protection is considered essential for sound competitive industrial policy. Elsewhere trademarks may be viewed as merely a tool to stimulate commerce. No single world policy has yet been developed that takes into account the perspectives of all nations.

No one knows exactly how big the market for counterfeit goods is, but trade associations generally agree that it is an estimated $750 billion-a-year business. About 80 percent of consumers worldwide regularly purchase counterfeit products.[26] Counterfeiting has become so widespread that *Fortune* has coined the term "brandnapping" for copying products and affixing illegal labels. This represents huge losses to legitimate owners of the brands. Pirated products range from computer software and designer goods to soap and candy. Packaging closely resembles that of the American-made counterpart, and often stolen logo designs are used. Individual firms may or may not choose to file an international suit against offenders.

Many problems with brand counterfeiting are occurring in China. In fact, China accounts for nearly two-thirds of all counterfeit goods. Recent investigations in China have turned up everything from fake Sony PlayStation game controllers, Sharpie markers, Cisco Systems router interface cards, even counterfeit elevators. When these components leave China, they sometimes end up in the product's legitimate supply chain, and can force companies to initiate expensive recalls.

However, many fakes today are getting so good that even company executives say that it takes a forensic scientist to distinguish them from the real thing.[27] For instance, the popular baby carrier brand Ergobaby has been fighting counterfeit versions of its carriers, which are often sold through online auction sites such as eBay. The company has released lists of known or suspected sellers of counterfeit carriers, along with suggestions for how to spot fakes.[28] Walk down a busy street in any large city of the world, and you'll likely find vendors selling knock-offs of Rolex watches, Gucci and Louis Vuitton purses, Tiffany necklaces, software and even pharmaceutical drugs, such as Viagra and Lipitor.

Unfortunately, some fakes can have very serious consequences. For example, it is estimated that in a single year, fake drugs led to the deaths of 192,000 patients in China who were given ineffective treatments. According to the World Health Organization, counterfeit drugs account for more than ten percent of the total global supply and can run as high as 50 percent in parts of Africa and Asia. Merck, a large pharmaceutical company, exclusively funded Global Pharma Health Fund (GPHF) in an effort to derail the counterfeit drug market. The organization will work in conjunction with various governmental and world health agencies.[29] U.S. trade negotiations have lessened the occurrence of infringements, but developing countries have little incentive to enforce laws. Efforts continue through such organizations as GATT (General Agreement on Tariffs and Trade) and the United Nations to develop international norms.

BRAND STRATEGIES

In addition to a generic or nonbranded approach, there are five common brand strategies: individual, family, manufacturer (national), private and hybrid. Each is described below.

GENERIC BRAND STRATEGY

Strategy in which no brand name is used.

Generic Strategy A **generic brand strategy** uses no brand name whatsoever. Firms generally select this approach when they want to gain a low-cost commodity market position. As mentioned before, pharmaceutical companies often adopt this strategy. Some grocery stores devote entire aisles exclusively to generic products, packaged in plain black and white. Many consumers prefer generics because they cost less than name brands.

INDIVIDUAL BRAND STRATEGY

Strategy in which there is a unique name for each major product or product line.

Individual Brand Strategy An **individual brand strategy** assigns a unique brand name to each major product or product line. There are three situations in which this approach is likely to be used. First, companies may have different product lines that compete against one another. For example, Ford Motor Company builds market share with several individual brands such as Ford, Lincoln and Mercury. Second, products within one line may be matched with unique market segment needs. For example, Procter & Gamble's thirteen laundry detergents appeal to different segments. Third, a company may make highly dissimilar products. For example, Kellogg markets breakfast cereals under its name, toaster pastries under the Pop-Tarts brand and pies under the Mrs. Smith's label.

FAMILY BRAND STRATEGY

Strategy in which a single brand name covers the entire group of products in the company's line(s).

Family Brand Strategy A **family brand strategy** uses a single brand name for the entire group of products in the company's line(s). This can be very cost-effective, because advertising, promotion and distribution resources can be focused to create a single image in the marketplace. The result is increased consumer awareness of the company and its products, such as Black & Decker tools.

The family brand strategy is used when products are similar. Dole markets more than 20 mainstream fruits and vegetables as well as numerous exotic fruits under one name. The Sony name covers hundreds of products, from high-priced stereos to inexpensive alarm-clock radios. The family brand approach has allowed Sony to introduce and eliminate products fairly rapidly while almost guaranteeing that its new products will at least be tried. Both Dole and Sony have sought to make their names synonymous with quality, regardless of the specific product.

MANUFACTURER'S BRAND (NATIONAL BRAND)

Brand named after the manufacturer.

Manufacturer's Brand Strategy **Manufacturer's brands** (**national brand**), as the term implies, are named after the maker. Sometimes they are called national brands or global brands, since the products often are found throughout the country or world. We've already mentioned a few in this chapter, such as General Electric, but manufacturer's brands also can be local, such as Hanover pretzels. The company's reputation is closely tied to the product. Benetton, McDonald's and Johnson & Johnson use public relations, advertising and other means to ensure that the public connects their products with the policies of the firm. Usually this means creating a singular image for the company and the products it makes. Samsung is known for electronics, Fisher-Price is known for products that relate to child development and safety, and Gerber is famous for baby food.

Private Brand Strategy When wholesalers or retailers place their own name on a product, it's called a **private brand** (or private label). Private brands are usually sold at a lower price than manufacturer's brands. They have become increasingly popular over the last two decades, as consumers have discovered that buying store brands not only saves money but gives them the taste, performance and innovation of more expensive national brands. In fact, store brand sales reached $118.4 billion in 2015, an all-time record and an increase of $2.2 billion over 2014.[30]

Private labels also allow the reseller to build and enhance its own reputation. For example, by carefully selecting suppliers and developing quality control mechanisms, Meijer can promote its line of private brands by meeting or exceeding the quality of national brands at a lower price.[31] Meijer also offers specialty labels such as Meijer Gold, Organics and Naturals, which give consumers more options to choose from. In addition, private brands enable retailers and wholesalers to differentiate themselves from competitors.

Meijer Organics is a private brand that allows the retailer to sell quality products at a low price.

Companies that use private brands attempt to understand consumers better than national marketers in several key respects, especially in their knowledge of local or regional consumer needs and shopping habits. Although they do not have the resources to innovate far beyond current brands, their goal is to increase in-store brand sales, which may carry strong margins. National brand competitors face the challenge of persuading consumers not to be drawn by lower-priced store brands. Some companies like Home Depot present particular challenges to manufacturers. It markets its own private brands, yet Home Depot is the major retail outlet for many manufacturers' brands. Essentially, these manufactures must cooperate with Home Depot while competing against its increasingly popular private brands.

The "battle of the brands" rivalry between in-store and national products is intense. The private label market is growing as consumers become more cost-conscious and as private label brands rival the quality of national brands. The "battle" started when large manufacturers gained power by selling products through a broad range of distribution channels, and their size allowed them to place many demands on retailers. Large retailers countered by creating private labels.

Hybrid Brand Strategy Many firms employ a **hybrid brand strategy**, which is a combination of two or more approaches. Often this happens when mergers and acquisitions join organizations that employ different strategies. In these cases, executives must decide whether to blend the acquired brands into the company's portfolio or let them maintain their identities.

In 2015, Kraft Foods and H.J. Heinz Co. merged, creating Kraft-Heinz, which is now the third largest food and beverage company in North America and the fifth largest food and beverage company in the world. The popular brands from each company kept their identity after the merger, so consumers can still find their favorites, including Kraft, Heinz, ABC, Capri Sun, Classico, Jell-O, Kool-Aid, Lunchables, Maxwell House, Ore-Ida, Oscar Mayer, Philadelphia, Planters, Weight Watchers Smart ones and Velveeta.[32]

BRAND EQUITY: THE VALUE OF A SUCCESSFUL BRAND

Brand equity refers to the assets linked with the brand name and symbol that add value to the product or service.[33] It indicates (in both denotative and connotative lights) how valuable the brand is to the parent company. It denotes (identifies) what the brand is, such as Head & Shoulders or Selsun Blue shampoo. It also connotes (produces an image of) the brand's relationship to the consumer's lifestyle. Connotative meanings, if properly supported, can strengthen over time. Names such as Gillette, Morton's Salt and Betty Crocker predate your grandparents. When people invest in a home and gradually purchase it from the mortgage company, we say that they are earning or gaining equity. In a similar fashion, companies must invest in developing brands. Through sustained communication of the brand's connotative qualities, value is increased. Brand equity is an intangible asset with five dimensions, as shown in Figure 9.5. Let's look at each dimension in more detail:

Brand Awareness **Brand awareness** is the extent to which consumers recognize the name and are likely to include it among the set of brands they consider. If consumers are familiar with a brand and like it, they will have positive attitudes about the product(s) with that name. Consider the warmth and reliability of the Betty Crocker mother figure or Pillsbury's Poppin' Fresh baker. Because strong brands are often global, they may be recognized around the world and provide traveling consumers with ready access to a familiar item. High brand awareness also represents the commitment of the company to maintaining long-term standards of excellence for the consumer.

Even established companies work to sustain brand awareness. One way Kraft does this is through its website, www.kraftfoods.com, which provides information on nutrition, cooking for specific occasions, mealtime tips, a personal recipe box and recipes customized to suit the user's available ingredients. Customers can also download apps to their smart phones and tablets that allow them to gain access to recipes and Kraft inspired games on the go. Online customers who choose to add their address to a marketing list will receive product information, promotions, a quarterly magazine and coupons through the mail.[34] This increased accessibility to Kraft's brand name is intended to heighten brand awareness.

Brand Equity

- **Brand Awareness**
  - Part of consumer's evoked (consideration) set
  - Greater familiarity and liking
  - Better recognition

- **Brand Loyalty**
  - Reduced marketing cost for repeat buyers
  - Leverage with distribution channel members
  - Attract new customers by word of mouth
  - Steady market share allows time to respond to competitors

- **Perceived Quality**
  - Reason to buy (value to customer)
  - Uniqueness
  - Better price

- **Brand Associations**
  - Help consumers process information
  - Create positive attitudes
  - Allow brand extensions and changes

- **Competitive Advantage**
  - Company can market value rather than compete on price
  - A barrier to entry
  - Supports promotion campaigns

Figure 9.5 The Five Dimensions of Brand Equity
Source: Adapted from David A. Aaker, Managing Brand Equity (New York: The Free Press, 1991), inside cover.

Brand Loyalty **Brand loyalty** occurs when consumers select a particular brand over others on a regular basis. Brand loyalty leads to lower overall marketing costs because it's much less expensive to persuade repeat buyers than to create new ones. Distribution channel members are more likely to provide a good location within their outlet for the sale of an item with high brand loyalty. Furthermore, companies with faithful customers tend to be less susceptible to economic downturns or new competitors because loyal buyers are not immediately inclined to look at other options; they'll stay with the brand even in times of economic hardship.

Cheerwine has carved out a niche market of extremely loyal customers in the Southeast. Its website offers delivery to the customers that are outside Cheerwine distribution areas, keeping loyal customers happy.

Brand loyalty is highest among more mature segments, who tend to find a brand they like and stick with it, while younger generations are more willing to experiment with various brands. However, studies show that brand loyalty may begin as early as the age of two. The nine to ten age group, usually referred to as "tweens," is the transitional generation, when "collective individualism" is a big trend; the 13-15 age group is more aware of what is "cool" and less affected by other advertisers.[35] Loyalty produces sales that enhance the earning power of the company. Cheerwine, created in 1917, is a nonalcoholic, carbonated drink produced by Carolina Beverage Corporation and sold mainly in the Southeast. Although Cheerwine does not even register in national market share polls, it has established itself as a Southern icon and has found its way of creating a niche of loyal customers. Carolinians are so loyal to the drink that those who relocate often write the company asking where they can find Cheerwine near their new location. Loyalists tell others about their favorite brand, often referred to as the "Nectar of the Tarheels" and the "Legend," and sales increase rapidly.[36]

Even Mother Nature's own fruits have been branded—bananas by Chiquita and oranges by Sunkist. While there is no critical difference between them and other bananas and oranges, consumers recognize and prefer the brand names. For a brand to be valuable to a company, a significant number of customers must prefer it over competitive brands.

The best kind of loyalty for a company is when consumers insist on the company's brand. **Brand insistence** occurs when consumers are unwilling to accept substitutes, an enviable position for the corporation, especially in the long run. This degree of loyalty is more likely for specialty items, such as polo shirts or branded pharmaceuticals, but in recent years, some unlikely products have gained brand insistence status. It used to be that technology products, such as electrical components, did not have much brand awareness, to say nothing of brand loyalty. Intel Corporation, the pioneering semiconductor company, gave technology branding a boost. It has persuaded consumers to insist on Intel microprocessors in their PCs and mobile devices. Apple has done the same; if you like your iPhone, you probably have, or want, an Apple computer. You likely use iTunes and FaceTime with friends. Most Apple users are not only brand loyal, they are also brand insistent.

BRAND INSISTENCE

A dimension of brand equity that makes consumers unwilling to accept substitutes for the brand.

PERCEIVED BRAND QUALITY

The degree to which a brand consistently produces satisfaction by meeting customer expectations.

Perceived Brand Quality The third dimension of brand equity is **perceived brand quality**, the degree to which brands consistently produce satisfaction by meeting customer expectations. This is one of the most important reasons consumers buy a product. The high or unique quality of a brand is directly related to what consumers are willing to pay and to whether the firm can charge a premium. For example, having and using a major accounting firm is associated with premium audit fees. However, a number of companies are willing to pay higher fees for the perceived higher quality of a Big Four audit, even though another firm could provide the identical service at a lower price.

BRAND ASSOCIATIONS

The positive attitudes and feelings a brand evokes in consumers' minds.

Brand Associations Brand equity also involves establishing **brand associations** that evoke positive attitudes and feelings in consumers' minds. This enables firms to create messages that gain consumers' attention more easily and extends the company's good reputation to additional products. For instance, Procter & Gamble marketed only 13 advertised brands in 1950. By 1991, there were more than 100, and there are more than 300 today. Twenty-five of these brands are called its "Billion-Dollar Brands," each generating more than $1 billion in annual sales.[37]

In a hard-hitting campaign against Yamaha motorcycles, Honda used brand associations with its automobiles. It quickly produced a great number of motorcycles of every type in an effort to crowd Yamaha out of the market. This was a feasible strategy because consumers already had a positive feeling about the Honda brand name.

Brand associations also can facilitate product changes. For example, Tide gradually altered its detergent from a bulky powder to concentrated powder and liquid forms, and most recently it introduced pods. Since 1985, Patagonia has donated more than $31 million to grassroots environmental activists and more than 1,000 organizations through its Environmental Grants Program. As a member of One Percent for the Planet, it contributes one percent of all sales to grassroots efforts. While encouraging a green lifestyle, Patagonia has also created affirmative brand awareness.[38] Positive brand associations help consumers make the transition to an altered product or a similar one with new features.

Competitive Advantage Finally, brand equity can lead to **competitive advantage**, since a company can sell value rather than compete on the basis of price alone. The firm can charge a premium for many of the intangible dimensions associated with the brand. Brand equity also creates competitive advantages by serving as a barrier to entry. In other words, it may be too risky or expensive for another company or brand to compete in the same market. In the 1980s, a battle of the brands among beer companies created an environment in which only the strong survived. Within only 10 years, hundreds of small and local breweries were put out of business by such companies as Anheuser-Busch, Stroh's, Miller and Coors. Nearly every beer company that relied on product processing and procedures rather than building brand equity fell out of contention.

MAINTAINING BRAND VALUE

How many times have you requested a Coke in a restaurant and been asked whether a Pepsi would be okay? Coca-Cola has gone to great lengths to make sure that the Coke brand does not become a generic name. Believe it or not, aspirin, escalator, kerosene, nylon and zipper were all brand names at one time. To prevent brand names from falling into the public domain, a company must continually announce and defend its exclusive ownership. Consequently, Coca-Cola waged court battles against retailers who substituted Pepsi when Coke was ordered. Without such efforts, Coke could have lost its trademark exclusivity.

Often, the first manufacturer of a new technology or product becomes synonymous with the entire product class. Did you grow up believing that Kleenex was another name for facial tissue? Do you ask for a Band-Aid when you want an adhesive bandage? Many people say they are going to Xerox something, but they may be using a Canon or some other brand of copier. To avoid the loss of its exclusivity, Xerox runs advertisements explaining that "Xerox" is its registered trademark and should be used only when referring to the company and its products as opposed to a general process.

DEVELOPING A SUCCESSFUL BRAND NAME

Choosing a brand name may not be easy. Americans file more than 500,000 trademark applications each year, a number that continues to increase. To keep pace, the U.S. Patent and Trademark Office staff includes more than 400 trademark-examining attorneys.[39] This poses a challenge to companies that want a memorable and meaningful brand name. Name Lab Inc., a specialist in this area, recommends choosing names that eliminate cultural associations or linguistic borders and can therefore succeed globally uninhibited. Names like Sony, Samsung and McDonald's do not show bias toward a particular language or region, and are also memorable, unique and distinctive.[40]

Some firms have chosen brand names that communicate product attributes or benefits. For example, Wheaties describes the ingredients of the cereal. When "Breakfast of Champions" is added, we get an image of wholesomeness or goodness. The name Weight

Watchers communicates a direct consumer behavior, and it carries strong associations with weight control and health.

Brand names must represent quality and commitment. That's why extensive research is usually conducted to identify whether the name is appropriate and can be used internationally. Standard Oil tested Exxon in multiple languages and foreign markets before making a final decision. Marketers must be acutely aware that not all brand names carry the same meaning when translated. For example, in the early 1990s, General Mills introduced a cereal called Fingos that was designed to be eaten with your fingers; however, it translated into a less than appetizing word for Hungarians. Also consider Chevy Nova, which in Spanish-speaking countries meant "no va," or "no go."

Some brand names are successful because of what they say about the user. Many convey a personality trait that makes the connection directly. Magazines such as GQ, Cosmopolitan and Vogue represent attributes that readers consider desirable.

JOINT MARKETING OF BRANDS

Joint marketing is cooperation between two companies, often two goods manufacturers, to sell their brands. Since coupons and short-term promotions (such as refund certificates) often cause disloyalty and confusion among customers, replacing those tactics with joint marketing can build business for the cooperating companies. It is important for marketers to understand how a consumer perceives the way a product, brand and the corporations fit together. Even more so, it is crucial to create a positive impression before marketing a co-branded product.[41] An example of this can be found in the partnership between the National Basketball Association (NBA) and YouTube which has led to the creation of a channel where NBA fans can watch videos of their favorite athletes online as well as post videos of themselves doing NBA moves for the potential to be shown on a weekly TV segment. The NBA also posts select, behind-the-scenes features on its channel to give fans a personal look into their favorite sports teams.[42]

When you buy concert tickets at Ticketmaster.com, you may be offered free Apple iTunes downloads. By establishing this partnership, Ticketmaster.com was encouraging customers to purchase tickets through its venue by promoting iTunes. This type of cooperation is expected to become more frequent.[43] Starbucks has also partnered with Apple. Many Starbucks locations offer free iTunes of selected artists in conjunction with a beverage purchase. Joint marketing efforts such as these are usually successful when the consumer has a positive image of both companies.

Packaging and Labeling

"People don't buy spray paint, they buy spray paint cans." That statement was made in a marketing research report for a major manufacturer in the industry to dramatize the importance of packaging. The research found that most buying decisions were made at the point of purchase. By looking at the color and design of the cans and by reading labels, consumers quickly determined which spray paint would best suit their needs.

Packaging and labeling once served simply to protect and identify the product inside. Arnold Palmer, golfing legend, has long been associated with his favorite refreshment, a mixed drink of half iced tea and half lemonade. Now the "Arnold Palmer" can be found at many golf pro shops, and on courses nationwide, recognizable in its distinctive bottle with the golf ball cap and Arnie's picture prominently displayed. Packaging has seven functions:

drinkarizona.com

Arizona's Arnold Palmer drinks have unique and attractive packaging that also functions well.

- Contain and protect items
- Be environmentally friendly
- Communicate messages to customers
- Contain product codes
- Make the product more convenient to use
- Protect against misuse
- Facilitate product storage.

LABELS

Information printed on a product's package to inform consumers and help promote the product.

The **labels** on a package inform consumers and help promote the product. The Fair Packaging and Labeling Act of 1966 requires that consumer products carry clear and easily understood labels, displaying the brand name and symbol, the manufacturer's name and address, the product content and amount, and recommended uses. The law also requires adequate information when value comparisons are made among competitive products.

In 1990, Congress passed the Nutritional Labeling and Education Act, which applies to food.[44] Excluded are meat, poultry and eggs (covered by U.S. Department of Agriculture regulations) as well as restaurants, delicatessens and infant formulas. Additional legislation that year required the FDA to develop standard definitions of terms commonly found on products, such as reduced calories, high fiber and low fat.[45] These laws affect about 15,000 U.S. food packagers as well as many importers. Food labels are required to display fat, saturated fat, cholesterol, carbohydrates, protein and the percentage of daily vitamin requirements contained. European standards on "diet" claims are even stricter. Research shows that the people most likely to read food labels are educated women who live with others, are relatively knowledgeable about nutrition, are concerned about the quality of food they purchase, and believe that current dietary recommendations are important to their health, while less educated men are the least likely to take a look.[46]

PRODUCT LIABILITY

The responsibility of marketers and manufacturers for injuries and damages caused by a faulty product.

The Labeling of Hazardous Art Materials Act (LHAMA) of 1990 addresses another product category. The U.S. Public Interest Research Group (PIRG) lobbied for this legislation because it believed that a wide variety of suppliers inadequately warned consumers of chronic and long-term health risks related to certain chemicals used in their products.[47]

Marketers must take care to ensure that packages are properly labeled. They benefit from this along with their customers, particularly when health and safety issues are involved.

Ethical Issues Surrounding Product Safety & Liability

The Consumer Product Safety Act of 1972 created the Consumer Product Safety Commission (CPSC) to police consumer goods. It has broad authority over the end product, can demand recalls and redesigns, and even inspects production facilities. For example, a massive toy recall was recently issued for high lead content in the paint on children's toys imported from China. In response, toymakers such as Mattel instated a comprehensive safety protocol for all of its products.[48] Of particular significance is the commission's ability to bring criminal charges against companies and individuals who develop unsafe products.

Product liability refers to the fact that marketers and manufacturers are held responsible for injuries and damages caused by a faulty product. In one case the CPSC found that more than 7,000 people were being injured monthly on three-wheel all-terrain vehicles (ATVs), most of them made by Honda and Kawasaki. Although the number of accidents was well known to dealers and distributors,

Three-wheelers were some of the first designs of ATVs made popular by Honda and Kawasaki. Companies were later pressured to develop a quad-wheel design for safety reasons.

only when the CPSC applied pressure did the makers agree to stop marketing the product in the United States. Many people believe consumers had the right to know about the ATV injuries. Clearly, wider publicity about the hazards would have meant lost sales.

The liability issue involves the right to safety and the manufacturer's responsibility for designing safe products and for informing the public about any dangers. Most companies fulfill this obligation through the product warranty and, in extreme cases, product recalls.

PRODUCT WARRANTIES

WARRANTIES

Written or implied expectations about product performance.

Warranties are written or implied expectations about product performance. An express warranty is a written statement about the content or quality of a product and the manufacturer's responsibility to repair or replace it if it fails to perform. For example, an express warranty may indicate that an item is handcrafted in the United States, or may use such general terms as "unconditionally guaranteed" or "fully guaranteed," or may be a technical description of the goods. In the past, when consumers made claims under a warranty, some unethical manufacturers made it very difficult for them to receive satisfaction, rendering many general warranty statements meaningless.

To address this problem, Congress passed the Magnuson-Moss Warranty–Federal Trade Commission Improvement Act in 1975. Essentially, the law requires that express warranties be written in clear language and indicate which parts or components are covered and which are not. If repair is included in the express warranty, it must occur within a reasonable time, free of charge. A full warranty states that either the merchandise will be repaired or the purchase price will be refunded if the product does not work after repair.

Many retailers pressure their suppliers to take back any product a customer returns for any reason. Companies such as Walmart have a very liberal return policy, allowing them to receive feedback on product performance and build good customer relations, which in turn helps to gain market share.

An implied warranty is an unwritten guarantee that the product or service will do the job it is intended to do. All products, even if not accompanied by a written statement, have an implied warranty based on the Uniform Commercial Code (UCC). Adopted in 1952, the UCC is a federal statute affecting the sale of goods and giving consumers the right to reject a product if it does not meet their needs. Many individual states also have laws protecting consumers.

Walmart has a very liberal return policy, providing feedback on product performance to the company and building good customer relations in the process.

PRODUCT RECALLS

PRODUCT RECALL

The withdrawal from the market, by either a manufacturer or the federal government, and repair, replacement, or discontinuation of a potentially harmful product.

A **product recall** is the withdrawal of a potentially harmful product from the market, by either a manufacturer or the federal government, for its repair, replacement or discontinuation. The Consumer Product Safety Commission (CPSC) is the federal agency responsible for protecting consumers from product-related injuries. It establishes standards for product design and requires that products meet those standards during testing. Manufacturers and retailers are required by law to notify the CPSC if they find a defective product that may result in injury.

When a manufacturer realizes a product is defective, its response can inspire consumer confidence and actually promote sales. In Chapter 2, we described the actions of Johnson & Johnson during the Tylenol scare in 1982. The unprecedented recall brought tremendous positive publicity to the company. When Tylenol was returned to store shelves, consumers made it the top-selling pain reliever.

Just because a company issues a recall does not guarantee that consumers will take action or that they will see the company in a positive light. Sometimes they aren't even aware of a recall if they didn't complete and return a product registration card after purchase. Sears sent a letter to registered owners of a particular dishwasher that was being recalled. The letter used large red letters for these words: "Important Safety Notice. Dishwasher Rework—Potential Fire Hazard. Please Give This Your Immediate Attention." After three days the response rate was only 20 percent.[49]

Even when a company meets its legal obligations, consumer awareness and other factors may have a lot to do with ethical considerations that must be addressed. It may be more devastating for a company to resist recalling a faulty product. Toyota recalled 4.3 million vehicles, including Avalon, Camry, Corolla, Highlander, Matrix, Prius, RAV4, Sequoia, Tundra and Venza models. Owners were experiencing sticking gas pedals that could cause unwanted acceleration. In less than four months, Google had more than 10 million hits about the situation. The first sites tended to be created by Toyota itself in efforts to manage the negative fallout from customers with concerns. In addition to experiencing one of the largest recalls in auto history, Toyota was confronted by angry shareholders who claimed the company misinformed the public, causing the stock price to rise initially and then fall, costing shareholders millions of dollars. Several class-action lawsuits claimed that Toyota publicly dismissed the seriousness of design flaws, knowing that public knowledge of the problems might have resulted in a large sell-off of Toyota shares. The suits claimed that initially the company blamed acceleration problems on floor mats, leading many consumers to believe that the problems were not as serious as the design problems that were identified later. The company eventually acknowledged that the problem existed without floor mats.[50]

Throughout this chapter, we have explored a wide range of strategies, from bundling products into special value units to assuring product safety, that marketers employ to build strong brand equity and give appeal to existing products. In Chapter 10, we'll take a look at the characteristics of goods, services and nonprofit marketing.

Chapter Summary

Objective 1: Describe the major dimensions used by marketers to differentiate products from competitors.

Products can be core, branded and augmented. The core product represents the most basic functions and benefits. Some call this the generic product. The branded product adds characteristics that help consumers differentiate it from others. The augmented product includes such features as delivery, warranty and customer service. A bundling strategy combines several products into one offering and sold together. When products are bundled, they provide more value to the buyer than if each were sold separately.

Objective 2: Define consumer and business product classifications based on how and why products are purchased and consumed.

Five categories are used to classify consumer products. Unsought products are bought on the spur of the moment. They include novelty, impulse and low-involvement items. Emergency products are bought because of unexpected events, such as an accident or theft. Convenience products are inexpensive and are usually purchased near home. Brand name and wide distribution are very important for these items. Shopping items are selected after comparisons are made. They tend to be carefully chosen and are kept for a long time. Specialty products have unique characteristics and value. They are often high-involvement purchases.

Business products are divided into capital, production and operations products, depending on their primary use. Capital products include installations, such as offices and factories, and equipment, such as delivery vans and computers. These products last for a long time. Production products become part of other products. This category includes raw and processed materials, components and subassemblies. Operations products help run the business. These include services such as accounting and waste removal, and office supplies such as business forms and cleaning products.

Objective 3: Know how organizations make product line decisions that determine what will be sold, including the degree of standardization chosen for global markets.
A product line may be comprised of one item or a number of related products. Companies may have one or more product lines, each with many or few items. The term depth refers to the number of items in a product line; the term breadth refers to the number of lines the company offers. Most companies with broad lines are relatively large; those with narrow lines may be large or small. The degree to which products should be standardized is a major consideration for global firms. Some organizations pursue standardization to benefit from the resulting economies of scale, whereas others use a local strategy to respond to local needs.

Objective 4: Recognize that branding and brand strategies are important aspects of building and maintaining a brand name.
A brand is distinguished from the product in general or other brands. Brands signify the "personality" of a product. The brand name and trademark can provide immediate recognition and credibility. Consequently, companies must register and protect trademarks. This is particularly challenging in global markets because stolen brand names and counterfeit products are so prevalent. There are several brand strategies. The generic approach involves no brand name. The individual strategy uses a unique name for each product line. The family brand is one name that covers all products in the line. Manufacturer brands are synonymous with the company that owns them. Private label brands are names used by wholesalers or retail-ers for products supplied to them. Combining two or more of these strategies is called a hybrid approach.

Objective 5: Explain how to create brand equity. A strong brand name is extremely valuable, but developing that name is not simple. First, the name must be selected with care. It should be acceptable globally, represent quality and commitment, and be protected legally. A good brand can easily be extended to additional products as they are developed. Second, brand equity must be created by devoting company resources to each of its five dimensions: brand awareness, brand loyalty, perceived quality, brand associations and competitive advantage. Third, care must be taken to protect the brand so it does not become a generic name for the product.

Objective 6: Discuss the legal and ethical issues surrounding brand and packaging decisions.
Federal laws and codes require that labels clearly identify the brand and manufacturer and warn consumers of safety hazards associated with use. Product liability holds marketers responsible for injuries and damages caused by a faulty product. Warranties refer to how products perform when used. In many cases, manufacturers are legally obligated to replace or repair faulty products. Express warranties are written. An implied warranty is unwritten. Essentially, a product should perform as it was designed. A product recall is instituted by the government or manufacturer to withdraw or modify a product. This occurs when a product is defective, especially if the potential for injury exists.

Review Your Understanding

1. What is a product? Give three examples.
2. What are core, branded and augmented products?
3. Explain bundling and unbundling.
4. What are five categories of consumer products? What are three categories of business products? Give examples.
5. Define product line, unit and SKU.
6. What is a broad and deep product line? What is a narrow and shallow product line? Give examples.
7. What are global products and brands?
8. What is joint marketing of products? Give an example.
9. What is brand equity? How is it developed?
10. Why is it important to secure trademarks?
11. Name and describe five brand categories.
12. What are the functions of packaging?
13. What is product liability?

Discussion of Concepts

1. Imagine that you are a marketing manager at IBM responsible for the sale of personal computers to individual consumers. How would you describe your product in terms of core, branded and augmented characteristics? Which of these do you feel is most important?
2. What are the advantages and disadvantages of a bundling strategy?
3. Name the five categories of products based on consumer buying behavior. Why is it so important for marketers to understand the category of their product?
4. Discuss the differences between product line breadth and depth. What are some advantages and disadvantages of each combination of breadth and depth?
5. Classify each of the following companies in terms of product line breadth and depth and explain your reasoning: Sears, 7-Eleven, Hallmark, Walmart, Kmart, Victoria's Secret.
6. If you were the marketing manager at a company with a broad product line, which of the six brand strategies would you likely select? What factors would affect your decision? What if the product line were narrow?

7. What are the most important activities involved in developing a successful brand name? Once the name is developed, how is brand equity formed?

8. Name the key functions of packaging. Which do you feel is most important? Does this vary by product?

9. The Consumer Product Safety Commission is a government entity with the power to bring criminal charges against companies and individuals who develop and market unsafe products. Is it fair to consider marketers criminals if consumers are injured by their company's products? Why or why not?

Key Terms & Definitions

1. **Augmented product:**   Product with characteristics that enhance its value beyond that of the core and branded product.
2. **Brand:**   A distinguishing name or symbol to identify and differentiate products from those of competitors.
3. **Brand associations:**   The positive attitudes and feelings a brand evokes in consumers' minds.
4. **Brand awareness:**   The extent to which consumers recognize the brand and are likely to include it among the set of brands they consider.
5. **Branded product:**   The core product plus the characteristics that allow the consumer to differentiate it from similar products.
6. **Brand equity:**   The assets linked with the brand name and symbol that add value to the product.
7. **Brand insistence:**   A dimension of brand equity that makes consumers unwilling to accept substitutes for the brand.
8. **Brand loyalty:**   A dimension of brand equity that causes consumers to choose one brand over others available.
9. **Breadth:**   The number of different lines a company markets.
10. **Bundling strategy:** A strategy in which several products are combined into a single offering.
11. **Capital product:**   A costly item that lasts a long time but does not become part of any finished product.
12. **Competitive advantage:**   A dimension of brand equity that permits the product to be sold on a value basis rather than a price basis and may serve as an entry barrier to competitive products.
13. **Convenience product:**   A relatively inexpensive item that consumers purchase frequently and with minimum effort.
14. **Core product:**   The essential physical item or intangible service that the customer receives.
15. **Depth:**   The number of items in a product line.
16. **Emergency product:**   A product purchased due to an unexpected event and for which the consumer has an urgent need.
17. **Family brand strategy:**   Strategy in which a single brand name covers the entire group of products in the company's line(s).
18. **Generic brand strategy:**   Strategy in which no brand name is used.
19. **Hybrid brand strategy:**   A combination of two or more brand strategies.
20. **Individual brand strategy:**   Strategy in which there is a unique name for each major product or product line.
21. **Item:**   A specific version of a product within a product line.
22. **Joint marketing:**   Cooperation between two companies to sell their products, which tend to be complementary.
23. **Labels:**   Information printed on a product's package to inform consumers and help promote the product.
24. **Manufacturer's brand (national brand):**   Brand named after the manufacturer.
25. **Operations products:**   Products purchased to help run a business that are not included in the finished products.
26. **Perceived brand quality:**   The degree to which a brand consistently produces satisfaction by meeting customer expectations.
27. **Private brand:**   The name wholesalers or retailers attach to products they resell for numerous suppliers.
28. **Product:**   Any physical object, service, idea, person, event, place or organization offered to satisfy consumers' needs and wants.
29. **Product liability:**   The responsibility of marketers and manufacturers for injuries and damages caused by a faulty product.
30. **Product line:**   Closely related products marketed by the organization.
31. **Product recall:**   The withdrawal from the market, by either a manufacturer or the federal government, and the repair, replacement or discontinuation of a potentially harmful product.
32. **Production product:**   Raw materials, processed materials, component parts and subassemblies that become parts of other goods.
33. **Shopping product:**   A purchase generally made only after the consumer has compared several alternatives.
34. **Specialty product:**   A product with unique characteristics that provides unusual value to the purchaser.
35. **Supplies:**   Consumable items used for business operations.
36. **Trademark (brand mark):**   A distinctive form or figure that identifies the brand.
37. **Unsought product:**   An item that consumers don't think about frequently and for which they don't perceive much need.
38. **Warranties:**   Implied or written expectations about product performance.

References

1. Allison Goodrich, "Harley-Davidson's electric bike gets mixed reactions," Northwest Herald, June 24, 2014.
2. Ibid.
3. Hannah Elliott, "If Harley-Davidson Makes An Electric Motorcycle Does That Make It Okay?," Forbes, June 23, 2014.
4. www.ustr.gov, website visited June 12, 2016.
5. "Best Global Brands 2013," Interbrand, www.interbrand.com, website visited June 12, 2016.
6. Patagonia, www.patagonia.com, website visited June 23, 2016.
7. www.prnewswire.com/news-releases/and-now-there-is-one-toyota-mirai-wins-2016-world-green-car-award-300241094.html, website visited June 26, 2016.
8. "Overview," Archer Daniels Midland, www.adm.com, website visited June 26, 2016.
9. Waller, Dave, "Dave's Eco-nomics: Stop the paper chase," Management Today, February 2008.
10. "UPS Helps Toshiba Shrink Service Time from 2 Weeks to 4 Days," www.thenewlogistics.ups.com, website visited June 26, 2016.
11. http://pantene.com/en-us/shop-products/all-products, website visited May 16, 2016.
12. http://www.statista.com/statistics/254608/global-hair-care-market-size, .website visited May 16, 2016.
13. http://www.brunswick.com/brands, website visited June 23, 2015.
14. Procter & Gamble Annual Report, 2014.
15. www.pepsico.com, website visited June 26, 2016.
16. http://ir.newellrubbermaid.com/annuals/cfm, Annual Report, 2009.
17. "China Crushes Caterpillar," Forbes, www.forbes.com, May 6, 2012.
18. Davis, Meredith, "Caterpillar cuts 2016 profit outlook, see China improvement," Reuters Business, April 22, 2016.
19. Aaker, David, A., Managing Brand Equity, (New York: The Free Press, 1991), pg. 7.
20. Jones, Glenda, S., "Your New Brand Image," Catalog Age, July 2000, pp. 175-178.
21. www.tns-mi.com, website visited April 14, 2016.
22. www.uspto.gov, website visited June 26, 2016.
23. Karen Haslam, "Many Apple Technologies Should be Shared Standards, Google Says," www.pcworld.com, July 23, 2012; Lou Hattersley "Massive Apple patent win could kill off Android completely," www.macworld.com, website visited July 19, 2016.
24. www.business.com/legal/5-trademark-cases-and-what-you-should-learn-from-them, website visited July 3, 2016.
25. Ibid.
26. "Study shows most consumers buy counterfeit goods with little remorse," International Chamber of Commerce, www.iccwbo.org, December 2, 2009.
27. "Fakes!" Business Week cover story, www.businessweek.com, website visited April 16, 2016.
28. http://store.ergobaby.com/Content/AboutUs_Counterfeits, website visited June 5, 2016.
29. www.gphf.org, website visited April 27, 2016.
30. plma.com/pressupdate/pressupdate.asp#ID105, website visited July 2, 2016.
31. www.meijer.com, website visited April 17, 2016.
32. www.kraftheinzcompany.com, website visited May 17, 2016.
33. Adapted from David A. Aaker, "Managing Brand Equity," Free Press, 1991, pg. 4.
34. www.kraftfoods.com, website visited June 27, 2016.
35. Gray, Rob, "Stages of Youth," Campaign, May 5, 2006, pg. 4-5.
36. www.cheerwine.com, website visited June 30, 2016.
37. Weilbacher, William M., Brand Marketing (Illinois: NTC Business Books, 1993), pg. 51; P&G Corporate Biographical Information, www.pg.com, website visited April 14, 2016.
38. "Environmental Grants Program," Patagonia, www.patagonia.com, website visited April 15, 2016.
39. www.uspto.gov, website visited April 4, 2016.
40. www.namelab.com, website visited April 12, 2016.
41. Helmig, Bernd, Huber, Jan-Alexander, Leeflang, Peter, "Explaining Behavioral Intentions Toward Co-Branded Products," Journal of Marketing Management, Vol. 23, No. 3-4, April 2007, pp. 285-304.
42. NBA, www.youtube.com, website visited June 30, 2016.
43. www.ticketmaster.com, website visited June 30, 2016.
44. Baum, Chris, "NLEA Compels Food Packagers to Redesign," Packaging, May 1994, pg. 21.
45. Dorfman, Andrea, "Less Bologna on the Shelves," Time, November 5, 1990, pg. 79.
46. Demetrakakes, Pam, "Packaging Field Gears Up for New Labeling Rules," Packaging, January 1993, pg. 3.
47. Hartley, Mark. "For the Sake of Invisible Ink," Occupational Health & Safety, December 1993, pg. 4.
48. Collins, Josephine, "Safety Zone: Massive Toy Recalls Have Rocked the Industry This Year — But Is Some Good Coming Out of the Bad?", License, www.licensemag.com, website visited April 16, 2016.
49. Recall letter from Sears, on file with authors.
50. DailyFinance: Betsy Schiffman, "Toyota's Second Shoe Drops: Shareholders Sue," www.dailyfinance.com, website visited March 22, 2016.

CHAPTER 10

Goods, Services & **Nonprofit** Marketing

connect to your future

Courtesy of College Summit

YouTube SCAN & WATCH

College Summit is a nonprofit organization serving more than 36,000 students.

College Summit is the nation's largest nonprofit organization dedicated to transforming the lives of over 36,000 low-income high school students each year by helping them learn the skills necessary to get into college and earn a degree. Why is this mission important? Low-income students who never attend or graduate from college have a hard road ahead. They're twice as likely to be unemployed. They'll earn less than half as much as college graduates. They're more likely to end up in poverty. Without these workers, we are affecting U.S. global competitiveness, so College Summit believes that America's future rests on its ability to develop the talents of all young adults.

This inspiring nonprofit is the largest of its kind, providing national services to train principals, teachers and students to boost college enrollment and create a college-going culture in their schools. It provides workshops and classes to high school students to teach them how to get a jump start on college academics and application processes. Students work with writing coaches and college counselors free of charge to complete a quality college essay and a universal college application. The company's statistics indicate that 95% of low income students want to go to college, but only 8% ever graduate with a college degree. In contrast, 95% of higher income students want to go to college, and 84% graduate with a college degree. Since 1993, College Summit has been nearly doubling the college enrollment rates of low-income students.

The company goes beyond just helping young adults apply to schools. It teaches students to make good decisions about which college to select, how to apply for financial aid, and which degree programs are in demand by employers. Students who make smart decisions on the front end are more likely to graduate and have less debt when they receive their degree.

Over the years, College Summit has generated revenue in a number of ways. It relies on the support of volunteers, individual donors, and corporate sponsors. Sponsors such as AT&T, Capital One, The Bill & Melinda Gates Foundation, New Profit, Google, Wells Fargo, Citi Foundation, Walmart and Deloitte all support College Summit with a good portion of the organization's funds. Many of these companies have donated more than $1 million at a time to the nonprofit organization. The organization also holds a series of roadshow meetings with finance executives to share the organization's objectives and seek their support." By doing this, College Summit raised another $15 million in just nine months.

The company also relies on federal grants and gifts. It was awarded $125,000 of President Obama's $1.4 million Nobel Peace Prize award, which supports students in communities across the country on the path to higher education. "College Summit is privileged that President Obama has made this commitment to our students and school partners," said J.B. Schramm, founder and CEO of College Summit. "We believe ensuring that the next generation is ready to create, thrive and compete in 21st Century jobs is the single best way to advance innovation, prosperity and peace." Financial support allows College Summit to continue achieving its mission with great success, one student at a time.

Sources: www.collegesummit.org, website visted July 2, 2016.

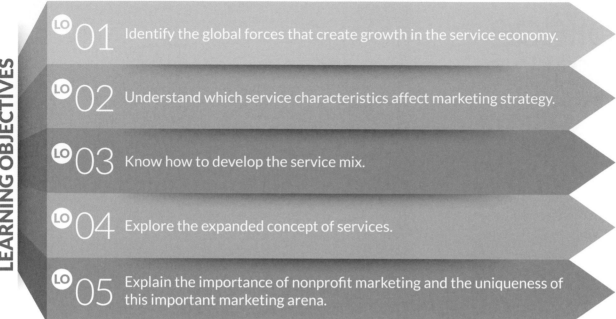

LEARNING OBJECTIVES

LO 01 Identify the global forces that create growth in the service economy.

LO 02 Understand which service characteristics affect marketing strategy.

LO 03 Know how to develop the service mix.

LO 04 Explore the expanded concept of services.

LO 05 Explain the importance of nonprofit marketing and the uniqueness of this important marketing arena.

The Concept of Services

SERVICE

An idea, task, experience, or activity that can be exchanged for value to satisfy the needs and wants of consumers and businesses.

Products can be either be goods (physical objects), or **services** (intangible ideas, tasks, experiences, performances or activities). A major difference between a good and a service is that services usually involve suppliers connecting directly with consumers for performance of the service. Your barber, your doctor and your professor all form a personal connection with you in order to provide their services. When you think about it, even goods are more valuable when accompanied by excellent service. Consequently, goods and services often go hand-in-hand.

To serve means to benefit a receiving party through personal acts. The marketing of services, by its very nature, concerns the development of beneficial relationships. Interpersonal skills are critical, because for a service to be performed well, these skills must help support the customer relationship. Marketers need to emphasize how well their company's service embodies these skills.

> The marketing of services, by its very nature, concerns the development of beneficial relationships.

For more than a quarter century, the dollar volume of services in the U.S. economy has grown steadily each year with no sign of decline. Developed countries such as the United States rely on the marketing of services for domestic growth.

Global services are also very important, representing about 60 percent of all trade among nations. The U.S. has emerged as the leader of services, with foreign countries spending more on American services than America spends on foreign ones.[1] Global marketing, therefore, is particularly important for many U.S. service providers. Burger King is already in many international marketplaces like Russia, Europe, the Middle East and Africa, and is now rapidly expanding in China. It is clearly focused on the global market; four-fifths of its new restaurants are opening outside of America.[2] Western companies like Burger King have a unique advantage in marketing themselves as brands of choice for younger Chinese. Helen H. Wang, award-winning author and expert on China's middle class, writes: "Sometimes, by simply keeping the locations

Services like those of KFC have found great success in the global marketplace.

clean, brightly lit, and air-conditioned, they can set themselves apart from competitors. This is one of the major reasons that many young Chinese have their dates at Starbucks and Kentucky Fried Chicken."

As you can see in Figure 10.1, this chapter begins by looking at forces that will continue to produce explosive growth for services. Following this is an in-depth look at services, which shows how they are differentiated, their relationships to goods, the attributes consumers use to judge them, and elements of service quality. Next, we will describe the aspects marketers consider when developing the service mix. You will extend what you learned in Chapter 9 to services by looking at core, augmented and branded services with the development of new offerings. Keep in mind that services are as important in business-to-business marketing as they are in consumer marketing. Such traditional services as health care, insurance, energy, telecommunications, garbage and snow removal, accounting and tax preparation, auto service and restaurants have been the backbone of the service economy for a long time. Finally, we will discuss the importance of nonprofit service marketing.

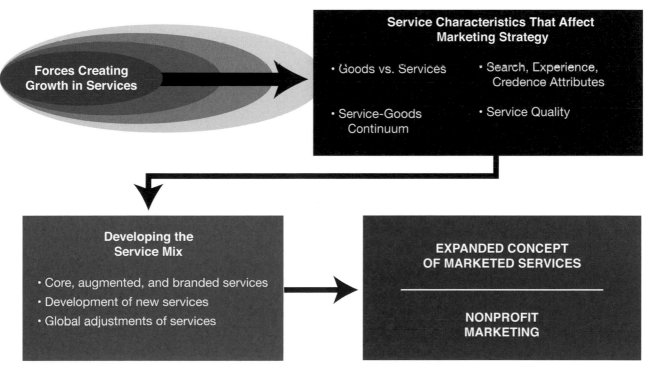

Figure 10.1   The Concept of Services

LO 01 Global Forces Creating Growth in Services

The service economy is not unique to the United States. As a nation develops and becomes more sophisticated, more and more of its total economic well being is based on services. The Industrial Revolution brought about productivity gains through the substitution of machines for human and animal labor. The technology revolution that followed then

Figure 10.1 Global Forces Creating Growth in Services

created products that exceeded human and animal capabilities. A century ago, who would have imagined that millions of business travelers would routinely fly six miles above the earth and use plastic cards to charge phone calls while in flight? Air transportation and telecommunications, including the explosion of the internet as a means of international communication, are examples of services that have brought the concept of a global community closer to reality. Figure 10.1 depicts the global forces that are influencing growth in services.

TECHNOLOGY

Until recently, even advanced nations were dedicated to the production of goods. However, technology is producing more sophisticated services rapidly, and today's technologies generally require highly trained professionals to educate consumers. Smaller percentages of the population are now able to produce greater quantities of more valuable goods, thereby shifting the emphasis to value-added services. Some of these services in the consumer sector include entertainment, travel, health and education, while consulting and environmental controls have risen to prominence in the B2B sector.

The technological revolution is making an information revolution possible, which facilitates nearly every human endeavor. An array of devices lets "lifeloggers" record nearly every aspect of their lives, from their sleep (with the Zeo) to their exercise (Fitbit and Motoactv) to their travel (smartphones and GoPro), then upload the information, sync it or share it with PCs, social media sites and more.[4] Each generation of microprocessors is replaced by technologies that operate millions of times faster, continually altering the commercial landscape. Technology continues to eliminate the need for face-to-face interaction between a buyer and seller. For example, according to the Federal Deposit Insurance Corporation, the number of commercial banks has declined from 12,343 in 1990 to about 5,800 today.[5] This is partially due to consumer preferences for automated teller machines, online banking and other services. Yet, the same technology has provided greater personalization through one-to-one connections. Electronic banking allows consumers the freedom to sit in their favorite coffee shop and conduct all of their banking, including real-time communications with customer service representatives. At tax time, the same systems provide financial information categorized for seamless integration into tax reporting programs.

Online shopping is putting added pressures on traditional brick-and-mortar stores. Online sales are increasing at more than double the rate of brick-and-mortar sales, and foot traffic is steadily declining. U.S. e-commerce sales accounted for only 4.9 percent of total retail sales five years ago, but has steadily increased to 7.8 percent today and will continue to climb.[6]

QUALITY OF LIFE

Quality of life is defined more by how people feel and experience life than by how much they consume. For example, our thinking about basic services such as health, education and mobility has expanded dramatically. Health once meant the absence of sickness, but today's perception of health has expanded to include fitness, increased physical performance and enhanced mental well-being. Education, once the domain of the elite few, has become accessible to a significant percentage of the population, particularly in emerging nations like China and India. Today people find expenditures at a theater as valuable as the purchase of a microwave oven was in the 1970s. Mobility, expressed in the 1950s by high-performance automobiles, now includes psychological mobility provided by movies, leisure activities, cellular phones and the internet. Internet cafes illustrate yet another change in the quality of life, providing customers with two popular services in one—specialty coffees and wireless access.

The fast pace of life has placed a tremendous premium on services that make life easier. Most people prefer to spend precious leisure time with their families and friends, enjoying activities rather than doing chores such as cleaning or grocery shopping. This attitude shift has created a plethora of opportunities for business marketing.

You might know someone who has a house cleaner. It might be an individual or a company franchise business such as Molly Maids, MaidPro, or Two Maids and a Mop. House cleaning services no longer cater just to the wealthy. Today, they're extremely popular with moderate income consumers as well, including those who work at home. In fact, the number of job opportunities for maids and housekeepers is expected to grow at 13% annually through 2022.[7] If you had the choice of going to work to make $100 a day and paying a house cleaner $75 a day to clean your house once in a while, would you do it? Why? What if you could take your kids to the park instead of cleaning all day? It's all about trade offs, and most people choose to enhance their quality of life if they can afford a house cleaning service.

Another service company enhancing lives of busy consumers is Peapod, "America's leading internet grocer."[8] Customers can go to peapod.com to select from more than 11,000 products, including groceries, flowers and wine. A personal shopper will then collect the items for front door delivery. Train commuters in cities like Boston, New York, Washington D.C. and Chicago can use the Peapod app to scan product barcodes from virtual shopping billboards that resemble life-size grocery shelves. The interactive billboards serve as advertising for Peapod and give consumers a fun and functional way to purchase groceries that can be delivered by the time they get home.[9] Customers can also choose to pick up their order, boxed and ready to go, at one of the many convenient locations in their area.[10]

Courtesy of Peapod

Peapod improves quality of life for busy consumers who don't have the time or desire to grocery shop.

Instead of spending valuable time in the evenings or on weekends shopping for groceries, busy consumers can place an order with Peapod and use their time for other things that are more personally rewarding. This service is extremely successful; the company has delivered more than 30 million orders across 24 U.S. markets on the East Coast and in the Midwest since 1989.[11]

GOVERNMENT DEREGULATION OF SERVICES

Another factor profoundly influencing growth in services is industry deregulation that has occurred over the past 20 years. This trend, started in the United States, has now spread throughout Europe and Asia. Understanding that competition provides vast opportunities for economic growth, legislators have deregulated many services that were traditionally controlled by government agencies. As expected, numerous private companies have stepped in to seize and create opportunities.

Competition stimulated by deregulation results in better selection at better prices, which improves demand and creates jobs. For example, when the government deregulated the airline industry, companies expanded the number, location and pricing approaches of airline flights, among other changes. The result has been better prices, better schedules and overall improved service levels for consumers. Increased competition has made it necessary for companies to deliver greater value to consumers, which in turn has stimulated demand for these services.

COMPETITION IN PROFESSIONAL SERVICES

Not long ago, doctors, lawyers and other professionals were prohibited from marketing their services in the media. They were dependent on sponsorships and word of mouth for advertising. All of this changed in 1974, when the Supreme Court ruled that a ban on lawyer marketing was unconstitutional. Today, nearly every profession engages in some form of marketing. Health care is a good case in point.

Hospitals, preferred provider organizations and health maintenance organizations compete vigorously for patients, and there are elaborate educational campaigns designed to teach doctors how to market services. The availability of information via technology has enhanced marketers' opportunities to promote health-care services. Users are able to access medical specialists and information as well as interact with visuals and audio. Since the health-care industry is complex and often confusing, consumers usually know very little about products and services offered. Without this knowledge about the industry, consumers must rely, to some degree, on marketers to inform them, making it extremely important for marketers to provide truthful and reliable information, even with well known and trusted websites such as WebMD. The recent explosion of drug companies advertising on television has caused some problems. The FDA regulates drug advertising and requires that advertisers name at least one approved use for the drug, the generic name of the drug and all the risks of using it.[12] For example, Pfizer and Pharmacia Corporation, the makers of Celebrex, an arthritis drug, were ordered to pull a TV advertisement by the FDA. The ad showed "Bill," a person with "arthritic knees," zipping around a park on a scooter. The FDA claimed that this ad overstated to consumers the actual efficacy of the drug.[13] The pharmaceutical industry claims that its advertisements serve to inform customers. In reality, ads often tug at emotions, and it is impossible to gain comparable knowledge to what a doctor would share by processing the information in a 30-second drug commercial.[14]

PRIVATIZATION

Privatization occurs when government services are contracted to private organizations for them to manage. The concept originated in the United Kingdom as an effort to revitalize the economy by shifting many bureaucratic services: railroad, telecommunications and transportation industries, among others, to aggressive private firms. Privatization also occurred in East Germany when the Berlin Wall came down and in Russia when the Soviet Union was dissolved. Both countries immediately began to transfer ownership of huge, government-controlled service institutions to private companies. Consulting organizations from the United States, Europe and Japan worked diligently to help these private companies succeed. In Greece,

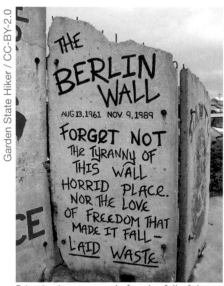

Privatization occurred after the fall of the Berlin Wall in 1989.

in the wake of the country's economic collapse, Prime Minister Antonis Samaras plans to privatize the country's train network and power company. The country's creditors say that taking these money-losing companies off its balance sheet will help stabilize Greece's finances and help its economy in the long term.[15]

In the United States, there is a definite trend toward privatization of local, state and federal government services. Private companies now operate many hospitals and jails, which were once the responsibility of city and county governments. A recent milestone in the privatization movement occurred when Los Alamos, the birthplace of the atomic bomb and oldest national laboratory, was handed to a private contractor.[16]

THE NEED FOR SPECIALIZATION

Specialization occurs when an organization chooses to focus its resources on core business activities. In order to utilize resources and build strength in the core business, many organizations rely on service providers for basic support of their business. Most companies find it economical to farm out some of the services they previously performed themselves. Personnel agencies hire and assess employees, accounting firms maintain the books, systems consultants set up the computer networks, and so forth. Accenture provides management consulting, technology services and outsourcing to other businesses. Corporations can hire Accenture to integrate sustainability approaches into their business strategies, industrialize application development or maximize IT security, for example. Companies realize that just as they specialize in a certain aspect of business, there are service providers who do the same.

GROWTH OF FRANCHISING

FRANCHISE

A contractual agreement whereby an entrepreneur pays a fee for the franchise name and agrees to meet operating requirements and use the organization's marketing plan.

A **franchise** is a contractual agreement in which an entrepreneur pays a fee and agrees to meet operating requirements in exchange for the franchise name and marketing plan. Franchising is another major trend influencing the service industry, with fast food, fitness and auto service sectors experiencing particularly aggressive growth, due to their ability to sustain many different locations. Chick-fil-A, for instance, operates more than 2,000 restaurants in 43 states and is quickly expanding its franchise. It is thriving in the Midwest, with 25 percent of the company's new restaurant openings in 2016 taking place in the region. The company is committed to growth in Michigan, where it plans to open three to four new restaurants each year over the next five years, adding a total of 15-20 new locations in the state.[17]

Another area of franchise growth is in the distribution channels for car sales. Since customers value pressure-free shopping when purchasing an automobile, online car sales have become increasingly popular. These alternatives have taken a fixed-price approach without aggressive sales tactics. However, customers rarely make the final sale without being able to personally see, touch and drive the car.

Chick-fil-A is a popular franchise that is experiencing aggressive growth.

Service Characteristics that Affect Marketing Strategy

Marketers have to consider several aspects of service when developing strategies. First, services are different than goods in several ways. Second, services should be looked at from the perspective of a service–goods continuum, not simply as services. Some products are all service, some are pure goods, and some are a combination of both. Third, consumers evaluate a service by looking at its attributes to find clues about its expected performance. Fourth, service quality plays a key role in success.

CONTRASTS BETWEEN GOODS AND SERVICES

When marketers refer to products, they are talking about both goods and services. In general, companies' products consist of a mix of the two, and marketing strategies for one generally work for the other. However, there are six sharp distinctions between the goods and services. The uniqueness of services lies in their intangibility, the relationship with the consumer, the importance of the service encounter, their simultaneous production and consumption, their perishability and the type of quality controls they require.

By the time you're experiencing the thrilling sensation of paragliding, it's too late to decide you don't want to use the service.

SeaDave / CC BY 2.0

Marketing Intangibles Physical goods have form and mass; they can be seen and touched. In contrast, services exist primarily as an offer or promise of some experience that will occur in the future. They don't become "real" until performed. Insurance, for example, simply offers a description of promised benefits that the policy contains. Only when the consumer suffers a loss is the product delivered—in the form of money or a replacement for an insured item.

Many services take shape in unexpected ways over time. With a home security system, for instance, it may be weeks, months or even years (hopefully never) before the potential benefit is realized. This intangibility makes it difficult to assess the value of services or to compare alternatives prior to purchase. After the service is performed, it is too late to change the decision. Paragliding is another example. By the time you are in the position to experience the thrilling sensation, it is too late to reject the service.

Relationship of Provider to Customer Services are performed for customers personally or for entities in their care—children (day care, youth sports camps), animals (vets, stables, feedlots), property (lawn care, car wash, auto repair), and so forth. Whereas most goods are manufactured at a plant far from customers, most services are created in their presence or with their personal knowledge of how they were performed, creating an inseparable bond between provider and customer. In some cases this interaction may be very personal, such as the relationship between parents and the provider of their child's care. Consumers can develop strong preferences for the work of a particular service provider, be it a doctor, dentist or hairdresser. As with loyalty to quality brands, customers also develop loyalty to service providers and are sometimes willing to pay more for services from providers they know and trust.

SERVICE ENCOUNTER

The interaction between the consumer and the seller.

The Service Encounter Connection One of the most important aspects of service marketing is the **service encounter**, the contact between the consumer and the seller. An early proponent of service as a strategy, Jan Carlzon, former president of Scandinavian Airline Systems (SAS), spoke of service encounters as "moments of truth." Carlzon led SAS toward a strong customer focus, pointing out that the airline came face-to-face with consumers 65,000 times each day. He estimated that each passenger had contact with five SAS employees over the course of a year. Although the typical service encounter lasted only about 15 seconds, the outcome of each one ultimately translated into success or failure for the company. His fervent conviction has made SAS one of the most customer-oriented carriers in the industry.

The service encounter concept reinforces the importance of customer relationships in marketing a service. Employees not only must have the interpersonal skills to treat consumers well but also must be oriented toward solving the customer's problem. At the most elementary level, service providers need to be cordial and gracious. At a more fundamental level, they have to be helpful in discovering and meeting service needs during the encounter. Each moment contributes to the customer's experience with the service.

Walmart greeters are a product of Sam Walton's insistence on "aggressive hospitality."

At SAS, Carlzon realized that in order to satisfy a customer in 15 seconds, his system needed to give frontline personnel the tools and authority to solve a wide range of consumer problems. Managers, who typically hold power and responsibility, became supporters for those employees. Walmart took up a similar policy, and the company receives letters daily from customers pleased with their service encounter, which may include an associate who remembers their name or carries out a purchase for them. Some customers write letters in appreciation of a simple smile. Sam Walton, the company founder, insisted that associates practice "aggressive hospitality" in order to offer better service, and the People Greeter program at Walmart is one example of this. The greeters have the job of handing out shopping carts, greeting customers with a smile as they enter the store, and welcoming them to Walmart. As customers leave, the greeter also thanks them for shopping at Walmart.

Simultaneous Production and Consumption The fact that many services are made and used at the same moment creates interesting situations. First, the buyer and seller have to cooperate, which often involves recognition of power dynamics. When you tell your stylist how you want your hair cut, you accomplish a managerial act. Second, since buyers vary and services depend on the recipient, the same service may be dramatically different from one situation to the next. A provider may interact in one way with one consumer and then adjust the service to meet the needs of another. A personal fitness trainer, for instance, must create a training program to suit each client's individual objectives and physical condition. Finally, since the buyer must be present in order for at least part of the service to be performed, consumers invest time. This places a premium on the speed of delivery and the importance of correct performance the first time. For example, factors like a car being ready when promised after service work, or a relatively short wait in a crowded physician's office, may have as much to do with satisfaction as the performance of the specific service itself.

PERISHABLE

The temporal nature of services, whose value exists for only a short time.

No Storage and Inventory Although most goods can be stored until needed, services can be extremely **perishable**, which means their value exists for a short time. When an airplane takes off with several empty seats, those fares can never be recovered. Therefore, accurate forecasting and the need to match supply with demand are important. When the demand for a service is stable, there is little difficulty in meeting supply requirements, but most services have erratic demand. For example, on very hot days, almost all consumers turn on their air conditioners, creating a surge in energy demand. Should the utility company build enough capacity to supply its peak load or its average load? In the first case, there will be many periods when resources are unused; in the latter case, blackouts can result. Similarly, cell phone use is often a problem at major sporting events, when a large number of people in one location try to make calls and send texts. If the service provider cannot meet the peak load, then customers are likely to get frustrated and consider changing providers. Have you ever encountered this situation at a football or basketball game?

Service Quality Control The quality of goods is usually monitored by human inspectors or the electronic eye of machinery, which is much more difficult to do with services. Unique quality control techniques, which are discussed in detail later in the chapter, are necessary for services. For now, it is important to remember that many services cannot be performed again if a mistake is made. An 18-year-old who emerges from high school poorly educated is unlikely to start all over again. In addition, because services are so people-intensive, quality can depend directly on service suppliers.

Service quality control is monitored by trained observers during and after service delivery. Chances are that you have called a company and heard a recording saying the call may be monitored for training purposes. This type of feedback, used by companies such as Amazon, lets the organization know whether service is being performed consistently as intended. Amazon also encourages feedback through its "contact us" page, which lets users choose to talk to a customer service representative via email, phone or online chat.[18] When there are difficulties, most customer-oriented service providers give employees additional training, supervision and help.

THE SERVICE–GOODS CONTINUUM

Although there are differences in marketing goods and services, there are also many similarities. In fact, few organizations market only one or the other. Most purchases fall somewhere along the continuum between almost pure goods and almost pure services, as illustrated in Figure 10.2.

Notice the word *almost* at each end of the continuum. Even in their purest form, goods and services still contain some aspect of the other. Almost pure goods are physical products that can be described by their form, mass and function. There are thousands of types, ranging from computer chips to ocean liners. A gym supplies several different products that can be considered almost pure goods, such as clothes, equip-

ALMOST PURE GOODS	GOODS WITH SERVICES	HALF GOODS, HALF SERVICES	SERVICES WITH GOODS	ALMOST PURE SERVICES
Physical products that are purchased and consumed with little or no service	Products supported with repair, mainten-ance, add-ons, and advice	Products that consist of both goods and services	Intellectual property or equipment to make goods work	Experiences that are consumed during delivery
Groceries Gasoline (self-serve) Steel	Autos Auto repair Video games	Restaurants Bookstores Movie theaters Prepared food delivery	Rental movies Training books Software Electronic mail Fax service	Health clubs Medical care Consulting Legal services Day care

Figure 10.2   Continuum of Goods and Services
Source: Valarie A. Zeithaml, "How Consumer Evaluation Processes Differ Between Goods and Services," in Marketing of Services, eds. James H. Donnelly and William R. George.

ment and health food.

Next along the continuum are goods with services. These are physical products accompanied by the supportive services required to make them work. For example, technology plays a major role in our economy not only because of its sales revenue but also due to the services it requires. Dell remains a very profitable computer company because of the extensive technical service it offers to support customers.

Half goods and half services are products that require both elements almost equally to succeed. Restaurants provide a certain level of service, which includes the wait staff, and goods such as food and beverages. Customers want to anticipate as well as enjoy their dining experiences, so marketers appeal to customer expectations about entertainment, a unique atmosphere or opportunities to interact with others. Dusty's Tap Room, an upscale Pub in Okemos, Michigan, is known for its food as well as its waiters and waitresses,

grilled cheese / CC BY-ND 2.0

Coffee shops are now fixtures in most leading bookstores to entice customers to spend more time at the location.

who make it a point to know the names of loyal customers. Bookstores provide not only products (books) but also guidance in seeking unique topics. In addition, their spatial arrangement, background music and atmosphere all contribute to the "feelings" that sell. Coffee shops are now fixtures in most leading bookstores to entice customers to spend more time at the location. A popular example is Barnes and Noble's partnership with Starbucks.[19]

Services with goods often entail intellectual properties and equipment required to make goods work. Examples include rental movies and software. A particular consideration with software is not only if it will run, but how well it will run. Microsoft once touted its Windows 8 operating system as designed to run on all hardware that can handle Windows 7, but beta testers noted that "Windows 8 is less kind to older, low-end graphics hardware" and "You should be using at least double the recommended amount [of RAM] to ensure headroom for additional programs and background services."[20] Beyond hardware issues, many people struggled with the new operating system's lack of familiarity to other upgrades. However, since the release of the newest operating system, Windows 10, Microsoft attempts to shorten development cycles, offering more frequent releases that may be less dependent on hardware updates.[21]

Almost pure services provide customers with experiences that are consumed during the delivery process. Among the many items in this category are health clubs, legal services and education. Although a haircut is considered the classic example of a pure service, even that ordinarily takes place in an establishment selling styling and beautification products. Services such as air and train travel involve such goods as meals and soft drinks as well as tickets that can be exchanged. Even though Southwest Airlines does not offer meals or assigned seats, consumers still have a reasonable perception of quality and service value, usually citing the good service, such as frequent departures, on-time arrival, friendly employees and low fares. According to statistics reported to the Department of Transportation (DOT), Southwest Airlines has consistently received the lowest ratio of complaints per passengers boarded of all Major U.S. carriers.[22] This is an almost pure service that passengers value highly, contributing to outstanding customer loyalty at Southwest.

CONSUMER EVALUATION OF SERVICES

Products can be viewed as having three types of qualities that affect consumer evaluation: search, experience and credence. Search qualities can be evaluated prior to purchase. Experience qualities can be assessed only during or after consumption. Credence qualities are almost impossible to evaluate even after purchase and consumption. As Figure 10.3 illustrates, most goods are high in search and experience qualities, whereas most services are high in experience and credence qualities.[23]

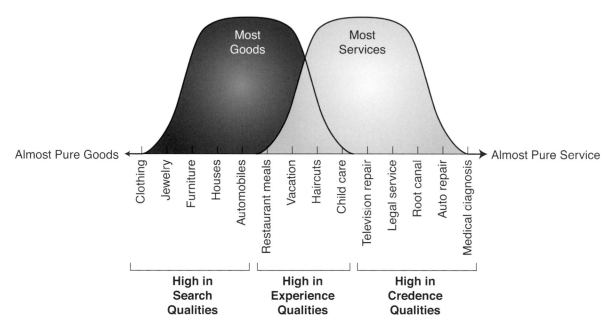

Figure 10.3 Search, Experience and Credence Qualities of Goods and Services
Source: Valarie A. Zeithaml, "How Consumer Evaluation Processes Differ Between Goods and Services," in Marketing of Services, eds. James H. Donnelly and William R. George.

Search Qualities Search qualities are found mostly in goods. They make it easy for consumers to judge one product relative to another. People can use their senses of smell, hearing, sight, touch and taste to note differences in attribute quality. Many products are compared and studied in detail before a selection is made. For example, if you are shopping for new stereo speakers, you can listen to different models at the retail store to decide which pair sounds best. Similarly, you can test-drive different cars or try out a pair of in-line skates in the store parking lot. Even after purchase, items high in search qualities allow the consumer to assess their value. Best Buy offers demonstrations of video games and other products in their stores. Since Best Buy offers a number of items high in search qualities, its format enables consumers to compare and contrast products easily.

Experience Qualities The combined categories—goods with services, half goods and half services, and services with goods—are high in experience qualities. Consumers cannot assess the amount of pleasure until they try them. Then they can decide whether the product meets or exceeds their expectations and can describe desired improvements or changes. As the name suggests, products high in experience qualities involve the customer, and promotional efforts usually show people taking part in the experience. For instance, photos on the Crystal Cruises website show travelers relaxing in a deluxe stateroom, families snorkeling and adults taking complimentary golf lessons onboard. Consumers can assess their experience only after the cruise has ended, but in this case, many are apparently satisfied; Crystal Cruises received the 2015 World's Best Award in Top Large-Ship Cruise Lines in a Travel + Leisure reader survey.[24]

Credence Qualities Credence refers to a person's belief that something is true or trustworthy. The credence qualities are found only in services and cannot easily be evaluated before, during or after consumption. A medical diagnosis, for example, is almost impossible for consumers to assess, since most people have little or no knowledge of pathology and must trust the ability of others. The outcomes of credence qualities are largely unobservable to the customer until indirect benefits emerge, such as feeling better after being treated by a doctor. Of course, there can also be negative effects from the service, such as continued or worsening symptoms. The more intangible the result, the higher the credence qualities involved. In other words, customers must have a high degree of confidence that the exchange has been worthwhile.

Consumer Evaluation and Buying Behavior

Because services are high in credence qualities, consumer buying behavior tends to be different for services than for goods. Specific differences, described next, range from the more personal nature of the information sources relied upon to the fact that the customer is often a competitor of the service provider.

> Because services are high in credence qualities, consumer buying behavior tends to be different for services than for goods.

The Personal Factor Services tend to be personal, so it's not surprising that buyers rely more on information from personal sources than anything else when selecting a service provider. Suppose you are going to court in an important lawsuit. Would you select your lawyer from an ad on television or a recommendation from a knowledgeable friend? Consumers not only relate better to personal information sources but also give them more credence.

Post-Purchase Evaluation Because services are not easily evaluated before purchase, most assessments are made during or after the fact. Reputable lawn care companies are careful not only to do a good job of mowing and trimming but also to clean away the clippings, leaving a well-manicured look with very little for the consumer to criticize. How a customer feels about a service will significantly determine if he or she purchases the service again.

Surrogates for Judgment When a product is high in credence quality, consumers use surrogate cues to make judgments. Many people equate high-priced services with greater value, for example. Another cue is physical features, such as how the service provider dresses or the location of offices. Some consumers may judge a car dealership by a detail like the cleanliness of the restrooms. An inefficiently run physician's office with new furniture may send off more positive cues than one that is better run but has poor lighting, outdated furniture and clutter. In this case, the cues are used to make judgments about the quality of medical treatment the consumer will receive, and the office decor is a surrogate for measuring the skill and success of the physician.

Small Sets of Acceptable Brands or Suppliers Because services are personal and difficult to judge, consumers are likely to consider a small set of providers when seeking a service. Since services have no search qualities, consumers will not benefit from elaborate comparisons. Furthermore, their personal sources of information are likely to yield relatively few options. Once consumers find a reliable provider, they tend to be loyal. For example, most of us use only one or perhaps two dry cleaners all the time. The same is probably true for hairstylists, tailors, party planners and other types of providers. Some business travelers limit their choice when selecting a hotel, booking only Marriott or Sheraton because they are brand loyal and confident they will receive acceptable service.

Slow Adoption Because pre-purchase evaluation is almost impossible, the risk of buying a service is greater than for goods. Therefore, new services take time to catch on, with most consumers waiting for word from the few adopters to hear how the service performs. Many consumers were initially reluctant to use the e-deposit feature many banks offer for depositing checks via a smartphone. They anticipated problems such as faulty deposits or theft and preferred contact with a human being or ATMs. With time, these fears are diminishing, and many consumers now e-deposit without hesitation. Shopping on the caused similar security concerns among consumers, but web developers and credit card companies developed security measures to ensure better consumer safety while shopping online.

Strong Brand Loyalty Services have a built-in loyalty factor. People show greater loyalty to other people than to things, and due to the participatory nature of services, they may blame an unsatisfying experience at least partially on themselves. For example, if your hairdresser cuts your bangs too short, you may think you were not explicit about what you wanted. Furthermore, the high degree of credence qualities in services makes it difficult to know whether the provider has done a poor job unless something goes wrong, such as your car failing to start the day after it was repaired. Without a negative signal, consumers are likely to assume that the provider did at least a good job. In general, there is less complaining behavior from consumers about services as opposed to goods. We know from earlier chapters, however, that it is very important to seek out and respond to consumer complaints about any type of product.

The Customer as Competitor Services usually involve activities that consumers can do for themselves. Parents may elect to stay home with their young children or have relatives take care of them, in which case, they are "competing" with day care centers. People can mow their own lawns, clean their own cars or homes, prepare their own tax returns, or prepare food for their own parties. In many instances the trade-off is between time and money, which is why so many providers stress the amount of time their services will save consumers. For example, the United States Postal Service now offers Pickup On Demand, a time-specific service giving customers the opportunity to conveniently schedule a pickup at their home or office on its website.[25]

CORE SERVICE

The basic benefit delivered.

Developing the Service Mix

Services, like goods, usually occur as a mix that relies on branding to communicate uniqueness. At the same time, several qualities must be considered when developing a new service. These include the service itself, the brand and factors that enhance the fundamental service. This section explores those dimensions in detail.

CORE, AUGMENTED AND BRANDED SERVICES

Services, like all products, have core, augmented and branded dimensions. We can use the example of a baby's birth in a hospital, as depicted in Figure 10.4. The **core service** is the basic benefit and main objective, in this case delivery of a healthy baby and safety for the mother. But, in today's competitive health-care arena, the augmented and branded product also plays a key role. The augmented service is the package of bundled goods and services that differentiates one provider from another. It has a great deal to do with how well service providers connect with customers. Since the core service is the same for all providers, the augmented features are critical.

Because a service is intangible, a customer comes to know its value through the symbols and cues around it. McDonald's has achieved name recognition not only because of the reliability of its products but also because of its customer service, personnel management, cleanliness, child-oriented image and so forth. Its brand equity reflects the interactive service element as well as the functional dimensions of the physical goods sold. Con-

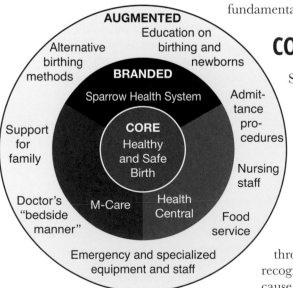

Figure 10.4 Example of a Core, Augmented and Branded Service

sider FedEx Office, with more than 1,900 branches worldwide and 400 centers open 24 hours a day, 7 days a week.[26] Other companies provide copy services, but FedEx Office has become synonymous with a customer-oriented philosophy. It has expanded services to computer rental and internet access, packing and shipping, convention center services, and marketing products such as banners, posters and signs. Customers associate the FedEx Office's name with value and service.[27]

Marriott extended its branded line by developing three chains with lower complexity than the original service. Courtyard has become an identifiable service mark associated with high-quality accommodations and limited services. Fairfield Inn is positioned as the least complex, no-frills part of the chain. Residence Inn caters to extended stay guests, such as business travelers and families who are relocating. With these three brand names, the company has developed services consistent with the target markets for which each is intended.

DEVELOPING NEW SERVICES

FUNCTIONAL ELEMENT

What a service is supposed to accomplished.

INTERACTIVE ELEMENT

The personal behaviors and atmosphere of the service environment.

SERVICE COMPLEXITY

The number and intricacy of steps involved in producing a service.

DIVERGENCE

The degree to which a service involves customization beyond routine or standardized procedures.

Certain functional and interactive elements are important when new services are created. The **functional element** is about accomplishing what is intended. (Does the orthodontist straighten a patient's teeth? Does an accountant prepare a client's tax return?) The **interactive element** involves the personal behaviors and physical atmosphere of the service environment.

Functional Elements in Service Development The functional element is influenced by the complexity and divergence of the service. **Service complexity** is the number and intricacy of steps involved in producing a service. The service a defense lawyer provides to a murder suspect is much more complex than what a real estate lawyer provides to a new home buyer. **Divergence** is the amount of routine procedure involved. A very customized service has high divergence, such as a consultant who tailors staff development advice to each person in a company. Fred Pryor Seminars Inc., a standardized service provider, gives a set presentation on various topics to groups representing many organizations, keeping divergence to a minimum. Crowd Management Strategies tailors strategic planning services for a broad range of clients in the entertainment industry, requiring consultants competent to deal with high complexity. The company focuses on addressing crowd management issues at concerts, festivals and other public assembly events through risk assessment, event planning assistance, crowd management training, on-site safety reviews and more.[28]

Figure 10.5 illustrates complexity and divergence for four services. Since most local hair salons do approximately the same thing, and cutting hair is not highly complicated, divergence and complexity are very low. Dentistry has low divergence due to standardized procedures, but it tends to be high in complexity. House cleaning is highly customized (divergent) but low in complexity, whereas litigation tends to be high in both divergence and complexity.

COMPLEXITY
(Degree of Intricacy)

		Low	High
DIVERGENCE (Degree of Standardization)	**Low**	Local barber	Dentistry
	High	House cleaning	Litigation

Figure 10.5 Complexity and Divergence in Services

Interactive Elements in Service Development The interactive element is often more important than the functional aspect in creating service excellence. Walt Disney Enterprises has attempted to produce a strong interactive service by using a stage (the environment) with actors (Disney employees) to involve the audience (consumers). Through extensive role-playing, the Disney organization has learned to connect in a way that produces strong customer satisfaction. One part of this interaction is simply to provide an enjoyable and entertaining experience for Disney guests.

Many companies use atmospherics, the environment in which the service is performed, to enhance the interactive element.[29] Originally applied to retail stores, atmospherics has important implications for all types of services outside the consumer's home. Such features as color, music and layout are all part of the atmosphere. They not only influence the selection of a service provider but also, and more importantly, they determine if service outcomes are satisfying.

The physical components of atmosphere have an emotional dimension. The mood created greatly influences whether consumers want to enter and explore the environment, communicate with personnel and gain satisfaction from the service encounter.[30] Retail stores such as Abercrombie & Fitch and Victoria's Secret emphasize music as a way to increase sales. DMX, a service provider to many retailers, researches the demographics and psychographics of a store's customers and then creates suitable sound. The music is designed to encourage customers to shop longer, and it also creates an atmosphere for each retailer.[31] The next time you visit an H&M, 24 Hour Fitness or DKNY location, note the music program created especially to appeal to you.

LO 04 An Expanded Concept of Services

In addition to the traditional offerings, service marketing is used to promote people, entertainment and events, places, political candidates and ideas, and different causes. It can even be used within an organization, through internal marketing, to promote one group's capabilities to another. The following sections describe additional types of service marketing

PERSON MARKETING

Person marketing involves promoting an individual's character, personality and appeal, which in turn may be used to promote a service or product. Ashton Kutcher, the model turned actor, has transformed himself into a social media mogul, using his own brand as a springboard. The "That '70s Show" star founded Katalyst, a production company that is a merger of three industries: film, TV and web. Kutcher uses his brand image to leverage his company through Twitter and Facebook. His Twitter feed, @ aplusk, is among the most-followed on Earth, topping 17 million in July 2015. Ashton's irresistible charm and fun-loving attitude have caught the attention of corporations such as Nikon, whose cameras he endorses, as well as Kellogg's and PepsiCo, who have both teamed up with Katalyst on social media projects through Twitter. Twitter was used as an interaction portal, urging users to post short commercials filmed with their Coolpix cameras.[32]

Many celebrities have agents who help market their exceptional appeal to various companies and consumers. While celebrities and athletes are admired for their skill or character, a great deal of their popularity is due to service providers marketing their personalities. Person marketing is often a two-way process, in which promotion of the individual increases his or her value as a product endorser. Public exposure that enhances reputation leads to more lucrative endorsement contracts, and vice versa.

Ashton Kutcher uses personality and appeal to help promote goods and services.

ENTERTAINMENT AND EVENT MARKETING

"Transformers: Age of Extinction" broke multiple box-office records in China in its first weekend of release and is the fifth highest grossing film in Hong Kong's history. Paramount Pictures cast several Chinese actors in the film, shot in Hong Kong and other cities, established multiple product-placement deals with Chinese consumer brands, and booked a snazzy premiere in Hong Kong. [33] The clever marketing helped the film gross more abroad than it did domestically; it is currently the 104th highest grossing movie in U.S. history.[34]

Television and radio also thrive on sophisticated marketing. Mark Burnett, creator and producer of "Survivor" and "The Apprentice," has a knack for marketing. His programs are successful because viewers can relate to the people cast as participants as well as the dramatic individual and team tasks that separate winners and losers. His shows are heavily promoted to inform viewers about each new series, and careful monitoring ensures that a show consistently reaches its target demographic.

EVENT MARKETING

Promoting an event in order to generate revenues and enhance the reputation of an organization.

Event marketing is the promotion of an event in order to generate revenues and enhance the reputation of an organization. It has become a huge factor in the entertainment world, with sporting events at the forefront. Ohio State University characterizes its athletic department as being in the entertainment business; the university has an annual athletics budget exceeding $100 million.[35] College athletics comprise a multibillion-dollar industry, generating revenue from game attendance, television and radio ratings, concessions, sponsorships and merchandising. Many universities earn several million in royalties annually.

One of the most successful event marketers is the National Basketball Association. Although most NBA games are played in the United States, the All-Star Game is broadcast in over 215 countries in more than 47 languages.[36] The NBA has assisted in basketball-themed movies as well: "Coach Carter" starring Samuel L. Jackson, "Finding Forrester" starring Sean Connery, "White Men Can't Jump" starring Wesley Snipes, "Space Jam" starring Michael Jordan and "Kazaam" starring Shaquille O'Neal.

Another event marketer, FIFA (Fédération Internationale de Football Association), is responsible for the organization of soccer tournaments like the World Cup, held every four years. It is also responsible for its promotion, which generates revenue from sponsorship. FIFA generates revenues of over 1.3 billion U.S. dollars, for a net profit of 72 million, and had cash reserves over 1.4 billion U.S. dollars.[37] The 2014 World Cup, held in Brazil, experienced a massive surge of viewership in the United States. ESPN reported record household ratings and averaged 3.7 million viewers per match. The increasing popularity of the sport domestically is nothing short of incredible. Viewership in 2014 rose 26 percent from 2010, and surged 116 percent from 2006.[38] Univision, a Spanish language broadcast television network in the United States, reported 10.4 million viewers during the Mexico vs. Netherlands match. The game was not only the most watched soccer game ever on Univision, but also the most watched telecast ever for the broadcaster—besting ESPN's broadcast of the match by 57 percent.[39] The 2015 FIFA Women's World Cup proved how American success in the sport swiftly increases viewership in the country. Fox Sports reported the first six US women's matches averaged 5.3 million viewers and Sports TV Ratings marked the championship game at a remarkable 15.2 rating, which translates to over 21 million viewers.[40] There is no shortage of excitement for a sport that is sweeping the nation.

The 2015 FIFA Women's World Cup championship game between USA and Japan was watched by more than 21 million viewers.

PLACE MARKETING

Place marketing enhances a location in order to appeal to businesses, investors and tourists. Vacation places receive tremendous marketing attention, which countries, states and cities are all eager to encourage. Michigan branded "Pure Michigan" to promote tourism with ads focusing on the state's 3,000 miles of shoreline, beautiful autumn colors and more than 100 lighthouses, among other highlights. The brand's national campaign launched with a $13 million dollar budget. Television commercials are aired on 20 cable channels along with NBC, CBS and ABC. Tim Allen, a Michigan native, narrates the 30-second spots. Its website, www.michigan.org, allows users to explore all the state has to offer, with featured destinations, special events, outdoor activities and package deals.[41]

Pure Michigan

The "Pure Michigan" campaign is an example of place marketing.

PLACE MARKETING

Promoting a geographical location in order to appeal to businesses, investors, and tourists.

POLITICAL MARKETING

Promoting an individual or idea motivated by the desire to influence public policy and voters.

CAUSE MARKETING

Gaining public support and financing in order to change or remedy a situation.

POLITICAL MARKETING

Political marketing involves the promotion of an individual or idea with the aim of influencing public policy and voters. Politicians use political marketing in order to present themselves and their ideas in the best possible way. Sophisticated political campaigns make efficient use out of virtually every marketing tool. The internet has provided an outstanding venue for political communication, often called web campaigning. Candidates in the 2016 U.S. presidential election will use more social networks than politicians of the past, in hopes of tapping the Millennial market. There are new social networks for campaigns to consider in advertising, including Snapchat and Instagram. These sites are particularly important because voters, especially Millennials, have shifted their social media preferences to video, live streaming and "disappearing post" apps, such as Snapchat. Millennials clearly don't want social-based political messaging to look like the age-old political ads they see on TV. They respond to authenticity.[42]

CAUSE MARKETING

Cause marketing involves gaining public support and financing for a cause in order to bring about a change or a remedy. You are familiar with many of the marketing campaigns to combat AIDS, drunk driving, drugs, domestic violence, and smoking among teens, as well as campaigns to prevent animal cruelty and to encourage the use of seat belts. Cause marketing is used for blood drives, Community Chest drives and charities that feed and clothe the homeless or combat various diseases. The overall objective is to remedy a situation by gaining public support for change.

Cause marketing is challenging because it usually confronts two very difficult tasks: raising money and providing help to those in need. For example, Walgreens won a 2014 Gold Halo Award for its "Give a Shot. Get a Shot" campaign. Partnering with the United Nations Foundation's Shot@Life program, it successfully increased flu shot volumes through its pharmacies. For every flu shot administered in Walgreens, it donated the value of the vaccine to children in developing countries.[43]

Eyewear company, Warby Parker, has a "Buy a Pair, Give a Pair" program; for

Warby Parker uses cause marketing in its "Buy a Pair, Give a Pair" program.

every pair of glasses purchased, the company provides funds for glasses to a nonprofit partner such as VisionSpring. Warby Parker also works with nonprofits to train low-income entrepreneurs and help them start their own businesses selling glasses in their home countries.[44]

INTERNAL MARKETING

Internal marketing occurs when one part of an organization markets its capabilities to others within the same firm. For example, imagine that you are a human resources manager. Your job, among other responsibilities, is to provide training and career development for employees in all the company's different divisions and departments. Using familiar marketing concepts can effectively achieve this; you're just aiming them at your own employees, rather than the target consumers of your organization's final product. This is not the same as internal communications, which are also important; internal marketing uses all the tools of the marketing mix, as well as techniques to insure customer satisfaction and loyalty.

INTERNAL MARKETING

The marketing of a business unit's capabilities to others within the same firm.

NONPROFIT MARKETING

The activities performed by an organization not motivated by profit in order to influence consumers to support it with a contribution.

The Marketing of Nonprofit Services

Marketing of nonprofit services is a huge area. According to the National Center for Charitable Statistics, there are more than 1.5 million nonprofit organizations in the United States.[45] **Nonprofit marketing** is performed by an organization that is not motivated by profit and is exempt from paying taxes on any excess revenues over costs. Churches, museums, foundations, hospitals, universities, symphonies and municipalities, among other institutions, regularly create marketing plans in an effort to gain funds and public support. Nonprofit organizations often use person marketing, entertainment and event marketing, and place marketing. Nearly all political and cause marketing, as well as marketing of the arts, fits the nonprofit description. Most nonprofit organizations have begun advertising and soliciting donations as well as volunteers on the internet, in an effort to maximize fundraising at little cost.[46]

TYPES OF NONPROFIT SERVICE PROVIDERS

Figure 10.6 shows several categories of nonprofit service providers and gives examples of each. As you can see, marketing skills are required by a very broad range of nonprofit organizations. For example, your university probably has a fairly elaborate marketing plan, and chances are that many of the administrators have attended American Marketing Association seminars on how to promote higher education. Many athletic directors and university presidents are currently being advised to view their positions as similar to that of a CEO of a major corporation.

THE NEED FOR EXCESS REVENUES

Nonprofit service organizations are usually tax exempt and may appear to be less concerned about pricing and cost structures, but they still have several reasons to generate

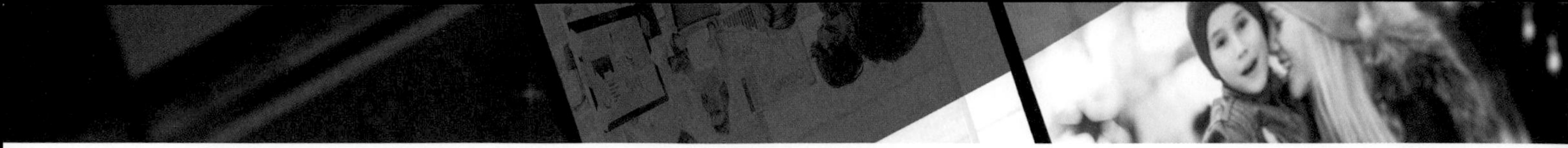

Category	Example	Product
Arts/Culture/Humanities	Metropolitan Museum of Art, New York	Exhibits
	Chicago Symphony	Musical programs
Education/Instruction	Michigan State University Executive Education	Executive programs
	University of Southern California Undergraduate Program	Classes, degrees
Environmental Quality/ Protection/Beautification	Smokey the Bear (U.S. Forest Service)	Fire safety
	Greenpeace	Saving the environment
Animal Related	San Diego Zoo	Species preservation
	People for the Ethical Treatment of Animals (PETA)	Animal rights
Health	Listening Ear	Cure for AIDS
	Alcoholics Anonymous (AA)	Stop alcoholism
Consumer Protection	Consumer Hotline	Legal aid
Crime Prevention	Neighborhood Watch	Discourage criminals
	Crime Tip Hotline	Catch criminals
Employment/Jobs	U.S. Army	Volunteer recruitment
Public Safety	State of Michigan	Drive safely
	State of Florida	Wear seat belts
Recreation/Sports	Silverdome	Football
	American Youth Soccer Organization	Youth sports programs
Youth Development	Boy Scouts of America	Scouting jamborees
	Big Sister/Big Brother programs	Companionship and role models
Community/Civic	Bring Your Company to . . .	Community enhancement
	Kiwanis Club	Economic development
Grant Agencies	Rockefeller Foundation	Arts development
	Robert Wood Johnson Foundation	Medical research
Religious Organizations	Catholic Church	Membership
	Evangelists	Spirituality
Other Cause-Based Groups	National Organization of Women (NOW)	Women's rights
	American Civil Liberties Union (ACLU)	Individual rights

Figure 10.6   Types of Nonprofit Service Providers

more revenue than cost. First, their revenues (money for services and from contributions) tend to fluctuate from year to year. For example, the Museum of Fine Arts in Boston relies on blockbuster shows every few years to boost revenues. For its all-star game, the NBA partners with local schools and youth serving community-based organizations in the host city to raise money. Tying a nonprofit event to a profit-making organization, especially a well-known one such as the NBA, can provide fund-raising opportunities.[47]

Second, organizations can't raise money if they are not solvent. The United Way wants the organizations it supports to have at least a three-month safety net, requiring the stern task of earning and setting aside a full quarter's worth of expenses. Fundraising operations must be run in a financially sound manner in order to gain support from large donors. That requires efficiency and documentation identifying the costs of items as well as the revenues received.

Third, nonprofits hire professionals to help the organization grow. Similar to any business, growth generally requires capital and the ability to access funds from financial institutions. Lenders look at nonprofits much the same way they look at any other organization. The Red Cross operates with positive cash flows (more revenues than expenditures), which not only attracts managerial talent but also affords the company access to lenders and all the services required by a for-profit company.

FUNDRAISING AND REVENUE GENERATION

Nonprofit organizations may raise revenues in two ways. First, they acquire funding from third parties, such as governments, private and public agencies and individual contributors. Second, they may expand into a number of business operations.

A considerable amount of funding comes from donations by individuals, families or businesses. Microsoft CEO Bill Gates is recognized for making substantial contributions to non-profits. The Bill & Melinda Gates Foundation works to reduce inequities and improve lives around the world.[48] Less well known is Microsoft co-founder Paul G. Allen, who has given more than $1.5 billion towards the advancement of science, technology, education, wildlife conservation, the arts and community services in his lifetime.[49]

Microsoft's co-founder, Paul G. Allen, has donated over $1.5 billion to various organizations.

Understanding donor profiles helps nonprofit groups target fundraising efforts. There are six categories of donors: communitarians, devout, investors, socialites, repayers and dynasts. The largest group is made up of communitarians, who believe in supporting their community. As government has decreased its support of social services and the arts, nonprofits in these areas must compete against one another for private dollars. Just as new ventures need a well-honed marketing strategy and innovative approach to entice venture capitalists, new nonprofits need to do the same to capture the attention of donors besieged by requests. For example, Shoestring bills itself as "the nonprofit's agency" and offers help with branding, media relations, strategy and more.[50]

In addition to fundraising, many organizations develop business ventures that provide substantial revenues. These are often unrelated to the basic nature of the core activity. Your high school band, drama club or sports team probably used some type of retail operation at one time or another—a car wash, a food stand at the local fair or a candy sale—to raise money for uniforms or a special trip. In fact, these activities often compete with the for-profit sector. Because the service labor is donated, the price charged by the nonprofit group can be substantially lower than the normal retail price, and the nonprofit group's cause often attracts consumer loyalty. In some cases, for-profit businesses simply cannot compete while a fundraiser is going on. Can you think of when nonprofits are customers of for-profit businesses?

Sometimes the revenue-generating venture fits nicely with the core activity of the nonprofit. For example, private schools and universities have bookstores and other merchandising operations. Museums and musical organizations (symphonies, opera companies) may have shops and mail-order catalogs. Some groups license their name or logo for a fee. Zoos, museums, sports teams and others often charge admission.

Finally, membership fees represent a large source of revenue. Most associations are formed for the benefit of members, whether individuals or organizations. For example, a member of the American Marketing Association pays $210 annually to the AMA in addition to chapter dues. This entitles the member to obtain AMA publications and attend conferences at substantially reduced rates. The AMA is the world's largest professional society of marketers, with more than 30,000 members worldwide; there are 78 professional chapters in the U.S. and Canada and dozens of collegiate chapters. The association works to promote education and assist in career development among marketing professionals.[51]

Most professions have a similar organization, and in many cases companies can be members. For example, firms interested in service quality are likely to join the Center for Services Leadership (CSL) at Arizona State University, North America's leading university-based program for the study of services marketing and management. The center conducts research, offers specialized education and training and works to provide firms with applicable principles, concepts and tools.[52]

PROVIDING POSITIVE SOCIAL BENEFITS

Another challenge for nonprofits is to provide maximum positive social benefits to their constituency. This can be difficult, because constituents may have differing objectives and needs. For example, the San Diego Zoo must balance the public's desire to see certain animals with the interests of environmentalists in species preservation. Expenses to house, care for and in some cases help rare animals reproduce can be very high.

Having a good understanding of constituent needs is not always easy, but the internet is a useful marketing tool for nonprofit groups. Many use it to communicate, share information, educate, collaborate and interact. It is an excellent format for publishing, sharing perspectives on issues, assisting in community development and increasing participation.

A good example of the importance of serving constituency needs can be found in the arts. These include a long list of services: museums, theaters, opera, symphonies, dance companies, exhibitions, public radio, public television and others. A major indicator of the quality of life in many communities is the availability of the arts. Numerous cities have a symphony orchestra, which can be an important factor in attracting businesses and people to the area.

Customers for the arts are called patrons. Attracting them is a critical aspect of marketing the arts, but that is only part of the challenge. Equally important is finding sponsors of all types, since revenues from ticket sales seldom generate enough money for sustained success. Yet patrons may have many choices about which arts events to attend, and sponsors may have a broad range of requests for donations. Ultimately, successful organizations are those that can clearly demonstrate the benefits they bring to their constituents.

ETHICAL ISSUES SURROUNDING NONPROFIT ORGANIZATIONS

Today, many types of organizations claim nonprofit status, which entitles them to tax exemption. While a majority of these benefit society, a growing number have little or no resemblance to traditional charities. In fact, of the 45,000 new organizations that apply for tax-exempt status each year, many make a considerable profit, which raises the question of whether it is ethical for money-making nonprofits to pay no taxes. The Journal News of New York state found that there were 33 private golf and country clubs in Westchester, Putnam and Rockland counties organized as tax-exempt nonprofits and thus not liable for federal income taxes. Initiation fees at some of the courses ranged from $35,000 to $200,000, and annual dues were $10,000 and $20,000.[53]

Although nonprofits are taxed on income from businesses unrelated to their function, fewer than five percent report such income. Nonprofit executives say they have shifted toward profit-making schemes, such as investments and business operations, in order to survive. Many others feel that there are too many nonprofits taking advantage of tax-exempt status, but efforts to change the law have failed repeatedly in Congress.

> Nonprofits are not limited to charity, and many can be found in retail, restaurant, hotel, insurance and even laundry services.

You may be familiar with many nonprofit organizations, such as the National Geographic Society, the Academy of Motion Picture Arts and Sciences (which presents the Oscars) and the Humane Society of the United States. Nonprofits are not limited to charity, and many can be found in retail, restaurant, hotel, insurance and even laundry services. Most nonprofits do not pay taxes on investment income either. Competitors of these orga-

The Nittany Lion Inn sits on one of the most valuable pieces of land on the Pennsylvania State University campus.

nizations are at a clear financial disadvantage, and several find the tax exemptions unfair and unethical. Consider the difference between a nonprofit hotel operated by a university and tax-paying hotels in an area. The Nittany Lion Inn, owned by The Pennsylvania State University, sits on one of the most valuable pieces of land on the university campus, within walking distance of nearly every event on campus from football and basketball games to lectures by outstanding educators and business leaders. Supported by the vast resources of the university, the hotel can develop marketing programs and charge prices that maximize occupancy regardless of costs.

The nation's nonprofit sector generates amazing revenues every year and controls a large percentage of all assets. While these organizations directly benefit their constituents, their tax-free status remains an ethical issue.

Chapter Summary

Objective 1: Identify the global forces that create growth in the service economy.

The service economy is growing at about twice the rate of the sale of goods. First, technological advances and the accompanying information revolution are creating vast opportunities in the service sector. Technology often can only be used with the help of service specialists who have the necessary knowledge and skills. Second, the quality of life is being measured by how people feel and experience life. Third, governments around the world have deregulated services. Fourth, professional service providers such as lawyers are turning to marketing as a way to conduct their business operations. Fifth, privatization of government functions is opening up service opportunities. Sixth, there is a need for outside specialists by companies that want to concentrate resources on their core business. Finally, there is a strong growth in franchising, which tends to focus on service-based products.

Objective 2: Understand which service characteristics affect marketing strategy.

Services are differentiated from goods on several key dimensions that must be considered in successful marketing. First, services are intangible, so evidence of benefits may occur long after purchase and may be difficult to assess. Second, there is a unique relationship between the service provider and customers, who are either present when the service is performed or have knowledge of how it was performed. Third, the service encounter is a crucial point of connection between provider and consumer, in which each moment must contribute to meeting customer needs. Fourth, since production and consumption often occur simultaneously, the same service may be different each time it is performed and may be adjusted to the unique circumstances of each consumer. Fifth, because there is no storage or inventory with a service, demand forecasting is im-

portant so that service providers are ready when needed. Finally, service quality control is extremely important, but it is complicated. It requires thorough training of personnel and careful monitoring.

Most products contain elements of both goods and services and can be placed on a service–goods continuum. Consumers tend to evaluate services differently from goods. Generally, services are high in credence qualities, which means it is difficult to evaluate them even after they have been consumed. Therefore, consumers tend to rely on personal references for information, engage in postpurchase evaluation, develop surrogates for judging quality, select providers from a small set of choices, and actually serve as a competitor to the service provider. They are slow to adopt new services but eventually develop strong brand loyalty.

Judgments of service quality usually have three aspects: the dimensions of service quality, consumer factors and quality perceptions. The dimensions of service quality include tangibles, reliability, responsiveness, assurance and empathy. Customer factors—word of mouth, personal needs, past experience and external communication—help form customer expectations. Quality perception is based on the difference between what is expected and what is received.

Objective 3: Know how to develop the service mix.

Service mix development requires understanding in two areas. First, services have core, augmented and branded dimensions similar to goods. Brand equity is equally if not more important for services than for goods. Second, when developing new services, marketers must give careful consideration to both functional and interactive elements. The functional element is influenced by the complexity and divergence of a service, which must provide benefits that match customer needs and wants. The interactive element involves such concerns as the consumer's personal behaviors and the atmosphere in which the service will be performed.

Objective 4: Explore the expanded concept of services.
There are many types of service marketing including person marketing, entertainment and event marketing, place marketing, political marketing, cause marketing and internal marketing. Person marketing promotes an individual, often a sports figure or movie personality, who in turn generally helps market another product. Entertainment marketing promotes movies, television programming and the like. Event marketing, like that for sporting events and concerts, is a major category. Through sponsorships of events, companies also market other products. Place marketing promotes a geographic location, such as a city, state or country. It is often connected to investment or travel products. Political marketing promotes politicians or political ideas and policy issues. Cause marketing attempts to gain support for a cause, such as research on HIV and AIDS. Internal marketing occurs when one business unit markets its capabilities to others within the same firm.

Objective 5: Explain the importance of nonprofit marketing and the uniqueness of this important marketing arena.
Nonprofit marketing accounts for more than seven percent of economic activity in the United States and is growing. It is performed by organizations that are tax exempt, such as churches, museums, foundations, hospitals, universities and orchestras. Even nonprofits need revenues in excess of their costs. These revenues provide service continuity from year to year and allow nonprofits to access the talent and funding required to serve their constituents. Consequently, fund-raising and revenue generation from donors, patrons and members are often a focal point. At the same time, nonprofits must provide benefits to all constituents, which can be difficult, because different parties have varying expectations and needs. Ethically, there is a question about tax-exempt status for at least some nonprofits, especially when they compete with for-profit organizations.

Review Your Understanding

1. List the seven forces that are producing substantial growth in services. Describe each.
2. What are the differences between goods and services?
3. What is the service–goods continuum? What are the categories of the continuum?
4. What are search, experience and credence attributes of services? List a product example in each attribute category.
5. What are the functional and interactive elements of services?
6. List three examples of person marketing.
7. What is entertainment and event marketing?
8. Give an example of cause marketing.
9. What is internal marketing?
10. What differentiates nonprofit services from other services?
11. Why do nonprofit organizations need more revenues than costs?

Discussion of Concepts

1. List three of the seven forces driving the explosive growth of the service economy. How will each force influence the nature of college education?
2. Select two differences between services and goods and detail how each affects marketing strategy development.
3. Do you think it is possible for a product to be either a pure good or a pure service? Why or why not?
4. What are the differences between search, experience and credence qualities of products? How does each affect marketing strategy development?
5. Name a service high in credence quality. What type of buyer behavior would you expect to encounter?
6. Select a target market and design the core, augmented and branded aspects of a restaurant.
7. Do you consider it appropriate for politicians to develop sophisticated marketing campaigns in order to be elected to office?

Key Terms & Definitions

1. **Cause marketing:** Gaining public support and financing in order to change or remedy a situation.
2. **Core service:** The basic benefit delivered.
3. **Divergence:** The degree to which a service involves customization beyond routine or standardized procedures.
4. **Event marketing:** Promoting an event in order to generate revenues and enhance the reputation of an organization.
5. **Franchise:** A contractual agreement whereby an entrepreneur pays a fee for the franchise name and agrees to meet operating requirements and use the organization's marketing plan.
6. **Functional element:** What a service is supposed to accomplish.
7. **Interactive element:** The personal behaviors and atmosphere of the service environment.
8. **Internal marketing:** The marketing of a business unit's capabilities to others within the same firm.

9. **Nonprofit marketing:** The activities performed by an organization not motivated by profit to influence consumers to support it with a contribution.

10. **Perishable:** The temporal nature of services, whose value exists for only a short time.

11. **Person marketing:** Promoting an individual's personality, character, and appeal, which in turn may assist in the promotion of a product.

12. **Place marketing:** Promoting a geographical location in order to appeal to businesses, investors and tourists.

13. **Political marketing:** Promoting an individual or idea motivated by the desire to influence public policy and voters.

14. **Service:** An idea, task, experience or activity that can be exchanged for value to satisfy the needs and wants of consumers and businesses.

15. **Service complexity:** The number and intricacy of steps involved in producing a service.

16. **Service encounter:** The interaction between the consumer and the seller.

References

1. World Trade Organization, www.wto.org, website visited April 7, 2016.

2. Helen H. Wang, "How Burger King Can Recover in China," Forbes, March 4, 2013.

3. Ibid.

4. "Dear digital diary – lifelogging in the Internet age," The Guardian, www.guardian.co.uk, August 12, 2012.

5. "Federal Deposit Insurance Corporation — Number of Institutions, Branches and Total Offices," FDIC Balance Sheet, www.fdic.gov, website visited June 13, 2016.

6. US Census Bureau, www.census.gov, website visited July 4, 2016.

7. Bureau of Labor Statistics, U.S. Department of Labor, Occupational Outlook Handbook, 2014-15 Edition, Maids and Housekeeping Cleaners, www.bls.gov, website visited June 23, 2016.

8. www.peapod.com/site/companyPages, website visited June 24, 2016.

9. Laura Evans, "Billboards at Metro stations provide a virtual grocery store for riders," myfoxdc.com, October 23, 2012.

10. www.peapodpickup.com, website visited June 24, 2016.

11. www.peapod.com/pdfs/PR-feel-good-non-profit-04032015.pdf, website visited June 24, 2016.

12. "Do Prescription Drug Ads Belong On TV?" The People's Pharmacy. www.peoplespharmacy.com, site visited April 7, 2015.

13. "Prescription Drug Advertising: Questions and Answers," FDA, www.fda.gov, website visited August 13, 2016.

14. "Do Prescription Drug Ads Belong On TV?" The People's Pharmacy. www.peoplespharmacy.com, site visited April 7, 2016.

15. "Greece faces difficult odds with privatization," Washington Post, www.washingtonpost.com, August 3, 2012.

16. "Privatization Gets an Endorsement from Smart Folks," Knight Ridder Tribune Business News, June 6, 2006, pg. 1.

17. "Chick-fil-A Announces Growth in the Midwest with Michigan Restaurants Opening in 2016," Chick-fil-A Press Release, April 19, 2016.

18. www.amazon.com, website visited June 16, 2016.

19. "The Book Superstore." Barnes and Noble, www.barnesandnobleinc.com, website visited April 21, 2016.

20. "Refining the recommended system requirements for Windows 8," Ars Technica, www.arstechnica.com, May 31, 2012.

21. Dave Altavilla, "Microsoft Learns From Windows 8 Backlash, Plans Windows Threshold Catering To Device Types," Forbes, June 30, 2014.

22. "Corporate Fact Sheet," Southwest, www.swamedia.com, web site visited June 13, 2016.

23. Zeithaml, Valeria A., "How Consumer Evaluation Processes Differ Between Goods and Services," Marketing of Services, (Chicago: American Marketing Association, 1981).

24. www.travelandleisure.com, website visited June 13, 2016.

25. www.usps.gov, website visited June 17, 2016.

26. "FAQ," FedEx Office, http://www.fedex.com, website visited June 14, 2016.

27. "Office Services," FedEx Office, http://www.fedex.com, website visited June 14, 2016.

28. www.pryor.com, website visited April 7, 2016.

29. Kotler, Philip, "Atmospherics as a Marketing Tool," Journal of Marketing 40 (Winter 1973-74, pg. 50).

30. Mehrabian, M.; Russel, J.A., An Approach to Environmental Psychology (Cambridge, Massachusetts: MIT Press, 1974).

31. www.dmx.com, website visited June 6, 2016.

32. McGirt, Ellen, "Want a Piece of This?" Fast Company, January, 2010; www.twitter.com, website visited June 6, 2016.

33. Julie Makinen, "'Transformers' breaks box-office records in China," Hollywood Reporter, Los Angeles Times, June 30, 2014.

34. www.boxofficemojo.com/alltime/domestic, website visited July 6, 2016.

35. Weinbach, John, "Inside College Sports' Biggest Money Machine," October 19, 2007, Wall Street Journal.

36. "Fans worldwide to enjoy NBA 2014 All-Star Game," NBA News by Official Release, www.nba.com, February 12, 2014.

37. "FIFA Financial Report 2013," FIFA.

38. Matt Yoder, "2014 World Cup viewership up 26% versus 2010, up 116% versus 2006," Bloguin, June 21, 2014.

39. Nancy Tartaglione and Dominic Patten, "World Cup Ratings Update: Univision Hits Highest Viewership Ever With Mexico Vs. Netherlands Game," Deadline, June 30, 2014.

40. Les Carpenter, "Huddles around TV sets prove US women's soccer is special in the world," The Guardian, July 4, 2015.; Jason Lisk, "Women's World Cup Final Draws Over 21 Million Viewers, Besting 1999 Final," www.thebiglead.com, July 6, 2015.

41. www.michigan.org, website visited June 14, 2016.

42. www.cio.com/article/2976083/social-networking/why- social-media- could-swing- the-2016- presidential-election.html, website visited July 14, 2016.

43. "2014 Halo Award - Best Health Campaign," Halo Awards, cause-marketingforum.com, website visited June 14, 2016.

44. Warby Parker, www.warbyparker.com, website visited July 6, 2016.

45. National Center for Charitable Statistics, http://nccs.urban.org, website visited June 15, 2016.

46. Bianchi, Alessandra, "The New Philanthropy," Inc., October 2000, pp. 23-25.

47. www.nba.com, website visited July 6, 2016.

48. www.gatesfoundation.org, website visited July 6, 2016.

49. Paul G. Allen, Philanthropy, www.philanthropicpeople.com, website visited July 6, 2016.

50. www.shoestringagency.org, website visited July 6, 2016.

51. www.marketingpower.com, website visited July 6, 2016.

52. http://wpcarey.asu.edu/csl, website visited July 6, 2016.

53. "(Loop) hole in one: 33 elite, private golf clubs do not pay federal taxes," Journal News, www.lohud.com, June 23, 2012.

CHAPTER *11*

Product
Innovation
& Management

Google

Courtesy of Google

Google's culture empowers employees to be more creative and innovative.

Today, Google (now officially known as Alphabet) offers more than 100 different products in over 110 languages, including YouTube, Picasa, Blogger, Chrome and Earth. With just one Google account, consumers are able to access Gmail, Google Docs, AdSense, and Google News. Each of these apps allows collaboration across the internet's data cloud, storing files and data on the Google servers, so users can access them from almost any device with an internet connection. Google adapts quickly and adds new products often. One upcoming offering is Google Fiber, a new internet and TV service coming to selected cities and promising speeds up to 100 times faster than the average household can currently run.

How does Google create and develop all these products? The answer lies in its corporate culture. One of Google's most famous management philosophies is called "20% time." Founders Larry Page and Sergey Brin highlighted the idea in their 2004 IPO letter: "We encourage our employees, in addition to their regular projects, to spend 20% of their time working on what they think will most benefit Google," they wrote. "This empowers them to be more creative and innovative. Many of our significant advances have happened in this manner." Essentially, Google employees are encouraged to take one day out of every five to brainstorm new product ideas.

While it might seem that creating new products is easy, the task can actually be quite daunting. Laura Holmes is a product manager who was accepted into Google's Associate Product Manager (APM) program and participated in the international launches of Google Instant. The APM program takes people with various experiences, lets them learn different functions of the company, then puts them in a situation where they get to build a product. Use the QR code to learn more about this unique rotational program and Ms. Holmes' experience collaborating with engineering, user experience and marketing teams to manage and launch new products—the Google way.

Plenty of these new Google products were revealed at the recent Google I/O annual developers' conference. One is a new computer chip with more than 10 times the capabilities of any existing chip. Called a Tensor Processing Unit, the chip will immediately read road signs on Google's StreetView, learn language idioms so Google Assistant will understand accents and dialects, and instantly make sense of Big Data.

Google is part of an industry with outstanding innovators. Apple combines technology with design; Facebook adapts technology to social e-commerce, and IBM invests in futuristic research. What makes Google different is its various innovation strategies, which allow it to introduce more innovations in a short period of time. The "20% time" philosophy contributes to this volume of innovation, and so does Google Brain—which has over a hundred researchers that work within Google product teams to brainstorm and develop new products.

Consider how many times you've said "Google it," and you'll appreciate the innovation and product management of this extraordinary company. In 2016, Fortune again ranked Google as the No. 1 company to work for—its seventh time in the top spot—and the #2 most valuable brand in the world. The company continues to reward all of its stakeholders, including employees, advertisers, consumers, shareholders, and communities across the globe.

Sources: fortune.com/best-companies/google-alphabet-1/, website visited July 3, 2016; Jillian D'Onfro, "The truth about Google's famous '20% time' policy," www.businessinsider.com, April 17, 2015; Satell, Greg, "Want to Do Corporate Innovation Right? Go Inside Google Brain," Harvard Business Review, June 01, 2016; www.wallstreetdaily.com/2016/05/25/google-chip-tensor-processing-unit, website visited July 4, 2016.

LO 01 Provide a framework to evaluate how existing or new products are marketed to new market segments.

LO 02 Understand how the characteristics of innovation influence the speed with which product innovations are accepted.

LO 03 Know the steps used to develop new products from the initial idea through commercialization.

LO 04 Show how the product life cycle concept can be used to build and adjust marketing strategies over time.

LO 05 Recognize how innovations are adopted by consumers by being spread from group to group.

The Concepts of Innovation & Product Management

A winning company doesn't sit idle while profits accumulate; it innovates! It researches markets, gathers customer feedback and develops its next introduction. New products invigorate organizations, and they are absolutely essential to competitive advantage. Companies that fail to innovate usually fail, period. Even those slower than competitors lose their customer connections as leading-edge organizations step in to vie for market share. At the same time, winning companies don't prematurely abandon their existing products. They nurture and support them like old friends. Organizations make direct connections with customers through products. Without these, no relationship can exist because products form the fundamental substance of all business exchanges. Whether these connections remain solid depends largely on the ability of marketers to introduce and manage products. This chapter explores how long-term connections are made through technological innovations and product management to fulfill market needs.

Speed and responsiveness—the ability to develop products quickly—is extremely important in gaining a competitive advantage. Companies are compressing the amount of time required to turn an idea into a marketable product. This vastly increases the number of products companies can offer, but also shortens the life of each product to make room for accelerated R&D. Because of these trends, executives are emphasizing the firm's **product mix**—all of the product lines a company offers. They are also adjusting the depth and breadth of product lines in response to rapidly changing market forces. Excellent product management is considered essential for creating superior customer value.

Organizations must be able to balance the management of existing products and the ability to identify, find or create new ones. In a classic study, the consulting firm of Booz, Allen & Hamilton found that 28 percent of company growth comes from products introduced in the past five years. So new product development is clearly important and necessary, but it also comes with a great deal of risk. About 56 percent

PRODUCT MIX

All the product lines and products a company offers.

of introductions fail within five years, and about 45 percent of new product development resources are spent on failures. In fact, companies usually have to come up with 13 new product ideas before they hit on one that works.[1] With the right strategy, products can generate profits necessary to reach the organization's objectives *and* cover the costs of cultivating new products.

Product Planning & Types of Innovation

PRODUCT PLANNING

Every business needs to develop a product plan consistent with its overall marketing strategy. **Product planning** outlines the focus given to core businesses (current products in current segments), market development (new segments for current products), product development (new products for current segments) or diversification (products totally new to the company for new segments).

    Product planning decisions are influenced by market segment strategies. Marketers must decide how to balance development of the existing product lines and segments with that of new products and markets. Figure 11.1 depicts these fundamental choices.

PRODUCT PLANNING

The focus given to core businesses, market development, product development, and diversification.

	Existing Products	New Products
Existing Market Segments	**Core Product Focus** Maintain, expand, or harvest current products	**Product Development** Improve products Add to product line
New Market Segments	**Market Development** Add new market segment(s)	**Diversification** Add new-product lines Expand into unrelated businesses

Figure 11.1   Product Planning Options

Core Business Focus A core business focus emphasizes the marketing of existing products to existing market segments. While this focus does not involve the risk and expenses of creating new products, it still requires careful decisions about whether to maintain, expand or eliminate current products, depending on market conditions, the age of the product and competitive factors. Firms that do not make these adjustments are often forced to downsize, consolidate or withdraw from some market altogether.

    Many strong companies achieve success by focusing on their core products and market segments. This does not mean to develop the core exclusively; rather, a successful core can generate revenues to support other ventures. Sometimes companies extend their core business to take advantage of additional product offerings supported by a unique competency. For example, Nikon opened in 1918 as a manufacturer principally of binoculars. It later expanded to cameras, microscopes, surveying instruments, measuring instruments and ophthalmic lenses. Today, its products range from imaging software to film scanners to cameras for everyone from kids to professional sports photographers.[2]

MARKET DEVELOPMENT

Offering existing products to new market segments.

Market Development **Market development** occurs when existing products are offered to new segments. Firms may sell directly to these or use new channels of distribution. They also may expand from local markets to regional, national, international or global markets. Many clothing companies and department stores are diversifying their product lines with plus-size clothing for women. I.N.C. label clothing, sold in Macy's and Bloomingdale's, is offering plus-size clothing that is designed exactly like regular-sized clothing, as well as styles designed to provide more coverage. Ralph Lauren has extended its products to include marketing to big and tall consumers through the Rochester Big and Tall retailing outlets.[3]

PRODUCT DEVELOPMENT

Offering new products to existing market segments.

Product Development **Product development** occurs when companies make new products for existing market segments. This may take the form of simple improvements to older products or extensions of the product line. Most companies are continuously introducing improved versions.

Whether in the consumer or business market, product lines are continuously expanding. Pizza Hut is always developing new products, many focused on stuffing, double-stuffing, even triple-stuffing cheese into crusts and breads in every way imaginable. Its most recent innovation is an old school throwback to traditional hand-tossed pizzas. The new hand-tossed pizzas feature a lighter, airier texture and contain imperfections in an attempt to appear more artisan, a trend popular with millennials.[4] Developing new products that are closely related to existing ones is called a **line extension**. In one recent example of a line extension, Dr Pepper rolled out its Dr Pepper TEN line, featuring 10 calories per serving. The soda was so successful the company has now come up with ten-calorie versions of its other core brands, like 7-Up, Sunkist, A&W, and Canada Dry.[5] Line extension is not limited to physical products: web-based companies frequently expand their product lines to keep up with a growing market.

LINE EXTENSION

A new product closely related to others in the line.

Diversification Diversification occurs when new products are introduced into new market segments. Sometimes this is done with extensions of the current business, and sometimes it occurs with new ventures. Nintendo engaged in product diversification through the release of the Wii. With more powerful processors and impressively realistic graphics, competitors Microsoft and Sony went after their existing market of established gamers. Nintendo went in another direction, focusing on simplicity and creating a system drastically different from any video-game console on the market. Rather than requiring a complex controller with multiple buttons, the Wii's wireless, motion-sensitive controllers allow users to mimic real movements.[6] Nintendo went a step further into expanding its market with the Wii Fit balance board. Wii Fit is meant to make fitness more fun for all ages and includes balance and aerobic games, and even yoga positions.[7] With accessibility and the ability to perform exercise while playing, the Wii has proven popular among markets that were previously not ex-

Nintendo uses diversification when entering new gaming units into the market.

perienced gamers. The Wii successor, Wii U, brought the revolutionary new Wii U GamePad controller with a second window into your gaming world.[8]

Another incredibly effective case of diversification was Apple's introduction of the iPod, iPhone and iPad. Apple ventured away from the computer arena and into uncharted territory. The result has been dramatic. Because of these ventures, Apple grew exponentially and gained significant ground on Microsoft.

TYPES OF PRODUCT INNOVATION

Marketers classify innovations according to the effect they are likely to have on consumers. **Continuous innovation** is a minor change to a familiar product, such as a new style or model that can be easily adopted without significant alterations in consumer behavior. For example, Adobe continually adds new features to its software products. Photoshop CS6 brought Content Aware tools to scale and improve aspect ratios in images, digital noise reduction tools, advanced 3D and video editing capabilities, and

CONTINUOUS INNOVATION

A minor alteration in an existing product, such as a new style or model, that can be easily adopted without significant changes in consumer behavior.

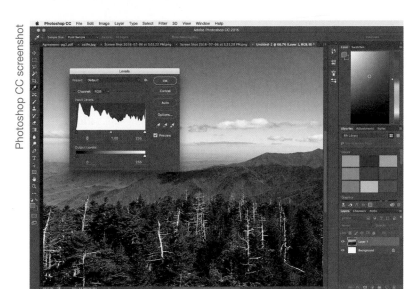

Photoshop CC screenshot

Adobe Photoshop has been a continuous innovation popular among professional and aspiring photographers for more than 25 years.

DYNAMICALLY CONTINUOUS INNOVATION

A familiar product with additional features and benefits that require or permit consumers to alter some aspect of their behavior.

DISCONTINUOUS INNOVATION

An entirely new product with new functions.

more.[9] Photoshop Creative Cloud 2015 includes a load of new mobile features and two new features of the most interest to professional and aspiring photographers—path-based blurs and focus-based selections.[10]

A **dynamically continuous innovation** endows a familiar product with additional features and benefits that require or permit consumers to alter some aspect of their behavior. When auto companies introduced the antilock braking system (ABS), consumers needed to relearn how they had been taught to react in an emergency. On slippery terrain, pumping the brake was the advised way to regain control, but brakes equipped with ABS work best when fully compressed. Manufacturers were careful to educate drivers about the benefits and requirements of ABS so that reaction to the new system would be positive. Another example is the transformation of music devices over time. From records to eight-track and cassette tapes to CDs to digital MP3s, each new device created a shift in how we listen to music.

A **discontinuous innovation** is an entirely new product with new functions. Sometimes called "new to the world," these products require behavioral changes by users. The high degree of novelty gives early potential adopters a great deal of costs and benefits to consider before making a decision. Examples include cellular phones, satellite-transmitted maps for autos, and heart pumps. When automobile airbags were introduced, buyers had to evaluate the benefits carefully before committing the additional funds for the optional purchase. Eventually airbags, became standard equipment and were included in the vehicle price.

The advent of the laptop computer is another example. Laptops created an opportunity for work to be done outside of the office, whether in a café or on an airplane. They have become almost obligatory for college students and are preferred over desktop computers for general use. Laptops are also becoming increasingly portable, as companies like Acer are decreasing the size and weight of their products. The Acer Aspire S7 weighs just 2.79 pounds and is only 12.9 millimeters thick—hardly even noticeable in a backpack.[11]

WHY INNOVATIONS SUCCEED

Research reveals that novelty itself is not as important as a new product meeting consumer needs.[12] Several specific factors influence consumer acceptance of new products: relative advantage, compatibility, complexity, trialability and observability.

Relative Advantage Relative advantage is the amount of perceived superiority the new product has in comparison to existing ones. Marketers must make it easy for consumers to recognize the benefits of switching from the old product, while making clear that any costs can be overcome. A new word-processing program may be easier to use but requires additional training. If consumers aren't convinced that the additional training will pay off, they are unlikely to purchase the new product.

In Apple's pursuit to gain market share over PCs, it is important to create a relative advantage over all other players in the industry. One way Apple attracts customers is through its claim of no-hassle software and ease of use, a claim that is demonstrated through its website. Visitors can not only review product information, but also access guided online tours demonstrating Apple products, such as how to download iTunes for use with an iPod. Apple.com also provides a wide array of support services and resources, so the customer can research and purchase products, and revisit the site for support later.

Compatibility Compatible products fit easily into the consumer's current thinking or system. Successful products are aligned with their consumers' thoughts and values, and are designed to meet their needs, not create problems. This is one reason many organizations now have 800 numbers to answer questions.

Most people consider safety important when deciding to purchase an automobile. Several companies understand the value of this and are working on high-tech ways to make driving safer. For example, GM's Delco division has created blind-spot radar to warn drivers when it's unsafe to change lanes. Texas Instruments has developed a thermal-image camera that eliminates glare from oncoming headlights. Since the products are included in the vehicle purchase, the issues of installation and additional purchase are avoided. Apple is especially successful at compatibility; its products synch so customers have their information and music on all their Apple devices.

Complexity Complexity is the degree to which a new product is easy to understand and use. Apple's Macintosh computers achieved great success by making personal computers accessible to anyone. Many people have sat down at a Macintosh, followed the simple instructions, and quickly learned to use elaborate programs. It wasn't until Microsoft developed its Windows interface that the DOS platform provided similar ease of use.

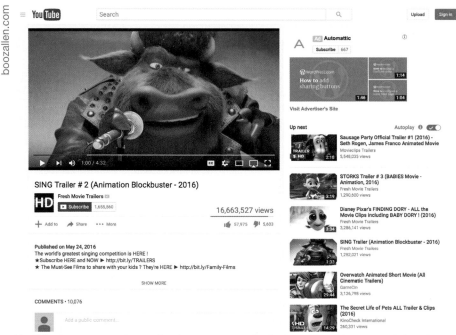

YouTube is easy to navigate, allowing users to easily find trending videos, search for other videos and view content specifically of interest to them.

Facebook makes social media easy to use even for the less-technically inclined. On Facebook, "liking," "commenting" or "sharing" a post is a simple click away. A search bar at the top invites users to "search for people, places and things," and another area invites users to share their status updates by asking, "What's on your mind?" The site is self-explanatory enough that 49 percent of seniors use it, according to a recent study by Forrester. YouTube also makes its site easy to navigate, with "channels" to choose from, such as trending videos, music, entertainment, sports and comedy. Select a video, and after it plays YouTube will recommend related videos you may enjoy.

Trialability Trialability refers to the ease with which potential users can test a new product at little or no expense. New product acceptance can be sped up through free samples, low-cost trials, interactive showroom techniques or loaners. Computer retailers usually place equipment on display so consumers can interact with it. Nearly every car buyer test-drives an automobile before purchasing it. General Motors offers an overnight test drive option on almost all of its vehicles to qualified drivers, providing the consumer doesn't drive more than 100 miles or leave the state. This promoted increased trialability of its products in a setting that's comfortable for the consumer.

Trialability is critical for software vendors, because only through use can potential buyers understand the features they would gain; software companies such as Adobe frequently offer free 30-day trials of their products. In the magazine world, free trial issues are common. Food companies often provide free samples in supermarkets.

Observability Observability means that a consumer can obtain a full appreciation for a product's features by watching someone else use it. When a new product has obvious benefits, it can usually be marketed at a rapid pace. When benefits are subtle, it's more difficult to gain acceptance. When the iPod was created, Apple realized it had low observability, because the device was frequently inside users' pockets or bags. To offset this, Apple made all of the iPod accessories white to create a differentiation in the market. When you see someone wearing white earbuds, the Apple iPod comes to mind even though the actual device cannot be seen. The white accessories help Apple increase the observability of its products.

The benefits of smartphone cameras have exploded into the cellular phone market. The continued growth of camera phones has been driven by improvements in imaging functions like flash, zoom and auto focus, and optics. The easily observable benefits of taking and instantly sharing a picture wirelessly, along with convenience and ease of use, are among the reasons these products have become so successful. Not to mention, the world's affection of taking and sharing selfies.

LO 03 The New Product Development Process

Success with new products depends on translating the organization's core competencies into goods or services that provide superior value to the customer. The competitiveness of most markets requires a stream of new products, processes and ventures. It's difficult to pinpoint exactly why some organizations are more innovative than others, but researchers suggest the following concepts encourage innovation success.

- A champion who believes in the new idea
- A sponsor high enough in the organization to provide access to major resources
- A mix of creative minds (to generate ideas) and experienced operators (to keep things practical)
- A team process that moves ideas through the system quickly so that they get top-level endorsement, resources and attention early in the game
- A focus on customers at every step.

Leading companies have a strategy for new product development. In forming that strategy, top executives must answer a number of questions: Will the organization be a market leader, close follower or also-ran? Will it have broad or deep product lines? How rapidly must the product stream flow, given competitive conditions and market expectations? How much will be invested in R&D over time?

Companies that do the best job of new product development have excellent market knowledge, including an understanding of customers and the competition.[14] They also use cross-functional collaboration among marketing, research and development, and other areas of the company.[15]

Fulfilling the company mission requires that marketers have the courage to introduce newer and more advanced technologies. The value statements of many corporations recognize the social responsibility of providing more functional, cost-effective, environmentally sound and safe products. How do those goals become a reality? Executives must be objective about the chances of product success. Since the costs of new product development increase as the product moves toward commercialization, companies will often implement a stage-gate method to prevent further investment into a product likely to fail.[13] Figure 11.2 describes the steps in the new product development process.

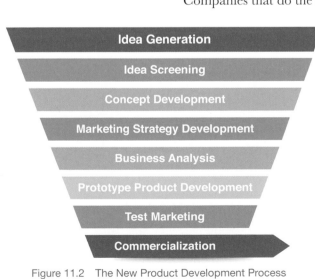

Figure 11.2   The New Product Development Process

IDEA GENERATION

IDEA GENERATION

The gathering of suggestions for new products from a number of sources using a range of formal and informal methods.

Organizations need idea-generation systems to find an adequate number of significant new product ideas. **Idea generation** is the use of a range of formal and informal methods to stimulate new product concepts from a number of sources.[16] Among the many possible sources are employees, customers, social media, technology analysis, distributors and suppliers, competitors, R&D, environmental trend analysis and outside consultants. Marketers often provide incentives to individuals who make significant contributions to idea generation.

A system based on the following four general principles seems to work quite well.

- Systematically seek and ask for new product ideas
- Insure that all ideas, no matter how trivial or elaborate, reach the individual or group responsible for collecting them
- Provide timely feedback to all people contributing ideas
- Build rewards and recognition into the organization scaled according to the number and quality of ideas

Good marketers will continually encourage employees to submit ideas. After all, employees have a great deal of experience working with the products, and can probably identify at least minor improvements that could make the product better. Customers are a logical source of new product ideas. This is particularly true in business-to-business marketing, since customers rely on suppliers to improve their own products and processes. By training salespeople to explore customer problems and creating a system for feedback (such as surveys and focus groups), companies are likely to discover many new concepts.

A technology analysis forecasts the speed and applicability of advances. Distributors and suppliers have a personal interest in the number of products a company makes. They are often asked to serve on the council that many organizations establish to generate new product concepts. Competitors can be a major source of ideas. Leading marketers observe the competition on many levels, analyzing market trends and how they will react to it.

For R&D personnel—scientists, engineers, designers and others—new product development is a major component of the job. Companies that encourage innovation make sure they provide ample opportunity for scientists to explore on their own. When a percentage of their time is free from routine tasks, an R&D staff will often forge major breakthroughs. This is why Google implemented their "20% rule." (See feature box.) And the 3M Corporation not only allows employees to work on projects they choose, but it urges them to seek new product ideas from everywhere, even failed experiments. The classic example, Post-it notes, came about from failed attempts to produce strong adhesive.

An environmental trend analysis estimates how major social forces may affect an industry. The organization can then use the results to project ways in which it can offer timely products. One example is to identify pollutants in a current product, find substitute ingredients and components, and develop a new version that will appeal to "green" consumers. Seventh Generation is a company that sells bathroom tissue made from 100 percent recycled paper rather than trees, as well as many other eco-friendly household products. The company's website states, "We create household and personal care products that are effective and safe for

seventhgeneration.com

Seventh Generation celebrates 27 years of creating powerful plant-based solutions for your home & family.

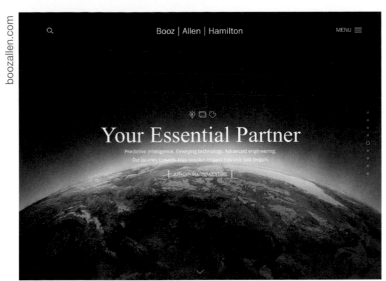

Booz, Allen & Hamilton has gained a global reputation for its ability to identify commercially viable solutions to customer problems.

IDEA SCREENING

Identifying the new-product ideas that have the most potential to succeed.

PRODUCT CONCEPT

A detailed version of the product idea stated in written descriptions, pictures and specifications.

the air, the surfaces, the fabrics, the pets and the people within your living home."[17]

Consultants make up a business that thrives on generating ideas that their consumers, other companies, can use. They use a broad range of techniques to help companies develop concepts: surveys, brainstorming, focus groups and others. Each method provides a structured way of discovering innovative products. The consulting firm Booz, Allen & Hamilton has gained a global reputation for its ability to identify commercially viable solutions to customer problems.

IDEA SCREENING

A good system will provide hundreds of new product ideas each year. More and more, companies are turning to their social media platforms to gather ideas from current consumers. Some even reward customers with free products and promotional opportunities if their idea is developed and implemented. The **idea screening** process identifies ideas with the strongest potential to succeed. Each company applies its own criteria to judge concepts, which can fall into several categories: the market, competition, required resources, technology, the environment, legal and liability issues, and financial factors.[18] Multiple scales measure how well a product performs on each dimension.

Usually, a cross-functional team examines the limited information about the idea, using both experience and subjective judgment. The team may weigh certain factors more than others, and a summary total is provided with qualitative comments to support the evaluation. Once this is completed, the team decides which products to develop further by how the evaluation scored them. The team then provides feedback to everyone who contributed an idea, including an explanation of why it was accepted or rejected. The various team members take different responsibilities over the course of a new product project. Involving several functions at the idea stage greatly increases the likelihood of choosing the best ideas and developing a great product. Each member of the team has specific skills (engineering, marketing, manufacturing) that contribute to product success.[19]

CONCEPT DEVELOPMENT

Once an idea is chosen, it must then be developed into a **product concept**. A product concept is a detailed version of the product idea stated in written descriptions, pictures and specifications. Since this product will be discussed extensively within the company as well as outside in various markets, marketing managers need to develop a definition of the product for internal and external communications. The definition becomes part of the product concept for on-going internal meetings.

An extension of the definition is the identification of how the product will be beneficial to consumers. Why would anyone buy the product? Marketers tackle this question by identifying the features, functions and resulting consumer benefits of the product. The benefits have to be more useful to consumers than what's already offered in the market. Based on this information, marketers then decide how they want customers to perceive the product—what image should they try to create in the minds of consumers? Is the product state-of-the art in technology? Is it a green product? Is it going to reduce costs? Is it attractive? Does it improve safety for children?

Once the product image is defined, then specifications for manufacturing a product prototype are developed. This requires communication and cooperation from employees in various functional areas throughout the company. The development of a product concept is fluid. It may be determined that the product concept needs to be tweaked a bit because

CONCEPT TESTING

Testing a new-product concept with target consumers, distributors and retailers, who provide input regarding the product's potential.

of manufacturing or supply logistics, in which case discussions continue until a fully-feasible concept is determined. At this stage, some companies choose to test the concept with target consumers, distributors and retailers, who provide input regarding the product's potential, as well as its description and visual representations. This is called **concept testing.** It gives marketers an idea of whether serious red flags exist, if one feature is disliked by many people, or if the concept is well received overall. It helps identify the facilitators and inhibitors to a product's success. While testing concepts to sell its new cake batters, Duncan Hines stumbled on the theme of moistness. After hundreds of hours of concept testing, one homemaker said the cake was so moist, it stuck to the fork, a phrase that inspired a successful campaign.

MARKETING STRATEGY DEVELOPMENT

MARKETING STRATEGY DEVELOPMENT

Creating an initial marketing strategy for a new product based on the product concept.

Once the concept is determined, marketers then begin creating an initial marketing strategy for the product's introduction. This is called **marketing strategy development**. It includes the contribution the product will make to overall company objectives, its costs, projected sales, anticipated market share and profit goals. If the product will affect other products in the company's line, those should be noted in the strategy. A timetable for the product launch is also part of the strategy, as well as identification of who will be monitoring the timetable to assure results are achieved on schedule. Finally, the strategy identifies market segments and, in particular, the target market(s) for the new product.

Target markets provide the information necessary to complete the last component of developing a marketing strategy—the marketing mix. How will price, product, place and promotion be established for this new product? As we discussed earlier, accumulating this information requires a lot of time and attention to detail. What will be the price structure of the product, including outright price, leasing options, discounts? How will the product be promoted, including print, retail, social media and digital marketing? How will the product be distributed? Will it be offered in retail stores or online? As you can tell, there are many pieces of work that go into strategy development for a new product.

BUSINESS ANALYSIS

BUSINESS ANALYSIS

Assessment of the attractiveness of the product from a sales, cost, profit, and cash flow standpoint.

Once the marketing strategy is developed, management needs to evaluate the new product from a business perspective. Does it make financial sense to go ahead with this new product? A **business analysis** reviews the product from a sales, cost, and profit standpoint. It determines if the projections for each of these are in line with the company's overall objectives. If they are, the product can proceed to the product development stage.

In order to estimate sales, the company may look at the sales history of similar products and conduct market surveys. From that information, financial analysts can estimate a range of projected sales, then marketers work with the analysts to prepare a sales forecast for the new product. After preparing a sales forecast, with profit and cost projections (costs include marketing, R&D, manufacturing, finance, accounting and logistics expenses, among others), management evaluates the financial attractiveness of the new product. If it is not a financially feasible venture, then the product is scrapped or sent back to the "Idea Generation" stage of the process to be reworked. If, however, the business analysis deems the new product viable from a business standpoint and congruent with company objectives, then it moves into product development.

PROTOTYPE PRODUCT DEVELOPMENT

A prototype is a working model of the product, usually created by a team of marketing, manufacturing, engineering and R&D personnel. Prototypes are typically made by hand, and can be vastly more expensive than the final product. Although costly, these models are necessary for the all-important next step, market testing. Openness among team members and a clear sense of direction, led by a product champion, greatly increase the chances for prototype success regardless of the competitive situation.[20]

Among the difficulties of developing new products is changing customer preferences and uncertainty about competitive products. When there is high uncertainty, organizations need to maintain flexibility in defining specific product characteristics. Often a core team of professionals is used to create product descriptions and supervise frequent interactions with customers, which help evolve product prototypes to meet latest marketing needs.[21] Once the prototype is refined and working well, then more development takes place to manufacture products for test marketing.

Trade shows are a great place for showcasing prototype products. Recently, at Tech World 2016, Lenovo introduced a prototype smart lifestyle running shoe capable of tracking steps, distance, and calories, while doubling as a mobile controller for playing games and interacting with smartphone apps. The smart shoe has LED lights for night running, a customizable insole, and a built-in, rechargeable battery. At the time of the show, neither an introduction date nor a price for the smart shoe was available, but the audience was extremely interested in the prototype. Shows like these are a wealth of information for marketers, who consider questions and comments from attendees in making final changes before manufacturing the actual product for test marketing.

The Verge "Lenovo's smart running shoe"

Lenovo showed off a prototype smart shoe at Tech World 2016 capable of tracking steps, counting calories, and doubling as a mobile controller.

TEST MARKET

A small geographic area, with characteristics similar to the total market, in which a product is introduced with a complete marketing program.

Figure 11.3 Top 20 Test Markets

Rank	City(s) / Regions	State
1.	Indianapolis-Carmel-Anderson	IN
2.	Cincinnati	OH
3.	Oklahoma City	OK
4.	Columbus	OH
5.	Jacksonville	FL
6.	Phoenix-Mesa-Scottsdale	AZ
7.	Nashville-Davidson-Murfreesboro-Franklin	TN
8.	Birmingham-Hoover	AL
9.	Charleston-North Charleston	SC
10.	Tulsa	OK
11.	Albuquerque	NM
12.	Greensboro-High Point	NC
13.	Kansas City	KS
14.	Charlotte-Concord-Gastonia	NC
15.	Orlando-Kissimmee-Sanford	FL
16.	Winston-Salem	NC
17.	Little Rock-North Little Rock-Conway	AR
18.	Richmond	VA
19.	New Orleans-Metairie	LA
20.	Baton Rouge	LA

Figure 11.3 Top 20 Test Markets
Source: "2016's Metro Areas That Most and Least Resemble the U.S.," wallethub.com, 2016.

TEST MARKETING

Test marketing is a limited trial of the strategy for the product under real or simulated conditions. Up to this point, champions may be able to push a weak product through the system. Now reality sets in. A **test market** is a small geographical area, with characteristics similar to the total market, where the product is introduced with a complete marketing program. Test marketing allows companies to implement the product strategy on a limited basis under real conditions. In fact, a test may involve trying two or more marketing strategies in separate areas to identify which works better.

In carefully designed test marketing, consumers are unaware that they are part of an experiment. Retailing, distribution and promotion activities are similar to what would occur at the national or international level. When the results are in, marketers can forecast how long it will take for the product to be adopted in the general market.

Marketers choose test market sites very carefully to represent the segments that eventually will be targeted. For example, manufacturers testing toys would avoid Sarasota, Florida, which has a large elderly population, and snowshoes would get a better reception farther north. Boise, Idaho is a particularly popular site, hosting tests that range from kitchen towels and oven mitts before they hit supermarkets. Audit services in more than 125 cities throughout the United States monitor test market results. Figure 11.3 lists the top 20 test markets with a population of 50,000 or more.

By the time an organization enters a test market, substantial funds have been spent on the new venture. There is a very strong probability of committing to a full-scale product launch at this point — unless the test is a total failure. The results rarely make or break the product; they simply help predict adoption rates among consumers and channel members. Testing products are very beneficial to companies that do not have large amounts of money to spend on research. Experiments also help identify factors that facilitate or hinder product adoption and may yield surprises about who the users will be.

There are several drawbacks to using test markets. First, it takes time, and product development costs rise with every delay in a full-scale launch. Second, marketers sacrifice secrecy and surprise, exposing their products to potential competitors. Sometimes a rival will jump in with a similar product or use tactics that spoil the results. For example, when a competitor test-marketed a new item, Vicks pulled all its similar products off the shelves, leaving no basis for judging whether the test was successful. Other tactics are flooding the market with unusual promotions, point-of-purchase displays and price cuts. Third, it's impractical to use test marketing for many products, like automobiles, because prototypes are too costly. Fourth, it is extremely expensive to make the trial products, stock stores, train salespeople, run ads and so forth.

A **controlled test market** uses consumer panels or other techniques to attempt to gain the same type of information obtained from real test markets. AC Nielsen's Scantrack and IRI's BehaviorScan monitor consumer behavior on new products. By combining information about consumer demographics and TV viewing behaviors with purchase data, it is possible to forecast product success. A controlled test market is often less expensive than conducting regular test marketing.

A **simulated product test** is an experiment in artificial conditions. This may be done before or instead of a full test. GHI, the most authoritative product-testing center in Great Britain, performed tests on vacuum cleaners by cleaning carpets and hard flooring covered with measured amounts of a sand and flour mixture that simulated actual conditions.[22] Such simulated product testing helps identify flaws and provides feedback. It can also be used to make evaluations against competitors. The food industry often sets up a replica of a supermarket, asks consumers to shop as if they were in a natural environment, and interviews them afterward. Although simulations are not as effective as a test market, they do provide useful information at dramatically reduced costs. Furthermore, competitors are less likely to find out about a company's plans prior to product launch.

CONTROLLED TEST MARKET

Consumer panels or other technique to gain similar information obtained from real test markets.

SIMULATED PRODUCT TEST

Experimentation with the marketing strategy in artificial conditions.

COMMERCIALIZATION

Final stage in the new-product development process, when the product is introduced into the market.

COMMERCIALIZATION

During the final stage of the process, **commercialization** introduces the product to the market. Launching consumer products requires heavy company support, such as advertising, sales promotions and often free samples. Consider the $30 million commercialization of Frito-Lay's SunChips brand, which included television spots and the company's largest ever direct-mail sampling program to more than 6 million households. After a decade of development, SunChips breezed through test marketing in six months, indicating to Frito-Lay executives that this multigrain snack had the potential for overnight success. In the snack food industry, new products rarely achieve even $40 million in sales, but Sun-

SunChips was a commercialization success, generating more than $100 million in sales in the first year.

sunchips.com

Chips topped $100 million in the first year and continues to bring in huge profits. Years later, Frito-Lay continues to develop the market for SunChips, attempting to prevent consumers from considering them "junk food." David Radar, executive vice president and chief financial officer, spoke at the University of Texas at Austin, stating that SunChips, which contain whole grains, can be considered a healthy product.[23] Frito-Lay has also engineered an environmentally friendly, 100 percent compostable bag for SunChips that will naturally decompose in about 14 weeks.[24]

The Ethics of Product Imitation

Some argue that since companies make substantial investments in new products, they should be protected from competitors who try to imitate their products. A huge number of intellectual property and patent laws have been created to address this concern. Others argue that imitation forces market leaders to keep up with technology, contend with lower-priced substitutes, and respond to smaller and faster challengers, thereby providing healthy competition. Organizations that want to remain competitive have to keep pace with a growing and changing market, which often requires emulating competitors' innovations.

Since product imitation has become a recognized business strategy, it is increasingly difficult for a firm to protect its products from being copied. Software development giant and market leader Microsoft has greatly benefited from the inventions of others. Its Windows operating system is considered very similar in accessibility and visual format to Apple's operating system. But it goes both ways; Apple's newest iOS 8 is certainly inspired by Microsoft's Windows 10 "flat design," a term given to a style of design in which elements like icons lose any type of stylistic characteristics that make them appear as though they lift off the screen.

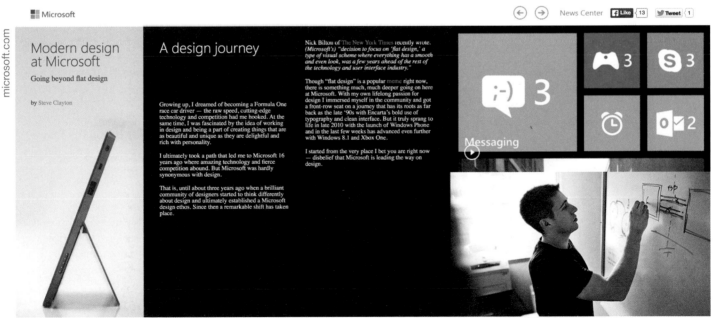

Microsoft designers are pushing the boundaries on modern design, paving the way for imitations to emerge in the market.

Not all imitations are created equally. Some are illegal duplicates of popular products, and some are truly innovative products merely inspired by a pioneering brand.[25] The makers of knockoffs or clones often copy original designs but may leave off important attributes. Clones are legal because protective patents, copyrights and trademarks are absent or have expired.

Some copies play on the style, design or fashion of a popular product. This type of imitation is common in the automobile industry. In the 1980s, several Japanese automakers introduced lines to challenge Mercedes-Benz and BMW. Toyota's Lexus, Nissan's In-

W.L. Gore, who was researching Teflon uses, left DuPont in 1958 and eventually developed Gore-Tex Fabrics.

finiti and Honda's Acura closely mirror the design and features of the German luxury cars. When technical products are copied, reverse engineering is often used to learn how the original was designed or made. Today, Hyundai is using the same approach but is now copying Toyota and other Japanese models.

Creative adoptions innovate beyond an existing product. These may occur as a technological development or as an adaptation to another industry. Initially, DuPont developed Teflon for the nose-cones of spacecrafts but soon extended its uses to coatings for consumer products. W.L. Gore, who was researching Teflon uses, left DuPont in 1958 and eventually developed Gore-Tex Fabrics, whose products are best known for being wind and waterproof. Gore-Tex fabric is frequently used in high-end sports clothing and has become the industry standard for outerwear comfort and protection.[26]

Organizational Structures and Product Management

Simultaneous new product development occurs when people from a number of functional areas work together. Marketing coordinates the team, which usually represents R&D, engineering, production, procurement, legal and human resources, financing and so on. This approach has many advantages over the old technique of **sequential new-product development**, which passes responsibility from one functional area to the next. Companies can produce better products at lower cost and gain returns more quickly when operating simultaneously, which is why the marketers should do their best to ensure all units of the business are working together effectively.

RECENT ORGANIZATIONAL TRENDS

There are many ways to manage existing and new products. Today, companies make creative use of computer and communications technologies to support a flexible organizational structure. This enables them to respond quickly to buyer demands. It also provides access to global technologies and the ability to adapt to competitive forces. There are three notable organizational trends.

1. **Downsizing:** Several product lines are brought under a single management team, or product offerings are reduced to those that generate strong and increasing revenues.

2. **De-layering:** The number of personnel and positions between top executives and those who manage market activities is reduced.

3. **Fewer functional silos:** When one function works in isolation from others, it is called a functional silo. Organizations are stressing cross-functional synergy and personnel with experience in multiple areas.[27] It is just as important that marketers and accountants be able to work with each other as it is with those in their own department.

SIMULTANEOUS NEW PRODUCT DEVELOPMENT

People from all functional areas work together to develop products.

SEQUENTIAL NEW PRODUCT DEVELOPMENT

People from various functional areas work on different stages of product development.

FUNDAMENTAL STRUCTURES

There are many acceptable organizational structures. Today, most companies prefer a structure that supports strategy changes. As strategies alter to meet new challenges, organizational structures need to change with them. The most fundamental structures for new product development are the product or market manager, the new product department, the new product committee and the venture team. Companies may combine elements of several of these and may use consulting organizations as well.

Product or Market Managers Some of the most successful organizations have used the product manager or market manager structure. A **product manager** oversees one or several products targeted at all market segments. A **market manager** is responsible for one or several similar product lines targeted at defined market areas. In either case, the manager works closely with individuals from a range of functions to build integrated strategies. The system was pioneered by Procter & Gamble, which developed teams of experts loosely tied but headed by a very strong manager. Each team was responsible for building the equity of a given brand. Product managers compete almost as strongly with other teams in the organization as they do with competitors on the outside. For example, the Crest product manager is in competition with the Gleem product manager. However, since each product is positioned to address a particular benefit — Crest for tooth decay prevention and Gleem for brightness — competition may not be direct.

Product managers or market managers have the following specific responsibilities:

- Achieve the sales, profit, market share and cash flow objectives for the product line.
- Develop the market strategy for the product.
- Prepare a written marketing plan, develop forecasts and maintain timely updates of progress.
- Integrate all functions necessary to implement a synergistic marketing strategy.

One difficulty with this system is that the manager has responsibilities beyond the traditional lines of authority. The product manager can be described as the hub of a wheel. Think of the spokes as all the functional areas that help make a good marketing strategy work. Product managers have no formal authority over these people, who report directly to managers in their own functional area.

What makes the system work? First, the product or market manager must have the necessary interpersonal and business skills to gain the team's respect without exerting too much authority. In this system, team play and networking are the most valued qualities of all involved, and strong product or market managers can use them to tap into very specialized talents from a range of people. Second, the manager must report to someone high enough in the organization to obtain the status required. Although unable to govern the activities of team members, product and marketing managers can make their presence known through communication with top executives and across functional areas of the company.

The system's strength is also its weakness. Product managers must rely on functional managers from various areas of the organization to help them build a strong team, and if everyone is not on the same page, this can lead to miscommunication or a lack of productivity. Experience has shown that without proper attention by top management, the product or marketing manager may be relegated to relatively mundane tasks. When there is appropriate executive leadership, the system can be a flexible, productive way to address numerous market situations.

New Product Department The **new product department** is responsible for identifying ideas, developing products and preparing them for commercialization. The members generally report directly to top executives and include individuals with experience in many aspects of the business. This structure separates the responsibility of new product devel-

PRODUCT MANAGER

A manager who oversees one or several products targeted at all market segments.

MARKET MANAGER

A manager responsible for one or several similar product lines targeted at specific market segments.

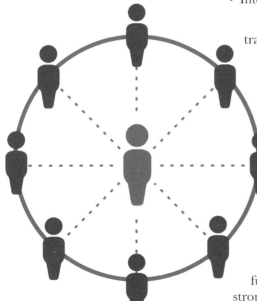

NEW PRODUCT DEPARTMENT

The organizational unit responsible for identifying product ideas and preparing them for commercialization.

opment from the rest of the organization. It also helps eliminate redundancies that occur when the same ideas are developed in different product areas. These personnel have a firm grasp of the methods and risks involved in developing new products. In reality, these departments are often formed with great expectations, but some quickly become a functional silo neglected by top management. This is particularly the case when top management is preoccupied with current products or when the new product department does not set aggressive goals regarding potential commercial products. Such a department usually operates best when it has strong executive involvement and concentrates its efforts on finding strategies to make product ideas successful.

New Product Committee The **new product committee** consists of key functional personnel who are brought together from time to time to develop new products. Because this activity is often not considered a strong factor in building a career, participants may give it less attention than required. Furthermore, the committee often lacks the authority to make things happen. However, it is flexible, allowing different people throughout the organization to contribute ideas and expertise, and committee members can come and go as needed in a project's development.

Venture Team A **venture team** (sometimes called a task force) is a group formed for a set period to accomplish a set objective. A venture team is headed by a manager who reports to someone very high in the organization. The manager selects team members from various areas of the company, and each is given release time so they may give the assignment their full attention. The very specific objectives and limited time frame are great incentives for the team to focus on completing its task. Strong leadership and decision-making power allow the team to commit resources in a timely fashion. Unfortunately, in many organizations, managers are unwilling to permit their best people to participate. In addition, the teams only remain assembled for the duration of the assignment, and a new team may be put together when another objective arises, stunting cohesive experience. Hewlett-Packard used a venture team to develop the first low-cost laser printer.

> The manager selects team members from various areas of the company, and each is given release time so they may give the assignment their full attention.

Consulting Organizations Organizations will sometimes hire full service or specialty consulting firms to set up new product development systems, facilitate the process or conduct the development task to some degree. In many cases, consulting groups have outstanding talent with experience in the area of new products. Because of that experience, companies can save vast amounts of time and money in the innovation process. Unfortunately, some companies leave their employees out of the decision-making process, which in turn can make the employees resentful and reluctant to implement the firm's ideas. Consulting organizations such as Booz, Allen & Hamilton and McKinsey and Company often make strong efforts to involve their clients in all phases of their new product consulting.

Product Life Cycles

One of the oldest and most useful concepts for marketers is the product life cycle, shown in Figure 11.4. Like living organisms, products move from birth through infancy, adolescence, maturity, old age and on to death. The **product life cycle** consists of four stages: introduction, growth, maturity and decline. It's important to recognize that this is only a conceptual tool, and not all products move through a complete life cycle. Some marketers question the usefulness of the idea, but it remains one of

NEW PRODUCT COMMITTEE

A group of key functional personnel who are brought together periodically to develop new products.

VENTURE TEAM

A group formed for a set period to accomplish a set objective.

PRODUCT LIFE CYCLE

The four stages a product goes through: introduction, growth, maturity, and decline.

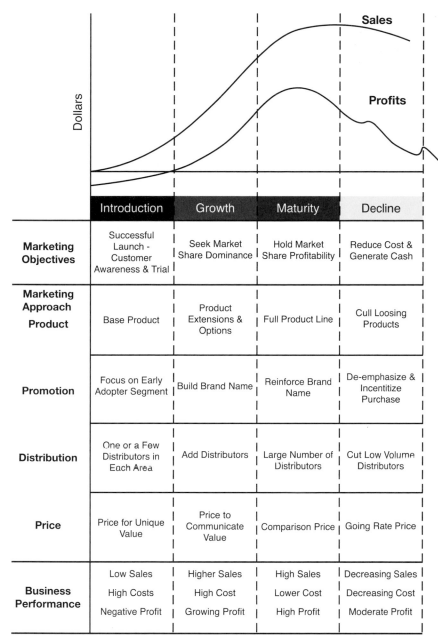

Figure 11.4   Traditional Life Cycle Curves and Marketing Approaches

	Introduction	Growth	Maturity	Decline
Marketing Objectives	Successful Launch - Customer Awareness & Trial	Seek Market Share Dominance	Hold Market Share Profitability	Reduce Cost & Generate Cash
Marketing Approach **Product**	Base Product	Product Extensions & Options	Full Product Line	Cull Loosing Products
Promotion	Focus on Early Adopter Segment	Build Brand Name	Reinforce Brand Name	De-emphasize & Incentitize Purchase
Distribution	One or a Few Distributors in Each Area	Add Distributors	Large Number of Distributors	Cut Low Volume Distributors
Price	Price for Unique Value	Price to Communicate Value	Comparison Price	Going Rate Price
Business Performance	Low Sales / High Costs / Negative Profit	Higher Sales / High Cost / Growing Profit	High Sales / Lower Cost / High Profit	Decreasing Sales / Decreasing Cost / Moderate Profit

the most common notions in marketing strategy. It has been applied to generic products, suppliers, industries and individual brands.

STAGES IN THE PRODUCT LIFE CYCLE

Each of the four stages in the product life cycle is associated with its own opportunities, costs and marketing strategies. In this section, we examine each stage in more detail.

Stage 1: Introduction During the introductory phase of the product life cycle, sales slowly take off and grow. Shipments from the factory may be high, and channels of distribution are filled as wholesalers and retailers stock the item. Since the product is new, marketers organize everything from heavy advertising campaigns and samples to educational sales techniques in order to create consumer awareness. During this critical period, marketers attempt to build share quickly to gain first-mover advantages. As numerous studies have shown, whoever introduces a product is likely to become the future industry leader in that area. Chrysler was the first to introduce minivans in the early 1980s, and its Chrysler Town & Country continues to be a market leader today.

Typically, there are few competitors during introduction, so marketers attempt to sell consumers on the new, unfamiliar concept, not focusing too intently on their own brands. When car phones were introduced, most advertising focused on selling the idea. Later advertising attempted to distinguish the various products from one another. Most organizations introduce only one or two items in a new product line so they can gain experience and monitor progress. Furthermore, global markets offer such vast opportunities for new products that some rivals may elect to avoid confrontations by selecting an untapped area.

As a rule, introductions represent advances in technology, manufacturing and service. Firms should make sure, however, that the design does not sacrifice accessibility. It's also important to have flexible manufacturing that can match production to highly uncertain demand. Distributors don't want to be left with unsold units, but if they don't produce enough to meet demand, consumers may lose interest or go to competitors' equivalents. Finally, customer service efforts must seek out and correct problems.

Profits may be negative during all or most of the introductory phase. Sales usually grow slowly, distribution channels need to be developed, and consumers need to learn of the product's existence and how it works.

Honda has grown substantially since its 1947 introductory Model A motorbike engine.

Stage 2: Growth

Stage 2: Growth During the growth stage, the pace of consumer acceptance and sales quickens. This is an especially critical time because rivals, noticing the increase in sales, will develop competitive products and aggressively pursue distribution channels. Consumers begin to make comparisons between competitive products, so companies (especially powerhouses like Microsoft or Apple) attempt to gain preferred status and brand loyalty. Many organizations believe that if they don't emerge from the growth stage as No. 1 or 2, then they should abandon that product. Honda, an automobile company which began in 1946 as a company successfully marketing 2-cycle motorbike engines, has continued to grow beyond its original product line. Honda is now famous for its automobiles, motorcycles, power equipment, marine motors and even jets.[28]

Product technology often enters its second generation during the growth stage. The first-generation technology applied to the original products is improved as companies gain experience, both costing the customer less and providing greater functionality. The first car phones had to be mounted permanently, and an antenna was attached to the vehicle's exterior. The next generation included bag phones that could be transferred from vehicle to vehicle. Now, mobile phones fit in your pocket, and many cars include Bluetooth integration that allows you to talk hands-free while driving.

With growth comes product designs that differ substantially from one manufacturer to the next. Building on the technology of short-range wireless connections and electronics, many companies have developed devices with Bluetooth or other wireless capabilities, allowing data to be transferred from mobile phones, computers and networked peripheral devices such as printers and scanners.

Manufacturing processes undergo change during the growth phase. The flexibility of the previous stage gives way to assembly lines and more automation. Higher sales volumes mean that standardized production can be used to achieve economies of scale and cost savings. Since markets are more predictable, just-in-time delivery and advanced quality control systems are possible.

Promotion and sales take on a whole new dimension during growth. Aggressive, head-to-head competition forces organizations to show their uniqueness, and the augmented product becomes extremely important. It remains critical that companies be cooperative with installation and training in product use, so customers don't have any reason to go to the competition. Advertising shifts to substantive messages that describe the benefits, functions and features of the product relative to competitors' offerings.

The companies that emerge as leaders tend to provide uncompromising customer service. They build trust in the distribution channel and with end users. Sometimes repeat purchases are based more on service satisfaction than on product performance and styling. Most consumers will forgive, and even expect, a problem with any product; it is the way the organization handles the situation that really impacts consumer relations. If service is performed correctly the first time, then consumers are likely to feel an affinity toward the supplier. In fact, loyalty may be strengthened when problems occur and are handled well.

Stage 3: Maturity

Stage 3: Maturity As products mature, sales level off and may remain flat for long periods. Overall market growth is relatively small, so a sales increase for one company usually comes at the expense of another, which is why firms with loyal buyers tend to have the greatest longevity. Yet, loyalty also indicates that consumer interest in the product is subsiding, which makes it very difficult and costly to build market share. Most firms are happy if they simply hold their own in this phase. Weaker competitors are likely to lower prices, while stronger rivals may sacrifice market share to maintain a satisfactory profit level. Strong rivals also engage in dramatic cost containment to preserve profits. Often this results in a standardized product design with less costly components and more efficient manufacturing.

At maturity, weaker rivals may drop out and use resources on more promising products. Even strong companies may exit if profit margins suffer too much. The maturity phase may last several months, years or even decades, and a low-cost position is critical for long-term success. This is particularly true if low-cost foreign competitors enter the business.

Product line size becomes especially important during the mature phase. Companies need to drop products with low-volume sales, high production costs or little competitive viability. But many buyers want to deal with a supplier who offers a full product line. This leads some organizations to outsource; that is, they purchase certain items from other companies and affix their own label. In this way they continue to mass-produce the lower-cost standardized items while relying on smaller firms to make the rest. Competitors may even buy from one another during the mature stage in order to gain an overall cost advantage, sometimes called co-competition.

The technology used for mature products tends to be older. Many firms have invested so heavily in past technology that they resist committing more resources to an aging product, choosing to focus instead on streamlining and improving the manufacturing process. For example, some organizations move from assembly-line and batch-oriented production to a continuous-flow system. This integrates people, paperwork, computerization and manufacturing into a seamless operation that maintains production at the greatest level of efficiency.

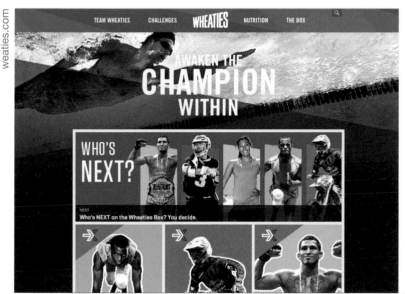

Wheaties actively advertises "the next" box cover athlete on its website.

Promotional campaigns focus more on reminder advertising than on new themes, since most buyers are now loyal to a particular brand or company. Sometimes companies resurrect messages that were used to build the brand's name. By adding a novel twist, the firm can keep its product in the forefront. For example, Wheaties, the traditional "Breakfast of Champions," regularly updates its package to show the latest sports superstars or to pay tribute to past champions. The objective is to create a link to younger consumers while maintaining its strong brand identity.

Service is usually standardized for mature products. In many cases, new service firms are formed to specialize in a particular product area. Even though Otis or Westinghouse installs most of the elevators we use, it is private service companies that keep them in optimal condition. Many organizations elect to hire local service firms to perform repairs. The marketing of replacement parts may become extremely profitable at this stage, especially during recessions, where consumers often prefer to repair an existing product than to replace it. In the United States, movable furniture systems from such companies as Steelcase, Herman Miller and Haworth have entered the maturity phase. Local firms are now purchasing and refurbishing the units for resale.

The rapid sales increase in the growth stage peaks during early maturity. Profits are likely to decline because of price competition, both domestically and internationally. Industries that would endure high costs to end a line of business (in other words, have a high exit barrier) are especially likely to run into this. Since it is costly to stop making the product, the companies often lower prices to maintain demand, sometimes using point-of-purchase sales or discounts. By the end of the maturity phase, a product may be losing money or have a very thin profit margin because of low demand.

Stage 4: Decline In the decline stage of the product life cycle, sales of new units diminish. For some products, such as earlier models of computers, the decrease may be very rapid. For others, it may be slow and steady, as with black-and-white television sets. Or it may be slow and then rapid, which was the case with vinyl records. Their sales dropped gradually and then plummeted as more and more titles became available on CDs. The speed of decline is related to the types and value of substitute products.

Most companies with a declining product want to maintain the lucrative replacement market but are willing to give up market share in exchange for earnings. Fierce price wars are likely to result in losses for all competitors. Low-cost producers that minimize new activities and standardize product design are in a much better position than high-cost competitors. Changes are intended to reduce the cost of components, which helps the company maintain earnings.

Companies are likely to return to a more shallow product line at this stage, focusing on the products that generate adequate cash flow. Old technology is kept in place, and manufacturing runs are limited, which frees up production capacity for more profitable items. To keep costs down, services are usually turned over to independents and very little promotional activity occurs, so buyers may have to seek out the product themselves. Because replacement parts still generate a profit, the firm is likely to maintain a supply that affords some level of earnings.

The profit life cycle implies that companies should have products in all stages at all times. Firms with only mature and declining products can expect dwindling profitability. A company with only products in the growing and mature stages will enjoy large profits, but they'll have to develop new products eventually, which will absorb a good deal of that profit. Strong companies, and ones that rely on patented products, plan ahead and add products at various stages in the life cycle to ensure a viable business. Pfizer faced a challenge when the patent on its biggest drug, Lipitor, expired in 2011, opening the door for generics. Analysts speculated that the company didn't have enough new drugs in the pipeline to offset the sales decline that would occur. Pfizer is awaiting Federal Drug Administration approval on several drugs, including the anticlotting drug Eliquis, in hopes they will fill the sales void left by the company's mature products.[29]

VARIATIONS IN PRODUCT LIFE CYCLES

The product life cycle is unique for high-tech products, fads, and styles, as shown in Figure 11.5. By understanding the different types, marketers can make general predictions about the challenges they face. Important aspects of product life cycles to consider include their shape, their length and how quickly consumers accept the product.

The first curve is typical of high-tech products, such as computers and computer software. Just when sales achieve a healthy pace, another generation hits the market. General acceptance of the product grows with each wave, however, which explains the successively higher peaks. Each generation usually lowers the cost to consumers. Microsoft's production of the Xbox is a good example. The Xbox 360 was launched in 2005 and was a hit with consumers. However, when the Xbox One was launched in 2013 and consumers switched to that generation, sales of the 360 dropped. Microsoft has recently stopped manufacturing the product.

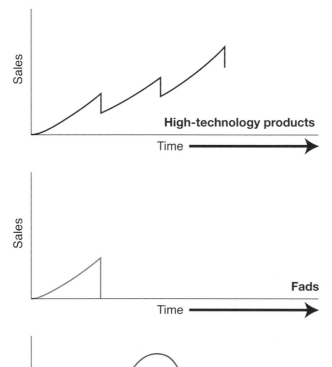

Figure 11.5   Life Cycles for Various Types of Products

The second curve illustrates the life cycle of a fad. Sales rise sharply in the introductory and growth phases and then quickly fall. Marketers realize such products are likely to be short lived and can't be considered a source of long-term sales. The overwhelming success of the young-adult trilogy, "*The Hunger Games*," sent publishers on a search for more novels about teens facing grim futures. However, just as this trend replaced the *Twilight*-inspired vampire craze, it will inevitably fade as well.[30]

Clothing fashions follow yet another kind of curve. When a style is first introduced, it is likely to experience relatively fast growth and then trail off, only to be resurrected a few years later. The width of neckties has gone from narrow, to medium, to wide, and back to narrow. Skirt lengths rise and fall. Marketers of these products must be aware of constantly changing consumer preferences and build strategies accordingly.

Although the product life cycle gives marketers a rule of thumb, it is not an exact science. To obtain more precise forecasts, researchers have developed mathematical and statistical models that examine market size, the number of initial buyers, and the time between first and repeat purchase. These can be very useful, particularly for products that behave similarly to those modeled.

EXTENDING THE PRODUCT LIFE CYCLE

Firms that resist change may keep products going far beyond their usefulness, but sometimes extending a product's life cycle is good business. The four most common ways to do this are to sell to new market segments, to stimulate more frequent use, to encourage more use per occasion, and to promote more varied use.

Selling to New Segments One way to give a product a new lease on life is to find new buyers. For example, in-line skates originally targeted primarily males, who typically wanted to simulate ice hockey, but now they have been adopted widely by females. Cosmetic surgery used to be thought of as primarily for celebrities and socialites, but middle-class moms are actually among the biggest buyers, opting for breast lifts, implants, tummy tucks and liposuction. The "mommy makeover" generally costs around $15,000 and isn't covered by insurance, but, as Dr. Jeffrey Ditesheim of Charlotte, North Carolina says, "Women don't want to look like pretty moms, they want to look like pretty women."[31]

Stimulating More Frequent Use After a decade of declining sales nationwide, the milk industry needed a marketing campaign to stimulate use. From this, the well-known "Got Milk?" campaign was born. Research indicated that the product played only a peripheral role in people's lives, with most only giving it a second thought when they ran out. The campaign theme chosen was "milk deprivation." One ad showed a man agonizing over a milk-free bowl of cereal, deciding whether to rob his baby's bottle or his cat's dish. Another ad had Santa entering a home, eating a brownie, finding no milk and taking the Christmas presents away. The campaign has also featured such celebrities as Nina Dobrev, Salma Hayek and the cast of "Modern Family." These award-winning ads not only heightened awareness of milk by more than 90 percent but also increased the sales of milk.[32]

gotmilk.com

got milk?
click and drag >>

Debuting in 1993, "Got Milk?" is still stimulating frequent use because of the great success of the campaign.

Encouraging More Use Per Occasion Have you ever purchased a Snickers bar offering 20 percent more candy for free? That is one way to encourage more use per occasion. Many companies promote on this basis. For years, McDonald's offered a "Super Sized®" meal, with a larger order of French fries and a larger beverage. Recently, McDonald's has shifted away from supersizing, perhaps because of public obesity concerns. Coca-Cola encourages greater consumption with 20-ounce sizes in vending machines. Claussen, a division of Campbell's, sells a giant crinkle-cut pickle slice to "blanket" hamburgers. Americans who enjoy pickles on their burgers now have a bigger option.

Arm & Hammer "Countless uses for pennies a day!" slogan is promoting more varied use.

Promoting More Varied Use Arm & Hammer dramatically extended the life cycle of baking soda by using it as an ingredient in toothpaste, laundry products, room fresheners, cleaners, and deodorant. Furthermore, ads recommend it for absorbing odors in refrigerators and closets. Once used only for cooking, today baking soda has far more applications. Even when it is being disposed of, it helps sanitize the drain. Another example is the "I could have had a V-8" campaign, which popularized the traditional breakfast drink as a refreshment for any time of day. And Yellowstone Park, traditionally viewed as a summer attraction, now advertises snowmobile trips in the winter.

THE PRODUCT LIFE CYCLE IN INTERNATIONAL MARKETS

A product's stage in the life cycle has important implications for international trade, not only in terms of marketing but also in terms of design and manufacture.

New products tend to be designed, manufactured and sold first in advanced economies, where there is sufficient wealth to underwrite development costs, and where markets accept innovation more readily. For example, personal computers were developed largely in the United States and sold primarily in the more upscale U.S. and Western European markets. As sales grew, however, Pacific Rim manufacturers developed clones, produced them with lower-cost labor, and became important competitors in Western markets. The lower prices that resulted in turn opened up new international markets in less advanced economies such as Russia and Eastern Europe.

A product at the peak of its popularity, with many brands competing for market share, may be manufactured far from its primary market if it can gain a competitive advantage through lower manufacturing costs. Athletic shoes, for example, were pioneered in the United States— which remains their largest single market. But as product sales burgeoned and new competitors entered the market, both Nike and Reebok moved their production to low-wage countries to reduce costs.

Maturing products tend to be exported to less advanced economies looking for lower-priced goods. As these markets grow, companies are likely to establish production facilities there, using their already standardized processes. We see this in Mexico, where both Nissan and Volkswagen have assembly plants that produce for the local market— and export to the United States as well. As manufacturing skills and processes are absorbed locally, the local companies may set up their own plants and begin producing for the home market, eliminating the need for foreign-owned manufacturing plants and thereby increasing competition.

Products that have reached the end of their life cycle in one economy may still be needed in another. Few U.S. households still do their laundry with washboards and tubs, but in other parts of the world, particularly in rural areas that have no access to electricity, such products remain useful and desirable.

Some countries are more suitable markets early in a product's life and others are more suitable later. Where products are made and marketed depends on their stage in the life cycle and on the economic characteristics of the location.[33]

Consumer Acceptance of Innovation

ADOPTION PROCESS

ADOPTION PROCESS

The steps an individual consumer goes through in making a product choice.

The **adoption process** refers to the five steps that consumers go through in making a product choice: knowledge, persuasion, decision, implementation and confirmation. First, the consumer becomes aware of the product and learns about it. Second, the person forms a favorable or unfavorable attitude toward the product. Third, the consumer chooses or rejects the product. Fourth, the consumer tries the product. Fifth, experience confirms or refutes the wisdom of the choice and whether the item will be purchased again.[34]

The speed of adoption depends on buyer characteristics and other factors, but it usually takes time. Because people are different, it is possible to categorize them according to how long it will take them to adopt an idea. We know, moreover, that product acceptance is passed from one group of consumers to the next. To explain this path, marketers have developed the diffusion process.

DIFFUSION PROCESS

DIFFUSION PROCESS

The spread of innovations from one group of consumers to another over time.

The **diffusion process** describes the spread of innovations from one individual or group to another over time. Marketers are keenly aware of how diffusion affects the introduction and long-term adoption of goods and services. We know that sales are influenced dramatically by the interaction of buyers, through word of mouth, as well as by promotions and messages from marketers. Often managers focus only on developing new or improved products, but they must also keep consumers' evaluations of these products in mind. Otherwise even very beneficial products may not be diffused throughout the market.[35]

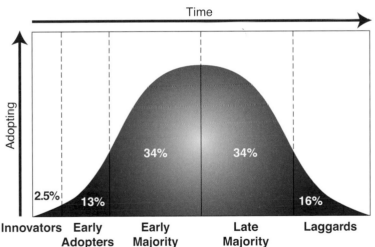

Figure 11.6   The Product Diffusion Cycle

Figure 11.6 illustrates the five groups of consumers who can be expected to purchase a product over time. The approximate distribution is 2.5 percent innovators, 13 percent early adopters, 34 percent early majority buyers, 34 percent late majority buyers and 16 percent laggards. The illustration is based on standard deviations, but the proportions may differ with various products.

INNOVATORS

INNOVATORS

The first group of consumers to purchase a new product.

Innovators The first consumers to purchase a new product are **innovators.** As you can guess, they are more adventurous than most of the population. They are technically competent and in some cases are almost obsessed with the details of new products, sometimes to the point of being eccentric. This small group has only minor influence over others, but their adoption provides proof that the product functions properly. Marketers can point to that experience in attempting to educate other buyers. The marketer of a new computerized vision system for detecting manufacturing flaws first installed the system at a small innovative firm that makes electronic parts. The company later cited successful use in selling the product to a leader in the industry.

EARLY ADOPTERS

EARLY ADOPTERS

The second group of consumers to purchase new products.

Early Adopters **Early adopters** are the second group to purchase new products and are critical to marketers. They have higher incomes, so they can afford to try relatively expensive introductions. They are the key to good word-of-mouth publicity and wider acceptance. They are well respected in their community, so other categories of buyers are likely to emulate them.

Early Majority Buyers

Early majority consumers tend to be more risk-averse than innovators and early adopters. They wait to see how something new works for others before purchasing it themselves. They also tend to read extensively about various products and compare different brands before reaching a decision. For the most part, these consumers are followers rather than leaders. For this reason, early majority consumers are likely to wait for new products to work out potential drawbacks before adopting them.

Late Majority and Laggards

The more skeptical consumers tend to fall into the **late majority** group. They have little faith in new products, so they wait until half the population has purchased them before they do. However, even more resistant to new products is the last group of consumers to purchase, the **laggards**; little, if anything, can be done to convince laggards to purchase new products.

U.S. farmers can be viewed using the diffusion cycle. Innovators and early adopters stay current on all developments in agriculture. They go to trade shows and read everything they can get their hands on. These consumers are the first to buy a new piece of equipment or pesticide. At the other extreme lie the laggards. They feel "if it ain't broke, don't fix it" and tend to stay brand oriented, influencing little to none of the market. Marketers have used different strategies to reach each group. The innovators and early adopters prefer advertising with a lot of good information or copy. Lag-

Laggards (pictured left) are less likely to stay current on developments in agriculture. Innovators and early adopters (pictured right) are more likely to adopt new technologies that improve efficiencies and production.

gards, on the other hand, need attention-grabbing ads and coupons as an incentive to purchase new products.[36] Since laggards often have low incomes and form a relatively small group, many marketers simply avoid marketing to them completely. The fact that they have low education and low income often makes them bad credit risks as well.

Here is an example of applying the diffusion cycle to the pharmaceutical industry. A pharmaceutical firm introduced a new pain reliever. Salespeople were asked to identify physicians who fit the early adopter profile: younger, heavy prescribers, on hospital boards, with modern offices and equipment. Special attention was given to these physicians through direct mail, sampling and sales calls. Because early adopters are more cosmopolitan than average, they are more inclined to accept information and interact with innovative firms. They agreed to test and evaluate the new product, quickly gave it their support and set in motion rapid diffusion throughout the medical community.

When we think of product innovation and new product introductions, our tendency is to think in terms of manufactured goods. Remember that services, too, are products—as you are aware from the marketing definition in Chapter 1 and the many examples of services we've discussed so far.

Chapter Summary

Objective 1: Provide a framework to evaluate the extent to which existing or new products are marketed to new market segments.

Every organization needs to develop a product mix consistent with its overall strategy. It must match current and new products with current and new segments. This produces four basic options for marketing mix management. A core business focus maintains, expands or harvests current products in current markets. Market development seeks new market segments for existing products. Product development improves or adds new products for sale to current segments. Diversification introduces new products into new market segments. Organizations can use this framework to help allocate resources to obtain the best overall performance.

Objective 2: Understand how the characteristics of innovation influence the speed with which product innovations are accepted.

There are three types of product innovations. Continuous innovations are minor changes in existing products that require no alterations in how consumers use them. Dynamically continuous innovations have added features and benefits that require minor changes in behavior. Discontinuous innovations are new to the world and may require major changes.

How rapidly a product is accepted depends on several factors. If its relative advantage over other products is high, then faster acceptance can be expected. If the product is compatible with current thinking, then quick adoption is likely. Also, less complex products and those that can be easily tried are more readily accepted. Finally, if the product can be observed in use by others, then it is more likely to be adopted rapidly.

Objective 3: Know the steps used to develop new products from the initial idea through commercialization.

The new-product development process has seven steps. First, a strategy is outlined by top management. This indicates the importance of new products to the organization. Second, idea generation provides a list of possibilities. These can come from numerous sources, especially if they are actively sought. Third, idea screening narrows the list to those most compatible with the organization's need. Several criteria are used in screening. Fourth, business analysis develops

a product concept and performs a financial analysis to assess feasibility and estimate profitability under numerous assumptions. Fifth, prototype product development involves all the steps leading up to and including the creation of a working model. Sixth, test marketing provides a limited trial of the marketing strategy under real or simulated conditions. The objective is to see whether the strategy will work or needs to be refined before full-scale launch. Seventh, commercialization occurs when the product is formally introduced into the market.

Objective 4: Show how the product life cycle concept can be used to build and adjust marketing strategies over time.

Products can be viewed as moving over a life cycle with several stages. In the introduction phase, sales usually take off slowly despite heavy promotion. Marketers concentrate on getting consumers to be aware of and accept the product class. During the growth stage, sales increase, and product technology often enters its second generation. Manufacturing and promotion are adjusted. Leading producers focus on customer service. At maturity, sales begin to slow and level off. Gains in market share for one company come at the expense of another. A few companies exit at this point. Low cost really counts now in manufacturing and marketing. The decline stage is marked by a downward sales trend. Although a good replacement parts market may exist for some products, many companies choose to exit or harvest.

Objective 5: Recognize how innovations are adopted by consumers by being spread from group to group.

People go through a series of steps in adopting a new product. The speed depends on personal characteristics. Individuals can be grouped into five categories that comprise the diffusion process. Innovators are the first to adopt. They are usually a small group and tend to be eccentric. Early adopters, a larger group, are next. They have high income and education levels, and others respect them. This group is key to the success of new products. The third category is early majority buyers, a larger segment that generally follows the leadership of the early adopters. The last two categories, late majority buyers and laggards, are the last to adopt. The late majority group is numerous, so it is important.

Review Your Understanding

1. What are the four product mix options? Describe each.
2. What are the three product innovation categories? What are the characteristics of each?
3. What product characteristics speed the adoption of an inno-

vation?
4. What are the steps in new-product development? Describe each.
5. What are test markets?

6. List five organizational structures for new-product development.
7. What are the differences between simultaneous and sequential methods of new-product development?
8. What is the difference between a product manager and a market manager?
9. What are the stages in the product life cycle? Identify and describe each .

Discussion of Concepts

1. Explain the differences among continuous innovation, dynamically continuous innovation and discontinuous innovation. What are the main activities for marketers when introducing each type?
2. Assume you are senior vice president of marketing for General Electric. What four product mix management options might you consider? Give specific examples of each.
3. Describe the typical profit scenario as a product moves through its life cycle. Do you think it's important for companies to have products in all stages? Why or why not?
4. What are some problems with using the product life cycle concept to make marketing decisions? Why do you think so many companies use the concept?
5. What are some ways to extend the product life cycle? Can you think of any companies that have used these techniques?
6. Many marketers use the diffusion cycle concept and the product life cycle concept. How are they different?
7. When introducing a new product, how may a marketer facilitate consumer acceptance?

Key Terms & Definitions

1. **Adoption process:** The steps an individual consumer goes through in making a product choice.
2. **Business analysis:** Assessment of the attractiveness of the product from a sales, cost, profit and cash flow standpoint.
3. **Commercialization:** Final stage in the new-product development process, when the product is introduced into the market.
4. **Concept testing:** Testing a new-product concept with target consumers, distributors and retailers, who provide input regarding the product's potential.
5. **Controlled test market:** Consumer panels or other techniques to gain similar information obtained from real test markets.
6. **Continuous innovation:** A minor alteration in an existing product, such as a new style or model, that can be easily adopted without significant changes in consumer behavior.
7. **Diffusion process:** The spread of innovations from one group of consumers to another over time.
8. **Discontinuous innovation:** An entirely new product with new functions.
9. **Dynamically continuous innovation:** A familiar product with additional features and benefits that require or permit consumers to alter some aspect of their behavior.
10. **Early adopters:** The second group of consumers to purchase new products.
11. **Early majority:** The third group of adopters, who are more risk averse in purchase decisions than innovators and early adopters.
12. **Idea generation:** The gathering of suggestions for new products from a number of sources using a range of formal and informal methods.
13. **Idea screening:** Identifying the new-product ideas that have the most potential to succeed.
14. **Innovators:** The first group of consumers to purchase a new product.
15. **Laggards:** Consumers who resist new products the longest.
16. **Late majority:** The more skeptical consumers who purchase products after the early majority.
17. **Line extension:** A new product closely related to others in the line.
18. **Market development:** Offering existing products to new market segments.
19. **Market manager:** A manager responsible for one or several similar product lines targeted at specific market segments.
20. **Marketing strategy development:** Creating an initial marketing strategy for a new product based on the product concept.
21. **New product committee:** A group of key functional personnel who are brought together periodically to develop new products.
22. **New product department:** The organizational unit responsible for identifying product ideas and preparing them for commercialization.
23. **Product concept:** A detailed version of the product idea stated in written descriptions, pictures and specifications.
24. **Product development:** Offering new products to existing market segments.
25. **Product life cycle:** The four stages a product goes through: introduction, growth, maturity and decline.
26. **Product manager:** A manager who oversees one or several products targeted at all market segments.
27. **Product mix:** All the product lines and products a company offers.
28. **Product planning:** The focus given to core businesses, market development, product development and diversification.

29. **Sequential new-product development:** People from various functional areas work on different stages of product development.
30. **Simulated product test:** Experimentation with the marketing strategy in artificial conditions.
31. **Simultaneous new-product development:** People from all functional areas work together to develop products.

32. **Test market:** A small geographic area, with characteristics similar to the total market, in which a product is introduced with a complete marketing program.
33. **Venture team:** Personnel from various areas of the company who are given release time to work on a specific assignment.

References

1. Christopher Power, "Flops — Too Many New Products Fail. Here is Why — And How to Do Better," Business Week, August 16, 1993, pp. 76-82.
2. Nikon, www.nikon.com, website visited July 2, 2015.
3. www.rochesterclothing.com, website visited July 2, 2015.
4. Maureen Morrison, "Pizza Hut Rolls Out 'Game Changer': Pie With Imperfections," AdAge, January 15, 2014.
5. Jane Wells, "Dr Pepper Thinks 10 Is the Magic Number'," CNBC, April 30, 2013.
6. "Nintendo Wii: A Gesture Toward Broader Entertainment," PC Magazine, Nov. 1, 2006, 25(21), p. 1.
7. www.wiifit.com, website visited April 22, 2015.
8. www.nintendo.com, website visited April 22, 2015.
9. Adobe, www.adobe.com, website visited June 13, 2015.
10. Ibid.
11. www.acer.com, website visited April 22, 2015.
12. Calantone, R.J.; DiBenedetto, C.A.; Bhoovaroghaven, S., "Examining the Relationship Between Degree of Innovation and New Product Success," Journal of Business Research 30, 1994, pp. 143-148.
13. Calantone, Roger; Schmidt, Jeffery; Song, Michael, "Controllable Factors of New Product Success: A Cross-National Comparison," Marketing Science, 1986-1998.
14 Luca, Luigi M. De; Atuahene-Gima, Kwaku, "Market Knowledge Dimensions and Cross-Functional Collaboration: Examining the Different Routes to Product Innovation Performance," Journal of Marketing, January 2007, Vol. 71, Issue 1, pp. 95-112.
15. Schmidt, Jeffery B.; Calantone, Roger, "Are Really New Product Development Projects Harder to Shut Down?", Journal of Product Innovation Management, 1998, pp. 111-123; Schmidt; Calantone, "Escalation of Commitment During New Product Development," Journal of the Academy of Marketing Science, Spring 2002; Power, "Flops"; Schlossberg, Howard, "Fear of Failure Stifles Product Development," Marketing news, May 14, 1990, pp. 1, 16.
16. Griffiths-Hemans, Janice; Grover, Rajiv, Journal of the Academy of Marketing Science, Winter 2006, Vol. 34, Issue 1, pp. 27-39.
17. "Seventh Generation, Inc.," Marketing News, April 25, 1994, pg. E8. www.seventhgeneration.com, website visited April 22, 2015.
18. Calantone, Roger; Schmidt, Jeffery; DiBenedetto, C. A., "Using the Analytic Hierarchy Process in New Product Screening," Journal of Product Innovation Management, 1999, pp. 65-76.
19. Calantone, Roger; Vikery, S.; Droge, C., "Business Performance and New Product Development Activities: An Empirical Investigation," Journal of Product Innovation Management 12, June 1995, pp. 214-223.
20. Haggblom, T.; Calantone, R.; DiBenedetto, C.A., "Do New Product Managers in Large or Hi-Market Share Firms Perceive Marketing R&D Interface Principles Differently?" Journal of Product Innovation Management 12, September 1995, pp. 323-333.
21. Bhattacharya, Shantanu; Krishnan, V.; Mahajan, Vijay, "Managing New Product Definition in High Dynamic Environments," Management Science, November 1998, Vol. 44, No. 11, Part 2, pp. S50-S54.
22. "Consumer: Suck It and See: Dyson Has Triumphed Over Hoover in the Great Vacuum Cleaner Legal War, but Which Are the Best Dust-Busters?" The Guardian, October 5, 2000.
23. Lawrence, Jennifer, "The SunChip Also Rises," Advertising Age, April 27, 1992, pg. S2; Lawrence, Jennifer, "Big Push for SunChips," Advertising Age, February 24, 1992, pg. 2; Taylor, Sandie, "Changing Perceptions of Frito-Lay Products Biggest Strategic Opportunity, Says Rader," Presentation at University of Texas at Austin, September 21, 2006.
24. www.sunchips.com/healthier_planet, website visited April 23, 2015.
25. Schnaars, Steven P.; Managing Imitation Strategies (New York: The Free Press, 1994), pg. 5.
26. W.L. Gore & Associates, Inc., Hoover's Company Records, March 15, 2008.
27. Song, X.M.; Montoya-Weiss, M.; Schmidt, Jeffery, "Antecedents and Consequences of Cross-Functional Cooperation: A Comparison of R&D, Manufacturing, Marketing Perspectives," Journal of Product Innovation Management, 1997, pp. 35-47.
28. www.honda.com, website visited March 31, 2015.
29. "Pfizer's Cost-Cuts Offset Loss of Lipitor," Wall Street Journal, www.wsj.com, website visited March 31, 2015.
30. "Spurred By Success, Publishers Look For The Next 'Hunger Games'," NPR, www.npr.org, March 6, 2012.
31. "More moms opting for 'Mommy Makeovers'," WBTV, www.wbtv.com, July 16, 2012.
32. Mergenhagen, Paula, "How 'Got Milk' Got Sales," American Demographics, www.marketingpower.com, website visited April 23, 2010; www.milkmustache.com, website visited August 7, 2012.
33. Vernon, Raymond, "International Investment and International Trade in The Product Life Cycle," Quarterly Journal of Economics, May 1986, pg. 199.
34. Rogers, Everett M., Diffusion of Innovations, 3rd ed. (New York: The Free Press, 1982), pp. 164-175.
35. Ohlshavsky, R.; Spreng, R., "An Exploratory Study of the Innovation Evaluation Process," Journal of Product Innovation Management 13, November 1996, pp. 512-529.
36. Blake, Brian F., "They May Be Innovative, But They're Not the Same," Marketing news, April 15, 1991, pg. 12.

CHAPTER 12

Integrated Marketing Communications

Allstate
You're in good hands.

Allstate Insurance

You Tube **SCAN & WATCH** ▶

Allstate targets sports fans through sponsorships of some of the biggest athletic events.

"You're in good hands with Allstate™" is the assurance that Allstate promotes to current and potential customers. The company provides a wide range of insurance services to approximately 16 million households and employs more than 38,000 professionals.

Allstate's marketing team has the challenge of advertising an intangible product. The team, along with agency partners, creates a seamless, integrated marketing communications (IMC) platform that combines national and local advertising, as well as sponsorship activities to connect with customers. One way that Allstate implements its IMC strategy is through the consistent use of a spokesperson to represent the brand. Dennis Haysbert, most commonly known for his role as President Palmer from the TV series "24," has been the spokesman for Allstate since 2003 and has become a voice synonymous with the brand. Click on the QR code to watch one of his Allstate commercials!

In combination with TV commercials and print ads, part of Allstate's integrated marketing includes an extensive sponsorship portfolio that includes the Mexican and U.S. national soccer teams, the FIFA World Cup, the U.S. Olympic Team, and a 10-year run of college football sponsorship. Allstate's presence in college football has been building over the last few years with Good Hands™ field goal nets in stadiums across the U.S. Televised football games display the nets for several seconds, showing them to millions of fans watching the game on TV. Allstate also owns the naming rights to the Allstate Sugar Bowl®.The beneficiaries are less-privileged partner schools.

Now, Allstate is adding a Twitter challenge to its IMC mix. Allstate will reward the school with the most fan conversation on Twitter an additional $10,000 in scholarship donations, for a total of $150,000 in scholarship giveaways. The overall program includes new advertising, creative, social and digital integration as well as public relations and promotional elements. The 30-second TV spot called "More Good" shows how Allstate's Field Goal Nets program delivers on the brand's promise of helping people live a good live by appealing to their interest of college football.

College sports fans are a target market for Allstate, says Pam Hollander, vice president, integrated marketing communications for Allstate."Having been a major sponsor in college football for a decade, we feel that we have some of the highest visibility not only in the category, but across all brands associated with college football." When people think about college football, we want them to visualize the Allstate Field Goal Net program.

Allstate has won numerous awards for its philanthropic, employee volunteerism and diversity efforts. The "Safe in My Hands" commercial is a touching story featuring an original song by Eli Lieb. A little boy with an abnormally large hand is shown as he grows up, feeling self-conscious and judged because he is different... until one day he finds another person like himself. The two cartoon men reach for each other, hold hands and begin to walk into the sunset while the cartoon fades to two real-life men holding hands. The words "Being visible should never leave you feeling vulnerable," and **"Everyone** deserves to be in good hands" appear as the screen fades to black. Using all the elements of IMC, Allstate continues to successfully connect with customers.

Sources: www.allstate.com, website visited July 1, 2016; www.mediapost.com/publications/article/234255/allstate-hosts-college-football-twitter-challenge.html?edition, website visited July 10, 2016.

LO 01 Describe the objectives of integrated marketing communications.

LO 02 Learn how the communication process provides the intended information for the market.

LO 03 Define about the communication mix, including personal selling, advertising, sales promotion, sponsorships and public relations.

LO 04 Know the factors that influence the communication mix.

LO 05 Describe the steps in developing an integrated marketing communication plan.

LO 06 Discuss how to address diversity, ethics and technology in communications.

The Concept of Integrated Marketing Communications

Which do you think would sell better: a poor product supported by great marketing communication or a great product supported by poor marketing communication? Actually, the product probably would not do well in either case. A good product that is poorly communicated is unlikely to be perceived well by consumers. A poor product, no matter how well it is promoted, will quickly become known for its lack of value. Both scenarios are detrimental for a company because negative opinions spread quickly on social media these days.

Marketers need to ensure that all four elements of the marketing mix—product, price, promotion and place—are working together. This chapter explores communication, a broad concept that encompasses promotion. Recall from Chapter 5 that a product's position is its image relative to competition in the minds of consumers. It would not make sense for Payless shoe stores to carry expensive brands. Nor would it make sense for Campbell's to charge less for its premium soup than its regular soup. Both images are inconsistent with consumer perception.

Nearly everything about a product communicates something to consumers. The gold label on Bumble Bee premium tuna communicates higher quality than the white label on its regular tuna. Even where you buy a product implies something; the very name Porsche is associated with expensive cars. Think of a doctor's waiting room: if it's dark, dirty, and you feel uneasy in it, you may decide to leave or change physicians altogether. That's why medical centers often hire interior decorators to enhance facility appeal with carpet, modern upholstery, art and other elements that communicate a professional and caring environment.

Communication is the process of sending and receiving messages. It is an exchange of meaning between parties which involves sharing points of view and con-

COMMUNICATION

The process of sending and receiving messages.

CHAPTER 12

PROMOTION

The process marketers use to inform, educate, persuade, remind, and reinforce consumers through communication.

INTEGRATED MARKETING COMMUNICATION (IMC)

The coordination of advertising, sales promotion, personal selling, public relations, and sponsorship to reach consumers with a powerful, unified effect.

necting with others to form relationships. **Promotion,** the process designed to influence consumers, can be used to inform, educate, persuade, remind and reinforce through communication. Although most marketing communications are aimed at consumers, some also address shareholders, employees, channel members, suppliers and society. In addition, we will see that effective communication is a two-way street: receiving messages is often as important as sending them.

Integrated marketing communication (IMC) is the coordination of advertising, sales promotion, personal selling, public relations, sponsorships and digital marketing to reach consumers with a powerful, unified effect. These six elements impact and enhance each other, and should be viewed as components of one whole package. A company combines these elements into a specific promotion mix to attract consumers to its products. The strategic use of television, newspaper, radio, direct mail and the internet can produce an extremely successful communication. The Coca-Cola Company uses nearly every form of media including television, print ads and the internet to market its products. It also maximizes brand awareness, especially in growing markets, through sponsorships such as the Olympic Games.

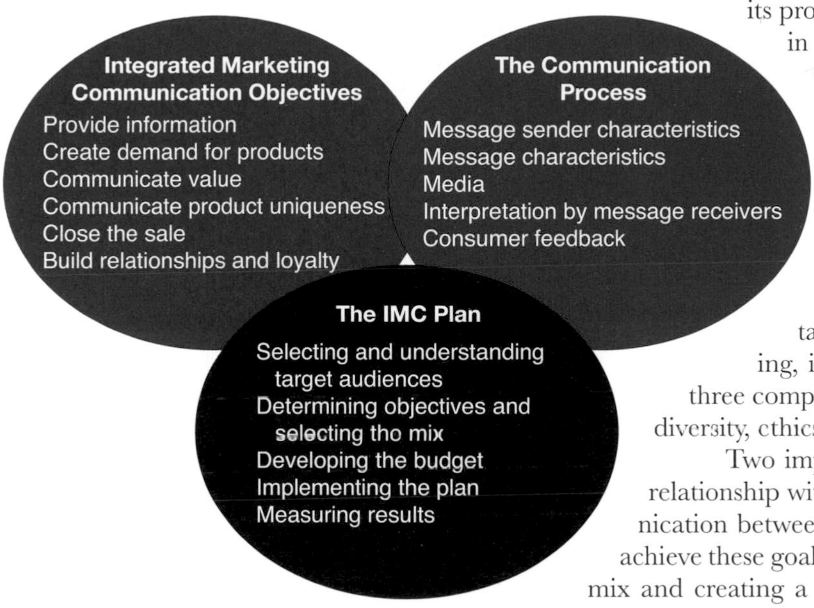

The IMC concept has three parts, as depicted in Figure 12.1. First, it is important to consider the objectives of IMC, which are related to the overall marketing strategy. Second, marketers utilize the communication process characteristics to improve communications. Third, each type of communication in the plan accomplishes a unique task. Using each effectively requires planning, budgeting, implementation and feedback. After outlining these three components of IMC, the chapter concludes with a look at diversity, ethics and technology issues pertaining to IMC.

Two important goals of IMC are to establish a one-on-one relationship with consumers and to encourage meaningful communication between a firm and its customers. Many companies try to achieve these goals by orchestrating various elements of the promotion mix and creating a brand experience that directly impacts consumers. Oprah Winfrey created exceptional experiences that forged valuable connections with millions of customers via her talk show, website and multimedia empire. Oprah's Angel Network opened 55 schools in 12 countries, created scholarships, as well as funded women's shelters and the building of youth centers and homes.[1]

Integrated Marketing Communication Objectives
Provide information
Create demand for products
Communicate value
Communicate product uniqueness
Close the sale
Build relationships and loyalty

The Communication Process
Message sender characteristics
Message characteristics
Media
Interpretation by message receivers
Consumer feedback

The IMC Plan
Selecting and understanding target audiences
Determining objectives and selecting the mix
Developing the budget
Implementing the plan
Measuring results

Figure 12.1 The Concept of IMC

Objectives of Integrated Marketing Communications

Integrated marketing communications has numerous objectives. The most notable are to provide information, create demand, communicate value and product uniqueness, close the sale and build loyal customer relationships.

PROVIDE INFORMATION

Ultimately, all communication is designed to provide some form of information. Proper marketing communication gives consumers what they need to know to make informed choices within a reasonable time frame. Depending on how familiar the target audience is with the product in question, communication can be dedicated to different degrees of explanation. Often this communication introduces consumers to the product's benefits and uses. When it is working most effectively, information helps consumers make the buying decision. It provides data on a broad range of topics, including product characteristics, uses, availability, prices and methods of acquisition.

Marketers need to be aware, however, that a consumer has many sources of information about a given product, so they need to select the most appropriate method

AT&T's "It Can Wait" commercial is a graphic reminder of why people shouldn't text while driving.

for their situation. In some cases, information is purely descriptive. For example, AT&T's "It Can Wait" awareness campaign focuses on the dangers of texting while driving. The company runs ads featuring young people who have suffered permanent disabilities or families who have lost loved ones because of texting-related accidents; it also has a Facebook page on which drivers are asked to pledge not to text and drive, then share the pledge with their friends and ask them to sign too. The campaign had collected 9,261,507 pledges as of July 1, 2016.[2] In addition, the AT&T site features a downloadable tool kit with public service announcements, advertisements and educational materials for schools and companies.[3] Marketers are challenged to create communications that contribute to the consumer's search for value in the marketplace and marketspace. Consequently, communications should be designed with consumer information needs in mind.

CREATE DEMAND FOR PRODUCTS

Communication helps create demand for products in global and domestic markets. It stimulates people to desire what they do not have and inspires them to earn the money to acquire items that improve their standard of living. Communication helps assure that products will be purchased in sufficient quantities to justify their development, production and distribution. Today, the speed of communication allows companies to attract worldwide demand in a short period. Many products marketed globally have coordinated IMC campaigns supported by high-tech information systems. The internet and corporate networks make it possible for companies to see what demand is being created by communication in different geographical areas and to adjust product availability accordingly. For example, smartphones and tablets have created a growing demand for Wi-Fi connectivity. Boingo recently acquired Wi-Fi advertising company Cloud Nine Media in an effort to add sponsored access to its managed wireless hotspots, which reach more than 1.4 billion people each year in such locations as airports, malls, restaurants and stadiums.[4] Communication infrastructures provide growing platforms for messages that build demand within society.

COMMUNICATE VALUE

The search for value is complicated because consumers need to assess the benefits of a product relative to many others. Marketers compete to provide value in keeping with consumers' willingness to pay. Consequently, a great deal of communication focuses on conveying a product's benefits in a memorable way. For example, Eaton Corporation technical sales representatives are trained to learn the various features and benefits of sophisticated electronics products, as well as how best to communicate those features to consumers. However, they first need to know how the customer intends to use the product. A contractor, for instance, would be installing equipment in a building. The sales representative can then point out cost-saving product attributes due to easy installation and reliable design.

Advertisers are careful to show scenes of consumers clearly benefiting from

You Tube **SCAN & WATCH**

This Beats by Dre headphones commercial adds perceived value to the product by suggesting that Beats can enhance mental focus and athletic performance.

products. Beats by Dre "The Game Before The Game" short film cleverly communicates value by depicting athletes using the product in pregame situations. Brazilian soccer star Neymar Jr., uses Beats by Dre headphones to help prepare for a game on the world's biggest stage, the 2014 FIFA World Cup. Neymar says, "Without Music, my preparation is not complete," communicating the impact Beats by Dre headphones has on his career. The five minute commercial, found on www.beatsbydre. com and YouTube, features cameos of Nicki Minaj, LeBron James, ESPN's Stuart Scott, Lil Wayne, Serena Williams, and music by Jay-Z.[5] Ironically, Beats by Dre headphones were banned from the tournament. FIFA's licensing agreement with rival Sony prevents players from wearing them inside stadiums or at media events. Despite Sony's efforts, even providing each player with a set of Sony headphones, players were spotted wearing Beats by Dre almost everywhere else.[6] Traditionally valued for sound quality and style, Beats by Dre added to its perceived value by suggesting that users could enhance their athletic performance.

COMMUNICATE PRODUCT UNIQUENESS

Marketers attempt to communicate uniqueness in order to differentiate their product from others. Burger King is broiled; McDonald's is fried; Southwest Airlines is less expensive because it has no frills; Titleist is used by more professional golfers than any other ball; and so on. Marketers also use persuasive communication to convince consumers to switch from one brand to another. Typical advertising messages compare a product's features, functions and benefits to those of the competition. In all of these cases, the ultimate goal is for marketers to illustrate the unique qualities of their brands and to build preference for them in their respective target markets.

Dr. Martens, an iconic boot manufacturer, has a historic culture of being different. Dr. Klaus Martens, the founder, injured his foot while skiing. He then invented a rubber-soled shoe that provides comfort to people who are on their feet all day. His shoes and boots quickly gained a reputation for being solid in construction and durable for years. Youth subcultures for decades have championed the brand: skinheads, punks, hardcore, psychobilly, goth, industrial, grunge, Britpop, and emos have all sported the working-man boot. Perhaps the next brave group of youths daring to be different will do so in a pair of Dr. Martens.

CLOSE THE SALE

Communication also helps close the sale. If purchasing a product results in a good experience for the consumer, chances are that same consumer will purchase it again or recommend it to others. IMC seeks to move buyers to action the first time and then reinforce their positive experience so they will become repeat customers.

Today, buyers are selective when they want to receive communications, and often that is just prior to purchase. Many people use the internet to look up information that will help them to make an informed first purchase. Current newspaper, magazine, billboard and television ads often include website information so consumers can learn more or refresh their memory of what they have seen. These websites are interactive, so communication is more personal and involves the consumer. Sometimes company websites will offer "free shipping" or "20% off" for a limited time as an incentive to close the sale faster with prospective buyers. Of course, once the sale is closed, the threat of a customer buying a competitive product is eliminated.

BUILD RELATIONSHIPS AND LOYALTY

Once consumers have tried a particular brand, marketers remind them why they chose it in the first place, reinforcing that behavior. Reminder communications reinforce the popularity of existing good by reassuring loyal customers that they have made the right choice. Because consumers tend to pay more attention to ads for products that they currently use, advertising often reinforces their ownership, which can bolster brand loyalty. For example, American Express builds loyalty and relationships with their cardholders by establishing "rewarding relationships" with them, such as travel packages and premier event tickets.

Recently, tickets for Chicago's theater presentation of the popular play "Hamilton" went on sale. Demand was so great that the ticket site actually crashed! American Express Gold members, however, were able to use a special code and secure premium seating—a reward for their relationship with American Express.

The Communication Process

The basic communication process is outlined in Figure 12.2. As you can see, messages move from the sender (marketer) to the receiver (consumer). Traditionally, communication has been seen as a one-way process. With the advent of one-to-one marketing through digital technologies and the internet, it is more useful to envision a two-way or continuous flow. Marketers need to start with a clear understanding of the target market, the objectives of the communication, and how to meet those objectives. They should also be aware that proactive customers have their own objectives and use the same process in reverse.

Let's look at the process. Effective communication can be difficult because consumers are bombarded daily by thousands of conflicting messages. Once marketers decide what to communicate, they must encode the message for the target market. It can be spoken, written, illustrated through pictures or diagrams, set to music or conveyed by a combination of these. The encoded message is then sent to consumers via channels: television, radio, newspapers, magazines, telephone, personal contact, or digital and social media.

Customers must decode, or interpret, the message that marketers send. Each customer's reaction will depend on personal background and experiences. One of the most important aspects of the communication process is feedback from the target au-

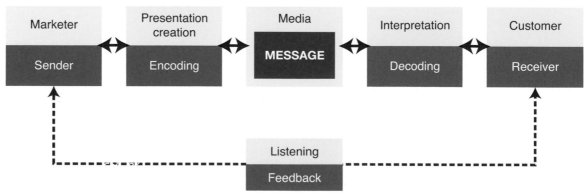

Figure 12.2   The Communication Process

dience. For example, if a campaign is designed to encourage product awareness, then positive feedback is an increase in the number of consumers who know about the product, and negative feedback is a flat or declining awareness. Such information is vital because it helps marketers judge whether the message accomplished its goal or needs to be adjusted.

One final element marketers should consider when communicating to consumers is noise, which can refer to anything that interferes with a message being received. For example, after talking to a salesperson about a new sports car, you may want to buy it. But then a friend says, "It's a piece of junk; my brother just bought one and has had nothing but trouble with it." Your friend obviously interferes with the marketer's message. Noise can also occur if you are distracted from receiving the message or if you're not sure who sent the message.

THE MESSAGE SENDER

Once marketers have determined that communication is in order, they initiate the process by formulating a message. As the sender, it is the marketer's responsibility to make sure the message is received by the targeted audience, is understood as intended, helps the audience become knowledgeable and elicits an appropriate response.

The reputation of the sender, be it a person, a company or some other organization, influences how consumers receive a message. In fact, when several sources communicate precisely the same message, it is received differently depending on the source, which is why selecting the right spokesperson for a message is very important. Different consumers have different beliefs and standards, so finding a single spokesperson that has high credibility with everyone is nearly impossible. Even within one segment, it's difficult to identify a single spokesperson to whom everyone relates. That is why the popular "Got Milk?" mustache appears on so many famous faces.

What makes a source credible with a target audience? Generally, spokespersons are judged according to their expertise, trustworthiness and attractiveness.

Expertise Consumers attribute expertise to a spokesperson for many reasons. They may believe he or she has specialized training, a great deal of experience or exceptional knowledge. Some companies hire engineers for industrial sales positions, believing that their academic degrees lend special credibility. Doctors are highly credible spokespersons in messages for pain relievers. Children's Tylenol, for example, is promoted as "the first choice of pediatricians." Robitussin notes that it is recommended by physicians, pharmacists and "Dr. Mom." Both campaigns are based on the credibility of their sources.

Consumers also tend to rely on someone with a lifestyle similar to their own, which accounts for the surge in advertising that features average, everyday people. "Real people" advertising uses "regular" people (not actors) who appreciate the products or services about which they are advertising. This creates instant credibility for the average consumer looking to purchase products or services. This is also why social media sites with company or product endorsements are so valuable: everyday consumers express their opinions without any scripts or fees involved. That equates to credibility and real-world expertise to other consumers.

Nike, like many companies, counts on star appeal, and signs large endorsement deals with the world's best athletes. Michelle Wie, a recent women's major golf champion, has endorsement contracts with Nike, McDonalds, Kia Motors, and Sony. [7] Golden Gate Warriors forward and former MSU Spartan, Draymond Green, has endorsement agreements with Nike, Foot Locker and Beats By Dre. [8]

Keith Allison / (CC BY-SA 2.0

Michelle Wie, a women's major golf champion, has endorsements from Nike, McDonalds, Kia Motors, Sony and others.

Trustworthiness Organizations such as the Underwriter's Laboratory, American Medical Association, American Dental Association, Good Housekeeping Institute and Consumer's Union have gained a great deal of credibility because of their trustworthiness. Not only do they have considerable technical knowledge, but most consumers perceive them as unbiased. People tend to discount messages from sources that stand to benefit in some way, but trust those from sources that appear "objective." Imagine that you are purchasing an new television and the salesperson constantly emphasizes the importance of an extended warranty. If you know the salesperson gets a commission on warranty sales, you are less likely to believe what he or she is telling you. If no commission is involved, you are more inclined to trust the person.

Pete Souza, White House photographer

President Barack Obama discusses the situation in Sudan with actor George Clooney during a meeting outside the Oval Office

Attractiveness (Personal Demeanor and Appeal) It's not surprising that many successful spokespersons are attractive, pleasant and likable. Attractiveness is not about good looks; a source is more attractive if he or she is reliable, pleasant to be around and helpful. Often celebrities gain credibility in areas outside their careers, such as movie stars who have influenced political campaigns. When famous endorsers are also informed, their power can be substantial. Actor George Clooney has been a longtime advocate of ending violence in Darfur and the Sudan, traveling to the region repeatedly, co-founding charities, and meeting with heads of state, including President Barack Obama. He even owns a private spy satellite that hovers over Sudan, tracking movements of the war criminal Omar Al-Bashir.[9] It's important to note that attractiveness involves all aspects of the source, from a company's reputation to its sales personnel to any others who represent the organization.

PRESENTATION CREATION: ENCODING

Encoding is the process of translating a message into terms easily understood by the target audience. We know from Chapter 6 that information processing is a complex but very important aspect of the purchase decision. Marketers must encode messages so they are interpreted appropriately by the people for whom they are intended. For example, marketers of fine jewelry have traditionally encoded their messages to reach men—once the main purchasers of engagement rings and other gems as gifts. Today, however, women have higher disposable incomes, and purchasing jewelry has become less associated with only special occasions. Generational encoding is also important: As the baby boomers reach milestone anniversaries and birthdays, jewelers expect them to celebrate with the purchase of jewelry. The De Beers Jewelry website allows visitors to create their own diamond engagement rings, encoding the message that buyers can be actively involved in creating their own dream jewelry.[10]

MESSAGE CHARACTERISTICS

There are countless ways to communicate a given message: one viewpoint or several can be presented. Recommendations or conclusions may or may not be included. Key points can be made at the beginning, middle or end. Humor or fear can be used. The product being described may or may not be compared with a competitor's.

One-Sided and Two-Sided Messages A **one-sided message** presents only aspects favorable to the source. A **two-sided message** recognizes the elements against a position and often provides the recipient with reasons why those arguments are invalid. For example, a message for a fast-food chain might mention only the positive aspects of the ingredients and cooking methods, or it might address a competitor's charge as well. When the source and receiver have relatively similar views, a one-sided message is more appropriate. When there is disagreement, a two-sided message often is more useful.

Recommendations or Conclusions A message can make recommendations, draw conclusions or leave those tasks to the receiver. Messages with conclusions are more easily understood, but those that allow the audience to draw their own conclusions are more likely to gain acceptance, particularly if the audience is highly educated. Repeated exposures give the target audience an opportunity to reach its own conclusions. If the marketer wants the message to have immediate effect, then the communication probably should draw direct conclusions. Rubbermaid launched a classic campaign in response to smaller competitors that were rapidly gaining market share. Since Rubbermaid wanted to influence consumers quickly, its ads were designed to focus on the numerous solutions its products provide to everyday problems. The company reinforced the campaign with an 89-page booklet, "1001 Solutions for Better Living."[11] Today, Rubbermaid's website, www.rubbermaid.com, provides a "Tips & Solutions" tab containing information to help customers organize with Rubbermaid products, an "Ask the Organizer" section, video tips and a blog. Customers can also register for the Rubbermaid Club to receive coupons, tips and new product announcements.[12] This type of promotional effort delivers product benefits directly to customers.

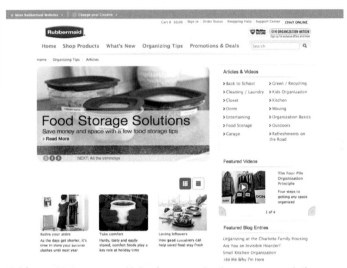

Rubbermaid does a good job of communicating recommendations and conclusions about its products.

Order of Presentation The placement of the key point of a communication affects how the message is interpreted and later recalled by buyers. People are more likely to remember messages at the beginning and end of a message, so advertisements often open and close with strong statements, leaving weaker arguments for the middle.

Humor Humor is effective when viewers find it novel and enjoyable, but it should not obscure the message. There are several things for marketers to keep in mind:

- Be sure to mention the brand name within the first 10 seconds. Otherwise, the communication runs the risk of inhibiting recall of key selling points.

- Subtle humor is more effective than bizarre humor.

- Humor must be relevant to the brand or the key selling point. Without this linkage, recall and persuasion are diminished.

- It is best not to use humor that belittles or makes fun of the potential user. Jokes about the brand, the situation or the subject matter are usually more effective.[13]

Evidence is still inconclusive as to whether or not a humorous approach is more effective than a serious one. Although humor tends to increase attention, it also may distract from or decrease acceptance of the message. TBS runs an annual special in which it counts down the funniest advertisements of the year from around the world. Its veryfunnyads.com website allows users to stream the nominees and offers additional ad exposure for companies.

Humor is constantly utilized to create a viral message. The intention of humor is to make people laugh enough to tell their friends, which is an efficient way to pass around the

YouTube **SCAN & WATCH** ▶

Options shown

Toyota's classic 2010 "Swagger Wagon" YouTube sensation is a classic example of how social media and a little humor can be a powerful combination.

message. Budweiser's "Bud," "Weis,"and "Er" frog campaign is one of the legendary paragons of advertising gone viral. Today, digital technology and social media sites like YouTube and Facebook facilitate the rapid growth of online viral advertising. Toyota's "Swagger Wagon," is a classic example of how social media and a little humor can be a powerful combination. It was so popular that Toyota attempted to relaunch the concept in a commercial with the release of the 2015 Sienna. The new version featured music by Busta Rhymes, but the video's 1.8 million views did not come close to the effectiveness of the original video's 13.2 million views.[14]

Fear Appeals Marketers sometimes use fear to gain the attention and interest of their audience. Campaigns by the American Dental Association warn that poor dental hygiene can result in tooth decay, gum disease and loss of teeth. In some instances, advertisers play on fear for the safety of loved ones. A Michelin spot shows a baby floating in a tire and reminds parents, "You have a lot riding on them." An advertisement for seat belt use by the Michigan Association for Traffic Safety pictures a wheelchair: "It's your choice."

In many instances, fear appeals are very effective. They can create higher attention and interest in the message. By Petty and Cacioppo's theory of persuasion, fear appeal works more successfully in a high-involvement product than in a low-involvement product. Furthermore, the reaction from audiences tends to be more uniform than reactions to other messages, since fear is a basic human emotion.[15]

Comparative Messages There have been sneaker wars, hamburger wars, beer wars, cola wars and many more. In each case, claims and counterclaims have been used in comparative messages. Burger King ran an unusual comparative ad against McDonald's, depicting the King breaking into McDonald's headquarters to steal the McDonald's Sausage McMuffin with Egg sandwich recipe. A voice-over in the ad proclaims, "It's not that original but it's super affordable." Burger King offers the sandwich on its dollar menu, while McDonald's has a higher price. These techniques engage the curiosity of audiences, but they do not guarantee success. Even though comparative messages allow marketers to present clear, objective arguments in favor of their products, many companies hesitate to use the technique. References to the competition may inadvertently cause the consumer to recall that product at the time of purchase. In addition, competitors may legally challenge claims of superiority or respond with comparative ads of their own. McDonald's has chosen to ignore the Burger King comparative ad, which is often the case with a market leader who does not want to give the contender's brand any ad time.

> Even though comparative messages allow marketers to present clear, objective arguments in favor of their products, many companies hesitate to use the technique.

In general, comparative messages may be more useful for companies with a lower market share, since they have little to lose by confronting the leader. For them, the potential gain in consumer awareness outweighs the likelihood that a large competitor will launch a counterattack.

MEDIA

Media are the means for transmitting messages from the sender to the receiver. There are three categories of media: personal, mass and mixed. Each has unique advantages and disadvantages, as summarized in Figure 12.3.

	Examples	Advantages	Disadvantages
Personal Media	Face-to-face Telephone	Two-way communication Allows for creative problem solving Flexible tailoring of messages Immediate response	Expensive Time-consuming Parties must be brought together at one time
	Television Radio	Messages can be developed prior to sending Low cost	Messages tend to be one-way
Mass Media	Magazines Newspapers Billboards Brochures	Many media choices Reaches most customers inexpensively	Preparations are expensive Harder to obtain feedback
Mixed (personal and mass combined)	Fax Internet Answering machine	Delayed or interactive Two-way communication Low cost	Receiver needs technology Lack of consumer experience

Figure 12.3   Media Advantages and Disadvantages

Personal media channels involve direct contact, such as face-to-face communication or telephone conversations. These two-way exchanges allow for creative solutions to the consumer's problem. Each party can assess characteristics of the other, granting opportunity for relationships to form. Although the phone does not provide physical contact, it has dramatic cost advantages over personal encounters. It also offers hotlines, which provide customer support after a sale. They not only help when problems arise with a product but also offer all kinds of advice that ultimately help to maintain customer loyalty. GoDaddy customers have access to technical support 24/7/365 via phone, through an email ticket system, or by real-time online chat.[16] The disadvantage of personal media is its expense. Each representative can only have a limited number of conversations, and the costs associated with hiring, training and motivating people can be very high.

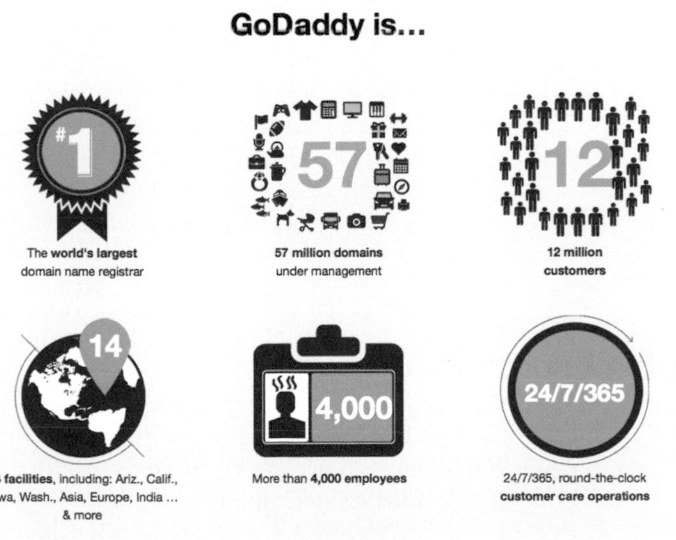

Mass media channels include television, radio, magazines, billboards, brochures and one-way internet. Services are readily available to help plan for and acquire space in most markets around the world. CIO Communications Inc., for instance, offers a resource center on the web to assist with media planning.[17] Messages can be developed prior to being communicated through a range of nonpersonal sources. With so many methods available to send a message, just about any customer can be reached at a reasonable cost. The downside of using mass media is the lack of interactive or two-way communication. Because it is impossible to get quick feedback, significant resources are spent beforehand on research to understand the customer. Furthermore, ad preparation can be expensive and take a long time.

The mixed media approach combines personal and mass communication channels and has many of the benefits of both. First, material can be developed well in advance and offered in both print (fax) and audio (via internet) formats. Many companies have adopted social media into their marketing mix, urging customers exploring Facebook or Twitter to

godaddy.com

GoDaddy is…

#1
The world's largest domain name registrar

57 million domains under management

12 million customers

14 facilities, including: Ariz., Calif., Iowa, Wash., Asia, Europe, India … & more

4,000 More than 4,000 employees

24/7/365, round-the-clock customer care operations

GoDaddy customer service uses personal media channels to allow customers to have direct contact 24/7/365.

follow them. For example, Ellen DeGeneres promotes her program, The Ellen Show, through her Twitter account. She often gives away tickets and other offers as an incentive for users to continue to follow and connect with her.

Sponsored Tweets, a company with expertise in social media promotion, is one of many places companies and advertising agencies can get help with a Twitter advertising campaign. Because Twitter is a free social networking service that allows users to send and read each other's updates, companies can engage large numbers of consumers in semi-orchestrated message campaigns. These can be stand-alone campaigns or more often part of a mixed media approach. Second, because mixed media can reach large numbers simultaneously, the technique is very cost-effective. Social media provides an outlet for companies to personally reach out to a wide base of consumers at once. However, it can only connect with customers who have the necessary technology, which some elderly people don't have.

INTERPRETATION BY RECEIVERS: DECODING

Strong communications begin with an understanding of target audiences. People are not passive receivers of communications. In fact, they resist persuasion by refuting arguments, attacking the source, distorting messages, rationalizing and tuning out. Many consumers regard marketing messages as "tricks" to make them purchase a particular product.

Refuting arguments is one way consumers resist persuasion. Weak messages may backfire as consumers create stronger counter-arguments in their own minds. Another defense mechanism is to attack the source. If a consumer doesn't trust an automobile, that person may reject all of its claims, whether they address comfort, prestige or gas mileage. Attacking the source rather than the ideas being communicated is common in politics. When politicians don't have a very convincing case, they are likely to strike out at the people who reject their arguments.

Intelligence and self-esteem have a lot to do with susceptibility to persuasion. Highly intelligent people are more likely to be influenced by logical, precise and complex information. Others have to be very carefully led through an argument. Depending on the audience, marketers should let some people draw their own conclusions. Unsurprisingly, people with low self-esteem are more likely to be easily persuaded by the suggestions of others. Messages designed for such people should avoid complex arguments.[18]

CONSUMER FEEDBACK

Listening is an important way to learn what consumers think. Feedback is essential to a customer-focused company, and it helps the marketer adjust communications. Today, leading organizations consider listening to be the first step in the communication process, even before the message is created. By listening to the consumer, they determine needs and wants, as well as how to structure communication.

LO 03   The Communication Mix

TYPES OF COMMUNICATION ACTIVITIES

The six main types of communication activities are personal selling, sales promotion, advertising, public relations, sponsorship and digital marketing. Figure 12.4 describes some characteristics of each type.

Personal Selling **Personal selling** requires person-to-person communication be-

PERSONAL SELLING

Face-to-face or other individual communication between a buyer and a seller.

	Personal Selling	Sales Promotion	Advertising	Public Relations	Sponsorship	Digital Marketing
Focus	Person-to-person interaction	Support of sales activity	Mass communication directed at target segments	Unpaid publicity that enhances the company and its products	Cash or resources in support of an event	Individual and group interaction through web-based technologies
Objective	Develop business relationship resulting in loyal customers	Obtain immediate sale and remind after the sale	Position the product and/or increase sales	Gain a favorable impression	Be associated with influential groups	Gain awareness and knowledge in real-time
Example	Pharmaceutical salesperson	Point-of-sale displays	Billboards	Press releases	Team sponsorship	Facebook promotion
	Computer and tele-communications sales	T-shirts with company name	TV ads	Charitable projects	Sport tournaments	LinkedIn job search
	Retail sales Consulting sales	Special sales 2-for-1 offers	Magazine ads Direct mail	Civic leadership Company spokesperson gives speech	Arts events Association events	Community and association connectivity
Appeal	Personal	Move buyer to action	Mass	Mass	Market segment	Personal
Cost per customer	Very high	Low	Low to high	Very low	High to low	Extremely Low
Amount and speed of feedback	A lot and immediately	A little and fairly fast	A little and delayed	A little and fairly fast	A lot and fast	A lot and immediately

Figure 12.4 Communication Mix Characteristics

tween buyer and seller. Generally, this occurs face-to-face, although it also may involve the telephone, video conferencing or interactive computer/mobile linkages. Despite its relatively high cost, personal selling continues to be the most important part of business-to-business marketing and is also significant in sales of big-ticket consumer items, such as autos, computers and housing. The objective of most personal selling is to build loyal relationships with customers that result in profitable sales volume. For example, physicians say that pharmaceutical salespeople are the most effective when they develop personal relationships and build rapport through their personal selling techniques. Since personal selling provides two-way communication, it is possible to engage in a dialogue that leads to problem solving, consulting and relationship building. Because this is generally the most expensive form of contact, salespeople are trained to do the best possible job of helping a customer find solutions through use of their goods and services.

ADVERTISING

Paid communication through non-personal channels.

Advertising **Advertising** is paid, impersonal communication from an identified sponsor using mass media to persuade or influence an audience. It includes newspapers, television, radio, magazines, direct mail, billboards, the internet and point-of-sale displays. It is considered mass communication because the same message is sent throughout the targeted audience as to the rest of the market. Advertising usually features the same basic theme regardless of where it is displayed. Depending on audience size, cost per consumer can be very low. In 2016, it was estimated that 111.9 million people watched Super Bowl 50, making it the third most-watched program in U.S. television history, just behind Super Bowl XLIX, and XLVIII.[19] Companies pay around $4 million for a 30-second ad, or $133,333 a second. However, these figures average out to a bargain low cost of a few cents per viewer.[20] Additionally,

Companies pay around $4 million for a 30-second ad, or $133,333 a second to be a featured Super Bowl commercial.

the Super Bowl is a unique arena for advertising on television since the dawn of the DVRs and TiVo. A recent survey found that 78 percent of viewers look forward to Super Bowl commercials more than the game itself.[21] The best ads often gain additional viewers when they are shared through social media. Because advertising plays a supportive role, it is sometimes difficult to determine just how well it works, in relation to other parts of the marketing mix. For example, the effects of accompanying shifts in product distribution and pricing are often felt more quickly.

Sales Promotion

Sales promotion is communication designed to stimulate immediate purchases using tools such as coupons, contests and free samples. Since the approach generally is designed to stimulate immediate purchases, its effectiveness can be easily measured. Costco uses free samples to encourage customers to buy products they might not have considered purchasing before. This method is very effective with food, lotions, perfumes, and aromatherapy products. Buy-one, get-one-free deals, often referred to as BOGO, is one of the most successful promotional methods. It might seem it is a liquidating tactic to clear stock to make room for something new, but it actually is designed to increase revenue. For example, if it costs 50 cents to produce a bag of chips that retails for $3.99, the company is still making money. Sometimes sales promotion is meant to remind customers of the organization after the sale, which contributes to relationship building. For example, a box of cookies may contain a discount coupon for the next box. Sales promotions usually last a short time.

Public Relations

Public relations (**PR**) is the strategic communication process that builds mutually beneficial relationships between organizations and their publics. Organizations need to anticipate, analyze and interpret public opinion, attitudes and issues that might impact, for good or for bad, the operations and plans of the organization. The most traditional public relations channel is the news media, but the presence of internet search engines and social media makes it more complex to handle negative publicity. When Toyota recalled over 8.8 million vehicles because of acceleration surges, social media and Google made the situation much more complex to handle.[22] A simple Google search for "Toyota" returned pages of news reports about the company's faulty accelerators linked to 19 deaths. Toyota's relatively slow and measured PR response to issues caused consumers deep concern about the company's trustworthiness. The crisis appeared to be on a downward spiral until Jim Lentz, Toyota's President of U.S. Sales, went on "The Today Show" to counter the negative news from media and owners alike. Toyota then coordinated a PR crisis management plan that saved the company by regaining consumer trust it had lost. The bounce-back plan included three steps: (1) extend warranties on vehicles, (2) increase marketing efforts and (3) create a page with information called "Toyota's Safety Recall." This page still exists today and allows owners to enter their Vehicle Identification Number (VIN) to obtain the latest recall news for their specific vehicle.[23] You will learn more about public relations in Chapter 13.

Sponsorships

A major form of communication is sponsorships, which are reaching 10 to 15 percent of promotion budgets. A **sponsorship** is the exchange of money (or some other form of value) in return for a public association with an event. Automobile companies sponsor many Professional Golfers' Association tournaments. PGA Tour events bear such titles as Wendy's 3-Tour Challenge, The

toyota.com/recall

Lookup Safety Recalls & Service Campaigns by VIN

Get information on open safety recalls and service campaigns released since 1999 for Toyota, Lexus and Scion vehicles intended for sale or sold in the U.S., U.S. Territories, and Mexico using our quick and easy recall and campaign lookup below.

This information was last updated on July 8, 2016

March 2016: Important Takata Airbag Safety Recall Information
More Information

Update May/June 2016: The National Highway Traffic Safety Administration (NHTSA) announced an industry-wide expansion of the Takata Inflator Recalls
More Information

Step 1:
Enter a 17-digit Vehicle Identification Number (VIN) below.

E.G., JTBKN3DU4BXXXXXXX

Where do I find my VIN? ▼

Step 2:
Please enter the four-digit validation code below, then click "Submit."

Submit

Contact Us ▲

Lexus Customer Assistance Center
1-800-255-3987
Contact Lexus

Toyota Customer Experience Center
1-800-331-4331
Contact Toyota
Update Ownership Information

Outside Continental U.S.

Saipan
Atkins Kroll
1-670-234-5911

Guam
1-671-646-1886

Hawaii
Servco
1-888-272-5515

American Samoa
ASCO Motors
(+685) 20800

Toyota's Safety Recall page was created as a Public Relations effort to provide timely information regarding all vehicle recalls.

Joey Logano was sponsored by Home Depot and created a loyal fan base for both himself and the sponsor.

DIGITAL MARKETING

Using tools such as Websites, social media, blogs, mobile apps, and email to immediately engage customers via their digital devices such as smartphones, tablets and computers.

Honda Classic and Hyundai Tournament of Champions.[24] Coca-Cola, PepsiCo, General Motors, Anheuser-Busch, United Parcel Service and Nissan are among the largest sponsors of sports. Corporate sponsorship is everywhere in NASCAR, from sponsors of individual drivers to official NASCAR products. One interview with a NASCAR fan had a die-hard stating, "I can tell you right now I wouldn't walk into Lowe's if I had a hole in my roof. …So I'll go to Home Depot and support Joey Logano as much as I possibly can."[25] Who knows if that person stayed a loyal customer after Home Depot dropped Joey Logano in 2012, or if the fan became a loyal fan to Pennzoil (the new sponsor), but for a time the sponsorship had dramatic impact on the consumer. Virtually all sporting events are sponsored now by either major products or corporations. The college football bowl season features games such as the Tostitos Fiesta Bowl, the Allstate Sugar Bowl, the Discover Orange Bowl and the Rose Bowl presented by Vizio, each explicitly showcasing its sponsor's name.

Sponsorships are usually integrated with all other aspects of the communications mix. General Motors takes its key dealers and business customers to the NASCAR racing events it sponsors, features the races in its magazine ads and cites testimonials from NASCAR drivers. This benefits both parties of the sponsorship.

Digital Marketing **Digital marketing** has evolved with the development of technology. It allows companies to connect with targeted and diverse audiences using digital devices such as smartphones, tablets and computers. From these devices, companies can communicate with customers on a variety of platforms such as Facebook, LinkedIn, Twitter, blogs, company sites, email, digital apps and more. The communication is often two-way, allowing for immediate response.

For example, Uber relies almost exclusively on digital marketing with customers who want local transportation. Uber uses your phone's GPS to detect your location and connects you with the nearest available driver who lets you know exactly when you'll be picked up. You don't even have to know your precise address because Uber will!

If you have the Foursquare app on your digital device, you enter a profile of what you like and it leads you to places with those characteristics. You prefer casual restaurants with outdoor seating that offer salted caramel deserts? No problem. It tells you the closest location that meets your desired parameters and also

Uber relies almost exclusively on digital marketing with customers who want local transportation.

tells you what your friends think about it if they've been there. The underlying theme: people have different tastes so why should they get the same search results?[26]

Another app, RetailMeNot, collects coupon codes and sale information from a range of retailers and lets you bookmark your favorite stores so you can check for any discounts while you're shopping. Instead of printing out coupons, the app lets you show the code on your phone while you're checking out to get the deal.

More generally, LivingSocial markets deals for restaurants, spas, fitness centers, and other experiences in cities around the world; specialized sites focus on a smaller target market, such as Zulily, which advertises items for children and women.

Many sites also encourage users to share deals with their friends on platforms such as Facebook or Pinterest. Other, more traditional companies like Nike are heavy players on Twitter and share comments by company spokespersons and paid athletes. It also gives them a platform to allow customers to RSVP for new products, eliminating long lines and the need to camp out at Nike stores to get the latest, coveted new release.

Finally, company blogs are proving to be significant forms of digital company communication. You may remember our highlight of Starbucks back in Chapter 1. The My Starbucks Idea crowdsourcing website has been engaging customers for over 3 years. The unexpected aspect of their blog is that it has minimal to do with coffee. Instead, Starbucks employs its blog as a global brainstorming platform. Customers submit ideas for new drinks, food items, packages, even store designs. It's brilliant marketing!

FACTORS AFFECTING THE COMMUNICATION MIX

Marketers must consider several factors in selecting the communication mix. The most important include whether the audience is the business-to-business or consumer market, whether a push or pull strategy is desirable.

Business Versus Consumer Markets All aspects of the communication mix can be applied to both business-to-business (B2B) and business-to-consumer (B2C) marketing, but different aspects are emphasized depending on the client category. Personal selling is most important in marketing to businesses, whereas advertising dominates in the consumer products arena. Sales promotion is equally important to both and outweighs advertising in business markets, while public relations is a relatively lower priority in both. Weighing costs against revenue reveals a lot about these differences. Per exposure, television advertising can cost less than a few cents; a print ad slightly more; direct mail, a dollar or two; a telephone call, about $10; and face-to-face personal selling in a B2B business, more than several hundred dollars. Although public relations involves few such expenditures, it cannot compare to the other forms in terms of effectiveness and the degree of message control.

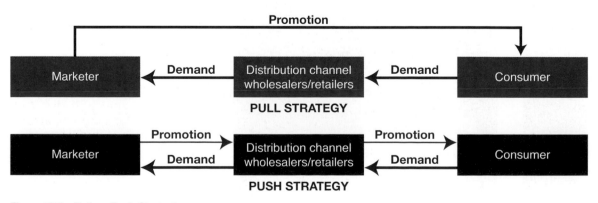

Figure 12.5   Pull vs. Push Strategies

PULL STRATEGY

An attempt to influence consumers directly so they will "pull" the product through the distribution channel.

PUSH STRATEGY

Communication to distribution channel members, which in turn will promote or "push" the product to the end user.

PUSH-PULL STRATEGY

Marketing directly to the channel and to the consumer or end user.

ONE-STEP COMMUNICATION

Communication in which all audience members are simultaneously exposed to the same marketing message.

MULTIPLE-STEP COMMUNICATION

Communication in which opinion leaders filter messages and modify positively or negatively their effect on the rest of the group.

OPINION LEADERS

An influential member of a target audience who first screens messages sent by marketers.

Pull Versus Push Strategies Marketers attempt to influence the market through either a push or pull strategy (or both), as illustrated in Figure 12.5. A **pull strategy** attempts to influence consumers directly. Communication is designed to build demand so consumers will "pull" the product through the channel of distribution. In other words, consumer demand is high, so retailers want to carry the product, who in turn ask wholesalers, who in turn contact the manufacturer. Many service firms use price discounts as pull strategies. But effectiveness of price discounts as a pull strategy has been suspicious.[27] For an airline company, dynamic pricing was proven to be the starting point for a competent pull strategy.[28]

Although pull strategies tend to be used often for consumer products, they also have a place in business-to-business marketing. For example, marketers of electrical control and distribution equipment often target the purchasing agent with their messages. Sales representatives call on design firms, which then specify that particular electrical equipment in the engineering design.

The **push strategy** involves communicating to distribution channel members, which in turn promote to the end user. This is particularly common in industrial, business-to-business or retail marketing. Marketers often train distribution channel members on the sales techniques they believe are most suited to their products. For example, many manufacturers who sell to Home Depot, such as cabinet manufacturers, train Home Depot in-store salespeople on the best way to sell their brand. They provide sales aids and literature to help Home Depot representatives entice consumers to their brands.[29]

Often, a **push-pull strategy** is appropriate. The combination approach markets directly to both the channel and end user, speeding adoption and the overall flow through the channel. This combination also helps address conflict that may arise between marketers and retailers. Retailers want to stock the most profitable products, which may not be marketers' biggest brands. Using a pull strategy to create strong demand at the consumer level makes channel members more willing to handle the product.

Opinion Leadership Marketing communications reach consumers directly and indirectly (Figure 12.6). In **one-step communication**, all members of the target audience are simultaneously exposed to the same message. **Multiple-step communication** uses influential members of the target audience, known as **opinion leaders**, to filter a message before it reaches other group members, modifying its effect positively or negatively for the rest of the group.[30]

Because of their important role, opinion leaders have often been called gatekeepers, to indicate the control they have over ideas flowing into the group. Competitive marketers make it a priority to identify opinion leaders. Opinion leaders tend to be well-informed on a wide variety of subjects, often as a result of research and direct communication with involved parties (in the case of marketing, salespeople). They can have a sort of multiplier effect, intensifying the strength of the message if they respond positively and passing it on to others. Consequently, the resources used to gain support from opinion leaders are probably well spent.

Public figures like celebrities are often opinion leaders. Some may not give much merit to Kim Kardashian's endorsement of Hillary Clinton for the 2016 election, but she might have significant influence among first-time voters. Kim recently posted an Instagram photo of her with Hillary, stating, "I got my selfie!!! I really loved hearing her speak & hearing her goals for our country!" The post has nearly one million likes and over 35,000 comments.[31] Pharrell Williams put his opinion out to his fans: "It's time for a

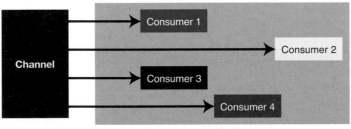

ONE-STEP COMMUNICATION (DIRECT)

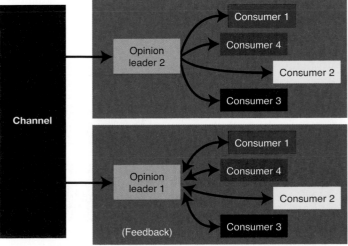

MULTI-STEP COMMUNICATION (INDIRECT)

Figure 12.6 Opinion Leadership

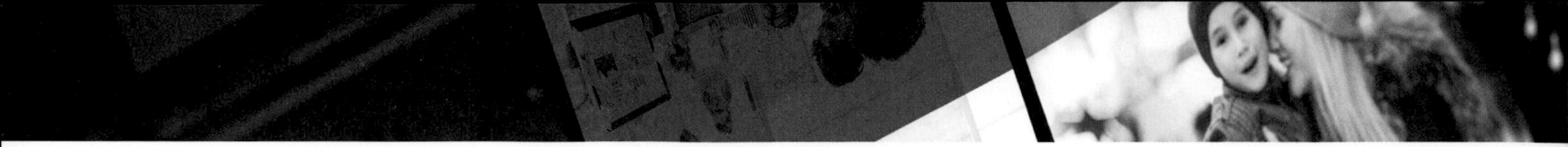

woman to be in there. Women think about things in a holistic way, it's not so individual." Donald Trump also has a long list of celebrity endorsements, including Mike Ditka, Stephen Baldwin, Azealia Banks and Kid Rock. Hulk Hogan says, "I don't want to be in the ring with any candidates, I want to be Trump's running mate."[32]

Developing the Integrated Marketing Communications Plan

LO 05

Now that we have examined the factors influencing the process, let us see how an integrated marketing communication plan is built. The steps are outlined in Figure 12.7. The IMC plan should never be developed in isolation from the strategic marketing plan. It's the responsibility of strategic marketing personnel to define the role of communication in the overall marketing strategy. The IMC plan is designed to position the organization and its products in a manner consistent with that strategy.

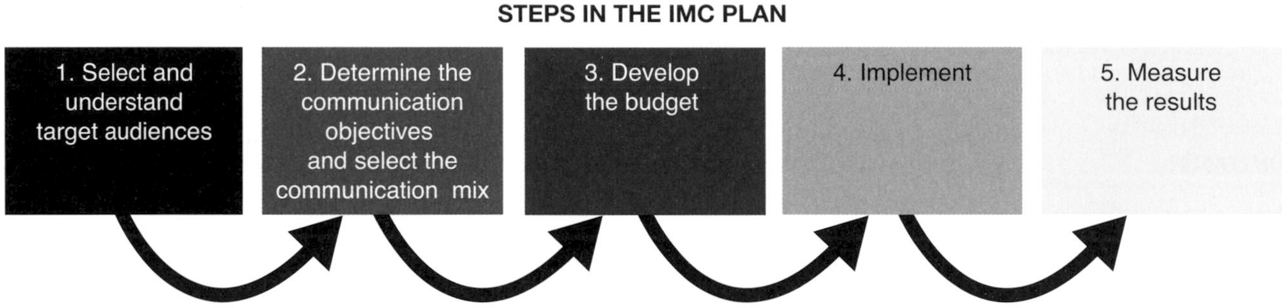

STEPS IN THE IMC PLAN

| 1. Select and understand target audiences | 2. Determine the communication objectives and select the communication mix | 3. Develop the budget | 4. Implement | 5. Measure the results |

Figure 12.7   Developing the Communication Plan

SELECTING AND UNDERSTANDING TARGET AUDIENCES

As we have discussed many times, selecting target markets is a critical step in nearly every aspect of marketing. The same thing is true regarding the development of an integrated marketing communications plan. Coke and Nike have outstanding communication programs that reach a very large portion of the population. However, these two leading edge marketers carefully segment markets and tailor specific integrated marketing communications for each target segment. For every target audience, communications experts generally have data to help understand key aspects of consumer behavior: where, how and why they obtain information. When market data and information are unavailable, for example in developing markets, companies sometimes use trial and error to get a grasp on media and buying habits. However, experimentation is expensive when a company doesn't know if it will hit the wrong audience, miss high potential customers or simply fail to resonate with the appropriate people.

DETERMINING OBJECTIVES AND SELECTING THE IMC MIX

Consumers move from a lack of awareness about brands to purchase and hopefully loyalty. This process of increasing involvement can be described by hierarchical models. The most straightforward of these is AIDA, which stands for attention, interest, desire and action.[33] Figure 12.8 depicts AIDA and a more detailed ver-

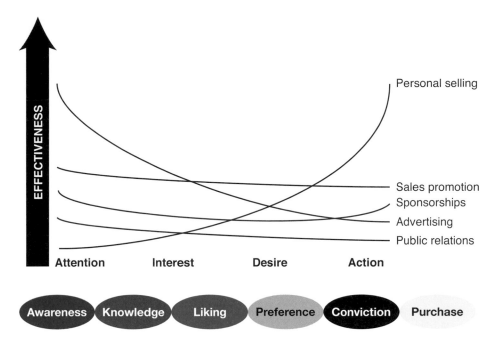

Figure 12.8   Effectiveness of Main Types of Communication at Different Stages in the Consumer Buying Process

sion that includes awareness, knowledge, liking, preference, conviction and purchase. For example, imagine you sit down to study but are distracted when you notice a friend's new Beats by Dre headphones (awareness). You ask how he likes them, then observe others wearing them around campus (knowledge). Perhaps you borrow a pair and are so amazed by the clarity and comfort over your stock iPod ear buds that you consider purchasing a pair of your own (liking). By talking to friends and watching ads, you decide you like Beats by Dre (preference). In-store displays and product guarantees convince you to buy the particular brand (conviction). Finally, you decide to put the headphones on your credit card (purchase).

As marketers plan communication activities, the objective must be foremost in mind. Is it to create awareness, build brand preference or encourage purchase? The IMC mix will vary considerably depending on the objective. To create awareness and product knowledge, advertising is very effective. It gains attention and even can lead to liking and brand preference. Once desire is created, however, sales promotion may be more useful. At this point the customer is more influenced by personal selling, sales promotions and sponsorships. Attending a sponsored event could make the product so immediately prominent that the consumer decides to buy. Sales promotions involving coupons, price incentives or in-store samples may move buyers to action by reinforcing their conviction to try the brand. The effectiveness of personal selling increases dramatically in the later stages of the buying process. This is especially true for high-priced items in consumer markets, but in some business markets, personal selling may be necessary just to gain attention. Although public relations appears to be least useful because it tapers off after the attention stage and remains low compared to the others, keep in mind that it has a lower cost. Other than the fairly minor expense of creating the public relations message, there is no cost for delivering it.

DEVELOPING THE COMMUNICATION BUDGET

The communication budget falls within expenditures for the entire marketing mix. Consequently, establishing the specific amount for IMC requires an understanding of the overall marketing strategy, the financial resources available and the contribution communication is expected to make. When allocating IMC money, organizations must remember that some activities can be started or stopped quickly, such as advertising and sales promotion. They often have to adjust personal selling more slowly, since time is required to hire, train and deploy the sales force.

The IMC budget is usually determined in two steps. First, the total allocation is decided. Second, the amount for each type of communication is assigned.

Determining the Overall Budget The first issue is how much it will cost to accomplish the objective. Generally, for existing products communication objectives are established once a year. Two-thirds of advertising budgets for the following year are submitted to top marketing management during September or October, and nearly 80 percent are approved by November.[34] Most IMC budgets are based on one of the following: percentage of sales, competitive budgeting, payout plan or cost of tasks that must be performed to accomplish objectives.

Allocating the Budget Communication works synergistically. In other words, investments in one type of communication may help other types accomplish their objectives. A salesperson benefits tremendously from awareness created by advertising and from purchase incentives due to sales promotion. The integrated aspect of marketing communication needs to be kept in mind when deciding the allocation for each activity. This process requires considerable and continuous dialogue among marketing team members. In many cases, data are fed into computer simulations that help determine the best allocations. In other cases, the team simply estimates what is required. In companies with major brands, many executives are usually involved, including senior management media and advertising staff, marketing personnel, brand marketing management and sales personnel. The allocations may be determined by very specific objectives. When Westinghouse process control wanted to increase name recognition, it shifted resources from the sales force to advertising.

IMPLEMENTATION

Implementation of an IMC plan tends to be done by functional specialists with considerable experience in their field. There are ample career opportunities in these areas including personal selling, advertising and public relations, because each is multifaceted and challenging. Marketers strive to obtain uniquely talented employees and suppliers to carry out communication programs. Even the best of plans will fail if not implemented by creative and professional team members.

The first decision is how much to do in-house and how much to outsource. For example, personal selling can be done by company personnel, manufacturer representatives (private salespeople) or distributors. Likewise, companies must decide whether to do their own advertising and sales promotion or hire outsiders. Most large and medium-sized firms outsource much of their IMC implementation. Often representatives from these advertising and promotion agencies work on-site with the client's marketing executives and personnel.

MEASURING IMC RESULTS

It was John Wanamaker, a famous 19th-century retailer, who first said: "I know that half of the money I spend on advertising is wasted, but I can never figure out which half." He was referring to the fact that many messages may never reach much of the target audience. This highlights two important questions to consider. First, who is reached by a communication? And, second, what does it accomplish relative to the goals established in the plan?

Why is it difficult to estimate the results of communication? The major problem is isolating the effects of one part of the IMC plan to determine its relative influence on product performance. Most marketers start by identifying criteria or measures. Performance measures are variables or factors that tell us how well the organization or product is doing. Common measures are market share, sales level and profitability. Other factors are often used, such as number of loyal customers, amount of brand recognition, brand image and knowledge of the product.

Once performance measures are selected, the task of assessing IMC influence can begin. Very seldom is only one part of the IMC mix adjusted at a time, and competitors' activities are virtually never stable, so determining the precise effect of communication is rarely possible. When Nike introduces a new model, how much of its success can be attributed to pricing, product distribution, customer service or promotion? Still, by monitoring IMC expenditures and performance measures for a large number of companies and then applying statistical analysis, researchers can get a good idea of the overall effect of IMC. This information is very useful in determining whether objectives are being met or whether changes need to be made.

LO 06

Issues in Communication

DIVERSITY

Effective communications are carefully targeted. The vast differences among consumers create opportunities for a wide variety of promotions to meet their needs. For example, 54 million Americans have some form of disability, and marketers are changing the way they communicate with these consumers. Long ignored, they represent several substantial target segments.[35] Marketers now have a new vehicle for communicating with many of these consumers—the internet.

Until recently, the web was not very user friendly for people with limited vision or dexterity. Now, however, the American Federation for the Blind (AFB) and Interliant Inc. have redesigned the AFB's website, www.afb.org, to better accommodate internet users with disabilities. Previous assistive technologies such as screen magnifiers or screen readers did not properly read site content, but the new site allows for a more thoroughly accessible site. Graphics are now labeled with text that can be read by screen readers, and all audio on the site is now available in text form so that it can be read by the hearing impaired. The AFB's site serves as a model for other government sites, which are required by the 1998 Rehabilitation Act to make the information they provide accessible to those with disabilities.[36]

AFB's site serves as a model for other government sites, which are required to make the information they provide accessible to those with disabilities.

LD OnLine is the world's leading website for learning disabilities and ADHD, serving more than 200,000 parents, teachers, and other professionals each month.[37] Visitors to the site can find relevant news articles, information on technology that can make living easier, issues related to schools and child disabilities, and health and medical information. In addition, site visitors can find stories about other people with disabilities who continue to lead fulfilling lives. Visitors can also become members of the site and receive e-mail updates and articles based on their interests. The site aims to assist people with disabilities who live independently.

Promotions in general are becoming more inclusive by depicting people with disabilities. Public tolerance of insensitivity toward people with disabilities is decreasing. When Nike ran ads that claimed its trail-running shoes would prevent a jogger from running into a tree and becoming a "drooling, misshapen, non-extreme-trail-running husk of my former self," it was met with swift opposition, and Nike removed the advertisement with a formal apology.

ETHICS

Marketers must be careful about how they communicate. The American Marketing Association Code of Ethics states that acceptable standards include "avoidance of false and misleading advertising, rejection of high-pressure manipulations or misleading sales tactics, and avoidance of communications that use deception or manipulation." Despite these guidelines, the ethical boundaries for promotion are not always clear.

Communications targeting children have long faced public scrutiny. Under pressure from consumer groups and the federal government, R. J. Reynolds agreed to stop using the Joe Camel character in its tobacco advertisements. Philip Morris Company pulled its tobacco ads from magazines with teenage readership. This decision removed ads from *Sports Illustrated* and *Rolling Stone*. The alcohol industry has also been accused of knowingly pushing products to minors. The Federal Trade Commission issued a report asking that beer, liquor and wine companies stop the promotion of alcohol in ads that would appeal to minors, including "promotional placement" in PG and PG-13 films, TV programs aimed at younger audiences and on college campuses. At the same time, Anheuser-Busch launched its "We All Make a Difference" campaign, which salutes those who have made a difference in fighting alcohol abuse.

Americans have voiced much concern about violence being marketed to children either through gun companies, video games, movies or television. Former U.S. Surgeon General David Satcher found that exposure to violent entertainment in childhood leads to aggressive behavior throughout life.[38] In response to attacks on the entertainment industry for marketing violence to children, ABC launched public service announcements featuring stars of the network's television series urging children to avoid violence.

TECHNOLOGY THAT BUILDS RELATIONSHIPS

In communication, marketers often use technology to reach consumers and establish relationships. Digital technology and the internet make it possible to connect with customers quickly. Almost every company has developed its own website to give consumers information about itself and its products, and also to use effective promotions. Today, email is an essential form of personal communication. Email communications can be targeted more directly to a select audience, providing information that will be useful for making a purchase. Microsoft invented its own email advertising application in a frantic race to catch Google's online advertising revenue with its own software.[39] However, a survey showed that 63 percent of people erase email advertising without reading it, and 56 percent think they receive excessive amounts of email promotions.[40] Therefore, marketers must be aware that sending messages indiscreetly may have a negative effect.

Digital marketing can also be aimed directly to consumers, especially appealing to younger generations. For example, a message containing a special discount coupon can be sent on a consumer's birthday, creating a positive company impression and helping to build relationships. The message might appear on Facebook, Twitter, or directly from a company. Mobile advertising continues to grow rapidly in the United States; spending reached $28 billion in 2015, and is projected to reach more than $40 billion in 2016.[41] Social media also has opened new doors for marketers; on Facebook, for example, marketers can "choose the location, gender, age, likes and interests, relationship status, workplace and education of a target audience."[42] Cookies and non-private browsing enables companies to track user site visits. While some people consider this an invasion of privacy, as long as it's legal it will continue to affect the way marketers combine and use communication activities to create the most effective IMC mix.

Chapter Summary

Objective 1:   Describe the objectives of integrated marketing communication.

Integrated marketing communication (IMC) is the coordination of all information to the market in order to provide consistent, unified messages. Since each of the six aspects of IMC—personal selling, advertising, sales promotion, public relations, sponsorships and digital marketing—tends to work synergistically, integration is very important. Marketing communication has six objectives. First, it should provide useful information that improves customer decision making and consumption. Second, it creates demand to ensure that products will be consumed in sufficient quantities to justify their development, production and distribution. Third, it supplies knowledge about the value of products, such as their benefits, features and functions. Fourth, it helps differentiate products by describing their uniqueness. Fifth, it helps close the sale by moving customers to action. Finally, it is critical in building the all-important relationship with customers and in securing their loyalty.

Objective 2:   Learn how the communication process provides the intended information for the market.

Traditionally, marketing communication was seen as a one-way process, from seller to buyer, without a feedback loop. Today, a two-way process is the norm. The sender needs to specify objectives, as discussed previously. The sender's characteristics are important determinants of how well messages will be received. Source credibility is determined by expertise, trustworthiness and attractiveness (or appeal). Encoding requires translating the message into terms that will be easily understood. Since message interpretation depends on consumer life experiences, a thorough comprehension of consumer behavior is required to do an adequate job of encoding. Message characteristics also play a major role. Marketers need to decide whether a one-sided or two-sided message is better; whether to supply conclusions; the order in which information will be presented; whether to use humor or fear appeals; and whether to use comparative messages. The choice of media—mass, personal or mixed—also influences communications. Today, mixed media channels such as social media and digital marketing are becoming more important. Audiences are not passive receivers; they interpret information by processing it.

Objective 3:   Define the communication mix, including personal selling, advertising, sales promotion, sponsorships, public relations and digital marketing.

The communication mix has six major components. Each has particular advantages. Personal selling involves face-to-face contact or two-way technology linkages, such as the telephone or internet. This allows dialogue and interactive problem solving. Advertising is paid, nonpersonal communication. It reaches all members of the audience with the same "mass" message. Sales promotion uses a one-way

message to motivate purchase, usually in the form of short-term incentives to buy. Sponsorship is paid support of an event. It associates the sponsor with the event and its participants. Public relations is non-paid communication (publicity) about a company and its products. These messages are sometimes broadcast by sources considered to be unbiased so they can have considerable credibility. Digital marketing includes online and social media, mobile marketing, brand websites, blogs and more. It allows companies to reach specific, more targeted markets and engage in two-way communication with customers.

Objective 4:   Know the factors that influence the communications mix.

The communication mix is influenced by several factors. First, business-to-business and consumer markets use different mixes. The former are dominated by personal selling, whereas the latter are dominated by sales promotion and advertising. Second, marketers use a push or pull communication strategy. A push strategy communicates to channel members, who in turn communicate to end users. A pull strategy communicates with end users, who in turn demand products from channel members. Third, communications must be suited to the product's stage in the life cycle in order to have the greatest effectiveness. Finally, marketing communications do not always work directly on consumers. There is often a two-stage process whereby opinion leaders filter information before it reaches others in the market.

Objective 5:   Describe the steps in developing an integrated marketing communication plan.

The IMC plan is an outgrowth of the marketing plan. It has five steps. First, select and understand target markets. Second, determine communication objectives and select the IMC mix. Third, develop the IMC budget in line with the overall strategic marketing plan. Fourth, implement the plan. Fifth, measure communication results and adjust accordingly.

Objective 6:   Discuss how to address diversity, ethics and technology in communications.

Many media are not accessible to physically impaired individuals, and other avenues must be used. Innovative software with voice recognition, and visual accessibility now makes it possible for most people to use the internet. Marketers must be careful not to cross ethical boundaries in their communications. They should avoid false and misleading ads and sales tactics as well as high-pressure manipulation. Targeting children is a questionable practice, because they may easily be misled or manipulated. Communication technology is providing better ways to connect with consumers and create relationships; email is one example. Fortunately, today's software makes interactive communication easier and quicker than ever before.

Review Your Understanding

1. What is integrated marketing communication?
2. What are the six objectives of integrated marketing communication?
3. What is the one-way communication process? How does it differ from the two-way process?
4. What are message sender characteristics, and why are they important?
5. What is encoding?
6. What message characteristics should be considered? How does each influence effectiveness?
7. What are personal, mass and mixed media? What are the characteristics of each?
8. What factors influence how messages are interpreted? Describe each.
9. What are the main categories in the communication mix?
10. What factors influence the communication mix? Describe each.
11. What are the steps in building an integrated communication plan?
12. How does diversity offer an opportunity and a challenge to communication?
13. What are some aspects of communication addressed in the American Marketing Association Code of Ethics?
14. Name one way that communication technology is helping to build relationships with consumers.
15. What effect does social media have on integrated marketing communication?

Discussion of Concepts

1. Describe the various goals of communication. What helps determine communication objectives?
2. Why is it so important for marketers to understand the communication process? How does that process affect the development and implementation of a campaign?
3. The way in which a message is communicated to consumers is critically important to its success. Name some of the issues involved in developing a message.
4. How do consumers distort messages? Have you ever distorted a message directed at you? How can marketers combat this problem?
5. Why is the source of a message so important? What are the three characteristics of a good spokesperson? Do you think one spokesperson can communicate effectively with the entire market? Why or why not?
6. Briefly describe the five steps in developing an IMC plan. How are the plan and the company's overall marketing strategy related?
7. List the pros and cons of each type of communication activity: personal selling, sales promotion, advertising, sponsorship, public relations and digital marketing. What factors help determine the appropriate combination to select?

Key Terms & Definitions

1. **Advertising:** Paid communication through nonpersonal channels.
2. **Communication:** The process of sending and receiving messages.
3. **Digital marketing:** Using tools such as websites, social media, blogs, mobile apps, and email to immediately engage customers via their digital devices such as smartphones, tablets and computers.
4. **Encoding:** Translating a message into terms easily understood by the target audience.
5. **Integrated marketing communication (IMC):** The coordination of advertising, sales promotion, personal selling, public relations and sponsorship to reach consumers with a powerful effect in the market.
6. **Media:** The channels through which messages are communicated.
7. **Multiple-step communication:** Communication in which opinion leaders filter messages and modify positively or negatively their effect on the rest of the group.
8. **One-sided message:** A message that presents only arguments favorable to the source.
9. **One-step communication:** Communication in which all audience members are simultaneously exposed to the same marketing message.
10. **Opinion leader:** Influential member of a target audience who first screens messages sent by marketers.
11. **Personal selling:** Face-to-face or other individual communication between a buyer and a seller.
12. **Promotion:** The process whereby marketers inform, educate, persuade, remind and reinforce consumers through communication.
13. **Public relations (PR):** Promotion designed to present the firm and its products in a positive light in the buyer's mind.

14. **Pull strategy:** An attempt to influence consumers directly so they will "pull" the product through the distribution channel.

15. **Push-pull strategy:** Marketing directly to the channel and to the consumer or end user.

16. **Push strategy:** An attempt to influence the distribution channel, which in turn will "push" the product through to the user.

17. **Sales promotion:** Communication designed to stimulate immediate purchases, using tools such as coupons, contests and free samples.

18. **Sponsorship:** The exchange of money (or some other form of value) in return for a public association with an event.

19. **Two-sided message:** A message that presents arguments that are unfavorable as well as favorable to the source.

References

1. www.oprah.com, website visited July 1, 2016.
2. www.itcanwait.com/pledge, website visited July 1, 2016.
3. Ibid.
4. "Boingo Acquires AWG, Combining Airport Industry's 2 Largest Wi-Fi Providers," AirportRevenueNews.com, August 26, 2013.
5. www.beatsbydre.com, website visited July 1, 2016.
6. Chris Harris, "Well This Is Awkward: FIFA Has Banned Beats by Dre Headphones From the World Cup," www.complex.com, June 17, 2014.
7. Patrick Rishe, "Michelle Wie, At Long Last A Major Champion, Should See Greater Endorsements," Forbes, June 22, 2014.
8. www.sportsbusinessdaily.com/Daily/Closing-Bell/2016/02/11/Draymond.aspx, website visited July 5, 2016.
9. "If George Clooney has a spy satellite, who else has one?," The Telegraph, August 30, 2013.
10. www.adiamondisforever.com, website visited July 1, 2016.
11. Narisetti, Raju, "Rubbermaid Opens Door to TV, Hoping to Put Houses in Order," Wall Street Journal Interactive Edition, February 4, 1997.
12. www.rubbermaid.com, website visited July 2, 2015
13. Ross Jr., Harold L., "How to Create Effective Humorous Commercials Yielding Above Average Brand Preference Change," Marketing News, March 26, 1976, pg. 4.
14. www.youtube.com/watch?v=ql-N3F1FhW4; www.youtube.com/watch?v=DHQ2sHyA9SI, websites visited July 7, 2016.
15. Cochrane, Lucy; Quester, Pascale, "Fear in Advertising: The Influence of Consumers' Product Involvement and Culture," Journal of International Consumer Marketing, Vol. 17, 2005, pg. 7.
16. www.support.godaddy.com, website visited July 3, 2016.
17. www.cio.com, website visited July 3, 2016.
18. Zelner, M., "Self-Esteem, Self-Perception, and Influenceability," Journal of Personality and Social Psychology 25, 1973, pp. 87-93.
19. Frank Pallotta and Brian Stelter, "Super Bowl 50 audience is third largest in TV history," CNN Money, February 8, 2016.
20. "The rising costs of Super Bowl ads in one chart," USA Today, February 1, 2014.
21. "Buzz Meter: Many just watch the Super Bowl for the ads," USA Today, January 15, 2014.
22. Nicole Briguet, "Crisis Management and PR Campaigns," www.crisismanagementpr.blogspot.com, February 13, 2013.

23. Ibid.
24. www.golf.com, website visited July 3, 2016.
25. "NASCAR Fans Have Unparalleled Awareness of Sport's Sponsors, New Study Finds," February 7, 2005.
26. https://foursquare.com/download#selected, website visited July 1, 2016.
27. Hu, Hsin-Hui; Parsa, H.G.; Khan, Maryam, "Effectiveness of Price Discount Levels and Formats in Service Industries," Journal of Service Research, July 2006, pg. 17.
28. Burger, Beat; Fuchs, Matthias, "Dynamic pricing — A future airline business model," Journal of Revenue and Pricing Management Leader, pg. 39.
29. www.homedepot.com, website visited July 3, 2016.
30. Sheth, Jagdish N., "Word-of-Mouth in Low Risk Innovations," Journal of Advertising Research 11, 1971, pp. 15-18.
31. www.instagram.com/p/6EUJcIuSw9, website visited July 7, 2016.
32. Christie D'Zurilla, Kyle Kim and Armand Emamdjomeh, "Celebrity endorsement tracker," Los Angeles Times, April 12, 2016.
33. Strong, E.K., The Psychology of Selling (New York, McGraw-Hill, 1925).
34. Russell, J.T.; Lane, Ronald; King, Karen, Kleppner's Advertising Procedure, ed. 17, 2007, (Prentice Hall).
35. www.ncd.gov, website visited April 5, 2016.
36. www.afb.org, website visited April 5, 2016.
37. www.ldonline.org, website visited April 5, 2016.
38. Leeds, Jeff, "Surgeon General Links TV, Real Violence Entertainment," Los Angeles Times, January 17, 2001, pg. A1; "Youth Violence on the Decline but Surgeon General Warns of Complacency," The Hartford Courant, January 18, 2001, pg. A10.
39. Nick Buchan, "Global dispatches," B&T Weekly (Sydney), June 9, 2006, pg. 11.
40. Greg Brooks, "Overcrowded Inbox," Marketing (London), July 13, 2005, pg. 40.
41. "Mobile Ad Spend to Top $100 Billion Worldwide in 2016, 51% of Digital Market," www.emarketer.com, website visited July 7, 2016.
42. www.facebook.com/advertising, website visited July 3, 2016.

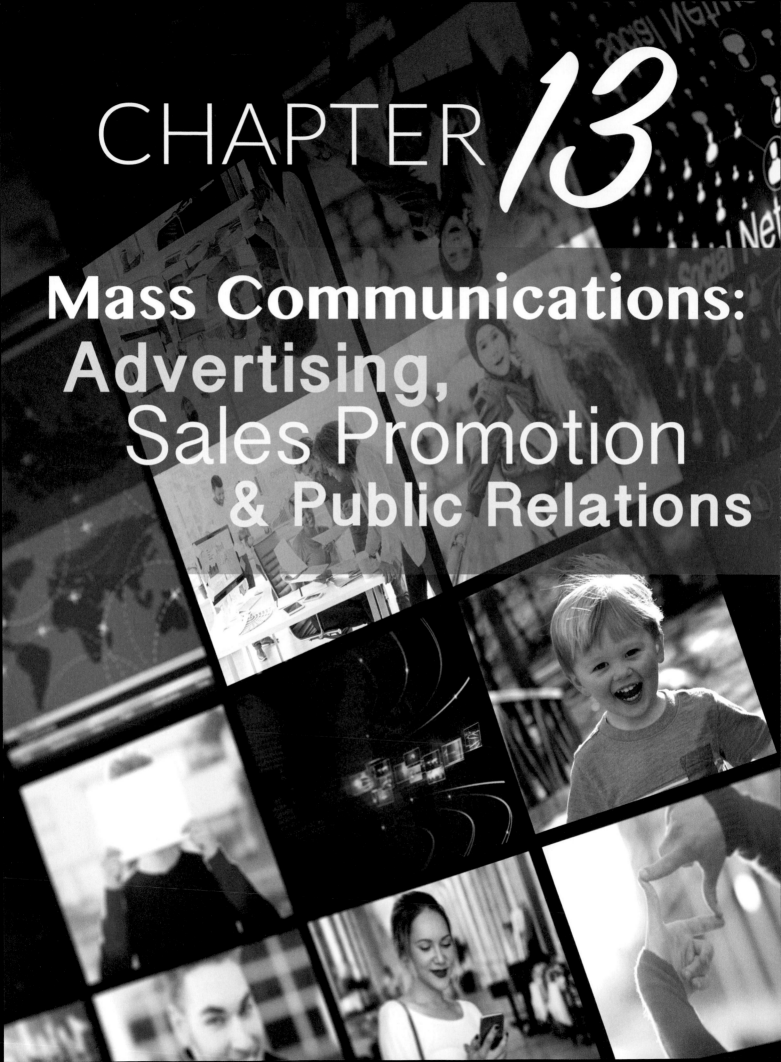

CHAPTER 13

Mass Communications:
Advertising,
Sales Promotion
& Public Relations

You Tube SCAN & WATCH ▶

Advertising during the Olympic Games offers repetitive exposure to the message.

Advertisements during the Olympic Games may not be as glitzy as the coveted Super Bowl commercials, but they are watched during a global event that draws millions of viewers over the course of weeks, instead of only a few short hours. While Super Bowl ads offer creativity and humor to be talked about the next day at work, the Olympics offer an opportunity to tap into human sentiment, spirit and achievement. Tone is an extremely important aspect to advertising, sales promotion and public relations. Knowing how to use humor and when to use emotion in advertising is no different than in everyday life.

The extensive media coverage of the Olympic Games, through television, online and social media, provides a perfect vehicle for mass communication—particularly for sponsors and their advertising. Procter & Gamble communicated a touching message with its "Proud Sponsor of Moms" campaign, honoring not just the Olympic athletes but also the mothers who sacrificed to help their kids realize their Olympic dreams. The ads were declared the best of the Olympics by London research firm Ace Metrix, and they were the social media winner by a mile; the ad videos were shared over 2.5 million times.

To extend a successful message, P&G created the newest installment of its award-winning "Thank You, Mom" campaign for the 2016 Rio de Janeiro Summer Olympics by releasing a new video called "Strong." The "Strong" campaign was inspired by the results of P&G's research for "The Global Mom Report." The campaign explores the courage moms show at critical times throughout their kids' lives. What's the connection to P&G other than goodwill and brand recognition? Think about how many moms buy diapers, laundry detergent, and paper towels. Do you think the heart-tugging strings embedded in their memories from this campaign might influence them to buy P&G brand Pampers, Tide or Bounty next time they're at the store? The company is betting on it.

The Olympic games are one of the most effective international marketing platforms in the world, reaching billions of people in over 200 countries throughout the world. Ten international marketing giants, including P&G, Coca-Cola, GE, Visa, Panasonic, Samsung and McDonald's held top sponsorship platforms at the Rio Games.

It's important to understand that the Olympic Games offer more to organizations than a single television commercial. They offer repetitive exposure, which can be extremely powerful when a brand is seen worldwide through television, digital media, social media, consumer goods, gear and apparel. Sponsors earn an exclusive right to place the Olympic rings on products and packaging, which can make a brand stand out from the competition. In return, sponsors provide support for the Olympic Games in the form of products, services, expertise, and staff, as well as for the training and development of Olympic athletes around the world. Finally, an Olympic sponsorship positions organizations to appear patriotic, supportive, and inspiring.

Sources: www.news.pg.com/press-release/pg-corporate-announcements/ strong-moms-inspire-latest-pg-thank-you-mom-campaign, website visited July 2, 2016; www.nbcolympics.com/news/how-watch-rio-2016-olympic- games, website visited July 2, 2016; www.stillmed.olympic.org/media/Doc- ument%20Library/OlympicOrg/Documents/IOC-Marketing-and-Broadcast- ing-General-Files/Olympic-Marketing-Fact-File-2016.pdf#_ga=1.9054863 4.1200019492.1468549707;

LO 01 Understand the concept of mass communications, including the relative use of advertising, sales promotion and public relations.

LO 02 Know the objectives, advantages and disadvantages of advertising, as well as the sequence of steps in creating an advertising campaign.

LO 03 Understand sales promotion objectives and what types of promotions are used to stimulate sales in business, trade, retailer and consumer markets.

LO 04 Understand the use of public relations in marketing.

LO 05 Learn how technology, globalization and ethics are playing major roles in mass communications.

The Concept of Mass Communications: Advertising, Sales Promotion & Public Relations

MASS COMMUNICATION

The communication of a concept or message to large audiences.

Today, mass communication helps companies connect with customers by providing information in exciting and creative formats. **Mass communication** is the communication of a concept or message to large audiences. The ability to inform large groups of people about available products in the global market is extremely important. It's so pervasive that most of us are exposed every few seconds to a message designed to influence our behavior.

Mass communications include advertising, sales promotion and public relations, as shown in Figure 13.1. Specific techniques for achieving success in those areas are constantly changing to incorporate advances in technology, globalization and ethics. This chapter looks at each component.

First, advertising and its purposes. We describe its categories, the agencies that create and place it, and the media that deliver it to the consumer. Next, sales promotion is described as a way to run trials, stimulate immediate sales and build customer relationships. Then a section on public relations and publicity addresses those roles in corporate communications. Finally, we discuss the three fluid forces of technology, globalization and ethics that affect mass communication in today's marketplace.

Figure 13.1   The Concept of Mass Communication in Marketing

Advertising

Advertising is paid, impersonal communication from an identified sponsor using mass media to persuade or influence an audience. The word is derived from the Latin advertere, "to turn toward."[1] Notice that advertising is paid for by an identified sponsor, so the audience knows the source of the message. In addition, it is a form of impersonal communication through mass media, such as newspapers, magazines, radio, television, the internet and social media, which each grant access to relatively large audiences. Traditionally there was no opportunity for the receiver to ask questions or for the advertiser to obtain immediate feedback. Advertising on the internet and social media, however, has changed that by allowing potential customers to directly contact sponsors with questions before placing orders for goods and services.

THE FOUR PURPOSES OF ADVERTISING

Although advertising itself is powerful, it also plays an important support role for other forms of communication. In a famous McGraw-Hill Publishing Company ad, a grumpy purchasing agent stares directly at the viewer, saying: "I don't know who you are. I don't know your company. I don't know your company's product. I don't know what your company stands for. I don't know your company's customers. I don't know your company's record. I don't know your company's reputation. Now, what was it you wanted to sell me?" The ad goes on to explain that the sales effort starts before a salesperson calls—with business publication advertising. Whether alone or in support of other promotion methods, advertising can be invaluable. There are four objectives in advertising, each of which accomplishes a different purpose: to inform, to persuade, to remind or to reinforce.

Informative Advertising **Informative advertising** is designed to provide messages that consumers can store for later use. For example, an art museum may place an informative advertisement to make the community aware that a particular exhibit is on display. Often, the more information an ad provides, the better the response will be. A 6,450-word ad for Merrill Lynch brought 10,000 inquiries from interested investors. An 800-word ad for Mercedes-Benz was headlined: "You give up things when you buy the Mercedes Benz 230S. Things like rattles, rust and shabby workmanship." Sales rose from 10,000 to 40,000 cars. Many consumers want to be provided with as much information as possible about items that interest them. Today, the internet provides a very effective format for informative advertising. An online ad can link customers to various pages that offer additional information they desire.

Persuasive Advertising **Persuasive advertising** is designed to change consumers' attitudes and opinions about products as well as create attitudes where none exist. These ads often list the product's attributes, pricing and other factors that influence the buying decision. They attempt to make the product choice important so consumers will think about the subject. In this way, the message recipient is asked to form an attitude first and then buy. For example, a Chevy Volt ad features an exasperated car owner explaining to aliens examining his car that the vehicle is electric but also has a gas tank that allows it to go farther when necessary. The consumer can draw the conclusion that driving a Volt won't leave him or her stranded if the charge runs out, because the car also runs on gasoline.[2]

Chevy Volt

YouTube SCAN & WATCH

This Chevy Volt ad is an example of persuasive advertising.

Reminder Advertising

Reminder advertising keeps the product at the forefront of the consumer's mind. In some cases, these ads simply draw a connection between the brand and some aspect of life. The ideal result, however, is to inspire action by the consumer. One major medium for reminders is outdoor advertising. McDonald's tried to move consumers into its restaurants with the slogan "You deserve a break today." The next campaign phrases asked, "Have you had your break today?" and "Did somebody say McDonald's?" "I'm lovin' it" is the most recent reminder slogan.[3] Product placement in television and movies is becoming a popular form of reminder advertising. Millions of viewers see "American Idol" judges sipping Coke, and Apple products are often featured on shows such as "Modern Family" and "30 Rock."

Reinforcement Advertising

To encourage repeat buying behavior, **reinforcement advertising** calls attention to specific product characteristics. The key here is to communicate with the consumer about product features that create the greatest amount of user satisfaction. These ads also reassure customers that they made the right choice. For example, classic ads for Dial asked, "Aren't you glad you used Dial? Don't you wish everybody did?"

ADVANTAGES OF ADVERTISING

Advertising has many advantages. By controlling what is said, how it is said and where it is said, marketers can develop standardized campaigns that run for extended periods. Over time, these help build a strong brand equity position. Moreover, advertising is a very cost-effective way to reach large audiences. For example, one 30-second network TV spot in prime time would currently cost less than one cent per customer and reach on average 12 million households. No other promotional method comes close to accomplishing that kind of exposure at such low rates.

The availability of advertising media such as television, radio, newspapers, magazines, the internet, social media and billboards makes it easy to reach most audiences. Because advertising is used so much, it's easy for marketers to find excellent agencies that can help research markets, develop campaigns and manage the entire process. The advantages of advertising can be summarized as follows.

istock.com / MaxOzerov

Coca Cola, Hyundai, Samsung and Pandora are seen on the famous screens at Picaddilly Circus in London, an excellent place for advertisement exposure.

Advertising:

- controls the content, presentation and placement of messages.
- builds brand position and equity over time.
- is cost-effective for large audiences.
- serves many communication needs—awareness, information, reminder.
- can reach most audiences.
- professionals are available to create effective advertising.

Advertising does have some disadvantages. First, it's difficult to direct an ad at only the target audience because many others may be exposed to it. Also, because consumers often distrust ads and try to avoid them, advertising campaigns may need to run for a long time, repeating the message so it is eventually absorbed. Finally, advertising is expensive; it's not unusual for some companies or industries to spend hundreds of millions of dollars on advertising. The disadvantages of advertising can be summarized as follows.

Advertising:

- reaches many nonusers.
- has a high level of audience avoidance.
- contains brief one-way messages.
- can be costly in the the long run.

CATEGORIES OF ADVERTISING

NATIONAL OR BRAND ADVERTISING

Advertising that focuses on brand identity and positioning throughout the country.

Advertising falls into various categories depending on its objectives, target audience and type of message. Most marketers use one or more of the eight types described in Figure 13.2.

Category	Description
National and Global (Brand) Advertising	Focuses on brand identity nationwide (globally). Aims to develop a distinctive brand image.
Retail (Local) Advertising	Focuses on local retail areas. Emphasizes positive attributes of retail outlets.
Directory Advertising	Company listings in a directory. Important to most businesses and retailers. Uses a short differentiating message.
Business-to-Business Advertising	Directed at professionals. Often communicates technical content. Common media include business publications and professional journals.
Institutional Advertising	Communicates corporate identity and philosophy. Describes social and ecological responsibilities of a company.
Direct-Response Advertising	Appeals directly to individual consumers. Usual delivery methods are telephone and mail.
Public Service Advertising	Supports public issues. Usually created for free and media donate space and time.
Political Advertising	Aimed at obtaining votes for issues or political candidates.

Figure 13.2   Categories of Advertising

National or brand advertising, as the name implies, focuses on brand identity such as Delmonte or Pepsi, and positioning it throughout the country. The aim is to develop a distinctive brand image in the mind of the consumer. While often known as national advertising, the same strategy can apply to a global market.

RETAIL (LOCAL) ADVERTISING

Advertising that focuses attention on nearby outlets where products and services can be purchased.

Retail (local) advertising attempts to draw attention to relatively nearby establishments, such as local restaurants. The emphasis is on attributes that will stimulate people to shop there, such as price, location, convenience or customer service.

DIRECTORY ADVERTISING

A listing of businesses, their addresses, phone numbers and sometimes brief descriptions in a publication.

Directory advertising is a listing of businesses, their addresses, phone numbers and sometimes brief descriptions in a publication such as the Yellow Pages. A short, differentiating message can be critical, since so many competitors also advertise there. Businesses usually consider directories extremely important because most consumers turn to them only when they have made the decision to buy a product.

BUSINESS-TO-BUSINESS ADVERTISING

Advertisements to businesses and professionals.

Business-to-business advertising sends messages, often providing technical information, to a variety of organizations ranging from healthcare providers to accountants, lawyers and manufacturers. In the health-care field, for example, publications such as the *Journal of the American Medical Association* carry extensive advertising of pharmaceutical products of all types.

INSTITUTIONAL ADVERTISING

Messages designed to communicate corporate identity and philosophy as opposed to product information.

DIRECT RESPONSE ADVERTISING

Targets individual consumers to get immediate sales.

PUBLIC SERVICE ADVERTISING

Free advertising that supports societal issues.

POLITICAL ADVERTISING

Advertising to influence voters.

ADVERTISING AGENCIES

A business that develops, prepares, and places advertising for sellers seeking to find customers for their products.

Institutional advertising is designed to communicate corporate identity and philosophy rather than messages about individual products. It describes the company's social and ecological responsibilities. The Environmental Working Group works to protect health and the environment; for example, its website features a "take action" tab where visitors can contact the FDA to protest Bisphenol A (BPA) being allowed in cans and bottles; support the Local Farms, Food and Jobs Act; and sign a petition for safer cosmetics.[4]

Direct response advertising targets individual consumers with the intent of obtaining immediate sales. Sales are stimulated through appeals by telephone, mail, the internet, social media, and TV infomercials; the product is then delivered to the customer's home or business. Companies such as Federal Express and UPS have helped to facilitate the dramatic increase in sales from direct-response advertising.

Public service advertising support societal issues like smoking cessation or the prevention of child abuse. These announcements are usually created free by advertising agencies, and the space or airtime is donated by the media. Sometimes they are partially supported by charitable organizations or the government. The Ad Council and the Free to Be Foundation recently teamed up for a new series of anti-bullying ads urging parents to "teach your kids how to be more than a bystander." The campaign uses television, print and online ads to convey its message.[5]

Political advertising is aimed at influencing voters in favor of individuals or particular ballot issues. It has come under harsh criticism for mudslinging, negative and sometimes false accusations against political candidates, and the lack of focus on substantive issues.

ADVERTISING AGENCIES

Advertising agencies are independent businesses that develop, prepare and place advertising in the appropriate media. Most companies, even large, established corporations, outsource some or all of these services. In fact, more than 90 percent of all advertising is placed through outside agencies. The cost-effectiveness of outside agencies makes this a good choice for most companies. There are more than 10,000 ad agencies in the U.S. alone, and as in any industry, some are very large and many are small. Big companies, such as WPP Group (UK) or Omnicom, have offices in nearly every major country to provide the services required for global marketers.

> There are more than 10,000 ad agencies in the U.S. alone, and as in any industry, some are very large and many are small.

In addition to full-service agencies, many specialize in certain advertising functions or in selected industries. For example, Creative Boutiques focuses primarily on developing ideas for advertising. In many cases, industries have certain unique needs. The health-care industry is a good example. Purohit Navigation of Chicago, Illinois, is an expert in that kind of advertising, which requires knowledge of extensive regulation of health-care ads by the Federal Drug Administration. Some agencies focus on certain target groups. L3 Advertising Inc. has expertise in the growing Asian market. It has helped major companies like Verizon and Pepsi to successfully reach the Asian demographic.[6] Other advertising agencies specialize in various minorities.

The Advertising Plan

When a company or agency develops an advertising plan, it follows the five major steps outlined in Figure 13.3. The process begins by setting objectives and determining the budget. Marketers then develop their message and a theme (creative concept) to convey it. Next, they select the media that will most effectively present their message and set a

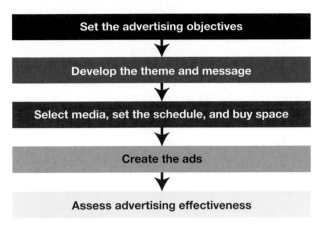

Figure 13.3 Steps in the Advertising Plan

schedule. At this point, they actually create the ads. Once they have had time for audiences to recognize them, the company evaluates their effectiveness.

SETTING OBJECTIVES

Each objective should be developed in such a way that its accomplishment can be measured. Remember that advertising should support the communications plan, which in turn supports the strategic marketing plan. As Figure 13.4 suggests, the goals of informing, persuading, reminding and reinforcing should be accompanied by specific objectives, such as: increase sales, establish brand position, increase awareness, support the sales force or distributors, maintain awareness or introduce a new brand.

DEVELOPING THE ADVERTISING BUDGET

Figure 13.4 Advertising Objectives

As we mentioned before, advertising can be expensive in total, although quite cost-effective on a per-person basis. In setting the budget, the first question to answer is how much will it cost to accomplish the objective? Most advertising budgets are determined using one of the following methods: percentage of sales method, competitive budgeting method, payout plan method or task method.

The **percentage of sales method** for developing the advertising budget involves simply estimating the desired sales level and then allocating a certain percentage of sales to advertising. Often this percentage is equal to the industry average. In some cases, the percentage of sales method is performed by taking a percentage of the previous year's sales and allocating it to advertising. The problem with this method is that sales are used to create the advertising budget when, in fact, advertising should be used to create sales. However, the method is used widely because it is very easy to administer.

The **competitive budgeting method** involves determining what competitors are spending and setting the advertising budget accordingly. Large companies use this method to maintain a strong presence in the eye of the consumer.

The **payout method** is generally used for new products that require high advertising expenditures. In this case, the marketer estimates future sales and establishes the advertising budget required to gain initial acceptance and trial of the product. Generally, these expenditures are very high relative to sales and in some cases even exceed sales. The large expenditures are deemed reasonable because of the payback that occurs in later years. This is similar to investing money in product development.

The **task method** sets specific sales targets or other objectives and then determines what advertising activities and amounts are required to accomplish those objectives. This approach can be extremely complex. Advertisers who use the task method rely on accurate information experience and extensive models developed for the purpose. It tends to be used by large organizations in highly competitive environments. It's superior to the other methods because so much attention to detail is given in determining how advertising contributes toward accomplishment of objectives.

PERCENTAGE OF SALES METHOD

Allocating a percentage of estimated sales to advertising.

COMPETITIVE BUDGETING METHOD

Setting the advertising expenditures relative to what competitors spend.

PAYOUT METHOD

Setting the ad budget to gain initial acceptance and trial.

TASK METHOD

Setting the advertising budget based on activities required to accomplish objectives.

DEVELOPING THE THEME AND MESSAGE

Once objectives are in place and the budget has been established, it is time to develop the theme and message—the **creative strategy**—that will govern and coordinate the development of individual ads and assure that their visual images and words convey precisely and consistently what the advertiser wishes to communicate. Be careful not to confuse this overall strategy with the creative work in putting a specific ad together. The message is a fairly straightforward outgrowth of the marketer's understanding of consumer behavior, information processing and the advertising objectives.

An **advertising campaign** is a series of different ads with the same creative strategy. Because one ad tends to have very little effect, campaigns are required to sustain the message and accomplish the objectives. There is usually an element of continuity across a campaign, with ads featuring recurring music, settings or characters, such as the pink Energizer bunny that keeps going and going through any number of ads. Other examples are Charmin's bears and Kellogg's Tony the Tiger commercials for Frosted Flakes. To be effective, an advertising campaign's theme and message must reach the consumer and be creative, understandable and memorable.

Reaching the Consumer Before an ad can benefit a company at all, it must reach its target audience. **Exposure** is the process of putting the ad in contact with the market. Once that is done, it's up to the ad's content to communicate the message. A good advertisement addresses nearly every aspect of consumer behavior in a package that captures interest and keeps it until the message is absorbed. Exposure does not ensure attention. As we learned in Chapter 5, the perceptual process filters out a great deal. The ad must have what marketers call **stopping power**—the ability to gain and hold attention. Ads with stopping power demand attention so effectively that they interrupt whatever the person is doing. The best ads gain and hold attention because the consumer finds them interesting and relevant to his or her lifestyle. Sometimes catchy music, humor or an association with a celebrity works. Some phrases may gain immediate attention from certain people: lose weight, quick cash, retire early, pay off debts, work at home, free, new, amazing, now and easy. On the other hand, some catch phrases have been so overused by advertisers that many people immediately tune out messages containing them.

Creativity Originality and uniqueness are very important in advertisements. On one hand, ads that are too unusual may not work, because people have difficulty relating to them. On the other hand, creative, humorous, upbeat ads that provide some novelty tend to gain more attention than the same old thing. Coca-Cola also captured viewers with its animated polar bears, which people considered to be heartwarming, creative and fun."

Once a consumer gives an advertisement his or her attention, he or she is likely to become aware of the message and internalize it. **Pulling power** holds the interest of the consumer to the end of the message. Most advertisers insist that the message must relate to some aspect of the recipient's life. Celebrities, for instance, have reference group appeal. Proactiv acne skin-care system ads in recent years featured entertainers such as Adam Levine, Olivia Munn and Julianne Hough.[7]

Understandability Although most ads don't attempt to say everything about a product, it's important that the information selected for communication be clearly under-

WHY HE TRIED PROACTIV+

" I'll be honest. **As a teenager, I had horrible breakouts.** I would hide from cameras, hide in my room. **I was just ashamed of my acne** ...Today, even though I'm a celebrity, I'm no different than anyone else. Acne just shows up and causes trouble. And it can mess with your confidence. "

WHAT HE LOVES ABOUT PROACTIV+

"This new Proactiv+ is awesome. It clears the acne blemishes, plus it can give you great-looking skin. Done and done .. Acne may be good at destroying self-confidence, but Proactiv+ is good at destroying acne."

Adam Levine has been a long-time celebrity endorser for Proactiv.

Slogan	Product or Brand
Now That's Better*	Wendy's Restaurants
Mobilizing Your World*	AT&T
Welcome In*	American Express
Just Do It	Nike
Live for Now	Pepsi
Innovation That Excites*	Nissan
Breakfast of Champions	Wheaties
Imagination at Work	General Electric
I'm Lovin' it.	McDonald's
Zoom Zoom	Mazda
Good to the Last Drop	Maxwell House
Obey Your Thirst	Sprite
Sometimes You Feel Like a Nut	Almond Joy
Let's Fly Together	United Airlines

*Used for 2 years or less

Figure 13.5   Modern Advertising Slogans

stood or it will not be remembered. Procter & Gamble communicated the benefits of its portable stain-removal pen, "Tide to Go," through a series of ads featuring "immediate results with a remarkable handy touch." Viewers have a clear understanding of what the product can do when the items are shown stain-free from the application of "Tide to Go."[8]

Memorability It's important that ads be memorable so that they are retained for some time. A high initial effect is useless if forgotten before the consumer actually purchases the product. One way to achieve this is through repetition. An ad usually must be seen at least three times before it moves into long-term memory. Jingles, slogans and tag lines also help ensure recall. How many of the popular slogans listed in Figure 13.5 do you recognize?

SELECTING AND SCHEDULING MEDIA

MEDIA

The channels through which messages are transmitted.

Media Options **Media** are the channels through which messages are transmitted from the sender to the receiver. Each medium has unique advantages and disadvantages, as described in Figure 13.6 on the next page.

Newspapers A highly credible and flexible medium, newspapers offer wide exposure to upscale adults. Many newspapers have prestige because of their positive impact on communities, and newspapers can also facilitate coordination between local and national advertising. Recently, however, newspapers have lost ground to television and the, so their effectiveness has declined. Daily circulation has declined 30 percent from 1990, to approximately 45 million today.[9] Newspaper companies have attempted to adapt by selling advertising on their websites and by sometimes requiring users to subscribe to access online articles.

Television Television is also a credible source and is extremely cost-efficient per person. It provides the creative flexibility to use both video and audio, allowing an unlimited range of spokespersons and themes. The disadvantages are high production costs and low recall of messages. Television is filled with advertising, which makes competition for the viewer's attention fierce and many consumers change the channel when commercials air. Additionally, with more people owning DVRs, the ability to bypass commercials altogether is compelling. Consequently, television ads need to be rerun often to be effective.

Radio Very low production costs make radio an attractive medium. Furthermore, marketers can be extremely selective in targeting U.S. consumers, because each market area averages 30 stations, each aimed at a specific audience. In the past, it was difficult to know how effective radio advertising really was, but technology is changing that. Software is available for post-purchase analysis so that ad agencies can estimate the ratings for stations and specific airtimes. Lacking visual content, radio spots require more repetition than television ads. As methods for audience rating improve, however, it should be possible to use fewer spots and more accurately evaluate each ad's effect on selected segments. Even online radio can be a medium. For example, Pandora, which allows users to customize their own radio stations, features ads between every few songs.

Magazines Magazines also target well-defined consumer segments, and professional journals reach very specific groups. Although about 93 percent of adults read magazines, overall magazine readership is declining. However, magazines still carry about $20 bil-

	Advantages	Disadvantages
Newspapers	Wide exposure for upscale adults Flexible; timely; buyers can save for later reference High credibility	Few ads are fully read Costs are rising Alternate media replacing Newspapers
Television	Creative and flexible Cost efficient Credible	Message quickly forgotten High production cost Difficult to get attention
Radio	Selective targeting possible Mobile—goes with listeners Low production costs	No visual content High frequency required to reach many people Audience research difficult
Magazines	Target narrowly defined segments Prestigious sources Long life—can be passed along	Audiences declining Long lead times to develop ads Need to use many different magazines to reach a lot of buyers
Outdoor Ads	Low cost per exposure Good to supplement other media With color, lighting, and mechanization gets attention	Can't communicate much Difficult to measure results
Internet	Considerable potential Medium for relationship marketing Customer driven and dialogue oriented Increasing number of users	Relies on consumers accessing the necessary technologies Revenues still small Difficult to target a specific audience Difficult to measure results
Social Media	High for relationship marketing Quickly growing Spreads quickly through viral channels	Rapidly changing and evolving Few guarantees for advertisers Must conform to rules set by privately owned companies
Mobile	Technological flexibility Excellent means to reach younger generations	Potential to annoy consumers Few standardizations in technologies

Figure 13.6   Advantages and Disadvantages of Various Media

lion worth of advertising, and more than three-quarters of Americans have purchased a product after seeing or reading about it in a magazine.[10] In the past few years, many "small" magazines have been introduced to appeal to unique tastes, which makes more finely tuned targeting possible. The disadvantages of magazines are long lead times and high production costs for ads. In efforts to target more finely, new techniques for producing special ads are being designed that will bring costs down. Magazines that focus on particular hobbies and interests allow advertisers to get very close to unique markets.

Outdoor Advertising Outdoor advertisements, primarily billboards, are very inexpensive per exposure, so they provide an attractive supplement to other media. With color, lighting and mechanization, some billboards have fantastic stopping power. Even though advertising in general has been declining, outdoor advertisements have increased steadily. Moreover, digital technology has been applied to outdoor advertising ,and this medium is expected to broaden vividly for several years. Digital outdoor advertising is managed by the internet and benefits from ads that can be changed in a short period of time; therefore, it is expected to be more useful than standard outdoor advertising to do strategic promotions.

The 2014 Tour de France began with Prince William, Prince Harry and the Duchess of Cambridge, Kate Middleton, cutting the ribbon to start a three-day tour of the United Kingdom, ending in front of Buckingham Palace. Transport for London (TfL) effectively used colorful outdoor advertisements to bring attention to the event while also warning Londoners about road closures and areas that would be affected. It also encouraged the use of its website, where travelers could plan and map out their trip. Miranda Leedham, head of marketing operations at TfL, said: "As well as capturing the excitement of such an iconic event, we also wanted to ensure the city is prepared for its arrival by informing our customers of the travel options available to them. This communication helps to build our reputation for hosting major sporting events by ensuring the city is ready for the impact on travel."[11] According to the NBC Sports Network broadcast, the event attracted nearly five million people to

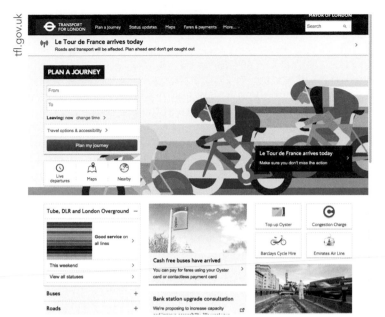

watch the race in person.[12] Bostik, a leading global adhesive specialist, renewed its sponsorship of the Tour de France cycling event in 2016. A series of marketing and promotional activities coincided with the sponsorship of the race, which included an outdoor advertising campaign in two prominent locations on Paris' 'peripherique' highway. This transit route is one of the Europe's busiest, which is traveled by an estimated 2 million vehicles each day.[13] Despite their flashiness, outdoor ads can't communicate a great amount of information, because people move past them so quickly. It's often difficult to measure the results of outdoor advertisements.

The Internet The internet provides a medium that is both customer-driven and dialogue-oriented. More than three-quarters of the U.S. uses the internet, and research of the products on the internet controls almost half of all retail purchases. This gives companies another way to develop relationships with customers through websites that provide many messages about their products or services, and other information that builds a good, solid relationship with customers. Oral-B's website has a learning center section where customers are able to access not only product information but tips for good oral care habits and most effective product use.[14] The internet allows advertising to occur in forms of banners, pop-up ads, pop-under ads and interstitials (web pages displayed before or after an expected content page).[15] Google Analytics and Google AdWords are two services that track visitors on a company's website and online banner advertisements, determining what keywords attract the most desirable prospects, what advertising copy pulled the most responses and what landing pages and content make the most money for a client.[16]

Transport for London used outdoor advertising to bring attention to the Tour de France, and also warned Londoners about road closures. Its website allowed users to plan their route while the event took place.

A major disadvantage of internet marketing is low click-through rates, as users ignore banner ads for the most part. However, the internet is the key tool in **viral marketing**, or diffusing a marketing message across several groups of people. Marketers can extend their message in a very limited, extremely cost-efficient format, ensure that a few people receive it and allow them to spread it through word-of-mouth discussion. As viral marketing develops, it becomes increasingly important to find an accurate method of tracking its effectiveness, which is what marketers are still attempting to discover.[17] Ford created a viral campaign for the Ford Fiesta with Fiesta Movement, an online competition in which 100 winners were given free gas and a brand-new Fiesta for six months, long before its release date. Winners were given a camera and a monthly challenge to complete and document in their Fiesta. Mission themes included travel, entertainment, social activism and adventure. Contestants submitted their videos to the Fiesta Movement website as well as their own YouTube pages. Ford has generated great promotion with this viral campaign and has helped to position the Fiesta as a fuel-efficient car for the hip and adventurous. Four thousand entrants submitted videos to Ford explaining why they were perfect for the Fiesta Movement challenge, and the winners have collectively generated millions of hits through their YouTube pages and the Fiesta Movement website.[18]

VIRAL MARKETING

Diffusing a marketing message across people.

Social Media Many companies have recently taken advantage of marketing through social-media sites like Facebook, Twitter and LinkedIn. Although social media has millions of participants, there are no guarantees for advertisers, many of whom have not yet found an effective method of cutting through the clutter. Some companies opt to scan sites like Facebook and Twitter looking for positive and negative mentions of their companies or brands. Many companies opt to use social media as a way of advertising, and some use it as a way of running contests and promotions, as well. Detroit's Faygo Beverages, Inc. introduced its newest flavor, Faygo Cotton Candy in 2014, with a summer contest using Instagram. Faygo fans are encouraged to photograph themselves and upload it to Instagram using hashtag,

#FaygoCottonCandy. The top three photos that generate the most "likes" will win prizes including Cedar Point tickets and a bicycle, valued at $699 from its promotion partner, Detroit Bikes.[19]

Mobile Mobile advertising means delivering text and video messages of ads to cell phones. Marketers are expecting to extend their messaging from offline to online and mobile handsets. Many internet advertisers have already tried mobile messaging marketing. According to eMarketer, mobile ad spending will grow faster than any other ad channel in the US this year, an 83 percent increase to reach $17.7 billion.[20] This trend is likely to continue as people spend more time on smartphones and tablets. If predictions are correct, mobile advertising will become the second-largest ad channel in 2018, behind only television.[21] Marketers expect this medium will be especially valuable for targeting younger generations.

Media Popularity Which media do the major advertisers select? Figure 13.6 illustrates a distribution of global advertising expenditures for 2013 and projected 2016. TV advertising is most popular, followed by newspapers, internet, magazines, radio, outdoor and mobile respectively. You will notice that the projected growth in mobile will most likely come at the expense of newspaper and magazine advertising.

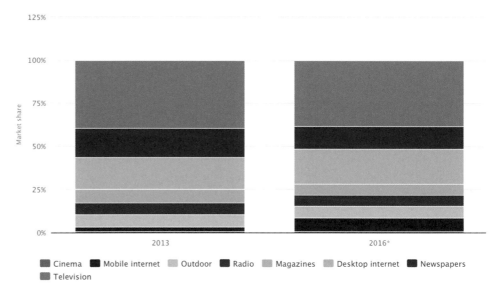

Figure 13.7   Distribution of Global Advertising Expenditure in 2013 and 2016, by Media.
Source: ZenithOptimedia, © Statista, 2014.

The Media Schedule Media scheduling can be viewed as a plan within the advertising plan. This very exact work involves a number of considerations: target audience analysis; reach, frequency and continuity balance; media timing; and budgeting.

Target Audience As you know, the marketing plan is always directed at specific market segments. Marketers have developed very detailed methods for defining their targets. For example, Claritas Corporation created PRIZM, which uses such variables as socioeconomic status, ethnicity, family life cycle, education, employment, type of housing and location of housing to describe 40 audiences. In turn, these data are correlated with media usage patterns. The information helps determine which media are likely to influence the respective segments at various times and locations.

Media scheduling usually is done geographically and demographically. For example, Taco Bell, McDonald's and Burger King all compete for the fast-food dollar in the United States, but Taco Bell targets males aged 19 to 24, whereas the other two include families with children.

Once decisions are made about target audience and geographic considerations, media planners calculate the cost of communicating with the audience through various media. Media costs are generally expressed in units of cost per thousand, abbreviated as CPM (M is the Roman numeral for 1,000). The CPM for reaching the target audience is calculated as follows:

$$CPM = \frac{\text{Advertising cost X 1,000}}{\text{Circulation to target audience}}$$

Suppose we are interested in reaching women with children younger than 2. We know that McCall's has 600,000 readers in this category, and an advertisement there will cost $60,000. The CPM of reaching our target audience is $100 ($60,000 times 1,000 divided by 600,000 = $100). We can then determine the cost per person by dividing CPM by 1,000. In this case it is $0.10 ($100 divided by 1,000 = $0.10).

Reach, Frequency and Continuity Balance Once media planners know the target audience and the cost of reaching it, they consider the reach, frequency and continuity of the advertising campaign. **Reach** is the number of consumers in the target audience who can be contacted through a given medium. In the preceding example the reach through McCall's is 600,000. **Frequency** is the number of times the audience is contacted during a given period, usually over four weeks. **Continuity** is the length of time the advertising campaign will run in a given medium. It is important to select a medium with enough reach, frequency and continuity to gain the desired effect. At the same time, agencies do not want to waste funds. **Overexposure** refers to reaching a prospect either after a purchase decision has been made or so frequently that the campaign actually wastes money.

Media Timing Products may be seasonal or purchased more frequently on certain days of the week. For example, sunblock is bought mainly during the summer and especially on weekends. Products such as soaps and cosmetics are purchased frequently all year round and may require constant advertising. Consider the importance of media timing for advertising weight-loss products. Companies such as Weight Watchers, Curves and Jenny Craig Inc. spend millions of dollars on television and print ads every January, since about half of all dieters initiate a program between January and April.

To complicate matters, it's important to look at the activity of competitors. Depending on the resources of the company, it may be necessary to counteract the competitions' campaigns or take advantage of times when they tend to promote less. Tactics include selecting media that competitors are not using or making adjustments to the scheduling, timing and frequency of various advertisements.

Media Budget Generally, the media budget is set according to the strategic marketing and communication plans. Marketers attempt to maximize the advertising effort within budget constraints, using one or a combination of media to achieve the most influence in the market. As part of the media plan, it's important to determine whether messages will be visual, verbal or both. The amount of information to be communicated will influence the choice of media and, consequently, the budget. Recently, the costs of all forms have been escalating, so careful attention must be paid to the trade-offs among them. Fortunately, media competition helps temper rising costs, since the media themselves have marketers that each hope to make their medium more attractive. To accommodate clients, they are willing to provide help in media selection and scheduling.

CREATING ADS

This step in the ad plan involves both science and art. Creating ads can be as complicated as making a movie. The key is to know your objectives and the constraints imposed by the

REACH

The number of consumers in the target audience who can be contacted through a given medium.

FREQUENCY

The number of times the audience is reached in a given period, usually per day or per week.

CONTINUITY

The length of time the advertising campaign will run in a given medium.

OVEREXPOSURE

Continuing to reach a prospect after a buying decision has been made or to the point that the campaign becomes tedious and actually turns off some potential buyers.

You Tube SCAN & WATCH ▶

Most people old enough to have watched the 2000 Superbowl, will likely relate the slang phrase "Wasssup?!" to Budweiser.

media, scheduling and budget. As with any creative process, it's difficult to determine precisely what people will like and remember. To help answer that question, Marketing, a British journal, conducts a survey each month called "ad watch." British consumers are asked whether or not they remember a specific advertisement.

In the U.S., there are certainly many classics. The California raisins who "heard it through the grapevine" combined humor, visual novelty and a great rock beat that caught the attention of millions in the 1980s. Most of the older generations still remember Mikey, who willingly ate Life cereal. And nearly everyone (if old enough) can recall the Budweiser "Wassssup?!" commercials.

When diverse segments are part of the target audience, the advertisement must be created in such a way that it appeals to various tastes and preferences. Marketers also need to be aware of language differences, acceptable behaviors, ethnicity and cultural norms. Many current promotional efforts are aimed at a global audience, and that means communicating in a variety of languages and dialects. To avoid costly mistakes, it is critical for marketers to research and understand the language(s) of a target market segment before advertising to it. For example, in Italy, a campaign for Schweppes tonic water referred to the product as Schweppes toilet water, and Kentucky Fried Chicken's slogan in China became "eat your fingers off" rather than "finger-lickin' good."[22]

ASSESSING ADVERTISING EFFECTIVENESS

The effect of advertising can be assessed at two different points: before running the ad campaign and afterward. This kind of measurement is extremely important to determine what does and doesn't work so that the campaign can be adjusted.

Individual ads and campaigns may be tested to evaluate effectiveness before committing more funds. Various recall and recognition tests are used on the sample audience to determine whether the ad content has been stored in the consumer's memory. One test asks the audience what it remembers about an ad after a limited run in a particular medium. These tests usually attempt to measure two types of recall. **Unaided recall** asks the viewer to identify any advertisements he or she can recall, such as "What commercials do you remember seeing for automobiles?" **Aided recall** refers to content that can be remembered without seeing the particular ad. An example is: "Do you recall seeing a commercial for Honda?" By questioning several respondents, researchers determine both the unaided and aided recall scores. These tests may be conducted immediately following exposure to the ad or up to several days thereafter.

Recognition means that you remember the ad when you see it again. This kind of remembrance is typically adequate for low-involvement products such as chewing gum or soup. To test recognition, audience members are shown an ad and later are asked if they remember it. In other words, the ad is a stimulus during the testing procedure. One of the most popular types of recognition test is the Starch test, which is usually conducted after an ad has been run. Respondents leaf through a magazine containing the ad and are then asked if they remember seeing it. Next, a series of questions determines whether they associated the ad with the advertiser's name or logo and whether they read at least half of the copy. Because Starch tests have been run on so many ads, marketers can compare the scores of their ad to similar types.

When persuasion is the objective of the advertisement, it is very important to go beyond simple memory tests and determine whether the ad influences attitudes or be-

UNAIDED RECALL

The viewer is asked to identify any advertisements he or she can remember.

AIDED RECALL

The viewer is given some specific piece of information about the ad before being asked if he or she recalls having seen it.

havior. For this, marketers use persuasion tests, which essentially measure attitude change. For example, respondents may be asked to preview a particular television show with ads embedded in it. They are then questioned about the program itself as well as brand preferences. Comparing the answers to measures taken beforehand, it's possible to determine the amount of attitude change.

Sales Promotion

Sales promotion is communication designed to stimulate immediate purchases using tools such as coupons, contests and free samples.[23] Notice that the definition focuses on immediate results and changes in the behavior of consumers or other channel members. In addition to its value as a short-term incentive, there is no doubt that sales promotion for many brands has a lot to do with long-term brand equity, particularly frequently purchased items like Coke and Pepsi. Sales promotion plays an important role in reinforcing continuous usage and offsetting gains made by competitors. When brand switching occurs, sales promotion is a valuable way to regain consumer loyalty.

> Sales promotion plays an important role in reinforcing continuous usage and offsetting gains made by competitors.

Sales promotion also stimulates trial. Many times buyers are reluctant to try a new product because it may not perform as well as their existing one. Sales promotion reduces the risk by lowering the price or creating other incentives. Car dealers are usually expected to offer test drives, and many food-based companies provide free samples.

Whereas advertising and public relations increase awareness, sales promotion prompts people to action, resulting in immediate sales. By either increasing the perceived value of a product or reducing its price, sales promotion motivates customers to make an immediate purchase decision. A promotion can increase value by providing a complimentary gift, an unusual warranty or other rewards. Price may be lowered directly, with an introductory offer, or through coupons and rebates. These concepts can also be combined by "bundling" products together for a lower total price than if purchased separately. In any case, the consumer recognizes an immediate opportunity and acts on it.

Although sales promotion generally has an immediate result, its long-term effects are less clear. It is most commonly used in conjunction with other forms of promotion, such as advertising, public relations campaigns or personal selling. Consequently, it is usually seen as part of the total promotion package designed by the marketing communication strategists.

SALES PROMOTION

Communications designed to stimulate immediate purchases using tools such as coupons, contests, and free samples.

BUSINESS-TO-BUSINESS PROMOTIONS

Tools designed to stimulate B2B purchases such as trade shows, conventions, sales incentives and specialty items.

TYPES OF SALES PROMOTION

Figure 13.8 depicts the relationship of four different types of sales promotion: business-to-business, consumer, trade and retailer promotions. Figure 13.9, found on the next page, lists typical activities in each category.

Business-to-business promotions usually involve trade shows, conventions, sales incentives and specialty deals, such as volume discounts and price sales. Manufacturers use two basic approaches to influence the consumer: the sales pull and the sales

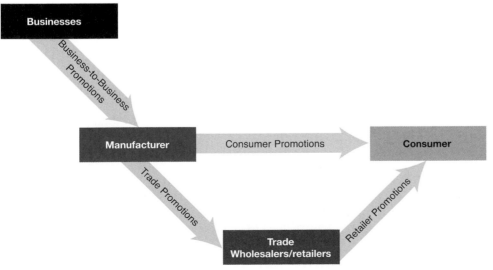

Figure 13.8   Relationship of Sales Promotions

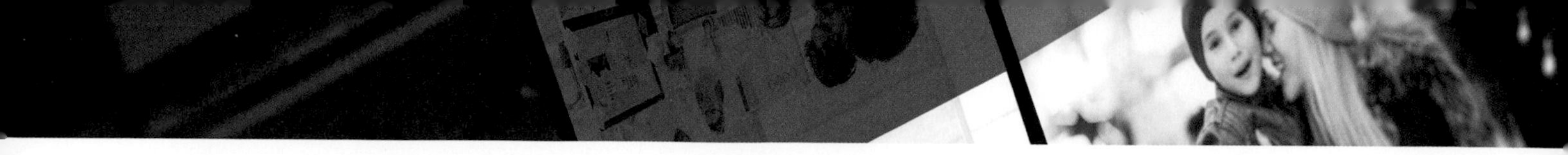

Business-to-Business Promotions	Manufacturer Trade Promotions	Manufacturer Consumer Promotions	Retailer Consumer Promotions
Trade shows Conventions Sales Incentives Specialty items	Discounts • off invoice • off list Allowances • advertising • display Financing incentives Contests Spiffs	Coupons Rebates (refunds) Samples Price packs ("cents off") Value packs ("2 for 1") Premiums (gifts) Sweepstakes (prizes and contests) Point-of-purchase displays Cross-promotion Continuity programs	Price cuts Displays Free goods ("trials") Retailer coupons Feature advertising Patronage awards

Figure 13.9   Major Types of Sales Promotion Activities

CONSUMER PROMOTIONS

Offer designed to pull the product through the retail establishment.

TRADE PROMOTIONS

An offer from a manufacturer to channel members, such as wholesalers and retailers.

RETAILER PROMOTIONS

An offer to the consumer that is sponsored by a retailer.

push. **Consumer promotions** are manufacturer incentives offered directly to consumers, largely bypassing the retailer. They are designed to pull the product through the retail establishment with coupons, rebates and other means that the manufacturer can control from headquarters.

Trade promotions are provided by manufacturers to distribution channel members. The objective is to give wholesalers and retailers an incentive to sell the manufacturer's brand. Essentially, these promotions make it worthwhile for the channel member to push the product to the consumer. Common incentives are advertising allowances and price reductions. For example, Ralston Purina may offer a three percent discount on Cat Chow to retailers, in hopes that retailers will pass the savings on to customers so more items are moved.

Retailer promotions are directed at the consumer by the retail outlet. They are often confined to a local area, although large chains such as Best Buy may run many of the same promotions at all locations. This provides a sales level sufficient to obtain quantity discounts from suppliers, which enables prices to be kept low.

Normally, the push and pull elements of the sales promotion strategy should work hand-in-hand. The sales force works to persuade customers (retailers or wholesalers) to purchase greater volume and push to consumers through retailer promotions. At the same time, the marketers are coordinating consumer promotions with ad messages about coupons and point-of-purchase displays tied into the advertising theme. This kind of one-two punch can produce dramatic results.

THE SUCCESS OF SALES PROMOTION

Sales promotion has become increasingly successful due to changing consumer lifestyles, improving technology and the evolving structure of the retail industry. Stores need to present themselves as destinations.[24] Today's busy consumers are looking for ways to simplify purchase choices in order to save time. In addition, they want value, and they view sales promotion as a way of getting more for their money.

Technology helps marketers target sales promotions more precisely than ever before. Checkout scanners can instantly identify a brand being purchased, sorting machines can trace the origin of coupons and other redemption items, and tracking devices identify the location and consumer involved in a purchase. It's now very easy for marketers to measure the effect of specific promotion activities on unit sales and profitability. The internet has also begun to track consumer spending patterns.

Another influence on the use of promotions is the changing structure of the retail industry. As large establishments such as Walmart gain market power, they can compete more effectively with manufacturers' brands. To counteract this power, manufacturers use sales promotion to create a pull through the channel to maintain their customer base. At the same time, they are engaged in competitive battles to maintain market share. A company that wants to hold onto market share is almost required to use sales promotions commensurate with those of other major competitors, whether retailers or other manufacturers.

CREATING CUSTOMER RELATIONSHIPS & LOYALTY THROUGH SALES PROMOTION

Sales promotion is an excellent tool for organizations that want to connect with customers through relationships. The purpose of relationship marketing is to create loyal, satisfied customers. Consumers can be very fickle, however, and marketers must keep that constantly in mind. Relational marketing and customer relationship management have received considerable attention by managers. One study finds that, among business managers, relationship marketing is becoming institutionalized. That is, relationship marketing has been so widely discussed that managers now perceive it is a standard practice to implement it in business-to-business exchange relationships.[25] Figure 13.10 describes the four main categories of buyers and strategies for marketing to each group.

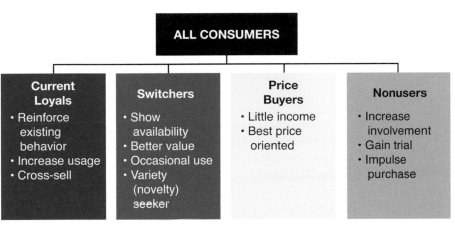

Figure 13.10   Types of Buyers

Current Loyals As the name implies, current loyals are presently purchasing a company's brand. They range from intensely loyal users who buy because of their relationship with the company to people who are loyal because of simple convenience or price factors. In either case, it is difficult to persuade this group to switch brands. One strategy used to maintain these customers is to reward their loyalty with personally targeted one-to-one promotions. This encourages them to continue using the brand, further forges a unique relationship with them, and reminds them about the product they have been purchasing. Many retail establishments send out e-newsletters and coupons, particularly for special occasions such as birthdays. Others will provide loyalty cards that reward the customer for making purchases.

Loyal consumers also may respond to sales promotions by buying a product in larger quantities or at a time when they normally do not purchase. For example, loyal users of Cheerios will likely view a promotion as an opportunity to stockpile the product. Users of Starkist tuna may buy several cans when the brand is on sale. If they have the product available at home, they are likely to use it more often.

When a manufacturer owns two or more brands, current loyal customers are excellent candidates for **cross-selling**, promoting another of the brands or using one product to boost sales of another, often unrelated product. In many cases the customer doesn't know they are the recipient of cross-selling. When you go to McDonald's and you are asked, "Would you like that 'super-sized'?" or, "Do you want to make that a 'meal deal'?" you are experiencing cross-selling in its most basic form. Amazon uses very sophisticated cross-selling techniques. When a visitor clicks on an item or adds it to a shopping cart, additional related products are displayed for purchase.[26]

Switchers Switchers purchase a number of different brands. In recent years, this category has increased in size as the amount of loyals declined. Consequently, many manufacturers and retailers focus on this group. In many cases, switchers cut their overall expenditures

CROSS-SELLING

Promotion in which the manufacturer of one brand attempts to sell another brand to the same customers, or the purchase of one product is used to stimulate the selection of another, often unrelated product.

by finding the best deal at the time. They may switch regularly or only when they see an opportunity to increase value or decrease price.

Switchers are not likely to wait for an out-of-stock brand, so they respond well to trade promotions that are designed to maximize inventory levels and store space. Since they are interested in price and value, they respond to even fairly complex purchase offers. For example, several units of the same product can be bundled together, the amount of product can be increased for the same price, or the price can be reduced.

Some switchers are simply seeking novelty or variety and change brands to alleviate boredom or monotony. Sales promotions work particularly well on them, since they are responsive to new purchase opportunities. If the product is noticed at the precise time the variety seeker is interested in buying, then the manufacturer benefits. 7-Up positioned itself in a way that distinguishes it not only from colas but also from other non-colas. A new Tropical flavor is in limited edition tall cans, and only available for the 2014 summer.[27]

Price Buyers The price buyer's only concern is cost. Most consumers in this category want low prices, but a few choose only the most expensive brand, equating price with quality. People in the latter category tend to ignore nearly all sales promotion, and they consider clipping coupons a total waste of time. In contrast, buyers after low prices are likely to purchase opportunistically, when they have funds and the product is on sale. They respond very well to price promotions: cents-off, two for one, buy a second one for a penny, limited-time offers and so forth.

Nonusers Nonusers do not currently purchase a particular brand. Sales promotions are designed to create involvement, which may stimulate purchase. Again, cross-selling supplies a trial opportunity. For instance, many Barnes & Noble bookstores have Starbucks cafes inside, encouraging nonusers to try a new drink. Some companies mail samples to nonusers, who will often at least try a free product with no strings attached. In other cases, nonusers are supplied a trial under captive circumstances. An example is the complimentary snacks offered on airlines, such as branded peanuts, pretzels and sodas.

BUSINESS-TO-BUSINESS PROMOTIONS

The four main types of business-to-business promotions are trade shows, conventions, sales incentives and specialty items. Often volume discounts and price sales occur in conjunction with these four activities.

JMPerez / CC BY-SA 3.0

Trade shows account for about 20 percent of the annual marketing budget in B2B companies.

Trade Shows Trade shows are designed to bring marketers and customers together at a given location for a short period. They occur around the world and provide opportunity for companies to display existing and upcoming product lines in ways that are convenient for customers. The majority of large firms use trade shows as a major promotion mechanism. On average, business-to-business marketers spend about 20 percent of an annual marketing budget on trade shows.[28]

Companies set up booths that are staffed by key personnel and salespeople, and it's not unusual for retailers and distributors to select the merchandise they will carry during the coming year. Since they play such an important role in future activity, business marketers may invest a large percentage of their promotional budget in trade shows. Specific shows are very cost-effective ways to meet a great number of potential purchasers.

Today, trade show information is accessible and heavily promoted on the internet. The Biz Trade Shows website is the largest directory of business events and trade fairs on the internet. Companies can quickly identify and select the event that will be the most beneficial in reaching potential customers.[29]

Conventions Conventions provide another opportunity for marketers and buyers to meet. They are often sponsored by professional groups, such as the American Hospital Association, the American Medical Association or the International Association of Certified Public Accountants. It is important to note that conventions are held around the world, giving marketers the chance to assess the level of global competition and gather ideas for new strategies. Although companies attend primarily to stimulate immediate sales, they also can take the opportunity to do long-range assessments of customer and industry trends. Marketing researchers often attend conventions and trade shows because so many qualified buyers are concentrated in one place. This provides a pool of readily available respondents, and schedules often permit in-depth interviews, focus groups and surveys. These events are considered prime opportunities for data collection.

SALES INCENTIVES

Awards for achieving defined goals or levels of activity, such as sales quotas.

SPECIALTY ITEMS

Gifts with the organization's name that are provided to customers, usually given through the mail or by the sales force.

Sales Incentives **Sales incentives** are awards for achieving defined goals or levels of activity, such as sales quotas. Most companies sponsor some type of sales incentive program for salespeople and dealers from time to time, awarding trips, gifts or cash, often at an annual sales convention. Volkswagen, for example, rewards top sellers of its featured models with free trips to exotic locations.[30] This type of sales promotion is designed to elicit immediate action by giving short-term rewards for short-term behavior. When incentives are tied to measurable and achievable sales objectives, they can be highly motivating. Sales contests are frequently tailored to specific product lines or market segments and are integrated into the company's overall selling and promotion strategy

Specialty Items **Specialty items** are gifts for customers, usually sent through the mail or handed out by salespeople, often with the organization's name imprinted on them. These are typically small office supplies or clothing items and do not require a purchase. During the holidays, it's common for businesses to also send food items, books, music or decorative items to their largest clients. Specialty items create goodwill with customers and reinforce brand exposure.[31] There are caveats marketers should understand about giving B2B gifts, however. For example, giving gifts during a bidding process is a definite no-no... even if a holiday happens to fall during this time. Also, it's important to know if either the giving or receiving company has policies regarding gifts; some companies prohibit gifts altogether, and others limit the value of gifts.

swissarmy.com

OUR PREMIUM CORPORATE GIFTS

CORPORATE GIFTS FROM VICTORINOX (B2B)

Victorinox offers customizable Swiss Army knives so businesses can create premium corporate B2B gifts.

TRADE PROMOTIONS

Trade promotions are offered by the manufacturer to wholesalers or retailers. The Dubai World Trade Centre in the United

Arab Emirates has become a focal point for international trade promotions, which are becoming increasingly common, by hosting a range of industry events including the Middle East International Motor Show.[32] You can expect nearly every type of trade promotion to be offered by the suppliers. Five common types are discounts, allowances, financing incentives, sales contests and spiffs.

Discounts One of the most popular trade promotions is discount or price-off arrangements, which reduce either the invoice or the list price. The invoice price is what the manufacturer charges to the distributor, whereas the list price is what the end customer is charged. If distributors choose to pass the price cut on to consumers, demand may increase. If not, distributor profit margins increase. Like all trade promotions, discounts encourage distributors to handle more of the company's product and to stimulate sales to consumers

ALLOWANCES

Funds given to retailers and wholesalers based on the amount of product they buy.

FINANCING INCENTIVE

An offer to finance the retailer's inventory prior to its sale.

Allowances **Allowances** are funds given to retailers and wholesalers based on the amount of product they buy. Two typical allowances are for advertising and display purposes. For example, a retailer who purchases $5,000 worth of product may receive a $500 allowance to help pay for advertising. Display allowances work the same way, except that the funds must be used for point-of-purchase displays in the retail outlet.

Financing Incentives **Financing incentives** help reduce the retailer's inventory carrying cost. This is commonly referred to as financing the "floor plan," which is the retailer's stock of inventory. For example, in the automobile business, dealers do not have to pay immediately for all the cars shipped to them, instead paying a fee for having them in their showroom. Financing incentives come in many forms, but all are designed to get the manufacturer's product into the retail establishment.

Sales Contests and Spiffs Two other types of trade promotion are sales contests and "spiffs." In this context, sales contests reward the retailer for selling a certain level of product and often extend to the salespeople within the retail establishment. Spiffs are like a commission paid to salespeople in retail outlets who sell the manufacturer's product rather than a competitor's brand. These cash incentives are not uncommon for such items as cameras, televisions, mobile homes and smartphones. Many people consider spiffs unethical because they encourage the promotion of one brand over others regardless of its value to the customer. Because consumers are not aware of the spiff, they may believe the salesperson's motives are more "pure" than is actually the case.

RETAILER PROMOTIONS

Retailer promotions are directed specifically at the end customer and originate within the retailing organization. They encourage consumers to purchase a product from a given location. Consequently, retailer promotions are often in-store or specific with regard to where the promotion can be exercised.

> Retailer promotions are directed specifically at the end customer and originate within the retailing organization.

The most common type of retailer promotion is cutting prices. Retailers are likely to use price cuts regularly to stimulate sales of certain product lines or to reduce inventory of older products. They will also direct attention to particular goods with display promotions. Large national retailers are likely to send teams on a seasonal basis to work with local outlets in developing similar displays across the country. Gap takes this approach for displays. Some retailers will promote their products with free trials, hoping to draw in future repeat customers. Retailer coupons are used relatively frequently and are often placed in local newspapers. Also popular is radio or television advertising that highlights discounted items, such as automobiles and mobile homes. Finally, patronage awards are very useful promotions. Generally, a card is punched or stamped each time the consumer shops at the retail outlet. When the card is filled, it's redeemed for free merchandise. Some coffee shops redeem not only their own loyalty cards but also those of competitors as a way to get new trials. Patronage awards, which stimulate loyalty to a given outlet, are particularly useful in local markets for creating a bond between regular customers and the retailer.

CONSUMER PROMOTIONS

Manufacturers use consumer sales promotions to influence their market share across all retailing outlets. There are several popular forms: coupons, rebates, samples, sweepstakes, price and value packs, point-of-purchase displays and continuity programs.

COUPON

Certificate that entitles a consumer to an incentive to buy the product, usually a price reduction or a free sample.

Coupons **Coupons** are certificates that entitle a consumer to an incentive, usually a price reduction or free sample. Trade coupons are redeemable only at a particular store or chain, whereas manufacturer coupons are redeemable at any outlet. They are particularly appealing to manufacturers because they can make a direct connection with consumers. Since manufacturers' coupons create work for retailers, they may be given incentives for handling them.

Coupons are one of the most popular forms of consumer sales promotion.

Coupons are one of the most popular forms of consumer sales promotion. Some consumers purchase a large percentage of their nondurable products through coupons and many plan their shopping lists around them. Other consumers do not want to take the time to search for and cut coupons, especially those who are loyal to particular brands and stores.

Paper coupons are generally distributed as freestanding inserts (FSIs) in newspapers or magazines. They can also be sent in special mailings or as bill stuffers. Another technique is on-shelf dispensers at retail outlets, placed near the manufacturer's brand. Only about two percent of regular coupons are redeemed, while checkout coupons see 8.5 percent redeemed, electronic coupons 9.8 percent and on-shelf coupons 13 percent. Marketers try to identify the level of price reduction that will stimulate coupon use. If a 25-cent incentive will do as much as a 50-cent reduction, then the 25-cent incentive should be used.

Mobile coupons are becoming extremely popular. Individual stores and chains usually have their own apps, and customers can also search for same-day coupons on general sites such as RetailMeNot, which carries over 500,000 coupons for more than 50,000 stores. As you're walking into a Sunglass Hut, you can check for coupons on the spot! Companies also tweet coupons to their followers, who forward the coupons onto *their* friends, and so forth. Digital marketing has reduced the cost to companies of coupon promotions, while reaching a larger consumer audience.

REBATE

Refunds given to consumers for the purchase of particular items.

> Rebates tend to be particularly effective in stimulating trial of brands that are priced higher than those of competitors.

Rebates **Rebates** are refunds given to consumers for the purchase of particular items. Psychologically, rebates make a larger impression than price reductions. For example, an automobile manufacturer offers a $1,500 rebate or a 10 percent reduction in price for a $15,000 car. Although the discount may be precisely the same, consumers are likely to see the rebate as greater, since the price discount from $15,000 to $13,500 is a perceptually smaller decrease than the $1,500 rebate. Since consumers usually have to mail a form to the manufacturer to get the rebate, they often will not bother if the amount is small. They also may lose or forget about the rebate, allowing the company to close the sale without paying the incentive. Another advantage of rebates is that they leave higher margins for intermediaries.

Rebates tend to be particularly effective in stimulating trial of brands that are priced higher than those of competitors. Hewlett-Packard frequently runs rebate offers on its printers and other electronic devices. To get the rebate, customers have to submit a completed rebate coupon in addition to a proof-of-purchase sticker. They receive their rebate six to eight weeks after the purchase.

Samples Generally, samples are distributed via direct mail, door-to-door or in stores. Sometimes coupons may be redeemed for free samples. This method is effective with new products or when targeted at people who lack experience with the brand. Occasionally, manufacturers attempt to renew an older product by providing samples. American Sampling Inc. sends gift packs to 3.8 million new mothers annually, and companies such as Market Source provide samples to college freshmen.

This kind of sales promotion requires very careful attention to detail, because the cost of samples is high. One study found that 51 million coupons for a free product distributed through freestanding inserts (FSIs) cost $7 per thousand, whereas 5 million samples distributed through direct mail cost $80 per thousand. But the FSIs only converted 367,200 people ($0.97 per convert), whereas the mail samples converted 800,000 ($0.50 per convert.)[33]

Sweepstakes A sweepstakes is a contest in which participants' names are pooled, and the winner is drawn randomly. Most of you have experienced a twinge of anticipation upon receiving an envelope stating that you may have won millions of dollars. The objective of the contest is to get buyers to purchase the products included in the sweepstakes offer, although laws prevent the sponsor from requiring a purchase in order to participate. Sweepstakes promoters must provide full disclosure of the requirements for entering as well as the probabilities of winning. Visa offers a sweepstakes for users of its credit cards, with the prize of lifetime trips to the Olympic Games. To enter, all you have to do is use your credit card during the games.[34]

Price and Value Packs Price and value packs are cents-off or two-for-one offers. The cents-off variety is easier to administer and receives a great deal of attention. The value pack, while more difficult to administer, gets more product in the hands of the consumer in a shorter period. Both are very flexible and relatively easy sales promotions to consumers. Value packs are different from premiums or gifts, which may not be related directly to the product. For example, in real estate sales, it's not uncommon for the purchaser of a home to receive a free airline ticket to a vacation spot.

Point-of-Purchase Displays

Point-of-purchase (POP) displays exhibit products at retail locations. Since up to 70 percent of purchase decisions are made in a store, the displays can be very important. Companies spend huge amounts annually on POP. More than 52 percent of carbonated beverage sales, 26 percent of candy/mint sales, and 22 percent of beer/ale sales have been attributed to such displays.[35] They work best when tied directly to other messages or advertising campaigns. Generally, POP displays need to have a lot of atten-

© BrokenSphere / Wikimedia Commons.

Some Niketown POP displays resemble what you might expect to see in a locker room.

Nearly every airline offers frequent flyer miles, and most hotel chains now have similar loyalty programs.

tion-getting power and must focus the consumer's interest on the sales promotion and product at hand.

Many stores are using POP to connect with customers in an interactive and exciting environment. For example, customers at Niketown will hear the sounds of bouncing tennis balls and squeaking tennis shoes. Displays of gear even mimic what you might see in a locker room, further connecting with consumers of the goods.

Loyalty Programs Loyalty programs reward people for continued and frequent use of a particular product. A good example is the frequent flyer miles offered in the airline industry. Although these usually don't stimulate more air travel, they are an incentive for a purchaser to continue to travel with a particular carrier. The programs are also recognized tools for increasing customer satisfaction. Nearly every airline offers frequent flyer miles, and most hotel chains now have similar programs. Hyatt, for example, offers free room stays after a certain number of regular stays. Loyalty programs tend to run longer than other types of sales promotion because their basic objective is to promote long-term usage.

Public Relations and Publicity

PUBLIC RELATIONS

As defined previously in chapter 12, public relations (PR) is the strategic communication process that builds mutually beneficial relationships between organizations and their publics. It is often confused with advertising, but, in fact, PR is very different. A company controls its advertising; it can only influence its PR. For example, a company can determine when to issue press releases and hold events, but it cannot control the press that independently decides whether to run the communication. Editors and news reporters serve as "gatekeepers;" They screen company-issued communication to ensure its accuracy so the public can have some confidence that the information it receives through public relations is truthful. In addition, PR provides editorial-type messages in language that can break through advertising clutter, which is usually visual. Public relations can be used to establish the social responsibility of a good corporate citizen; it builds trust because it must be earned, whereas advertising builds exposure that a company buys. Furthermore, there are few legal restrictions on PR activities, making it a way to address numerous issues in a more balanced light than may be possible with advertising.

> Public relations is likely to focus on many publics, including employees, shareholders, community members, news media and government.

Public relations is likely to focus on many publics, including shareholders, community members, news media and government. Rather than directly promote a particular product or brand, most PR messages have the appearance of objectivity. Many PR promotional campaigns center on social issues, taking local markets into account. For example, Avon supports breast cancer awareness in the United States, the prevention of violence against women in Malaysia, child nourishment in China, and AIDS prevention in Thailand. Recently, Kentucky Fried Chicken ran its Buckets for the Cure campaign. The company's red buckets were changed to pink, and the chain donated 50 cents to the Susan G. Komen Foundation for every bucket sold, raising $1.9 million in the first week alone.[36] These cause marketing campaigns are generally supported by major PR activities including visibility of company executives and other spokespersons.

Public relations supports the marketing function in several ways:

- *Corporate communication.* Messages promote a better understanding of the organization among employees, shareholders and other relevant publics.

- *Media relations.* Newsworthy information, such as new activities and personnel promotions, are provided to the media on a timely basis.

- *Lobbying.* Communication with legislators and government officials to promote or defeat legislation is a major activity for heavily regulated industries.

- *Product publicity.* Newsworthy innovations or new attributes of products can be promoted at little cost through the media.

PUBLICITY

Publicity is what is communicated about an organization in the public news media. Negative publicity detracts from the organization's image and can have serious effects on its market position. Most PR groups attempt to generate positive publicity through news stories and public service announcements. The more common avenues are press releases, news conferences and event sponsorship. The internet is increasingly being used by marketers, both to spread publicity and to respond to crisis situations.

Sponsors of the 2014 Sochi Olympics weren't prepared for the backlash of criticism they received for sponsoring the games in Russia, a country with anti-gay laws. Soon after McDonald's launched a twitter feed with the hashtag #CheersSochi, which was intended to send messages to the athletes, activists flooded it with tweets that used the hashtag to challenge McDonald's sponsorship of the games. McDonald's eventually relented and withdrew the hashtag altogether. They, like other sponsors, simply didn't expect the backlash.

For marketers, the implications were broader than just the reaction of the LGBT community. More than ever before, marketing is battling with social activists, interest groups and politics. Marketers need to aware of and responsive to public issues in advertising and all communications.

Press Releases and News Conferences A **press release** is a statement written by company personnel and distributed to various media for publication at their discretion. It includes information about the organization or product that marketers believe will be of interest to the public. The advantage of a press release is that the marketer has control over what information is provided. Many large organizations issue press releases regularly. Organizations will use them almost invariably when negative publicity needs to be countered. Rather than leave it to the media to track down the facts, companies provide the same information to all members of the press simultaneously. Press releases must be accurate, to the point and based on hard evidence. If not, then the media will become skeptical about any material the company issues.

News or press conferences occur when reporters are invited to a meeting at which company officials make a public statement and usually respond to questions. As with press releases, companies have some control over news conferences.

Wimbledon tennis tournament in London included organizations like IBM, Ralph Lauren, Evian, and Jaguar.

Sponsored Events or Activities A very popular type of publicity is sponsored events or activities, especially for local promotion. Many companies sponsor rock or symphony concerts, sports teams or youth groups. This gets the company's name into the public while contributing to the community. Sponsors of the 2016 Wimbledon tennis tournament in London included organizations like IBM, Ralph Lauren, Evian, and Jaguar. The final match up between Andy Murry and Milos Raonic should be seen by about 9 million viewers. Peak viewership for the 2015 championship game between Novak Djokovic and Roger Federer was over 9 million viewers, giving sponsors a massive amount of publicity in exchange for their funding.[37] IBM provides technology to the event in addition to funding. A team of 48 IBM analysts capture data, from ball speed to player statistics, to provide insights in real time. The data is then pushed to broadcasters so TV graphics are updated instantly. Match analysis videos are given to coaches and players for more detailed stats on their performance.[38]

The Internet The internet can be an ideal medium for publicity, having already spawned a new group of PR companies. Edelman Public Relations Worldwide is a leading creator of websites. Its services can be especially helpful when companies need to minimize negative publicity. For example, less than three hours after several bottles of Odwalla apple juice were found to contain E. coli bacteria, Edelman created a site to provide consumers with information. Ford has also used the internet when it needed to recall defective tires.

Marketers who skillfully blend public relations and publicity into their communications mix can underscore and intensify the positive feelings created by other mass communications activities. In Chapter 14 we will turn our attention to the most personal and individualized form of marketing communication—personal selling. Although one-on-one relationship building is key to effective personal selling, mass communication provides important support. It lays the groundwork for personal sales by creating deeper receptivity toward the company and its products.

Factors that Influence Mass Communication

The three main components of mass communication—advertising, sales promotion and public relations—are continually influenced by three additional factors: technology, globalization and ethics.

TECHNOLOGY

The history of mass communication mirrors a number of technological advances. Before the age of printing, street criers shouted merchants' messages, and shop signs often used pictures to identify their trade to a largely illiterate public. Movable type was invented around 1440, helping to spread literacy, and 32 years later an advertisement for a prayer book was tacked to church doors. The word advertisement appeared in about 1665, when it was used as a header to describe announcements of commercial significance. By the mid-1700s, newspapers were popular and carried publicity and ads.

By the 1800s, mass communication through newspapers and handbills was abundant. When the magazine was introduced in the mid-1800s, it provided an excellent way to communicate commercial messages. The birth of magazines provided a medium for the professions of copywriting and advertising to develop. By the mid-1930s, great ad agencies such as J. Walter Thompson, Rubicam and BBDO were successful. During that era, the growth of radio provided yet another medium for promotion and quickly surpassed magazines as the leading vehicle. Although television came along in 1939 when NBC was established, it did

eMarketer recently released a study showing that online ad spending is expected to surpass TV spending in 2017.

not surpass radio as the primary promotional medium until the '50s. Once marketers adopted it, they were able to take advantage of the combination of video and voice, addressing consumers with famous spokespersons, such as actor (and later president) Ronald Reagan. Television now dominates, but magazines, newspapers, radio and the internet still carry a significant proportion of promotional messages. In recent years, marketers have been budgeting fewer advertising dollars to traditional media and more to internet advertising. This increased popularity is due in part to the fact that online advertising is easier to measure than traditional means. Better measurement allows for more efficient assessment and adjustment, leading to a higher marketing ROI.

eMarketer recently released a study showing that online ad spending is expected to surpass TV spending in 2017, for the first time in U.S. history.[39] Whereas traditional media once revolutionized advertising and public relations, it has taken a back seat in recent years to exciting new digital technology that allows for information systems, including social media, to contribute dramatically to sales promotion. Technology makes it possible to track product sales in a variety of ways so marketers can evaluate the effectiveness of a sales promotion regionally, nationally and globally. Clearly, the internet is doing for mass communication what the telephone did for interpersonal communication.

GLOBALIZATION

Global advertising, sales promotion or public relations occurs when a marketing team standardizes key elements of these activities across national boundaries. Since campaigns are usually used to support global brand strategies, companies such as Coca-Cola, PepsiCo, Procter & Gamble, BMW, Nike, Toyota and Nestlé are leaders in this arena. Today, all the large advertising agencies have offices worldwide to support clients who seek global coordination. You may recall this was exactly the goal of Coca-Cola in creating its current One Brand strategy (Chapter 2). Due to cultural differences, marketers need to assess the benefits of standardized versus localized promotion. Sometimes global strategies require some adjustment at the local level to appeal to different segments of a diverse market.

Because standardization provides numerous economies, the cost of developing creative promotions can be shared across many markets. For example, when Gillette introduces a new product, a worldwide campaign often uses the same actors dubbed in various languages. Using LeBron James' to promote Nike costs millions, but they have the same appeal in Italy or Russia as in the United States.

Global standardization works best when customers, not countries, are the basis for identifying segments and when the product is compatible across cultures. It is also important for the firm to have similar competitors and an equivalent competitive position in most of the markets. Finally, promotion management should be somewhat centralized so that global marketing can occur.[40] Since every culture has a different view of marketing, global standardization cannot be applied to every concept. Although this attitude is changing, Singaporeans tend to regard promotion negatively, whereas Russian consumers are even more positive about it than Americans.[41]

Sales promotion and publicity often have a very local flavor. Each country has a unique promotional style, and most have legal as well as other restrictions. For example, Procter & Gamble (P&G) found it was legal to mail free samples to consumers in Poland, a practice prohibited in many countries. What surprised P&G's marketers was that thieves stole the samples from mailboxes before they reached intended recipients. In Germany, however, the government regulates the size of samples sent through the mail; another law prohibits advertising via personal letter.[42] In England, Hoover Ltd. gave away free round-trip airplane tickets to New York or Orlando with the purchase of £250 in merchandise. The company underestimated demand and spent several million pounds more than it had budgeted.

ETHICS

DECEPTION

When a false belief is created or implied and interferes with the ability of consumers to make a rational choice.

The most serious ethical issue surrounding advertising, sales promotion and public relations is deception. These communication methods are designed to be persuasive, but too much of the wrong type of persuasion can be misleading.

Deception occurs when a false belief is created or implied and interferes with the ability of consumers to make rational choices.[43] Purely descriptive information is seldom deceptive, but what about embellishment or omissions? At what point does it become deception? Marketers must use sound judgment to avoid being deceptive. An ad may show Michael Jordan soaring hundreds of feet to make a slam dunk in his Nikes, but no one is likely to believe that shoes make this possible. The exaggerated message is that Nike shoes will significantly improve the performance of the common athlete. But Nike lets you know that playing basketball well is also based on ability, training and skill building. Nike campaigns have featured athletes as role models for children, not as superstars. By depicting the athletes as serious, compassionate and hardworking, Nike is able to convey that being an athlete is about more than just the sport. How exciting would it be to see Nike or Reebok simply describe the materials and design for their shoes? Most would not consider Nike's more outlandish "fluff" to be deceptive, and many see it as creative or clever.

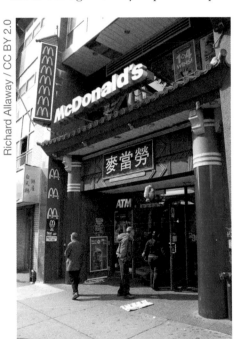

Richard Allaway / CC BY 2.0

McDonald's global standardization attracts its target market across cultures in more than 100 countries.

Marketers have to walk a fine line between producing creative, stimulating messages and being deceptive. Even company slogans can come into question when they evoke strong emotions or make comparative comments. Verizon reminds us, "We never stop working for you." Navy recruiting ads say, "It's not a job. It's an adventure." Is Verizon really at our beck and call 24 hours a day? Does joining the Navy really involve zero work? While they are not necessarily true, consumers probably would not think these slogans seriously interfere with their ability to make informed choices. Are these catchy phrases provocative or misleading?

When false information or exaggerated claims are used, deception is clear...and illegal. Kentucky Fried Chicken (KFC) used deceptive communication by leaving some information out: The FTC charged that KFC provided false information about the relative nutritional value and healthiness of its fried chicken in a national television advertising campaign. KFC publicized that its fried chicken, in particular two Original Recipe fried breasts, was healthier than a Burger King Whopper, due to less total fat and saturated fat. However, its product has more than three times the trans fat and cholesterol, more than twice the sodium, and more calories. So is it really ethical for KFC to claim it's healthier?[44]

Chapter Summary

Objective 1: Understand the concept of mass communication including the relative use of advertising, sales promotion and public relations.

Mass communication helps companies connect with customers around the world. It adds value by providing information about the goods and services available. Expenditure on mass communication—advertising, sales promotion and public relations—is increasing at about 7 percent annually in the United States and at a slightly higher rate globally. Roughly the same amount is spent on sales promotion and advertising, but sales promotion is slightly ahead and is growing at a faster rate. Public relations is a distant third.

Objective 2: Know the objectives, advantages and disadvantages of advertising, as well as the sequence of steps in creating an advertising campaign.

Advertising is highly controllable and works over time to build brand equity. It is cost-effective for reaching large audiences. Its primary objective may be to inform consumers, to persuade them to buy, to remind them of the product or to reinforce buying behavior and positive feelings about the brand. Advertising media are readily available, and it's easy for marketers to find help in creating effective campaigns. But advertising reaches many people outside the target audience, encounters a high level of avoidance and can be costly. It also can communicate only brief, one-way messages. There are several different types of advertising: national, retail (local), directory, business-to-business, institutional, direct response, public service and political. Generally, there are six steps in developing the advertising plan: set objectives, establish the budget, create the theme and message, select and schedule media, create the ads, and assess effectiveness.

Objective 3: Understand sales promotion objectives and what types of promotions are used to stimulate sales in business, trade, retailer, and consumer markets.

Sales promotion is used to prompt consumers to action, resulting in immediate sales results. It is generally used with other forms of promotion, such as advertising, public relations or personal selling. There are four types of sales promotion: business-to-business, trade, retailer and consumer. Business-to-business promotions include trade shows, conventions, sales contests and specialty deals. Trade promotions, which are offered by manufacturers to wholesalers or retailers, include discounts, allowances, financing incentives, sales contests and spiffs. Retailer promotions, offered to consumers, include price cuts, displays, free trials, coupons and patronage awards. Consumer promotions are manufacturers' offers, including coupons, rebates, free samples, sweepstakes, price and value packs, POP displays and continuity programs.

Objective 4: Understand the use of public relations in marketing.

Public relations activities are used primarily to influence feelings, opinions, or beliefs about a company or its products. An attempt is made to develop messages that at least have the appearance of objectivity. PR supports the marketing function in the following ways: corporate communication, press relations, lobbying and product publicity. Common publicity-generating activities are press releases, news conferences and sponsorship of events or activities. Because public relations messages are placed through public channels, the messages tend to be more credible and believable than advertisements. They also tend to break through the advertising clutter and are relatively low in cost. Public relations can publicize the social responsibility of a good corporate citizen.

Objective 5: Learn how technology, globalization and ethics are playing major roles in mass communication.

The history of mass communication coincides with the development of communications technology, particularly print, radio and television. Today, the internet is adding an interactive medium. Global mass communication occurs when key elements of messages are standardized across regions and nations. Standardization has cost advantages when the same customer segments are found in many countries, but it has several limitations. The primary ethical issue in mass communication is deception. Puffery may be used to make a point, but care must be taken not to be deceptive. Some countries have very strict legislation that does not allow exaggerations of any sort.

Review Your Understanding

1. Why is global standardization of mass communication useful?
2. How do deception and puffery relate?
3. What is advertising? What is its overriding goal?
4. What are the four objectives of advertising? Describe each.
5. What are some of the advantages and disadvantages of advertising?
6. List the eight types of advertising. What is the focus of each?
7. Name the six types of advertising media. What are the advantages and disadvantages of each?
8. What is sales promotion? How is it different from advertising?
9. Briefly describe the four different types of sales promotion. What are the most common promotional activities within each

category?

10. How does sales promotion help build relationships?

11. What is public relations? How is it unique from other forms of mass communication such as advertising and sales promotion?

12. What are the pros and cons of public relations?

Discussion of Concepts

1. Describe the five steps in developing an advertising plan. On which ones would you most enjoy working? Least enjoy? Why?

2. Why is it important to develop a creative strategy before creating specific ads?

3. What are the critical issues in selecting and scheduling the appropriate advertising media?

4. As with any creative process, it's difficult to determine precisely what people will like. When it comes to developing an advertisement, what are some of the characteristics that will tend to make the ad successful? Why?

5. In business, it's important to measure how well the organization performs certain tasks in order to make adjustments as necessary. How do marketers measure the effectiveness of advertising campaigns?

6. Marketers sometimes divide consumers into four categories of buyers. Briefly describe each type and the promotional activities that are likely to be successful with each.

7. List the most popular types of trade promotions. When is each type appropriate?

8. How do the advantages and disadvantages of public relations compare to those of other forms of promotional activities?

Key Terms & Definitions

1. **Advertising:** Paid communication through impersonal channels from a sponsor trying to persuade or influence an audience.

2. **Advertising agency:** A business that develops, prepares and places advertising for sellers seeking to find customers for their products.

3. **Advertising campaign:** A series of advertisements with a main theme running through them.

4. **Aided recall:** The viewer is given some specific piece of information about the ad before being asked if he or she recalls having seen it.

5. **Allowances:** Funds given to retailers and wholesalers based on the amount of product they buy.

6. **Business-to-business advertising:** Advertising to business and professionals.

7. **Business-to-business promotions:** Tools designed to stimulate B2B purchases such as trade shows, conventions, sales incentives and specialty items.

8. **Competitive budgeting method:** Setting the advertising expenditures relative to what competitors spend.

9. **Consumer promotion:** Offer designed to pull the product through the retail establishment.

10. **Continuity:** The length of time the advertising campaign will run in a given medium.

11. **Coupon:** Certificate that entitles a consumer to an incentive to buy the product, usually a price reduction or a free sample.

12. **Creative strategy:** The strategy that governs and coordinates the development of individual ads and assures that their visual images and words convey precisely and consistently what the advertiser wants to communicate.

13. **Cross-selling:** Promotion in which the manufacturer of one brand attempts to sell another brand to the same customers, or the purchase of one product is used to stimulate the selection of another, often unrelated product.

14. **Deception:** When a false belief is created or implied and interferes with the ability of consumers to make a rational choice.

15. **Directory advertising:** A listing of businesses, their addresses, phone numbers and sometimes brief descriptions in a publication.

16. **Direct response advertising:** Targets individual consumers to get immediate sales.

17. **Exposure:** The process of putting the ad in contact with the consumer.

18. **Financing incentive:** An offer to finance the retailer's inventory prior to its sale.

19. **Frequency:** The number of times the audience is reached in a given period, usually per day or per week.

20. **Informative advertising:** Messages designed to provide information that consumers can store for later use.

21. **Institutional advertising:** Messages designed to communicate corporate identity and philosophy as opposed to product information.

22. **Mass communication:** The communication of a concept or message to large audiences.

23. **Media:** The channels through which messages are transmitted.

24. **National or brand advertising:** Advertising that focuses on brand identity and positioning throughout the country.

25. **Overexposure:** Continuing to reach a prospect after a buying decision has been made or to the point that the campaign becomes tedious and actually turns off some potential buyers.

26. **Payout method:** Setting the advertising budget to gain initial acceptance and trial.

27. **Percentage of sales method:** Allocating a percentage of

anticipated sales to advertising.

28. **Persuasive advertising:** Messages designed to change consumers' attitudes and opinions about products, often listing product attributes, pricing and other factors that may influence consumer decisions.

29. **Political advertising:** Advertising to influence voters.

30. **Press release:** A statement written by company personnel and distributed to various media for publication at their discretion.

31. **Public Service Advertising:** Free advertising that supports societal issues.

32. **Pulling power:** The ability to maintain the interest of the consumer to the end of the advertising message.

33. **Reach:** The number of consumers in the target audience who can be contacted through a given medium.

34. **Rebate:** Refunds given to consumers for the purchase of particular items.

35. **Reinforcement advertising:** Messages that call attention to specific characteristics of products experienced by the user.

36. **Reminder advertising:** Messages that keep the product at the forefront of the consumer's mind.

37. **Retail (local) advertising:** Advertising that focuses attention on nearby outlets where products and services can be purchased.

38. **Retailer promotion:** An offer to the consumer that is sponsored by a retailer.

39. **Sales incentives:** Awards for achieving defined goals or levels of activity, such as sales quotas.

40. **Sales promotion:** Communications designed to stimulate immediate purchases using tools such as coupons, contests, and free samples.

41. **Specialty items:** Gifts with the organization's name that are provided to customers, usually given through the mail or by the sales force.

42. **Stopping power:** The ability of an ad to gain and hold the consumer's attention.

43. **Task method:** Setting the advertising budget based on activities required to accomplish objectives.

44. **Trade promotion:** An offer from a manufacturer to channel members, such as wholesalers and retailers.

45. **Unaided recall:** The viewer is asked to identify any advertisements he or she can remember.

46. **Viral marketing:** Diffusing a marketing message across people

References

1. Wells, Burnett, and Moriarty, Advertising, pg. 10.
2. www.youtube.com/user/Chevrolet, website visited July 5, 2016.
3. McDonald's, www.mcdonalds.com, website visited July 5, 2016.
4. "Get Involved: EWG's Action Center," ewg.org, website visited August 14, 2012.
5. www.adcouncil.org, website visited July 5, 2016.
6. C2 Advertising, www.c2advertising.com, website visited May 12, 2010.
7. Proactiv, www.proactiv.com, website visited July 8, 2016.
8. www.tide.com/en-us, website visited May 12, 2016.
9. www.naa.org, website visited June 8, 2016.
10. "Testimony from Hearst's Ellen Levine on the Postal Crisis," Association of Magazine Media, www.magazine.org, website visited June 30, 2016.
11. Gillian West, "Transport for London warns commuters of possible disruption with Tour de France creative," The Drum, July 9, 2014.
12. "2014 Tour de France," NBCSN, Stamford, Connecticut. July 9, 2014. Television.
13. Bostik Renews Tour de France Sponsorship for 2016," Bostik Press Release, June 30, 2016
14. www.oralb.com, website visited June 30, 2016.
15. Huang, Chun-Yao; Lin, Chen-Shun, "Modeling the Audience's Banner Ad Exposure for Internet Advertising Planning," Journal of Advertising Vol. 35, Summer 2006, pg. 123.
16. www.google.com/analytics, website visited June 30, 2016.
17. Watts, Duncan J.; Peretti, Jonah, "Viral Marketing for the Real World," Harvard Business Review Vol. 85, May 2007, pg. 22.
18. www.fiestamovement.com; www.youtube.com, websites visited July 2, 2016.
19. Kathy Blake, "Detroit's Faygo now offering cotton candy flavor," Oakland Press, July 3, 2014.
20. Ben Fox Rubin, "Mobile ad spending expected to jump 83% this year," CNET, July 3, 2014.
21. Ibid.
22. "International Marketing Nightmares," Marketing Update Newsletter, www.exton.com, website visited August 15, 1996.
23. Bennett, Peter D., Dictionary of Marketing Terms (Chicago, American Marketing Association, 1988), pg. 179.
24. "The changing face of retail," Deloitte, www.deloitte.com, February 2012.
25. McNally, Regina C.; Griffin, Abbie, "An Exploratory Study of the Effect of Relationship Marketing Institutionalization and Professional and Organizational Commitment in Business-to-Business Exchanges," Journal of Business-to-Business Marketing, 2005, 12(4), pp. 1-39.
26. "Examples of Cross-selling," http://crosselling.org, website visited July 5, 2014.
27. 7-Up, www.7up.com, website visited July 5, 2014.
28. Alex Kantrowitz, "B2B Marketing Budgets Set to Rise 6% in 2014: Forrester," Ad Age, January 21, 2014.
29. www.biztradeshows.com, website visited July 5, 2016.
30. Alonzo, Vincent, "Showering Dealers with Incentives," Sales and Marketing Management, October 1999, pp. 24-26.
31. Hernandez, Andrea, Free Gifts Work as a Marketing Tool, McClatchy-Tribune Business News, December 18, 2007.
32. Bawaba, Al, Dubai World Trade Centre Receives Trade Promotion Award, November 28, 2007.
33. Lefton, "Try It: You'll Like It."
34. www.visa.com, website visited July 5, 2016.
35. Heath, Rebeca P., "Pop Art," Marketing Tools, April 1997.
36. "Cause & Effect," Department of Business Administration, College of Business at Illinois, http://business.illinois.edu, February 2012.
37. Tom Eames, "UK TV ratings: Novak Djokovic's Wimbledon 2015 victory scores peak of 9.1 million," Digital Spy, July 13, 2015.
38. www.ibm.com/innovation, website visited July 7, 2016.
39. "Digital Ad Spending to Surpass TV Next Year," eMarketer, March 8, 2016.
40. Jain, Subhash C., "Standardication of International Marketing Strategy: Some Research Hypotheses," Journal of Marketing 53, January 1989, pp. 70-79.

41. Darley, William K.; Johnson, Denise M., "An Exploratory Investigation of the Dimensions of Beliefs Toward Advertising in General: A Comparative Analysis of Four Developing Countries," Journal of International Consumer Marketing 7, No. 1, 1994, pp. 5-21; Andrews, J.C.; Durvasula, Srinivas; Netemeyer, Richard G., "Testing the Cross-National Applicability of U.S. and Russian Advertising Belief and Attitude Measures," Journal of Advertising 23, March 1994, pg. 21.

42. Wessel, David, "Memo to Marketers: Germany Wants to Import American Junk Mail," Wall Street Journal, December 10, 1999, pg. B1.

43. Boatright, John R., Ethics and the Conduct of Business (Upper Saddle River, New Jersey, Prentice Hall), 1997, pg. 277.

44. Anonymous, "KFC Plucked," Cently, Multinational Monitor, May/June 2004. Vol. 25, Iss 5/6; pg. 45.

CHAPTER *14*

Personal
Selling

AVON

Ever since Avon unveiled its first product more than 125 years ago—the Little Dot Perfume Set—the company has found ways to make direct selling relevant to consumers. Avon continues to innovate its direct sales model to fit into Representatives' and customers' lives.

In 1886, direct selling at Avon provided a way for women to earn their own money at a time when not many women worked outside the home. It connected women, who were otherwise isolated and immersed in domestic life, in what the company calls "the original social network."

With Avon on the scene, many women no longer had to travel long distances to the closest department store or drugstore to purchase beauty products. A visit from the Avon Lady meant the store would come to them. A customer could shop, chat with her Representative and receive free beauty advice addressing her specific concerns—somewhat of a novelty at the time.

Since then, Avon Representatives have made the personal relationship the core of their businesses. It's impossible to tell just how many women have bonded while selecting the perfect Avon lipstick shade or fragrance. But there's no doubt that this intimate, consultative selling approach works; by 1920, sales topped $1 million, reaching $1 billion by 1972 and $10 billion by 2013.

Historically, the whole premise of Avon's business had been door-to-door selling. So what happens when no one is home to answer that door? It's a question the company had to address in the 1970s, once more women were working outside the home. One answer was the Advance Call Back brochure, a packet that could be left on a doorknob and included samples. A second solution came in 1986: workplace selling. This was a way to move the Avon "store" to a customer's work location so she could browse during breaks. But nothing in recent history has changed the way people interact and shop more than the internet; the creation of a digital, virtual world has altered fundamental behavior.

The 1954 "Ding Dong, Avon Calling" ad campaign is one of the longest running and successful in advertising history.

Avon's challenge was to find a way to adapt to this enormous change while preserving the personal attention component of its direct-selling model. The company needed to merge high tech with high touch. And it did. Today, Avon Representatives still make personal contact whenever possible, and they supplement that contact with digital marketing.

Representatives have access to a "Social Media Center" on their sales dashboard, and they regularly share customized communications with clients based on product preferences to maintain a personal connection. When Avon participates in fashion runway shows, videos with professional make up tips and interviews with makeup artists backstage (see QR code), may be sent out to clients via Facebook, Twitter, Pinterest and Tumblr.

The Little Dot Perfume Set is long gone, but Avon's commitment to direct selling is as strong as ever. The company is currently focusing efforts on using the same direct selling strategy to develop markets in Russia, Brazil and Mexico. Its ability to continue connecting with the consumer in person, at Avon.com and through social media guarantees that Avon still places the highest value on relationship-based sales and service to the customer.

Source: www.avoncompany.com, website visited July 8, 2016.

LEARNING OBJECTIVES

LO 01 Identify the five types of selling and describe the three selling approaches.

LO 02 Describe the responsibilities of salespeople and sales managers.

LO 03 Identify and explain the seven steps in personal selling.

LO 04 Identify the characteristics of strong salespeople.

LO 05 Describe the three steps involved in developing a sales team.

LO 06 Explain the six elements of sales action plans.

The Concept of Personal Selling

Successful people usually manage to "sell" their ideas. Broadly speaking, any time one party attempts to motivate the behavior of another party through personal contact, some form of selling takes place. When was the last time you tried to influence someone by expressing your point of view? Did you try to convince a friend to go to a movie you wanted to see or to a restaurant you wanted to visit? While this kind of communication is not always considered personal selling, it shares many of the same characteristics. It's through interpersonal contact that leaders influence the behavior of others. What makes personal selling a profession and not just interpersonal influence? It focuses on creating the economic exchange that is at the center of marketing. Salespeople often sell customers on products in very similar ways to how you sell your friends on your desired movie.

Personal selling is one of the most prevalent and highest-paid occupations in the United States. For every person employed in advertising, there are many more jobs in sales; about 11 percent of American workers are employed in sales in some capacity.[1] Furthermore, personal selling pays well, and compensation is rising dramatically. Income varies according to industry and position, but the median salary of top sales executives is $235,034 a year.[2] It is not unusual for salespeople to make hundreds of thousands—sometimes more than a million dollars annually.

Whether you are planning a professional sales career or simply want to sell your ideas more effectively, you'll find this chapter very helpful. It encompasses the essentials of personal selling, a tool in the promotion component of the 4Ps. We begin by describing the different types of sales personnel and selling situations. Next, we emphasize the importance of relationship selling by comparing various selling approaches. We follow this with a section on the responsibilities of a salesperson, both to the customer and to the company. We then explore each of the steps involved in personal selling—from planning and prospecting to closing the sale and providing follow-up, customer-care service. The final personal selling section, which describes the four characteristics of strong salespeople, may help you determine if you think sales might be a good career choice for you.

Although a salesperson in a small start-up company may work fairly independently, as a company grows, its management must begin to think in terms of a sales force, sales teams and sales managers. Good sales force management is needed to coordinate and inspire the efforts of these personnel, as well as to integrate them with the overall marketing plan. In the second half of the chapter we examine the five key functions of sales management: organizing the sales force, developing diverse sales teams, preparing forecasts and budgets, implementing sales actions, and overseeing sales force activities.

Personal Selling

Figure 14.1 diagrams the topics in personal selling. We will examine each of these in turn.

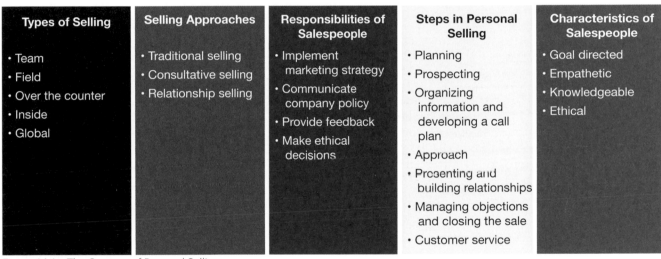

Types of Selling	Selling Approaches	Responsibilities of Salespeople	Steps in Personal Selling	Characteristics of Salespeople
• Team • Field • Over the counter • Inside • Global	• Traditional selling • Consultative selling • Relationship selling	• Implement marketing strategy • Communicate company policy • Provide feedback • Make ethical decisions	• Planning • Prospecting • Organizing information and developing a call plan • Approach • Presenting and building relationships • Managing objections and closing the sale • Customer service	• Goal directed • Empathetic • Knowledgeable • Ethical

Figure 14.1   The Concept of Personal Selling

TYPES OF SELLING

The many titles for sales positions tend to describe the type of activity performed: sales executive, sales engineer, sales consultant, sales counselor, representative, account executive, account representative, territory representative, management representative, technical representative, marketing representative, agent and sales associate. Many times the title of vice president is conferred on top-level salespeople who have important sales responsibilities but may have few, if any, people reporting to them.

Some common categories of salespeople are described in Figure 14.2 on the next page. **Direct sales** occur when a salesperson interacts with a consumer or company in order to make a sale. **Missionary sales** are made by people who do not take orders but influence purchase by recommending or specifying a product to others. For example, textbook salespeople influence professors, who then require students to purchase a particular book for a class. Likewise, physicians prescribe drugs, golf professionals endorse a brand of clubs and travel agents help select vacation packages.

There are five specific types of selling, each differentiated by the circumstances in which it occurs: executive and team selling, field selling, over-the-counter selling, inside selling and global selling. Because each category involves a different setting, the activities of salespeople differ accordingly.

DIRECT SALES

Sales that result from the salesperson's direct interaction with a consumer or company.

MISSIONARY SALES

Sales made indirectly through people who do not obtain orders but influence the buying decision of others.

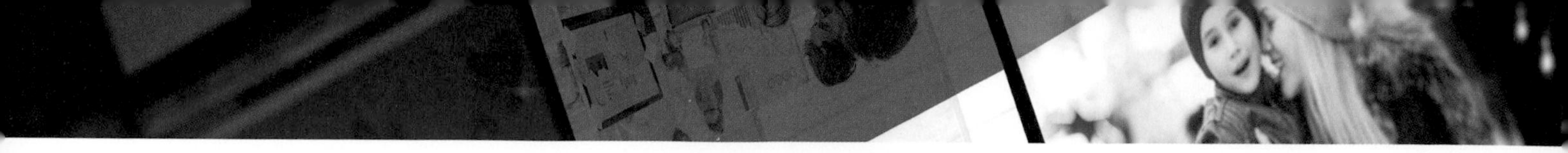

	ACTIONS	EXAMPLE
Telemarketing Representative	Uses telephone to contact customers to receive orders.	People who respond to callers of 800 numbers (Gateway 2000).
Inside Sales Support	One-to-one contact with customers via the internet or telephone.	IBM salesperson who sells without traveling to a customer's site.
Field Salesperson	Meet face-to-face with customers.	Nike salesperson calling on retail sporting goods chain.
Technical Salesperson	Meets face-to-face with customers to sell very technical products.	Square D salesperson (engineering background) calling on an electric utility.
Detail Person	Meets with people who influence the sale of a company's products but may not purchase directly.	Eli Lilly salesperson who calls on doctors to increase prescription rate for Lilly products.
Service Salesperson	Sells intangible products, such as insurance and real estate, to a broad range of customers.	Prudential salesperson who sells a life insurance policy.
Retail Salesperson	Associates or clerks selling items in a retail outlet.	Saturn salesperson working in showroom.

Figure 14.2   Types of Sales Personnel

Executive and Team Selling Although many people are employed in personal selling, the statistics don't count the numerous individuals with non-sales titles who spend much of their time on sales activities. Many executives, regardless of their departments, view personal selling as one of their primary functions. They not only communicate with the board of directors and employees in order to "sell" corporate policies but also frequently interact with major customers and suppliers.

TEAM SELLING

Selling that involves people from most parts of the organization, including top executives, working together to create a relationship with the buying organization.

Team selling involves people from most parts of the organization, including top executives, who work together to create relationships with the client's buying organization. Boeing recently won a $14.7 billion order for 150 737 jets for United Airlines, and in late 2011, the company had a record $22 billion sale of 230 737 models to Indonesia's Lion Air.[3] Many top corporate executives were deeply committed to the effort, although most of the responsibility still remained with the sales force. In a high-technology business such as aircraft manufacturing, nearly every function gets involved in the sales process. At Boeing it is the salesperson's job to coordinate contact between the company and the technical, financial and planning personnel from the airline. Even if the CEO is brought in, it is not unusual for the salesperson to remain in charge of the sale, using the CEO when appropriate. The salespeople perform the leadership function because they know all aspects of their customers' business. They also must be thoroughly familiar with Boeing's services. This includes cost-per-seat calculations, computerized route simulations and many other analysis tools Boeing uses to show how it can fulfill customer needs.[4]

Field Selling Field selling occurs at a customer's place of business. Field representatives spend most of their time, as the name implies, away from their company and near customers. Their job is to discover prospects, make contacts and create relationships. By working with customers in their own environment, field reps have ample opportunity to understand the customer's circumstances in depth. The best performers in field selling are often skilled at learning about the customer's situation and problems. Field sales in consumer markets (B2C) include products such as real estate, home building and remodeling, landscape maintenance and even computers.

Field selling to businesses (B2B) is also common. It is used for nearly every imaginable industrial product, from pharmaceutical sales to physicians and hospitals, to services such as consulting, accounting and business management for manufacturers and retailers. Merck, a leader in health-care products, sends sales reps to hospitals, clinics, government agencies, drug wholesalers and retailers, among others. In the 2015 fiscal year, Merck salespeople sold $38.77 billion in goods and services to other businesses and organizations including hospitals, physician clinics and pharmacies.[5]

Courtesy of Best Buy

Best Buy relies on quality salespeople to assist customers and provide knowledgeable information about its products.

Over-the-Counter Selling Sales that take place in retail outlets (such as clothing, furniture or jewelry stores) are examples of over-the-counter selling. Customers are drawn to the salesperson by the attraction of the store itself or by advertising and sales promotion. Salespeople need to be skilled at identifying customers' requirements quickly, often in a single encounter, and at providing the appropriate service at the point of sale. Providing first-time consumers with quality service entices them to return, which creates the opportunity to gain a loyal customer. It also creates positive word-of-mouth (WOM) promotion, which attracts friends and relatives of satisfied customers. Successful over-the-counter salespeople tend to build loyal relationships by working with customers multiple times over a long period and becoming knowledgeable about their unique tastes, particularly in personal care items such as cosmetics, and higher-end apparel items such as business suits.

Inside Selling Inside sales involve one-to-one contact with a customer via the telephone and internet. Mail-order companies are a good example. At Nordstrom, sales representatives know the products, how they fit, how to ship them quickly, how to care for them and how to expedite repairs if necessary. The section of the company website called "Nordstrom Live Help" offers customers an opportunity to chat with knowledgeable salespeople. Customers are given three options regarding the type of online assistance needed: customer service representative, beauty specialist and designer specialist. Nordstrom's customer friendly, interactive website encourages return visits.[6] Another example is the banks of telephone sales representatives who take orders in response to advertisements and infomercials. Sometimes they perform only a clerical function, since the consumer already is sold on the product, but many of these people do an excellent job of answering questions and selling additional items. Telephone marketers perform similar tasks, either attempting to sell a product or arrange a home visit for field salespeople.

Another form of inside sales is to work with established clients primarily by phone. Stock brokerage firms conduct much of their business this way. Many manufacturers and distributors have field reps and inside salespeople who work together with large customers. The reps solicit business at the customer's site, and inside sales personnel are ready at all times to provide technical support and take orders via the phone. This form of inside sales can be critical for industrial companies.[7] These inside sales people are increasingly educated and trained about products, acting more as consultants for the customer. This position requires crucial skills for recruiting and retaining customers, and can serve as a first job for many technical salespeople, since they learn about company policies and products while receiving help with their first customer contacts. Once experience is gained inside, these people often take a field sales position.

Global Selling It is difficult to overstate the importance of personal selling in global markets. Many of these sales involve millions or even billions of dollars. Kathy Sacks, Vice President of Communications for Infusionsoft, compares selling to dating and says, "You have to attract leads by playing up your positives; you have to differentiate yourself from the competition; and you have to spend time building meaningful relationships—ultimately choosing one person for what you hope will be lifelong wedded bliss."[8] Even as today's communication becomes increasingly more technological, many cultures adhere to personal relationships as the foundation of business.

In the domestic arena, companies and their representatives often become accepted in a short period, but this may take years in a foreign environment. To overcome this resistance, many companies use domestic personnel from the host country to represent them, but if that culture does not consider personal selling a prestigious occupation, this is not an ideal solution. Furthermore, finding and training qualified people can be challenging and expensive. As a compromise solution, companies often rely on nationals to provide information and make initial customer contact, but then they send salespeople from headquarters on regular visits to establish relationships and negotiate larger contracts.

SELLING APPROACHES

All employees are important in building and maintaining customer relationships, but salespeople are critical, because that is their primary responsibility. There is a growing trend to move from building short-term sales to building long-term satisfaction and loyalty. By establishing personal, long-term and loyal relationships with customers, salespeople can increase customer retention and repeat sales, furthering their company's competitive advantage. If salespeople do not have the skills and desire to build relationships one customer at a time, then no amount of support from all the other company employees can compensate.

Business strategies should focus on creating relationships rather than simply selling products. Companies are entering into joint activities in record numbers, and selling organizations must work closely with customers to help them accomplish their goals. Sellers must understand the consumer's lifestyle or how the customer's business works. Consequently, sales organizations are shifting from traditional ways of doing business to a new emphasis on building relationships. The three basic sales approaches are shown in Figure 14.3—traditional sales, consultative sales and relationship selling.

TRADITIONAL SELLING

Focuses on persuading consumers to buy a company's product.

	Traditional Selling	Consultative Selling	Relationship Selling
Focus	Understand your product	Understand customer's problems	Understand customer's business or lifestyle
Role of the customer	Prospect	Target	Asset of the business
Salesperson focus	Persuasion	Problem solving	Partnering
Salesperson role	Obtain sales volume	Advise customers	Building win-win circumstances
Objective	Profit through sales volume	Profit through problem solving	Profit through strategic relationships and customer satisfaction

Figure 14.3 Major Selling Approaches

Traditional Selling Approach
Traditional selling focuses on persuading consumers to buy a company's product, thereby raising sales volume. Remember that the Industrial Revolution produced goods in record quantities, and supply consistently exceeded demand. Therefore, the purpose of personal selling was to stimulate sales. Firms focused on selling more in order to keep up with increased production. The salesperson's focus was on pushing the company's products, especially features and functions, to persuade prospects to buy them

and increase the sales volume. Techniques for persuasive selling, which taught salespeople how to negotiate, were often the dominant subject of sales training courses. Essentially, sellers and buyers tried to see who could get the best deal.

Consultative Selling Approach

For many organizations, the traditional sales era continued well into the 1990s. As the marketing function became more important, however, the sales function also took on new responsibilities. Marketing began to focus on serving customers, and selling had to change with it. That's how consultative selling evolved. **Consultative selling** means working closely with customers to help solve problems. Salespeople are expected to advise customers on how their company's products can solve problems and fulfill needs rather than beat a competitor's price. In order for this type of selling to be successful, salespeople must work closely with the customer over an extended period. Customers on all levels, from individuals to businesses, are extending the buying cycle through spending more time in the decision-making process.[9] At some companies, salespeople act as consultants to their customers and may even suggest a competitor's product if it would better suit the customer. Consultative selling stops just short of relationship selling.

Relationship Selling Approach

Relationship selling creates bonds between buyers and sellers in an effort to gain loyalty and mutual satisfaction.[10] Because it promotes loyalty, it parallels the strategic nature of marketing, recognizing that sellers and buyers benefit from one another's success. In today's consumer markets, people like to buy based on relationships with companies that consistently enhance their lifestyle. Businesses, meanwhile, are looking for partners who will help them compete. Relationship selling recognizes that the salesperson's role is to create value for the customer as well as the company. Typically, a great deal of work on both sides goes into building and maintaining relationships.

Understanding the Customer's Business Strategy

The focus of relationship selling is to uncover strategic needs, develop creative solutions and arrive at mutually beneficial agreements.[11] Salespeople must recognize that companies buy products to help them run their businesses more efficiently. By understanding the customer's business, salespeople are more likely to communicate in meaningful ways with the potential buyer. Dow Chemical Company, a supplier of plastics and adhesives to the global automotive industry, "lends" technical sales engineers to assist clients with product and program development. They help create product strategies and are very familiar with confidential aspects of the client's business, effectively becoming a core part of the customer's marketing team.

Cisco Systems demonstrated its customer-focused structure when it entered into a deal with Wachovia, the parent company of the nation's fourth-largest bank and third-largest brokerage firm. Wachovia wanted to improve its key business drivers, including business growth, higher productivity and employee engagement. Cisco provided its TelePresence system to Wachovia to enhance collaboration by providing ultra high-definition, "in person," virtual communications, ultimately increasing individual productivity and reducing corporate travel costs.[12]

Cisco Systems GmbH / CC BY-ND 2.0

Cisco's TelePresence system can enhance collaboration by providing ultra-high-definition "in person" virtual communications.

The Customer as an Asset

Loyal customers should be viewed as an asset by the firm. Long-term contracts and repeat sales produce predictable sources of revenue. In fact, the worth of many businesses can be calculated by the size of the customer base, such as the number of subscribers of a cellular phone company. Companies with foresight do not treat

---

CONSULTATIVE SELLING

An approach to selling in which sales personnel work closely with customers to help solve problems.

RELATIONSHIP SELLING

An approach to selling in which bonds are created between buyer and seller to gain loyalty and mutual satisfaction.

customers as prospects for a single sale, but as partners in a long-term relationship. In the highly competitive hotel industry, Marriott International restructured its sales program to make it possible for individuals to earn reward points at one hotel and then take their families on vacation at another. After implementing the program, customer loyalty and frequency of stays increased.

Partnering Under the traditional approach, salespeople use persuasion to obtain orders, whereas consultative selling emphasizes the ability to solve customers' problems. Relationship selling, however, focuses on partnering. Some partnerships are contractual, established through long-term written agreements. Some are non contractual; that is, the buyer and seller enter into an implied agreement to do business together over time. In either case, a sharing of power occurs. In traditional sales, the balance of power is typically with the salesperson; in consultative selling it is with the customer. Relationship selling involves a symmetrical relationship—both parties have equal authority and responsibility. Both share information to help the other party succeed.[13]

> Relationship selling replaces short-term thinking with a perspective that ensures value long after the sale is made.

Relationship selling replaces short-term thinking with a perspective that ensures value long after the sale is made. Consequently, just as much work is needed after the sale as before. A strong follow through insures that partnerships are honored.

NEGOTIATION

Discussion between two or more parties to arrange a transaction.

Building Win-Win Opportunities Historically, buying and selling have involved negotiation. **Negotiation** can be defined as discussions by two or more parties to arrange a mutually beneficial transaction, with some degree of compromise. To some it means that each party tries to maximize its own benefit relative to the other through a power position obtained during the interaction. To others, negotiation is a way to build relationships. Instead of being seen as conflict or struggle, negotiations can be regarded as information sessions that lead to win-win opportunities.[14]

Figure 14.4 describes negotiation outcome possibilities. When any party loses, the foundation for building a relationship diminishes greatly. When one party gains a great deal more than the other, a relationship will not grow or will dissolve over time. A sound relationship requires that each party perceives it has gained value; the best negotiations are win-win situations. Even in early meetings with customers, both parties need to win.

	Buyer Gains	Buyer Loses
Seller Gains	Win-Win	Buyer negotiates poorly
Seller Loses	Seller negotiates poorly	Lose-Lose

Figure 14.4 Buyer-Seller Negotiations

Managing Strategic Relationships Account management refers to the activities of a salesperson or sales team to build and support the relationship with a customer. Many companies assign an account manager to each large customer (often called a major account) to provide personal service. Consulting firms, advertising agencies and manufacturers often have account managers. Delphi assigns them to work with the Ford, Toyota, Volkswagen and BMW accounts, as well as with GM assembly divisions. These managers concentrate their energies on maintaining the bonds between Delphi and the client. Account managers are particularly effective when the product supplied is important to the overall strategy of the buying company. For example, Delphi's components are critical to their customers' product designs. For some auto brands, Delphi produces most of the electrical systems, brake systems and other components. Account managers spend considerable time with customers and carefully monitor satisfaction with products and delivery.

Walgreens Health Systems sells pharmacy benefit programs, home health care and specialty pharmacy programs to employer groups, managed-care organizations, hospitals and government agencies. Some clients want basic services such as an on-site pharmacy and others want complete benefit programs. According to Katie Lestan, Walgreens regional vice president of sales: "In the health-care industry, which is rapidly changing, many services such as contracting for retail pharmacy service are being viewed as commodities. Most clients are looking for the best services at the lowest cost. Our strategic account managers are trained to help customers to align their business priorities with the requirements needed and the criteria in which to measure their success. If the customer and Walgreens can align priorities with the proper solutions, everybody wins. Our goal is to provide the best services that meet the needs of the client at the lowest net cost." Win-win occurs when both parties accomplish its objectives. Generally this requires careful understanding of the other party's needs, cooperation and compromise.

LO **02** RESPONSIBILITIES OF SALESPEOPLE

Salespeople do not simply increase sales volume. Today, most salespeople are considered marketing reps or marketing managers of a territory. This can be a geographical area, such as a city or region or a single large account. Essentially, a **sales territory** is all the actual and potential customers for whom the salesperson has responsibility. As marketing manager of a territory, the salesperson has several functions. He or she must implement the company's marketing strategy in that territory and communicate company policy to clients and potential customers. The salesperson must also provide the company with feedback about the marketing environment, including the competition and customer needs and wants. While accomplishing all of this, salespeople must operate ethically.

Implement the Marketing Strategy In order to translate the company's marketing strategy into action, the sales force needs to have a basic understanding of all marketing functions. In many companies, salespeople have considerable flexibility in applying the entire marketing mix to their territory, including which products to emphasize, which prices and discounts to offer, and which promotional materials to distribute. In other words, although their primary responsibility is to carry out the company's strategic marketing plan, they can use their own judgment in determining *how* to do it. Constant communication between sales teams and marketers is essential to success. Salespeople are able to provide the customer with information gathered by the marketing team's surveys and focus groups. Sales calls are often made by representatives from both marketing and sales divisions, particularly to major accounts.

SALES TERRITORY

All the actual and potential customers, often within a specified geographic area, for which the salesperson has responsibility.

©iStockphoto.com/Notorious91

A salesperson should implement the company's marketing strategy, communicate company policy, provide feedback about the marketing environment and operate ethically.

Communicate Company Policy As agents of their organization, salespeople are responsible for communicating company policies to customers. A policy is a guide or set of rules the company uses in conducting business. For example, Urban Outfitters allows customers to return or exchange any unworn, unwashed or defective merchandise. Within 30 days, their original method of payment will be refunded; after 30 days, they receive a merchandise credit.[15] Although company policies are relatively straightforward in most consumer sales situations, they can be extremely complex in business-to-business selling. For example, pharmaceutical sales representatives usually educate doctors about the proper use of certain drugs or medical equipment, and sometimes

> By communicating such policies and enforcing them, salespeople help shape customer expectations, create goodwill and maintain positive customer relationships.

they are present when surgeons operate in order to answer questions about products should the need arise.

Companies are likely to specify exactly what technical and corporate information salespeople can communicate. Also common are policies on appropriate product use, warranty issues, delivery and pricing. By communicating such policies and enforcing them, salespeople help shape customer expectations, create goodwill and maintain positive customer relationships.

Provide Feedback Another important role of the sales force is to provide their company with information about customers, competitors and market conditions. Salespeople are in constant contact with the market, and many companies have formal systems for collecting their information rapidly. Examples are portable personal computers with elaborate, user-friendly programs or arrangements with customers to contact their computer systems directly.

Most salespeople have an array of sophisticated communication capabilities, including voicemail, email, internet, smartphones, and social media. This keeps them in touch 24 hours a day, seven days a week. Customer inventory levels (stock on hand), purchase orders, price quotations, shipping data and promotional offers can be shared in both directions very efficiently. In addition, salespeople usually help forecast opportunities by describing the plans of current and potential customers that may affect future sales. Many times these estimates require careful analysis of a client's strategic plan.

Salespeople also provide valuable information about competitors. By collecting and assembling this input from around the globe, Lear Corporation can identify nearly every initiative competitors make. Let's say a salesperson in Germany identifies a rival's product introduction, new promotional campaign or altered pricing strategy in that territory. The information can be evaluated at Lear Corporation headquarters to determine the likelihood that markets elsewhere will be affected. Because auto suppliers like Lear need to develop automotive systems to sell to global auto companies like Ford, Suburu and Toyota, this type of feedback is critical.

Make Ethical Decisions Other than specific technical and corporate policies, salespeople rarely have restrictions on what they do and say, so they have a responsibly to act with sound, ethical judgment. Because performance evaluation is frequently tied to sales levels, however, there may, at times, be temptations to put self interests ahead of customer interests. Successful sales people resist this temptation! A good company anticipates ethical dilemmas and instills a win-win philosophy for its salespeople, in which value is created for the customer as well as the organization.

Why does independence from supervision pose ethical issues? The company usually goes to great expense to hire, train and support a salesperson. If he or she does not work hard, then the company may lose sales. The amount of time spent selling is an issue of personal ethics. Most employers recognize that the job may require spending time on evenings or weekends with customers or doing paperwork. To compensate, there tends to be some flexibility regarding working hours, but an unethical salesperson may take advantage of the situation. For example, it may be relatively easy to shorten the workweek without being missed or to play golf repeatedly with clients, with more concern for stroke count than for building a relationship. A salesperson may take on another job rather than devote full energy to the primary employer. What about taking an MBA class during work hours without telling the company?

Other ethical issues arise with regard to performance objectives. Most salespeople are evaluated at least partially on sales volume or profitability. This creates several temptations, including overstocking, overselling or pushing brands that yield higher commissions. Overstocking occurs when customers purchase more than is required for a given period, which results in unnecessary inventory-carrying charges. Imagine that you are a few thousand dollars short of your monthly sales objective. Suppose there is a distributor who relies on your estimates to restock inventory. If you put in an order for more than is needed, then you may gain a better performance evaluation, but you have acted unethically. Overselling occurs when customers request a lower-priced product that suits their needs and budget, but the salesperson supplies a much more expensive and profitable product. Similarly, some companies offer spiffs (immediate bonuses) for selling their product rather than a competitor's. Another unethical practice is to promise delivery when the salesperson knows the product will be late. The customer is prevented from ordering a competitor's brand, and when the delay becomes apparent, it is too late to obtain a substitute.

What salespeople communicate can also be an ethical issue. Puffery, or sales rhetoric so obviously excessive that customers recognize it as such, may not be in good taste but is rarely considered dishonest. Misrepresentation is far more serious. Salespeople are unethical when they give incorrect information, such as claiming their product is the same as another when it is not. Selling often involves verbal communication, and there may be little documentation other than an invoice after the sale, so actions like this can be difficult to prove. Whether spoken or written, intentional misrepresentation is illegal and can result in criminal or civil suits. Unintentional misrepresentation is at best a sign of incompetence in the salesperson and is grounds for canceling a contract. Ethical salespeople say, "I don't know, but I'll find out," rather than guess at the facts.

LO 03 STEPS IN PERSONAL SELLING

Personal selling can be divided into seven stages, as outlined in Figure 14.5 and explained below.

Planning Sales planning translates the company's marketing strategy into territory plans and account plans. Territory management is extremely important. Salespeople must determine how the company's target marketing and positioning can best be applied in their territory. Because each area is different, it is important to make adjustments based on local

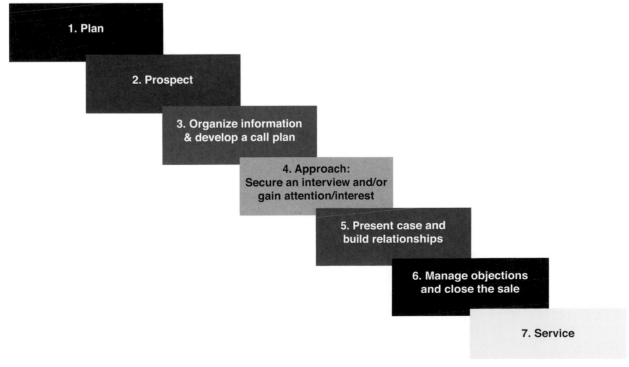

1. Plan

2. Prospect

3. Organize information & develop a call plan

4. Approach: Secure an interview and/or gain attention/interest

5. Present case and build relationships

6. Manage objections and close the sale

7. Service

Figure 14.5   Steps in Personal Selling

TERRITORY PLANNING

Identifying potential customers, their sales potential, and the frequency with which they will be contacted about various products.

ACCOUNT PLANNING

Establishing sales goals and objectives for each major customer.

PROSPECTING

Looking for potential customers within the company's target market.

LEADS

Names of all those who may have a need for a company's products.

PROSPECT

A potential customer interested in the seller's product.

QUALIFYING

Examining prospects to identify those with the authority and ability to buy the product.

QUALIFIED PROSPECT

A potential buyer interested in the seller's product who possesses the attributes of a good customer.

conditions. Exceptional sales skills are of little use if calls are not made on the appropriate accounts with the right frequency and intensity. **Territory planning** determines the pool of customers, their sales potential and the frequency with which they will be contacted about various products. The fundamental objective is to allocate sales time and use company resources to obtain the best results. Territory management is so important that many companies calculate, to the minute, how their salespeople should use their time.

Account planning establishes sales goals and objectives for each major customer, such as the sales volume and profitability to be obtained. Increasingly, account objectives include customer satisfaction, often measured by loyalty (repeat business). Account plans are based on an understanding of the customer's business and how the seller's products contribute to it. Elaborate account plans for major customers are common. For example, the AT&T sales team responsible for Ford Motor Company has a detailed description of its entire communication picture. This required a massive effort to develop, but the millions of dollars generated in revenues make it worthwhile. The plan provides all the information necessary to build and maintain the AT&T relationship with Ford.

Prospecting As the name implies, **prospecting** is looking for potential customers within the company's target markets. As illustrated in Figure 14.6, it involves three steps: obtain leads, identify prospects and qualify them. **Leads** are the names of all those who might have a need for the product, a large pool that must be narrowed down to the most likely buyers. **Prospects** are potential customers who may have an interest in the product. Perhaps they currently buy from a competitor, are former customers or have shown interest in some way. **Qualifying** is the process of determining which prospects have the authority and ability to buy the product, as well as whether they are desirable customers. A **qualified prospect** is a potential buyer interested in the product and likely to be a reliable customer.

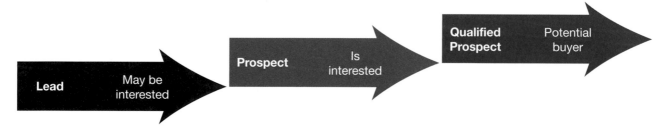

Figure 14.6   Potential Customers

COLD CALLING

Contacting a lead for the first time.

CENTER OF INFLUENCE

An opinion leader who can be quickly qualified as a potential customer because of his or her standing in the community.

A number of methods are used in prospecting: cold calls (canvassing), referrals, exhibiting at trade shows, networking, telemarketing, secondary data, and coupons and ads. These are shown in Figure 14.7.

Cold calling (canvassing) is contacting the lead for the first time, either by telephone, fax or in person. The salesperson has no idea whether the person will be interested. A few prospects are likely to be found, some of whom may be qualified. Cold calling is warranted when there is little information about the market or when the product is likely to have universal appeal. Many consumer products are sold door-to-door, and cold calling is also used in business-to-business selling. It is not very popular with customers, but it can be a useful method if not abused.[16]

A variation of cold calling is the **center of influence** method, which identifies leads by contacting opinion leaders. Opinion leaders are open to communications with salespeople and are considered reference group models. It is common knowledge that the pharmaceutical industry has profiled every physician in the country according

Cold Calls (Canvassing)	Going door-to-door
Center of Influence	Identify opinion leaders and contact them for leads.
Referrals	Get customers or prospects to provide names of others.
Exhibitions and Demonstrations	Exhibit at trade shows or give speeches.
Networking	Contact friends, relatives, and associates to obtain leads.
Telemarketing	Phone people on lists.
Secondary Data	Obtain lists from companies such as Dun & Bradstreet.
Coupons and Ads	The prospect responds to an ad or redeems a coupon.

Figure 14.7 Prospecting Methods

REFERRAL

A lead provided by a qualified prospect.

NETWORKING

Contacting friends, relatives, and associates to obtain leads.

TELEMARKETING

Making telephone calls to leads provided by marketing services or from other lists.

to opinion leadership. The leaders are more open to new products and also are more likely to influence colleagues.

Referrals are names of leads provided by a qualified prospect. This method can be very effective, since qualified prospects tend to associate with those who have similar attributes. Furthermore, compared to cold calling, the referral is likely to be receptive when the salesperson mentions the name of someone they both know.

Exhibitions and trade shows are an important way to obtain leads. About 85 percent of attendees significantly influence buying within their firm. It also costs 70 percent less to close a sale with these leads than with others.[17] In 2016, more than 815,000 people attended the North American International Auto Show in Detroit.[18] More than a million are drawn to North America's largest auto show, held in Chicago.[19] Participants include both domestic and foreign automakers as well as specialty manufacturers and retailers. Nearly every industry sponsors a trade show. Large halls such as Madison Square Garden in New York City, the Omni in Atlanta, and McCormick Place in Chicago provide facilities for thousands of organizations to display their products and obtain leads. Though networking through the internet is increasing, there is no substitution for the human element of exhibitions and trade shows.[20]

Networking involves contacting friends, relatives, previous customers and associates to obtain leads. Successful salespeople in most fields find this an important part of their business. Amway Corporation, a part of the Alticor family of companies, has had great success obtaining sales through networking. The company uses a system of independent agents who sell home care products directly to consumers. The agents ask customers for names of additional leads to contact. Amway is an incredible global success, with distributors in Asia, Africa, Latin America and North America. Its worldwide sales are about $10 billion annually.[21]

Telemarketing uses phone calls to contact lists of leads provided by marketing services and various directories. Organizations, such as Dun & Bradstreet and Information Resources Inc., provide listings of nearly every private and public organization as well as the name and title of executives, managers and buying influencers. Many marketing services contact these leads to determine the types of products they purchase and other information. These interviews are then turned into lists of prospects and sold to various marketing organizations. For example, AT&T has its own staff of telemarketers to find small business prospects for its products.

Secondary data sources can provide thousands of lists. Categories of secondary data can range from local libraries to company databases. Today, the information highway provides access to the names of nearly all U.S. companies and most international organizations. By using

©iStockphoto.com/Zsolt Nyulaszi
Telemarketing can be a very effective method to nurture leads and increase sales.

database technologies, companies can effectively filter to find qualified prospects. In some cases, the selling organization manages the database, but this is a highly specialized field. Because of the very costly technology and expertise required, most secondary data searches are outsourced.

Coupons and ads form another method for obtaining leads. Generally, coupons are placed in newspapers or magazines or sent through the mail. People who take the time to respond tend to be very interested and may have the attributes of a qualified prospect. A trend in magazine advertising is response cards that consumers mail in for free information after circling a number that corresponds to a specific ad. These cards give the seller a list of leads to pursue.

Organizing Information and Developing a Call Plan

Pre-approach refers to preparing for the initial meeting by learning about the prospect. For consumers, just their address can yield socioeconomic information, such as the likelihood of sufficient income to purchase the product and even some general idea of tastes and preferences. Columbia TriStar Home Video has developed its own software for its sales force to use in learning about the large retail chain outlets they visit. In the case of businesses, the salesperson can obtain copies of the organization's literature and annual reports. These contain data on the firm's financial strength, organizational structure, objectives, plant locations and sometimes even its purchasing philosophy. The salesperson's goal is to obtain enough information to develop an initial strategy for each call.

Once the preapproach phase is completed, a call plan is developed to save time and minimize travel expenses. The **routing schedule** identifies which prospects will be called on and when. Companies sometimes form routes with computerized programs, or they can elect to do it informally.

Approach

The **approach** is the salesperson's first formal contact with the potential customer. The objective is to secure an initial meeting and gain customer interest. It's usually a good idea to schedule an appointment; it will save time, and it puts the prospect in the frame of mind for a sales call. Many times, a letter of introduction before calling to schedule will help in obtaining the first appointment.

Many techniques have been developed for the initial approach. The most successful ones focus on the potential customer's business, such as a brief explanation of how the salesperson's company has been able to help other companies similar to theirs. As you'll learn later in this chapter, once a current customer is satisfied, it's always good to ask him or her for referrals to other people who might be willing to meet briefly. It's a lot harder for a prospective customer to reject an appointment request if someone he knows recommended him as a contact. He might not be interested in the product, but will usually agree to an initial meeting out of respect for the person who referred him. Organizations with a strong reputation generally have an advantage in the approach stage. For example, Xerox or IBM salespeople may have more success in gaining an initial appointment than representatives of an unknown company. That's why successful sales people are tenacious and creative at getting appointments! Once an appointment is secured, the sales person should confirm the date, time, duration and objective of the meeting.

Presenting and Building Relationships

The sales **presentation** is a two-way process: the salesperson listens in order to identify customer needs and then describes how the company can fulfill them. It is often said that successful selling is 90 percent listening and 10 percent talking. Unfortunately, many salespeople don't place proper emphasis on the importance of listening, and they end up doing most of the talking during valuable contact time. Instinctively they want to tell prospects about their products in the hope of making a sale. However, by asking open-ended questions, they empower the customer to talk and participate and demonstrate that they have the customer's best interest in mind. The first contact is the most important opportunity to connect with

PRE-APPROACH

Preparation by the salesperson for the initial meeting with a prospect.

ROUTING SCHEDULE

A travel plan for calling on prospects that is developed to save time and minimize expenses.

APPROACH

The salesperson's first formal contact with the potential customer.

PRESENTATION

A two-way process in which the salesperson listens to the customer to identify needs and then describes how the product will fulfill them.

a customer.

Few people are naturally good listeners, so sales organizations invest significant resources in training their sales people to become effective listeners. The training identifies ways to learn about the prospect's situation. It also teaches how to show that the salesperson is listening and is concerned about the customer's needs and wants. **Empathy** occurs when a salesperson understands precisely how the prospect feels. Only when prospects know that the seller understands their needs and wants are they receptive to solutions the salesperson offers.

A popular technique for interfacing with customers is SPIN selling. It stands for situation, problem, implication and need payoff.[22] The approach resulted from research into what makes people successful at large sales. Companies such as Xerox and IBM supported the study and have used the system successfully for years. Considerable training is required for people to become proficient with the technique. Essentially, it employs a sequence of probing questions that enlighten the salesperson and the client at the same time.

Situation questions help discover facts about the buyer's environment. Some of this information can be learned before the appointment but in most cases the salesperson is actively listening to the client's description of the present situation. Problem questions identify dissatisfaction with the current circumstances.[23] For example, the salesperson may ask: "What makes it difficult to use this type of product?" Implication questions follow, and these are crucial. They highlight the consequences of current problems and reveal important needs. For example, in response to questions about product safety, one customer began to realize that high insurance costs, low morale and ethical issues were consequences or hidden costs.[24] Need payoff questions then explore why it is important to solve the problem. In the SPIN process, the buyer and seller establish the need for a product and the benefit of its ownership.

The first contact is not only an opportunity for the salesperson to make the case for a product; it is also the first step in building a relationship. Although sales are sometimes made on the first visit, most occur later. Over time, the salesperson assumes different roles as the relationship develops.

Managing Objections and Closing the Sale

It's almost a given in any sales process that a potential customer will raise objections. Perhaps the office manager doesn't have time to see you, or your product costs too much, or the color doesn't match the office decor, or it looks too complicated, or whatever. One of the most important skills a salesperson can learn is the ability to overcome objections. These may be raised subtly in many cultures. In the United States, for example, they are often disguised as questions. A consumer may say, "I can't afford to purchase that automobile," but he or she is really asking about what financing is available, or how much it costs, or about the trade-in terms. Assertive salespeople do not let the first objection stop the dialogue; they use it to advance the discussion. Most organizations have training programs to teach salespeople how to manage objections.

Closing means getting the order. In many cases this is simple, such as asking directly if someone wants to buy the product or whether they will use cash or credit. In other cases,

EMPATHY

An interpersonal connection in which the salesperson understands precisely how the prospect feels and communicates that understanding.

CLOSING

The point at which the salesperson obtains the first order from the customer.

it involves elaborate contracts. Good salespeople know how important it is to help the buyer toward the final decision. You have probably tried on a suit or dress and heard the salesperson say, "Shall I have that measured for alterations?" or "Shall I wrap that for you now?" In business-to-business situations, the salesperson may ask if the purchaser is ready to make a decision or would like to discuss the issue more thoroughly. It is important to use caution in closing.[25] If a buyer is not ready to make the commitment, then asking for an order prematurely can make the salesperson appear pushy and unconcerned with the buyer's needs. A great deal of sensitivity is required to accurately read the buyer's state of mind.

Customer Service There is a big difference between making a sale and gaining a customer. One sale equals one sale. The word "customer" implies something more than a single sale. In order to maintain relationships, salespeople spend significant time servicing accounts. They make sure products are delivered on schedule and operate properly. When there is a problem, the salesperson makes sure that it is resolved quickly and satisfactorily.

FOLLOW-UP

After-sales service to ensure customer satisfaction in order to obtain repeat business.

Follow-up occurs when a salesperson ensures after-sale satisfaction in order to obtain repeat business. If a salesperson effectively provides information that supports the purchasing decision, it can alleviate buyer's remorse. If that evidence is not forthcoming, then customers may quickly become dissatisfied, especially with more expensive purchases. Follow-up also offers a way to identify additional sales opportunities. After the first step is taken, the second is easier. The salesperson who continues to work closely with the buying organization can uncover other needs to fulfill. Good service builds strong customer loyalty, which is the goal of partnership selling.

CHARACTERISTICS OF SALESPEOPLE

Hundreds, perhaps thousands, of studies have been done to determine what makes a good salesperson. Figure 14.8 describes the characteristics noted most often: goal direction, empathy, strong knowledge of applications and ethics.

First, strong sales performers tend to be goal directed. They spend focused time on planning and then work according to those plans. They use their time effectively, which allows them to manage their territory efficiently. They are also highly competitive and obtain results in the face of stiff competition.

Second, because strong salespeople are empathetic, they are aware of the concerns and feelings of others. This means they can understand buyer behavior and see things from the customer's perspective. Most have very good listening and questioning skills that help them get this information.

Third, strong salespeople know how their products apply to the customer's situation. This requires technical competency as well as a good understanding of the customer's business. That combination allows the salesperson to creatively solve problems for the customer. Since each customer has a specific set of needs, each requires special attention. A salesperson must customize or assemble a mix of products that best addresses the specific customer's needs. In essence, the strong salesperson works with

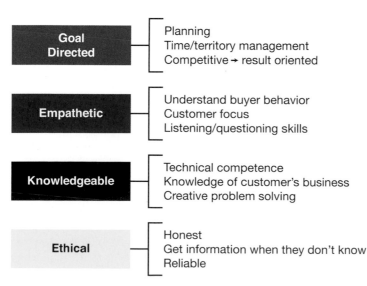

Figure 14.8 Characteristics of Successful Salespeople

the customer to tailor a solution.

Fourth, salespeople must be ethical. The nature of the job often places them in difficult situations. Since good salespeople build relationships, they must be viewed as trustworthy. They find the appropriate information when they don't know the answer to a question. They provide pertinent information and don't waste a customer's time with irrelevant information. They try to help customers solve problems, whether or not a sale is involved. They have a reputation for keeping customers informed, for admitting mistakes and for promising only what they can deliver.

Relationship selling requires that salespeople be more versatile, creative and visionary than ever before. A strong salesperson works to harness all company resources for the customer's benefit.

Sales Force Management

SALES FORCE MANAGEMENT

The marketing function involved with planning, implementing, and adjusting sales force activities.

The sales organization places great emphasis on forging personal relationships with customers. Managers develop and guide the sales organization to make sure connections are made in the right ways with the right customers. They lead others in order to carry out the overall personal selling portion of the communications mix. **Sales force management** is the marketing function involved with planning, implementing and adjusting sales force activities. It is a tremendously important function for companies that stress customer relationships. Nearly every dimension of how salespeople behave with customers is influenced by how they are managed. Sales management teams keep this in mind when they recruit, train and motivate salespeople. And sales force management helps salespeople create lasting connections with customers by directing company resources to support relationship building.

©iStockphoto.com/Jirsak

Managers develop and guide the sales organization to make sure connections are made in the right ways with the right customers.

SALES MANAGER

The person responsible for the leadership and management of salespeople in order to accomplish the sales objectives established in the marketing plan.

Sales managers are responsible for the leadership and management of salespeople in order to accomplish the sales objectives established in the marketing plan. Sales managers are more than very good salespeople. They are vital in implementing the marketing strategy in companies such as General Electric, Intel, Xerox, Eaton Corporation and thousands of others. Many marketing executives, especially in technology-driven firms, have made their way up through the sales manager route. To be effective, sales managers need a full understanding of the marketing strategy and planning, each aspect of the marketing mix and personnel management, in addition to the principles of selling and sales management.

Sales managers need to handle their teams with care, however. One study published in the Journal of Marketing showed that, especially when selling a new product, it's more important to focus on "strengthening a salesperson's selling intentions by creating positive attitudes about the launch and heightened feelings of self-efficacy" and treating sales staff as the first "customers," rather than merely exhorting them to sell. Perceived pressure by management can actually reduce a salesperson's ability to influence buyers.[26]

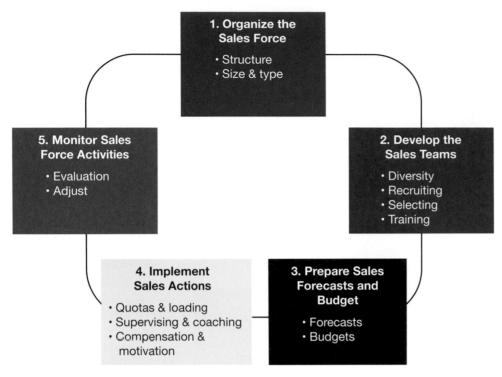

Figure 14.9 Sales Management Functions

Sales force managers perform many functions in support of the marketing strategy. Figure 14.9 describes the most important ones: organize the sales force, develop sales teams, prepare sales forecasts and budgets, implement sales actions and oversee the sales force. These functions may be performed alone in a smaller organization or by a team of people in a larger company. The sales management team is composed of representatives from personnel, who help with recruiting, training and personnel records; from marketing (management) information systems, who provide necessary sales data; and from customer service, who connect the sales force and their customers with manufacturing and logistics. Yet the overall responsibility for all the functions described in Figure 14.9 belongs to sales management.

ORGANIZING THE SALES FORCE

The characteristics of sales managers and the chain of command are important considerations in organizing the sales force. These and other concerns are of particular importance in global settings. Both the structure and the size of the sales group have a lot to do with sales coverage.

Sales Manager Types The sales manager position can be executive, mid-level or first line, depending on responsibilities and scope of operations. At the top are national and international sales executives, often with the title of vice president. They usually report to the top marketing executive. In most companies, only one or a few people are in this position. Their management scope covers several products across a broad territory. In large companies, executive sales managers may have several other sales managers reporting to them and they ultimately are responsible for several thousand salespeople. Mid-level managers, called regional managers when the sales force structure is geographic, supervise several other managers in a large area, such as all of the states in New England or the southwestern U.S. First-line managers oversee several salespeople who handle certain products or types of accounts in a limited geographic area. First-line managers who supervise field reps and retail salespeople usually have a sales force of eight to 12; those who supervise inside sales or telemarketing personnel are likely to have more. As a first assignment, some sales managers supervise only three or four people.

SALES FORCE STRUCTURE

The organization of the reporting relationship between sales managers and sales people.

Sales Force Structures A **sales force structure** is the organization of the reporting relationship between sales managers and salespeople. Sales organizations can be structured by geography, product or division, by market segment, or by individual account. In some cases, all four are used. Figure 14.10 shows a typical geographical structure, topped by a general sales manager who reports to the vice president

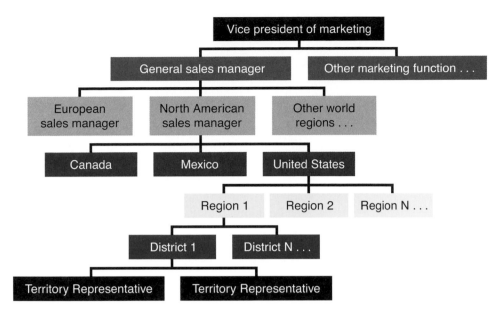

Figure 14.10 A Geographic Sales Force Structure

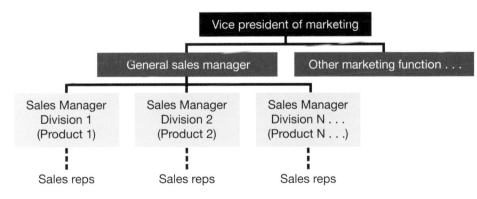

Figure 14.11 A Division or Product Line Sales Force Structure

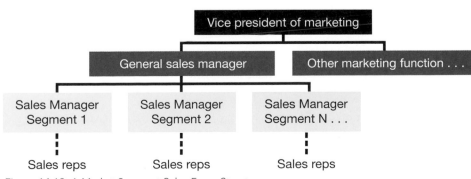

Figure 14.12 A Market Segment Sales Force Structure

of marketing. Sales managers in the various geographical areas report to the general sales manager. Below them may be sales managers at the regional and district level, then territory representatives (salespeople).

Figure 14.11 illustrates the division or product line structure. Many companies are organized into divisions, and each may have a sales organization. Companies with very technical products are likely to use this sort of structure. For example, companies within the auto industry often have a sales organization structured according to the components of an automobile: interior, exterior, electronics and so forth. Each area requires a great deal of interaction among salespeople, designers, manufacturing personnel and individual customers.

The third approach is to structure the sales force by market segment, as shown in Figure 14.12. Salespeople are focused on a given target segment, as outlined in the marketing plan. IBM has historically operated in this manner. It has one sales organization that sells to the financial community, another for universities and yet another for manufacturing firms. The advantage is that salespeople focus on and truly understand the needs of a particular market segment. A company with a limited product line that has differing applications by segment would prefer this arrangement.

Many companies have a few customers who represent extremely large volume, called key accounts, house accounts, national accounts or global accounts, depending on how they are managed. Major accounts may fit the 80-20 rule: About 80 percent of a company's sales volume comes from only 20 percent of its accounts. Although the percentages may differ considerably, the point is that major accounts are large, usually have unique sales needs and are so important to volume and profitability that they require special emphasis. Major ac-

counts are often managed by a separate sales group of a few very experienced people who report to the top sales executive. In other cases, they may be allocated to the mid-level area in which they are located. In some companies, major accounts are assigned to sales managers who split their time between these customers and their management duties.

DEVELOPING THE SALES TEAM

In order to develop the sales team, a good sales force must first be recruited, selected and trained. Recruitment is the activity of attracting qualified prospects for the sales job. Selection involves choosing the strongest recruits for employment in the sales force. Training provides education and disbursement of equipment/tools so salespeople are prepared for the job.

Recruiting Although the structure and size of the sales force are important, nothing is more critical for relationship marketing than the diversity of the sales organization. A sales force that represents various groups has a greater ability to be sensitive to the needs of more individual customers, which improves the company's relationship-building capacity. A diverse sales force provides a variety of insights, ideas and perspectives, all of which make it easier to accommodate a dynamic and multicultural customer base.[27] Strong managers consider diversity in all stages of their sales force development, particularly during recruitment, selection and training.

> Although the structure and size of the sales force are important, nothing is more critical for relationship marketing than the diversity of the sales organization.

Whirlpool, for example, recruits many of its new sales reps from colleges or related sales-education programs. In the company's "Real Whirld" program, the recruits live and learn together in a nine-bedroom house dedicated to their new careers. The program helped Vice President of Sales, Sam Abdelnour, recruit a more diverse sales force; 60 percent are women or minorities.[28]

Effective recruitment attracts a qualified pool of candidates to fill the sales positions. The first step is to develop a job description specifying activities and qualifications. This written document spells out organizational relationships, responsibilities and duties of the position.

The convenience of the recruiting site is important, which is why college campuses are often chosen. Strong organizations devote time to finding experienced candidates through recruiting companies. Many companies have increased college hiring with aggressive e-recruiting online. Some companies also offer mock interviews, career fairs and resume critiques on university campuses. To learn more, contact your college placement office or visit company websites directly.

Selecting Because good sales talent is in high demand, strong candidates have some choice in where they work. Sales managers must demonstrate sound judgment in selecting from a broad range of talent, and they need to sell top candidates on opportunities with their organization. FedEx sales managers see recruitment and selection of sales candidates as one of their most important functions. FedEx is considered to have one of the best global sales forces, selecting candidates who can build relationships with a dynamic customer base spread over 220 countries.[29]

In the selection process, managers of U.S. companies are required to comply with the federal Equal Employment Opportunity Act. Hiring discrimination based on age, sex, race, national origin, religion, ethnic background and physical handicap is illegal. Similar restrictions exist in other countries.

Although there is no definitive list of attributes that can accurately predict who will become a successful salesperson, the attitudes, skills and knowledge of some individuals set them apart. Important personality traits include empathy, which allows a salesperson to understand problems from another's perspective; ego drive, which ties self-image and identity to job performance; and resilience, which allows a salesperson to bounce back from defeat. Also important is the ability to communicate, think analytically and effectively organize and manage time. Knowledge of and experience with a product, industry, competitor or company territory are also valuable qualities. Others include self-discipline, intelligence, creativity, flexibility, self-motivation, persistence, a personable nature and dependability.

Training Even the most qualified salespeople need continuous education. New hires need the most, but seasoned veterans also can benefit from advanced training and formal practice. Many sales executives believe training is critical for developing individual and team skills. Many companies find that it increases morale, reduces turnover, improves relationship-building skills and develops a stronger sense of teamwork, all of which combine to increase sales dramatically. Total U.S. training expenditures were $70.6 billion in 2015 according to Training magazine's 2015 Training Industry Report.[30] Training programs are usually conducted regarding company policies and procedures, product and customer applications knowledge, sales skills and territory and account planning.

Company policies and procedures can be very elaborate, specifying the exact relationship that salespeople are expected to have with customers. Policies range from mundane matters, such as sales account and entertainment budgets, to complicated issues, such as the types of special customer requests the company will honor. In today's sales environment, procedures are often highly complex. Among other things, they may involve understanding how to enter orders, how to service accounts and how to create and maintain reporting systems between the selling and buying organizations.

Training is necessary to understand the product's attributes and benefits. In technical sales jobs, products are often very sophisticated. In some cases, training builds background information, such as knowledge of electricity for electrical products or pharmacology for drug products. Salespeople learn not only about the technologies behind the product but also about how the product works. Teaching salespeople about new items is critical to the success of a pharmaceutical company such as Merck. There is very little time between a product's FDA approval and its introduction to customers.

Most organizations train new hires in basic relationship-selling skills and experienced salespeople in more advanced techniques. The objective is to help the sales force do a better job of working with customers, listening and finding ways to develop profitable relationships for each party. There are companies that specialize in sales training that provide sales certification programs to enhance the skills and credibility of a sales force. In this form of training, salespeople must attend classes or in some cases take distanced learning courses offered over the internet. Certificates are given according to the competency level attained.

Jim Larrison / CC BY 2.0

Training can occur in small company meeting rooms, in the field, or in large conferences with many different organizations networking and trading insights.

More than 50 percent of managers believe that a certification program would benefit their company, and 66 percent of consumers believe certified salespeople are more credible, skilled and competent. Although such training is expensive, many organizations consider it a good investment.[31]

SALES FORECASTING AND BUDGETING

Forecasting and budgeting are important steps in allocating sales resources. The forecast estimates the potential sales demand based on likely responses of buyers to future market conditions, sales force and other promotional activities and marketing actions. Sales force budgets are generally set with the sales forecast in mind. Accuracy in the forecast and budgets is important, since production is scheduled to meet demand. When forecasts are lower than actual demand, customers go unserved. When they are higher than demand, high inventory-carrying costs dramatically reduce profitability. Estimation methods vary from elaborate computer programs to fairly simple questioning of potential buyers. Even small companies, which are known for their ability to adjust quickly, depend on accurate forecasts.

Sales Forecasting Most companies go through three basic steps in estimating demand: an environmental forecast, an industry forecast and a company sales forecast. An **environmental forecast** examines the economic, political and social factors likely to affect the level of spending for a product. Factors include unemployment, consumer spending, interest rates, business investments and inventory levels. In general, information of this type helps determine whether economic conditions for the company's products are likely to be positive or negative. Environmental forecasting can estimate not only global, international, national and regional trends but also very localized trends. Every year, Sales and Marketing Management prints a "Survey of Buying Power," a tool that helps marketers predict sales of products based on environmental conditions, consumer age, wealth and distribution channels.

Sales forecasts often use the industry outlook as a key element. An **industry forecast** estimates the amount of overall demand expected based on such factors as the industry business condition, amount of spending, number of new products and communications budgets anticipated for competitors. In other words, this forecast projects the level of sales and mar-

> Industry forecasts project the level of sales and marketing activity for the industry as a whole, as well as for competitors likely to affect the company most directly.

keting activity for the industry as a whole, as well as for competitors likely to affect the company most directly.

The **company sales forecast** is a prediction of unit or dollar sales based on the overall marketing strategy. It forecasts unit sales and must be in line with marketing, financial and operations plans. If not, then the sales forecast is revised. The marketing plan is particularly critical. For example, a product positioned as a high-priced specialty item may have a low expected sales volume. For a product positioned as a low-priced commodity, the sales volume estimate will probably be higher. In addition, in order to do a good job of developing objectives, it is important to estimate demand with other departments in mind. Sales managers communicate about forecasts with many areas of the company to reconcile any differences. Since various departments may have specific objectives, such as cost containment, brand growth and financial targets, this interaction is necessary. Estimates may be made for the entire company, a particular product, a geographic region, a market segment or on some other basis.

ENVIRONMENTAL FORECAST

An estimate of the economic, political, and social factors likely to affect the level of spending for the types of products or services being forecasted.

INDUSTRY FORECAST

An estimate of the amount and type of competitive activity likely to occur in an industry.

COMPANY SALES FORECAST

A prediction of unit or dollar sales based on the overall marketing strategy.

Forecasting and budgeting are important steps in allocating sales resources.

It's important to remember the more dynamic the situation, the more difficult the prediction is likely to be. Consequently, businesses in new fields may have to spend more time estimating demand than do businesses with mature product lines. Yet, even in innovative, highly competitive industries, it is important to obtain reliable forecasts.

Some marketers mistakenly associate good forecasting with strong marketing. In fact, there are many examples of organizations that have forecast low sales volume and created less aggressive marketing strategies. Although they met their forecasts, they probably would have reached much higher sales levels if they had pursued an aggressive strategy. Most organizations recognize that perfect sales projections may mean the company is operating much too conservatively. Whirlpool Corporation believes a perfect forecast is possible only when a marketing group is performing below potential.

Forecasts are very important in deciding how to allocate company resources. Divisions that foresee high levels of sales are often given ample resources, such as additional salespeople, large advertising and promotion budgets, and lots of attention from product development and manufacturing. Consequently, the forecast can become a self-fulfilling prophecy. When forecasts are low, fewer resources are provided, and lower sales result.

Sales Force Budgets One of the most important tasks of the sales manager is to create and administer the sales budget. The three most common methods for setting the budget are: as a percentage of overall sales, relative to competitors' budgets, and as projected costs for the sales tasks. The first method establishes the sales budget as a percentage of the historical sales level. Although simple to use, this method has a major flaw. The estimated increase over past sales results in a larger sales budget, but perhaps the situation should be the reverse: A larger sales budget should result in improved sales volume. Despite this problem, many sales organizations base the budget on past performance. Essentially, a sales force that produces more is rewarded with increased resources in the future for its past success. A variation on this is to use the sales forecast to establish the budget. This is more acceptable because it looks at the future rather than the past.

The second way to determine the sales budget is through comparison with a competitor's budget. Industry data provide the number of salespeople and sales offices as well as sales expenditures for other companies. The sales budget is then set accordingly. One advantage of this method is that it emphasizes competitive activity in the marketplace. A disadvantage is that it is not based on an understanding of the actual costs of one's own sales activities.

Finally, task-based budgeting looks at the tasks salespeople must perform in order to accomplish ob-

One of the most important tasks of the sales manager is to create and administer the sales budget.

jectives. Careful thought is given to each aspect of the sales process and to estimating the associated costs. The items usually considered are salaries, recruiting, training, travel, sales promotion, staff and clerical expenses, dues and supplies.

IMPLEMENTING SALES ACTION PLANS

Once the sales forecast and budget have been established, sales activity can take place. Sales managers set quotas, measure performance, determine compensation and supervise, coach and motivate the sales organization, and establish ethical expectations in such a way that objectives are accomplished.

Quotas **Quotas** are quantitative performance standards used to direct sales force activity. They also provide a way to evaluate performance. Whereas forecasts estimate results, quotas provide guidelines. They are one of the most important methods sales managers use to set and meet objectives. When quotas are exceeded, the sales force has produced beyond objectives; when quotas are not met, the sales force has fallen short of objectives. Overall, quotas are set in line with the strategic marketing plan. Most sales organizations use one of three types: sales volume, profit or activity quotas.

Sales volume quotas establish unit or dollar objectives. Usually these are set for a market segment, product or service line, and average volume per customer. Typically, a quota for the entire sales organization is determined and then divided among the various sales regions and salespeople. During this process, salespeople and others are likely to provide feedback to sales executives regarding potential in their territory, the level of competition and what goals they think are realistic. That information is combined with the sales forecast.

Sales profit quotas establish profitability objectives for customers, products and market segments. Rather than volume, the focus is on the overall profit that can be made. This kind of quota is particularly important when sales actions such as price negotiations or the ratio of repeat to new customers influence profit. It is also important when different products yield different profits.

Activity quotas encourage salespeople to engage in certain tasks, such as prospecting calls, service calls, sales calls, demonstrations and visiting new accounts. The focus is on customer contacts that will allow the company to implement its overall marketing strategy.

Quotas are generally used to determine some portion of a salesperson's compensation. The simplest procedure is to set the same quota (such as amount of sales) for all salespeople and provide bonuses to those who exceed it. This tends to be inequitable, however, because sales potential and competition are likely to differ from one sales territory to another. Consequently, sales quotas usually vary for different parts of the organization and different salespeople. Compensation is covered in more detail in a later section.

Performance Measures Volume, profit and activity quotas can be combined to measure performance, as shown in Figure 14.13. In this example the quota is based on sales volume, profit margin percentage, number of new accounts obtained, percentage of accounts retained, level of customer satisfaction and number of new leads. Each factor is weighted in terms of importance. At the end of the sales period, the percentage of quota reached in each category is multiplied by the weight to determine the contribution of that category to achieving the total quota. In the example, sales are weighted at 40 percent, the quota is $500,000, and performance is $25,000 above that, leading to 105 percent of quota on that item. Multiplying by the weight, we get a 42 percent contribution to the total quota. Notice that when all these items are put together, this particular salesperson achieved 110 percent of quota (exceeded objectives by 10 percent). Performance exceeded the quota in all areas except the number of new accounts.

The performance measurement shown in Figure 14.13 can be used for several

QUOTAS

Quantitative objectives used to direct sales force activity and evaluate performance.

SALES VOLUME QUOTAS

Unit or dollar objectives, usually set by market segment, product or service line, and average volume per customer.

SALES PROFIT QUOTAS

Profitability objectives for customers, products, and market segments.

ACTIVITY QUOTAS

Action objectives that encourage salespeople to engage in certain tasks, such as prospecting calls, service calls, sales calls, demonstrations, and visiting new accounts.

	(1) Weight	(2) Quota	(3) Performance	(4) % of Quota	(5) Contribution to Total Quota: (4) 3 (1)
Sales in dollars	40%	$500,000	$525,000	105%	42%
Profit margin	20%	30%	33%	110%	22%
Number of new accounts	15%	25%	20%	80%	12%
Number of accounts retained	20%	100%	120%	120%	24%
Number of new leads	5%	25%	50%	200%	10%
					TOTAL: 110%

Figure 14.13   Quotas as a Measure of Performance

purposes. First, this person maintains loyal customers but seems to do little to increase the number of new accounts. The sales manager should discuss the situation to see whether training is needed or whether the territory has minimal potential for new customers. Second, since quotas can be used to motivate the sales force, the salesperson could be compensated for performing so well. Third, although the example provided here focuses on dollar volume, organizations often use this method to emphasize certain products or market segments consistent with their overall marketing strategy and positioning plan.

Compensation   A well-designed compensation plan should be geared toward the needs of both the company and the sales force. It should be developed with the overall sales strategy in mind. A compensation system not only helps motivate salespeople but is also important in keeping loyal employees. Satisfied employees are less likely to leave the company and will probably work harder to develop loyal customers. It is almost impossible to build customer loyalty with a dissatisfied sales force.

The three basic elements of sales force compensation are salaries, commissions and bonuses. A **salary** is a fixed amount paid regardless of specific performance. Salaries are usually based on education, experience, longevity and overall professionalism. A **commission** is an amount paid in direct proportion to the accomplishment of specific short-term sales objectives. It usually is given for meeting or exceeding a broad range of criteria, including volume and profit by product, or according to customer type and loyalty. A **bonus** is a percentage of salary or fee paid in addition to other compensation for meeting long-term or unique goals. Bonuses are often given to the entire sales team for an outstanding effort, usually quarterly or annually. Compensation plans can be based on salary only, commission only, or both, and sometimes bonuses as well.

Supervision and Coaching   Supervision and coaching are face-to-face interactions between the sales manager and a salesperson. Most managers spend considerable time working with their people in the field. Good managers communicate well and help salespeople determine appropriate sales actions. They provide guidance to keep the sales force operating according to the company's philosophies, policies and marketing plans.

The three components to central coaching are: "supervisory feedback, role modeling and salesperson trust in managers."[32] Essentially, sales coaching occurs when the manager assists in the development of skills. Similar to a voice coach or athletic coach, the sales manager gives advice and demonstrations that enable salespeople to do a better job. Feedback should be objective and balanced, and positive incentives should be used as progress is made. Coaching usually involves visits with customers by the manager and salesperson. The sales manager observes and gives pointers afterward on sales techniques. Good coaches also address all aspects of selling — from time management to customer sales support to interaction with other company employees, sometimes involving role-playing. Henry Mueller, former vice president of new business partnerships at American Express, said: "The sales manager's role is to add value, whether it's with the customer or whether it's helping your salespeople prepare for their next round of sales calls. It's keeping an eye out for those common problems and opportunities that are coming up. ... You're always coach-

SALARY

The fixed amount of compensation paid regardless of performance.

COMMISSION

A form of sales force compensation in which the amount paid is in direct proportion to the accomplishment of specific objectives.

BONUS

A percentage of salary or a fee paid in addition to other compensation for meeting long-term or unique goals.

ing, coaching, coaching."[33]

There are many appropriate coaching styles, but good coaches usually don't simply take over. They observe, ask questions and listen. They communicate clearly and provide positive reinforcement for the activities that salespeople carry out well. Feedback from sales managers is invaluable because it helps salespeople understand their strengths and weaknesses.

Motivation Most top salespeople are motivated by the very nature of the job. They find selling fascinating and want to excel in a competitive environment. Still, good sales managers can add to motivation by providing a positive organizational climate as well as financial and career incentives. Since many salespeople spend little time under direct supervision, the systems for motivation must work well without the constant presence of the sales manager. A positive organizational climate exists when salespeople feel good about their opportunities and rewards. A positive climate also helps salespeople perform at the highest professional level. Many companies use financial incentives. Money is a strong motivator, but companies are increasingly incorporating different forms of incentives.

Progressive companies are starting to account for individual differences in salespeople when determining how to motivate. The Harvard Business Review categorized salespeople into three distinct groups: stars, core performers and laggards. Each group is motivated by different kinds of incentives. For stars, it is best to not cap commissions, because they are very self-motivated but will stop selling if they have reached compensation limits. Core performers can be motivated by offering prizes, contests, and multi-tier targets. Laggards can be motivated by creating more frequent bonus structures and applying some ethical social pressure to increase performance.[34]

Ethical Issues in Motivation and Compensation In striving to produce peak performers, sales managers may use several motivational approaches. If they push too hard in the wrong ways, salespeople may be pressured to compromise ethical standards. When performance is poor, rewards may be withheld, or in extreme cases punishment may be used. Proper motivational techniques generally reward people for good performance. A key part of the management job, however, is to establish expectations not only in terms of sales volume but also regarding acceptable behavior. When managers focus exclusively on sales volume objectives, they are telling salespeople that the ends justify the means. This lack of attention to appropriate behavior in combination with pressure to perform can be considered unethical in itself. Let's look at three questionable practices.

- *Family pressure*: High-performing salespeople are rewarded publicly with free trips, gifts or monetary bonuses. For average or under-performing salespeople, however, it's clear to family members that they are low producers. Do you think family dynamics change as a result? Is the company interfering in family relationships for the purpose of elevating sales?

- *Peer pressure*: The sales manager broadcasts performance results to all salespeople or, in announcing sales contest winners, points out a few low producers. Rather than private communications between the manager and the salesperson, overt peer pressure is being used to gain behavior changes. This would be like posting student names along with grades in the student newspaper. Is that an ethical way to motivate you to learn? Could this increase the pressure on students to cheat?

- *Termination*: All salespeople are rank ordered, and the lowest performers are asked to leave, even though they may be performing very profitably for the company. This keeps all salespeople pushing for fear of losing their job. Since termination is devastating for most people, to avoid it they may put undue or unscrupulous pressure on buyers.

Even quotas, though less extreme than these scenarios, can be troublesome. They are generally considered useful tools, but some sales managers believe they lead to high-pressure tactics and thus are harmful to relationship building.

MONITORING SALES FORCE ACTIVITIES

Once sales operations are in effect, management needs to take the final steps of its process: evaluation and adjustment. Sales activities can almost always can be improved. In fact, some of the strongest sales organizations are very flexible in meeting business challenges and competitive situations, an especially useful attribute in industries subject to rapid change. In general, most evaluation programs look at efforts and results, assess the company's influence in supporting performance, identify problems and opportunities and take corrective action.

Salesperson performance can be evaluated behaviorally or by outcome. Behavioral performance is based on skills and the ability to meet the demands of the job. This includes such aspects as sales presentation, planning, teamwork, relationship selling and technical knowledge. Outcome performance is measured by such customer-related factors as sales volume, market share, customer loyalty and satisfaction and number of new accounts.[35]

In addition to evaluating individual salespeople, managers must regularly assess the entire sales force. This tells whether overall performance is strong. It may result in territory shifts, the addition of people or other adjustments. The process gives both field reps and management an opportunity to learn whether the level of activity has produced the expected results. This often means doing productivity analysis to determine whether sales volumes have been reached, market shares have been accomplished, and the appropriate product mix has been sold to targeted segments. Usually, good evaluation requires looking behind the numbers to determine where the strongest and weakest results occurred and under what conditions.

Today, many companies use 360-degree evaluations; that is, salespeople are asked to evaluate their sales managers as well. This supports the team concept and helps break down the old barriers to joint progress. Since managerial success depends on working through others, this type of feedback is seen as absolutely critical in many companies.

Chapter Summary

Objective 1: Identify the five types of selling and describe the three selling approaches.
Direct and missionary sales encompass five types of selling: team selling, field selling, over-the-counter selling, inside selling and global selling.. Team selling involves people from different parts of an organization working together to make sales. Field selling occurs at a customer's place of business. Over-the-counter selling takes place in retail stores. Inside selling involves sales made from within a company's location, often through phone or internet contact. Finally, global selling occurs in foreign markets, and salespeople may be from the home office or from the host country.

There are three distinct personal selling approaches: traditional selling, consultative selling and relationship selling. Traditional selling is persuasive in nature and focuses on simply moving product.

Consultative selling focuses on working closely with customers to solve problems. Relationship selling is strategic in nature and involves developing long-term relationships that are mutually beneficial for buyer and seller. It requires that the selling organization understand the customer's business or lifestyle and treat loyal customers as assets of the firm. Typically this leads to partnering that creates value for the customer and the selling organization.

Objective 2: Describe the responsibilities of salespeople and sales managers.
Most professional salespeople are responsible for implementing their company's marketing strategy within a territory. They also communicate company policy to customers and potential customers. They are important sources of feedback and have a responsibility to convey this information to their organization. Salespeople must have

excellent ethical judgment since they often operate without much direct supervision, are under pressure to boost volume and have flexibility in what they say to customers.

Sales managers are responsible for planning, implementing and adjusting sales force activities. First, sales managers work with others in their company to organize the sales force, including its structure, size and type. Second, they develop diverse sales teams through recruiting, selecting and training. Third, they prepare forecasts and budgets. Fourth, they implement actions by establishing quotas, assessing performance, determining compensation and supervising, coaching and motivating the sales force. Finally, they evaluate sales activities and make any necessary changes.

Objective 3: Identify and explain the seven steps in personal selling.

The seven steps in personal selling are planning, prospecting, organizing information and developing a call plan, approaching a prospect, presenting a case and building relationships, managing objections and closing, and customer service. Sales planning translates the company's marketing strategy into territory and account plans. Prospecting involves looking for new customers within the company's target markets. Next, sales personnel organize information and develop a call plan. To do this, they learn about prospects and prepare a routing schedule to identify which prospects will be called on and when. The approach is the first formal contact with the customer. The objective is to secure an initial meeting and gain customer interest. The next step is making the case and building relationships. This is done through the sales presentation. Sales personnel then manage objections and close the sale. One of the most important sales skills is the ability to overcome business objections. Closing means getting the first order. Following through with customer service after the sale is essential for developing customer loyalty.

Objective 4: Identify the characteristics of strong salespeople.

First, strong salespeople are goal directed.. They use time well, manage their territory efficiently and like to compete to obtain results. Second, they are empathetic; they understand buyer behavior, are customer-focused and possess excellent listening and questioning skills. Third, they are knowledgeable. They are technically competent, know their customers' business and are good at creative problem solving. Fourth, excellent salespeople are ethical and trustworthy; they are honest, seek additional information when they don't know the answer and make reliable partners.

Objective 5: Describe the three steps involved in developing a sales team.

To develop a sales team, a good sales force must be recruited, selected and trained. Recruitment entails looking for exceptional, diverse candidates and often takes place on college campuses. Selection is a choice process for both the company and the candidates, as both seek a good match. Training involves educating salespeople about company policies and procedures, product and customer knowledge, relationship selling skills and the seven-steps of personal selling.

Objective 6: Explain the six elements of sales action plans.

Implementing sales action plans involves six steps on the part of a sales manager. First, quotas are set to establish the sales volume, profit and activities expected from each salesperson. Second, performance measures are established. Third, a compensation plan is designed which usually includes salary, commission and bonus elements. Fourth, supervision and coaching involves managers working with salespeople to improve performance, build self esteem and increase skills. Fifth, motivation must be created to make employees feel rewarded for their efforts. Finally, ethical issues related to motivation and compensation must be discussed to insure that salespeople don't use unethical techniques to achieve quotas.

Review Your Understanding

1. List several types of personal selling situations. Give an example of each.
2. What is relationship selling?
3. List the responsibilities of a salesperson.
4. What are the seven steps in personal selling?
5. What characterizes a strong salesperson?
6. What does closing mean?
7. Give three reasons why ethics are important to salespeople.
8. List the types of sales forecasting. Briefly describe each.
9. What are three methods for setting a sales force budget?
10. What are quotas?
11. What is coaching?
12. What are three ethical issues surrounding sales force management?

Discussion of Concepts

1. What are the key differences among the traditional, consultative and relationship sales approaches? Which do you feel is most appropriate in a majority of circumstances? Why?
2. List the seven types of sales personnel. Under what circumstances would it make sense to have each type?
3. Why is it important for the salesperson to support the company's strategic marketing plan?
4. What is most important about each of the seven steps in personal selling? How do they form a process?
5. Describe some of the ways salespeople find new customers.

Under what circumstances might each be appropriate?

6. Do you have the characteristics of a strong salesperson? Do you believe people are born with these, or can they be learned?

7. The job of the sales manager is to support the strategic marketing and communications plan of the organization. What are the key responsibilities of a sales manager?

8. Describe the methods a sales manager can use to set the sales budget. Which one do you feel is most effective? Why?

9. Is it acceptable to use family pressure to motivate salespeople? Why or why not?

Key Terms & Definitions

1. **Account planning:** Establishing sales goals and objectives for each major customer.

2. **Activity quotas:** Action objectives that encourage salespeople to engage in certain tasks, such as prospecting calls, service calls, sales calls, demonstrations and visiting new accounts.

3. **Approach:** The salesperson's first formal contact with the potential customer.

4. **Bonus:** A percentage of salary or a fee paid in addition to other compensation for meeting long-term or unique goals.

5. **Center of influence:** An opinion leader who can be quickly qualified as a potential customer because of his or her standing in the community.

6. **Closing:** The point at which the salesperson obtains the first order from the customer.

7. **Cold calling:** Contacting a lead for the first time.

8. **Commission:** A form of sales force compensation in which the amount paid is in direct proportion to the accomplishment of specific objectives.

9. **Company sales forecast:** A prediction of unit or dollar sales based on the overall marketing strategy.

10. **Consultative selling:** An approach to selling in which sales personnel work closely with customers to help solve problems.

11. **Direct sales:** Sales that result from the salesperson's direct interaction with a consumer or company.

12. **Empathy:** An interpersonal connection in which the salesperson knows precisely how the prospect feels and communicates that understanding.

13. **Environmental forecast:** An estimate of the economic, political and social factors likely to affect the level of spending for the types of products or services being forecast.

14. **Follow-up:** After-sales service to ensure customer satisfaction in order to obtain repeat business.

15. **Industry forecast:** An estimate of the amount and type of competitive activity that is likely to occur in an industry.

16. **Leads:** All those who may have need of a company's product.

17. **Missionary sales:** Sales made indirectly through people who do not obtain orders but influence the buying decision of others.

18. **Negotiation:** Discussion by two or more parties to arrange a transaction.

19. **Networking:** Contacting friends, relatives and associates to obtain leads.

20. **Pre-approach:** Preparation by the salesperson for the initial meeting with a prospect.

21. **Presentation:** A two-way process in which the salesperson listens to the customer to identify needs and then describes how the product will fulfill them.

22. **Prospect:** A potential customer interested in the seller's product.

23. **Prospecting:** Looking for potential customers within the company's target markets.

24. **Qualifying:** Examining prospects to identify those with the authority and ability to buy the product.

25. **Quotas:** Quantitative objectives used to direct sales force activity and evaluate performance.

26. **Referral:** A lead provided by a qualified prospect.

27. **Relationship selling:** An approach to selling in which bonds are created between buyer and seller to gain loyalty and mutual satisfaction.

28. **Routing schedule:** A travel plan for calling on prospects that is developed to save time and minimize expenses.

29. **Salary:** The fixed amount of compensation paid regardless of performance.

30. **Sales force management:** The marketing function involved with planning, implementing, and adjusting sales force activities.

31. **Sales force structure:** The organization of the reporting relationship between sales managers and sales people.

32. **Sales manager:** The person responsible for the leadership and management of salespeople in order to accomplish the sales objectives established in the marketing plan.

33. **Sales profit quotas:** Profitability objectives for customers, products and market segments.

34. **Sales territory:** All the actual and potential customers, often within a specified geographic area, for which the salesperson has responsibility.

35. **Sales volume quotas:** Unit or dollar objectives, usually set by market segment, product or service line, and average volume per customer.

36. **Team selling:** Selling that involves people from most parts of the organization, including top executives, working together to create a relationship with the buying organization.

37. **Telemarketing:** Making telephone calls to leads provided by marketing services or from other lists.

38. **Territory planning:** Identifying potential customers, their sales potential and the frequency with which they will be contacted about various products.

39. **Traditional selling:** Focuses on persuading consumers to buy a company's product.

40. **Qualified prospect:** A potential buyer interested in the seller's product who possesses the attributes of a good customer.

References

1. "Occupational Employment and Wages News Release," Bureau of Labor Statistics, www.bls.gov, website visited August 10, 2012.
2. www.salary.com, website visited July 10, 2014.
3. "Boeing Commercial Airplanes Achieves 2009 Delivery Target, Maintains Strong Backlog," http://boeing.mediaroom.com, January 7, 2010.
4. "Boeing wins $14.7 billion jet order from United," CNN Money, http://money.cnn.com, July 12, 2012.
5. www.marketwatch.com/investing/stock/mrk/financials, website visited July 16, 2016.
6. "Live Help," Nordstrom, http://shop.nordstrom.com, website visited July 10, 2014.
7. Boyle, Brett A., "The Importance of the Industrial Inside Sales Force: A Case Study," Industrial Marketing Management, September 1996, Vol. 25, Issue 5, pp. 339-348.
8. "Five Relationship Blunders to Avoid in Your Sales and Marketing," MarketingProfs, www.marketingprofs.com, February 14, 2011.
9. Graham, John R., "Successful Selling: Learn the Customer's Buying Cycle," The American Salesman, March 2000, Vol. 45, Issue 3, pp. 3-9.
10. Chapman, Joe; Rauck, Stephanie, "Relationship Selling: A Synopsis of Recent Research," Developments in Marketing Science, no. 18, ed. Roger Gomes (Coral Gables FL, Academy of Marketing Science, 1995), pg. 163.
11. Del Gaizo, Edward R.; Corcoran, Keven J.; Erdman, David J., The Alligator Trap (Chicago, Irwin Professional Pub) 1996, pg. 21.
12. "Wachovia Chooses to Innovate With Cisco TelePresence," Cisco News Release, www.newsroom.cisco.com, June 4, 2007.
13. Ellram, Lisa M., "Partnering Pitfalls and Success Factors," International Journal of Purchasing and Materials Management, April 1995, Vol. 31, Issue 2, pp. 35-44.
14. Foster, Dean A., "Negotiating and 'Mind-Meeting,'" Directors and Boards, Fall 1992, Vol. 17, Issue 1, pp. 52-54.
15. "Returns and Exchanges," Urban Outfitters, www.urbanoutfitters.com, website visited July 10, 2014.
16. Astarita, Mark J., "Cold Calling Rules and Procedures," 1995, www.seclaw.com/coldcall.htm, website visited July 10, 2014.
17. Peterson, Roger S., "Go Modular, Be Flexible to Control Exhibit Costs," Marketing News, December 2, 1996, Vol. 30, Issue 25, pg. 11.
18. Stafford, Katrease, "Attendance up at this year's Detroit auto show," Detroit Free Press, January 24, 2016.
19. "2016 Chicago Auto Show: Big and lean," www.KBB.com, website visited July 16, 2016.
20. Karen E. Klein, "Wring the Most Out of a Trade Show", Bloomberg Businessweek, April 12, 2012.
21. "Amway reports 2015 sales of $9.5 billion USD," Amway Press Release, http://globalnews.amway.com, February 2, 2016.
22. Rackham, Neil, SPIN Fieldbook: Practical Tools, Methods, Exercises, and Resources (New York, McGraw-Hill) 1996.
23. Ibid, pp. 11-12.
24. Role-playing with executives witnessed by the author.
25. Hawes, Jon M.; Strong, James T.; Winich, Bernard S., "Do Closing Techniques Diminish Prospect Trust?" Industrial Marketing Management, September 1996, Vol. 25, Issue 5, pp. 349-360.
26. Frank Q. Fu, Keith A. Richards, Douglas E. Hughes and Eli Jones, "Motivating Salespeople to Sell New Products: The Relative Influence of Attitudes, Subjective Norms, and Self-Efficacy," Journal of Marketing, Vol. 74 (November 2010), pgs. 20-21.
27. Labich, Kenneth, "Making Diversity Pay," Fortune, September 9, 1996, Vol. 134, Issue 5, pp. 177-179; Wah, Louisa, "Diversity at Allstate: A Competitive Weapon," Management Review, July/August 1999, Vol. 49, Issue 3, pp. 24-30.
28. "How One Enterprise Sales Force Works With Channel Partners to Maintain and Build Sales," Selling Power, June 27, 2012.
29. Brewer, Geoffrey; Galea, Christine, "Best Sales Forces: The Top 25," www.fedex.com, website visited June 26, 2010.
30. "2013 Training Industry Report," Training, www.trainingmag.com, website visited July 12, 2014.
31. Honeycutt, Jr., Earl D.; Attia, Ashraf M.; D'Auria, Angela R., "Sales Certification Programs," Journal of Personal Selling and Sales Management, Summer 1996, Vol. 16, Issue 3, pp. 59-65.
32. Rich, Gregory A., "The Constructs of Sales Coaching: Supervisory Feedback, Role Modeling, and Trust," The Journal of Personal Selling and Sales Management, Winter 1998, Volume 18, Issue 1, pp. 53-63.
33. Brewer, Geoffrey, "Meeting of the Minds," Sales and Marketing Management, November 1996, Vol. 148, Issue 11, pp. 72-74.
34. Thomas Steenburgh and Michael Ahearne, "Motivating Salespeople: What Really Works," Harvard Business Review, July-August 2012 Issue.
35. Grant, Ken; Cravens, David W., "Examining Sales Force Performance in Organizations That Use Behavior-Based Sales Management Processes," Industrial Marketing Management, September 1996, Vol. 25, pp. 361-371.

CHAPTER *15*

Supply Chain
Management
& Channels

amazon

Courtesy of Amazon

Scan to see how Amazon has become a global leader in supply chain management.

When Jeff Bezos, CEO of Amazon, delivered his first letter to shareholders in 1997, he committed to providing compelling values, reduced delivery times and tailored customer experiences. In that year, Amazon's main focus was selling books. It served 1.5 million customers and earned revenue of $147.8 million. Today, Amazon is the leading multi-product e-retailer in the United States with more than 304 million active customer accounts worldwide and $107 billion in 2015 net sales. Industry analyst Gartner's 2016 rankings position Amazon as the third best company in the world for global supply chain management.

Amazon's dominance of e-commerce through digital marketing is astounding. Consider this: of every additional $1 Americans spent online in 2015 (compared with 2014), Amazon captured 51 cents! This massive growth can be attributed in part to the company's Prime marketing strategy. A whopping 25% of American households now belong to Amazon Prime, and Ben Schachter, a retail analyst at American investment bank Macquarie, suggests that at least half of American households will subscribe to it by 2020.

Why is Prime so important to Amazon? Because data from Consumer Intelligence Research Partners indicate that Prime members in the U.S. spend an average of $1500 a year with the company, as opposed to $625 for nonmembers. Membership costs $10.99 per month or $99 per year. Subscribers willingly pay the fee in return for speedy shipping. The company has refined its delivery from 48 hours, to next day, to the evening of the same day. Now it's investing in drone technology to deliver packages within 30 minutes. Consumers love the service!

Amazon has invested billions of dollars to create an infrastructure that makes this all possible. Behind the scenes, there's a massive, incredibly fine-tuned supply chain management system running 24/7. What happens from the time an order is placed on Amazon until it arrives at a customer's door? A lot! First the or-der shows up with a bar code on an Amazon employee's hand-held scanner showing the exact location of where the product sits in one of the company's million-square-foot fulfillment centers. The employee physically finds the product in the appropriately labeled bin of the warehouse, takes it out, scans it so it can automatically be reordered for inventory, and places it in a crate, which travels on a conveyor belt for miles to the packing area of the warehouse. There, the product is packed, sorted into trucks according to geographical destination, shipped and tracked by bar code until it arrives at its destination.

Amazon's success is a result of its dedication to connect with customers through innovation and technology. From its choice of suppliers, to its systems for order management, warehousing and distribution, to materials handling, inventory control, transportation choices and customer response programs, the company is always considering what consumers want. In fact, Amazon is working to get a patent for predictive purchasing—delivering products to customers before they even order them! Amazon tracks its performance against about 500 measurable goals, and nearly 80% relate to customer objectives. This customer attention, coupled with a precisely managed supply chain, has buoyed Amazon to become one of the world's most valuable brands.

Sources: Simpson, Paul, "The secrets behind Amazon's success," *Supply Chain, Technology,* January 21, 2016; www.forbes.com/global/2012/0507/global-2000-12-amazon-jeff-bezos-gets-it.html, website visited July 10, 2015; www.gartner.com/newsroom/id/3053118, website visited July 10, 2016; www.statista.com/topics/846/amazon, website visited July 10, 2016.

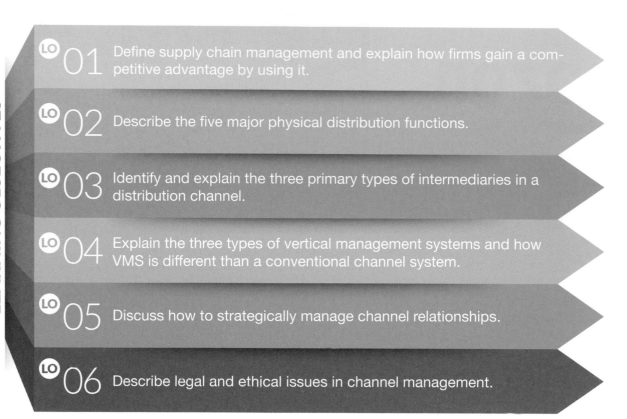

LEARNING OBJECTIVES

LO 01 Define supply chain management and explain how firms gain a competitive advantage by using it.

LO 02 Describe the five major physical distribution functions.

LO 03 Identify and explain the three primary types of intermediaries in a distribution channel.

LO 04 Explain the three types of vertical management systems and how VMS is different than a conventional channel system.

LO 05 Discuss how to strategically manage channel relationships.

LO 06 Describe legal and ethical issues in channel management.

The Concept of Supply Chain Management & Channels

Supply chain management helps companies link upstream suppliers of raw materials, components and expertise required to make a product, with all of the downstream distribution of products by wholesalers, retailers and other organizations. Historically, marketers focused primarily on marketing channels used to distribute products. Today, information systems provide the data required to manage the entire supply chain to create outstanding customer value. For example, as soon as you buy a product from Walmart, a supplier from as far away as China knows the product has left the store, and all other members of the chain that produce and ship that product get the same information. This allows the product to be replaced in the quickest and most efficient way possible.

Figure 15.1 illustrates supply chain management and channels in the most elementary way. Notice that supply chain management deals with the total chain, while channels are a very important part of the chain. In this chapter we extend the concept of supply chain management to include the consumer. Channels are included in two places of figure 15.1

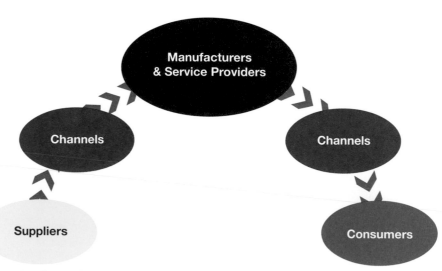

Figure 15.1 Supply Chain Management & Channels

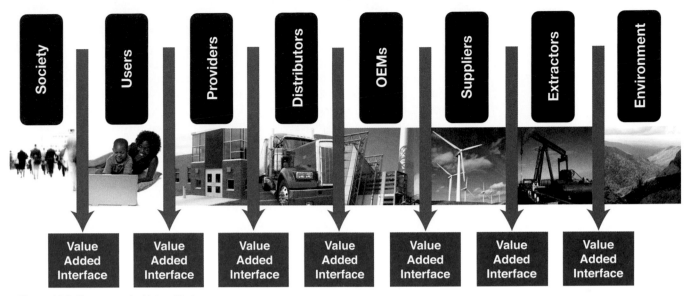

Figure 15.2 Elements of a Value Chain

because channel strategies are equally important in B2B (business-to-business) and B2C (business-to-consumer) marketing.

The value chain in Figure 15.2 shows the linkage of actions performed by suppliers, producers and all channel members to create and deliver value to customers. Members of the value chain extend from the environment, including all of the natural resources, to society, which consumes and disposes of products. Members include extractors, suppliers, OEMs, distributors, providers and users. At each link in the chain, marketing helps connect the specific organizations by forming beneficial relationships. These are the value added interfaces along the chain. The types of organizations that are linked for a particular product form the supply chain for the product's industry. An individual company generally refers to its supply chain as that part of the value chain which is most important to its overall business. In some cases it only refers to upstream elements, but both upstream and downstream members are critical.

Supply Chain Management, Logistics & Physical Distribution

SUPPLY CHAIN MANAGEMENT

Incorporation of all activities concerned with planning, implementation, and control of sourcing, manufacturing, and delivery of products and services.

SUPPLY NETWORK

All of the organizations from which components, semi-finished products, and services are purchased.

Supply chain management incorporates all of the activities concerned with planning, implementation and control of sourcing, manufacturing and delivery for products and services.[1] The development of a network of supply and distribution organizations involved in acquiring and moving products, as well as the flow of information about these activities within and across different firms, is important because these business activities impact customer satisfaction and profitability. First, we will discuss supply chain management. We will then cover integrated logistics management, which deals mostly with the physical management of raw materials, components and finished products. Finally, we will address physical distribution in detail.

SUPPLY CHAIN MANAGEMENT

Excellent supply chain management can typically lower a company's costs by three to seven percent and increase cash flow as much as 30 percent.[2] One important aspect of supply chain management is the development of a supply network. The **supply network** consists of the organizations from which components, semi-finished products and services are purchased. It is important to develop a network of suppliers that can provide the support required to develop excellent products. For example, Ford has a supply network of more than 2,000 companies, not including a large set of independent Ford dealers.

Firms employ different strategies to obtain a competitive advantage in supply chain management; many firms form strategic alliances with suppliers and distributors to optimize performance and increase customer satisfaction.[3] Raytheon, a leading contractor of defense and commercial electronics, uses a program to help its suppliers reduce costs and increase efficiency. This may or may not lead to a larger profit margin for Raytheon, but it invariably results in a lower cost for its end customers, which encourages customer loyalty.[4]

Some companies use vertical integration to control the supply chain. **Vertical integration** occurs when a company controls or owns the supplier or customer, which gives the organization a lot of control over the supply chain but is expensive to maintain. General Motors spun off Delphi, the world's largest auto supplier, and Ford spun off Visteon, the nation's second-largest auto supplier. Now General Motors and Ford have no direct management responsibilities for these spin-offs and as a result can focus attention on other aspects of their respective companies.

VERTICAL INTEGRATION

Ownership or control of suppliers by a buying company.

Supply Chain Management Activities and Objectives Figure 15.3 shows supply chain management activities, objectives and business performance elements. The activities are movement of products and information management, while objectives include increased efficiency and improved customer service. The resulting business performance improvements are described in the four cells.

Supply Chain Management Activities

Supply Chain Management Objectives	Movement of Products	Information Management
Low Cost (Efficiency)	Improved profit	More relevant information which improves coordination and decision making
Customer Service (Effectiveness)	Rapid product delivery which improves customer satisfaction and loyalty	Better understanding of customer needs to satisfy unique customer requirements

Figure 15.3 Supply Chain Activities, Objectives and Business Performance Improvements

Business Performance Improvements Overall, there are four types of business performance improvements: decreased costs, which improves profit; more relevant information, which improves coordination and decision making; rapid product delivery, which improves customer satisfaction and loyalty; and better understanding of customer needs to satisfy unique customer requirements.

Activities: Movement of Products and Integration of Information The movement of goods in the supply chain starts with raw materials and ends with the final consumption of the product. An important part of this process is the selection of suppliers. In the case of cereal, the chain would start with the farmer and end with the family that finally consumes the cereal. Information management includes the collection, storage and processing of data from different departments and across firms to provide real-time knowledge of the flow of goods from all sources. It also provides feedback on whether schedules are being met, potential obstacles and their remedies. This information links all parties; therefore, integration provides consumers with what they want, when they expect it, in a location that is most convenient and at a reasonable cost.

Objectives: Efficiency and Customer Service Better efficiency occurs when unnecessary steps are avoided, delays are eliminated and the actions of all companies are coordinated at the lowest cost while supplying the customer with precisely what is intended. Customer service is all of the actions taken to meet customer expectations, including rapid and satisfactory resolution of any problems. A firm that focuses on customer service is dedicated to its customers and their needs. The initial increase in costs to the firm to meet those needs will allow it to capture greater rewards in the future through customer loyalty.

LOGISTICS

LOGISTICS

The movement of raw materials, components, and finished products within and between companies.

INTEGRATED LOGISTICS MANAGEMENT

The coordination of all parts of the logistics process.

Logistics is the movement of raw materials, components and finished products within and between companies. Physical distribution is the part of logistics that involves only finished products. **Integrated logistics management** coordinates all parts of the process. If the movement of inputs is not properly managed, then physical distribution to customers will be hindered. Coordination is equally important when goods move between plants, distribution centers, warehouses, wholesalers and retailers. A firm must excel at integrated logistics management to have superior supply chain management.[5] Integration requires effective communications among companies, departments and people whose decisions affect logistics. Any company is subject to internal problems, and proper communication can address or even circumvent these issues. Salespeople may be so worried about late deliveries that they pad their forecasts. Concern about costs may lead firms to make conservative sales projections. In many companies, the people deepest in the organization and farthest from the customer are production planners, who develop the final estimates used to hire workers and build inventory.[6]

Integrated logistics management is only as strong as a company's understanding of its customers and the ability of its people to work together. Cross-functional teams in purchasing, production-warehousing, marketing and sales often produce excellent results. By sharing information on purchasing, production schedules, marketing and sales plans, customer service standards and customer preferences, the team can make logistical decisions that are truly integrated and beneficial to the company. Even without teams, integration can occur if communication from and about customers flows throughout the company in the form of market research reports, sales activity, forecasts and orders. This information can be refined into specific purchasing and manufacturing plans.

LO 02

PHYSICAL DISTRIBUTION

PHYSICAL DISTRIBUTION

The movement of finished products through channels of distribution to customers.

Physical distribution is the movement of finished products to customers. Although the concept is simple, accomplishing this task effectively and efficiently is often complex. The primary objective of physical distribution is to get the right products to the right locations at the right times at the lowest total cost. An effective distribution system can contribute to customer satisfaction and, in turn, increased sales revenues, while a poor performance will alienate customers and may even drive them to switch allegiance to competitors.[7]

While revenue generation is important, no less significant is careful control of the costs of processing orders, maintaining warehouses, carrying and handling inventory, and shipping products. Physical distribution can account for up to 40 percent of total cost and more than 25 percent of each sales dollar.[8] Achieving high customer service levels at the expense of company profitability makes no sense. Therefore, physical distribution management involves a delicate balance between effective customer service and efficient operations.

Toyota's Lexus division is an excellent example of striking the right balance. The typical car dealer has more than $200,000 in parts inventory, a heavy financial burden. At the same time, stockouts frequently occur. Understanding this, Lexus designed a system that better serves the company, its dealers and its customers. Lexus requires dealers to have AS400 computers and satellite dishes that connect them to company headquarters in Torrance, California. Specialized inventory control software helps dealers

Lexus uses inventory control software to reduce stock costs at dealerships and ensure customers receive the parts they need.

keep track of which parts they need on hand. If an item is unavailable in inventory, then it can be ordered electronically one day and received by air freight the next. Although Lexus dealers have only $100,000 tied up in parts inventory, there are few stockouts, and customer satisfaction levels are higher.[9] The system-wide costs of computers, satellite dishes, software and air freight are more than offset by lower inventory costs and increased sales through better customer service.

Physical distribution has five functions which will be described in this section. The functions need to be followed up with efficient customer response, which we'll discuss next, to ensure customer value. **Order Management** refers to how the company receives, fills and delivers orders to customers. The design of the physical distribution system—including order processing, warehousing, materials handling, inventory control and transportation functions—determines how well the company manages orders, as outlined in Figure 15.4. New technologies, such as electronic data interchange and bar coding, have had a remarkable effect on system design, which in turn has improved the effectiveness and efficiency of order management. **Electronic data interchange (EDI)** is a process which allows one company to send information to another company electronically in standard format.

Customer service standards will have a major bearing on the design of a physical distribution system. Companies that want high marks on order fill rate, order cycle time, delivery reliability and invoice accuracy must be prepared to invest heavily in network design. Often, managers find they must lower desired standards somewhat because the costs of achieving an ideal level are prohibitive. One approach is to recognize that all customers are not equal. As a general rule, a small percentage of a company's customers, often 20 percent or less, provide over 80 percent of its revenues. This is often called the Pareto Principle, after Italian economist Vilfredo Federico Damaso Pareto, who noticed 80 percent of the land in Italy was owned by 20 percent of the population. After realizing 80 percent of his peas were produced by 20 percent of the pea pods, he concluded this noteworthy ratio applied to many areas of life.[10] Customer service standards can be set higher for the firm's most important customers. Scarce resources can be saved by lowering customer service standards, at least to some extent, with less important customers.

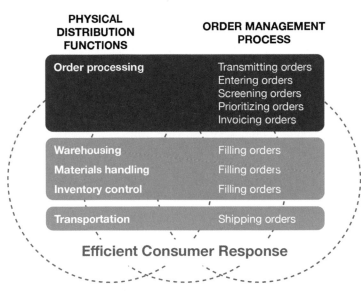

Figure 15.4 The Order Management Cycle

Order Processing The distribution of products cannot begin until the company receives an order. Order processing includes all the activities and paperwork involved in transmitting and entering, screening and prioritizing and invoicing orders.

Orders received from customers, channel members or company personnel are entered into the company's record-keeping system. Traditionally, salespeople wrote the orders by hand and delivered them to the office in person or by mail, phone or fax. New technology has dramatically changed all that. EDI connects many companies directly with customers, who key in the order and submit it electronically, significantly cutting down cycle time. Furthermore, invoices are more accurate, because only the customer needs to enter his or her information. Labor and material costs for printing, mailing and handling paper-based transactions are lower. Virtually all companies that have field sales reps now supply them with laptop computers or tablets. They have instant access to pricing and delivery schedules; they can enter an order and transmit it within seconds, even providing the customer with a receipt on the spot. Inside salespeople also use the internet to input telephone orders directly into a company's system. Order cycle time, invoice errors and order-processing costs are all reduced.

Caller ID integrated with computer IT systems enables an inside salesperson to know who is calling before picking up the phone. A variety of information about the caller appears on a computer screen, including payment history and credit information. If a problem is apparent, then the salesperson can notify the customer before entering the order, which saves time on everyone's part. After screening, many companies prioritize orders based on the importance of the customer or the order cycle time requested. For example, often customers can request same-day delivery on orders at a premium price. The computer system transmits these orders to distribution ahead of next-day orders. Bills are prepared once it is known how much of the order can be filled from available inventory.

Warehousing **Warehousing** is the storage of inventory in the physical distribution system. Many companies perform this function with a mix of distribution centers and warehouses. **Distribution centers** are where the bulk of a company's finished-goods inventory is maintained before being routed to individual sales outlets or customers. There are two types: **private warehouses** are fixed costs owned and operated by the company, and **public warehouses** are variable costs for rented space to store products. Preferences for fixed versus variable costs help determine a company's mix of private and public warehousing.

WAREHOUSING

The storage of inventory in the physical distribution system.

DISTRIBUTION CENTERS

A location where inventory is maintained before being routed to individual sales outlets or customers.

PRIVATE WAREHOUSES

A storage facility owned and operated by the company.

PUBLIC WAREHOUSES

A storage facility owned and operated by businesses that rent space.

Benetton Group uses an Automated Distribution System that can handle 40,000 incoming and outgoing boxes per day.

With technology, many companies can provide better customer service with fewer warehouses. Benetton Group, Italy's integrated fashion manufacturer and retailer, ships 150 million items each year directly to more than 6,000 shops in 120 countries. The company does so with its unique Automated Distribution System. Spanning more than 20,000 square meters, this system can handle 40,000 incoming and outgoing boxes per day and has a total capacity of 400,000 boxes. The Automated Distribution System operates efficiently, employing 24 people to take on what would traditionally require a workforce of 400.[11]

Cross docking involves sorting and reloading an incoming shipment from a supplier for delivery to customers without its being stored in any warehouse. The method is used most frequently in truck transport. EDI and specialized information systems allow for the close coordination that makes cross-docking efficient. This practice is on the rise because it reduces inventory carrying costs and order cycle time. Furthermore, the fewer times the product is handled, the lower the potential for damage. Jacobson Co. is an example of a transportation company that specializes in cross-docking. The company can build a custom-designed plan for its customers in order to enhance the bottom line.[12] The technique affects warehousing design; larger parking lots are needed for transferring products from truck to truck, and buildings are smaller.

CROSS DOCKING

Sorting and loading an incoming shipment from a supplier for delivery to customers without it being stored in any warehouse.

MATERIALS HANDLING

The moving of products in and around a warehouse in the process of filling orders.

Materials Handling **Materials handling** is the moving of products in a warehouse while filling orders. Traditionally, the facility manager would receive the paperwork and assign it to a worker. With a handcart or motorized forklift, the worker would go through the warehouse, picking up products and checking them off on the order forms. If some were unavailable, that would be noted on the form, and the facility would produce a back order, filling and shipping it when a new supply arrived. New technology significantly reduces the time it takes to find the inventory. Kiva Systems, a Massachusetts-based robotics company, has created small robots that transport inventory shelves to workers. The person processing the order pushes a button, and moments later the shelf with the needed product is within reach. When multiple robots operate at the same time, products from all corners of the store can be brought to one place simultaneously instead of one worker going through the entire warehouse. Zappos and Walgreens both use these revolutionary and time-saving robots.

Bar codes, radio frequency technology and hand-held scanning devices have remarkable effects on materials handling. Bar code labels for identification purposes can be placed on everything from cardboard boxes to plywood sheets. Hand-held scanners with display panels receive orders directly from the mainframe computer through radio waves and guide workers to the appropriate locations. Workers then scan in the bar codes to make sure the right product and quantity are selected. If not, the scanner will beep. This system reduces errors and order cycle time, while filling back orders much more quickly. It is a must for any company interested in boosting quality control and customer satisfaction.

RFID, or radio-frequency identification, is one of the most useful automatic identification methods. It is used in supply chain management because it allows users to store and retrieve data remotely, saving them a great deal of time and preventing errors from re-entering data. Volkswagen uses RFID in its supply chain to improve the flow of supplies. The company worked with IBM to strategically place RFID tags in shipping containers. Information is collected by RFID readers at key locations throughout the entire supply chain.[13]

This RFID chip is used by Walmart on label cases and pallets.

INVENTORY CONTROL

Management of stock levels

Inventory Control **Inventory control** is the management of stock levels. For each product, company management must decide how much inventory will be carried in each distribution center and warehouse. Carrying too little inventory leads to poor order fill rates, too many back orders and poor customer service. Carrying too much leads to higher than necessary costs. Many companies fail because they have too much capital tied up in inventory; this reduces cash flow, which means that bills cannot be paid.[14]

Inventory levels are often determined with the help of the ABC classification approach. Stock keeping units (SKUs) are divided into three categories based on their sales volume and profitability. Inventory levels are kept relatively high for the A category, moderate for B, and relatively low for C. The trap to avoid is a large inventory of less profitable SKUs purchased by fringe or non-core customers.

Part of inventory control is to determine reorder points and order quantities. A reorder point is the inventory level at which a replenishment order is generated. The standard formula is:

Reorder point = Demand or usage rate x order cycle time + safety stock

In other words, there should be enough inventory to supply customers during the time required to get more stock, plus a margin of safety. More formally, safety stock is the inventory kept on hand in case of forecasting error or delayed delivery of replenishment stock. For example, if the average daily demand rate is 50 units, order cycle time is 4 days, and safety stock is 20 units, then the reorder point is (50 x 4) + 20 = 220 units. Whenever inventory drops to that level, a replenishment order should be made.

ECONOMIC ORDER QUANTITY (EOQ) MODEL

A method of determining the amount of product to be ordered each time.

The **economic order quantity (EOQ) model** is a method for determining how much product to order each time. It compares ordering costs to inventory carrying costs, with the objective of minimizing total costs. The standard formula is:

$$EOQ = \frac{2 \times CO \times D}{CI \times U}$$

CO = Cost per order
D = Annual sales volume in units
CI = Annual inventory carrying cost
U = Unit cost

The cost per order is calculated by determining purchasing costs, computer costs, and accounts payable costs associated with placing individual orders. Annual inventory carrying costs are calculated by summing expenses associated with warehouse space, insurance, taxes on inventory, obsolescence and shrinkage, materials handling (including wages and equipment) and costs of money invested. The lower the cost per order relative to inventory carrying costs, the lower the order quantity.

The EOQ method should be used only as a guideline. It works particularly well for products with consistent demand patterns throughout the year. For seasonal items or for products on which suppliers give discounts at certain order quantities, EOQ estimates need some adjustment. A just-in-time (JIT) system also skews the EOQ method. In a JIT system, the necessary unit is delivered in the necessary quantity at the necessary time. The fundamental objective is to eliminate waste of all sorts, especially excess inventory. Products are delivered in just enough quantity to cover demand for a short period. Shipments are made frequently and are scheduled precisely; 100 percent delivery reliability is sought because little safety stock is carried. Emphasis is placed on total cost of ownership; per-unit price is less important than the costs associated with extra handling, warehousing and inventory management. JIT requires companies to meet specific deadlines, supply exact quantities and adjust deliveries and quantities to meet changing needs, all with a minimum of paperwork. Strong relationships between the companies, including high trust, are critical to the success of such systems.

Transportation In a physical distribution system, transportation is the movement of goods to channel members and customer locations. It is the largest distribution expense for many manufacturers, especially if heavy, bulky products are involved, since transportation fees are charged by the pound. The cost of transporting weight-training equipment and exercise bicycles, for example, might approach the cost of the equipment itself. Deregulation of the transportation industry increased competition among carriers, which has led to greater efficiency and real cost savings for U.S. manufacturers, wholesalers, retailers and consumers.

The methods for moving products are motor vehicles, railroads, airlines, water carriers and pipelines. Figure 15.5 contrasts the advantages and disadvantages of the various modes of transportation. Managers choose among them based on customer service versus

	Trucks	Railroads	Air	Water Carriers	Pipeline
Transportation cost	high	average	very high	very low	low
Door-to-door service	high	average	average	low	high
Speed of service	high	average	very high	very low	low
Dependability in meeting schedules	high	average	very high	average	high
Availability in different locations	very high	high	average	low	very low
Frequency of shipments	very high	low	average	very low	high
Need for intermodal transfer for door-to-door service	no	often	almost always	often	often
Primary advantage	door-to-door service and speed	low cost for long hauls of bulk commodities	fastest and highest quality	low cost for long hauls of bulk commodities	low cost and dependability

Figure 15.5   Comparison of Different Modes of Transportation

cost trade-offs. Different modes can be used to serve different clients. For example, orders to core customers may go via fast, reliable air service, whereas orders to non-core customers may be delivered by less expensive ground transportation.

Walmart's new fuel efficient prototype is designed to lower transportation costs and its carbon footprint.

Trucks The major advantages of trucks are door-to-door service and speed. Trucks also are dependable and widely available, making frequent shipments possible. Their major disadvantage is cost. Given these characteristics, trucks are ideally suited for high-value manufactured products. Companies can purchase and operate their own fleet of trucks or use the services of independent companies. The trade-offs have to do with level of control and fixed versus variable costs. When uncertainty is high, the use of independents is preferable. Walmart recently debuted a very futuristic truck to improve the overall fuel efficiency of its fleet and lower the company's carbon footprint. Walmart trucks log millions of miles every year, so sustainability and fleet efficiency are taken very seriously by the company.[15]

Railroads Railroads represent the most efficient mode of land transportation for bulky commodities, such as chemicals, coal, grain, iron ore, lumber, sand and steel. Major U.S. railroads haul more than 40 percent of all freight, more than any other mode of transportation. Coal is the most distinct commodity carried by rail, accounting for more than 70 percent of the coal used by power plants.[16] The major disadvantages of railroads are transit time and lack of door-to-door service, although rail spurs can reach some customer locations. Unit trains are known for running back and forth between a single loading point, such as a coal mine, and a single destination, such as a power plant, to deliver one commodity. Leading U.S. companies providing rail transportation include Burlington Northern, CSX and Union Pacific.

Air Transport Air transport is offered by the airlines and cargo service companies. Relative to other modes of transportation, it provides great speed and reliably adheres to schedules. Air is the most costly transportation method, however. Fashion merchandise, fragile and highly perishable items, emergency shipments and expensive industrial goods account for the majority of products shipped as air freight.

Water Carriers Water carriers include transoceanic ships as well as barges used on inland waterways. Their transportation cost is the lowest among the various options. However, they are relatively inaccessible, and only channel members and customers in port cities can be reached directly. Water carriers are used for bulky commodities, such as cement and petroleum. Ore barges, for example, are a common sight on the Great Lakes. This mode also is used to carry mass-produced goods, such as automobiles and toys, overseas.

Pipelines Pipelines transport natural gas and petroleum by land from production fields to refineries. Up to 40 different grades of product can be shipped through the same pipeline simultaneously and separated at destination points. Pipelines are very dependable and offer door-to-door service. They are the least labor-intensive of any mode, and maintenance expenses are low. They can be used only for a narrow range of products, however, and delivery speed—less than five miles per hour—is slow.

INTERMODAL TRANSPORTATION

The combination of two or more modes in moving freight.

Intermodal transportation **Intermodal transportation**, the combination of two or more modes in moving freight, is gaining popularity. The objective is to exploit the major advantages of each. Piggybacking truck trailers on rail cars, for example, joins the benefits of long-haul rail movement with the door-to-door service of trucks. Express delivery often uses trucks and air to rush shipments from source to destination. Federal Express, the pioneer in overnight delivery, has developed a thriving business running transportation services for such clients as National Semiconductor, Laura Ash-

Grolltech / CC BY-SA 3.0

This map visually represents the global commercial shipping density. The data collected for the map is used by the University of California Santa Barbara to study human impacts on marine ecosystems.

ley and Vanstar. Other companies offer a variety of intermodal options. For example, CNF Transportation, headquartered in Palo Alto, California, owns and operates Conway Transportation Services, which focuses on trucking services, and Emery Worldwide, which offers global air freight, ocean transport and air charter.

The transportation modes used by companies are sometimes influenced by laws and government pressure. Some companies use three-wheeled motorbikes for deliveries in Shanghai, China, because truck use is restricted during daylight hours. New York City, Tokyo and many metro areas have strict laws about truck deliveries because of extreme traffic congestion. Many companies use bicycles to deliver products in Europe because of pollution concerns, and a few cities in the United States have begun delivering goods this way for the same reason.

New technologies are having a major influence on transportation. Progressive trucking companies install on-board computers in vehicles. UPS, which provides transportation services to companies globally, gives its drivers electronic data that informs the driver exactly where to go, which route to take, and how much time to spend getting there.

Satellite communication systems also have an important role, providing a fast and high-volume channel for information movement around the globe. Many companies use a real-time global positioning system in their fleets of delivery trucks. The drivers and dispatchers can contact each other while the truck is in transit, and dispatchers always know where a truck is on the delivery route. The real-time interaction provides up-to-date information to customers regarding location and delivery time. Furthermore, dispatchers can redirect trucks in response to need or traffic congestion. Federal Express, UPS, Roadway and DHL are among the many companies that track shipments electronically to ensure that all customers remain fully informed about deliveries.

EFFICIENT CONSUMER RESPONSE (ECR) PROGRAMS

Programs to improve the efficiency of replenishing, delivering, and stocking inventory in the distribution channel, while promoting customer value.

Efficient Customer Response **Efficient consumer response (ECR) programs** are designed to improve the efficiency of replenishing, delivering and stocking inventory while promoting customer value. Enhanced cooperation among channel members in order to eliminate activities that do not add value is a primary goal. A study found that excellent ECR could yield as much as $24 billion in operating cost reductions and $6 billion in financial savings. Potential savings ranged from about three percent for manufacturers to 12 percent for retailers.[17]

Traditionally, retailers and wholesalers have used professional buyers to decide what and when to order from suppliers. Suppliers frequently offered buyers price deals. Forward buying became commonplace: a large order for a product at a special price per carton and then a long delay until the next order, which resulted in inconsistent order patterns for manufacturers and general uncertainty. Because of inefficiencies, stockouts occurred much too frequently, even though inventory levels for many products were high throughout the channel.

ECR requires a change in the roles played by channel members. Wholesalers and retailers give up some of their buying authority. On a daily basis, they send information on stock levels and warehouse shipments to their suppliers over EDI networks. Personnel in the supplier organizations use this information to decide what and when to ship. Order quantities are determined with the objectives of providing sufficient safety stock, minimizing total logistics costs and eliminating excess inventory in the channel. Before shipments go out, wholesalers and retailers can review and edit orders if they desire via EDI. Fewer special prices are offered by suppliers to reduce the incentive for forward buying, which is disruptive to ECR. Instead, everyday low pricing may be used.

If administered effectively, ECR can reduce inventory costs and stockouts in the channel. Furthermore, wholesalers and retailers can reduce the number of professional buyers they employ, since suppliers assume more ordering responsibilities.

GLOBAL PHYSICAL DISTRIBUTION

Any challenge that domestic business presents is multiplied when taken abroad. Uncertainty increases because of greater transport distances, longer lead times and complex customs requirements and trade restrictions. The most important factor from a physical distribution perspective, however, is a country's infrastructure, which influences how products are stored and transported.

Due to its extremely high economic growth rate, China is now the world's second-largest economy after the United States. Many foreign companies have established supply relationships with China. The Chinese government has spent billions of dollars building and updating road and rail access, as well as water treatment plants. Moreover, the government has established very advanced e-commerce and business-to-business links, making China a huge market opening for non-Chinese businesses.

Of course, a major challenge for many companies is moving products into other countries. Organizations will often use cargo specialists, or **freight forwarders**. Domestically, they pick up partial shipments at the customer location, consolidate all of these into truckload or carload size, and arrange for delivery at destination points. Their gross margin is the difference between the rates they charge customers and what they pay carriers. Many exporters rely on freight forwarders to handle the documentation, insurance and other aspects of delivery abroad. For example, they ensure that letters of credit are issued at the buyer's bank and properly transferred into the seller's account. Leading global freight forward-

FREIGHT FORWARDERS

Service companies specializing in the movement of cargo from one point to another, often country to country.

nipponexpress.com

Nippon Express connects companies beyond national and regional boundaries, integrating land, air, and marine transport.

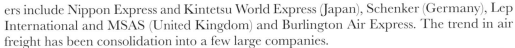

ers include Nippon Express and Kintetsu World Express (Japan), Schenker (Germany), Lep International and MSAS (United Kingdom) and Burlington Air Express. The trend in air freight has been consolidation into a few large companies.

Regardless of geographic location, the ultimate goal of distribution is to make the product readily available to the consumer or end user. For the majority of consumer products, this has traditionally meant delivering goods to the retail outlets where consumers shop. Today, however, direct marketing—including sales via the internet—is a growing force in consumer as well as business-to-business sales.

Distribution Channels

LO 03

DISTRIBUTION CHANNEL

A set of interdependent organizations that help make a good or service available for purchase.

A **distribution channel** is a set of interdependent organizations that help make a good or service available for purchase by consumers or businesses. The distribution channel serves to connect a manufacturer, such as Coach, or a service provider, such as AT&T, with consumers or users. In simple terms, a distribution channel is a pipeline or pathway to the market.

Distribution channels are needed because producers are separated from prospective customers. Mattel's star product, Barbie, is made available to consumers in countries around the world through a host of different retail establishments. Walmart, Toys "R" Us and Target account for nearly 45 percent of Mattel sales.[18] These retailers are members of Mattel's distribution channel, and they are customers of Mattel.

A distribution channel consists of at least a producer and a customer. Most channels, however, use one or more inter-mediaries to help move products to the customer. **Intermediaries** are independently owned organizations that act as links to move products between producers and the end user. The primary categories are brokers, wholesalers (distributors) and retailers. **Brokers** do not purchase the goods they handle but instead actively negotiate their sale for the client. A familiar example is real estate brokers, who negotiate the sale of property for their customers. Companies have more control over the activities of brokers, including the final price to the customer, because brokers do not own the goods they sell. **Wholesalers** (also referred to as distributors) take title to products and resell them to retail, industrial, commercial, institutional, professional or agricultural firms, as well as to other wholesalers. A good example is Ingram Micro Inc. The company, based in Santa Ana, California, is the world's largest technology distributor and logistics company for the IT industry worldwide. With approximately 190,000 customers, Ingram Micro distributes to retailers such as Walmart, Staples and Office Depot.[19] **Retailers** take title to products for resale to the ultimate consumer. These range from discounters such as Walmart and large department stores to specialty chains such as Victoria's Secret and local boutiques.

> Distribution channels are needed because producers are separated from prospective customers.

INTERMEDIARIES

Independently owned organizations that act as a links to move products between the producer and the end user.

BROKERS

A firm that does not take title to the goods it handles but actively negotiates the sale of goods for its clients.

WHOLESALERS

A firm that takes title to products for resale to businesses, consumers, or other wholesalers or distributors.

RETAILERS

A firm that takes title to products for resale to ultimate consumers.

DIRECT CHANNELS

A distribution channel in which the producer uses its own employees and physical assets to distribute the product directly to end users.

INDIRECT CHANNELS

A distribution channel in which the producer makes use of independent organizations to distribute the product to end users.

CHANNEL STRUCTURE, DYNAMICS & FUNCTIONS

Direct & Indirect Channels There are two fundamental types of channels. In **direct channels** (also called integrated channels) companies use their own employees (i.e., salespeople) and physical assets (i.e., warehouses and delivery vehicles) to serve the market. For example, IBM's sales force sells information technology systems directly to large companies such as Bank of America. Sherwin-Williams owns and operates a majority of the outlets where its paint is sold. With **indirect channels** (also called nonintegrated channels), companies make use of independent agents to serve markets. General Motors sells aftermarket components through a variety of channels such as independent parts distributors, auto

CHANNEL LEVELS

The number of distinct units (producers, intermediaries, and customers) in a distribution channel.

body repair shops and independently owned dealerships.

Distribution channels can be described by the number of **channel levels** or the number of distinct units (producers, intermediaries and customers) in a distribution channel. A direct channel has two levels: the producer and its targeted customers. Indirect channels are longer, with at least three levels. Figure 15.6 illustrates common channel arrangements for consumer goods, business-to-business goods and services.

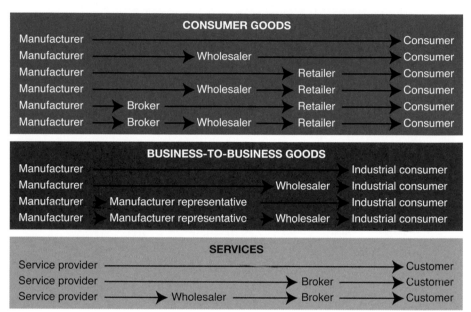

Figure 15.6 Common Channel Configurations

Companies must decide whether to use direct channels or intermediaries. Direct channels are more attractive when the following conditions apply:

- Customers and orders are large, especially if concentrated in a few geographical areas.

- Resource constraints are not severe.

- Environmental uncertainty is low to moderate.

- Investments in direct distribution will produce a high return.

- Significant value-added activity is required in the channel, including specialized investments.

- Customers prefer or demand to deal directly with manufacturers, Walmart being a prime example.

Many markets are simply too small to make it economically feasible for companies to establish a direct channel. Consider independently owned convenience stores, whose average order from a company such as Procter & Gamble would be tiny relative to supermarket or discount chains. The manufacturer's costs of selling, processing orders and delivering products to mom-and-pop stores would be larger than the revenues generated. The problem is intensified because convenience stores are so geographically dispersed.

Intermediaries assemble merchandise from a variety of manufacturers and sell in smaller lots at a regional or local level. Therefore, an order from a small convenience store represents a relatively larger sale to a wholesaler than to an individual manufacturer. Moreover, wholesalers often have greater cost efficiencies than manufacturers due to their smaller size (lower overhead) or proximity to customers (lower selling

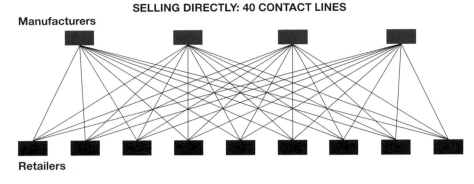

SELLING DIRECTLY: 40 CONTACT LINES

Manufacturers

Retailers

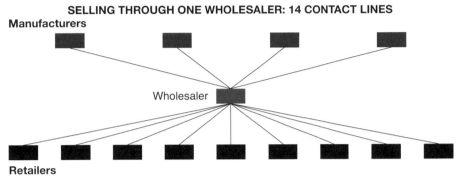

SELLING THROUGH ONE WHOLESALER: 14 CONTACT LINES

Manufacturers

Wholesaler

Retailers

Figure 15.7   Contractual Efficiency
Source: Louis Stern, Adel El-Ansary and Anne Coughlan, Marketing Channels, 6th ed. © 2001.

and logistics costs). The result is that wholesalers can make money serving smaller customers whereas manufacturers cannot. The same rationale applies to retailers. Figure 15.7 shows that four manufacturers selling directly to 10 retailers would need to make 40 contacts to conduct business, compared to four contacts if they do business with one wholesaler, who in turn makes 10 contacts with the retailers for a total of 14. Establishing each contact requires resources, so this is a significant difference.

Intermediaries tend to require less of the company's resources. They make investments in inventory, offer credit to customers and manage accounts receivable. They also pay for sales personnel and other employees, allowing the producer to avoid these costs. More and more companies such as General Electric, Intel and Texas Instruments are relying on the use of intermediaries rather than company-owned or direct channels.

The use of intermediaries is attractive to companies when it is difficult to make accurate predictions about the future. This lowers the risk level for the company because the intermediary is sharing the investment burden. Adapting to change is also easier, since companies have less fixed investment and, therefore, more financial flexibility. For instance, if a company owns its own warehouse facilities and the economy flounders, the company incurs a significant toll dealing with building, equipment and personnel costs.

Multiple Channel Systems   Often, manufacturers want to connect with customers in as many ways as possible. **Multiple channel systems** make use of more than one channel to access markets for the same product. For example, Ben & Jerry's distributes its premium ice cream through company-owned stores, wholesalers that resell to supermarkets and convenience stores, and franchised outlets. Most distribution channels flow from the manufacturer to the end user, but goods sometimes move in the opposite direction. A **reverse channel** flows from the end user to the wholesaler or the manufacturer. An example is the recycling of bottles and cans.

CHANNEL ALIGNMENT

In a **conventional channel system,** efforts to coordinate actions are seen as unimportant by channel members. Loosely aligned and relatively autonomous manufacturers, wholesalers and retailers bargain aggressively with one another over each transaction.[20] Once a deal is reached, there is not much concern about what others in the channel are doing. Most giftware, furniture and motion pictures move through conventional channels, where channel members tend to follow traditions.

In contrast, **vertical marketing systems (VMS)** are networks that emphasize

MULTIPLE CHANNEL SYSTEMS

The use of more than one channel to access markets for the same product.

REVERSE CHANNEL

A distribution channel that flows from the end user to the wholesaler or producer.

CONVENTIONAL CHANNEL SYSTEM

A channel system in which efforts to coordinate the actions of channel members are seen as unimportant.

VERTICAL MARKETING SYSTEM (VMS)

A system in which channel members emphasize coordination of behaviors and programs.

channel coordination. VMS have grown in importance over the past two decades, as more and more companies realize that customer satisfaction is impossible without efficient and effective distribution. There are three types of VMS: administered, contractual and corporate.

Administered Channel Systems

Administered Channel Systems Members of an **administered channel system** coordinate with others in the channel and facilitate activities. Marketing programs, such as cooperative advertising and sales training, are developed and offered to channel members.[21] Black & Decker, General Electric and Sealy (the mattress company) are among the manufacturers known for their administered channel systems. Among retailers, Walmart is among the heaviest investors in coordinating relationships with suppliers. The internet has selling spaces in which companies and wholesalers can develop strong relationships, such as the shopping sites in Yahoo! or America Online. When channel members have roles that are rather complex and challenging, greater coordination is needed.

Contractual Channel Systems In a **contractual channel system**, relationships are formalized, often with a written contract. Retail cooperatives, wholesaler-sponsored voluntary chains and franchises are three common forms.

A **retail cooperative** unites a group of small retailers into a wholesaling operation to increase buying power. Compare a hardware retailer who buys 20 Black & Decker power drills a year to 100 stores that buy 2,000. Obviously, the group will have more clout in negotiating price. Ace Hardware and SERVISTAR are major retail cooperatives. The grocery industry is a common ground for cooperatives, such as Associated Grocers and Topco Associates.

In a **wholesaler-sponsored voluntary chain**, a wholesaler takes the initiative to unite a group of retailers. Again, enhanced buying power is the main objective. Such channels are prominent in the automotive accessory market (Western Auto), the grocery trade (Independent Grocers Alliance, Red and White, and Super Value), and the hardware arena (Pro, Sentry). More than one-third of all U.S. pharmaceuticals used each day are delivered by McKesson Drug Co., a wholesaler of pharmaceuticals and health-care products.[22]

In a **franchise system**, a formal contract ties the franchiser to franchisees. The franchiser holds the product trademark and licenses it to franchisees. They pay royalty fees and promise to conform to standards and guidelines laid out in the contractual agreement. This usually covers such issues as the fees required, rights and responsibilities of both parties, transfer of the franchise and grounds for termination.

There are two types of franchise systems. In product and trade-name franchising, the franchisee acquires some of the identity of the franchiser. Automobile dealerships, gas stations, motorcycle dealerships and soft-drink bottlers are a few examples. Business format franchising involves not only the product and trademark but also the entire business concept — marketing, strategy, training, merchandising and operating procedures.[23] This is especially prevalent in the service arena: fast-food restaurants (McDonald's and Burger King), hotels and motels (Holiday Inn), diet programs (Nutrisystem), real estate (Century 21), travel services (Uniglobe) and vehicle rental (Hertz).

About 760,000 franchise outlets in the United States account for more than $1.5 trillion in annual sales. About 40 percent of all U.S. retail sales flow through a franchise system, and a new franchise is opened every eight minutes of every business day.[24] Business format franchising is growing at a particularly phenomenal rate. U.S. franchisers have been very successful in establishing indirect channels in global markets. For

> About 760,000 franchise outlets in the United States account for more than $1.5 trillion in annual sales

Coca-Cola has a long relationship with independent franchised bottlers.

example, Coca-Cola has a long relationship with independent franchised bottlers in each market, who buy the syrup concentrate and then carbonate, package and sell the product to retailers. Its anchor bottlers, a breed of regional intermediaries, have deep local ties, huge capital budgets and finely tuned distribution systems. On a broader scale, McDonald's has developed an excellent program for recruiting and developing a diverse mix of franchisees.

In a **corporate channel system**, the corporation runs and operates organizations at other levels in the channel. It is very similar to a direct channel, and great emphasis is placed on coordinating activities.

INTENSIVE, SELECTIVE & EXCLUSIVE DISTRIBUTION

The number of locations through which a company sells its products in a given market area is an important strategic consideration. There are three strategic options. **Intensive distribution** uses many outlets in each geographical area. **Selective distribution** uses several outlets per area. **Exclusive distribution** uses only one outlet in each trading area.

The choice is driven to some extent by the nature of the product. Many consumer and business-to-business products are relatively low in price and are purchased frequently, requiring little value-adding activity in the channel. Commonly referred to as convenience goods, they require intensive distribution. Numerous sales outlets per trade area will minimize travel time and acquisition costs for customers. Examples are most brands of coffee, detergent, chewing gum, motor oil, soft drinks and toilet tissue. Other products, referred to as shopping goods, require some search on the part of the customer. Different brands are compared on price, quality and other features at the time of purchase. Selective distribution is appropriate for these goods, which include bicycles, cameras and motorcycles. Finally, specialty goods, or luxury items, have unique qualities that induce high customer loyalty. Since people are willing to exert considerable effort to find and purchase them, exclusive distribution can be used.

The brand strategy of the company also will influence the decision. Different brands of the same product can have widely differing distribution patterns. High-priced brands that are intended to be high in quality require more selective distribution, because broader markets may be swayed by lower-priced competitors.[25] Generally, the more prestigious the brand, the fewer the number of outlets a manufacturer will use.

When a company has independent wholesalers and retailers in its channel system, selective and especially exclusive distribution breeds considerable loyalty. For example, Caterpillar uses only 178 independently owned dealers worldwide. They are like extensions of Caterpillar, willing to support the company in any way they can. Recently, Caterpillar recognized that many of its dealers have been missing important new opportunities, which it believes is costing the company between $9 and $18 billion. Because of this, Caterpillar is giving dealers until the end of the year to develop a three-year plan identifying how they will capture those lost sales.[26]

Companies that use independent intermediaries must be careful in moving from a selective to a more intensive strategy. The loyalty of traditional channel members can quickly vanish. For example, Vidal Sassoon hair care products used to be distributed only in beauty salons. When the company decided to distribute through major supermarket and drugstores, the salons dropped the line in a flash. Calvin Klein sued licensee Warnaco for selling goods bearing his name to discount outlets such as Costco; he was trying to prevent

CORPORATE CHANNEL SYSTEM

A vertical marketing system in which a company owns and operates organizations at other levels in the channel.

INTENSIVE DISTRIBUTION

Making the product available through every possible sales outlet in a trade area.

SELECTIVE DISTRIBUTION

The use of a limited number of sales outlets per trade area.

EXCLUSIVE DISTRIBUTION

Distributing a product through only one sales outlet in each trading area.

his own brand from being devalued in a similar fashion. Wider distribution is also likely to invite price competition, reducing profit margins of current channel members.

LO 05 — STRATEGICALLY MANAGING CHANNEL RELATIONSHIPS

Companies must think strategically about relationships with intermediaries. Interdependence, trust and support are important elements in managing channel relationships. Figure 15.8 outlines these guidelines for channel management.

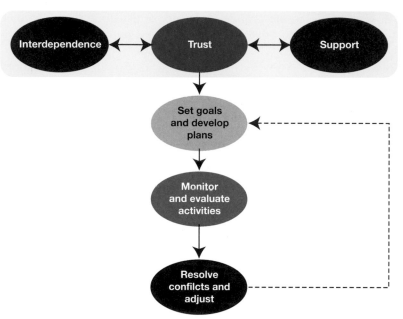

Figure 15.8   A Process for Managing Channel Relationships

Interdependence Each channel member depends to some degree on other channel members to achieve desired goals. This need is high when a large amount of a channel member's sales and profits can be attributed to the arrangement.[27] High interdependence means that each has the potential to influence the decisions of another. Gaining attention and support is easier in that case because each party has a vested interest in continuing the relationship. For example, Pepsi and Walmart have a highly dependent relationship, and both commit considerable effort and resources to ensuring that it works smoothly.

When a channel relationship is unbalanced, one firm is more dependent on the other for success, granting a power advantage to one of them. If the producer has the advantage, then the buyer is likely to be very receptive to its salespeople and their plans. In the semiconductor industry, Intel has that kind of power over wholesalers such as Arrow Electronics and Hamilton-Hallmark. When the supplier is dependent, because a particular buyer purchases the majority of its output, for instance, the supplier must be willing to make concessions. The buyer is likely to demand very low prices.

When dependence is low for all parties, each lacks power in the channel relationship, and they are unlikely to offer each other much support. Therefore, producers need to establish channel systems in which the dependence of associated firms is reasonably high.

Trust Another important factor in channel relationships is trust, or confidence in the reliability and integrity of channel members.[28] High trust is the belief that another's words and promises can be relied upon. Each member of the channel relationship has no need to question others' credibility, so coordination is much smoother. Lack of trust creates serious problems. When Anthony Conza, a cofounder of Astor Restaurant Group, discovered he was losing the trust of many of his 600 Blimpie franchisees, he responded by improving communications. He established a franchisee advisory council, a newsletter called *No Baloney News* and a toll-free hot line for franchisees. These changes increased trust, sales and franchisee satisfaction.[29]

Courtesy of Blimpie

Blimpie established a franchisee advisory council, a newsletter called *No Baloney News* and a toll-free hot line for franchisees, increasing trust, sales and franchisee satisfaction.

Support A company may lack power with an intermediary because of low dependence, but it can grab attention with the right kind of support. Cooperative advertising is a common means. The producer reimburses intermediaries for expenses when they submit proof of the ad along with media invoices, if the ad meets certain standards. For example, motorcycle manufacturers do not reimburse dealers if ads mention more than one brand. For eligible ads, half the expense is normally reimbursed, although limits are set on the amount per year, which are ordinarily based on the intermediary's percentage of annual sales for a product. Many manufacturers supply prepared advertising material to ensure quality.

Another form of support is to invite intermediaries to sales conferences to mingle and attend sessions devoted to new products or marketing techniques. Although some business is conducted at these events, the main purpose is to socialize and build personal relationships. As another way to foster goodwill, many companies help fund sales conferences sponsored by intermediaries. Support also may be offered through inventory management and sales training programs, hotlines and toll-free numbers.

> Channel management is facilitated when members meet formally to set joint goals and develop plans for the coming year.

Set Goals and Develop Plans Channel management is facilitated when members meet formally to set joint goals and develop plans for the coming year. This works best when interdependence and trust are high. During these sessions, intermediaries make a commitment to a set of goals, often including accounts and products that will get special emphasis. Specific business plans are developed regarding the activities and investments intermediaries will make to help achieve the goals. At the same time, the producer agrees to assist intermediaries through support programs and marketing efforts.

Monitor and Evaluate Performance Once the business plan is in place, company sales personnel must keep abreast of the marketing and selling efforts of each intermediary. Deviations from the plan must be noted. How well the intermediary is doing in reaching the goals established must be constantly evaluated.

For example, McDonald's has corporate employees visit franchisee locations and order food as regular customers. Then they rate the particular facility on a variety of dimensions, including friendliness of the staff, quality of the food and cleanliness. Similarly, Holiday Inn evaluators stay overnight and rate performance. Monitoring such as this gives a company valuable feedback as well as leverage in channel relationships.

Conflict Resolution Channel conflict occurs when members disagree about the course of their relationship. It often arises due to business pressures, policy changes and the use of coercion. Some conflict is inevitable. Channel members recognize that some policies will not be changed and get on with their business. Sometimes company sales personnel can help by explaining policies to intermediaries. In other cases, companies recognize they made a mistake and try to correct it.

LEGAL AND ETHICAL ISSUES IN CHANNEL MANAGEMENT

U.S. antitrust laws and other regulations designed to promote competition and consumer welfare affect distribution practices. Legislation in other countries varies widely.

Resale Price Maintenance Resale price maintenance is an attempt by companies to compel channel members to charge certain prices. The practice is illegal when title to the product changes hands. Since wholesalers and retailers normally purchase the products they sell, they can charge any price they choose. If manufacturers cross the line between persuasion and coercion, then legal problems can arise. For example, a manufacturer should never threaten to take a product line away if prices are not raised.

Collusion among channel members to pressure a wholesaler or retailer to charge higher prices is against the law, so company personnel should never consult with channel members to find out whether any are discounting prices. They also should not solicit the support of intermediaries in persuading another channel member to maintain a certain price level.

Differential Pricing and Support Programs

Differential Pricing and Support Programs A company must give prices and support programs on proportionally equal terms to competing channel members unless two conditions are met. First, a price differential is justified if it costs less to serve one channel member versus another. Costs are usually lower in dealing with large distributors and retailers due to economies of scale, so quantity discounts are justified in those cases. Second, variations are legal if they are required to meet a competitive offer.

Companies can provide differential pricing and support programs to intermediaries who are not in competition. For example, a computer manufacturer can charge one price to a local wholesaler in San Diego and another to a local wholesaler in Seattle. Whether this makes good business sense is another matter.

Territorial and Customer Constraints

Territorial and Customer Constraints A territorial constraint exists when a company assigns an intermediary a specific geographic area in which to sell its products. That is, it can sell there but nowhere else. Such constraints are legal, as they are seen as protecting the investment of all neighboring intermediaries who sell the company's products.

A class-of-customer constraint is a company limit on the customer groups to which an intermediary can sell its product. For example, a manufacturer of medical equipment may direct a wholesaler to sell to physicians and nursing homes in New York City but not to hospitals. This constraint is illegal, as the courts have found that it limits competition and harms consumer welfare. A company is allowed to suggest that an intermediary focus on certain targets: "We are looking for you to cover primarily these customer groups."

Exclusive Dealing

EXCLUSIVE DEALING

Restricting intermediaries from carrying competitive lines.

Exclusive Dealing **Exclusive dealing** occurs when a company restricts intermediaries from carrying competitive lines. Such constraints are legal, unless they are proved to be a substantial limit on competition in the marketplace. Furthermore, terminating intermediaries for failure to perform can be difficult if exclusive dealing is a requirement. The intermediary may have passed up opportunities to add other lines and may be very dependent on the channel relationship as a result.

Tying Arrangements and Full-Line Forcing

TYING ARRANGEMENT

The purchase of a superior product is conditioned on the purchase of a second product of lower quality.

FULL-LINE FORCING

Requiring intermediaries to carry and sell the company's complete line.

Tying Arrangements and Full-Line Forcing A **tying arrangement** exists when a company conditions the purchase of a superior product on the purchase of a second and less desirable product. For example, a copier company may refuse to sell a high-quality machine unless the customer buys a service agreement. Such arrangements are illegal.

Full-line forcing occurs when a company requires intermediaries to carry and sell its complete line. This practice has been generally upheld in the courts, especially when it is common within an industry. It may be challenged, however, if it entails quantities to be purchased and inventory levels to be maintained. It also may be challenged as an illegal tying arrangement if it involves unrelated product lines.

Intermediary Termination

Intermediary Termination In many channel systems, agreements commonly allow either party to terminate the relationship with 30 days' notice. In franchise systems, contracts are more complex. Whatever the case, companies need to document the reasons for termination. Usually, the intermediary fails to meet standards or is a poor credit risk. The termination may be challenged if based on intermediary noncompliance with illegal restraints on trade.

Ease of termination varies considerably by state. Wisconsin has a very strict law.

If a company's product comprises 12 percent or more of an intermediary's sales volume, then the company cannot terminate it. This has led many manufacturers to establish direct channels in Wisconsin, though they generally use indirect channels elsewhere.

Ethics It is illegal for companies to impose certain constraints on channel members. Other practices may not be against the law but are ethically questionable. For example, franchisers often confront the issue of how close to place outlets. Market coverage improves with a greater number, but existing franchisees may be hurt. They have committed time and money to building their business, and they do not want to be crowded out by competition from their own company.

Another ethical issue arises when companies set territorial constraints and then choose to ignore them. They lack the courage to confront large intermediaries for selling outside their assigned territory. Such intermediaries often claim they will drop the product line and switch to competitors if they cannot broaden their market area.

Company executives must carefully consider the consequences that each strategic move will ultimately have on the company. Competitive pressures aside, what is good, ethical business practice and what is not must be carefully spelled out to all employees. All employees and constitutes of the distribution channel must know that bribery and unethical gifts for favorable treatment are unacceptable. Successful companies recognize that spikes in short-term sales make no sense if they weaken existing channel members. To maintain the integrity of the entire channel system, companies need to enforce policies and terminate violators.

Chapter Summary

Objective 1: Define supply chain management and explain how firms gain a competitive advantage by using it.
Supply chain management incorporates all of the activities involved with planning, implementation and control of sourcing, manufacturing and delivery for products and services. It involves acquiring suppliers and moving products, as well as the flow of information about these activities within a firm and across different firms. The movement of goods in the supply chain starts with raw materials and ends with the final consumption of the product. An important part of this process is the selection of suppliers. Information management includes the collection, storage and processing of data from different departments within and across firms to provide real time knowledge of the flow of goods from all sources. The objectives of supply chain management are cost efficiency and customer service.

Objective 2: Describe the five major physical distribution functions.
The five major physical distribution functions are: order processing, warehousing, materials handling, inventory control and transportation. New technologies have dramatically changed the way orders are transmitted, entered, screened, prioritized, invoiced and filled. Most orders are now sent electronically. Hand held scanners with display panels often are used by warehouse workers in filling orders (refer to the Amazon feature at the beginning of this chapter). There are automated distribution centers with mechanized picking

equipment controlled by computers in conjunction with conveyor systems. Inventory control is essential to assure maximum fill rates at minimum cost. In transporting orders to customers, the major advantage of trucks and airplanes is speed, but they are relatively costly. Railroads and water carriers are the most efficient modes for the movement of bulky commodities. Gaining in popularity is intermodal transportation, the combination of two or more modes in moving freight.

Efficient consumer response programs attempt to eliminate activities that do not add value in distribution channels. Wholesalers and retailers give up some of their buying authority. They send daily information via EDI to their suppliers on stock levels and warehouse shipments. Personnel in the supplier organization then decide what and when to ship.

Objective 3: Identify and explain the three primary types of intermediaries in a distribution channel.
Primary intermediaries include brokers, wholesalers (distributors) and retailers. Brokers actively negotiate their sale for the client, but they do not purchase the goods they handle. Wholesalers, also referred to as distributors, take title to products and resell them to retail, industrial, commercial, institutional, professional or agricultural firms, as well as to other wholesalers. Retailers take title to products for resale to the ultimate consumer.

Objective 4:   Explain the three types of vertical management systems and how VMS is different than a conventional channel system.

A conventional channel system places little importance on coordination; members bargain aggressively with each other about every transaction. In contrast, vertical marketing systems (VMS) are networks that emphasize channel coordination, realizing that customer satisfaction is impossible without efficient and effective distribution.

There are three types of vertical marketing systems: administered, contractual and corporate. An administered channel system is one in which channel members devote effort to coordinating relationships. A contractual channel system is one in which relationships are formalized, often with a written contract. Retail cooperatives, wholesaler-sponsored voluntary chains and franchises are three common forms of contractual channel systems. A corporate channel system is one in which a company owns and operates organizations at other levels in the channel.

Objective 5:   Discuss how to strategically manage channel relationships.

Coordinating relationships within the distribution channel is a challenge. The company must think strategically and develop a management plan. Interdependence, trust and support will influence the success of coordination. Channel management is facilitated when

members meet to set joint goals and develop plans for the coming year. Once the plan is in place, company sales personnel need to monitor and evaluate the performance of each intermediary, noting deviations from the plan. Finally, conflict resolution is necessary when channel conflict occurs.

Objective 6:   Describe legal and ethical issues in channel management.

U.S. antitrust laws and other regulations designed to promote competition and consumer welfare affect channel management and distribution practices. These include resale price maintenance, differential pricing and support programs, territorial and customer constraints, exclusive dealing, tying arrangements and full-line forcing, and intermediary termination. Sales and marketing personnel need to be completely familiar with laws and regulations affecting these areas.

Ethical issues include the fact that it is illegal for companies to impose certain constraints on channel members. For example, franchisers often confront the issue of how close to place locations. Another issue arises when companies set territorial constraints and then choose to ignore them. All employees and constitutes of the distribution channel must understand that bribery and unethical gifts for favorable treatment are unacceptable.

Review Your Understanding

1. What are intermediaries? List three primary categories of intermediaries.
2. What is a reverse channel? Give an example.
3. What are the guidelines for managing channel relationships?
4. What is a wholesaler? Briefly explain why wholesalers are important.
5. What is integrated logistics? What is physical distribution? Name the primary objective of physical distribution.
6. What is order management? Name a technological advance that has improved its effectiveness and efficiency.
7. What is warehousing? Name two types of distribution centers.
8. List five modes of transportation used in a physical distribution system.
9. What is efficient consumer response?
10. Name an important factor in global physical distribution.

Discussion of Concepts

1. What is a distribution channel? Why are distribution channels so important to companies and consumers?
2. How do direct channels differ from indirect channels? Under what conditions are indirect channels preferred to direct channels?
3. Why do channels vary in length or number of levels? What are multiple channels? Why are they being relied on by more and more companies today?
4. What are vertical marketing systems? Discuss the three types of VMS.
5. Describe the three distribution intensity options available to companies and give examples of each.
6. What is interdependence? Why is it such an important concept

in managing channel relationships? What role do support programs play in the distribution channel?
7. Explain how conflicts can be resolved in channel relationships.
8. What is EDI? How is it influencing the effectiveness and efficiency of order processing?
9. Explain how bar codes, radio frequency technology and scanning devices are improving the effectiveness and efficiency of the materials handling function.
10. How are efficient consumer response programs changing the way business is conducted between manufacturers and retailers?
11. What is the major challenge to integrated logistics management? How can companies overcome this challenge?

Key Terms & Definitions

1. **Administered channel system:** A vertical marketing system in which channel members devote effort to coordinating their relationships.
2. **Broker:** A firm that does not take title to the goods it handles but actively negotiates the sale of goods for its clients.
3. **Channel levels:** The number of distinct units (producers, intermediaries and customers) in a distribution channel.
4. **Contractual channel system:** A vertical marketing system in which relationships among channel members are formalized in some fashion, often with a written contract.
5. **Conventional channel system:** A channel system in which efforts to coordinate the actions of channel members are seen as unimportant.
6. **Corporate channel system:** A vertical marketing system in which a company owns and operates organizations at other levels in the channel.
7. **Cross docking:** Sorting and loading an incoming shipment from a supplier for delivery to customers without its being stored in any warehouse.
8. **Direct channel:** A distribution channel in which the producer uses its own employees and physical assets to distribute the product directly to end users.
9. **Distribution center:** A location where inventory is maintained before being routed to individual sales outlets or customers.
10. **Distribution channel:** A set of interdependent organizations involved in making a good available for purchase.
11. **Economic order quantity (EOQ) model:** A method of determining the amount of product to be ordered each time.
12. **Efficient consumer response (ECR) programs:** Programs to improve the efficiency of replenishing, delivering and stocking inventory in the distribution channel, while promoting customer value.
13. **Electronic data interchange (EDI):** Process which allows one company to send information to another company electronically in standard format.
14. **Exclusive dealing:** Restricting intermediaries from carrying competitive lines.
15. **Exclusive distribution:** Distributing a product through only one sales outlet in each trading area.
16. **Franchise system:** A type of distribution channel in which the franchiser holds the product trademark and licenses it to franchisees who contract to meet certain obligations.
17. **Freight forwarders:** Service companies specializing in the movement of cargo from one point to another, often country to country.
18. **Full-line forcing:** Requiring intermediaries to carry and sell the company's complete line.
19. **Indirect channel:** A distribution channel in which the producer makes use of independent organizations to distribute the product to end users.
20. **Integrated logistics management:** The coordination of all logistical activities in a company.
21. **Intensive distribution:** Making the product available through every possible sales outlet in a trade area.
22. **Intermediary:** An independently owned organization that acts as a link to move products between the producer and the end user.
23. **Intermodal transportation:** The combination of two or more modes in moving freight.
24. **Inventory control:** Management of stock levels.
25. **Logistics:** The movement of raw materials, components and finished products within and between companies.
26. **Materials handling:** The moving of products in and around a warehouse in the process of filling orders.
27. **Multiple channel systems:** The use of more than one channel to access markets for the same product.
28. **Order management:** The means by which a company receives, fills and delivers orders to customers.
29. **Physical distribution:** The movement of finished products through channels of distribution to customers.
30. **Private warehouse:** A storage facility owned and operated by the company.
31. **Public warehouse:** A storage facility owned and operated by businesses that rent space.
32. **Retailer:** A firm that takes title to products for resale to ultimate consumers.
33. **Retail cooperative:** An alliance of small retailers for wholesaling purposes.
34. **Reverse channel:** A distribution channel that flows from the end user to the wholesaler and producer.
35. **Selective distribution:** The use of a limited number of sales outlets per trade area.
36. **Supply chain management:** Incorporation of all activities concerned with planning, implementation, and control of sourcing, manufacturing, and delivery of products and services.
37. **Supply network:** All the organizations from which components, semi-finished products and services are purchased.
38. **Tying arrangement:** The purchase of a superior product is conditioned on the purchase of a second product of lower quality.
39. **Vertical Integration:** Ownership or control of suppliers by a buying company.
40. **Vertical marketing system (VMS):** A system in which channel members emphasize coordination of behaviors and programs.
41. **Warehousing:** The storage of inventory in the physical distribution system.
42. **Wholesaler:** A firm that takes title to products for resale to businesses, or other wholesalers or distributors, and sometimes consumers.
43. **Wholesaler-sponsored voluntary chain:** A group of retailers that have been united by a wholesaler.

References

1. Bowersox, Donald J.; Closs, David J.; Cooper, M.B., Supply Chain Logistics Management, (McGraw-Hill), 2009.
2. Ibid.
3. Bowersox, Donald J.; Closs, David J.; Stank, Theodore P., 21st Century Logistics: Making Supply Chain Integration a Reality, Council of Logistics Management, 1999, pg. 6.
4. Reeves, Collin, Raytheon, from a talk given on March 12, 2001, at Michigan State University.
5. Bowersox, Donald J.; Closs, David J.; Cooper, M.B., Supply Chain Logistics Management (McGraw-Hill), 2009.
6. Shapiro, Benson; Rangan, V.K.; Sviokla, John, "Staple Yourself to an Order," Harvard Business Review, July/August 1992, pp. 113-122.
7. Bowersox, Donald J.; Closs, David J., Logistical Management.
8. Stern; El-Ansary; Coughlan, Marketing Channels, pg. 119.
9. Reichheld, Frederick F.; Teal, Thomas; The Loyalty Effect; The Hidden Force Behind Growth, Profits, and Lasting Value, (Harvard business school press) 2001, pg. 263.
10. Bryan Eisenberg, The Pareto Principle: Applying the 80/20 Rule to Your Business, www.clickz.com, March 11, 2002.
11. "Distribution," Benetton Group, www.benettongroup.com, website visited July 13, 2015.
12. "Cross Docking," Jacobson Companies, www.jacobsonco.com, website visited July 13, 2015.
13. "Volkswagen drives RFID use through its supply chain," Computing. Co.UK, www.computing.co.uk, March 24, 2009.
14. Graham, Distributor Survival; Reichheld, Frederick F.; Teal, Thomas, The Loyalty Effect; The Hidden Force Behind Growth, Profits, and Lasting Value, (Harvard business school press; 2001), pg. 25B.
15. "Walmart Debuts Futuristic Truck," Walmart Press Release, March 26, 2014.
16. "Overview of America's Freight Railroads," American Association of Railroads, April, 2014.
17. Stern, El-Ansary, and Coughlan, Marketing Channels, pg. 119.
18. Hoover's Company Records, July 13, 2014.
19. Ingram Micro, www.ingrammicro.com, website visited July 13, 2015.
20. Davidson, William, "Changes in Distribution Institutions," Journal of Marketing, January 1970, pg. 7.
21. Rosenbloom, Bert, Marketing Channels, 8th ed., (Cincinnati, South-Western College Pub.), February 1, 2007.
22. www.mckesson.com, website visited July 13, 2014.
23. Coughlan, Anne; Anderson, Erin; Stern, Louis W., Marketing Channels, 7th ed., (Upper Saddles River, NJ, Prentice Hall), December 29, 2005.
24. International Franchise Association, www.franchise.org, website visited July 13, 2014.
25. Frazier; Lassar, "Determinants of Distribution Intensity."
26. James B. Kelleher, "From dumb iron to Big Data: Caterpillar's dealer sales push," Reuters, March 20, 2014.
27. Gundlach, Gregory; Cadotte, Ernest, "Exchange Interdependence and Interfirm Interaction: Research in a Simulated Channel Setting," Journal of Marketing Research 31, November 1994, pp. 516-553.
28. Morgan, Robert; Hunt, Shelby, "The Commitment-Trust Theory of Relationship Marketing," Journal of Marketing 58, July 1994, pp. 20-38.
29. Touby, Laurel, "Blimpie Is Trying to Be a Hero to Franchises Again," BusinessWeek, March 22, 1993, pg. 70.

CHAPTER 16

Retailing,
Direct Marketing
& Wholesaling

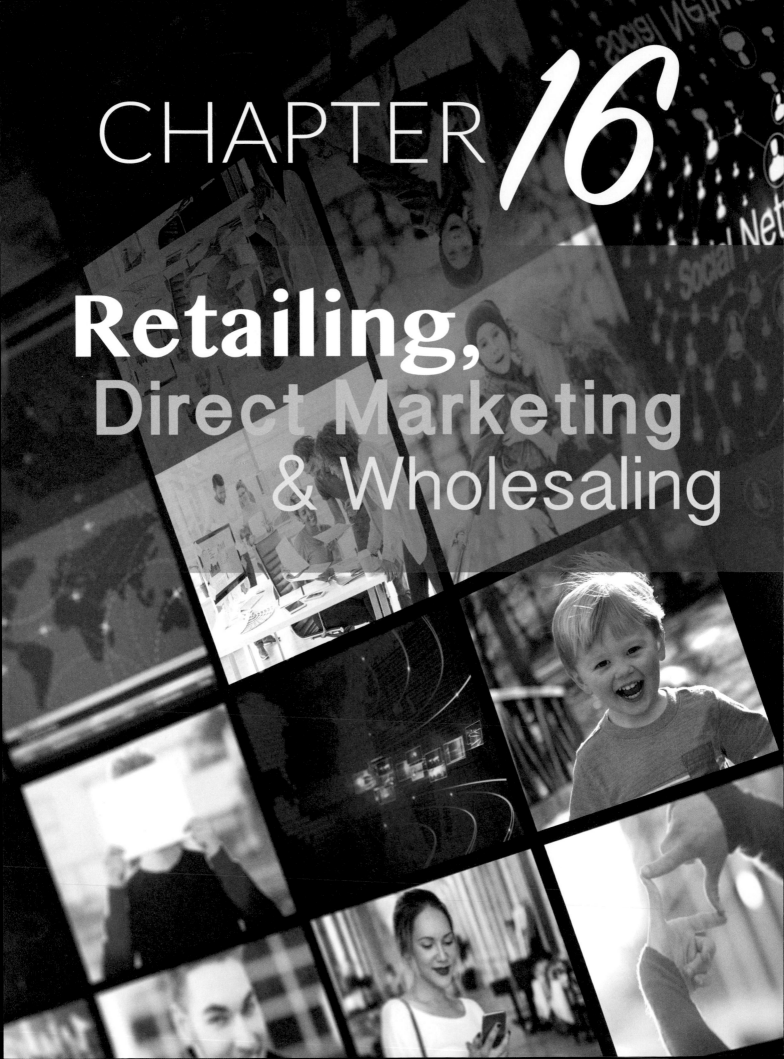

YouTube SCAN & WATCH ▶

IKEA has over 590 million visitors a year! Scan above to see how IKEA markets to homeowners.

IKEA is the world's largest furniture retailer, with more than 375 gigantic stores in 27 countries. Its concept of "offering a wide range of well-designed, functional home furnishing products at prices so low that as many people as possible will be able to afford them," has over 600 million annual visitors purchasing more than $35 billion in products each year. To keep prices affordable, IKEA uses flat packaging and customers assemble the products at home.

Targeting the global middle class, IKEA has found success by creating a culture built for a community of trendy shoppers. Using clever promotions, IKEA creates a frenzy with each new store opening, becoming a global phenomenon. Before the Atlanta opening, IKEA managers accepted essays from local customers describing why they thought they deserved $2,000 in store vouchers. Five winners would each receive $2,000, but only after they lived in the store for three days before the opening. IKEA's press generated enough buzz to draw in even more shoppers than expected on opening day.

The company continues to expand around the world; it recently asked India for permission to begin retail operations and plans to invest $1.9 billion in the nation. IKEA also expects to expand operations into China and Russia.

Selling products through its huge superstores is not the only way IKEA reaches its target market. Catalogs are used as a primary marketing channel, produced in 27 different languages and distributed to more than 198 million homes worldwide. IKEA also uses digital marketing and social media to reach even more potential customers.

Video is one of IKEA's core content marketing approaches, and Alia Kemet, U.S. media and web manager, likes to show—not tell—customers how to improve their lives. When she first started with IKEA, she says the goal was to extend the message by telling a story bigger than a commercial allowed. The videos tell the IKEA story in funny, instructional, and inspirational ways. They also target a variety of market segments—from adults and older Millennials to college students and singles establishing their first homes.

Measuring the effectiveness of video storytelling is based on engagement goals and changes in consumer perception. Consumers viewing videos on IKEA's YouTube channel are surveyed in real time so marketers can quickly change the marketing mix if necessary, depending on customer reaction. Scan the QR code above to watch one of IKEA's story telling videos.

IKEA has achieved success in the U.S. market despite early challenges. Steen Kanter, a former IKEA employee, said, "We got our clocks cleaned in the early 1990s because we really didn't listen to the consumer." U.S. managers were not paying close enough attention to details. "Americans want more comfortable sofas, higher-quality textiles, bigger glasses, more spacious entertainment units," says Pernille Spiers-Lopez, head of IKEA North America. There is no doubt, with revised products in the U.S. and closer attention to other regional markets, consumers will continue to make IKEA one of the most successful retailers in the world.

Sources: "Facts and Figures," IKEA, www.ikea.com, website visited July 10, 2016; "IKEA Completes Expansion of Round Rock, TX Store," IKEA, www.ikea.com, website visited July 14, 2014; "Swedish giant IKEA close to getting approval for entry into India: report," China Post, www.chinapost.com, website visited July 14, 2014; www.hoovers.com, website visited July 14, 2014; Albee, Ardath, "IKEA Executes B2C Video Storytelling with Style," Content Marketing Institute, September 8, 2015.

LO 01 Appreciate the important role retailers play in our economy.

LO 02 Identify the steps in creating a retail strategy.

LO 03 Recognize the diverse array of retailers that compete with one another.

LO 04 Learn what direct marketing entails, its value, and how it differs from mass communication.

LO 05 Describe the different types of direct marketing media.

LO 06 Know the different types of wholesalers and the distinct roles they play.

The Concepts of Retailing, Direct Marketing & Wholesaling

Retailing, direct marketing and wholesaling touch our lives daily. Retailing is involved whenever you purchase a burger at McDonald's, select a cell phone at Verizon or buy a pair of jeans at The Gap. Direct marketing is involved whenever you receive a catalog from IKEA, watch QVC on TV, or place an order for Maroon 5's latest single on iTunes. Wholesalers enter the picture by supporting retailers and direct marketing with product assortments that match the needs of the vast array of target customers. Retailers, direct marketers and wholesalers help connect us with the goods and services that support our diverse lifestyles.

Retailing

RETAILING

The activities involved in selling of products to end users for use and consumption by the purchaser.

Retailing refers to the selling of products to end users for use and consumption by the purchaser. It does not include the sale of products to other resellers, which is the domain of wholesaling. Best Buy sells primarily to consumers, while retailers like Staples have a large business clientele. Home Depot does significant business with each group. Typically, a retailer is a firm that makes the majority of its sales to consumers, although many also sell to small businesses. Home Depot sells a large percent of its volume to independent contractors such as builders, painters, plumbers and electricians. Many discounters and warehouse clubs sell to small businesses as well, such as restaurants and small independent stores. OfficeMax and Staples are also examples of retailers that have a significant amount of sales to business customers.

Retailers generally use direct mail and catalogs to supplement their store sales. Texas-based Neiman Marcus sends out a Christmas Book every October to its credit card customers. Over the years it has included exotic products such as camels, his-and-her airplanes, mummy cases, windmills and submarines. A study by technology and market research firm Forrester projects that online retail sales will reach $327 billion in 2016. Clearly, it is a key part of most retailing businesses.[1] Companies can increase customer profits through add-on services that encourage multi-channel shopping. For example, customers who order a product online but pick it up at a store location are exposed to multiple services and therefore expected to be more satisfied.[2]

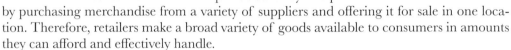

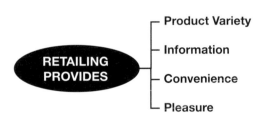

The Neiman Marcus Christmas book has evolved into the ultimate wish book.

THE IMPORTANCE OF RETAILERS

Retailers are vital to our economy. Retail sales in the United States represent about two-thirds of our gross domestic product annually. Retailing also is one of the largest U.S. employment industries—about 14.4 million people work in retailing.[3]

Figure 16.1 Functions of Retailing

RETAILING PROVIDES
— Product Variety
— Information
— Convenience
— Pleasure

Retailing is the final stage in the distribution channel for the majority of products sold to consumers...everything from chewing gum to insurance to automobiles. As retailing practices develop and become more refined, better products are provided to consumers at better prices in more creative ways. Retailers perform a variety of functions described in Figure 16.1 that increase the value of products to consumers. Similar to wholesalers, they play two critical roles in the mix of goods. They perform an allocation function by purchasing products in large quantities from suppliers (manufacturers, wholesalers, or brokers) for resale to consumers in smaller quantities. They also perform an assortment function by purchasing merchandise from a variety of suppliers and offering it for sale in one location. Therefore, retailers make a broad variety of goods available to consumers in amounts they can afford and effectively handle.

Although packaged goods such as cereal, detergent, milk and toothpaste are purchased off the shelf by consumers, retailers still provide information about such products through advertising, displays and unit prices posted on the shelves. Other consumer products, especially durable goods and services such as insurance, require retailers to use salespeople who can provide information and answer questions about product benefits.

Well located stores increase the convenience of shopping for customers through physical locations and integrated web e-tailing. Furthermore, many retailers facilitate transactions by investing in scanner technology and offering credit. They also may customize products, as do clothing retailers who alter suits or insurance agents who develop specialized packages. Repair services are provided by retailers such as Sears, Best Buy and Radio Shack.

Without retailers, acquiring basic necessities would be difficult in terms of both time and money. Retailers bring convenience to customers by supplying them time, place, possession and form utilities.

The **wheel of retailing** is one way to describe how retailers emerge, evolve and sometimes fade away. According to the theory, new retailers locate their no-frills stores in low-rent areas to keep costs down. When they experience success, they add more services, move to more expensive real estate, upgrade facilities and raise prices. This makes them

WHEEL OF RETAILING

A descriptive theory about how retailers emerge, evolve, and sometimes fade away.

vulnerable to new low-price entrants, and the wheel goes round and round. If a retailer carefully develops and implements a strategy to satisfy its target market, it can escape the wheel. Upgrading services, locations and prices is justified only if that is what the target market demands.

RETAIL STRATEGY

The steps in formulating a retail strategy are shown in Figure 16.2. Invariably, successful retailers have a sound retail strategy.

Target Markets and Positioning Like any business, retailers must understand their customers to be truly successful. As a first step, they carefully analyze the general market and decide the segment or segments to target. For example, Autozone, based in Memphis, is an auto parts retailer that targets lower-income consumers who repair their own cars. Nordstrom's, headquartered in Seattle, is a department store chain that targets middle- to high-income households desiring superior service. Wet Seal Inc., based in Foothill Ranch, California, operates 532 apparel stores in 47 states and Puerto Rico with a target market of young women ages 13 through 18.[4]

Whatever the overall targeting strategy, individual outlets may face different mixes of customers. The primary trade area is the geographic territory in which the majority of a store's customers reside. The trade area can vary in circumference from less than one mile for a convenience store to 20 miles for a specialty store such as Toys "R" Us. Each store manager must understand primary trade areas and operate accordingly. For example, Walmart uses AC Nielson and census information to locate stores in areas with large multicultural populations and tailors merchandise for these locations specifically to the customer base.[5]

Retailer positioning is the mental picture consumers have of the retailer and the shopping experiences it provides in relation to competitors. Retailers decide what image they want to establish with customers—high prestige, superior service, friendly atmosphere, low prices, etc. Then they must determine how to instill this image in the minds of their customers. Decisions on service level and pricing, merchandise assortment, and store location all influence the retailer's image.

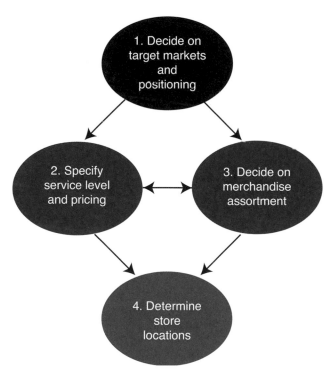

Figure 16.2 Developing a Retail Strategy

Service Level and Pricing There are three different strategies that relate to service level and pricing, and which one a company chooses to use is influenced by its target market and positioning. Many retailers follow a discount-oriented strategy, offering products and service of acceptable quality at low prices. The objective is to keep service costs and overhead down in order to make prices competitive. Lucky Stores is a supermarket chain in southern California that offers low prices and few amenities. Walmart and Kmart have a discount-oriented strategy. Crown Books offers a standard 10 percent discount in addition to discounts up to 40 percent on New York Times hardback bestsellers.

A service-oriented strategy emphasizes quality products and value-added functions with prices to match. It is successful to the extent that this is what the target mar-

Mikimoto is well known around the world for its quality of pearls and level of service.

ket wants. In the jewelry business, Mikimoto offers some of worlds' finest cultured pearls, and its well-trained sales force caters to the specific needs of each customer. After each purchase, a sales associate personally follows up with the customer with a handwritten letter, thanking them for their business. Nordstrom is well known in the Northwest for its quality of service, such as ironing shirts for customers immediately after purchase. Successful companies work to differentiate themselves from competitors by offering unique and quality service.

Other retailers follow a hybrid strategy, combining quality products, value-added services, and low pricing in some manner. Autonation, Carchoice and Carmax offer huge inventories of used cars marked with low, no-haggle prices. Their stores have such amenities as child care centers, coffee bars and touch-screen computers. The well-known booksellers Barnes & Noble offers more services than just selling books. The stores also feature coffee shops, sell music and toys, have special promotions and host in-store special events. The company also offers the Barnes & Noble membership program to enhance customer loyalty and distinguish Barnes & Noble from its competition.[6]

Merchandise Assortment Retailers must take great care in deciding what merchandise to offer. Those with the right assortment have greater sales revenues and customer satisfaction. Merchandise breadth, the variety of product lines offered, and merchandise depth, the number of products available within each line, must be determined. Department stores have considerable breadth but only moderate depth, while retailers such as Best Buy have limited breadth but great depth.

A **scrambled merchandising** strategy means that the product lines carried seem to be unrelated. The goal is to facilitate one-stop shopping for customers and achieve competitive advantage. For example, Kmart introduced "Super Kmart" stores to combine its traditional goods with typical supermarket products. Meijer, a chain in the Midwest, has used this strategy since its inception.

As discussed in Chapter 9, part of the assortment of many retailers is private label merchandise. JCPenney's St. John's Bay jeans and Sears' Canyon River Blues jeans are two examples. Private labels are especially common in the apparel, food, home appliance and drug industries. In apparel, private labels serve to build the image of the retailer rather than the manufacturer. Ann Taylor and Gap have taken this a step further, designing, manufacturing and marketing their own products in their own stores. Private label sales are growing quickly in supermarket chains that feature their own products. You may notice Kroger brand orange juice placed next to the popular Tropicana brand with prices displayed side-by-side. Once supermarket retailers realized customers would buy private label products if they believed they were of good quality, the quality and marketing of these products improved. A Nielsen Company study shows that private label sales in U.S. supermarkets total about $77 billion, 15.9 percent of total sales.[7] Globally, private label products represent more than 20 percent of grocery sales and are expected to grow to 30 percent by 2020.[8]

> The location decision can be a source of competitive advantage if it preempts competitors from moving to an area with high sales and profit potential.

Store Location The location decision is very important for any retailer. Among other things, it affects how convenient shopping will be for customers. The target market dictates the choice to some degree. Autozone, for example, places its stores directly in low-income neighborhoods.[9] In contrast, specialty toy stores and clothing boutiques locate in well-to-do suburbs or high-end urban shopping districts such as the Gold Coast Magnificent Mile in Chicago. The location decision can be a source of competitive advantage if it preempts competitors from moving to an area with high sales and profit potential. Walmart's strategy was to establish stores in small towns that could not support more than one large discount operation. It froze out competition while building a strong sales base. Once it had this firm foundation, Walmart spread to larger suburban areas.[10]

Some retailers use a destination location strategy; that is, stores are put in low to mid-rent areas off highways and some distance from other retailers. Because the store is off the beaten path, consumers make it their destination when they want to shop there. In contrast, a competitor location strategy puts stores near those of major competitors, rationalizing that more consumers drawn to the area results in more likely to shop at any store there. Wherever you find McDonald's you are very likely to see Burger King. Diamond merchants cluster along 47th Street in New York City, antique stores line the Place du Grand Sablon in Brussels, and a Planet Hollywood usually can be found near a Hard Rock Cafe. In general, retailers with large stores, a large amount of merchandise, and attractive pricing can use a destination location strategy effectively. Retailers selling goods that consumers want to compare for quality and price are usually wise to locate close to competitors.

Of course, many retailers choose a local or regional shopping mall rather than a freestanding location. A shopping mall or center is a group of retail stores in one place marketed as a unit to shoppers in a trade area. Shopping malls, especially regional ones, provide a wide array of merchandise and immense pulling power. Merchants can pool resources to provide entertainment, such as pianists or clowns or even a supervised indoor playground, as at the huge Mall of America in Minneapolis. This supermall has 2.5 million square feet of retail space, equivalent to four regional shopping malls, features more than 520 specialty stores and brings in more than 40 million visitors annually, including many of whom charter flights from all over the world. It also has development rights for up to an additional 5.6 million square feet of mixed-use space.[11]

TYPES OF RETAILERS

There are several ways to classify retailers. Form of ownership distinguishes between small independents (often called mom-and-pop stores) and **chain stores**, which are groups of centrally owned and managed retail outlets that handle the same product lines. Level of service can be used, whether full, limited or self-service. Price level can be used as well. However, the most informative classification is based on the merchandise assortment, whether retailers sell a limited line or general merchandise. Within each category, different types of retailers exist based on their service level and pricing strategy, as outlined in Figure 16.3. A number of successful companies have stores of more than one type, such as Macy's and Walmart.

Limited Line	General Merchandise
Specialty stores Franchises Category killers or superstores Automatic vending retailers	Department stores Convenience stores Supermarkets Warehouse clubs Discount stores Variety stores Hypermarkets Big Box

Figure 16.3 Classification of Retailers

Limited-Line Retailers Limited-line retailers focus on one product category. The four types are specialty stores, franchises (defined in Chapter 10), superstores and automated vending retailers.

Specialty stores offer merchandise in one primary product category with considerable depth. Examples are Wet Seal, The Limited, Florsheim, Women's Foot Locker, Champs Sports, and Roller Skates of America. Goods are of moderate to high quality, and prices tend to also be high and comparable to department stores.

Automated vending is extremely popular in Japan and is a growing market in many parts of the world.

SUPERSTORE

A retailer that focuses on a single product category but offers huge selection and low prices; also called a category killer.

AUTOMATED VENDING

The use of machinery operated by coins or credit cards to dispense goods.

DEPARTMENT STORE

A retailer with merchandise of broad variety and moderate depth with a relatively high level of customer service.

Many specialty stores are run by franchisees, who sign a contractual agreement with a franchiser organization to represent and sell its products in particular retail locations. Examples include Blockbuster Video stores, the vast majority of fast-food restaurants (some outlets are company-owned) and automobile dealerships.

Superstores, sometimes called category killers, focus on a single product category but offer huge selection, low-to-moderate service levels and low prices. Examples include Barnes & Noble, Home Depot, IKEA, Staples and Office Depot. Superstores have been particularly successful in taking business away from traditional discount stores as well as wholesalers.

Automated vending retailers use machinery operated by coin or credit card to dispense goods. The placement of machines is critical, and airports, hospitals, schools and office buildings are among the most popular locations. Traditionally, vending has focused on beverages, candy, cigarettes and food, but the industry is expanding into new areas, such as life insurance policies in airports, movie rentals in supermarkets, and lottery tickets. ARAMARK and Canteen Corporation are two leading automatic vending retailers.

In Japan, vending machines are more important in retail trade. Homes and apartments have little storage space, and consumers often travel on foot or by mass transit. The convenience of location, wider variety of products, and small quantities are appealing. Roboshop Outlets allow customers to look through displayed items, punch in the desired product's number, and then receive their purchases through a trap door. More than a dozen of these shops exist in Tokyo alone, and the Vending Machine Manufacturers Association of Japan reports that there is one vending machine for every 23 people in Japan. These vending machines sell everything from alcohol to pagers to underwear.[12]

General Merchandise Retailers
General merchandise retailers carry a number of different product categories. There are seven types: department stores, convenience stores, supermarkets, warehouse clubs, discount stores, variety stores and hypermarkets.

Department stores carry a broad array and varying depth of merchandise, and the level of customer service is relatively high. Merchandise is grouped into well-defined departments. Both soft goods, such as apparel and linens, and hard goods, such as appliances and sporting goods, are normally sold. The intention is to provide one-stop shopping for most personal and household items. While often situated in downtown areas at a stand-alone location, department stores also are prevalent in shopping malls, where they are considered anchor tenants that draw customers.

Target markets and pricing strategies vary considerably among department stores. Some companies seek the upscale customer, such as Bloomingdale's, Neiman Marcus and Saks Fifth Avenue. Their decor is plush, with an ambiance and prices to match. Others, such as Kohl's and Target, appeal to a somewhat broader middle-income

Saks Fifth Avenue is a department store targeting higher income customers.

clientele and focus on mainstream tastes, increasingly offering popular brands at lower prices.[13] Still others, such as JCPenney and Sears, seek an even broader array of customers. Specialty stores provide the most competition to upscale department stores, while discounters pose a threat to lower-end department stores.

Convenience stores are small and have moderately low breadth and depth of merchandise. Sandwiches, soft drinks, snack foods, newspapers and magazines, milk, and beer and wine are among the most popular products carried. They are open long hours, prices are high, and their location is their primary advantage. Some are part of large corporate chains, including 7-Eleven and Circle K. Some large oil companies have established their own operations, such as Speedway and Texaco's Food Mart. Many convenience stores are mom-and-pop businesses, family-owned and operated.

Supermarkets are large, departmentalized, food-oriented retail establishments that sell a wide variety of foods and beverages, as well as many non-food items, typically cosmetics and toiletries. Many have in-store bakeries and delicatessens. Merchandise breadth and depth are moderately high. Since gross margins are generally low, supermarkets attempt to maximize sales volume. In the United States, regional chains dominate, such as Kroger, Safeway, and Winn-Dixie.

Recently, the east-coast regional supermarket Wegmans ranked in the No. 33 spot on Fortune's Best 100 Places to Work List. Operated in New York, Pennsylvania, New Jersey, Maryland, and Virginia, Wegmans' 75 supermarkets cater to those who want a complete upscale shopping experience. Wegmans stocks more than 60,000 products, including specialty cheeses, fine dinnerware, and ready-to-cook entrees.[14]

Warehouse clubs are large, no-frills stores that carry a revolving array of merchandise at low prices. They are typically 60,000 square feet or more. Consumers must become members before shopping in these clubs. Brands carried vary by day and week, depending on the deals arranged with suppliers, so product selection is somewhat limited. By carrying only the most popular items in a merchandise category, clubs strive for high asset turnover (net sales divided by total assets) with gross margins as low as 8 percent. There are approximately 4,000 warehouse clubs and superstores in the United States, accounting for $410 billion in annual revenue. A recent First Research Industry Profile reveals that the U.S. industry is highly concentrated: the top four companies hold over 90 percent of sales.[15] These retailers give supermarkets stiff competition. Examples include Costco, BJ's and Sam's Club.

Courtesy of Sam's Club

Sam's Club is an example of a successful warehouse club in the United States.

Discount stores offer a broad variety of merchandise with limited service and low prices. Merchandise depth is low to moderate. Service levels are minimal. Operating costs, including payroll, are normally 20 percent or less of total sales.[16] Discounters concentrate on low- to middle-income consumers, and their goal is asset turnover and sales volume per store. Some large discount stores are also considered hypermarkets or big box retailers, such as Walmart and Kmart.

There are two specialized types of discounters. **Off-price retailers** sell brand-name clothing at low prices. Their inventory frequently changes as they take advantage of special deals from manufacturers selling excess merchandise. Examples are Loehmann's, Marshall's, Men's Warehouse and T. J. Maxx.

Variety stores offer an array of low-priced merchandise of low to moderate quality. There is not much depth. These retailers are becoming more scarce because of

Hypermarkets are giant shopping facilities that offer one-stop shopping.

HYPERMARKET

A giant shopping facility with a wide selection of food and general merchandise at low prices.

BIG BOX RETAILERS

A large retail establishment, usually part of a chain, selling either general merchandise or specialty items (such as electronics) and focusing on large sales volume.

intense competition, mainly from larger discounters. Examples of variety stores are Everything's A Dollar and Pic'N'Save.

Hypermarkets are giant shopping facilities offering a wide selection of food and general merchandise at low prices. They have at least 100,000 square feet of space, some of them three times that. The concept was developed by a French company, Carrefour, which is very successful throughout Europe and Latin America.

Big box retailers are large establishments, usually part of a chain, that focus on high sales volume. These stores, often considered large discount stores or hypermarkets, boomed in the 1990s, with chains such as Walmart, Home Depot and Best Buy expanding across the United States. Many stores, such as Target, offer one-stop shopping; you can get groceries, clothes and a new camera all in one location. In addition, big box stores often make it easy to find an item locally that smaller stores may not stock. Looking for a new Samsung Galaxy tablet? You can visit BestBuy.com, enter your ZIP code and see which nearby stores have it in stock. You even pay online and the store will have it ready for you to pick up at your convenience. Sales in some of these stores, however, have declined in recent years because of shifting demographics and more customers buying items online and shipping directly to their homes.

ISSUES IN RETAILING

Retailing changes rapidly. Retailers must address such important factors as diversity, ethical issues, and global retailing.

Diversity Because retailers deal directly with consumers, most of them realize that staffing and marketing programs must reflect the nature of the population they serve. Recognizing diversity and its implications for business practice is a must for top-performing retailers. Sears, Roebuck and Co. is at the forefront in connecting with diverse markets. Some of its stores in Florida have a customer base that is 90 percent Hispanic, and Sears has bilingual signs, sales staff, in-store posters featuring minority models, and four apparel lines designed for multicultural women.[17] With the Spanish-language media market growing twice as fast as the rest of the market, companies are investing significant amounts of money in advertising to attract the Hispanic population.[18]

Ethical Issues Ethical dilemmas often arise over the goods sold by retailers. Consumer action groups may lobby them to stop carrying certain products. More than 10 years ago, Target, under pressure from the growing stigma attached to smoking, eliminated cigarette sales in its stores.[19] Depending on community standards, many stores do not carry certain magazines, or they keep them in locations inaccessible to children. Walmart stopped carrying guns in its stores in 1994. It still sells them through catalogs, though, and it sells many shooting accessories such as gun cases as well. This, predictably, offends many consumer advocates.

Employee relations are another area in which ethical questions arise, such as steps taken to prevent unionization or reduce employee theft. Whatever the issue, if employees are not treated with fairness and respect, then major problems can result. One recent survey found that a two-way performance review is an excellent way to retain good workers. This way, both the management and the employee can comment on the employee's performance, as well as on the management's performance, ensuring the review can be just that,

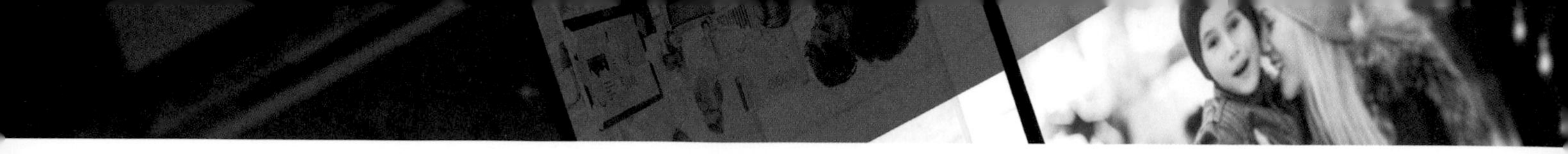

a "review," and not a "criticism." This plan aims to confront problems in the employee-employer relationship before they cause problems for the company.[20]

Global Retailers For years, a number of U.S. retailers have had successful ventures in global markets. McDonald's, along with KFC and Burger King, have brought fast food retailing to most mature and emerging markets for the past couple of decades. Each of these retailers uses a similar approach with adjustments to local requirements. For example, you will find beer in McDonald's in Germany and Cadbury chocolate sticks in its ice cream cones in the United Kingdom.

Today, retailers from other countries are finding the U.S. to be an excellent market, as well. Recently, European retailer Zara opened its largest flagship store in the United States in Chicago. This three-story clothing and accessory shop boasts 16,000 square feet of retailing space. Situated on Michigan Avenue, Zara engages in competition with other clothing stores like H&M, Banana Republic, and Forever 21.[21] As with most growth-oriented companies, leading-edge retailers emphasize the global nature of business.

LO 04

Direct Marketing

DIRECT MARKETING

Uses various methods to communicate with consumers, generally calling for a direct response on their part.

Direct marketing uses various methods to communicate with consumers, generally calling for a direct response on their part. It is part of the promotion component of the 4Ps in the marketing mix. Direct marketing is an extension of retailing that occurs outside of a retail store through activities that involve various levels of consumer response. There are six types of direct marketing: direct mail, internet, catalogs, telemarketing, print and broadcast media, and television home shopping.

Many organizations can benefit from direct marketing. A growing number of companies are direct marketers, who conduct business primarily or solely with this method. This kind of direct marketing is most powerful when it communicates product and pricing information, along with guidance for placing orders. The sale is completed by delivery of products via computer (such as software) or through services such as UPS, DHL and FedEx.

According to industry research conducted by Winterberry Group, spending for direct marketing will total $163 billion in 2016—52.1 percent of total advertising spent in the U.S. Clearly, direct marketing is very significant in generating sales and is becoming even more important. There are 1.3 million direct marketing employees in the country, and their sales efforts directly support 7.9 million other jobs.[22]

According to industry research conducted by Winterberry Group, spending for direct marketing will total $163 billion in 2016.

In comparison, total direct marketing expenditures are approximately equal to total expenditures for mass advertising. About 52 percent is spent by B2C businesses, and the remaining 48 percent is directed at the B2B arena. However, the B2B expenditures are growing at a faster rate. Because the B2B arena is larger, direct marketing represents about 4.4 percent of business sales and about 12 percent of consumer sales. Direct marketing is also slightly more productive in generating sales for consumer businesses:

- $1 spent on consumer direct marketing yields $12.66 in sales;
- $1 spent on business direct marketing yields $10.10 in sales.[23]

Direct marketing offers consumers a convenient way to shop from the comfort of their home or office. The fast-paced lifestyle of many people leaves little time or energy for shopping trips. Rising gas costs, traffic, parking and retailers' decreased staffing all reduce the convenience of physically traveling to stores. The widespread availability of credit cards, toll-free numbers, digital technology including social media, and overnight delivery service has made direct marketing to consumers even more viable. Convenience is also important in business-to-business markets. Direct and digital marketing allows business customers to gain information on products and place orders instantly—much more efficiently than having to meet with several salespeople.

Direct marketing may yield better quality and pricing, too. For example, mail-order florist Calyx & Corolla claims that its flowers have superior blooms that last five to 10 days longer by eliminating long truck or retail cooler times. Instead, it partners with growers to send flowers directly using UPS.[24] Another advantage of direct marketing is competitive prices. A company can operate out of an unadorned warehouse in an inexpensive location, keeping overhead low and passing the savings onto its customers.

Direct marketing is of increasing value to many entrepreneurs as retailers cut back on inventory. For example, many music stores feature only mainstream artists and compilations, because consumers can find exactly what they want on internet sites such as iTunes. Large organizations also benefit from direct marketing. Some use it as their primary means of doing business; others use it in combination with different channels.

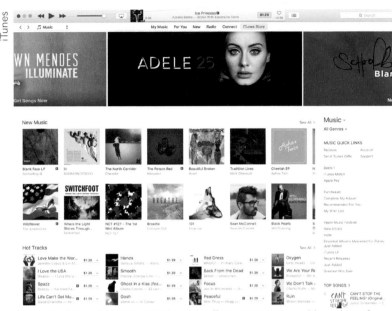

iTunes is a form of direct marketing that offers consumers a wide variety of options.

All companies that conduct direct marketing maintain a database with customer names, addresses and purchase history. These are often supplemented with lists purchased from market research companies such as Zeller's and Dun and Bradstreet. Some direct marketers have taken the art of database management to a new level. Access Innovations has software called Data Harmony, which helps publishers, corporate libraries and online directory producers design and manipulate databases. The company's Thesaurus Master allows users to tag their own phrases and keywords in a database's thesaurus, and it gives searchers more accurate results by using individualized terms relevant to a specific company, industry, and scientific discipline.[25]

DIRECT MARKETING MEDIA

Direct marketers use many media; some choose only one, but many combine several media in attempts to connect with customers. Figure 16.4 identifies the most popular media which are described in this section. The following sections describe each type of direct marketing media in more detail.

Direct Mail Direct mail is among the most popular methods of direct marketing. It brings products and services to consumers without them ever leaving their homes. Each year, billions of paper-based pieces are sent to prospective customers through the U.S. Postal Service. Bed, Bath and Beyond is famous for its 20% off direct mail coupons, Express for its NEXT rewards program coupons, and Victoria's Secret for its Angels mailers offering free lingerie. Some companies like J.Crew and Macy's even personalize birthday coupons that arrive within two weeks of a loyal customer's birthday! Others include samples, DVDs, even customized note pads and return address labels. Each presents an offer that will hopefully entice the recipient to respond with a purchase. According to the Direct Marketing Association, 3.7% of households that receive a direct mail campaign actually respond to it.[26] Direct mail is a popular type of direct marketing because it reaches a select market at a reasonably low cost.

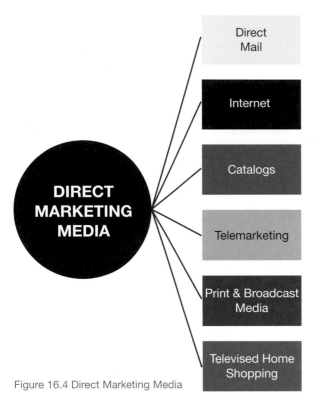

Figure 16.4 Direct Marketing Media

Direct Mail

Internet

Catalogs

Telemarketing

Print & Broadcast Media

Televised Home Shopping

DIRECT MARKETING MEDIA

Internet The majority of companies have e-commerce websites, encouraging consumers to make purchases directly online. However, some people are reluctant to provide credit card numbers over the internet because they don't want their private information intercepted, misused or stolen. The overwhelming benefit of digital marketing is its ability to reach huge markets. Beyond our borders, however, the heavy American influence grates on some in other cultures. Adaptable marketers can use this as an opportunity to provide an inviting environment to people in those cultures.

Companies choose whether to set up and maintain their own websites or turn to a provider. Clearly a company maintains greater control and circumvents fees by creating its own, however, professional website developers can craft a dynamic and exciting site to encourage customer visits. They can even run it! An annual fee plus some percentage of the company's online sales, typically two percent, is paid to the online service. Individuals who do not have their own websites, or who wish to sell their items through larger sites, can use services such as eBay, which allows users to bid on items and then charges the seller a set amount based on the purchase price.

In the consumer market, Amazon sells over 480 million products in the U.S. Its product selection has expanded by 235 million in the past 16 months. That's an incredible average of 485 thousand new products each day![27] Amazon owns no inventory; instead it relies on a network of wholesalers to ship orders, normally within 24 hours, but as you learned in the Chapter 15 opener, Amazon Prime gets a product in to a customer's doorstep within 24 hours, and its new droid technology is expected to deliver within 30 minutes. Since some companies can' handle large volume shipping, Amazon created one of the most advanced fulfillment networks in the world, offering to pack and ship products for them. The fulfillment centers are so impressive and sophisticated that public tours are offered at several U.S. locations.

Many companies' profits are increasingly coming from internet sales. By 2017, 60 percent of U.S. retail sales will involve the internet in some way, either through digital marketing, or as the initial source for providing research and user reviews.[28] The booming of the internet in direct marketing has led to a growth of digital printing with personalized targeting possibilities. The Target Marketing's Media Usage Forecast indicates that of the top media channels marketers will use in the year ahead, email is the most favored at 94 percent, then direct mail at 91 percent, and social media at 89 percent.[29]

Amazon owns no inventory but has some of the largest shipping fulfillment centers in the world.

Catalogs Catalogs present product and price information in paper form, and deliver it to consumers in attractive, colorful layouts to encourage purchase. According to the Direct Marketing Association, about 90 million Americans make purchases from catalogs each year, and nearly 60 percent of them are women.[30] Some catalogs feature general merchandise, such as J.C.Penney, and others focus on a narrow range of products. Omaha Steaks sells beef, seafood, pork, lamb, chicken, pastas and desserts in its catalog. Eddie Bauer catalogs include men and women's apparel, luggage, footwear and accessories.

Like direct mail, catalogs offer several advantages to companies. First, they don't require costs for property space, physical display equipment and sales clerks. Second, they can be targeted to select audiences based on known preferences and historical buying patterns. Have you ever placed a first-time order from a particular catalog, and then found that you regularly receive the catalog thereafter? It's because marketers know that if you liked something enough to purchase it once, you'll probably at least open their catalog in the future and glance through it, possibly placing another order. You become part of a target market for the catalog's company.

A major disadvantage of catalog marketing is the expense. Victoria's Secret recently announced it will no longer publish its popular catalog to save the $100+ million a year it spends on printing. L Brands, the parent company of Victoria's Secret, explained that its marketing strategy will focus on loyalty programs and brand-building engagement rather than traditional catalogs. J.C.Penney is another example. It discontinued its catalog in 2010 to save costs, then brought it back in 2015 when CEO Myron "Mike" Ullman said, "We lost a lot of customers."[31] The company learned that many shoppers browse catalogs then go online to make their purchases. When the catalog was discontinued, sales dropped. Despite the expense of producing catalogs, they create emotional connections with customers; even the overall style of a catalog can draw a customer to the brand.

IKEA is a perfect example. Its unique, simple design attracts a lot of customers to the brand. Even if there's not an IKEA store close by, shoppers will spend hours looking at a 300-page IKEA catalog and then plan a trip to the nearest store, which is often hours or states away. The company will deliver more than 250 million copies of its 2016 catalog in 49 countries, 71 printed versions, and 34 languages.[32]

To eliminate printing and mailing costs, many companies are producing digital catalogs. Unlike printed catalogs, online catalogs have no space limitations for product presentations, so instead of just showing a picture, marketers can promote a product with video, and actual applications. It's also easy and inexpensive for marketers to make changes to a product online; price increases/decreases, additional features, new colors...all can be made at the touch of a keystroke. Finally, digital catalogs can be accessed on smartphones and mobile devices, which enables a consumer to comparison shop from anywhere.

The 2016 IKEA Catalog is available in 71 printed versions, 34 languages and distributed in 49 countries.

Telemarketing As we learned in Chapter 14, telemarketing occurs when salespeople make telephone calls to leads provided by marketing services or from other lists. The timing of calls is very important. Late morning and early afternoon are normally the best times for reaching businesses, while evenings between 7 p.m. and 9 p.m. are best for contacting households—from the marketer's standpoint. You probably have had more than a few interruptions at that time from telemarketers. Telemarketing has a higher cost per contact than direct mail or catalogs. Furthermore, many consumers view unsolicited telephone calls as an annoyance and resent unwanted clutter on voice mail. Salespeople may not directly answer consumer questions or handle objections well. In fact, they may be instructed not to deviate from prearranged scripts regardless of what they are asked.

Automated telemarketing uses machines to dial numbers, play recorded messages and take orders either via answering machines or by forwarding calls to live operators. Outbound automated calls meet with strong resistance, and the system is better used for incoming calls—that is, consumers are reached by other means and then place orders through the automated systems.

Precise list selection and development are critical for telemarketing. The sales message must be simple and strong. Salespeople need to receive at least some training on how to make calls and handle customer concerns. Person-to-person telemarketing is best used in the consumer market with current customers who prefer this mode of communication from a company. In business-to-business markets, especially when targeted at employees outside the purchasing area, telemarketing is not very successful. Sometimes services like Skype can be effective if that is indicated as a contact method on a business person's business card or LinkedIn page. In the business setting, it is especially important that telemarketers be carefully selected, well trained and adequately compensated.

Print and Broadcast Media   Print ads in magazines and publications are used a great deal in direct marketing. Along with information on products and prices, a call to action is usually used to draw attention to a phone number or website for further information. Direct marketers also rely on television and radio spots, usually ranging from 10 to 60 seconds. Television is the most powerful medium in the United States, reaching 80 percent of the population daily. Radio is the second most powerful medium, reaching 59 percent. In comparison, 49 percent are reached by the Internet and 13 percent by print media.[33]

Drawing on the power of television, many companies are creating Infomercials to sell products. **Infomercials** are long advertisements that resemble documentaries. They range from 15 to 60 minutes in length and often include celebrity endorsers and testimonials from satisfied customers. Products like smoking cessation, weight-control programs, cosmetics and exercise equipment are promoted this way. Established companies such as Chrysler and Mattel are beginning to use this technique to communicate in depth about product benefits. Some direct marketers use it to obtain distribution in retail stores. For example, pitchman Billy Mays started selling cleaning products like OxiClean for Orange Glo International on the Home Shopping Network in the 1990s. In no time, sales skyrocketed and products were available at retailers across the country. His legendary pitches were so successful, the Discovery Channel show "PitchMen," featured Mays as he attempted to sell various products.

Televised Home Shopping   In the past several years, home shopping via cable television has become popular with television audiences. Dedicated shopping channels feature products displayed by hosts and celebrities. The two largest marketers are Quality Value Channel (QVC) and Home Shopping Network (HSN). Themed programs are telecast 24 hours a day, seven days a week, to more than 248 million households worldwide. Program hosts, including such celebrities as Suzanne Somers, Tori Spelling, Heidi Klum and Kourtney Kardashian offer products ranging from books to computers, jewelry to lamps, clothing to power tools. Often celebrities use the opportunity to sell their own line of products. Customers can either order through an 800 number or online, enabling companies to adjust inventory minute by minute, not just season by season. Orders are usually shipped within 48 hours. Recently, HSN reported sales of almost $2.5 billion, and QVC's net sales totaled more than $8.7 billion.[34] QVC and HSN also have websites that allow customers to shop online, track purchases and chat with other users.

While keeping their foundation of television audiences, these companies are rapidly extending their markets through digital technology. QVC is already ranked as the 6th largest e-commerce player among multi-category retailers, and 7th in social commerce sales, according to Internet Retailer's Top 500 list.[35] Now, consumers can still enjoy the traditional benefits of shopping from home...or *wherever* they may be.

Ginsu knife demo on the home shopping channel QVC.

DIRECT MARKETING DECISIONS

Direct marketers make several decisions when developing a marketing strategy. The most important relate to target markets, database management, merchandise assortment, pricing, choice of media and other channels, message design, and payment

INFOMERCIAL

A long advertisement that resembles a documentary.

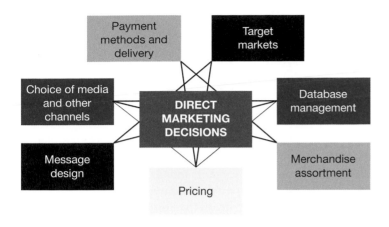

Figure 16.5 Direct Marketing Decisions

methods and delivery. The steps are depicted in Figure 16.5.

Target Markets Every excellent marketing strategy begins with an understanding of the intended audience, whether the audience is baseball hobbyists, newlyweds, cooking buffs or outdoor enthusiasts. Therefore, segmenting the market and selecting a target market is critical.[37] Many direct marketers are small companies content to serve a narrow group of customers in their home territory. Others expand nationally or globally once a strong business foundation is established. Dell Computer Corporation began in 1983 by serving small and medium-sized businesses in Austin, Texas, that needed upgrades on IBM-compatible computers. Dell branched out to serve large businesses and government agencies throughout the United States in the mid-1980s. Today, Dell has regional business units all over the world and is considered one of the world's most valuable brands (see Chapter 6).[36]

Database Management Maintaining a strong customer database is essential. The database should contain current and accurate names, addresses, email addresses, social media addresses, product preferences, and notations of any customers with poor credit histories or who no longer desire contact.

Another critical function of a database is tracking. For example, a retailer of sports-oriented hats developed a database that tracks the performance of individual stores and shows which ones are falling short of company goals. Because of the stores' limited product line, the company could not afford to overlook missed opportunities for improvement.

Merchandise Assortment The choice of target markets goes hand-in-hand with decisions on merchandise assortment. Baseball enthusiasts will be attracted to fantasy baseball camps and memorabilia. Cooking buffs are interested in exotic ingredients and hard-to-get equipment. Companies need to review and adjust the assortment in light of economic trends, competition and changes in preferences of the target market. Omaha Steaks initially sold beef but responded to the trend toward lower-fat foods by offering seafood, lamb, and chicken. Dell, which focused on desktop computers for years, had to add laptops and local area network (LAN) servers when it expanded to many user segments and began selling numerous handheld devices. It has also started to produce storage, appliance servers and network switches.[37]

Pricing Direct-marketing companies often follow a low-price strategy, facilitated by their low overhead. In contrast, some companies emphasize merchandise quality and follow a premium price strategy. Brigandi Coin Company in New York City has a strong direct-marketing business in baseball cards, team-signed baseballs and autographs. It has developed a reputation for selling only the finest-quality, authentic memorabilia. This is particularly important, since fraud is a major problem in the industry. Many collectors will pay Brigandi's high prices because of their confidence in the company.

Media and Channels Direct marketing companies normally start with one promotion medium and then branch out to multiple media over time. Some companies prefer to use traditional channels such as direct mail, catalogs, telemarketing, print and broadcast, and televised home shopping channels. Others use digital marketing channels exclusively, including email, pop-up ads and banners on internet sites, social media sites, mobile marketing, coupon direct mailers and direct response online. Most companies, however, use a combination of both once they get established.

Dollar Shave Club's YouTube video went viral and gained over 22 million views to date.

Dollar Shave Club, a young company you learned about in Chapter 8, is a good example. It's a member-based business that helps save time and money by delivering razors right to consumers' doors. The company launched in 2012 with a single media channel: a YouTube video that went viral and has gained over 22 million views to date. The company began growing as its sales increased, and it added radio as a promotion medium. Some of you might have heard the advertisements on the popular sports talk radio show hosted by Jim Rome. That, too, was a success for the company. As sales continued to increase, the company decided to hire a consulting firm, Convertro, to determine what promotion media it should use next. Adam Weber, vice president of consumer marketing at Dollar Shave Club, had this to say about hiring an outside consulting firm: "Dollar Shave Club had great success with online video marketing, but we didn't want to make the leap into broadcast without the ability to test, measure and improve our campaigns. Convertro determines which radio and TV buys are profitable for our brand and recommends strategic adjustments that continue to improve our results."[39]

Message Design Whatever medium is used, message design and presentation are most important. For paper-based mail, attention must be paid to the envelope, the cover letter and the product brochure. Envelopes of standard size and appearance are often discarded unopened, especially when mailing labels are used. An illustration or an important reason for opening the envelope often helps. The cover letter should be short and clear, using bold type to identify key product or service benefits. Brochures must be of high quality in appearance and content.[40]

Catalogs vary in quality of production depending on the company, its merchandise and its targeted customers. For example, West Elm sells high-quality home furnishings, targeted to a young and upscale market, and it reflects that through high-quality paper, design and photographs. In contrast, Hello Direct sells telephone productivity tools, such as cordless headsets and speaker phones, to businesses. It emphasizes low prices, and its catalog is produced at low cost.

On the internet, the home page must be eye-catching and provide different categories of information the user can access. Sites must be easy to navigate, and returning to the home page should always be simple. One rule of thumb is that content should never be more than three clicks away. The site must provide a clear overview of the company and why its products are a good buy. Testimonials from satisfied customers are a good idea. Finally, sites must be updated regularly so that users will keep coming back to see what's new.[41] A recent study indicates that the use of lifelike characters, or avatars, can have a significant impact on customers during their online shopping experience. Lifelike characters can engage users and enhance perceptions of social interaction often missed in online shopping, which leads to positive feelings and higher perceptions of value.[42]

Finally, the diversity of a company's customers must be considered when designing direct-marketing messages. A study by Skunkworks of New York said that companies can average a 20 percent increase in sales simply by advertising on Spanish-language network television instead of on English-language broadcast networks.

By directly targeting Hispanic communities in ways that appeal to them, companies can increase both sales and increase customer loyalty.[43]

Payment Methods and Delivery Direct-marketing companies serving the consumer market often offer several different payment methods—check, money order, or credit card. Installments also may be possible, especially when the product is relatively expensive, although the final cost to the consumer is greater under that option. Tempur-Pedic company allows a free trial period of 90 days for its mattresses.[44]

In B2B markets, customers often have an account with the direct marketer and pay on a monthly basis. Typically, if the invoice is paid within 10 days, a two percent credit will be applied to the next bill. Payment is normally due within 30 days unless special terms are negotiated.

Customers usually have several delivery options as well. The standard mode at Sharper Image is Federal Express second-day air; the delivery charge is based on the dollar value of the order. For an extra fee, customers can select next-day air or Saturday delivery. Dick's Sporting Goods offers standard delivery (three to six days), two day, and one day shipping at progressively higher charges.[45]

THE TERMS OF THE OFFER

HONESTY AND CLARITY OF OFFER: All offers should be clear, honest, and complete. Before publication of an offer, marketers should be prepared to substantiate any claims or offers made. Claims that are untrue, misleading, deceptive, or fraudulent should not be used.

ACCURACY, CONSISTENCY AND CLARITY: Simple and consistent statements or representations of all the essential points of the offer should appear in the promotinal material. Representations which, by their size, placement, duration, or other characteristics are unlikely to be noticed or are difficult to understand should not be used.

ACTUAL CONDITIONS: All descriptions, promises, and claims of limitation should be in accordance with actual conditions, situations, and circumstances existing at the time of the promotion.

DISPARAGEMENT: Disparagement of any person or group on grounds addressed by federal or state laws that prohibit discrimination is unacceptable.

DECENCY: Solicitations should not be sent to consumers who have indicated to the marketer that they consider those solicitations to be vulgar, immoral, profane, pornographic, or offensive in any way and who do not want to receive them.

PHOTOGRAPHS AND ART WORK: Photographs, illustrations, artwork, and the situations they describe should be accurate portrayals and current reproductions of the products, services, or other subjects they represent.

DISCLOSURE OF SPONSOR AND INTENT: All marketing contacts should disclose the name of the sponsor and each purpose of the contract. No one should make offers or solicitations in the guise of one purpose when the intent is a different purpose.

ACCESSIBILITY: Every offer should clearly identify the marketer's name and street address or telephone number, or both, at which the individual may obtain service. If an offer is made online, the marketer should provide its name, an Internet-based contact mechanism, and a street address. For e-mail solicitations, marketers should comply with Article #38 (Commercial Solicitations Online).

SOLICITATION IN THE GUISE OF AN INVOICE OR GOVERNMENTAL NOTIFICATION: Offers that are likely to be mistaken for bills, invoices, or notices from public utilities or governmental agencies should not be used.

POSTAGE, SHIPPING, OR HANDLING CHARGES: Postage, shipping, or handling charges, if any, should bear a reasonable relationship to actual costs incurred.

Figure 16.6 Summary of Direct Marketing Association Guidelines for Ethical Conduct
Source: "Terms of the Offer," Direct Marketing Association

ETHICS IN DIRECT MARKETING

There are a number of ethical problems that confront direct marketers and consumers, including important issues involving fraud, the right to privacy and confidentiality of personal information. Misrepresentation happens often. For example, contests and sweepstakes are sometimes worded so people believe they have won a prize only to find out that their call to a 900 number has cost a lot with no prize in sight. In other cases, sales are made and shipments don't occur. Every time you enter a sweepstakes, buy a magazine subscription or register your name online, chances are your name goes into a database that will be accessed by many organizations. It's becoming more common for these databases to be stolen and accessed by people interested in identity theft. All of these ethical issues can complicate the business environment for legitimate direct marketers and consumers. Consequently, the Direct Marketing Association has developed a rigorous set of 53 guidelines for ethical business practice. If you read the complete guidelines, you will probable recognize many situations in which your rights have been violated with direct mail. Figure 16.6 shows some of the guidelines.

Additional ethical guidelines fall into the following categories:

- Advance Consent Marketing: Guidance for credit card usage, advance payments, reminders, refunds, etc.

- Marketing to Children: Suitable communications, parental involvement, information from and about children, marketing by age (i.e., under 13).

- Special Offers and Claims: The meaning of free, price comparisons, and guarantees.

- Use of Test or Survey Data: Valid, reliable, including source and methods.

- Sweepstakes: Prizes awarded by chance (no skill required) without participants rendering anything (including no purchase required), can't represent that the participant has already won, clear representation of prizes vs. premiums, and disclosure of all of the rules.

- Fulfillment: No shipments without permission, product availability, and free test periods.

- Collection, Use, and Maintenance of Marketing Data: Consumer must be told if their information will be rented, sold, or exchanged, provided with source of data upon request, confidential maintenance of data, health-related data use guidelines, promotion and sale of lists, who in the firm sees and uses data, and information security.

- Online Marketing: Notice of online listeners, honoring time of contact, online access for problems, online data security, age restrictions, accountability procedures, commercial email solicitation restrictions and information required, email authentication, use and installation of software on others' computers, getting online leads from people, appending emails to consumer records.

- Telephone Marketing: Calling during reasonable hours, taping only with notice (and a beeping device), not calling unlisted numbers, interfacing with caller ID, limited ring time on automated dialing equipment, diary of call success, appropriate use or prerecorded voice messaging so consumers can gain feedback, use of facsimile machines, promotion with toll-free and pay-per-call numbers, disclosures, fundraising, and compliance with all laws.[46]

WHOLESALING

Selling of goods for resale or use to retailers and other businesses.

Sharese Ann Frederick / CC BY-SA 2.0

Inside a wholesale market in Guangzhou, China.

Wholesaling

Wholesaling affects our lives every day, but we rarely notice. We may buy aspirin at Walgreens, not knowing it was purchased from Bergen Brunswig Corporation, a large pharmaceutical wholesaler. We order a pepperoni pizza at a small neighborhood restaurant, not knowing most of the ingredients were acquired from SYSCO, a large wholesaler of food products. ToyDirectory.com Inc. provides a web service that helps retail stores access toys from 2,200 toy importers (wholesalers) and manufacturers. One reason parents and kids can find a broad range of toys at many price points, including the latest dolls or Spider-Man action figures, is because organizations like ToyDirectory.com or WholesaleCentral.com, business-to-business services, provide information for retailers about the vast number of toy wholesalers.[47] Most of us never see these intermediaries, but they are very important to us. **Wholesaling** is selling goods for resale or use to retailers and other businesses. Producers have a number of options in making sales to retailers and other businesses, including company-owned sales branches, brokers and wholesalers.

Many wholesalers are relatively small, filling a certain niche. Others are multibillion-dollar companies serving global markets. Wholesalers help thousands of companies connect with millions of customers. Whatever their size or scope, they all face competition. Their ability to make decisions about target markets, service level, pricing, business locations, merchandise assortment, credit management, use of technology, and image will influence their survival.

A wholesaler is an intermediary that takes title to the products it carries and makes a majority of sales to retailers or other businesses. Many wholesalers make no direct sales to consumers. For others, direct sales may be a significant part of revenue. For example, Smart and Final Inc., sells food products and related merchandise to small businesses and to some consumers. Since more than half of its sales come from small businesses, it is classified as a wholesaler. A pure wholesaler organization does not manufacture any goods. Only firms that sell goods they purchase from manufacturers or other intermediaries are considered part of wholesale trade. As a marketing ploy, many retailers that sell mostly to the general public present themselves as wholesalers. For example, "wholesale" price clubs, factory outlets and other organizations are retail establishments, even though they sell their goods to the public at wholesale prices.

For wholesalers of consumer goods, the primary customers are retailers and service businesses, such as restaurants, hospitals and nursing homes. In business-to-business markets, the primary customers are manufacturing organizations and service firms, such as accountants or contractors.

THE IMPORTANCE OF WHOLESALERS

Wholesalers play an important role in the economy. The roughly 375,000 such organizations in the United States employ approximately 6 million people, with annual sales reaching about $2 trillion.[48]

Wholesalers are prominent in a wide variety of product categories, including beverages, climate control equipment, computer hardware and software, electrical products, electronic components, fabrics, flowers and florist supplies, food, gift ware, medical supplies, movies, pharmaceuticals, telecommunications, tools, and toys. They provide value to customers and suppliers, as depicted in Figure 16.7. We will also see that they provide value for one another.

Wholesalers are important for product assortment and allocation. They fulfill their **assortment** function by purchasing merchandise from a variety of suppliers for resale. This makes a range of products available in one place for the convenience of customers. They fulfill their **allocation** function by purchasing large quantities to resell in smaller amounts. This means savings for customers in both purchase price and storage costs. In essence, wholesalers make a wide variety of goods available in amounts that can be afforded and handled effectively. Wholesalers also perform other functions, depending on customer needs. They may provide credit, education on product benefits, training in product use, and technical assistance.

Figure 16.7 Wholesalers Add Value for Suppliers and Customers by Performing Important Channel Functions
Source: Adapted from Bert Rosenbloom, Marketing Functions and the Wholesaler-Distributor (Washington, DC: Distribution Research and Educational Foundation, 1987) p. 26.

ASSORTMENT

A wholesaler function that entails selling a range of merchandise from a variety of sources.

ALLOCATION

A wholesaler function that entails purchasing products in large quantities and reselling them in smaller quantities.

Some believe that wholesalers only add to the price of goods. Actually, their price is lower than what individual manufacturers would have to charge on most orders if they were made directly. Wholesalers get a discount for buying in quantity, and part of that is passed on to consumers. Furthermore, overhead is normally lower for wholesalers than for manufacturers. Therefore, wholesalers can serve small or medium-sized companies and still make a profit, whereas most manufacturers cannot.

Wholesalers will do business with one another, often as a matter of courtesy. A wholesaler may need a Black & Decker power drill for an important customer and can get it most quickly by calling a nearby wholesaler. In other cases, the transactions are systematic. Small wholesalers may find it easier to do business with large wholesalers than with manufacturers. As a result, in a number of industries other wholesalers are a primary target market.

Master distributors are wholesaling companies given the right by manufacturers to develop certain geographical areas and recruit other distributors. These, in turn, are called sub-distributors. All sales to sub-distributors go through the master distributor. The system is often used by manufacturers entering a global market, especially if they lack the resources to serve it directly.

TYPES OF WHOLESALERS

Full-service wholesalers perform a wide range of tasks for their customers. **Limited-service wholesalers** provide only some of the traditional channel functions, either eliminating others entirely or passing them on to someone else to perform. Within each category, several types of wholesalers can be identified. Figure 16.8 summarizes the functions performed by different types of wholesalers.

Full-Service Wholesalers *General Line Wholesalers* General line wholesalers carry a wide variety of products and provide a full range of services. Bosler Supply of Chicago and W. W. Grainger are good examples. They stock thousands of different industrial products, provide technical advice on product applications, and expedite shipments when necessary. Another example is SYSCO, which sells a broad array of frozen, dry and refrigerated products to the food industry. It can provide special packaging and delivery schedules. Its cruise ship customers, for example, can receive plastic-wrapped pallets of food at any time of day or night.

FULL-SERVICE WHOLESALER

An intermediary who performs a wide range of functions or tasks for its customers.

LIMITED-SERVICE WHOLESALER

An intermediary who performs only some of the traditional channel functions, either eliminating others or passing them on to someone else.

Type of Wholesaler	Personal Selling	Carry Inventory	Product Delivery	Offer Credit	Specialized Services
Full Service					
General line	yes	yes	yes	yes	yes
Specialty	yes	yes	yes	yes	yes
Rack jobbers	yes	yes	yes	yes	yes
Limited Service					
Cash and carry	yes	yes	no	no	no
Drop shippers	yes	no	no	yes	no
Truck jobbers	yes	yes	yes	no	no
Mail order	no	yes	no	sometimes	no

Figure 16.8 Functions Performed by Different Wholesalers

Specialty Wholesalers Specialty wholesalers focus on a narrow range of products, carry them in great depth and provide extensive services. Ryerson is the largest metals wholesaler in the world, with 50 distribution centers across the United States. It performs a variety of specialized services for customers, such as cutting metals to specification. Ingram-Micro and Tech Data focus on computer hardware and software products, while providing many customer services.

Rack Jobbers Rack jobbers, who sell single product lines to retail stores on consignment, set up product displays and keep them stocked with goods. Retailers pay for the goods only after they are sold to consumers. Krispy Kreme doughnuts are distributed this way. Rack jobbers are common in the music industry, having stepped in to take back new albums with offensive language. For example, Walmart learned of a singer's lyrics suggesting that it sold guns to children and pulled the album from its shelves.

Limited-Service Wholesalers *Cash-and-Carry Wholesalers* Cash-and-carry wholesalers are located near customers. They do not extend credit and do not use an outside sales force. Customers perform certain functions for themselves, such as bagging their own goods and delivery. Costs are tightly controlled in order to offer excellent prices.

Drop Shippers Drop shippers arrange for shipments directly from the manufacturer to the customer. They do not physically handle the goods but take title to them, assuming all associated risks (such as damage and theft) while in transit. In addition, they offer credit terms to customers. Drop shippers are prominent in the lumber, chemical and petroleum industries, where goods are bulky and sold in large quantity.

Truck Jobbers Truck jobbers specialize in the speedy delivery of perishables or semi-perishables, such as candy, bakery goods, fresh fruits, potato chips and tobacco products. They use their own vehicles and offer virtually all services except credit. They focus on smaller customers that full-service wholesalers tend to ignore.

Mail-Order Wholesalers Mail-order wholesalers sell through catalogs distributed to retailers and other businesses. They are most popular among small businesses in outlying areas that are not regularly contacted by salespeople. These wholesalers are prominent in the clothing, cosmetics, hardware, office supply, jewelry, sporting goods and specialty food industries.

Chapter Summary

Objective 1: Appreciate the important role retailers play in our economy.

Retailing is the final stage in the distribution channel for a majority of products sold to consumers. Time, place, possession and form utilities are provided to consumers by retailers. In addition, retailers may promote the general welfare of society through efforts to recruit a diverse workforce. A number of U.S. retailers have been very successful in global markets by understanding important variations in consumer tastes across cultures.

Objective 2: Identify the steps in creating a retail strategy.

Retailing strategy must cover a variety of issues. Each retailer must decide on the target market(s) and positioning, then adopt a distinct service level and pricing approach, and decide what type of merchandise assortment it will offer. The geographical location of stores is a very important decision. Some retailers locate stores in low-rent areas off highways and at a distance from other retailers, whereas others place stores close to competitors. Well-run shopping centers have immense pulling power and are good locations for many retailers. New technologies, such as sophisticated computer systems that allow merchandise to be tailored in individual stores, help improve retailer performance. Furthermore, effectively managing relationships with suppliers—whether manufacturers, wholesalers, or agents—is critical.

Objective 3: Recognize the diverse array of retailers that compete with one another.

Limited-line retailers include specialty stores, superstores and automated vending operations. General merchandise retailers include department stores, convenience stores, supermarkets, warehouse clubs, discount stores, variety stores and hypermarkets. An understanding of each type is useful in tracking and predicting competitive trends. A number of successful retailers have stores of different types.

Objective 4: Learn what direct marketing entails, its value, and how it differs from mass communication.

Direct marketing is a powerful selling approach, especially when media are used to communicate information on products and prices and how to place orders. Growth in sales through direct-marketing channels is outpacing growth in U.S. retail sales by about two to one. Direct marketing offers consumers and businesses a convenient way to shop. It enables many small companies to access markets they could not reach through traditional retail and wholesale organizations. It is popular in many parts of the world. In fact, the largest direct-marketing companies are based in foreign countries. International direct-marketers must adjust their strategies to the unique characteristics of each country they serve.

Objective 5: Describe the different types of direct marketing media.

A large number of direct marketing media are available. Paper-based mail, fax, email, and voice mail are options. Mail-order catalogs are used by many companies, and electronic versions are gaining popularity. Telemarketing is a major force, especially in business-to-business markets. Advertisements in print and broadcast media are important in direct-marketing activities. Infomercials can be used effectively to sell products and gain distribution through retailers. Television shopping channels have done well, as has the Internet. Each medium has its strengths and weaknesses that must be considered by companies choosing which one or which mix to use.

Objective 6:   Know the different types of wholesalers and the distinct roles they play.

A wide range of functions is performed for customers by full-service wholesalers, a category that includes general line wholesalers, specialty wholesalers and rack jobbers. In contrast, limited-service wholesalers perform only some of the traditional channel functions. In this category are cash-and-carry wholesalers, drop shippers, truck jobbers and mail-order wholesalers.

Review Your Understanding

1. What is retailing? What is a retailer?
2. What are the steps in developing a retail strategy?
3. What are the four types of limited-line retailers? What are the seven types of general merchandise retailers?
4. List three ethical issues in retailing.
5. What is direct marketing?
6. List several ways direct marketing provides value to customers.

7. List several media used in direct marketing.
8. List the seven decisions direct marketers make when developing a marketing strategy.
9. What are two ethical problems in the direct-marketing industry? Briefly explain each.
10. What is a full-service wholesaler? What is a limited-service wholesaler? List three types of each.

Discussion of Concepts

1. Is following a hybrid strategy on service and price more difficult for a retailer than either a discount-oriented or service-oriented strategy? Explain.
2. What are the pros and cons of following a destination location strategy? Under what conditions would locating stores close to the competition be preferable?
3. Among the various types of limited-line and general merchandise retailers, which have the strongest competitive positions? Why?
4. Some experts view Internet shopping as a major threat to retailers. Do you agree or disagree?
5. What are the major reasons for the growing importance of direct marketing in the United States?

6. What are the pros and cons of using fax, email, and voice mail? Would you recommend their use to a direct-marketing company? Why or why not?
7. What are infomercials? Can they be misused? How?
8. Explain how effective database management can improve the performance of a direct marketing company.
9. Are the efforts of the Direct Marketing Association to promote ethics among its members worthwhile? What else can be done to encourage ethical behavior in the industry?
10. Compare the businesses of limited-service and full-service wholesalers. Can limited-service wholesalers be just as successful financially as full-service wholesalers?

Key Terms & Definitions

1. **Allocation:**   A wholesaler function that entails purchasing products in large quantities and reselling them in smaller quantities.
2. **Assortment:**   A wholesaler function that entails selling a range of merchandise from a variety of sources.
3. **Automated vending:**   The use of machinery operated by coins or credit cards to dispense goods.
4. **Big Box Retailers:** A large retail establishment, usually part of a chain, selling either general merchandise or specialty items (such as electronics) and focusing on large sales volume.
5. **Chain store:**   One of a group of centrally owned and managed retail stores that handles the same product lines.
6. **Convenience store:**   A small retailer with moderately low breadth and depth of merchandise.
7. **Department store:**   A retailer with merchandise of broad variety and moderate depth and with a relatively high level of customer service.

8. **Direct marketing:**   The use of various communication media to interact directly with customers and generally calling for them to make a direct response.
9. **Discount store:**   A retailer offering a broad variety of merchandise with limited service and low prices.
10. **Full-service wholesaler:**   An intermediary who performs a wide range of functions or tasks for its customers.
11. **Hypermarket:**   A giant shopping facility with a wide selection of food and general merchandise at low prices.
12. **Infomercial:**   A programmatic advertisement of considerable length that resembles a documentary.
13. **Limited-service wholesaler:**   An intermediary who performs only some of the traditional channel functions, either eliminating others or passing them on to someone else.
14. **Off-price retailer:**   A seller of brand-name clothing at low prices.

15. **Retailing:** The activities involved in selling of products to end users for use and consumption by the purchaser.

16. **Scrambled merchandising:** A retail strategy that entails carrying an array of product lines that seem to be unrelated.

17. **Specialty store:** A retailer offering merchandise in one primary product category with considerable depth.

18. **Supermarket:** A large, departmentalized, food-oriented retail establishment that sells beverages, canned goods, dairy products, frozen foods, meat, produce and such nonfood items as health and beauty aids, kitchen utensils, magazines, pharmaceuticals and toys.

19. **Superstore:** A retailer that focuses on a single product category but offers a huge selection and low prices; also called a category killer.

20. **Variety store:** A retailer offering a variety of low-priced merchandise of low to moderate quality.

21. **Warehouse club:** A large, no-frills store that carries a revolving array of merchandise at low prices.

22. **Wheel of retailing:** A descriptive theory about how retailers emerge, evolve and sometimes fade away.

23. **Wholesaling:** Selling of goods for resale or use to retailers and other businesses.

References

1. Lauren Indvik, "U.S. Online Retail Sales to Reach $327 Billion by 2016," Mashable Business, www.mashable.com, website visited February 27, 2016.

2. Venkatesan, Rajkumar; Kumar, V.; Ravishanker, Nalini, "Multichannel Shopping: Causes and Consequences," Journal of Marketing Vol. 70, No. 2, April 2006.

3. Barbara Farfan, "2014 US Retail Industry Overview - Info, Facts, Research, Data, Trivia," http://retailindustry.about.com, website visited July 14, 2016.

4. Wet Seal Inc., www.wetsealinc.com, website visited July 14, 2016.

5. CNW Group, "For the First Time Walmart Canada Stores Add Authentic Merchandise to Help Asian Customers Ring in the New Year," www.newswire.ca, website visited July 14, 2016.

6. Barnes & Noble, www.barnesandnoble.com, website visited July 14, 2016.

7. "Higher Unit Prices, Not Volume, Behind Rapid Growth of U.S. Private Label Sales," Nielsen, www.us.nielsen.com, June 04, 2008

8. Phillips, David, "Not Your Father's Store Brand," Dairy Foods Vol. 107, Issue 6, June 2006, pg. 8.

9. Bolotsky; Fassler, Hard Goods Specialty Retailing, p. 2-4.

10. Levy; Weitz, Retailing Management, pg. 258.

11. www.mallofamerica.com, website visited July 15, 2016.

12. www.japan-guide.com, website visited July 15, 2016.

13. Frank, Robert J.; Mihas, Elizabeth A.; Narasimhan, Laxman; Rauch, Stacey, "Competing in a Value-Driven World," McKinsey & Company Report, February 2003.

14. www.wegmans.com visited July 15, 2016.

15. "Warehouse Clubs and Superstores: Industry Profile," Research and Markets, www.researchandmarkets.com, website visited July 15, 2016.

16. Stern; El-Ansary; Coughlan, Marketing Channels, pg. 43.

17. Smith, Joyce, "Chain stores change focus," Knight Ridder Tribune Business News, Washington, pg. 1, April 8, 2006.

18. Wentz, Laurel, "Expect More Growth in '07," Advertising Age Vol. 78, Issue 17, April 2007, pg. S1.

19. White, George; Levin, Myron, "Target Stores to Stop Selling Cigarettes," Los Angeles Times, August 29, 1996, pp. A1, A28.

20. Steinberg, Jules, "Worker Performance Reviews Can Be a Two-Way Street," Twice, September 4, 2000, pg. 28.

21. Zara Opens Largest Store in the United States in Chicago, October 30, 2009.

22. www.winterberrygroup.com/our-insights, website visited July 10, 2016.

23. "NMA Releases New 'Power of Direct' Report; DM-Driven Sales Growth Outpace Overall Economic Growth," Direct MYarketing Association, www.the-dma.org, October 2, 2011.

24. www.calyxandcorolla.com, website visited July 15, 2016.

25. "Access Innovations Enhances Thesaurus Master," Information Today 22(7), July/August 2005, pg. 38.

26. www.marketingcharts.com/traditional/direct-media-response-rate-cpa-and-roi-benchmarks-53645, website visited July 5, 2016.

27. www.export-x.com/2015/12/11/how-many-products-does-amazon-sell-2015, website visited July 9, 2016.

28. Amy Dusto, "60% of U.S. retail sales will involve the web by 2017," Internet Retailer, October 30, 2013.

29. "Media Usage Forecast 2013," www.targetmarketingmag.com, website visited July 15, 2016.

30. "Catalogs, After Years of Decline, Are Revamped for Changing Times," New York Times, website visited January 25, 2016.

31. Safdar, Khadeeja, "Victoria's Secret Turns Its Back on the Catalog," The Wall Street Journal, April 8, 2016.

32. www.ikea.com/us/en/about_ikea/newsitem/fy16_catalog_release, website visited July 11, 2016.

33. "Statistics and facts on the U.S. Radio Industry," www.statista.com/topics/1330/radio/, website visited July 13, 2016.

34. www.qvc.com, website visited July 11, 2016.; www.hsn.com, website visited July 11, 2016.

35. www.qvc.com/AboutQVCFacts.content.html, website visited July 10, 2016.

36. Stone, Robert, Successful Direct Marketing Methods (Lincolnwood, Illinois, NTC Business Books) 1994.

37. www.dell.com, website visited July 15, 2016.

38. Ibid.

39. "Dollar Shave Club Translates Its Online Video Success To Radio and TV," www.convertro.com/case-studies/dollar-shave-club, website visited July 13, 2016.

40. Stone, Successful Direct Marketing Methods.

41. Judson, NetMarketing.

42. Wang, Liz C.; Baker, Julie; Wagner, Judy; Wakefield, Kirk, "Can a Retail Website Be Social?" Journal of Marketing Vol. 71, No. 3, July 2007.

43. Cunningham, Dwight, "One Size Does Not Fit All," Media Week, November 15, 1999, pg. 54.

44. www.tempurpedic.com, visited July 15, 2016.

45. Shipping Methods and Costs, Dick's Sporting Goods, www.dickssportinggoods.com, visited July 15, 2016.

46. "Direct Marketing Association's Guidelines for Ethical Business Practice," Direct Marketing Association, September 2006.

47. www.toydirectory.com; www.wholesalecentral.com, websites visited March 19, 2012.

48. "Wholesale Trade," Bureau of Labor Statistics, www.bls.gov, website visited July 15, 2016.

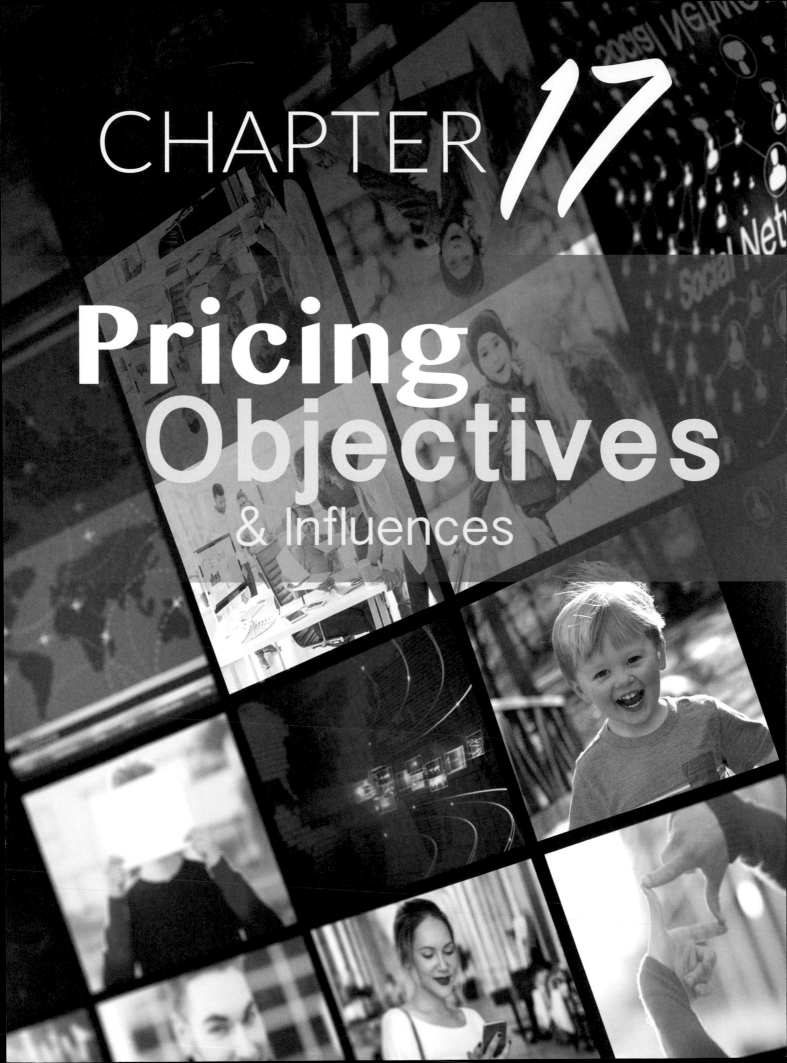

CHAPTER *17*

Pricing
Objectives
& Influences

ALDI stores may be small in scale compared to competitors, but its low-price strategy has been very successful.

ALDI Foods, a German-based supermarket chain, entered the U.S. market in 1976 with a goal of offering customers an alternative to the expansive and mega-sized strategies of its competitors. ALDI has mastered the art of selling its select assortment of groceries at prices that are, on average, 40% less than competitors' prices. Carrying a mere 1,400 items, ALDI is miniature in scale compared to the 40,000 products of a typical grocery store, but the small stores pack a big punch with rock bottom prices on the fastest-moving grocery items.

The niche grocer is a stickler when it comes to top quality products. ALDI only carries its own national brand products and each product is typically packaged in an average size container. Limiting its stock to primarily its own brand gives ALDI serious buying power with its suppliers–and savings that it passes onto customers. The company also believes so highly in the quality of its products that it will replace a product AND refund the purchase price if a customer is not satisfied.

In order to maintain its commitment to quality while offering the lowest prices possible, ALDI involves customers in its unique business model. For example, ALDI customers pay for each bag (or bring their own) and bag their own groceries. The grocer also has a unique cart system. Customers insert a quarter to release a shopping cart from the cart corral before they begin shopping. When they finish, they return the cart and receive their quarter back. The savings in labor costs are passed along to customers in the form of lower prices.

While the German company has taken a 'no-frills' approach in many areas of its business model, hiring top quality talent employees and maintaining consistent customer service are two areas in which the company will not cut corners. In order to ensure it attracts the best of the best, the company is at the top of its industry in pay and benefits. With quality employees and high job satisfaction, an ALDI store runs much more efficiently than many other retailers.

The German company already operates over 10,000 stores in 17 countries, and it is the world's ninth-largest retailer overall. ALDI received the 2015 Supermarket News Retail Achievement Award for its ongoing business expansion. Its goal to open 650 new stores across the U.S. by 2018 will bring the number of U.S. locations to nearly 2,000. This expansion alone will create more than 10,000 new jobs at ALDI stores in the United States, and will serve a customer base of more than 45 million people each month.

The company challenges consumers to switch from competitive grocers with this ALDI Truth: "Switching to ALDI will save you up to 50 percent of your grocery bill. Your taste buds won't know the difference, but your wallet will." Shoppers are clearly responding! With its everyday low-pricing strategy and high-quality products, ALDI is quickly becoming a fixture and favorite in neighborhoods everywhere. Click on the QR code to learn more!

Sources: Saabria Chaudhuri, "Aldi Details U.S. Expansion Plan," The Wall Street Jounal, June 11, 2015; www.aldi.us/us/html/company, website visited June 4, 2016.; www.corporate.aldi.us/en/newsroom/awards/2015-supermarket-news-retail-achievement-award, website visited July 13, 2016.

LO 01 Describe how pricing works with the other parts of the marketing mix.

LO 02 Learn how economic factors such as demand and supply influence prices.

LO 03 Understand the legal and ethical constraints on pricing decisions.

LO 04 Use industry structure concepts to understand how competitors determine price in different types of industries.

LO 05 Use competitive factors surrounding industry structure concepts to understand how pricing works in different types of industries.

LO 06 Recognize the conditions that make international pricing complex.

The Concept of Pricing

You can purchase a tote bag for as little as $2, or you can purchase a trendy Louis Vuitton bag for $5,000. A scarf can cost as little as $10, but a luxury Hermes may cost over $1,000. Ginseng roots grown for tea in Korea and other Pacific Rim nations sell for a few dollars, but a couple of ounces found in the wild will cost nearly $50,000. New cars range from around $13,000 for a 2016 Chevrolet Spark LS to the $4.8 million 2016 Koenigsegg CCXR Trevita.[1] Even college tuition can cost anywhere from several thousand dollars a year to well over $50,000 at a select private university. So why do some people pay more than others for an item that serves the same function?

Pricing plays a critical role in the allocation of resources in free market economies. Since prices fluctuate according to competitive forces, their rise and fall directly influence the amount of goods and services consumers are willing to purchase. Pricing is also critical for the firm. The price of a unit multiplied by how many units are sold determines the total revenue a company receives. Long before a product is introduced, marketers forecast consumer demand at varying prices. This influences the allocation of resources used to create, promote and distribute products. Prices have a dramatic effect in determining the overall profitability of the firm. Consequently, pricing is one of the most important and complex areas of marketing.

Price is also a concept described by many

The 2016 Koenigsegg CCXR Trevita goes from 0-62mph in 2.9 seconds and is priced for the world's wealthiest thrill seekers.

names. These euphemisms "soften" the unpleasant feeling people may have when paying a price for something. How many can you think of? Tuition is what you pay to go to school. Rent is what you pay for your apartment. An honorarium is paid for a speech. A retainer is paid to a lawyer. A fee is paid to a doctor. A premium is charged for insurance. Highways charge a toll. Dues are charged for membership. Assessments are used to calculate property taxes, the ongoing price for real estate ownership. A wage or salary is the price paid for work, and interest is the price paid for using money. Fares are charged for public transportation. Salespeople receive a commission for achieving a certain level of sales, and a bonus is the price paid for extraordinary performance. Whatever the name, price still signals that an amount is exchanged for something.

We have mentioned before that value comes from both the marketing organization and the buyer. In each case, value is given up and received. **Price** is the exchange value of a good or service in the marketplace. We tend to think of price as a set amount of money that can be exchanged for a particular product, but a good or service can also be bartered or traded for other products. Bartering simply bypasses the monetary system.

PRICE

The exchange value of a good or service in the marketplace.

Price as a Part of the Marketing Mix

We have discussed many decisions concerning the four elements of the marketing mix. Products, place, and promotion create value for buyers. Price, on the other hand, captures value for the seller. Price should cover a company's costs for other parts of the mix *and* produce a profit. All parts interact to establish the firm's positioning. In fact, good pricing decisions require analyzing what target customers expect to pay even before products are developed, distributed and promoted. Marketers need to understand ahead of time what customers perceive to be good value. If products cost too much, customers think that they are losing value, and they'll spend their money on other products or purchase the minimum amount necessary. If products cost too little and the company loses money as a result, it will eventually become uncompetitive and go out of business. As you've learned earlier in this text, if a product is priced to low, customers may also perceive the value is low.

Objectives of Price Setting

Prices are set with four objectives in mind: profit objectives, volume objectives, competitive objectives and customer objectives. Businesses need to charge enough to make a profit, which satisfies owners (shareholders) and creates the financial resources needed to grow. Even nonprofits must have excess revenues over costs in order to keep pace with inflation and expand operations. Prices are also tailored to the amount of product sold. Like profit, volume maintains or increases the size of the business. In addition to pleasing owners, financial health creates opportunities for employees to progress and prosper. Third, price is often a deciding factor when consumers have to choose among competing brands. Finally, proper pricing helps build customer relationships by satisfying wants and needs.

As with the chicken and the egg, it's difficult to determine what comes first; profit, volume, competitive and customer objectives are all linked. Figure 17.1 shows that the satisfaction of all parties to the business is in some way affected by price. Most important, when an organization meets relationship objectives, it gains satisfied, loyal customers who consistently produce revenues and profit. Yet it takes satisfied shareholders, contented employees and a strong competitive position to make customers happy. Let's look at each set of objectives.

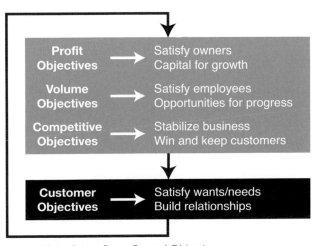

Figure 17.1   Prices Serve Several Objectives

PROFIT OBJECTIVES

Profit is critical for every business. Without it, investors will take their money elsewhere, and the business will cease to exist. In other words, businesses need to price appropriately so they make money. In the simplest terms, revenue minus cost equals profit. Price has a direct impact on revenue: multiplying price by volume yields revenue. Later, we will see how price affects volume, which in turn affects cost. The point is that price plays a role in all the major factors that influence profit. To change profit, you simply increase or reduce price, volume or cost. Since these three elements are so closely connected, the situation is very intriguing. Exactly how they interact is a big issue for marketers. Let's say a business makes a 10 percent profit on sales. If nothing else changes, then a three percent price increase means that profits also increase by three percent. A price decrease will have the opposite effect.

> Satisfactory profits are based roughly on how much the company has historically made, how much similar companies make, and the risks involved in the business.

Profits are required to cover the risks attached to marketing a product. Price may be designed to create maximum profits, but more often satisfactory profits are the objective. Essentially, satisfactory means that the expectations of investors are met or exceeded. Satisfactory profits are based roughly on how much the company has historically made, how much similar companies make, and the risks involved in the business. Profits are usually stated in terms of return on sales, return on investment, or profit margin. A minimum return on investment is the amount you make when you put your money in a financial institution and earn interest. Companies with significant profit margins will typically be successful. Satisfactory profit goals are designed to reflect what shareholders, management, employees and customers believe are fair for all parties involved.

Profit maximization is often stated as the goal of pricing, but since price is intertwined with volume and cost, it's difficult to project the ideal price for maximized profits. Furthermore, there are limits to what people will pay, and analysis needs to take into account the long-term picture. Customer demand fluctuates with changes in economic conditions and shifts in the marketing mix. Competitive pressures also make it difficult to know exactly what price will maximize profit in dynamic markets.

VOLUME (SALES) OBJECTIVES

The price charged often affects the number of units purchased. Firms must price in such a way that production is maintained at a stable or growing level. Too high a price may result in layoffs, and too low a price may cause difficulty in meeting demand, which means lost sales and damage to the company's reputation. In either situation, employees will be unhappy. As you have learned, too low a price can even reduce the units demanded. Because it influences the overall amount to be consumed, price must be carefully set.

COMPETITIVE OBJECTIVES

Volume translates into market share, which creates market power. Many firms have specific market share objectives and price accordingly. Of course, many factors other than price contribute to high share. Although lowering price to increase share may reduce profits in the short run, it may cause competitors to restrict activities or withdraw from markets. Prices can sometimes be raised later in the absence of competition. But certain predatory pricing is illegal, as discussed later in this chapter.

STATUS QUO PRICING

When a competitor makes a price change, rivals follow suit.

Aside from gaining share, pricing also can help the organization maintain its market position. Leaders try to establish the market price, while followers have to react to the leaders' change. If either party wants to prevent pricing from being used to adjust demand, then it may choose one of two strategies. **Status quo pricing** maintains

NONPRICE COMPETITION

Price is unchanged but adjustments are made to other parts of the marketing mix in response to competitor's price change.

the same relative position: Every time a competitor makes a price change, rivals follow suit. This happens frequently in the airline industry. **Nonprice competition** leaves price at a given level and adjusts other parts of the marketing mix, adding or subtracting value when appropriate. For example, advertising may be increased or decreased, extra products may be piggybacked on packages, or container size may be reduced. Of course, in the short term it is always easier to adjust price than alter other marketing mix variables.

RELATIONSHIP (CUSTOMER) OBJECTIVES

One of the most direct ways to engage in relationship marketing is to establish prices with customer loyalty in mind. The objective is to create sufficient value over time to develop repeat business. In this case, pricing signals the relationship the company desires with customers. This is called value-based pricing and is a major topic in the next chapter. Fundamentally, prices are set to provide value for the customer in both the short term and the long run. Your most loyal customers should benefit to some degree from the extra profit generated through the relationship. You can accomplish this by lowering the price for loyal buyers or by adding value to the product they receive. Most importantly, you must understand your customers thoroughly to learn what value means to them.

LO 02

DEMAND CURVE

A depiction of the price elasticity demand for a given product.

Major Factors Influencing Price

Pricing according to value concepts requires a grasp of several elements, as outlined in Figure 17.2. First, economic factors explain how the demand for and supply of products relate to price. Second, legal and ethical constraints affect pricing decisions. Since price plays a major role in determining how economic resources are distributed, the government and courts have taken a particular interest in pricing. Third, the competitive environment influences price. Marketers must understand how competitors differentiate their products and the effect that substitutes have on price. Fourth, understanding how the company's cost structure is influenced by price decisions is very important. Finally, numerous global factors affect pricing in domestic and international markets. Each of these areas is addressed in the following sections.

ECONOMIC FACTORS: DEMAND AND SUPPLY

Economists have developed elaborate theories about the effect of consumer demand and product supply. Both have a significant influence on pricing.

The Demand Curve Demand is determined by the amount of product customers need, plus their willingness and ability to buy. Demand has a major influence on price. It is usually depicted by a **demand curve**, which is a graph showing quantity along the horizontal axis and different prices along the vertical axis. Marketers use the curve to estimate changes in total demand for a product based on differing prices. The demand curve describes the price elasticity of a

Figure 17.2   Factors Influencing Price

given product. **Price elasticity** is a measure of the sensitivity of demand to changes in price. It is used to forecast buying demand in response to price changes. Knowing the price elasticity for company and competitor products is important in determining a pricing strategy.

When price has a major effect on demand, the product is price elastic. When price has little effect on demand, the product is price inelastic. Figure 17.3 shows two demand curves, one for a price-elastic product (everyday blue jeans) and the other for a price-inelastic product (heart surgery). Blue jeans are useful but not a necessity. If their average price is high, then consumers will demand very few and search for alternatives like khaki pants; if the price goes down, then demand will increase dramatically. In contrast, most consumers who need heart surgery do not care about the price, especially if government or private insurance will cover the cost. Price changes in heart surgery are not likely to influence the total demand to any large degree.

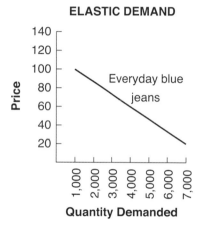

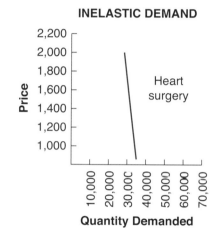

Figure 17.3   Demand Curves

When demand is elastic, prices tend to decrease over time to maintain or increase revenue. As Figure 17.3 shows, when the price of everyday blue jeans drops from $100 down to $20, sales increase from 1,000 units to more than 7,000 units, reflecting elastic demand. For heart surgery, as the price drops from $2,000 to $1,000, demand stays roughly the same. In the elastic case, total revenue rises from $100,000 to $140,000 as increased volume more than compensates for the lower price. In the inelastic case, revenue declines from about $60 million to $35 million.

Demand Sensitivity by Market Segment In addition to the type of product, differences in market segments explain some of the variation in demand. Because the airline industry believes that the overall demand for business travel is less sensitive to price than the demand for leisure travel, pricing policies are designed specifically for each segment. Business travelers often purchase tickets at the last minute and are likely to pay full fare, while those on vacation can plan well in advance and pay discounted rates. Fares are also lower for trips that include at least one weekend night, which seldom applies to business travelers. Their demand is inelastic because a certain amount of travel is required for the functioning of their firms. Leisure travelers not only have more elastic demand but also are more sensitive to price differences among airlines. Just before spring break, student newspapers are full of ads offering trip packages at greatly reduced prices. StudentBreaks.com, for example, is a website dedicated to offering a great variety of destinations for students for as low as $300 per person.[2] Several travel websites now allow users to view airline prices from hundreds of other sites all in one place. Kayak.com even has a function to track flight prices and notify you when a plane ticket in your price range becomes available.[3]

Cross-Price Elasticity of Demand We find **cross-price elasticity of demand** when the quantity demanded of one product changes in response to price changes in another product. For example, an increase in the cost of lumber in the building industry increases the demand for substitute products made of plastic and steel. At the brand level, an increase in the price of Dasani increases the demand for Ice Mountain. Marketers use demand curves to describe price elasticity for a product class (all brands) or for a single brand. Price elasticity may differ for the total industry (that is, for all brands) versus an individual brand. Because gasoline is a necessity, variations in the average price charged by all producers may not affect demand dramatically. But British Petroleum-Amoco may find that its demand is elastic if it charges a lot more than the industry average. In other words, cross-elasticity refers to the amount of demand for one company's product based on its difference from the average price. Therefore, the concept of elasticity applies to the total industry, whereas cross-elasticity applies to preferences for individual brands or substitutes. Several marketing factors are likely to have a significant effect on cross-elasticity. For example, customers who are brand loyal to a particular gasoline company, especially those who buy the premium grade, are less likely to buy gasoline elsewhere because of a two- or three-cent difference in price; those with little or no loyalty, and who buy the lowest grade, are more likely to shop around for the lowest price.

Many marketing plans are designed to produce inelastic cross-elasticity for the brand. That means price is less important to buyers than brand attributes, which prevents price competitors from luring them away. Consider Seven for All Mankind jeans, which typically retail for around $200 per pair, whereas Levi's often sell for less than $40. Many consumers are willing to pay more for the Seven brand to satisfy their need for esteem and prestige or because they like its features.

Seven for All Mankind jeans retail for around $200 per pair. Some consumers are willing to pay this much for the prestige and status associated with the brand.

To reduce the cross-price elasticity of their products, marketers may use any of the following approaches:[4]

- *Position the product relative to costly substitutes.* General Motors attempted this when it priced its Aurora to be competitive with BMW, Audi, Lexus and Infiniti in the $40,000 price range.

- *Focus attention on unique features.* Boston Whaler commands a premium for its line of recreational craft due to the company's reputation for safety. The boats can't sink, which is a major reason the U.S. Coast Guard selects the brand.

- *Make it costly or difficult to switch.* ABB Robotics trains users of its systems in programming and maintenance. Retraining on another system is expensive and time consuming.

- *Make cross-brand comparisons difficult.* Prudential says "get a piece of the rock," implying that its size and stability is an asset in financial planning.

- *Use price to signal status, image or quality.* The name Rolex is synonymous with high price. One jeweler says: "If customers have to ask the price, they can't afford it."

- *Put price in the context of high value.* Volvo emphasizes family protection. Assuring the safety of loved ones is a benefit that customers are likely to value more highly than the money they could save by purchasing a cheaper brand.

The Supply Curve Price, which influences profit, also has an important influence on the willingness to produce. When price is higher, producers are willing to supply more. When profit margins are low, companies are likely to produce less. The supply curves shown in Figure 17.4 depict these relationships. In the elastic curve, an increase in unit price from $20 to $140 causes a dramatic increase in everyday blue jean production, from 1,000 units to 7,000 units. In the inelastic curve, price hikes cause only a moderate increase in supply; there are relatively few trained heart surgeons, and they can squeeze only so many procedures into each day's schedule.

SUPPLY CURVE

A depiction of the price elasticity of supply for a product.

The **supply curve** reveals the amount that producers are willing to provide at each price. Theoretically, it operates very much like a demand curve, but different factors are at work. For example, companies with high fixed investment find it extremely difficult to exit the industry, so supply is inelastic. Another example is lawyers, who are generally reluctant to switch careers because they have invested heavily in education. When the price of legal services drops dramatically because of competition, lawyers are still willing to produce the same amount, reflecting the highly inelastic supply curve. When industry entry and exit are easy, supply tends to be more elastic. As prices rise, firms are willing to produce more; as prices decline, firms produce less or switch to other products.

Equilibrium Price In theory, price plays a role in balancing supply and demand. In Figure 17.4, the equilibrium price for everyday blue jeans--the point at which the supply and demand curves cross--is $60. At prices below that point, producers are increasingly reluctant to supply everyday blue jeans; at prices above it, consumers are increasingly reluctant to buy. Market forces work to help balance supply and demand so that products do not go unused and customers do not pay more than is required. Economic theory suggests that, over time, most product prices are somewhat elastic. When prices are high, supply is likely to outstrip demand. Suppliers then lower prices until supply and demand come into equilibrium. When prices are too low, less is produced. Consumers are willing to pay more for scarce products, so supply increases until it is in balance with demand. In other words, supply and demand are related because changes in price affect how both suppliers and consumers respond. The demand for cranberries rose sharply after 1994 after a Harvard University study showed that cranberry juice soothed urinary tract infections, and cranberry growers increased their acreage by 176 percent over the next few years to match the new demand. In 1999, however, the new acreage yielded a record harvest and the supply of cranberries surpassed the demand, resulting in the low price of $11 a

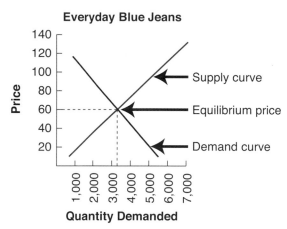

Figure 17.4   Equilibrium Price

barrel. Some cranberry farmers went out of business because the price of their product did not cover the costs of growing it, much less produce a profit. With cranberry production scaled back as a result, in 2003 its price rebounded up to $38, and by 2012 it had increased to around $69.90. In 2013, prices plummeted once again to $15.50 because of a near-record 210 million pound supply.[5]

It is important to remember that supply and demand curves work perfectly only in economic theory, which assumes that most variables are held constant. In reality, the marketplace changes rapidly. Indeed, a main purpose of marketing strategy is to alter the supply and demand characteristics of an industry in the company's

It is important to remember that supply and demand curves work perfectly only in economic theory, which assumes that most variables are held constant.

favor. Unfortunately, this does not always work positively for all competitors. For example, Toyota, Honda and Ford have increased their hybrid car production; environmental concerns among consumers and increasing gas prices have yielded higher demand for these products. As a result, vehicles with poor gas mileage have slowed in sales.[6] In many industries, the tremendous diversity in market segments and individual firms introduces more variables than can reasonably be taken into account. Furthermore, it is very difficult to forecast demand and to predict what competitors will do. For all these reasons, attempts to influence elasticity through marketing strategies may not always work as well in practice.

LEGAL AND ETHICAL INFLUENCES ON PRICING

Both federal and state laws affect pricing decisions. In fact, pricing is one of the most legally constrained areas of marketing. Most regulations are designed to allow prices to fluctuate freely so that market forces can work. Some, however, protect consumers from unfair prices—those that are higher than the value created due to the manipulation of market forces. Pricing practices that are legislatively restrained or regulated include price-fixing, price discrimination, minimum prices (unfair sales), price advertising, dumping and unit pricing, each of which is described later. Figure 17.5 summarizes federal legislation on pricing.

Although marketers certainly must take care to avoid outlawed pricing practices, many companies are equally concerned to avoid unethical pricing that could tarnish their reputation and erode consumer trust. "Pricing Ethics," the last topic in this section, describes a number of questionable practices.

Act	Key Aspects
Sherman Antitrust Act 1890	Restricts predatory pricing (to drive competitors from the market) and makes it illegal to price fix.
Federal Trade Commission Act 1914	Set up the Federal Trade Commission, which is responsible for limiting unfair and anticompetitive practices in business.
Clayton Act 1914	Restricts price discrimination and purchase agreements between buyers and sellers.
Robinson-Patman Act 1936	Restricts discriminatory pricing that diminishes competition, particularly among resellers.
Wheeler-Lea Act 1938	Allows the Federal Trade Commission to investigate deceptive pricing practices and to regulate advertising of prices to help ensure that it does not deceive consumers.
Consumer Goods Pricing Act 1975	Eliminates price controls vertically and horizontally in the market so that channel members cannot set prices and so that retailers do not have to sell according to manufacturer or other channel member price schedules.

Figure 17.5 Major Federal Price Legislation

PRICE-FIXING

An attempt by one party to control what another party will charge in the market.

VERTICAL PRICE-FIXING

An attempt by a manufacturer or distributor to control the final selling price at the retail level.

HORIZONTAL PRICE-FIXING

Agreement among manufacturers and channel members to set prices at the retail level.

Price-Fixing **Price-fixing** occurs when one party attempts to control what another party will charge in the market. There are laws against vertical and horizontal price-fixing. **Vertical price-fixing** is an attempt by a manufacturer or distributor to control the final selling price at the retail level. The Consumer Goods Pricing Act of 1975 made all interstate use of unfair trade or resale price maintenance illegal. Retailers cannot be required to use the list price (suggested retail price) set by manufacturers or resellers. Freedom for retailers to adjust prices enhances competition, thereby reducing the overall average price to consumers. The passage of this law was controversial because manufacturers and wholesalers often want to control retail prices in order to maintain consistent positioning. Several practices for controlling retail prices are legal. The manufacturer or distributor may do any of the following:

- Own the retail outlet and establish its pricing policy.
- Suggest and advertise a retail price.
- Preprint prices on products.
- Sell on consignment (own items until they are sold).
- Screen channel members, choosing only those with a history of price maintenance in their retail outlet.

Horizontal price-fixing is an agreement among manufacturers and other channel members to set prices at the retail level. The Sherman Act and the Federal Trade Commission Act outlaw these practices even if the prices are "reasonable." Violations of

The U.S. Supreme Court recently ruled that Apple was guilty of price-fixing e-books.

either statute can be severely punished with steep fines and prison sentences. For example, the Department of Justice investigated several corporations for price-fixing through business-to-business exchanges. Apple was put under federal investigation for possible price-fixing in the e-book industry. The D.O.J., along with the European Commission, launched a price-fixing probe of Apple and five major publishers. Apple was alleged to have placed deals with publishers to raise prices of e-books sold through its iBooks app. Traditionally, the book publishing business sells books to retailers at wholesale prices and retailers set the prices to consumers. In this case, the U.S. Supreme Court found Apple guilty of conspiring with publishers to force Amazon to raise its prices. Apple is ordered to pay $450 million to end the antitrust suit, complying with a settlement of $400 million to e-book consumers, $20 million to the states, and $30 million in legal fees.[7]

Signs of price-fixing include cooperation among competitors on discounting, credit terms or conditions of sale; any discussions about pricing at association meetings; plans to issue price lists on the same date or on given dates; plans to withhold or rotate bids on contracts; agreements to limit production in order to increase prices; and any exchange of information among competitors on pricing. The intent is to prohibit communication among competitors about pricing or any aspects of the business that may influence pricing levels.

On the international level, there are few antitrust sanctions to ensure fair competition. For example, in most countries impartial bidding processes are required, but in others the winners are secretly predetermined. In Japan, this practice is called *dango* and is a common occurrence. In the United States and many other nations, it is known as *bid rigging*, and is responsible for substantial business loss. For example, U.S. builders have been prevented from competing for their share of the $500 billion Japanese construction market. The United States hired a Japanese law firm to file for $35 million in damages against 140 Japanese companies accused of rigging bids. This action resulted in a $32.6 million settlement.

Price Discrimination **Price discrimination** occurs when a manufacturer or other channel member charges different prices to retailers competing in the same marketplace. The Robinson-Patman Act of 1936 was designed to enhance competition by protecting small retailers from discounters or larger retailers that might obtain favorable treatment from suppliers. Today, this law is a major restriction on how manufacturers price. Essentially, the act permits manufacturer discounts only if the seller can demonstrate that they are available to all competing channel buyers on the same fair basis. Price fluctuations must be developed in such a way that both small and large buyers can qualify for discounts, or the discounts must be cost justified. The law specifies that it is illegal not only for sellers to engage in unfair

> The Robinson-Patman Act of 1936 was designed to enhance competition by protecting small retailers from discounters or larger retailers that might obtain favorable treatment from suppliers.

practices but also for retailers to purchase products when they know that discrimination toward other retailers is occurring.

The Robinson-Patman Act involves a relatively complex issue. Differential pricing is allowed in many circumstances in which manufacturers are competing to gain or hold business. The law was designed to enhance competition by preventing restraint of trade. Essentially, violation occurs when manufacturers or other channel members charge differential prices that inhibit the ability of one retailer to compete with another. Acceptable price discrimination occurs when the differences are based on time, place, customer characteristics or product distinctions. In other words, any time the marketing mix has been altered, price may reflect those changes.

Consider the annual fees associated with different credit cards. The issuer may charge affluent customers $100 a year for premium gold cards but suspend all fees for students. American Express charges annual fees for many of its cards. The Platinum has a $450 annual fee but comes with extra benefits such as access to airline lounges and a concierge to assist with dinner reservations or concert tickets.[8] The top-tier customers, who charge more than $250,000 annually, may hold the black American Express Centurion Card. This card has a $7,500 initiation fee plus an annual fee of $2,500. There is no interest rate for this card because cardholders must pay off the balance at the end of each month.[9] Discounts for senior citizens, such as a percentage off on a particular day of the week, are another acceptable form of price discrimination. These practices demonstrate how price deviates among consumer segments.

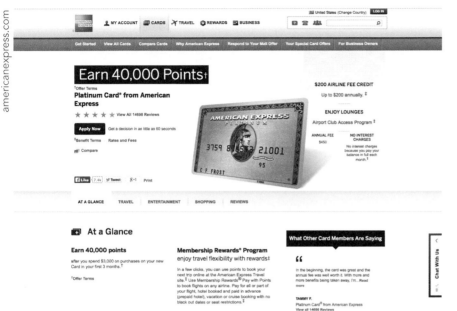

American Express Platinum has a $450 annual fee but comes with benefits like access to airline lounges and a concierge to assist with dinner reservations or concert tickets.

Minimum Prices Laws against so-called minimum prices, often called unfair sales acts, have been enacted in a number of states. These prevent retailers from selling merchandise for less than the cost of the product plus a reasonable profit. Many states have such laws in order to protect smaller retailers and agricultural industries from larger competitors. **Predatory pricing** occurs when large firms cut prices on products in order to eliminate small local competitors. Walmart was recently accused of violating predatory pricing laws when it began offering $4 generic prescription drugs. However, other competitors such as Costco and Kroger were able to match Walmart's low price.[10] At the national level, the Sherman and Clayton acts prevent this. Other laws apply to intrastate commerce.

Loss leaders are items priced below cost to attract customers. In some states this practice is restricted. In others it is legal, particularly when it is not designed to injure specific local competitors. Most loss leaders are heavily advertised brands with strong appeal, ensuring volume that compensates for the low price. For example, supermarkets may feature a special on brand-name laundry detergents that have wide appeal. Once in the store, customers are likely to purchase additional goods at normal or even elevated prices. McDonald's and other fast-food chains can lower prices on burgers to increase traffic because its margins on soft drinks and fries make up the difference. Victoria's Secret uses the five pair for $27.50 deal on its Pink underwear to attract a younger market into its stores to buy its more expensive underwear.[11] Even investment companies use loss leaders; many waive fees on money funds to attract business, hoping that customers will later invest in other areas.

Black Friday, the day following Thanksgiving in the United States, is traditionally

PREDATORY PRICING

Price-cutting by large firms to eliminate small local competitors.

LOSS LEADERS

Items priced below cost to attract customers.

BlackFriday.com brings most major advertised deals together in one spot. Users can register to be notified when new deals are released.

BAIT AND SWITCH

An unethical practice in which sellers advertise items at extremely low prices and then inform the customer that the items are out of stock, offer different items, or attempt to sell the customer more expensive substitutes.

DUMPING

Selling a product in a foreign country at a price lower than in the producing country and lower than its cost of production.

> In the international market, one of the most common regulations relates to dumping, which is a form of price discrimination.

PREDATORY DUMPING

Pricing below cost to drive local firms out of business.

known as the beginning of the Christmas shopping season. Many large retailers offer steep discounted loss leaders to lure consumers into their stores. While thousands line up at the door early in the morning to get the best deals, others are finding similar door-buster deals online. For some, Black Friday shopping has become an important annual tradition to be carefully planned and orchestrated. Websites like BlackFriday.com allow shoppers to pinpoint the best advertised deals year-round.[12]

Price Advertising The Federal Trade Commission has set up permissible standards for price advertising. Essentially, these guidelines prohibit marketers from communicating price deceptively. Firms may not claim that a price is reduced unless the original price has been offered to the public regularly and recently. A company can only make price comparisons with the competition if it verifies its claims. Furthermore, pre-marked prices cannot be artificially increased as a point of comparison unless products are actually sold at that price in substantial quantities. In addition, a retailer cannot continuously advertise the same product as being on sale when that price has become standard at that outlet.

Bait-and-switch promotions are specifically outlawed by the Federal Trade Commission Act and various state statutes. **Bait and switch** occurs when the seller advertises an item at an extremely low price and then informs the customer it is out of stock, offers a different item, or attempts to sell the customer a more expensive substitute. In other words, when there is no intent to sell the advertised item, retailers are being dishonest.

Dumping In the international market, one of the most common regulations relates to dumping, which is a form of price discrimination. **Dumping** occurs when a product is sold in a foreign country at a price lower than in the producing country and lower than its actual cost of production. Because global organizations cover many of their costs in domestic markets, they do this to maximize volume and profit abroad. Dumping is illegal because it puts manufacturers in the local foreign market at a disadvantage. The U.S. Department of Commerce recently placed an anti-dumping tariff on certain steel products imported from China and the United Arab Emirates. The importers were penalized as much as 118 percent of the product value. Often, emerging economies are the source of dumping in the United States because of lower labor costs.[13]

Predatory dumping is pricing designed to drive local firms out of the market. The organization gains strong market share and pushes competitors out of business with low prices, then raises them after establishing this power.[14]

Unit Pricing Container sizes for the same item can vary considerably. In some cases the package may have similar wording, such as "giant" or "large economy" size. This makes it difficult for consumers to compare the price of products based on the size and type of packaging. The unit pricing legislation enacted two decades ago requires that certain types of retail outlets, especially food stores, display price per unit of measure as well as total price. For example, a four-ounce can of tuna selling for $1 is also priced at 25 cents per ounce. In this way, consumers can clearly see whether a larger size makes a price difference. The law is designed to help cost-conscious consumers make wise decisions at the retail level. In fact, according to a survey of customers, the most important attribute in stores is unit pricing signs on the shelves.[15]

Pricing Ethics   Ethical issues in pricing abound. For price-sensitive (elastic) products, they revolve around the creation of demand and delivery of value based on price. For price-inelastic products, particularly because of the captive audience, gouging is an issue.

Although laws protect customers against unscrupulous pricing, companies still find questionable ways of using price to increase demand. For example, an ad for dramatically reduced airfares states (in tiny print) that some restrictions may apply. When you call, you learn that so many restrictions apply that your choices are limited to a few seats and times. Italy's airline Alitalia was fined €30,000 for misleading consumers with an ad on round-trip flight fares showing only the one-way ticket cost.[16]

Another way to increase demand is to make the product seem less expensive than it really is, sometimes by not clearly disclosing all costs. For example, a car salesperson may quote a price for the car you're considering. Yet, when you decide to purchase it, you find additional charges, such as administrative expenses and delivery fees, on the invoice. The salesperson tells you that these are standard costs and are stated in small print on the contract.

Perhaps you have noticed that your favorite brand of paper towel or pudding seems to disappear faster than it once did. Check the package. There is a good chance that the price remained the same but the size was reduced. Rather than pass on increased costs to customers, some manufacturers reduce the amount of product contained in a package. To obscure the issue, words like "new convenience package" are printed in small type. You're getting less value but may not be aware of it, because basic package design and price stay the same.

The captive customer creates a tempting target for some marketers. Because demand is already there, the question is how much to charge. Consider the cost of automobile parts. After an accident, you find that replacing one door will cost 20 percent of what you paid for the car. Are you likely to scrap it? It is true that the fee for handling and stocking inventory has to be included in prices, but many companies make a much greater percentage on replacement items than on the original product.

Another way to reduce the amount delivered is to price on an all-you-want basis and then limit the supply. For example, a golf course or tennis club has a monthly fee for unlimited usage, but there are so many customers that you must wait an exorbitant amount of time for space. Some e-retailers experienced a similar circumstance during Christmas, when many online stores did not have enough products, or an efficient system of delivery, to deliver items already bought and paid for by consumers. A number of orders arrived late or did not arrive at all, and hence the Federal Trade Commission fined stores that failed to make good on their delivery promises. As a result, during the next Christmas season, many online retailers improved ordering and shipping practices to meet the consumer demand for their products and services.

COMPETITIVE FACTORS THAT INFLUENCE PRICE

When making pricing decisions, marketers must take the competitive environment into consideration. More specifically, it's important to look at industry structure and the potential for differentiating products through pricing strategies.

Industry Structure   The basic definition of industry is a group of firms offering similar products. However, this definition can be applied broadly or narrowly. For example, Pizza Hut executives may view their industry as only establishments that sell pizza, or as all restaurants in a particular price range. As with most other tools, marketers must make sure that the industry concept they use is relevant to the situation at hand.

To understand how competition affects price, we must look at industry structure as well as the behavior of individual firms. Industry analysis examines such aspects as the number of firms, whether products are differentiated, and the freedom of firms to enter and exit. Economists have identified four basic industry structures: perfect competition, monopoly, oligopoly and monopolistic competition. Figure 17.6 shows how each type is likely to affect pricing and other forms of competition.

Type of Structure	Number of Firms	Product Differentiated or Homogeneous	Firms Have Price-Setting Power	Free Entry	Distinguishing Characteristics	Examples
Perfect Competition	Many	Homogeneous	No	Yes	Price competition only	Wheat farmer Textile firm
Monopoly	One	A single unique product	Yes	No	Constrained by market demand	Public utility Brewery in Taiwan
Oligopoly	Few	Either	Yes	Limited	Strategic behavior	Cereal maker Primary copper producer
Monopolistic Competition	Many	Differentiated	Limited	Yes	Price and quality competition	Restaurants Music industry

Figure 17.6 Industry Structure and Competition

PERFECT COMPETITION

The industry structure in which no single firm has control over prices.

MONOPOLY

The industry structure in which one organization makes a product with no close substitutes.

Perfect Competition In an industry with perfect competition, each firm has little if any control over prices. None is large enough relative to others to control factors of production or market demand. Usually, many small firms produce precisely the same product. Because they cannot dictate prices, their primary decisions revolve around how much to produce and how to produce it. Since firm size is small, it is generally easy to enter and exit the market. Profits tend to be generated not through price but economies of scale and cost reductions.

Monopoly At the opposite end of the spectrum from pure competition is monopoly, an industry structure in which one organization makes a product with no close substitutes. As the only firm in the market, the monopolist has a great deal of freedom in establishing price. Most monopolies exist because there are barriers to entry for competing firms. For example, governments in many countries establish sole providers for certain services, such as communications or public transportation. Generally, these are heavily regulated to prevent abuses, and prices are set by governing boards rather than company executives. Public utilities that are established as monopolies usually must have their rates approved by a commission whose job is to protect the public interest.

From time to time, private enterprises can achieve monopoly status through control of a patent or scarce raw material. Sometimes entry barriers, such as the sheer size of initial investment, may keep competitors out. Intel has been called a monopoly because of its dominance as a technology supplier. Legal experts often refer to companies such as Microsoft and Intel as essential facilities because customers have to buy their products. However, in 2000, federal court judges decided that Microsoft constituted a monopoly because the company illegally tied its Internet browser to the Windows operating system, making it difficult for consumers to buy separate operating and Internet systems.

Wanting lower concert prices for fans, Pearl Jam once contended that Ticketmaster inflated the cost with an unwarranted charge, which added as much as 30 percent to the face value. The company argued that the service charge was used to secure venue arrangements, to guarantee performances, and sometimes for marketing purposes. It claimed that its activities may be misconstrued as anti-competitive because small-scale ticket services are unable to duplicate them. Increased competition, however, has not led to an elimination of the service charge. A number of websites sell concert and event tickets, such as TicketWeb.com, Ticketmaster.com, and Tickets.com, and they charge a service fee. But the fee has fallen from the almost 30 percent Ticketmaster was charging in the early 1990s to a price as low as $2. Most ticket sellers now charge a variable fee based on the event, the face value, the demand for the tickets, and the delivery method chosen.[17]

Oligopoly An oligopoly exists when an industry has a small number of companies competing for the same customers. Firms may behave in unusual ways to gain business, such as introducing a new technology, or they may combine a number of factors that can affect their use of price as a strategic tool. They tend to be large, and old rivals engage in strategies and counterstrategies over long periods. The global auto industry, for instance, consists of seven major companies around the world that produce nearly all motor vehicles, and each firm is large enough to commit considerable resources to differentiate itself. Each gains competitive advantage over the others from time to time. A few small firms in a local market also can be considered an oligopolistic situation.

Because oligopolies are usually well established and have strong market position, it is difficult for new firms to enter. The incumbents also get to know one another well. Through intelligence gathering, they learn about their competitors' cost structure and gain insight on their potential for profit. Because members of oligopolies engage in moves and countermoves, planning is essential. This has become evident over the last several years with Boeing and Airbus, as they jockey to win business from airline companies. Together, these two companies control the majority of the commercial airline manufacturing industry.[18]

Monopolistic Competition The industry structure known as monopolistic competition occurs when many firms compete for the same customers by differentiating their products. It falls between monopoly and pure competition but is much closer to the latter. Companies create brand loyalty to gain some of the benefits of monopoly. They control price by creating unique market offerings, such as non-fast-food restaurants in urban areas. Both price and quality are important in attracting customers and differentiating the product. Often there are numerous firms that are small or similar in size. Entry and exit are relatively easy, and the success of incumbents invites additional competitors. That's why several similar restaurants are likely to spring up when one starts doing well.

Strong marketing plans help organizations gain monopolistic advantages in highly competitive markets. They do this by creating subtle product differentiation. Rock groups are in this category. Stylistic differences enable you to differentiate between Radiohead, Neon Trees, Coldplay and Maroon 5. Each group also commands a price differential for concerts. Monopolistic competition can be found in the athletic footwear industry as well. Nike, Reebok, New Balance, Adidas and a few others make up the bulk of the competition, with subtle product differences among them.

Differentiation and Price Competition
Nonprice competition usually involves a differentiation strategy. **Differentiation** occurs when product attributes are stressed. Marketers try to demonstrate value and avoid any price reductions. In its purest form, a differentiation strategy relies on little or no mention of price. BMW is positioned as the "ultimate driving experience" to differentiate from competitors, reducing the need to rely on price to influence demand.

Price competition adjusts prices to gain more customers or to establish a dominant position in the market. Recall that nonprice competition occurs when other marketing mix variables, such as product quality and promotion, are adjusted in response to competitors' pricing practices. Marketers need to understand the general approaches to price taken

OLIGOPOLY

The industry structure in which a small number of firms compete for the same customers.

> Because oligopolies are usually well established and have strong market position, it is difficult for new firms to enter.

MONOPOLISTIC COMPETITION

The industry structure in which many firms compete for the same customers by differentiating their products and by creating unique offerings.

DIFFERENTIATION

A strategy in which product attributes that provide value are stressed.

PRICE COMPETITION

A strategy that employs price adjustments to gain more customers or to establish a dominant position in the market.

by their key competitors. This helps them anticipate overall market prices and what rivals are likely to do in response to price competition.

Marketing strategists study competitors in order to predict what they are likely to do under various conditions. Most companies respond in fairly consistent ways to price situations. Those that can produce at lower costs are more inclined to engage in price competition. Southwest Airlines cut costs by removing services such as assigned seating, and therefore it can charge less per ticket than other airlines. Furthermore, it sells most of its tickets on the Internet, which eliminates travel agency fees. Because of these differences, Southwest Airlines can offer lower prices and still sustain a profit, whereas companies with higher costs are likely to lose money as prices drop. In countries where wage rates are below average, such as South Korea and Taiwan, production costs are low for many types of goods.

COST FACTORS THAT INFLUENCE PRICE

Although cost alone should not determine price, it is a critical part of determining the profitability of pricing decisions. By understanding costs, marketers can judge profitability in advance. They can move resources to the highest-profit opportunities, avoid losing money, and gain better control of internal processes. By comparing costs with those of competitors, it is possible to assess production efficiency and estimate the relative profits each competitor can expect at various prices. This, in turn, helps to anticipate the pricing choices available to competitors.

Types of Costs Costs are categorized in several ways. Most simply, accountants look at fixed and variable costs. Marketers also should consider marginal and incremental costs.

FIXED COST

A cost that does not vary with changes in volume produced.

VARIABLE COST

A cost that changes depending on volume.

Fixed and Variable Costs **Fixed costs** are expenditures for items such as production facilities, equipment, and salaries. Regardless of a product's sales performance, fixed costs will not change very much, especially in the short term. Often these are called sunk costs because, once committed, nothing can be done to lower them. In service industries, salaries account for a large portion of fixed costs. For example, hospitals pay nurses regardless of how many patients they serve. In the airline industry, expenses for aircraft, hangar space and salaries are fixed costs. The best a company can do is manage these fixed costs more effectively. McDonald's did this when it introduced its breakfast menu, as well as its McCafe menu, so its facilities could produce more revenue during the same business hours.

Variable costs change depending on how much is produced or sold. They are usually calculated for each unit of production. These costs include raw materials, warranty costs and the aspects of payroll (such as commissions) that rise or fall depending on the units sold. In the airline industry, for example, variable costs include the commissions paid to travel agents and food served on planes.

Total costs (*TC*) for a given period are calculated by multiplying the variable cost (*VC*) per unit times the quantity (*Q*) of units and adding the fixed costs (*FC*):

$$TC = VC \times Q + FC$$

Total revenues *(TR)* for a period are calculated by multiply-

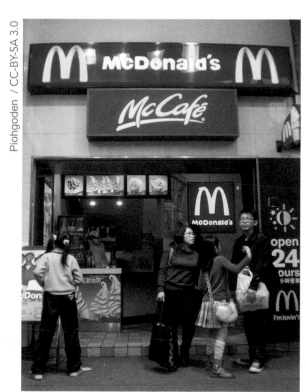

McDonald's manages fixed costs effectively with the introduction of the McCafe menu. Facilities could produce more revenue during the same business hours.

ing the price *(P)* per unit times the quantity *(Q)* of units sold:

$$TR = P \times Q$$

Profits *(PR)* are the difference between total revenues *(TR)* and total costs *(TC)*:

$$PR = TR - TC$$

The average cost *(AC)* of each unit is the total cost *(TC)* divided by the quantity *(Q)* of units:

$$AC = TC/Q$$

The average cost of each unit doesn't provide very much useful information for pricing decisions, however, because average costs are sensitive to volume. The more units sold, the lower the average cost.

MARGINAL COST

The expenditures incurred in producing one additional unit of output.

MARGINAL REVENUE

The income from selling one additional unit of output.

Marginal Costs Unlike many accountants, economists look at marginal costs and marginal revenues. Marginal costs (MC) are expenditures incurred in producing one additional unit of output. These costs often go down with each unit sold and stabilize at a volume of production near full capacity. **Marginal cost** then increases because additional fixed costs must be added, such as more production machinery. Imagine an airline with a plane that normally flies half full. It would not cost much to add one passenger — the cost of another meal and the commission paid to the travel agent who sells the ticket, so that single passenger's price would likely generate profit. The price of the new ticket sold would be the **marginal revenue** (MR), the income from one more unit of the product sold, usually the product price. But let's say the plane is full. Would you add another aircraft to take one more passenger? Obviously not, unless that passenger is willing to pay a huge price.

Economic theory shows that profits are maximized when *MR* equals *MC*. In the airline example, we can continue to lower the price until all seats are gone, or *MC* (the price of food and commissions) equals the price of a ticket. Airlines do this to a degree by offering a few discount seats. But selling a ticket for the cost of food and the agent commission (about $35) is impractical. In reality, you won't often find many marketing executives sitting in their offices looking at graphs of marginal revenues and costs. Yet, like most good theories, this concept provides useful insights.

It was noted that fixed costs do not change with prices and sales volume. Many people assume that these are the costs of being in business. Also called overhead, these fixed costs may be higher or lower for different competitors. For example, the pharmaceutical industry has high fixed costs because of the research and development necessary to yield one profitable drug; of the 5,000 compounds tested in the laboratory, only five make it to the clinical trials, which are expensive and time-consuming to conduct. Of those five drugs, only one is approved by the FDA for patient use. Fixed costs are extremely important in determining the profitability of a firm.

In practice, companies with high overhead may justify high prices if these reflect added value. Often they do not, yet decision makers push prices higher in an effort to obtain maximum revenue. The result may be even lower volume or reduced profit. If fixed costs do not add value for customers, they probably should not be a factor in pricing decisions. This is very difficult for many executives to accept because pricing to cover all costs (cost-based pricing) is initially most lucrative for the company.

The income generated when an airline fills an extra seat is considered marginal revenue.

Costs that increase or decrease based on volume, including variable costs and certain fixed costs.

Incremental Costs Relevant costs for pricing decisions are **incremental costs**: costs that increase or decrease based on volume. Like variable costs, incremental costs are related to pricing because the price can affect the volume sold. Variable costs are always incremental, whereas only some fixed costs are incremental. For example, if a low price will increase demand to the extent that a new factory will have to be added to satisfy it, then the factory is an incremental cost and becomes a factor in the decision of whether to lower the price. Once the factory is built, the cost becomes fixed or sunk. It has to be paid for regardless of how much is produced.

Cost-Oriented Pricing Both cost-plus and rate-of-return pricing are based on the company's costs. Cost-oriented pricing adds an amount to the product cost, called a markup, which is designed to yield a profit. A percentage markup can be added directly, or additional calculations can be made to determine what percentage rate of return the seller will receive. Either approach has serious problems because each tends to ignore the customer and, to varying degrees, the competition as well.

Cost-Plus Pricing Because of its simplicity, the cost-plus approach is popular. But, as the following example shows, it doesn't necessarily assure a profit. A local furniture store pays $750 to a wholesaler for a sofa and sells it to the consumer for $1,500, a markup of 100 percent. On the surface, it appears that the store has gained $750. But it has many costs to meet, such as salaries and overhead. When these are taken into account, and depending on overall sales volume, the retailer might actually lose money on this sofa and other items. Clearly, to determine whether the sale is profitable and precisely how much is made on the sofa, a portion of the retailer's costs has to be allocated to each of the products sold.

> Markups are popular because they are perceived to be fair or equitable for both the buyer and the seller.

Markups are popular because they are perceived to be fair or equitable for both the buyer and the seller. Standard markups have evolved in many industries to help indicate what amount is "fair." Manufacturers or wholesalers often suggest prices to retailers, or retailers form their own conventions. For example, an auto parts dealer may mark up brake assemblies by 40 percent and consumables such as oil by 25 percent. Since all similar retailers use the same basic markup structure, all have approximately the same retail price. Notice that the calculation is based on the wholesale price, which itself is a markup on the manufacturer's price.

Government contracts and some industrial contracts often specify that the seller must use cost-plus pricing. This is full-cost pricing because the markup is based on all costs, including allocations of overhead and other fixed costs. Sellers are expected to provide an accounting upon request. The difficulty lies in determining which costs to assign to which products. Again, even full-cost pricing largely ignores the value of the product to the customer.

Rate-of-Return Pricing A variation on cost-plus pricing, rate-of-return pricing is based on the break-even point. Essentially, the method determines how many units must be sold at a particular price in order to cover fixed costs plus a profit on the investment made. The break-even point is the amount sold at a given price on which the business neither makes nor loses money. Any volume beyond that point makes money.

As an example of rate-of-return pricing, assume that you decide to start a small business that will offer house-painting services to homeowners during summer vacation. You calculate that you will have to invest $10,000 in fixed (sunk) costs, including advertising and promotion, insurance, equipment, truck rental, and a salary for yourself. You feel that you should earn a 20 percent return ($10,000 x 20% = $2,000) for having the idea, taking the initiative, and assuming the risk of losing your invested capital. Furthermore, you estimate that labor, paint, and other variable costs for each house will average $2,100, and with four workers your company can paint eight houses in four months. What is the average price you should charge for each house?

To answer this question, you first add your desired return to your fixed costs ($2,000 + $10,000 = $12,000) to determine the total revenue contribution required. Then you divide that sum by the number of houses (units) to find the amount that each unit must contribute ($12,000 / 8 = $1,500). Since the variable cost to paint a house is $2,100, you determine that you must charge $2,100 + $1,500 = $3,600 per house.

Notice that rate-of-return pricing ignores the customer and the competition. If homeowners consider $3,600 to be too expensive, then they may hire someone who charges less or choose to do the work themselves. If they believe the price is very low, then they may be willing to pay even more. The pricing of competitors is important. Whether competitors are willing to paint a house for $3,000 or $9,000 will influence how consumers perceive your price.

Rate-of-return pricing also tends to ignore the scale of operations you could have. For example, if eight painters rather than four were employed, the fixed costs could be spread across 16 houses rather than eight. That would lower the price, but you would have to supervise more workers while not making more profit. A major problem with the rate-of-return approach is that price will increase when demand declines. For example, if only six houses are painted, the price for each rises by $500, to $4,100.

International Pricing

Pricing in global environments is affected by several factors not experienced in domestic markets. With markets functioning differently in different countries, international pricing is a complex process. Marketing executives must be knowledgeable about many issues and remain flexible in adjusting to unforeseeable circumstances. The major influencers on global pricing are market, cost and financial factors, as outlined in Figure 17.7.

Market Factors	Cost Factors	Financial Factors
Local demand	Distance and transportation	Exchange rates
Competitive conditions	Tariffs and homologation	Inflation
Availability of substitutes	Export duties, subsidies, and controls	Government price controls
Gray marketing	Transfer pricing	

Figure 17.7   Influences on Global Pricing

GLOBAL MARKET FACTORS

Market factors such as local demand, tastes and preferences, competitor activities, and gray marketing are important. All of these elements must be considered in international pricing.

Local demand can vary dramatically due to demographic, geographic and political conditions. For example, China is the world's most populous country and is experiencing economic growth at a staggering rate. Yet few Chinese have enough income or even the space for most of the durable goods so common in the West. Consequently, many products for the Chinese market must be designed to be priced very low.

Subtle competitive differences can influence demand, even in fairly similar economic environments. With the advent of the euro, for example, price gaps have narrowed between the countries that adopted it in the past years. Differences in price between countries still exist, however. In Amsterdam, a bottle of whiskey costs almost 80 percent more than in Rome; in Brussels, Pampers cost 56 percent more than in Frankfurt, and a movie ticket costs 170 percent more than in Madrid, but Brussels is the place for Levi jeans—43 percent less than in Paris.[19]

Globally, tastes and preferences also vary dramatically. A nationalistic bias for domestic products can make them less cross-price elastic relative to imports. Generally, people in

Heinz Salad Cream has been a popular condiment in Britain since 1914. When Heinz considered scrapping the product because of declining sales in the 1990s, there was such an outcry from loyal consumers that Heinz kept it and sales surged again.

countries where domestic brands are preferred have high incomes and tend to be much less price sensitive across the board, which allows more latitude for premium pricing. For example, companies selling consumer food products in Europe have found themselves in a difficult position recently. The economic unification of the European Union means that many global food retailers want to reduce the number of brands to streamline production processes and lower prices. Customers, however, tend to want to continue buying familiar, specific brands and products, regardless of price.

For example, Heinz Salad Creme is a type of salad dressing that Heinz designed specifically for the British market in 1914. It became known as "the English sauce," and developed into somewhat of a monopoly. In the 1990s, however, sales were declining and Heinz considered scrapping the product. Consumers revolted! There was such a protest from loyal users, particularly older Brits, that Heinz decided to continue production and invest in new advertising to stimulate demand. The strategy worked; Heinz captured 75 per cent of the Salad Cream market and customer demand remains high. [20]

The availability of substitute products also varies widely. The most obvious case is the substitution of automation for labor. Japan, with its high education level, high labor rates, and low unemployment, is very automated, while Chinese producers use readily available low-cost human labor whenever possible. The market for high-priced robotics is mature in Japan, where many competitors are constantly seeking an edge, but buyer demand is weak within China.

GRAY MARKETING

GRAY MARKETING

Importing products made in a foreign country back to the company's home market without approval.

A notable feature of many foreign economies is the gray market, which has a significant effect on pricing. Many global companies manufacture in local markets so they can sell at lower prices there, but this also may lead to gray marketing.[21] **Gray marketing** occurs when pirated products made in a foreign country are imported back to the company's home market without approval. They are then sold at reduced prices, usually by unauthorized channel members. The importation of gray market goods is prohibited in the United States by a law that forbids bringing products into the country without permission of the trademark owner. Elsewhere in the world, restrictions vary, may not exist, or may not be well enforced. Many times the foreign-made product is of a different quality but bears the company label, so consumers are confused or deceived. In other cases, prices differ because of manufacturing costs, exchange rates or other reasons.

Companies that want to ensure selective or exclusive distribution must take steps to eliminate gray market problems. If they do not, then the strength and motivation of the authorized channel will be seriously impaired. The company must clearly communicate to all members of the authorized channel the importance of following policy and upholding contracts. They should also monitor activity, especially when dealing with known gray market areas, and be prepared to terminate contracts with those who violate agreements.

GLOBAL COST FACTORS

In calculating the costs of doing business internationally, it is not just distance that matters but the expense of moving goods from one country to another. Transportation and insurance costs escalate when borders are crossed, as do tariffs and red tape. Risks also increase, so prices must cover potential adverse circumstances.

TARIFFS

A tax levied against a good being imported into a country.

Tariffs—taxes levied against incoming goods—contribute to costs and are sometimes added to price. They affect imports in nearly every country. In Turkey, for instance, vehicle prices are elevated nearly threefold by tariffs. In the United States, importers pay an average of less than 10 percent on all items, much more for some. Recently the World Trade Organization—the entity that regulates importing and exporting—ruled against the European Union's import tariffs for bananas from African and Latin American countries.[22]

> Bureaucratic red tape often makes it difficult and expensive to enter a market.

Bureaucratic red tape often makes it difficult and expensive to enter a market. The Japanese use it as a barrier to foreign competitors. For example, they lock out international construction companies by claiming that Japan's dirt is unique, or they require considerable testing at border entry points for all sorts of products. Vietnam operated in a similar way. There was so much red tape involved with doing business in Vietnam that many multinational companies decided the hassle wasn't worth the benefit, and they withdrew. In the end though, Vietnamese officials decided that the country needed the investments more than it needed to protect its own industries. The country rescinded hundreds of bureaucratic procedures and tariffs that had prevented foreign firms from doing business in Vietnam. Finally, some European pharmaceutical companies claim that FDA regulations impede their access to the U.S. market. The U.S. federal health agency has streamlined its system, cutting the time needed to help speed the approval process to bring certain new drugs to market from years down to months.[23]

EXPORT SUBSIDY

Funding by a government to encourage businesses to export goods.

The opposite of a tariff is an **export subsidy** paid by a government to encourage businesses to export. When you compete against these companies, essentially you're competing against their governments as well. When they target a certain market, their prices can be more competitive because the subsidy covers much or all of their export costs, which can put nonsubsidized exports and domestic products at a pricing disadvantage. In other cases, governments may restrict exports by adding costly duties, which raises prices in importing countries. Many countries in the world subsidize big national industries; Canada, Brazil, France and Great Britain all subsidize their aircraft manufacturers, for example.

Risk is also a factor in international business. When risk is high, a company must raise its prices. For example, selling in Russia is risky because of an unstable economy and the possibility of political takeovers. Anywhere in the world, a change in government can affect economic regulations and market access. Furthermore, a weak or indifferent government may permit greater corruption or lawlessness, which can mean that warehousing and distribution channels are insecure.

TRANSFER PRICES

The amount a company charges its foreign affiliate for a product.

Transfer prices are the amounts that companies charge their foreign affiliates for products. This causes some interesting price variations across countries. By altering the transfer price, both local prices and profits can be dramatically affected. In this way, companies can manipulate their price in markets globally, affecting competition and their sources of revenues. For example, Japanese auto supply companies can charge higher transfer prices for components going to assembly plants in the United States, which increases Japan's profit and lessens the United States'. In turn taxes are paid in Japan, where the rate may be lower than in the United States. Ultimately, the tax savings mean that a lower price can be charged for the product in the United States.

GLOBAL FINANCIAL FACTORS

The primary financial factors influencing international prices are exchange rates, inflation and government price controls. Exchange rates and inflation alter the value of currencies, whereas government price controls prohibit companies from moving prices upward at will. Controls are particularly troublesome when a rapid shift in exchange rates or inflation devalues the price put on a product.

Even money has a price, which is reflected in the exchange rate. The **exchange rate** is how much one currency is worth relative to another. If the Chinese yuan has risen about five percent against the U.S. dollar over the past 18 months, Chinese goods will be more expensive in America. Currency exchange rates can fluctuate considerably over time, affecting prices for imported and exported products. Recently, economic conditions in Europe have caused the Euro to decline in value relative to the dollar, making it cheaper for people in the U.S. to purchase European products or travel in that part of the world. At the same time, U.S. products tend to be more expensive in Europe. To avoid these fluctuations, many marketers set pricing in local currencies.

Inflation is the tendency of a currency to be worth less over time. When inflation occurs, product prices along the supply chain increase. These are passed on in higher prices, so consumers have to spend more money to buy the same item. Most advanced nations now have low inflation rates, often around three percent or even less per year. In some countries inflation is extremely high and escalates monthly or even weekly. In extreme cases, companies may need to raise prices twice a month, by 20 or 30 percent, just to keep up with inflation.

Governments often use **price controls** in an attempt to keep inflation in check. Essentially, the maximum price increase allowable is set by law. Sometimes the controls are applied to all goods, sometimes they are selective, and sometimes they apply only to imports. In any case, they can make it difficult to earn a profit, so companies may not want to sell in that market. It is not uncommon for people to buy key raw materials, such as coal, cheaply on the local price-controlled market and sell them on the world market for a huge profit, instead of selling the products locally at a price controlled by the state.

Companies consider many factors when making pricing decisions locally or globally. All of these factors are likely to influence price. However, as we will see in the next chapter, the actual pricing strategy must be well grounded in an understanding of how pricing captures value from the market. This requires knowing how customers define value.

EXCHANGE RATE

The worth of one currency relative to another

INFLATION

The tendency of a currency to be worth less over time.

PRICE CONTROLS

Government restrictions on the price that can be charged for a product.

Chapter Summary

Objective 1:   Describe how pricing works with the other parts of the marketing mix.

Pricing is an important element of the marketing mix. Price decisions are made along with product, promotion and logistics decisions. Pricing is influenced by profit, volume, competitive and customer relationship objectives. Consequently, pricing is important for nearly all aspects of the business.

Objective 2:   Learn how economic factors such as demand and supply influence prices.

Demand is determined by the amount of product customers need, plus their willingness and ability to buy. The availability of substi-

tutes, necessity, the portion of income spent on the product and the timing of price changes affect the price sensitivity of demand. Supply tells how much product firms will provide at various prices. Usually, more is produced when prices are expected to rise.

Objective 3:   Understand the legal and ethical constraints on pricing decisions.

Both legal and ethical factors affect price. Laws prohibit both vertical and horizontal price-fixing by U.S. firms. It is also illegal for manufacturers to sell to different parties at different prices, although some forms of price discrimination are acceptable. To control unfair price competition, many states regulate pricing minimums and the use of loss leaders. The Federal Trade Commission sets permissible standards for price advertising. For example, you cannot advertise a sale price unless it is really a sale and the items are available. International firms must sell at a high enough price to avoid violating anti-dumping laws. Finally, unit pricing regulations help consumers make comparisons. To be ethical, prices should reflect a fair exchange of value, and marketers must be careful not to misrepresent the terms of an exchange. This requires clear communication of both price and value.

Objective 4:   Define the four industry structures and describe how they set market prices.
The four basic industry structures are perfect competition, monopoly, oligopoly and monopolistic competition. In perfect competition, many firms vie to provide goods at the going price. A firm with a monopoly can set prices as high as the market will bear, although pricing by public utility monopolies is generally regulated in the public interest. In an oligopoly, a small number of competitors make pricing decisions based on their knowledge of one another's cost structures. Monopolistic competition tends to be based on product differentiation rather than price.

Objective 5:   Use competitive factors surrounding industry structure concepts to understand how pricing works in different types of industries.
Pricing decisions must consider variable and fixed costs, marginal costs and incremental costs. Incremental costs, which are the most important, include variable costs and, often, some fixed costs, such as the cost of building a new factory to meet increased demand. Cost-oriented methods, such as cost-plus pricing and rate-of-return pricing, have serious drawbacks because they tend to ignore the consumer and competitors.

Objective 6:   Recognize the conditions that make international pricing complex.
Market, cost and financial factors unique to global business must be considered in pricing. Market factors include local demand, competitive conditions, tastes and preferences, the availability of substitutes and gray marketing. Important cost factors are transportation distance, tariffs, red tape and export subsidies. Major financial considerations are inflation, exchange rates, and price controls. Risk is another influence on international pricing.

Review Your Understanding

1. List 10 names for price.
2. Which constituents of a firm can be pleased with profit objectives, volume objectives, competitive objectives and relationship objectives?
3. What are the major factors that influence price?
4. What is elastic demand? Inelastic demand?
5. What factors influence price elasticity?
6. What is supply and demand equilibrium?
7. What are the laws that affect pricing practices? Describe the restrictions.
8. Describe dumping.
9. What are two ethical issues regarding pricing? Explain.
10. What is industry structure? What are four structures that have price implications?
11. What are fixed and variable costs?
12. What are incremental costs?
13. What is cost-plus pricing?
14. What factors influence pricing in global settings?

Discussion of Concepts

1. Prices are set with several objectives in mind. What are they, and how are they important to a company?
2. A company's pricing strategy is influenced by many factors: legal and ethical issues, economic conditions, the company's costs, the global environment and competitors. What major effect does each category have on pricing decisions?
3. Product demand is influenced by price elasticity. What does this mean, and what effect does it have on a marketer's pricing policy?
4. Federal and state laws in the United States prohibit unfair pricing. What is meant by "unfair"? Give specific examples of laws and briefly describe their objectives. Do all countries prohibit unfair pricing? Explain.
5. How does the type of competition within an industry affect a company's ability to set prices? Briefly describe the major competitor-based pricing approaches.
6. What types of costs are relevant for pricing decisions? Which are irrelevant? Why? What are some of the main problems with cost-oriented pricing?
7. Despite its drawbacks, cost-oriented pricing is still used by many companies. Briefly describe the two types of cost-oriented pricing.

Key Terms & Definitions

1. **Bait and switch:** An unethical practice in which sellers advertise an item at an extremely low price and then inform the customer that the item is out of stock, offer different items, or attempt to sell the customer a more expensive substitute.

2. **Cross-price elasticity of demand:** The extent to which the quantity demanded of one product changes in response to changes in the price of another product.

3. **Differentiation:** A strategy stressing product attributes that provide value.

4. **Demand curve:** A depiction of the price elasticity demand for a product.

5. **Dumping:** Selling a product in a foreign country at a price lower than in the producing country and lower than its cost of production.

6. **Exchange rate:** The worth of one currency relative to another.

7. **Export subsidy:** Money paid by a government to encourage businesses to export goods.

8. **Fixed cost:** A cost that does not vary with changes in volume produced.

9. **Gray marketing:** Importing products made in a foreign country back to the company's home market without its approval.

10. **Horizontal price-fixing:** Agreement among manufacturers and channel members to set prices at the retail level.

11. **Incremental costs:** Costs that increase or decrease based on volume, including variable costs and certain fixed costs.

12. **Inflation:** The tendency of a currency to be worth less over time.

13. **Loss leaders:** Items priced below cost to attract customers.

14. **Marginal costs:** The expenditures incurred in producing one additional unit of output.

15. **Marginal revenue:** The income from selling one additional unit of output.

16. **Monopolistic competition:** The industry structure in which many firms compete for the same customers by differentiating their products and by creating unique offerings.

17. **Monopoly:** The industry structure in which one organization makes a product with no close substitutes.

18. **Nonprice competition:** Price is unchanged but adjustments are made to other parts of the marketing mix in response to competitor's price changes.

19. **Oligopoly:** The industry structure in which a small number of firms compete for the same customers.

20. **Perfect competition:** The industry structure in which no single firm has control over prices.

21. **Predatory dumping:** Pricing below cost to drive local firms out of business.

22. **Predatory pricing:** Price-cutting by large firms to eliminate small local competitors.

23. **Price:** The exchange value of a good or service in the marketplace.

24. **Price competition:** A strategy that employs price adjustments to gain more customers or to establish a dominant position in the market.

25. **Price controls:** Government restrictions on the price that can be charged for a product.

26. **Price discrimination:** A legally restricted practice in which a manufacturer or other channel member charges different prices to different retailers in the same marketplace.

27. **Price elasticity:** A measure of the sensitivity of demand to changes in price. .

28. **Price-fixing:** An attempt by one party to control what another party will charge in the market.

29. **Status quo pricing:** When a competitor makes a change, rivals follow suit.

30. **Supply curve:** A depiction of the price elasticity of supply for a product.

31. **Tariff:** A tax levied on a good being imported into a country.

32. **Transfer price:** The amount a company charges its foreign affiliate for a product.

33. **Variable cost:** A cost that changes depending on volume.

34. **Vertical price-fixing:** An attempt by a manufacturer or distributor to control the retail selling price.

References

1. "Most Expensive Cars In The World: Top 10 List 2014-o2015," www.supercars.com, website visited June 5, 2016.
2. Student Breaks, www.studentbreaks.com, website visited May 18, 2016.
3. www.kayak.com, visited May 23, 2016.
4. Nagle, Thomas T.; Hogan, John; Zale, Joseph, The Strategy and Tactics of Pricing 5/E (Upper Saddle River, New Jersey, Prentice Hall), 2011.
5. "U.S.: Banner year predicted for cranberries," Fresh Plaza, www.freshplaza.com, website visited May 20, 2010; Winter, Greg, "Growers Sue Ocean Spray, Seeking Possibility of Sale," New York Times, November 29, 2000, Section C, pg. 6; Lord, Robin, "Massachusetts Cranberries," New England Agricultural Statistics, March 15, 2012; Waterhouse, Gail, "More cranberries mean lower prices for growers," The Boston Globe, October 11, 2013.
6. Ferriss, Paul, Marketing, Toronto, February 11, 2008.
7. Greg Stohr, "Apple Rejected by U.S. Supreme Court in $450 Million E-Book Case," Bloomberg Politics, March 7, 2016.
8. www.americanexpress.com, website visited June 4, 2016.
9. Ibid.
10. Shlachter, Barry, "$4 Generic Drugs Often Loss Leaders for Big Retailers," McClatchy-Tribune Business News, Washington, March 1, 2008.
11. www.victoriassecret.com, website visited May 31, 2016.

12. www.blackfriday.com, website visited May 31, 2016.

13. Addison, Bill, "Nail Dumping Tariffs Approved," New York, February 11, 2008.

14. Associated Press, "Japanese Company Defends Sale of Supercomputers," USA Today, May 12, 1997.

15. "Consumers Are Skeptical Again," Progressive Grocer, April 1996, pp. 40-46.

16. "Alitalia Fined for Misleading Advertising," Airline Industry, December 14, 2005, pg. 1.

17. www.ticketmaster.com, website visited June 2, 2016.

18. Newhouse, John, Boeing versus Airbus, Vintage Books, New York, 2007.

19. "Finance and Economics: The Flaw of One Price; Price Differences in Europe," The Economist Vol. 369, Issue 8346, October 18, 2003, pg. 97.

20. Corcoran, Caroline, "Heinz Salad Cream celebrates its 100th anniversary next week - but is it just a poor man's mayonnaise?," Independent, June 5, 2014. Also see www.independent.co.uk.

21. Lansing, Paul; Gabriella, Joseph, "Clarifying Gray Market Gray Areas," American Business Law Journal, September 1993, pp. 313-337.

22. "WTO Rules Against EU on Bananas," Wall Street Journal, February 9, 2008.

23. Gertzen, Jason, "Official Promises at Biotech Convention to Help Speed Up Drug Approval Process," Knight Ridder Tribune Business News, June 8, 2004, pg. 1.

CHAPTER 18

Pricing Strategies

Southwest.

Southwest Airlines emerged nearly 46 years ago when two Texans decided to launch a revolutionary airline. Rollin King and Herb Keller believed they could entice travelers with three simple objectives: get passengers to their destinations on time, provide the lowest possible fares, and ensure customers have a good time. The recipe was a success! Today Southwest flies more than 100 million passengers to 98 destinations across the United States and seven additional countries each year. As a Fortune 500 company with revenues of more than $19.8 billion, Southwest is a major competitor in the airline industry. Fortune magazine has named Southwest to its World's Most Admired Companies list for the 21st consecutive year; in 2015 it was ranked seventh.

A major factor of this success is Southwest's mission: dedication to the highest level of customer service delivered with a sense of warmth, friendliness, individual price and company spirit. A major component of its company spirit is delivering fun, something all Southwest employees strive to ensure customers. Southwest flight attendant David Holmes became a YouTube sensation when a passenger uploaded a video showing Holmes rap the standard emergency announcements while passengers clapped the beat. Were executives at Southwest upset when they saw the video? Of course not! Employees are given the flexibility and authority to make a flight more enjoyable—as long as they stay within safety regulations—and passengers clearly enjoyed the performance by Holmes.

Another factor driving the success of Southwest is its pricing strategies. It created "Trans**fare**ncy," a philosophy which treats customers honestly and fairly, and in which low fares actually stay low. Recently, SmarterTravel awarded Southwest a Readers' Choice award for "Best Airfare Prices." With an industry-leading website that lets customers easily find the best fares, and email alerts for exclusive offers, Southwest's average passenger airfare was $154.85 for a one-way flight in 2015.

An extension of its pricing strategy is the "Freedom From Fees" promotion. When oil prices began to rise, airlines began imposing additional fees for checked luggage and even in-flight snacks—but not Southwest.

Scan the QR code above to watch Southwest flight attendant David Homes rap the standard emergency announcement.

The airline also waives the $200 fee charged by competitors if customers want to change their travel plans once they have a reservation. And while other airlines currently charge passengers $25 to $35 for each bag, Southwest lets a passenger check two bags completely free. Pricing strategy clearly differentiates Southwest from other airlines.

In a New York Times article, David Ridley, Southwest's senior vice president for marketing and revenue management, said, "We decided to make a strategic business decision that customers would rather deal with transparent pricing. The charges at other airlines are just a brand violation for us." That decision has made a positive impact on the bottom line, returning value to stakeholders, and it's another way Southwest delivers outstanding service to its customers. It's also why customers are flocking to the airline.

With its first flights in 1971, Southwest Airlines created an unprecedented era, dubbed "The Southwest Effect," a lowering of airfares by competitors and an increase in passenger traffic whenever the airline enters a new market. Rightfully so, it's pricing strategies and customer service are continually recognized with awards, among them being named the top airline employer and one of the top 20 America's Best Employers of 2015 by Forbes.

Sources: "Fact Sheet," Southwest Airlines, www.swamedia.com/corporate-fact-sheet, website visited July 13, 2016; "World's Most Admired Companies," Fortune, www.fortune.com, website visited March 30, 2016; "David Holmes - Southwest Airlines - Rapping Flight Attendant," YouTube.com, website visited July 13, 2016; Maynard, Micheline, "At Least the Airsickness Bags Are Free," New York Times, www.nytimes.com, August 16, 2008.

LO 01 Understand why an appropriate customer value proposition is a useful guide to pricing strategy.

LO 02 Know what factors to consider when using customer- and competitor-oriented pricing methods.

LO 03 Learn how pricing strategy is implemented by setting prices and communicating them to the market.

LO 04 Explain how some pricing practices are unethical.

The Concept of Price Strategy

Customers should feel they've received a good value for the price they pay, and marketers should earn a satisfactory return. The objective of marketing is not simply to sell a product but to create value for the customer and the seller. Consequently, marketers should price products to reflect the value produced as well as received. Innovative marketers create value by offering, for example: a better product, stronger branding, faster delivery, better service, easier ordering and more convenient locations. The greater the value perceived by customers, the more often they demand a company's products, and the higher the price they are willing to pay.

The firm will likely, but not always, incur higher costs when producing increased value. For example, it often costs more to make innovative products, create better distribution systems or develop service facilities. Gillette can command higher prices because it invests in regular new product development of razor blades. In some cases, companies produce value by reducing their costs relative to those of competitors so that they can pass savings on to the customer in lower prices. That's how Walmart became a leading retailer. It developed very focused marketing strategies that allowed dramatic cost reductions compared with rivals. By passing most of the savings on to customers, Walmart gained considerable competitive advantage.

> Whether a company improves its position through innovative products, distribution, communication or cost cutting, the challenge is to find a balance between what customers are willing to pay and the costs associated with the strategy.

Whether a company improves its position through innovative products, distribution, communication or cost cutting, the challenge is to find a balance between what customers are willing to pay and the costs associated with the strategy. Essentially, the price charged is what marketers think their product is worth, and the price paid is what the customer thinks the product is worth. If both parties have a similar price in mind, there is a strong likelihood that each party will believe it is worthwhile to trade.

It is not easy to establish precisely what price both buyers and sellers agree is appropriate. We need to look at how customer value is derived, recognizing that people place different values on the products they buy as well as their relationships with companies. Several pricing strategies may work. It all depends on how price is perceived, how competitors act, and how a strategy is designed and implemented. This chapter

is devoted to these issues. First we explore the use of value as the basis for pricing, which is critical for relationship marketing. Next, we discuss the methods used for customer, competitor and global pricing. Finally, we discuss how marketers implement the pricing strategy.

Value as the Basis for Pricing

To arrive at the proper balance between the needs of the market and the needs of the firm, it is important to understand a marketing decision approach called value-based pricing. **Value-based pricing**, depicted in Figure 18.1, recognizes that price reflects customer value, not simply costs. Traditionally, firms assessed the costs of doing business, added a profit and arrived at the price. Once it was set, the marketer's job was to convince customers that the product was worth the price. If the marketer was not successful, then the price was lowered. If demand turned out to be higher than anticipated, the price was raised. An important point is that the customer was the last person to be considered in this chain of events.

Value-based pricing begins by understanding customers and the competitive marketplace. The first step is to look at the value customers perceive in owning the product and to examine their options for acquiring similar products and brands. In other words, how much satisfaction do they gain from owning the product, compared with what similar items or substitutes cost? Next, the marketer estimates the costs of production and necessary profit. To the extent possible, a similar analysis is usually done for each major competitor. Finally, product, distribution and promotion decisions can be made. Notice that price is defined before developing the rest of the marketing mix. That way the marketer has a better chance of supplying products at a volume competitive with rivals and of earning profits that satisfy the firm's financial objectives.

Although cost-based pricing is easier, it ignores the customer and the competition. Marketers know that it is impossible to predict demand or competitors' actions simply by looking at their own costs. Consequently, cost-based pricing is becoming less popular.

VALUE-BASED PRICING

A strategy that reflects customer value, not simply costs.

Understand Customers & The Competitive Marketplace

Make Aligned Marketing Mix Decisions

Know What Customers Value Relative To Choices

Access Costs & Profits

Develop The Pricing Strategy

Figure 18.1 Value-Based Pricing

VALUE IN USE

The consumer's subjective estimate of the benefits of a particular product.

VALUE IN EXCHANGE

The objective worth of a product in the competitive marketplace.

SOURCES OF VALUE

What is value? Generally there are two sources: value in use and value in exchange. **Value in use** is the customer's subjective estimate of the benefits of a particular product. **Value in exchange** is the product's objective worth in the competitive marketplace. Figure 18.2 describes these two concepts. Value in use is what economists call utility. The use value of a product is based on the buyer's needs and his or her understanding of the marketplace at a given time. For example, under normal circumstances a Snickers candy bar may sell for 99 cents. But after working several hours in a location where food is unavailable, a person may be willing to pay $2 or $3 for it. In this case, the use value is high because of the

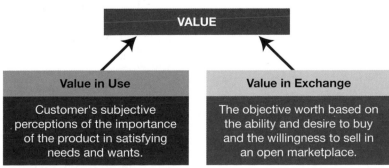

VALUE

Value in Use

Customer's subjective perceptions of the importance of the product in satisfying needs and wants.

Value in Exchange

The objective worth based on the ability and desire to buy and the willingness to sell in an open marketplace.

Figure 18.2 Sources of Value

"The Excellence Child Seat Concept" by Volvo is revolutionizing future car design by the automobile company known as the industry leader of safety.

buyer's circumstances. The exchange value is still 99 cents, the price established by competitive forces in the market.

Although general prices are based on value in exchange, companies also need to manage buyer perceptions of the value of their products in use. When a product is perceived in a use situation, its perceived value increases. Volvo has captured buyers at relatively high prices for years because of a reputation for durability and safety. The Volvo Saved My Life Club is not an advertising gimmick. On their own initiative, Volvo owners who had survived accidents wrote to the company about their real-life stories. Volvo then developed a campaign of testimonial print and television ads to promote the safety and reliability of the car and enhance value-in-use perceptions of consumers.[1] Volvo continues to take vehicle safety very seriously. It has recently announced its ambition to prevent all fatalities and injuries in its cars by 2020 through the development of sophisticated sensory devices.[2] Recent plans by Volvo reveal a radical design of a car interior featuring a child seat concept that places the child in the front passenger seat instead of a rear seat. The child sits facing the rear of the car, which allows a passenger parent to keep eye-contact with the driver and the child.[3]

CUSTOMER VALUE IN PRICING

Because prices send powerful messages, it is extremely important that they reflect the customer value the company delivers. Customer value is derived from the product itself, the services surrounding it, the company-customer interaction and the image the customer associates with the product. First, we will examine the connection between price and customer value. Second, we will find out how market leaders create customer value.

Price and Customer Value Strategies The relationship between price and customer value is illustrated in Figure 18.3. FedEx, with its reputation for delivery 100 percent of the time by 10 a.m. the next day, is perceived by many consumers as having a high price and high customer value. The U.S. Postal Service (USPS) scores low on both dimensions. When FedEx introduced overnight delivery, it charged 25 times more than the USPS. Rather than undercut price, it redefined expectations of high customer value.

Two hypothetical price strategies are indicated in Figure 18.3. Most consumers would be unwilling to take to strategy A and pay a high price for something they don't see as worthwhile. How about strategy B -- low price and high value? Buyers would leap at the opportunity, but the company would be pricing at less

Figure 18.3 Price and Customer Value Strategies Example

BUYING MARKET SHARE

A strategy in which prices are set low for the short run to pull buyers away from competing brands.

than buyers are willing to pay. A strategy of this sort is called **buying market share** — that is, setting prices low in order to pull buyers away from competing brands. Trader Joe's wine brand Charles Shaw, better known as "Two Buck Chuck," recently received three gold medals for various wines at a prestigious wine-tasting competition in California. Charles Shaw outshone more than 2,500 Californian wines, nearly all of which were more expensive. "With this month's Consumer Reports Magazine making our Chardonnay a Best Buy and ranking it third of 10 wines rated costing up to ten times as much, it's been a great month for Charles Shaw," said Fred Franzia, CEO of Bronco Wine Company, producer of Charles Shaw. "We thank the American people for recognizing our quality and value and also thank our retail partner, Trader Joe's."[4] The $2.49 price tag is so low that it is taking market share from other labels. The company gives up potential profit it could gain from a higher price in order to gain market share. The payoff—the company sells about 5 million cases of wine per year.[5]

A company will select the strategy that best compliments its target market and the number of buyers who want to purchase at each value/price position. Any price strategy has the potential to produce profit or loss depending on the volumes it obtains and the marketing costs associated with it.

Customer Value Propositions Product leadership, operational excellence, and customer intimacy are the three strategies that deliver customer value. Because different customers buy different kinds of value, it isn't necessary to be the best in all these areas. However, an organization should be excellent in one area and good enough in the other two to deliver what buyers want. Essentially, the customer value proposition for each of the three areas is (1) customers want the best products (product leadership); (2) customers want the best price (operational excellence); and (3) customers want the best solution (customer intimacy).[6]

Figure 18.4 describes how companies gain leadership in customer value by matching their strategy with what buyers want.

PRODUCT LEADERSHIP

The value strategy that builds value by differentiating the product.

Figure 18.4 Leadership in Customer Value

Product Leadership The **product leadership** strategy builds customer value by differentiating the product. Nike and Intel, for instance, both provide products whose design and functionality have high perceived value. Both invest heavily in R&D and lead the pack in innovation. Customers have grown to rely on their leadership and are willing to pay extra, knowing they will benefit from the product's supremacy. At the same time, these leaders can cut prices on old models, keeping even price competitors in check. For example, Intel's release of new products like the Core series i3, i5 and i7 processors will result in lower prices for older ones like the Quad-Core Xeon processor series.[7] Each company has very good operations that keep costs in line, but neither is striving to be the absolute lowest cost producer. Both also have good customer relationships, but some might question whether or not they pursue customer intimacy strategies.

OPERATIONAL EXCELLENCE

The value strategy designed to produce lower costs than competitors while achieving high quality.

Operational Excellence An **operational excellence** strategy is designed to produce lower costs than competitors while achieving consistent quality. Why can Casio sell a calculator for less than Kellogg can sell a box of cornflakes? For one thing, Casio's operational competencies translate into some of the lowest costs imaginable for manufacturing small objects. This means that no one can offer a lower price and sustain the same margins as Casio. Casio leads with price, its product design is adequate, and its customer service is equitable.

Many companies have trained employees on Six Sigma, a program designed to help companies achieve operational excellence. The rigorous standards of Six Sigma, which was

DHL has eliminated services the customers do not really want, while customizing services they desire.

pioneered by Motorola, begins with setting goals such as less than two late deliveries per month, one customer complaint per year, and manufacturing all parts within design tolerances. Six Sigma has been embraced by many leading companies. For instance, Starwood Hotels uses Six Sigma to drive and foster innovation and then rapidly disperse new ideas across the company. Utilizing this strategy enables Starwood to build a sound foundation to continually serve and delight its customers while still improving the bottom line.[8]

Customer Intimacy The **customer intimacy** strategy is about creating very close relationships. DHL grew very quickly when it acquired Xerox Corporation as a client with a customer intimacy strategy. By carefully targeting a few accounts and working closely with them to identify and serve their specific needs, DHL has eliminated services the customers do not really want, while customizing services they desire. The company shares the rewards of intimacy by passing some of the savings on to customers, so both parties win.

LO 02 Customer, Competitor, and Global Pricing

Customer-oriented, competitor-oriented or global pricing describe the three ways to set prices.

CUSTOMER-ORIENTED PRICING

Marketers should keep in mind the effect of prices. Customers can't purchase everything they want, so they have to determine what will give them the "best value"—or, at least satisfactory value—for the money. But value is relative, not absolute, which is why exact prices are not nearly as important as price differences. Among the most important influences on customers are reference prices, price awareness, the association between price and quality, the perception of odd-even prices, limited offers, and target pricing.

Reference Prices Consumers try to obtain satisfactory value, not necessarily the best value. They try to determine how much satisfaction will be gained by comparing the benefits and price of one product relative to another. In most situations it is simply not worth the time to make all the calculations necessary to identify the absolute best value. Instead, buyers use reference prices and a price range. The **reference price** is what consumers expect to pay, and the **acceptable price range** is all prices around the reference point that consumers believe reflect good value.

In many airports, the price of food often so far exceeds consumers' reference points and acceptable range that they are dissatisfied with purchases. The Greater Pittsburgh Airport Authority requires concessionaires to use prices consistent with those in "typical" retail settings. The result is a unit volume of sales and a percentage of satisfied customers much higher there than in many other airports. An important point is that consumers respond more to price differences than to absolute prices. A reference price provides a standard to judge different prices against. For example, if a brand price is greater than a reference price, then the consumer perceives a loss in purchasing that product. If the brand price is less than the reference price, then the

CUSTOMER INTIMACY

The value strategy designed to create close relationships with customers.

REFERENCE PRICE

The amount that consumers expect to pay for a product.

ACCEPTABLE PRICE RANGE

All prices around the reference price that consumers believe reflect good value.

consumer perceives a gain.[9]

Researchers have found that consumers are likely to accept a price range for products and adjust their reference price accordingly. The brands lying outside the range will be rejected, and their prices won't be used in creating the reference price.[10] For example, you are looking for a mountain bike to go trail riding and expect to pay about $500 to $600. You find several bikes similar to what you want with price tags from $375 to $450. Your range shifts to about $400 to $500, and your reference price drops to around $425. You also see bikes at $100 and $900 (a midpoint of $500), but those extremes do not figure in your calculations.

The reference price gives consumers an idea about the value they can expect. A reference price is generally based on one or more of the following:

When purchasing a mountain bike, you might not consider bikes priced on extremes of the reference price.

- the last price paid
- the going price (amount paid most frequently)
- the believed fair price
- the average price
- the price limit (what most buyers will pay)
- the expected future price (price based on trends).[11]

Marketers also look at the differentiation value of their product's attributes to determine whether their brand is seen favorably or unfavorably. The buyer looks at the relative price and relative quality. If consumers tend to evaluate a product as better than others, then it has a positive differentiation value. This means that it may have higher demand or command a price on the upper end of the range. The opposite is true if a brand has a negative differentiation value.

Marketers often help consumers establish reference prices. How many times have you seen ads with the original price (manufacturer's suggested retail or list price) and a sale price? In this way, marketers attempt to create favorable differential price impressions. Other methods are "cents off," "everyday low prices," "new low prices" or promotions such as "2016 models at 2015 prices." Marketers must be careful, however, about price changes. If the frequency, length and level of price promotions are not carefully managed, consumers can grow accustomed to the lowered prices and lower their reference price.

Price Awareness Business-to-business customers must be very price conscious. Each item they buy contributes to their costs and, thus, impacts their profits and competitiveness. Many businesses keep extensive records using formalized purchasing systems designed to obtain the best value for the price. Consumers tend to be less aware of actual prices. Studies of grocery shoppers have found that people are inaccurate about the exact price they paid for an item 90 percent of the time, and the range of error is approximately 20 percent.[12]

Price/Quality Association and Product Categorizations When buyers have little information about a product, they often assume a relationship between its price and its

The Nike Air Jordan 1, released in 1985, retailed at $65. At the time, it was the most expensive basketball shoe on the market.

PRICE CEILING

The top end of a price range.

quality. In other words, price is a surrogate for quality. A traveler who doesn't know the local hotels may select a medium-priced property, expecting an average room, or the highest-priced hotel, expecting luxury accommodations. Ordinarily, the product delivered should be consistent in quality with its price relative to the competition.

Sometimes putting a very low price on a high-quality item may reduce demand by signaling low quality. Nike found that higher prices on many of its signature lines increased sales because consumers perceived that the price tag matched the company's image. Would it make sense to price Michael Jordan's signature Air Jordan shoes lower than any others? Price indicates not only what we expect to pay but also the value that we expect to gain. If these two are highly inconsistent, we distrust the seller, our own judgment or both. Nike decided not to do business with Sears Holdings, the combination of Sears and Kmart, because the retailers are discounters, which could undermine the premium image that Nike holds. Nike did sell to Walmart, but only its swoosh-free Starter brand, which is now owned by Iconix Brand Group.[13]

Marketers often refer to the top end of a price range as the **price ceiling**. Many companies establish ceiling prices from which prices can be reduced.[14] In a product line with several levels of quality, there may be several ceiling prices. When consumers make few or no comparisons among brands, companies can charge prices at or near the ceiling. Companies with strong brands also justify high-end prices, which is why a Samsung cell phone priced just under a $200 ceiling works. It would be less profitable for Verizon to charge $182.99 rather than $199.99. In theory, the $17 difference could increase revenue through more sales, but it doesn't change the consumer's perception of value.

We know from experiments that price comparisons are made on a ratio rather than an absolute basis. If a Honda Insight has a sticker price of $20,000 and is sold for $1,000 less, then that is seen as roughly a five percent discount. The same discount on an Insight with a sticker price of $15,000 is seen as slightly larger, approaching seven percent. Although consumers may not actually compute the percentages, their perception works as if rough calculations were made.[15] Pricing policy must take this into account.

Consider the error made by a discount copying service that didn't understand how prices are perceived. Major copy centers had established copy prices of approximately four cents per page. The discount firm offered the same service for three cents a page. This attracted a lot of customers and produced a substantial amount of sales. The difference of "approximately 25 percent" was enough to entice many students. When the major centers increased price to five cents and then six cents, however, the discounter followed with two one-cent increases. Offering a discount of five cents instead of six was not nearly as enticing, as the differential was only about 17 percent. The discounter's sales volume declined with each price increase, although the one-cent absolute differential in price was maintained.

Performance Pricing Performance pricing provides a warranty that the product will perform as expected. It is generally used with new and uncertain products. Johnson & Johnson has negotiated with Britain's National Health Service using performance pricing, offering money back if its cancer drug Velcade doesn't work. If a patient on the $48,000 per year drug doesn't obtain expected results, Johnson & Johnson will refund the cost. Like in the U.S., British health-care providers are looking for new ways to justify spending great amounts on products that promise outstanding value in use. Likewise, providers such as Johnson & Johnson are looking for ways to charge higher prices for extremely innovative, high value products.[16]

Odd-Even Price Perceptions Prices that end in odd numbers tend to be perceived differently from even-numbered prices. Consumers have learned that discounters tend to use prices ending in a nine, seven or five. Before sophisticated computer systems and inventory control systems were available, retailers used these endings as a code: nine identified a markdown, seven a second markdown, and five a third markdown. Early discounters adopted the odd numbers for all their products to suggest sales prices. Today, odd numbers connote lower quality and price, while even numbers connote higher quality and price.[17]

Limited Offers Limited offers are often used by marketers to encourage consumers to buy types or quantities of products they had not planned to purchase. The special prices are meant to persuade consumers to stock up. Consider for example, the psychology behind a limit on sales. A special promotion for sugar may read "limit four." Why? A study has found that people are more likely to buy an item that has a limit. This is similar to children who want candy because they are told they cannot have any. Furthermore, one study showed that shoppers are more likely to buy an item with a limit of four rather than two.[18]

Target Pricing Customer-oriented pricing focuses on buyers' psychological information processing and their perceptions of value in use and value in exchange. **Target pricing**, which uses price to reach a particular market segment, is a very important strategy. It is a way of matching price with the value perceived by each segment. Burton manufactures and sells snowboards that are marketed towards various types of snowboarders. Distinct lines are priced in relation to an individual's level of interest, ability and income. The Ripcord is a value board priced at $299.95 for beginners and price-sensitive customers, while freestyle riders can choose from more than a dozen boards, including the modestly priced Custom and Restricted models, which sell for about $500.[19] For the ultimate enthusiasts, Burton offers the Mystery Flying V Snowboard for $1,499.95. Burton also markets boards designed especially for women, such as the Feelgood at $549.95, and boards for kids priced at $249.95 or less.[20]

Burton manufactures and sells snowboards that are priced according to an individual's level of interest, ability and income.

COMPETITOR-ORIENTED PRICING

Competitor-oriented pricing focuses primarily on prices set by rivals. Leader-follower, going rate, discount or premium, and competitive bids are all price schemes of this type. Carried to its extreme, competitor-oriented pricing can lead to mutually destructive price wars.

Leader-Follower Pricing When manufacturers of major household appliances were faced with rising commodity costs from oil and steel shortages, Whirlpool decided to raise prices by up to 10 percent. Competitors like Electrolux followed by increasing prices. Although material and energy costs were squeezing profits, all were able to produce additional profits through retail prices, which more than compensated for cost increases.[21]

Competitor-oriented pricing often involves such scenarios. The leader-follower situation tends to occur in oligopolistic industries whose products have relatively inelastic derived demand. The leader usually has considerable strength—high market share, a loyal customer base, an efficient cost structure, moderate inventory, and a technological edge. Leaders generally can exercise power, but often that is not necessary. The reason is that they create competitive environments, which benefit followers by providing fair profits for all. Good followers can also help create a positive industry pricing climate. In a lot of industries the small and medium-sized companies copy the products and pricing policies of larger competitors. Price leaders must show a willingness to defend their position when price becomes an issue. Yet, across-the-board cuts may hurt larger companies more, so it's important to be selective.

Discount or Premium Pricing Discount or premium pricing positions the company relative to competitors based solely on price. In most markets, there are buyers who seek the cheapest products and those who seek the most expensive. Consider the sale of store-brand hair coloring at very low prices and L'Oréal at higher prices. A L'Oréal model will say she uses the product because "I'm worth it." The Meijer food chain establishes the lowest price possible and asks: "Why pay more?"

Going Rate Pricing The **going rate** price evolves over time when no competitor has more power than others, so they all price at a similar level. This is often the case in monopolistic competition when product differentiation is very minor and firms attempt to gain loyalty while pricing at the going rate. For example, lawyers in the same community will often charge a standard hourly rate. The rate might vary considerably from one community to another, but consistency within a geographical area tends to avoid price wars. Because all providers charge approximately the same, and these prices are broadly communicated, they usually meet buyers' expectations.

Competitive Bids We tend to think of bids as related to the purchasing function, but they also are a prevalent form of competitive pricing. Sealed bids are opened at a certain time, and the low price usually is the winner. An alternative is for buyers to look at bids as they are received and perhaps give feedback to sellers indicating they are too high. This is called open bidding, and it is intended to get suppliers to lower prices.

By understanding competitors, a company can greatly enhance its ability to win contracts at the highest possible price while still being the low bidder. Competitors often scale prices up or down to meet their own volume or cost objectives. By knowing competitors' capacity and cost structure, marketers can adjust their own bids. At priceline.com, a commonly used web auction site, customers can "name your own price" for airline tickets, hotel rooms, rental cars, cruises and vacation packages. The customer's price is either accepted or rejected. Upon rejection, the customer is able to submit another bid at a higher price.[22]

At Priceline.com customers can "name your own price."

Price Wars **Price wars** occur when price cuts by one company spur similar reductions by competitors. These price-slashing battles can substantially lower profit margins. The consumer benefits, since products can be purchased below their value. The company most successful at cutting costs is usually the victor—if it can survive despite the meager profit margins. Large organizations with ample reserves have an obvious advantage.

Price wars have been especially common in the airline industry, with the success of low-cost carriers like Southwest and JetBlue. A classic price skirmish ensued one day after JetBlue announced a flight from Boston to New York for $69 round trip; American and Delta followed suit, cutting prices by as much as 80 percent. This heavy discounting technique was pioneered by Southwest and has been very successful. If these price wars continued to different routes, profits for American and Delta would undoubtedly take a large tumble. JetBlue, on the other hand, experienced positive moves in market share with better than expected results.[23]

GLOBAL PRICING

Global pricing is complicated by many factors. One of the most important is when a government mandates that imported products cannot be paid for with cash; **countertrade** requires companies from the exporting nation to purchase products of equivalent value from the importing nation. Countertrade affects up to 30 percent of all world trade. When a nation's banking system is poor, countertrade may be the best form of pricing. It also provides governments with a mechanism for stimulating exports. It is common for developing countries to require foreign companies to purchase goods from domestic companies as part of any major trade agreement. In other words, countertrade is a simple barter, the exchange of one good for another.

Although technically the term refers to government-regulated exchanges, countertrade also may be initiated by trading partners. There are many arrangements similar to barter that can benefit both parties. Agreements to purchase like values but without exchanging money can increase demand, and avoiding the use of cash can be advantageous when considering taxes. A countertrade deal that covers an extended period can provide a lot of flexibility in scheduling, manufacturing and shipping. Japanese and Dutch trading companies may have hundreds of these arrangements going at one time. The Japanese keiretsu system relies on cross-ownership, cross-ties in banking, and discrimination against outside buyers and sellers to form huge trading organizations.[24] By locking suppliers into the organization, enormous cost savings result. The major keiretsu are Mitsui, Mitsubishi, Sumitomo, Fuyo, Sanwa and Daiichi. However, these arrangements between closely knit Japanese manufacturers, suppliers and distributors are eroding.[25]

International pricing is also complicated by the need to transfer funds. Payment is seldom direct, and generally a bank must be involved. This often requires a letter of credit that specifies the bank will pay a seller under various conditions. Because a good deal of time may pass between the settlement of an international deal and the transfer of products and funds, financing is critical. If it is poorly executed, then a lot of money can be lost.

Exchange fluctuations also influence global pricing. Companies that use value-based pricing tend to treat these fluctuations differently from those that use cost-plus pricing. As exchange rates go up and down, profit margins tend to vary. The cost-plus method simply increases or decreases price to keep the same margins, which changes what buyers pay. The value-based method tends to leave prices the same, varying instead the level of profit. Japanese companies exporting to the United States tend to maintain stable prices, reflecting their tendency to keep them in line with the market as well as profit objectives.[26] This works unless exchange rates fluctuate widely. For example, if the Japanese yen depreciated in relation to the dollar, Japanese companies such as Honda, Sony and Nissan could lower prices on their U.S. products. Many companies benefit when the dollar is strong because foreign-made products and components are cheaper. However, this can also create challenges for domestic companies attempting to keep up with the lower prices offered by foreign competitors.

Implementing the Pricing Strategy

Once the overall pricing strategy has been chosen, it must be implemented. Since prices are easier to adjust than any other part of the marketing mix, they tend to fluctuate. Even companies with consistent pricing based on customer value make changes. Whether initiating a new strategy or adjusting an existing one, the first step in implementation is to set prices. The second step is to communicate them to the market. At both stages, ethical issues are involved.

SETTING PRICES

Fundamental Strategies for Price Setting
Price strategies are often categorized according to the following six approaches: skimming, penetration, sliding down the demand curve, the price umbrella, everyday low prices and promotional pricing. Companies can price high, low or in between. Whatever the decision, it is sure to affect buyers and competitors. Figure 18.5 describes the fundamental strategies for price setting.

Skimming and Penetration Pricing
These two approaches are discussed together because they are opposites. **Price skimming** is designed to obtain a very high price from relatively few consumers with the desire to buy regardless of price. The name is taken from the practice of dairy farmers, who once skimmed the valuable cream off the top of non-homogenized milk and discarded the remainder or fed it to farm animals. Today, skimming is used by companies with certain innovations or fads. Marketers charge a very high price, thereby attracting only a small part of the total market. Because use value is high in a product's introductory period, a premium can be obtained. When more producers enter the market, prices tend to move downward as exchange value declines.

Strategy	Objective	When Typically Used
Skimming	High short-term profit without concern for the long run	No competitive products Innovation or fad Block competitor entry due to patent control, high R&D costs, high fixed costs, control of technology, government regulation, or high promotion costs Uncertain demand and/or cost Short life cycle Price-insensitive buyers
Penetration Pricing	Stimulate market growth and capture market share; become entrenched to produce long-term profits	Large markets Products of broad appeal Long product life cycle Very price-elastic demand
Sliding Down the Demand Curve	Gain short-term profits before competitors become entrenched without sacrificing long-term market share	Launch of high-technology innovations Slight barriers to competitive entry Medium life cycle
Price Umbrella Leadership	Encourage competitors to promote the product category to stimulate purchase of all brands and encourage competitors to follow the price leader	Several comparable competitors Growing market Stable competitors One or a few dominant competitors
Everyday Low Prices or Value Pricing	Appeal to buyers willing to shop for the "greatest" benefits for the money	Component parts in industrial markets Repurchased consumer products Mass merchandisers Established products
Promotional Pricing	Stimulate demand to introduce or reintroduce a product, neutralize a competitor, or move excess inventory	Demand fluctuates seasonally or for a certain period Marketing "wars" or head-to-head competition Mass merchandisers Fashion items

Figure 18.5 Fundamental Strategies for Price Setting

PRICE SKIMMING

A strategy designed to obtain a high price from relatively few consumers with the resources to buy regardless of price.

PENETRATION PRICING

A strategy seeking the maximum number of buyers by charging low prices.

If companies perceive they can obtain a monopoly position for a short time, then they might skim to generate profits that provide investment capital for further innovations. To sustain skimming, companies must offer unusual products of the highest quality or artistic value. Many times this strategy does not produce loyal customers, since subsequent entrants eventually will offer a better value at lower prices. In contrast to skimming, **penetration pricing** seeks the maximum number of buyers by charging a low price. This approach is used for products that are very price elastic. If costs are sensitive to volume, then these will drop dramatically as share increases relative to competitors. This is a way to keep rivals from entering the market, since many companies avoid situations in which overall prices are extremely low.

The problem with penetration pricing is that losses are likely, especially in the short term. Because profit margins tend to be very small, demand must meet expectations in order to generate enough earnings. Furthermore, when customers buy only because of price, loyalty tends to be low. They are likely to switch to competitors offering an even lower price or innovations of higher value at a higher price.

SLIDE DOWN THE DEMAND CURVE

A strategy that involves setting a high price when a product is introduced and lowering it significantly as competitors enter the market.

Sliding Down the Demand Curve To **slide down the demand curve** means to descend from higher to lower prices when competitors enter. Texas Instruments has used this strategy when launching its industrial control products. First, management establishes a high price for an innovative product to skim the market. Second, when a major competitor follows with its version, Texas Instruments drops its price—sometimes only slightly, often considerably. This aggressive strategy discourages or delays market entrants, and Texas Instruments obtains high short-term profit margins without sacrificing its long-term objective of penetrating the market.

PRICE UMBRELLA

The leader maintains the price at a high enough level that competitors can earn a profit at the same price or lower levels.

The Price Umbrella DuPont is known for its leadership in innovations. It produces innumerable plastics, fibers and chemicals used to create thousands of products, and is doing so in more and more sustainable ways. Because of its strength, the company is in a perfect position to use the **price umbrella**; that is, the leader selects the highest price. Competitors can make fair profits at that level or even lower, especially if their costs are relatively low. Price leadership occurs when one or two companies price in such a way that others follow them. In DuPont's case, marketers launch innovations after careful study of the product's likely contributions to customers and society. By assessing the use value relative to substitutes and other brands, DuPont establishes a price commensurate with the high value it typically offers. Along with the product, buyers receive DuPont's uncompromising customer support, which is based on an advanced distribution system, consultative and relationship selling, and service.

Generally, DuPont's price is high enough to encourage other healthy companies to participate in the market. At the same time, because several competitors are promoting a similar product, demand is stimulated for the product category. DuPont even licenses its products to rivals in exchange for a percentage of sales revenue. Since these competitors do not have to engage in basic R&D, DuPont's leadership in product innovation is protected.

EVERYDAY LOW PRICES

Prices, on average, are consistently lower than those of competitors.

Everyday Low Prices Walmart is famous for its "**everyday low prices**," which on average are consistently lower than those of competitors. Sometimes this strategy is called value pricing (not to be confused with value-based pricing). In order for it to work, retailers need to develop extremely efficient (low-cost) operations. Walmart has the most advanced computerized restocking system imaginable. Rapid turnover (products don't sit on the shelves for long) and aggressive purchasing power provide the basis for keeping prices low. Walmart has approximately $475 billion in annual sales and is the largest retailer in the world.[27] Target and Toys "R" Us also use this strategy—and pledge to meet or beat any competitor's price on any item. In this way, they maximize volume and keep customers from shopping around. Riesbeck's Food Market, an independent supermarket chain in Ohio, Toronto and West Virginia, moved to an everyday low price strategy after noticing the rise in popularity of supercenters and dollar stores. The company was quite successful with this strategy until Walmart stores nearly doubled in surrounding areas and a head-to-head battle ensued. Riesbeck, finding it difficult to

Courtesy of Walmart

Walmart is famous for its everyday low prices.

square-off with the giant, shifted back to injecting savings into value programs, including multi-day specials promoted in weekly ads.[28]

Everyday low pricing can be highly competitive on an international scale as well. For example, Zellers, Canada's low-price leader, used the slogan "lowest price is the law." Its profit margins shrank when Walmart entered the Canadian market, and the two now compete intensely with their value-pricing strategies. Zellers proclaims, "There's more than low prices," while Walmart continues to implement cuts in order to offer the lowest regular prices to consumers. In an effort to keep its own customers and lure customers from its rival, Zellers became the first retailer in the world to seek and gain from the International Organization for Standardization in Geneva its certification that it meets world-class standards of efficiency and quality. Walmart has run into problems with price controls, strict labor laws, tough zoning regulations and fierce competition. Historically, mature rivals such as Aldi and Lidl have been more than ready to compete on low prices and are familiar with thin profit margins.[29]

Promotional Pricing Competitive companies such as Coca-Cola and PepsiCo, Burger King and McDonald's, and Toyota and Nissan are nearly always engaged in some form of **promotional pricing**. These battles serve three purposes. First, the price discount is a way to make consumers notice the product. Second, immediate purchase is encouraged because promotional pricing gives consumers the impression that the price is likely to rise in the near future. Third, consumers are kept aware of the entire product category. The "wars" between Coke and Pepsi keep buyers loyal to cola at the expense of other soft drinks. Marketers in these two companies expect continuous challenges from one another as price interacts with other parts of the marketing mix to stimulate demand and produce minor market share shifts.

Burger King offers promotional priced 2 for $10 Whopper Meals.

PROMOTIONAL PRICING

A strategy in which price discounts are used to gain attention and encourage immediate purchase.

One kind of promotional pricing is loss leaders, used by retailers to lure consumers into their store. As you'll remember from the previous chapter, these products are priced at or below the retailer's cost. For example, Meijer often prices milk very low compared to competitors. Because this item is purchased regularly by most consumers, most tend to remember its price. For that reason, milk and similar repeat purchase items provide shoppers with a ready source of comparison among rivals. The theory behind loss leaders is that once customers are in the store to buy the lower priced product, they'll do additional shopping at regular prices. Retailers make up for loss leaders by increased volume or additional purchases made by the customer.

There are many other forms of price promotion. Although we usually assume that price reduction is most likely to stimulate demand, sometimes any message drawing attention to the product, including a price differential, will lead to purchase. Marketing research by a major pharmaceutical company revealed some surprising news. For many years, price promotions had been used to boost sales of selected prescription drugs. Each time the product was promoted at a reduced price by sales representatives, physicians prescribed it more. The assumption was that these products were price elastic for doctors, but the research found that most of them didn't know the price of these drugs and did not especially care. Then why the increase in prescriptions? The study found that the price reduction gave salespeople a reason to discuss the product with physicians; drawing their attention to the product was what increased prescriptions. Subsequent research revealed that nearly any relevant sales message led to a rise in sales because, for established and commonly used drugs, many doctors prescribe the brand that first comes to mind—often the one most recently discussed with a sales rep. The point is that price decreases often stimulate sales, but the attention drawn to a product by price promotions also may be a factor.

PRODUCT LINE PRICING STRATEGIES

Consumers tend to use all products in a company's line as a way of making comparisons. Consequently, marketers use several strategies: product array, bundling, optional product and captive product pricing.

Product Array Pricing Most companies sell several products. These may be offered within the same brand, such as different GMC trucks, or in several lines, such as Buick, Chevy and Cadillac. Prices need to be established across the entire product array. Apple prices its lines of devices so prices go up arithmetically while storage increases exponentially. For example, the new 32GB iPad Pro costs $799, the 128GB costs $949, and the 256GB costs $1099.

Toyota takes the competition one step further by challenging the entire auto industry on its website. Customers can go to the company's website and click on a tab for cars, trucks, SUVs and vans, and hybrids, then use a side-by-side feature to compare specific Toyota automobiles to three competitive companies. It lists key rivals of each of its car models, ranging from Ford to Lexus. Once you click to compare, it assesses important factors like fuel economy, features, measurements, performance, safety, warranty and price. The website then highlights the advantages that Toyota has over its opposition. Toyota's competitive strategy leads the market by expecting continuous challenges as price interacts with other parts of the marketing mix to stimulate demand and produce minor market share shifts.[30]

Apple prices its lines of devices so prices go up arithmetically while storage increases exponentially.

Bundled Pricing Products can be bundled or unbundled for pricing purposes. The bundled approach, which gives a single price for the entire package, is used for standardized products, whereas unbundling is often used for customized products. For example, home builders use each method depending on the offering. House prices in a subdivision are usually bundled to include carpeting, fixtures and landscaping, while various items will be listed separately for custom homes. Even property and land preparation cost will be specified. The unbundling helps custom buyers assess the value of each item and make choices according to tastes and budgets. Comcast offers packages that bundle digital cable, high-speed Internet and Comcast Digital Voice®. Other telecom companies also offer discounts to customers that buy more than one service.[31]

Optional Product Pricing Many products are sold as base units with optional add-ons. Cars are an obvious example. The 2016 Jeep Wrangler has a base price of $23,895—but by selecting options to make the vehicle more aggressive and powerful, a Wrangler can cost you more than $45,000.[32] Add-ons for automobiles include satellite radios, sunroofs, security features and alloy wheels. Companies often price the base product low as a platform for selling other items.

The 2016 Jeep Wrangler has a base price of $23,895, but with optional product options and upgrades, the car can cost $45,000 or more.

Captive Product Pricing It is pretty obvious why Gillette prices its razors low. Once you own one, you will buy blades—perhaps for years. In a sense, you're a captive customer, but since razors and blades are not very expensive, the cost to escape is minor. But consider the cost of moving from Xbox to PlayStation video games. You need to purchase a new system (at a price of $350 or more), and your current games will not work with the new system. The average consumer might decide that switching console systems is far too costly and continue to purchase Xbox products. The captive product strategy is used by many marketers. Internet-access cellular phone companies price with a variation on the captive theme. They have an installment fee, then a fixed rate plus a variable usage charge. Often the fixed rate is set very low in order to obtain the more profitable usage fees.

Communicating Price

An important step in price implementation is to communicate with the market. This involves more than just advertising a figure. The price may have several components that are quoted in differing ways, and various kinds of price reductions can be offered.

Price Components Let's say that Joan Martin purchased Rossignol skis, poles and boots at the California Ski Company outlet. The package cost $800, and the total including tax was $848. Her roommate purchased the same package at a Winter Sports Equipment store for $800, but the total including tax was $893. She was charged $30 extra for binding installation and $15 for tuning the skis. Whether the buyer or seller pays for "extras" can make a substantial difference in price.

In consumer markets, there is wide variation in what is included in the price. Playmakers, a sports retailer in Okemos, Michigan, has won national awards for its customer service. Playmakers will return your money if a shoe does not meet your expectations. If the support breaks down before you think it should, then you can take the shoes back for a refund or a new pair, no questions asked. Although Playmakers' price may be similar to that of other retailers, few provide the same level of customer service. Playmakers' return policy is added value. The most common additions to price include:

- finance charges
- installation fees
- warranty charges
- 800-number assistance
- replacement parts inventory
- shipping and handling
- training.

It is important to clearly communicate the components that are included within a price quotation. If buyers are hit with unexpected charges for items they thought were included in the original price, they are likely to be dissatisfied. This is because many consumers believe hidden charges constitute unethical behavior on the part of the seller.

Price Quoting Price quoting is how prices are communicated to buyers. Some companies offer a price quoting service. For example, Progressive Auto Insurance uses online comparative shopping by showing quotes from its competitors as well as its own. This establishes rapport with consumers and makes them feel confident they are getting a fair and reliable price.[33] Sometimes prices are stated clearly and directly, but often an indirect method is used. The **list price** (or suggested retail price) set by the manufacturer usually provides the reference point by which consumers judge the fairness of the market price. The **market price** is the actual amount buyers must pay for the product, and is often much lower than the list price. For example, when Sony introduces a product, the list price may be more than double the market price. The market price is likely to result from several types of reductions, including discounts and rebates.

Price Reductions Discounts are often given for cash payment, for purchasing large quantities, or for loyalty. Cash discounts are offered to consumers, business-to-business customers, and nearly all channel members. Many buyers look at the non-discounted price as a penalty for delayed payment. Discounts are incentives to speed cash flow from buyer to seller, and they are standard in many industries. It is common for cash discounts to be quoted in terms of a percentage reduction and a specific time for payment, most often 2/10, net 30. This says the buyer has a two percent discount if paid in 10 days, and full payment without a discount is due in 30 days. Many buyers pay within the first 10 days because a two percent discount figured over the remaining 20 days is equivalent to an interest rate of about 36 percent on an annual basis. Sellers use the discounts to speed payment and reduce losses due to bad debts. Many industries have increased their prices by nearly two percent to offset these cash discounts.

Quantity discounts, which are reductions for large purchases, are justified because the seller has lower unit costs when handling larger orders. That is, selling, order processing, billing, shipping and inventory carrying costs are averaged over a greater volume. It is common for a supplier to use quantity discounts to entice buyers to purchase more and to achieve economies of scale for transportation and processing costs.[34] These can be offered at one time or on a cumulative basis. Victoria's Secret PINK sells its name brand underwear for $9.50 per piece. However, a customer can save a substantial amount of money by taking advantage of the ongoing "5 for $25" deal.[35] Another example is pricing of financial mutual funds, which often charge differing commissions, or "loads," depending on the amount purchased. One popular fund charges 4.25 percent for orders less than $50,000, 3.5 percent for $50,000 to $100,000, and 2.5 percent for more than $100,000. The buyer has up to one year to meet the commitment.

> Quantity discounts, which are reductions for large purchases, are justified because the seller has lower unit costs when handling larger orders.

LIST PRICE

The price set by the manufacturer and used by consumers as a reference point. Also called suggested retail price.

MARKET PRICE

The actual price buyers must pay for a product.

Patronage discounts are very similar to cumulative quantity discounts, and they reward buyer loyalty. Starbucks offers My Starbucks Rewards; American Eagle offers AEREWARD$; after accumulating a certain number of "points," customers are rewarded with a free coffee or gift card. Another variation is Sam's Club, a no-frills retail buying center developed by Walmart, which offers discounts only to fee-paying members. Discounts should not be used, however, as the sole means for achieving customer loyalty. Customers who buy a product solely because of price are likely to switch to a competitor for the same reason.

Rebates reduce prices through direct payments, usually from the manufacturer to the consumer. In today's competitive car market, rebates are a popular way to move cars off the lot. Rebates may have a greater psychological effect on customers than discounts. A discount is a small percentage of the total price; a rebate is a large amount of money. Remember that price differentials make the largest impression on buyers. With rebates, manufacturers also are more assured that the savings will not be partially absorbed by dealers. Sometimes, when discounts are given to dealers with the idea that they be passed along to consumers, part of the difference is kept by the dealer.

LO 04   Unethical Pricing Practices

When marketers develop a pricing strategy, it should reflect the value perceived and received. This does not always happen. Abuses can occur through manipulation of the consumer's reference price, quoting overcharged or misleading prices, or using discriminatory pricing practices. Unethical pricing can have legal repercussions, not to mention the risk of losing valuable customers.

As mentioned earlier, the reference price serves as a guideline to consumers. What happens when marketers manipulate that price in order to change the consumer's perception of what is "fair?" Three studies have addressed this issue.[36] When a reference price is set at an implausibly high level, it can influence perceptions about a fair price as well as the highest price. Another study indicates that plausible reference prices can strongly influence customers' estimates of the highest and lowest prices for a given item, but implausible reference prices have little impact on their estimates.[37] Therefore, it is important for marketers to establish reference prices with care.

Another unethical practice is to raise prices to profit from tragedy or natural disaster. Many states have laws to prevent price gouging in the event of a disaster or state emergency. In general, price gouging is the act of raising rates of more than 10 to 25 percent, depending on the state. A Long Island hotel that raised its rates 185 percent after the 9/11 disaster was required to pay $9,500 in restitution, fines and legal costs. Oil companies also gouged consumers on 9/11, spiking gas prices close to $6 per gallon. Other natural disasters such as tornadoes and hurricanes have spawned unethical pricing practices for items such as food, water and construction supplies.[38]

Discriminatory pricing practices are often very controversial. Is it fair to charge a woman more than a man for dry-cleaning a shirt or for a haircut? This depends on a number of circumstances. Are the shirts similar, or is the service more difficult to perform for one gender versus another? Since most women have longer hair than men, perhaps it is more difficult or time-consuming to cut. Nevertheless, studies have found that women do pay more than men for products ranging from haircuts to cars.[39] In 1995, with the Gender Tax Repeal Act, California became the first state to prohibit gender discrimination in pricing for similar services. Even so, a number of California businesses continue to use different prices. Three years after the passage of the act, the California Public Interest Research Group reported that many dry cleaners and hairdressers continued to charge higher prices for services to women than to men. Because of the small amounts involved in these price differences, however, very few women have chosen to take costly legal action against businesses that violate the law.[40]

Chapter Summary

Objective 1: Understand why an appropriate customer value proposition is a useful guide to pricing strategy.
Pricing strategies are complex and must balance the needs of both the customer and the company. Value-based pricing, which includes the concepts of value in use and value in exchange, is increasingly popular. Since customers seek differing types of value and competitors have a broad range of choices in how to price, other strategies are viable as well. In devising a pricing strategy, it is important to identify a customer value proposition that matches the capabilities of the organization. The three types of capabilities are product leadership, operational competence, and customer intimacy.

Objective 2: Know what factors to consider when using customer and competitor-oriented pricing methods.
Pricing strategies may focus on customers, competitors or global factors. Customer-oriented pricing requires an understanding of reference prices, price awareness, price/quality association, odd-even perceptions, limited offers and target pricing. Competitor-oriented pricing considers leader-follower scenarios, going rates, discounting and competitive bids. Some companies engage in price wars that can seriously affect industry and company profits. On a global scale, pricing may include countertrading or barter. Funds transfer and exchange rates also affect international pricing.

Objective 3: Learn how pricing strategy is implemented by setting prices and communicating them to the market.
Implementing a price strategy requires setting and communicating prices. One of six fundamental approaches can be used to set prices: skimming, penetration pricing, sliding down the demand curve, price umbrella, everyday low prices and promotional pricing. Product line pricing complicates matters. Options are product array, bundled, optional product and captive product pricing. When prices are communicated, various components may be specified or only the overall price, and various reductions may be offered. Price communication requires company-wide commitment to avoid unethical practices, such as false impressions about price or unfair discrimination.

Objective 4: Explain how some pricing practices are unethical.
There are several pricing practices that are unethical and should be avoided. One is when manufacturers or sellers misrepresent a reference price to consumers. This creates an unfair guideline upon which consumers base purchase decisions. A second is when prices are raised in the wake of a tragedy or natural disaster. This is unethical because it takes advantage of consumers when they're vulnerable. A third is when prices discriminate based on sex or race. Companies need to set pricing strategies with the highest regard for ethical standards if they expect to develop loyal customers.

Review Your Understanding

1. What is value-based pricing? How does it differ from cost-based pricing?
2. What is value in use? Value in exchange?
3. What three leader strategies match what buyers want?
4. What are reference prices? Give several categories.
5. What is a ceiling price, and how is it used in setting prices?
6. How are odd and even prices perceived?
7. When is going rate pricing used?
8. How is pricing used to attract senior citizens?
9. What are price skimming and penetration pricing?
10. What is umbrella pricing?
11. List three aspects of product line pricing.
12. How are prices quoted?
13. What is discriminatory pricing?

Discussion of Concepts

1. How are price and value related? What are the advantages of value-based pricing over the traditional cost-based approach?
2. What is the difference between value in use and value in exchange? How could a marketer use these concepts to improve profitability?
3. What is required if a company wants to use product leadership, operational competence or customer intimacy as the basis for establishing a customer value proposition? Give examples of each.
4. How does competition affect a company's prices? Briefly describe the major competitor-based pricing approaches.
5. We know that several factors influence consumer responses to prices. What psychological factors should marketers keep in mind when using consumer-oriented pricing? Describe each.

6. How is a company's market position related to price leadership? What does this have to do with price wars?
7. Describe the six fundamental ways to set price. In what situations is each strategy typically used?
8. How does the communication of price present ethical dilemmas? Give examples of several questionable practices.

Key Terms & Definitions

1. **Bait and Acceptable price range:** All prices around the reference price that consumers believe reflect good value.
2. **Buying market share:** A strategy in which prices are set low for the short run to pull buyers away from competing brands.
3. **Countertrade:** Government mandates that imported products cannot be paid for with cash; instead, companies from the exporting nation are required to purchase products of equivalent value from the importing nation.
4. **Customer intimacy:** The value strategy designed to create close relationships with customers.
5. **Everyday low prices:** Prices that, on average, are consistently lower than those of competitors.
6. **Going rate:** The price that evolves over time when no competitor has power over others and all price at a similar level.
7. **List price:** The price set by the manufacturer and used by consumers as a reference point. Also called suggested retail price.
8. **Market price:** The actual price buyers must pay for a product.
9. **Operational excellence:** The value strategy designed to produce lower costs that competitors while achieving high quality.
10. **Penetration pricing:** A strategy that seeks the maximum number of buyers by charging low prices.
11. **Price ceiling:** The top end of a price range.

12. **Price skimming:** A strategy to obtain a very high price from relatively few consumers, who have the resources and desire to buy irrespective of price.
13. **Price umbrella:** The leader maintains the price at a high enough level that competitors can earn a profit at that or lower levels.
14. **Price war:** A cut by one company spurs similar reductions by competitors, resulting in price slashing that can lower profit margins.
15. **Product leadership:** The value strategy that builds value by differentiating the product.
16. **Promotional pricing:** A strategy in which price discounts are used to get attention and encourage immediate purchase.
17. **Reference price:** The amount consumers expect to pay for a product.
18. **Slide down the demand curve:** Set a high price when a product is introduced and then lower it significantly as competitors enter the market.
19. **Target pricing:** The use of price to reach a particular market segment.
20. **Value-based pricing:** A strategy that reflects value, not just cost.
21. **Value in exchange:** The objective worth of a product in the competitive marketplace.
22. **Value in use:** The consumer's subjective estimate of the benefits of a particular product.

References

1. www.volvocars.com, website visited March 19, 2016.
2. "Volvo Crash Test Lab photos: Crashing cars, saving lives," Cnet, May 7, 2010.
3. "Volvo Cars adds a little luxury with Excellence Child Safety Seat Concept," Volvo Press Release, July 2, 2015.
4. "Charles Shaw Wins Triple Gold in Orange County ," http://www.winebusiness.com, June 27, 2013.
5. Erica Ho, "Trader Joe's Two-Buck Chuck Gets a Price Hike," Time, January 25, 2013.
6. Treacy, Michael; Wiersema, Fred, The Discipline of Market Leaders (Reading, Massachusetts, Addison-Wesley), 1995.
7. Intel Microprocessor Quick Reference Guide, www.intel.com, website visited May 12, 2016.
8. Starwood Hotels, www.starwoodhotels.com, website visited January 24, 2016.
9. Kopalle, Praveen; Rao, Ambar G.; Assoncao, L. J., "Asymmetric Reference Price Effects and Dynamic Pricing Policies," Marketing Science 15, no. 1, 1996, pp. 60-85.
10. Urbany, Joel E.; Bearden, William O.; Weilbaker, Dan C., "The Effects of Plausibile and Exaggerated Reference Prices on Consumer

Perceptions and Price Search," Journal of Consumer Research 15, June 1988, pp. 95-110.
11. Morris, Michael H.; Morris, Gene, Market Oriented Pricing (Lincolnwood, Illinois, NTC Business Books) 1990, pp. 5-8.
12. Urbany, Joel E.; Dickson, Peter R., Consumer Knowledge of Normal Prices: An Exploratory Study & Framework (Cambridge, Massachusetts: Marketing Science Institute, 1990), pp. 7-8.
13. "Nike, with little explanation, has decided not to do business with Sears. Whose image suffers?", New York Times, May 5, 2005.
14. Chen, Yongmin; Rosenthal, Robert W., "On the Use of Ceiling Price Commitments by Monopolies," Rand Journal of Economics 27, Summer 1996, pp. 207-220.
15. Harrell, Gilbert D., Consumer Behavior (New York: Harcourt Brace Jovanovich), 1986, pg. 68.
16. Pollack, Andrew, "Performance Pricing: Drug Company Offering a Money-Back Guarantee," New York Times, July 14, 2007, pg. B1.
17. Harrell, Gilbert D., Consumer Behavior (New York: Harcourt Brace Jovanovich), 1986, pg. 68.
18. Staten, Vince, "Can You Trust a Tomato in January?", Library Journal, July 1993, pg. 179.

19. Burton, www.burton.com, website visited July 16, 2016.
20. Ibid.
21. "Whirlpool lifts prices to offset commodity costs," Financial Times, February 4, 2005.
22. www.priceline.com, website visited March 24, 2016.
23. "American, Delta cut JFK air fares to match JetBlue," Knight Ridder Tribune Business News, October 2005.
24. Hesna, Genay, "Japan's Corporate Groups," Economic Perspectives 15, January/February 1991, pp. 20-30.
25. "Japan: Just the facts," Journal of Commerce, June 2005.
26. Onkvisit and Shaw, International Marketing, pg. 614.
27. http://investors.walmartstores.com, website visited February 3, 2016.
28. "Why Follow the Leader Isn't Best Pricing Game," www.supermarketnews.com/blog, website visited February 12, 2016.
29. "How big can it grow," The Economist, March 2016.
30. Toyota, www.toyota.com, website visited May 3, 2016.
31. Comcast, www.comcast.com, website visited March 24, 2016.
32. "Build Your Jeep," Jeep, www.jeep.com, website visited July 13, 2016.
33. Progressive, www.progressive.com, website visited March 24, 2016.
34. Benton, W.C.; Park, Seungwook, "A Classification of Literature on Determining the Lot Size Under Quantity Discounts," European Journal of Operational Research, July 19, 1996, pp. 219-238.
35. Victoria's Secret, www.victoriassecret.com, website visited June 5, 2016.
36. Suter, Tracy A.; Burton, Scot, "Believability and Consumer Perceptions of Implausible Reference Prices in Retail Advertisements," Psychology and Marketing 13, January 1996, pp.37-54.
37. Alfor, Bruce L.; Engelland, Brian T., "Advertised Reference Price Effects on Consumer Price Estimates, Value Perception, and Search Intention," Journal of Business Research Vol. 28, No. 2, May 2000, pg. 96.
38. White, Martha, "Travelers Charged $1,000 by Hotel in Irene's Wake, http://moneyland.time.com, August 3, 2011.
39. Myers, Gerr, "Why Women Pay More," American Demographics 18, April 1996, pp. 40-41.
40. Bazar, Emily, "Women Pay More for Services, Study Finds," The Nando Times, October 29, 1998.

Credits

Photo credits are listed throughout the text adjacent to the appropriate image. Images not credited in the text are property of the author, GNU Free Documentation License, Non-Attributed Creative Commons (CC) license or deemed public domain.

Index

Q

R

W

Y

Z

NOTES

NOTES

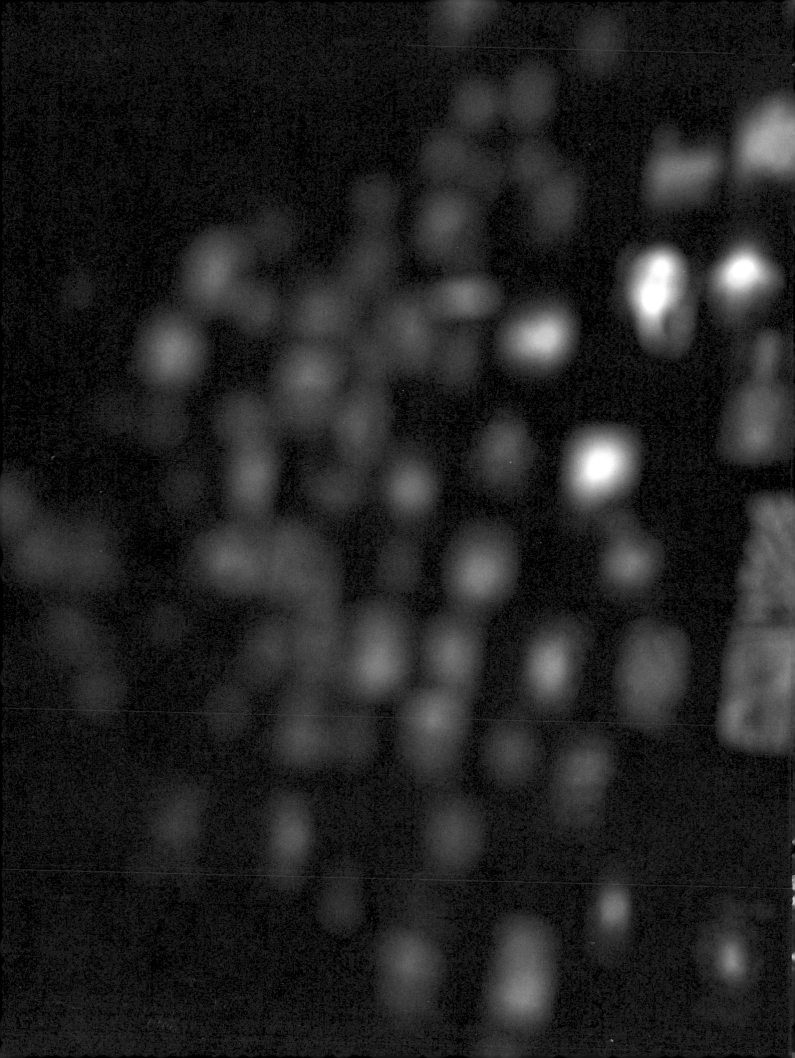